Supervisory Management

Principles and Practice

Fifth Edition

David Evans BA, DipM, MCIM, MISM, MInstAM
formerly Senior Lecturer in Management Studies,
West Oxfordshire College,
Witney, Oxon
NEBSM Course Tutor

CASSELL

Cassell
Wellington House
125 Strand
London WC2R 0BB

370 Lexington Avenue
New York
NY 10017-6550

First edition 1981
Second edition 1986
Reprinted 1988, 1989 (with corrections), 1990
Third edition 1992
Reprinted 1993 (with corrections) (twice)
Fourth edition 1995
Fifth edition 1999

ISBN 0–304–70611–6 (paperback)

Typeset by Pantek Arts, Maidstone, Kent
Printed and bound in Great Britain by Redwood Books, Trowbridge, Wiltshire

Contents

Acknowledgements

I must express my grateful thanks to all those who provided help and criticism during the preparation of this book, including Bernard Caswell, Senior Lecturer, Oxford Brookes University, over the references to work study; the publisher's reviewers, and their staff, who, over the years, have done so much to ensure the books success.

NEBS Management were kind enough to permit me to quote from their publications, and they would, of course, welcome enquiries from prospective students at their address, 1 Giltspur Street, London, EC1A 9DD.

Finally, I acknowledge the support and encouragement of my wife, Wendy, and my family, who did without my company for many hours during the preparation of the book, and subsequent revisions.

*To every student
who reads this book*

Preface to the Fifth Edition

This fifth edition carries on the tradition of previous editions in attempting to marry together both the theory and practice of supervision and management.

Theories are important as they help us to make sense of the world in every area of life. So it is with management and supervision. How can we hope to look at practical problems such as training people, or introducing change in the workplace, without first trying to understand the reasons why people behave as they do?

Of course there are incomplete, inadequate and misleading theories: the history of science is littered with them. But it is still useful to study theories (even if they are dated) provided we can learn from doing so; to judge a good or bad theory when we see one. The study of outmoded ideas about supervision and management even becomes essential when we realize that managers at every level are still, years later, being profoundly influenced by them.

Then there is the job itself. The functions of individual managers and supervisors vary inevitably from organization to organization and within them, but closer examination reveals such variation is in *emphasis* not in activity.

This book is therefore intended to assist both students and practising managers at every level to examine these common functions. And to consider the problems of organizing, controlling and motivating a work group in a time of considerable and continuous technological and social change.

The various sections aim first to cover the majority of the topics included in the NEBSM Certificate in Supervisory Management under the headings of 'Managing Products and Services', 'Managing Human Resources' and 'Managing Information'. Much of the material is also suitable for both the remaining BTEC National Certificate in Business Studies and the more recently introduced GNVQ Advanced level. Students following similar level programmes in Scotland (produced by SCOTVEC) have also found the book invaluable.

Even later arrivals have been the revised Management NVQs (at levels 3 and 4), which became available in 1997. Several examination boards are offering them, including NEBS Management and Edexcel/BTEC. Candidates for these and similar programmes (such as the Edexcel/BTEC Professional Development Award in

Supervisory Management) will find *Supervisory Management* useful in underpinning their knowledge, experiences and existing competences. In particular, Unit VI, *Management and Supervisory Competences* (originally added to the third edition to enhance this kind of support) has now been further updated.

A completely revised Chapter 36 now caters in considerable detail for the supervisory competences and the extensive knowledge and understanding required of candidates working towards the current level 3 Management NVQ. It was pleasing to find when re-writing this chapter that so many of the skills and items of knowledge and understanding required for the NVQ can be related back to specific sections of this book. Indeed, the NVQ requirements – in both knowledge and understanding (K&U) and personal competences (PCs) – are a useful summary of the K&U and PCs a manager at any level should possess.

As well as the awards already mentioned, others students of management and associated topics should find the book useful, particularly those on programmes leading to:

> The Certificate in Management Studies/Professional Development Certificate
> The Diploma in Management Studies/Professional Development Diploma
> Edexcel/BTEC Higher Diplomas or Certificates in Management and Business Studies (and associated topics)
> The Certificate of the Institute of Supervision and Management
> The Certificate and Diploma of the Institute of Administrative Management Programmes and courses at Universities and Institutes of Higher Education, containing Management modules
> Open learning and short courses in management subjects

In this latest edition every effort has been made to ensure the book can be seen to relate as much to the many thousands of successful (and potential) female directors, executives, managers and supervisors, as to their male colleagues.

Further up-dating has also been necessary to accommodate the many changes to health and safety legislation and industrial relations law in recent times. Other changes to the content and coverage of the text have been inspired by those of you who have taken the trouble to put forward constructive suggestions. This edition has benefited considerably from these very welcome inputs, and any further comments or suggestions you may have should be sent to the publishers direct.

Finally, I would like to reiterate to all users of this book, the emphasis is on *supervisory and management principles and practice* (hence the book's sub-title) and *not* on economic/financial or technical/management information aspects. These areas are covered in the appropriate specialist texts.

Witney, April 1999   David Evans

About This Book and How to Use It

THE BOOK

This book has several significant features:

1. It is clearly divided into self-contained and distinct parts.
2. Its scope is broad enough to apply to most managers and supervisors.
3. It can be used equally well by individual students for home study, or by lecturers and students as a classroom textbook, or as supporting material for short courses.
4. Examples are drawn from situations likely to be readily understood by most students.

HOW TO USE IT

Students

1. Each chapter should be studied until the content has been understood.
2. You should then tackle the questions and exercises at the end of each chapter before passing on to the next topic.
3. The initial questions at the end of each chapter are to test your understanding of the text. Further questions and exercises widen the topic areas, and you would benefit from tackling them on a class basis.

Lecturers

Finally, the case studies can be considered by the whole class, in small groups or by students individually. By ensuring that each group elects a chairman, secretary and spokesman for the group in any subsequent report-back session, you can aid the development of social and communication skills as the course progresses.

UNIT I

Introduction to Supervision

All supervisors work in organizations. At the beginning, therefore, we ask 'Are there common features to all organizations?' We shall find that we can identify the essential features of organizations of different types.

In the same way, all supervisors can be found to be doing essentially the same job, even if the individual tasks they do are different.

We shall spend this unit, therefore, in examining organizations, and the managers and supervisors who work in them.

1
Organizations

1.1 TYPES OF ORGANIZATIONS

One of the problems of the modern world is the lack of consistency in the agreed use and meaning of words. Just think how words such as 'democracy' meant and mean different things to different peoples—Athens at the time of Plato, 18th century England, modern America and Russia. So many people use words differently, that untold confusions can arise. So it is with *organization*. Scientists using the term could apply it to crystals, molecules, atoms, or even sub-atomic particles. The way in which the different parts of a thing—molecule, crystal, atom are arranged is called its 'organization'. Similarly, on a larger scale we can talk of the 'organization' of the solar system.

We must be careful, then, from the start to show how we are going to use this word. Sociologists and management writers—even if they do not attempt a definition[1]— tend to use it to mean social units or human groupings, that is organizations consist of groups of *people*. While appreciating that some organizations own things like buildings and machinery, and some would want to include these things as well as the people, the basic definition we shall use is: *'organizations are groups of people working towards a common objective, or set of objectives.'*

Now, as you go about your daily business, you find yourself surrounded by organizations. Indeed, most of us begin life as a member of a family—a very special type of organization—or some kind of similarly organized group. Very soon we begin to get involved with other organizations—weekly visits to the local clinic, perhaps introduced as an infant into a religious group, later being enrolled in a play group. Then, at the age of five, we join a complex set of organizations we call the 'educational system'. We start school.

In fact, your life and mine are heavily dependent upon a multitude of organizations—we talk about living in a 'highly organized society'. The Electricity and Water Boards combine to help us wash in warm water on dark mornings,

---

[1] Indeed some sociologists (e.g. Amitai Etzioni) would want to restrict the definition further to what I call 'formal organizations', and to exclude any other kinds of social units altogether.

cornflake manufacturers provide us with part of our breakfasts, oil companies sell the fuel needed to help most of us get to work. We work or study in organizations during the day, and even when we relax at home in the evening, we watch television provided for us by broadcasting organizations. Indeed, even when we sleep, emergency services remain in a constant state of readiness, so we can call upon them if needed.

We must not imagine, however, that organizations are a modern invention. Consider what organization was required to build the Pyramids, the Aztec cities, or the tall tops of Troy. Much earlier still, Stonehenge presented not only the problems of site planning and the erection of the stones, but the transportation over great distances of the stones themselves. We can say, however, that as we go back farther into history there were considerably fewer large and complex organizations than there are today, partly owing to the small numbers of people available to form groups, and partly owing to a lesser need for organizations on the grand scale.

So smaller social units and human groupings were dominant in earlier societies. Indeed, they have not disappeared, and are still of vital importance today. There are often organizations in which you participate that you might not immediately recognize as such. For example, perhaps you are friendly with colleagues in another department, or on another course, and meet regularly, say, at lunch time; maybe you have a 'turn and turn about' arrangement of car-sharing with a neighbour when travelling to work or college; or perhaps you are sometimes involved with a few others in arranging for a collection for someone leaving the firm. All these activities are *organized* to a greater or lesser degree, and those involved belong to the same organization.

1.1.1 Why do organizations exist?

We must now ask why organizations exist at all. How did they start, and why have they continued to grow in number and complexity? The answers are complicated because:

1. There are so many different organizations;
2. They satisfy so many different kinds of human needs—emotional, physical, mental, economic. However, we can consider at least the following reasons:

Organizations enlarge individual activities

Human beings are limited biologically as to what they can do as individuals. 'Many hands make light work' is not the whole story: some work could not be done *at all* without many hands. Single individuals cannot build pyramids or pay return visits to the moon. Even when one person performs a spectacular feat like sailing round the world on his own, he does so with the help of countless organizations who built his boat, navigational gear, and provided his food and clothes.

Organizations satisfy social needs

'Man', said Aristotle, 'is a political animal', that is to say people like to be involved in group activities, outside the immediate family circle. Even a small company can provide its employees with many satisfying contacts both inside and outside the firm. For others, the companionship of people with similar tastes leads to the formation of clubs, societies, and unions, for example.

Organizations save time

An organized and numerous group can obviously accomplish a task much more quickly than either a lone individual or isolated individuals. Sometimes the need exists for muscle power for jobs such as hauling in a boat, or helping with the harvest. Sometimes the need exists for group members to specialize in particular tasks ('division of labour' as economists call it), and divide the work out accordingly. Primitive agricultural settlements must have learnt these lessons early on in their development.

Organizations pool and conserve knowledge

Instead of everyone having to work everything out for themselves, and be limited to what they have learnt from experience, members of organizations can and do share both (intellectual) knowledge of facts about situations, and 'know-how' or skills. Indeed, many organizations now have highly developed facilities for retaining in more or less permanent form records of this knowledge.

Organizations are power centres

'In union there is strength'; 'the whole is greater than the parts'; both are true of organizations. The individual rarely has power to influence events on a large scale. Joined, however, with others in a union, political party, protest or pressure group, people can bring pressure to bear on those individuals or other organizations they want to influence. While, of course, most organizations are not pressure groups or lobbies, all have the potential to influence events—creating demand, winning orders, creating wealth, helping the balance of payments, and so on. In this sense organizations are power, or influence centres.

Organizations can cater for man's needs and wants more effectively

People working in groups can provide more effectively for their needs and wants, and those of others. Not only can larger quantities of goods be provided more quickly, as we have already seen, but what economists call 'economies of scale' (in essence this means the more of an item you can produce, the cheaper the unit price is) lead to a lowering of costs, or a rise in the standard of living.

Organizations tend to increase efficiency

This follows on from the previous point. Despite the constant (and often justified) criticism of the efficiency or otherwise of private firms, nationalized undertakings, or government departments, all these are patently more efficient than isolated individuals ever could be; and more efficient than their ancient or mediaeval counterparts.

Added to this, we live in an age in which most political systems from extreme right to the left approve of—at least in principle—planning, order, co-operative achievement, and efficiency.

Organizations provide greater security for the individual

Isolated human beings are vulnerable. Wild animals, other people, the weather, natural disasters (earthquakes, etc.) were ever present threats in earlier days. The ability of a group to cope with such potential dangers more effectively is self-evident; today we still react to danger by forming groups. Whether it is on a small scale (a union at a workplace), or of an international character, where things are taken a stage further with groups of groups (NATO or the United Nations for example), a basic aim behind the formation of such groups or groupings is to enhance the security of individuals or states—which are of course made up of the individuals who belong to them.

It is thus not surprising, for reasons of the kind we have considered, that the number, size and complexity of organizations have grown, and will continue to grow. People have joined organizations for the simple reason that they consider that they will be more successful, satisfy more needs and wants, be generally better off by so doing.

1.1.2   Classifying types of organizations

There are various ways in which we can classify something like, say, motor cars; by engine size, by horse power, by fuel consumption, overall dimensions—the list is endless. We choose the classification to suit the purpose we have in mind, while we are aware they are different ways of grading motor cars. So the classifications set out below are neither final nor exhaustive—just useful for our purpose.

1.1.3   Formal-informal classification

Here we attempt to classify organizations according to their structure. Note, however, that the words 'formal' and 'informal' represent extremes, and in the same way that we are unlikely ever to find an economy either totally capitalist or totally state controlled, we are unlikely to find either a totally formal, or totally informal organization.

1.1.4 Formal organizations

The major characteristics of formal organizations are:

Well-defined structure

In formal organizations we can usually see a clearly defined relationship between the members of the organization—there are the rulers and the ruled; status, ranks and different levels of power and authority can be identified.

Rules exist to regulate the ways in which the members of the organization can or may communicate with each other; expected types of behaviour exist, and often written instructions on how tasks are to be performed (or not to be performed) are issued to members.

Precisely identified beginning

We can usually pinpoint precisely when a formal organization came into being. There are normally written documents (copies of which are kept by the organization in its files) to mark the event, and evidence may be found elsewhere in central or government archives, of the organization's existence.

If the organization disbands, there is again, usually written evidence of its demise.

Longer life span

Formal organizations usually last for a long time. Many associations, clubs and firms are proud to print the year of their foundation prominently on their notepaper. Agreed, the buildings and the people who belong may be completely changed after a lapse of years, but in the majority of cases a definite continuity of purpose can be traced.

Membership (by choice)

Members of formal organizations—except where say, the law lays down you *must* join (e.g. going to school, being called up for military service)—join by choice. Even where we have little choice in whether we join or not—e.g. school, the army, etc.—there is often some choice of which school, which regiment, which trade we join. Joining is usually formal—and a *contract* exists between the member and the organization. Employees have contracts of service with their firms, club members get services or privileges in return for their subscriptions.

Definite aims (goals)

Formal organizations have definite aims (or goals). By this we mean they try to make particular things happen. Societies have aims—the name itself may give us a clue (the Society for the Propagation of the Gospel)—which are circulated to members; and every limited company in the UK is required by law to produce a list of its goals (the Articles of Association). The latter are necessary because they enable shareholders (the providers of the money with which the firm is run) to see clearly what they are investing in.

Criticisms are sometimes made that organizations do not always follow their stated goals. Worse, they may have secret goals, or even conflicting ones at the same time. For example, a political party might publicly state it is really in favour of free collective bargaining at the moment it brings in (just as a temporary measure) a rigid incomes policy.

These comments are, of course, true but do not alter the basic notion that formal organizations have definite (usually stated) purposes which you can find out by investigation in the right places.

Division of work

Conscious efforts are made by those belonging to formal organizations, and in particular by those running them, to share out the work required to achieve the aims of the organization. While these efforts do not always succeed, there is a general attempt to enable the group members, nearly all of whom specialize in one particular job, to function as a unit, each doing his own part, without getting in the way of the others.

Examples of formal organizations are: British Telecom, Yorkshire County Cricket Club, Westminster City Council, Unison, and the pop group 'Oasis'.

1.1.5   Informal organizations

The opposite in many ways to formal organizations, the major characteristics are:

Loosely defined structure

In contrast to that of formal organization, we can usually see a much less defined relationship between the members of an informal organization: who is 'boss', or takes the lead at any one time may vary; levels of power or authority are difficult to define.

If rules of conduct do exist, they are rarely written down.

Beginnings not clearly identifiable

In an informal organization membership may grow over a period of time. At first, you may be occasionally invited by more senior colleagues to join them at lunch time; later on, you might become accepted as a regular member of the lunch group. Nobody in the group could point to a particular day when you became a 'full member'.

Except, say, in a private diary, records are unlikely to be kept either of the beginning or ending of an informal group.

Shorter life span

While it is true a friendship, a card school or family can last for many years, on the whole, informal organizations tend to have a shorter life span than formal ones: indeed some organizations like a group of passers-by who arrange themselves to rescue people from a car crash, and summon emergency services, may only form and function for half an hour or so.

Less conscious membership

Very often informal groups form without a seemingly conscious effort by everyone to form the group. Membership is rarely formally confirmed. This is especially true of 'ad hoc' or temporary groupings to cope with, for example, an emergency.

Less well-defined goals

There is much less evidence of a consistent and constant pursuit of specific goals over time in an informal organization. The lunch group may meet and discuss work problems on Monday, football on Tuesday, politics on Friday. It is in fact more than likely different members of such a group have their own peculiar, individual reasons for belonging. Such a group is really a 'coalition' of goals.

Flexibility

As a result of the less precise nature of the group it is infinitely more flexible; can adopt new ideas, react spontaneously and very quickly to new situations. Members can take on new roles or duties without much discussion or loss of status.

For example, during a week-end trip into the country, everyone in the group could drive in turn, have a share in the cooking or washing-up.

Smallness in size

Informal organizations tend to be small in size, and by their very nature all the members are likely to know each other. This contrasts with formal organizations which can be either large or small.

Examples of informal organizations are: a friendship, a dinner party, a 'clique' or 'set' at school or college, a game of dominoes in the saloon bar, or a group of people giving someone with a jammed starter a 'push start' to assist a quick getaway.

1.1.6 Organizations—change of status

Organizations which start as informal ones may change to formal ones in time. A group of friends interested in railway modelling as a hobby could form a society with rules and a constitution; or even go as far as to start a business. Similarly, a formal organization like an old comrades' association could decline as the ex-soldier members died off, leaving a few elderly veterans meeting each other informally on an irregular basis.

1.1.7 Co-existence of formal and informal organizations

It is very important for managers and supervisors to appreciate that a formal organization—such as a firm—can have within it a number (perhaps even a large number) of informal organizations with overlapping memberships. Small work groups on the shop floor can form, with special and individual practices, customs and values; and at higher levels of the organization managers and supervisors of different levels can form powerful networks, the membership of which may be difficult to discover, and even if known may well not resemble the official, formal structure of the ranks and gradings in the organization.

In addition, there can exist in formal organizations smaller (but still very formal) organizations such as trade unions, works' councils or boards of directors.

1.2   BUSINESS, ADMINISTRATIVE AND RELATED (FORMAL) WORK ORGANIZATIONS

1.2.1   By organization goals

A way of classifying organizations, particularly formal ones, is to establish the organization's goals—what is the organization trying to do?

Business (or what we loosely call 'firms') are endeavouring *to make a profit* (a primary goal), by doing one or more of three things:

1. Taking raw materials, or partly-finished items, working on them, and producing products to sell at a price higher than the total costs (i.e. the cost of the raw materials, the labour charges, and all other expenses—including selling—combined).
    Examples: car manufacturing, baked bean canners, or farmers.

2. Providing a service for organizations or individual customers, and selling the service at a price higher than the total costs (i.e. the cost of labour, expenses and parts supplied).
   Examples: accountants, TV maintenance, laundries.
3. Buying completed items, and reselling them at a price which is greater than the cost of buying the goods, plus all the selling expenses involved.
   Examples: shops, wholesalers, petrol stations, or car showrooms.

Some organizations may do *more* than one of these things at the same time: the local electrical retail shop may service TVs; a garage may sell and repair cars; a manufacturer may have a repair service.

Another class of organizations are *non profit-making,* but have as a primary goal the provision of a service at a specially reduced rate, or even free. Most of these are state financed, or provided by local government out of the Community Charge.

Examples are: educational establishments—schools, colleges; hospitals (run within the National Health Service) and the police.

1.2.2 By ownership

Another way of classifying organizations is by *ownership*.

Private ownership

Private enterprises are owned by clearly identifiable people, who also collect the profits that are available for distribution at the end of each year of operation. There are several types.

Sole traders. These are people in business on their own. This is a very common form of business organization and is also the simplest. The sole trader starts the business from his or her own savings (or obtains a loan from a bank), and provides his or her own labour, plus that of one or two employees. There are few formalities in starting.

Sole traders take all the profits as their reward, and enjoy the freedom of running the business as they like. Against these advantages are set the disadvantages of long hours and competition from larger units. Other unpleasant factors are *unlimited liability* for *debts*,[2] the inclusion of the business in an owner's private estate at death, meaning that he or she could incur high death duties, as a result of which the owner could face difficulties in raising extra capital while still alive.

Examples can be found in the classified advertisements of your local newspaper—builders, plumbers, hairdressers, and the like, plus a host of corner shops, newsagents and market traders.

Partnerships. Partnerships may grow out of two sole traders combining to form a bigger unit, to acquire more capital and expertise, but often businesses start life as a

---

[2] The concept of unlimited liability is explained below under limited companies.

partnership. A partnership exists where two or more (up to 20, in fact in the UK, except in *professional* partnerships—accountants for example—where there is no upper limit) people join *together* to run a business. Such an arrangement is eminently suitable for service organizations such as, for example, doctors, solicitors or accountants, each with their own workload, and specializations. A greater area of service can be covered—a veterinary partnership could include a member specializing in horses, another in smaller animals, and a third in cattle and sheep.

However, partners still have the problem of being liable for the debts of the partnership, and for death duties on their share of the partnership. The death of a partner could have a significant effect on the business.

Examples of partnerships: shops; professional groups such as doctors, lawyers, business consultants; farmers and small engineering concerns.

Limited companies.   A very popular form of business organization—over half a million are in the UK alone, the vast majority being private companies. We have already seen sole traders and partners are liable for the debts incurred by the business to the extent that if the business fails and owes more than it can repay the sole trader or partner could be made bankrupt. He might have to sell his car, even his house, as well as his business, to repay his creditors.

However, the principle of *limited liability*, introduced in 1856 to stimulate the formation of new companies, allows people to start a business with less fear of the financial consequences. Provided the company is formed in particular ways as laid down by various Acts of Parliament (and in respect of public companies, in accordance with Stock Exchange rules), then a large number of people can contribute to an enterprise without risking their homes or other possessions. The basic idea is that if a business owes money which it cannot repay, those contributing to the company's funds (shareholders) could lose what they put in originally, *but no more*.

Thus if you put £1000 into a company (i.e. becoming a shareholder), and the company failed owing many times this amount, you could lose all of the £1000 stake you had in the company. However, you would not be called upon to provide any more money.

As a safeguard, limited companies must state in an official document—the Memorandum of Association—what the goals of the company are, so intending shareholders can ascertain with a fair degree of precision what kind of business they are investing in. They could in fact have a claim against the company if their money is used for anything else.

Limited companies can be either *private*[3]—with from two to 50 shareholders, or *public*[4]—with from two shareholders upwards with no upper limits. The private limited company has the attraction that it has independent legal status, limited liability; the founders can usually keep control of the business by taking a majority of shares, and can control the transfer of shares from existing shareholders to a new, potential, shareholder.

With up to 50 shareholders, a reasonable amount of capital can be raised to help finance the business; and its affairs remain reasonably private.

---

[3] Signified by 'Ltd.', e.g. Waitrose Ltd.
[4] Signified by 'PLC', e.g. Barclays Bank PLC.

This type of company is usually quite a small, family affair, although it could be very large; Sainsburys were a private limited company until comparatively recently.

The public limited company, having satisfied both the legal and Stock Exchange requirements, can advertise for the general public to invest in the company (i.e. become shareholders), and while there must be seven original shareholders, there is no upper limit. What is fixed at the start is the *amount* of capital that can be subscribed.

Recent figures show there are in the region of 15 000 public limited companies in the UK. Many are very large with sales turnover figures in excess of £10 million per year.

Despite the considerable legal problems and expenses involved in starting a public limited company, for example, the restrictions placed upon its operation by the Government, the right of access to information about the company by both share-holders and trade unions representing workers in the firm; the ability to raise money from the public at large and the advantages of a large-scale operation more than outweigh the disadvantages.

Examples: British Aerospace PLC, Britoil PLC, United Biscuits (Holdings) PLC.

In view of the fact that there are so many limited companies (adding public and private together the figure is over 510 000), they can be regarded as the 'typical' firm. Their internal structure is discussed in Chapter 2.

Multinationals.   A complex type of organization, with many problems for governments, as well as for supervisors and other workers. A multinational enterprise is a firm (or more usually a large corporation) that owns (in whole or part), controls and manages income producing assets in more than one country. It often engages in international production.

Multinationals can be British companies with overseas operations (Shell, for example); companies jointly controlled by boards in more than one country (Unilever with both British and Dutch ownership); or be British subsidiaries of foreign companies (IBM UK Ltd).

Working for such an enterprise can be challenging and interesting especially where different management philosophies are practised—for example by most Japanese firms in the UK. In some multinationals promotion prospects are greater and 'overseas postings' a possibility. However the minuses in the situation include the fact that it is difficult for Governments to control multinationals—they can quite quickly and easily reduce investment, or switch production from one area or country to another to take advantage of lower labour costs. In 1978 the Chrysler Corporation sold off (without prior warning to anyone—including the UK Government) its entire European interests including Chrysler UK to the Peugeot-Citroën group.

Other problems have been the inability of local management to react quickly to environmental changes, and decisions may often have to be referred to 'Head Office' which might be in Detroit or Chicago.

Co-operative societies

These fall into two categories:

Retail societies.   The retail co-operative movement can be traced back to Rochdale in 1844. The essential principle was the banding together of a group of people to buy essential foodstuffs from farmers and wholesalers, and selling the produce to the members at a profit. However, at each year's end profits were divided between members in proportion to their purchases.

Today's co-operative societies are much more sophisticated and complex; and to the casual customer little different from other stores, but there are members of each society who provide capital, elect a management committee and receive interest payments. The rebate on purchases is now by trading stamps.

Producers' co-operatives.   Producers such as farmers join together to buy and share expensive pieces of farm machinery, or achieve economies by linking together to market their produce.

Public sector organizations

While a great deal of economic and commercial activity is conducted by the types of organizations mentioned above, many goods and services are provided by central or local government.

Central government.   A variety of different organizations come under this heading:

1. The Government as trader. This is where, as in the case of Her Majesty's Stationery Office, trading activities are under the control of the Treasury.
2. The Government as large shareholder, in what in every other respect is a normal limited company.
3. Public corporations (the nationalized industries). A prominent public sector organization is the Post Office. Since there are no shareholders in the ordinary sense special arrangements are made both to provide capital, and to make each corporation ultimately responsible to Parliament.
4. Other organizations. These provide a service but do not charge directly—the BBC, the Arts Council and the Forestry Commission are typical examples.

Local government.   Local government has had a long history of providing services out of the rates—waste collection, pest control, for example, but business operations like Birmingham Airport, swimming baths, dance halls, golf courses also figure in the list. However, even here, income from the services is often insufficient, and the deficits have to be made up from the Council Tax or from income received from central government.

Social service organizations

These can be both publicly and privately owned.

Publicly owned.   Probably the most important of these are hospitals, and medical services (Department of Health), social services and benefit payments (local authorities and Department of Social Security), and schools, colleges, universities (local authorities and the Department of Education and Science). Many of these are large-scale organizations employing large numbers of personnel, and spending large amounts of capital on their equipment.

Privately owned.   There is an overlap with the publicly owned: schools, colleges and even a university, as well as hospitals. In addition, charities like Oxfam, or religious institutions, such as the Salvation Army, provide useful social services.

Regulatory organizations

These are organizations which help to regulate society, and consist of the police forces, the Army, the Navy, the RAF, the customs service, the inland revenue, conservation, development planning organizations and the civil service. All are owned and controlled by national or local government.

Non-profit-making organizations

These are organizations like cricket and tennis clubs, sports and social clubs, workingmen's clubs which exist to provide services to members in return for a subscription. While a 'profit' (in terms of an excess of income over expenditure in a year) may be made, it is either shared out amongst the members or ploughed back into the club in the form of improved facilities.

All these organizations are important to us, not only as users of their services, but because most of them employ managers or supervisors of one kind or another. Thus, when we consider the job of the supervisor, we must not forget that there are many other types of supervisory or managerial jobs with different problems, different conditions of work and with differing status.

1.3   THE ORGANIZATION AND ITS ENVIRONMENT

If someone asks the question 'Where does a physical object end?', the answer seems simple: the outside. But when we look more closely at an object like, for example, the sun, we find it has no finite boundary, but just becomes tenuous as we move further into space. Consideration of a more mundane example, the motor-car, brings out a further point: we cannot really consider the role and function of the car—to transport people and goods from point to point—without considering its *environment*. We cannot isolate the car from its surroundings: if we describe it in motion we can talk about its suspension, its road-holding abilities and its speed—all of which will be related to and affected by such characteristics of its environment as road surfaces, weather conditions, the amount of traffic on the road and the time of day.

So it is with all organizations, including manufacturing ones. To talk about a firm without considering its location, its customers, its suppliers and a great deal more is only to tell part of the story. It is how a firm or organization *copes* with its environment—importing inputs from outside, working on them, and re-exporting them—which is of significance, just as the fuel/mileage ratio or road-holding performance of a new car is of significance to its purchaser.

Systems theory was born out of the Second World War. A team of scientists assembled at the Massachusetts Institute of Technology—a 'think-tank' of mathematicians, engineers, biologists and others—worked to improve the functioning of anti-aircraft guns and similar weapons. Soon the team realized they were all working to the same end: a theory of *control*. From this research the science of control, *cybernetics,* was developed in 1947, and in 1950 came general systems theory (GST), based on the notion that there were basic similarities in the ways that *all* systems function, and that a system is a related group of elements organized for a purpose.

It is clear that the definitions of a system as used in GST include all human and social systems, including manufacturing ones. Thus what can be said of systems can be applied to organizations.

1.3.1 Classification of systems

Systems can be classified under various headings, but the most important for our purpose is the major division into closed and open systems, and the relations of these two kinds of systems with their environment.

Closed systems

A completely closed system is one with sealed boundaries against any influence from or interaction with the outside environment. Nothing enters or leaves a closed system. A characteristic of such systems is an inherent tendency to move towards a static equilibrium and random state in which there is no potential for work (entropy). A closed system will tend to increase in entropy over time. Possibly the only *totally* closed system is the whole universe.

Open systems

An open system, on the other hand, while it can have or be given boundaries, does have relationships with its environment (other systems). When an open system is acted upon by other systems it is said to go through an *import process* or, to use a term from computer language, it receives inputs. When it acts upon the *inputs*, the open system is said to carry out a *conversion* or *transformation* process, and when it *reacts outwards* to the environment (other systems), this is called the *export process,* or *outputs.*

The organization or firm can be considered in terms of a general open-system model as illustrated in Fig. 1.1.

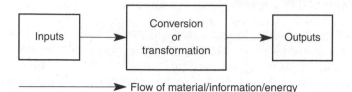

Figure 1.1 An open system.

Such a system is in constant interaction with its environment, and at the same time strives to achieve a *dynamic* equilibrium: the biochemistry of the human body tries to maintain an equilibrium between its inputs (food, water, information, etc.) and energy expended/work done and waste products. The survival of an open system ultimately depends upon a continuous inflow, transformation and outflow process. It goes without saying that the system must receive sufficient inputs at a suitable rate of entry to maintain the rest of the cycle.

Adaptive systems

Adaptive or *self-adjusting* systems adapt themselves to changes in the environment that is, they contain some mechanism which enables them to respond to increased or decreased inputs, or the demands for increased or decreased outputs. Human beings are able to adapt in this way, for example in dealing with temperature changes by putting on or taking off clothes, perspiring and shivering. It is not surprising that organizations—groups of people—share this adaptive ability.

Probabilistic systems

These are systems in which certain events can be predicted but not others, even given large amounts of information about them. With a roulette wheel in motion, for example, you can predict that *some* number will come up, but not which one.

Contrived systems

Contrived systems are not naturally occurring ones like biological systems, but are deliberate, artificial creations.

Industrial firms

We can now see that firms and business organizations are examples of open, adaptive, probabilistic and contrived systems.

1.3.2 The manufacturing system

It is clear that manufacturing systems are many and varied and it is therefore difficult, except at a very general level, to establish what the inputs and outputs of manufacturing systems are.[5] However, it can be said that all manufacturing systems interact considerably with their environment (other systems). Some of the factors operating on them are shown in Fig. 1.2.

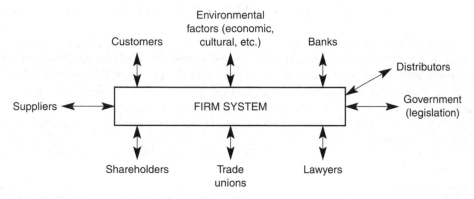

Figure 1.2 Factors operating on the firm/system.

Inputs to the systems

The major inputs can be classified as follows:

Information. No open system can continue to function without information from its environment. In the case of the manufacturing system, inquiries, opinions and orders from customers (particularly the latter) are of extreme importance. Data and standards accepted throughout the industry (e.g. British Standards), legal requirements (health and safety legislation), known fashion trends, market research information, information on competitors and the like must also be treated as essential inputs. Raw material availability and cost must also be known.

Money (capital). Contrived systems need an initial impetus to start them off, equip the conversion processes with adequate technology and provide other necessary inputs. The almost universal way of doing this for manufacturing systems is to borrow money from shareholders or banks.

---

[5] See Parnaby, J. 'Concept of a manufacturing system', in Open Systems Group (ed.) *Systems Behaviour.* London: Harper & Row and Open University, 1981.

Cash inputs will be required constantly once the system is functioning. Much of the necessary finance will come from the sale of the outputs, though further loans may be necessary to expand the business, and to be used for the purchase of raw materials, labour, etc.

Raw materials. This term covers not only the basic products used in the manufacturing process but also bought-in components, sub-assemblies and finished items (i.e. outputs of other firms).

Consumable items. These are items which are used up or 'consumed' during the manufacturing process—lubricating oils, rags, etc.

Labour. Staff, both manual and non-manual (i.e. technical, administrative and managerial), are needed to operate and manage the conversion processes within the system.

Assets (plant and equipment). 'Assets' covers a wide range of items including the premises in which the processes are housed, computers, machinery (large and small), spares, tools and transport vehicles. These assets are purchased from capital.

Services. A constant supply of energy in the form of gas, electricity, oil, etc. will be needed. Other services, such as water, sewerage and drainage, specialist maintenance by outside contractors, telephones, and mail collection and delivery, are also examples of essential inputs.

Business environment. The general climate of business opinion (for example about the current economic situation) and the values, norms and ideals of other firms will affect to a greater or lesser extent the way the manufacturing system behaves.

Social pressures. Firms are usually keen to create a 'good image' of themselves. Criticisms in respect of dangerous practices, unsightly buildings, chemical additives or nasty smells can affect the technology and conversion processes operated.

Trade union pressures. The attitudes, aspirations and policies of trade unions and their members can produce sudden and traumatic inputs to a manufacturing system.

General economic/political environment. The current state of the economy, interest rates, political stability, etc. can affect *all* business systems.

Outputs from the system

The major outputs can be classified as follows:

Finished products. These are the result of the conversion process being applied to the raw materials, and undoubtedly are the most important tangible output from the system. They can be measured in terms of *quantity, quality* and *sales value*.

Profit (or loss). This is the amount of money left over after all the expenses incurred in paying for inputs, the conversion process and facilitating outputs have been paid out of sales revenue. A loss is a 'minus profit'.

Information. Contrived open systems generate considerable amounts of information (usually by design). Provided available data are captured and ordered into significant information, much can be learned about the nature of the outputs, for example whether they have met the targets set. Provided this information is fed to a control process in the system, it can be used to help improve the control and general running of the system.

Reputation. Every manufacturing organization will strive to establish and maintain a good reputation. Such a reputation will be one of the outputs, provided the firm fulfils orders promptly, to specification, in the right quantity at the right price. However, if the firm supplies poor-quality goods at uncompetitive prices, with delays in delivery, a less acceptable output—a bad reputation—will result. A good reputation (hard earned and easily lost) is a key factor in obtaining both new and repeat business.

Inputs and outputs: an overall view

The manufacturing system can now be represented diagrammatically as in Fig. 1.3.

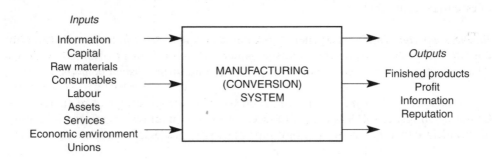

Figure 1.3 An overall view of inputs and outputs: manufacturing system.

1.3.3 Controlling the system

As mentioned already, a significant output is information. Some of this information will in fact be taken back into the system for control purposes. It has been noted that 'controlling' involves the setting or establishment of standards of performance, devising and using methods of measuring and monitoring performance, comparing the standards set with actual performance, and (where necessary) making appropriate adjustments to the system to correct significant deviations from the standards set.

In systems language this is described as measuring the *outputs* of the system against some predetermined standard and *feeding back* the results of this measurement process to a monitor/controller (i.e. some person or piece of equipment capable of noting and dealing with the information appropriately). If deviations or variances from the desired outputs are noted, the controller can make necessary adjustments to the *inputs*. For example, the quality control department could be regarded as the 'monitoring' process. If the chemical analysis of a product reveals the product is not up to standard, then changes to inputs can be made, for example new manufacturing instructions (information), the use of better-quality raw materials, or more highly trained labour.

In this way there is a loop in the system known as a *feedback loop*. The process is illustrated in Fig. 1.4.

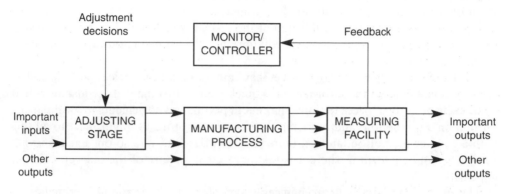

Figure 1.4 A system with a feedback loop (for control).

This then gives supervisors and managers an insight into what lies behind every successful control system. First, we need ideals—standards to go by; these could be specification standards, quantity targets, quality levels, performance indicators and so on. We would use these standards to assess whether the outputs from the operation we controlled were up to the standards selected. The measurement systems should be sufficiently accurate to spot significant deviation from the *norms* or standards chosen. We can then investigate these deviations (sometimes called 'variances'), to discover the reasons for them, so that we can modify the output to bring it to the required standard. There could, however, be a time lag before the corrections can be made.

1.3.4 Non-manufacturing organizations

General Systems Theory (GST) maintains that *all* systems display the kind of characteristics discussed in respect of manufacturing organizations. Thus we can apply the model to a hospital, a college of further education, a travel agency—in fact any business or public sector activity.

All that changes from the basic model of the system is that the inputs and outputs will vary. In the case of an FE college the inputs will include: information, capital, revenue money (from the funding authority), consumables, staff, services, students, teaching materials, and so on; and outputs would include students successfully completing courses (for finished products), information, reputation, etc.

Similarly, changes in the environment (e.g. an increased or decreased demand for existing courses, demands for entirely new courses) disturb the system's equilibrium and the organization reacts by redeploying its resources in terms of teaching staff, rooms, equipment, or even purchasing new equipment or hiring more staff in certain areas, as appropriate.

1.3.5   Interaction with the environment

We can now begin to understand how the organization reacts with its environment. Each of the inputs (we have not really considered yet how many there are) will have the effect of disturbing the equilibrium of the system, which will then react by doing things which it hopes will restore the equilibrium. The following examples will make this clearer.

Rival supermarkets in the High Street may embark on a bitter price war. As soon as store A cuts its prices, the information is quickly passed to the district manager of B who reacts by cutting prices too; this may entail putting advertisements in local papers, putting on a promotion, and repricing the items in the store. A might react to all this with a counter-promotion, and yet more selected price cuts, and so on. Each is trying to achieve an equilibrium where it is taking as great a share of the market as it can cope with.

The effects of the arrival in an engineering company of a large and unexpected order include the disturbance of the ordered life of the system. Because, perhaps, the order cannot be met from stock, the whole company is galvanized into action to restore the situation to more normal levels, where the company is keeping pace with its order book. The sales department will pester the production department to keep to promised delivery dates; the production department in turn will press the purchasing department to obtain the raw materials in the quickest possible time. Extra workers may be needed, in which case the personnel department will telephone advertisements to local papers and Job Centre. The accounts department may be unaware of the customer's credit rating, and put out enquiries to credit rating agencies. Longer term effects could include the recalculating of stock levels of particular raw materials, the purchase of new machinery, the hiring of new workers.

Thus we see the interdependence of the different systems, the company, its suppliers and customers; and their reactions one to another. What is true at this level is also true of the different departments, or sub-systems of the firm.

SUMMARY

In this chapter, we have noted:

1.   Organizations are groups of people working towards a common objective or set of objectives. (It is true some would want to include the things owned by the organization, as well as the people.)

2.   We are surrounded by organizations of all kinds, big and small, formal and informal. Indeed most of us belong to several organizations at the same time.

3.   People have needs or goals, and feel they can fulfil or achieve them better in groups because organizations

   (a)   Enlarge human activities.
   (b)   Satisfy social needs.
   (c)   Save time.
   (d)   Pool and conserve knowledge.
   (e)   Lead to greater efficiency.
   (f)   Provide greater security.

4.   An important classification of organizations is into *formal* and *informal*. *Formal* organizations have a well-defined structure, a definite beginning in time, a long life, definite aims, are joined by people voluntarily (usually) and are characterized by the division of labour, or specialization of their members. *Informal* organizations, are, on the other hand, characterized by a loosely defined structure, vaguely defined beginnings, endings and aims, less conscious membership, and are more flexible and smaller.

5.   Informal organizations can become formal and vice versa.

6.   Informal organizations can exist within formal ones. Such informal organizations are both important and significant.

7.   Business organizations can be classified in one of two ways: By organizational goals:

   (a)   Profit-making: manufacturing, providing a service, or re-selling items at a profit.
   (b)   Non profit-making: social/state service organizations.

   By ownership:

   (a)   Private ownership: sole traders, partnerships, private and public limited companies.
   (b)   Co-operatives.
   (c)   Public sector organizations.
   (d)   Social service organizations.
   (e)   Regulatory organizations.

8.   A *system* is a related group of elements organized for a purpose.

9.   Systems can be classified as:

    (a)   Closed systems—no interaction with environment.

    (b)   Open systems—interaction with environment, by receiving *inputs,* acting upon the inputs (conversion process), and exporting the converted or transported to the environment as outputs; the survival of a system depends upon a continuing receipt of a sufficient number of inputs.

    (c)   Adaptive systems—those which possess a self-adjustive mechanism which enables variations in output to be coped with.

    (d)   Probabilistic systems—those about which only general predictions can be made; with degrees of uncertainty about inputs and outputs.

    (e)   Contrived systems—those constructed by people.

10.   Industrial firms (and other commercial and public sector organizations) are open, adaptive, probabilistic and contrived systems.

11.   Control of a system involves measuring its outputs against predetermined standards, and comparing the two. Variances or differences between the two are noted; and if significant, the adjustments necessary are made by the control element. This process is known as a feedback loop.

12.   Organizations interact, the outputs of one organization forming the inputs to others.

13.   Systems are usually composed of sub-systems, which sub-systems similarly interact with each other.

REVIEW QUESTIONS

1.   What are the basic differences between formal and informal organizations?

2.   Why do people join organizations?

3.   What is meant by the idea of 'specialization' or 'division of work'?

4.   Using the 'ownership' basis of classification, who 'owns' the following: (a) the local town hall; (b) The Post Office; (c) Lloyds TSB Group; (d) a private limited company?

5.   What is meant by the principle of limited liability?

6.   Explain what is meant by the terms: 'inputs', 'conversion process', and 'outputs', in the context of a business organization? Give suitable examples in each case.

7.   What do we mean by 'sub-systems'? Make a list of the sub-systems you can identify in any organizations with which you are familiar, e.g. school, college, firm or club.

8.   Explain the idea of 'feedback'. How useful is 'feedback' in a control process? How does a teacher use feedback when teaching a class?

9.   Compare and contrast open and closed systems. Is a prison a closed system? If so, why?

DISCUSSION TOPICS

1.   Suppose a person told you he did not belong to any organizations whatsoever. If this were a true statement, what sort of person would he be; and what would his life be like?

2.   Discuss the *disadvantages* of belonging to formal organizations.

3.   What do you think are the major goals (or objectives) of the following:

        (a)   The Royal Air Force.
        (b)   Your local football club.
        (c)   Tesco (supermarket chain).
        (d)   A pop group.
        (e)   Ford (car manufacturers).
        (f)   The classes in which you are using this book.

4.   'In the modern world organizations have become larger and more numerous.' Discuss the truth of this statement, and advance reasons for your opinions.

5.   What would happen if a business organization stopped receiving most of its inputs (for example during a postal/telephone strike)? What would happen to the equilibrium of the organization: could it be restored?

6.   In what ways are a college, hospital, a railway and a food supermarket similar as systems (i.e. in terms of the flow of information and/or materials through the systems)? Discuss how the inputs, outputs and conversion processes differ.

ASSIGNMENTS

A1.1   By looking at dictionaries and management textbooks try and find out at least *two* other definitions of organization other than the one used in this book. Compare and contrast their usefulness.

A1.2   Make a list of all the organizations to which you and your fellow class members belong. Besides classifying organizations on your list into *formal* and *informal*, can you find other useful ways of classifying them?

A1.3   Identify a major sub-system of an organization with which you are familiar. Make as complete a list as you can of *all* the inputs, outputs and conversion processes which go on in the sub-system.

Case studies

A1.4   Barbara Smith and Joan Edwards were two friends who met at a local dressmaking class. Barbara soon found she was a skilled maker-up of garments, while Joan discovered she had a talent for designing clothes.

  When the course was over, each found time on her hands, but already they had had several enquiries from other friends and acquaintances for coats and dresses, and from time to time they got together to help each other out. One day, Joan said 'Look here, Barbara, why don't we organize ourselves on a regular basis and try to make some extra cash as well as helping our friends out?' Barbara was a bit doubtful. 'It's true,' she replied, 'I'm quite good at making up, and you've quite a flair for design, but what about keeping accounts, and VAT? And there's another thing, if we're going to do this properly I'll need a new sewing machine.'

  Joan was now less confident: 'I hadn't thought of that—and what do we do when we've run out of orders—I don't see myself as a saleswoman. We'd need help.'

  (a)   What kind of organization exists at present between Barbara and Joan? In what way would the change they discussed enlarge their individual possibilities?

  (b)   Joan and Barbara recognize the value of the division of labour. In addition to selling and book-keeping, what other talents would they either have to buy or develop if they did get started?

A1.5   Last Wednesday was a black day in the board room of Bar Products Ltd, makers of equipment used in hotels and bars throughout the country. A Government Bill had just been published which, if passed, would make it illegal in two years' time for any one to sell draught beer, except through automatic beer dispensing machines, a half pint at a time. Bar Products had been making and selling traditional hand operated pumps for 75 years.

'This will ruin us,' said Alan Brewer, the managing director, 'beer pumps are our major selling line, and now the market will dry up overnight. We'd better begin the meeting by working out the redundancy position.'

'Just a minute, Al' replied Bill Newman the recently appointed technical director, 'this is our chance to make a great deal of money fast—a captive market awaits us if we can design and produce the new pumps on time.'

(a) What will happen to Bar Products if Al's view prevails at the meeting? Why?

(b) If the meeting decides to follow Bill Newman:
   (i) What kinds of changes to the material inputs and outputs of the organization would you expect?
   (ii) Discuss the ways in which the manufacturing and purchasing sub-systems would have to adapt and change to meet the new situation.

2
The Structure of the Organization

The kinds of organization we are going to consider in this chapter are those likely to be encountered by managers and supervisors in their daily work: industrial, business and commercial organizations; the armed forces or the public sector. All of these are, of course, formal organizations—though we must not forget that informal organizations do exist *inside* formal ones.

Before the 20th century, most organizations were smaller and simpler than those of today, so small and simple that the unifying power of one man—the owner manager—was such that he alone made decisions, and the success (or failure) of the whole enterprise depended upon him. Today, even small firms have more than one manager; power is shared, decisions are decentralized. The primary objectives, the tasks undertaken decide the form of the organization: a change in the market-place, a different kind of raw material (substituting plastics for metal for making car heaters, for example), can dictate a change in the organization's form.

Thus, most organizations have developed structures (consciously or unconsciously) to cope with the problems that they face. We must look, therefore, at such structures in more detail.

2.1 THE USE OF MODELS

Models aid understanding. Sometimes the purpose of a model is to *remind* ourselves of something with which we are familiar—a model railway locomotive; sometimes to *assist discovery*—a model aeroplane in a wind tunnel can be used to test various theories about the behaviour of a full-scale aeroplane in flight; and finally, sometimes as *explanation*; to make an idea clearer. Lists of statistics about the sizes, distances and orbital speeds of planets can, with concentrated thought, be transformed into a mental picture of the solar system. However, if all this information is turned into a working model the relationship of time (and perhaps space) becomes much easier to grasp. We say we can 'see' the connections, or the relationships at once.

While it is possible to make *exact* copies of things, models are usually less than exact and are loose in complexity compared with the original. This loss of detail is irrelevant as the usual purpose of the model is to highlight certain, selected aspects of a situation rather than *all* of them. In fact, the human mind ignores the imperfections: our model of the solar system could be full of cogs, wheels, handles, levers and wires, but all the observer looks at are the 'billiard ball' planets circling the 'sun'.

Diagrams and maps are also models, except they are only two-dimensional. As with all models, maps sacrifice complexity to concentrate on a particular aspect: *relief* maps describe the hills and valleys; *road* maps concentrate on the road communication networks; and *weather* maps show fronts, wind speeds and areas of high or low pressure. When we look at organization structure maps, we must realize these, too, are two-dimensional models and they do not illustrate the real factory. On a visit to the factory, you will see people who are moving around performing tasks. However, the casual observer, or newcomer cannot always make sense of what he sees, he fails to understand the relationships that exist between the people working around him and appreciates even less the underlying structure of the organization.

So, although the 'structure map'—we usually call this an 'organization chart'—is very different from the factory's personnel, it does help us to 'see' the whole and how it fits together, more clearly. From one point of view, it could be said the structure exists *apart* from the people, for while a particular employee may leave and be replaced, the job or *position* in the structure remains. Indeed, even if jobs remain unfilled, the organization may well go on functioning.

2.2   ORGANIZATION CHARTS

Organization charts are very similar to the maps we use to plan holiday journeys. Just as maps concentrate mainly on the road network, they concentrate on only a few aspects of the network of communication which exists between various managers and officials in the organization. They often have 'keys', 'legends' or 'conventions' (explanations of the symbols used). Both, of course, are two-dimensional representations of three-dimensional situations.

Maps also come in all sorts of shapes and sizes, have different scales, signs and symbols. So it is with organization charts. Contrary to popular belief, the 'family tree' type of organization chart is not the only kind of chart to be used.

2.2.1   Types of organization charts

As we aim normally to model (or map) only the *formal* structure of the organization, a chart can be seen as a network, and described in spatial terms. Important people can be at the top of the chart, and those seeming to be less important at the bottom. In another version of a chart, the manager, the important person, is shown at the centre, and the subordinates at the circumference of a circle.

The examples of different types of organization charts which follow are all based on either an up-down or left-right relationship, with the exception of the circle charts.

All use a spatial relationship (i.e. a *distance* between) to illustrate differences in rank, power, authority or status.

Basic

The basic relationship is that between superior and subordinate, and usually this is shown *vertically*, as illustrated in Fig. 2.1.

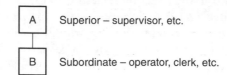

Figure 2.1 Superior/subordinate relationship.

Scalar chain

Most organizations that a manager or supervisor is likely to encounter will have more than two members. Henri Fayol (whom we shall meet in Chapter 3) produced what he called the 'scalar chain', or 'chain of grades or steps', and his chart looked like a triangle without a connecting base line. (See Fig. 2.2.)

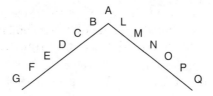

Figure 2.2 Henri Fayol's scalar chain.

This chart looks odd to our eyes; as we have seen, we do not often meet a situation where nearly every manager (i.e. F, E, D, C, B, L, M, N, O, P) has only one subordinate. However it would appear Fayol's chart was even more abstract than the type of charts we use commonly today. It does however help to understand that:

1. Authority and power flow from the top (A) downward.
2. Accountability flows upward.

Authority is the right or power to make decisions or give instructions or orders. *Accountability* is the obligation to give an account of the stewardship of the authority given, to a superior. Such superiors in turn are accountable to *their* superiors. This reporting, or accounting chain is what Fayol refers to as the scalar chain, and some contemporary writers the 'job task pyramid'.

The 'T' chart

The job task pyramid idea becomes a little clearer if we use a 'T' chart, the most widely used and understood map of the organization.

In its most basic form it consists of a series of inverted letter 'T's (see Fig. 2.3). (Taking a ruler, we can quite quickly draw a pyramid shape around the chart.)

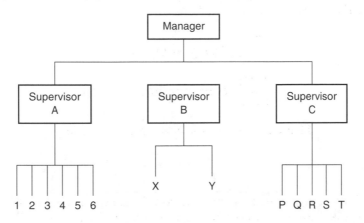

Figure 2.3 Basic 'T' chart or job task pyramid.

Of course, we will only get a result like this if the three supervisors are of pretty equal status, and the numbers of staff each control are similar. Even in Fig. 2.3, there is some doubt about the perfect pyramid; and if we transferred supervisor B to the outside, to replace either A or C, the 'pyramid' shape becomes somewhat distorted.

Wheel charts

Sometimes it is more useful to indicate, in addition to a superior/subordinate relationship, a geographical one. Consider a firm with a head office in Birmingham and factories in London, Bristol, Liverpool, Glasgow, Newcastle and Ipswich. We could envisage such an organization as a *wheel* with the group production director (A) in the centre, and the factories at the ends of the various spokes.

The form of the wheel would not be exactly geographical (the well-known map of the London Underground is neither strictly 'geographical' nor to scale), but would represent the 'structure' in a very appropriate way (see Fig. 2.4).

Modified 'T' charts

There are many different ways of setting out relationships, and we are at liberty to combine 'T' charts with wheel charts (or any other variety) (see Fig. 2.5).

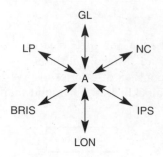

Figure 2.4 Wheel chart.

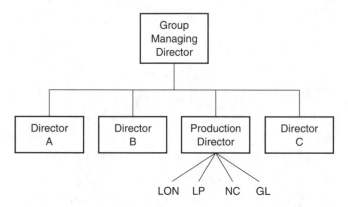

Figure 2.5 Modified 'T' chart (1).

The implication here is that London, Liverpool, Newcastle and Glasgow *do not* communicate with each other: had they been expressed as illustrated in Fig. 2.6. then we might feel that London, Liverpool, etc. *do* communicate.

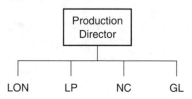

Figure 2.6 Modified 'T' chart (2).

Circular (concentric) charts

Finally, in this brief survey, we come to the *circular* chart, a slightly different idea from the wheel or circle chart (Fig. 2.7). Here we place the top person in the centre, and jobs at different levels are shown in concentric circles surrounding the central job.

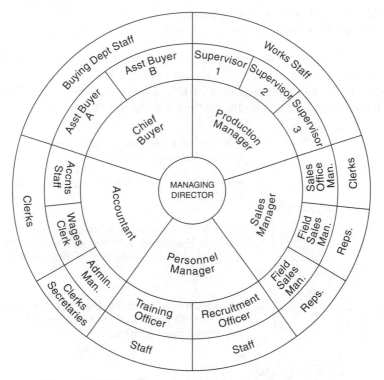

Figure 2.7 Circular or concentric organization chart.

The spatial implication here is the nearer the centre you are, the greater your position, power and authority; conversely, those at the outside of the circle have lower status and position (see Fig. 2.10).

This brief survey does not cover all the possibilities. You can use any device you like to 'picture' or model the organization, always provided the chosen method is:

(a) appropriate;
(b) accurate (about the aspects to be shown);
(c) easily understood.

However, as long as we realize that charts should *describe,* not *prescribe*, and that there are inherent shortcomings in every model, we can make much fruitful use of organization charts.

2.2.2 Essential features of organization charts

Charts are used to show:

(a) the whole business;
(b) the individual constituent companies or divisions of the whole;

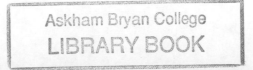

(c) the departments or sections in a company;
(d) the details of one department or section only.

Compared with a map, the first could be a map of the world, the second the British Isles, the third counties, and finally a street plan of a town.

At present there are no international or BSI standards covering the symbols used, but certain conventions are normally followed, as is shown in Fig. 2.8.

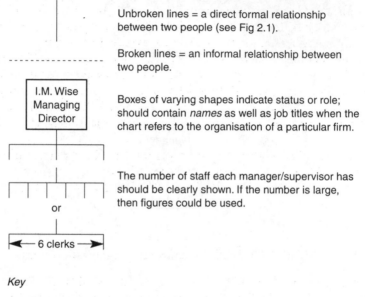

Figure 2.8 Conventional symbols used for organization charts.

We have already noted that models often highlight only a few aspects of the thing they model. So it should be with organization charts: too much detail or too many symbols, lines or colours could confuse rather than aid understanding.

2.3   TYPES OF ORGANIZATIONAL STRUCTURE

Now we have seen how organization charts can be used to model organizational structures, we must next consider what kinds of structures the charts attempt to model. As with much in management, it is dangerous to set everything under neat headings, and although we shall review some basic structures, any given organization may exhibit any or even all of the structures at the same time. A further difficulty we have to overcome is that not everyone is agreed on the definitions used for the basic structures.

2.3.1 Line organization

Joan Woodward[1] carried out of a study of a number of firms in Essex in the early 1960s. She came to the conclusion that each firm had two kinds of function: *task* and *element*.

1. Task functions. These, she maintained, were those functions vital to the achievement of the organization's *primary* objectives. Most firms would have four such functions: production, sales, accounts/finance, and research and development. (There could be differences in firms like transport contractors, and in those where there is no production, for example in a wholesale warehouse.)
2. Element functions. Functions of lesser importance such as quality control or personnel are not in existence to meet the primary objectives, but rather to *help* by acting as 'back-ups' to task functions. By taking, for example, inspection problems away from direct production, quality control offers a service; the services the personnel department offers are too numerous to mention here.

'Line organization' is that part of the organization which relates to task functions. 'Line managers' are the managers of task functions: works managers, chief accountants, managing directors and sales managers would all, under this definition, be line managers. A simple form of line organization is shown in Fig. 2.9.

2.3.2 Line and staff organization

The first problem with 'line and staff' is the use of the word 'staff'. Sometimes it means the whole labour force of a firm, but more often it means that part of the labour force which has better terms of employment, is paid monthly rather than weekly, and has a

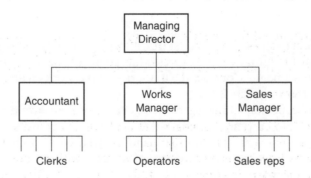

Figure 2.9 Line organization

---

[1] Woodward, J. (1965) *Industrial Organization: Theory and Practice.* Oxford University Press.

pension partly provided by the firm. 'Being on the staff' is an expression of status, if not of extra income.

'Staff' in 'line and staff' does not mean either of these things. Staff personnel are, in fact, people employed in the 'element' functions, such as personnel or quality control officers, or as special helpers to managers or supervisors. Figure 2.10 illustrates this definition.

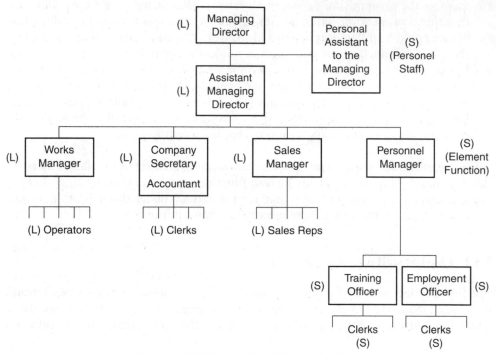

Figure 2.10 Line and staff organization.

Another explanation of 'line' and 'staff', differing from Woodward's analysis of task and element functions, can be expressed in terms of the *authority* vested in the manager of a department.[2] Consider the authority of the works manager and the personnel manager shown in Fig. 2.10.

While, of course, personnel managers are in charge of their own departments, their authority is limited to carrying out policy laid down by the board and/or the managing director; works managers, on the other hand, may have wide executive powers and may make their own decisions on a variety of matters without necessarily referring such decisions to the managing director.

---

[2] Bullock, Lord and Stallybrass, O. (1977) *Fontana Dictionary of Modern Thought*. London: Fontana: A useful book for all interested in science and technology which defined 'line positions' as those in the chain of command for decision and action. A line manager is part of the direct line from managing director to shop floor.

2.3.3 Functional authority

The matter is, however, complicated by the fact that certain managers (usually 'staff' managers) actually have and exercise authority *outside* their own departments. While such authority is limited and refers to specific areas, it does affect the line manager. A clear-cut example would be the firm's safety officer, who might walk through a workshop and find an operator using a machine which was, in the safety officer's opinion, in a dangerous condition. The safety officer, without reference to a supervisor, could order the worker to stop work and switch off the offending machine. But there the authority would end. The safety officer could not instruct the worker to start another job or another machine. Similarly, the personnel department may have authority to discipline workers when certain grades of punishment—dismissal, suspension, etc.—are involved. Such authority, once the prerogative of the manager, is now transferred to the specialist. Perhaps we should call 'functional authority' 'specialist authority'.

2.3.4 Line and staff problems

Managers and supervisors quite rightly feel that the employment of such specialist staff and departments does take away authority, the more so when certain 'staff' personnel are introduced into their departments (from quality control, for example). The fact that personnel and other specialists have invented their own jargon does not help.

Some managers are eccentric, wilful or just non-conformist, and while being excellent servants to the organization and 'good' managers, they may bend a few rules or fail to fill in the right forms, achieving the right ends by totally unorthodox means. The specialist who works 'to the book' or likes to see everything run exactly may object to the irregular behaviour of such managers, and even report them to top management.

Another cause of friction is that, rightly or wrongly, line managers often consider themselves (and their departments) as being 'more important' than the 'staff' managers, who cause overheads, because the line staff are engaged in accomplishing the organization's primary objectives. Conversely, the specialist (functional) staff are becoming ever more qualified and may be culturally distinct from the line managers, particularly if the latter have been promoted from the shop floor.

2.3.5 Delegation

Delegation is an important concept, and very much related to the organization structure. If we look at a typical organization chart, we see the seemingly all-powerful managing director at the top, but we must quickly realize that he or she cannot take all the decisions and do all the work: that is what the managers are for. However, subordinates cannot do what is required of them without the necessary authority and power to act.

Delegation, then, is where one person, A, gives someone else, B, the power and authority to perform work or to give orders to others on behalf of A. B accepts the power and authority, but in return also accepts the need to justify his or her steward-ship, to 'be accountable' to A in due course. Delegation is usually *downwards,* although in a trade union it could be argued that the power of the branch (and other) officers is delegated *upwards* by the members.

In Fig. 2.11 one can see the chain of delegation, starting with the shareholders, who are the owners of the business, but who in many companies are too numerous, too widely dispersed to take decisions about the day-to-day running of the firm. The shareholders *delegate* the running of the business, both policy-making and the implementation of policies to a committee, called the board of directors (all, of course, shareholders), but require the board to be *accountable* at the company annual general meeting.

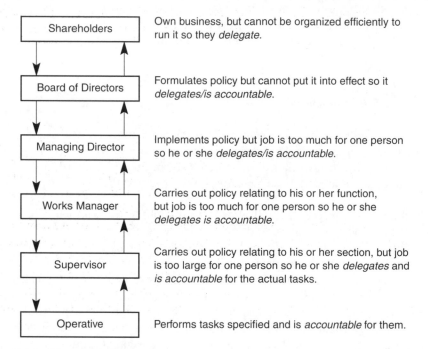

Figure 2.11 Chain of delegation. *Note.* Downward arrows = delegation; upward arrows = accountability.

The board decide on policy, but *delegate* the carrying out of the policy to the man-aging director, who, besides being a shareholder and director, is usually a full time employee of the company. However, even in a relatively small firm, the task of super-vising every job, and making decisions in sales, purchasing and production, is too much for one person to do effectively. So the managing director *delegates* the running of the separate functions of the company to senior managers (only the works manager is shown here in Fig. 2.11) who take upon themselves the job of carrying out company policy in their function (usually called a department). The senior managers, however, must *account* to the managing director for all the decisions they take.

In the same way the works manager is unable to oversee every job done in the factory, and will need to *delegate* to junior managers (supervisors), who supervise, say, 25 operatives, the task of running a particular section, for example a press shop. The supervisor is, in turn, *accountable* to the works manager (see the next section).

At the end of the chain are the operatives. The supervisor delegates to them the actual performance of various tasks in the shop. In turn, the operatives are *accountable* to the supervisor for the work they turn out.

Delegation is practised much less than it should be; some managers are insecure, and feel that others may do jobs better than they can, if given the chance; others perhaps genuinely believe their subordinates are incapable of doing certain jobs, and only the 'big white chief' can cope. Inevitable consequences flow from a serious failure to delegate: at best, an enormous workload leading to inefficiency on a large scale; at worst, a nervous breakdown or an ulcer; and a demoralized, untrained workforce.

2.3.6 Accountability

Authority and accountability must go hand in hand (see Fig. 2.11). A fair system demands that every manager or supervisor should be answerable for his or her actions. People given authority without accountability can become either ruthless dictators, acting on unchallenged whims, or lazy and uncaring in their work. Conversely, people given responsibility without authority either do nothing, or assume authority they do not have. Both situations are obviously unsatisfactory.

Just because a manager delegates a job to someone else, it does not mean the manager ceases to be accountable for the carrying out of the job. For example, imagine a supervisor who is responsible, in addition to organizing production, for the security of his department. As the supervisor knows a meeting he is to attend is likely to last until late, he deputizes Tom Smith, a charge hand, to close the windows, lock the filing cabinets, and see the workshop door is shut at the finish of work. Late that night, an intruder gains entry, and makes off with important documents as well as loose tools.

Tom Smith has failed in his job, and is accountable for this failure. However, the supervisor is still accountable in turn to his boss, and cannot evade the issue by saying 'It's Tom's fault!'

2.3.7 Spans of control

By 'span of control' we mean the number of people reporting *directly* to one superior. This number can vary enormously from one department to another, from firm to firm and from industry to industry (Fig. 2.12).

How many people can a manager or supervisor control? Unfortunately, the answer is not simple. The limits are set by a number of different factors, all of which are important.

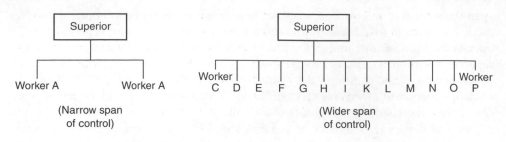

Figure 2.12 Narrow and wider spans of control.

The nature of the job

This is a significant factor. If the job is relatively simple, and most employees in the department are doing the *same* job, then larger numbers can be handled easily. On the other hand, if the jobs are complex, fewer people can be supervised effectively.

Imagine a managing director with 25 senior managers reporting directly to him or her, all with vastly different areas of work and with vastly different problems! In contrast, think of a manufacturing department where all the employees have been with the company a long time and know the job and the machines; in this situation a supervisor could comfortably cope with such a number.

The time available

The less time managers actually have in which to manage, the fewer people they can control effectively. This applies where managers have special duties which frequently take them away from their nominal job, or when they run more than one department.

The nature of the employees

The amount of experience, training and expertise possessed by the workforce is crucial. New entrants, untrained personnel and inexperienced workers all need extra care and attention. Effective control depends to a great extent on the nature of the employees.

How many employees?

Many writers on management have expressed opinions on the correct number of subordinates a manager should have. In 1937 V. Graicunas suggested that six direct subordinates could be effectively supervised; in 1938 L. Urwick was more cautious, with five or six at the most. A famous general, Sir Ian Hamilton, maintained that four was the ideal figure. From what we have already considered, such statements are questionable, to say the least. The total situation dictates the span of control.

Joan Woodward found South Essex firms in the mid-1950s with spans of control for the first-line supervisors which varied from seven to 90.

Assuming, however, that the ideal number could be determined, a manager could be faced with more subordinates than the ideal (too wide a span), or alternatively, fewer subordinates than the ideal (too narrow a span). Too wide a span entails lack of control. Too narrow a span can lead to a waste of personnel, too many grades of staff and more levels of communication. Both situations lead to increased costs.

2.4   SYSTEMS DIAGRAMS

So far we have used the organization chart model to discuss and describe organizations. Systems diagrams such as those encountered in Chapter I can not only highlight different aspects of static organization structure but can also indicate *movement* or *flow,* this enabling complex and interrelated situations to be understood in broad outline. (See Fig. 2.13.)

By tracing the inputs and outputs of each department the systems diagram can construct a picture of the interreactions throughout the organization. This picture can be studied objectively and used to enhance the *control* of the system.

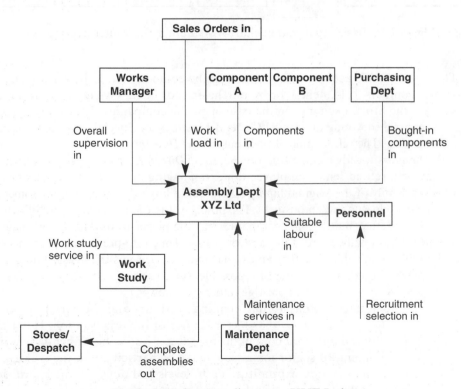

Figure 2.13 Systems diagram—XYZ Ltd.

2.5   THE ORGANIZATION OF A TYPICAL FIRM

Talking about a 'typical' firm is rather like talking about the 'average' person; we are dealing with something which does not exist, but for our purposes we will designate a medium-sized engineering firm, with a factory and offices on one site, as typical. Even so straightforward a choice could lead to a confusing chart, so for the sake of clarity, we will first look at an overall view of the divisions, or departments, and then consider each department separately. (See Fig. 2.14.)

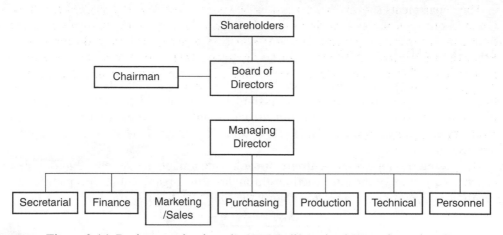

Figure 2.14 Basic organization chart—Medium-sized Manufacturing Co.

The *Shareholders* acquire their interest in the company either by buying shares when the company is launched, or by purchasing (or being given) shares at a later stage—via the Stock Exchange in the case of public companies. They exercise their right of control by voting at Annual General Meetings, or Special General Meetings of the company. They elect some of their number as *Directors.*

The *Directors* together constitute the *Board of Directors.* They elect a Chairman, who may be a retired senior employee (an ex-managing director), a member of the controlling family (if the original family still retains a large shareholding), or someone with considerable standing in business. The power of the *Chairman* is often difficult to determine or define, but in some companies has the power to dismiss the Managing Director. (Occasionally, there is in addition a President, Life-president, or Honorary President. This individual is either an ex-chairman, or perhaps the actual founder of the company who takes little interest—possibly due to age—in the daily running of the company. Such a post carries prestige rather than power.)

The board delegates the day-to-day running of affairs and the carrying out of policy to the *Managing Director*, the chief executive of the organization. He or she has great authority and influence both in the boardroom and in his or her daily work. He or she will appoint all senior managers, make or participate in the making of major decisions and sanction expenditure up to levels laid down by the board. Job security is often greater than that of other directors: the job may have a five- or ten-year contract, with redress for early termination of contract. Typically, the Managing Director is either an employee who has been with the company some years and worked his or her way up, or a nominee of a dominant group among the shareholders, or someone appointed from outside the company.

Clearly, the relationship between the Chairman and the Managing Director is crucial, the Chairman acting as advisor and confidant to the Managing Director. In some companies both posts are filled by the same person: or alternatively there can be a Chairman, and two (or even more) Joint Managing Directors.

The departments shown reporting to the Managing Director in Fig. 2.14 are those found in our typical, medium-sized firm. Students may find their own organization is different—a separate organization and methods/work study section, a Business Data Processing (or Electronic Data Processing) Department; or there may be even a Research and Development Department distinct from the Technical side. The permutations are endless.

2.5.1 The secretarial function

The secretarial function is headed by the *Company Secretary.*

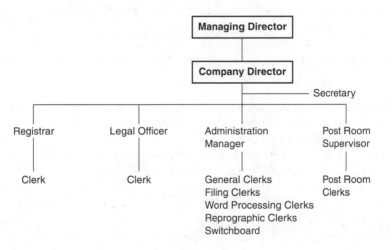

Figure 2.15 Secretarial function.

By law, every limited company must have a Company Secretary whose functions as laid down in various Acts of Parliament are somewhat restricted to the legal and financial sides of the business, but in recent times the Company Secretary's department has taken over other administrative duties. These include:

1. Ensuring enough capital is available for the company.
2. Recording share transactions (through the Registrar).
3. Matters relating to company meetings.
4. Matters relating to shareholders.

5. Legal matters.
6. General administration, office organization.
7. Provision of services (telephones, reception, reprographics, etc.).
8. Compiling or supervising compilation of books of account, statistics, financial statements for the board.
9. Policy statements.
10. Distribution (including transport department).

The Secretary acts as secretary to board meetings, but unless elected a director is *not* a member of the board. (Note: in smaller companies the Company Secretary may even fulfil other roles, such as transport manager, etc.)

2.5.2 Finance/accounting function

The finance/accounting function is headed by the *Accountant* (almost certainly these days with a professional qualification). (See Fig. 2.16.)

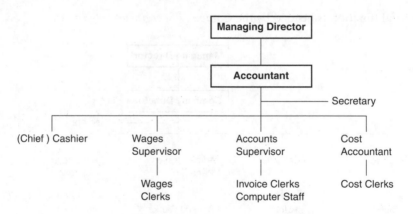

Figure 2.16 Accounting function.

The Accountant's responsibilities include:

1. Financial accounting (the 'book-keeping' aspect).
2. Cost accounting (keeping a check on the costs of running the firm, especially the manufacturing process).
3. Management accounting (provision of financial information on the past, present and possible future activities of the firm—budgeting etc.).
4. General financial management, including the provision of adequate finance to run the business; credit control.
5. Wages (although in most organizations the actual calculations and payment arrangements will be computerized).

(Note: in smaller firms the Accountant may also be the Company Secretary.)

2.5.3 Marketing/sales function

The marketing/sales function (see Fig. 2.17) is headed by the *Marketing Manager* (increasingly a person with a professional qualification). Some companies regard this function as so vital that the title is often *Marketing Director*.

Figure 2.17 Marketing function.

It must be clearly understood that the precise allocation of responsibilities in the marketing/sales function varies enormously from company to company (indeed, some firms do not have a marketing manager at all—the Sales Manager is supreme). Some companies do their own advertising, others use agencies etc. Basically, however, the marketing function is concerned with bargaining or selling, contracting, supplying; and generating, stimulating, facilitating and charging correctly for such transactions.

Typical responsibilities include:

1. Market research (trying to establish what the customer wants and what the present state of the market is).
2. Advertising, and sales promotion.
3. Sales, and the management of the sales force, both at home and abroad, including: territory planning, establishing commission rates, promoting sales, dealing with complaints.
4. Sales administration, order processing, estimating, quotations, possibly invoicing, compiling sales statistics.

2.5.4 The purchasing function

The purchasing (or buying) function (see Fig.2.18) is headed by the *Chief Buyer* (sometimes called 'Head Buyer', or 'Purchasing Manager' or even 'Chief Purchasing Officer').

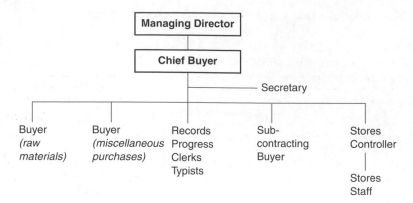

Figure 2.18 Purchasing function.

Often the purchasing function is an independent department, buying materials and equipment for *all* aspects of the business, as shown here. In some firms, however, the production department or division would include purchasing as a part of its province. Raw materials purchasing will often call for great skill and knowledge, especially where prices (say in the metal market) fluctuate rapidly and erratically. In addition, consumable items, such as oils, rags, drill bits, etc., used in production and office equipment and stationery will be required. The purchasing function may also include subcontracting the work that the company cannot undertake to other companies.

In some organizations the stores function is either completely independent, or comes under the production function (the argument here being that as the stores in the main is there to serve production, production should control stores). In our example, we see the stores controller reporting to the Chief Buyer, which does make sense where a close liaison is essential between purchasing and storage of expensive materials.

2.5.5 The production function

The production (or manufacturing) function is headed by an executive who could be variously titled *production director, production manager, works director* or *works manager,* depending upon the size of the company. Where there is a production director or manager, his or her deputy could be called works manager.

The organization of production is so varied from firm to firm, or industry to industry, that it is impossible to describe a 'standard' organization layout. To give some idea of the possibilities, the following three examples cover a medium-sized engineering firm, a 'process' manufacturing company and a small, specialist set-up. (It must never be forgotten that the majority of manufacturing organizations employ fewer than 50 people.)

Medium-sized firm

The production function illustrated in Fig. 2.19 is split into two. The works branch, headed by the works director, is responsible for:

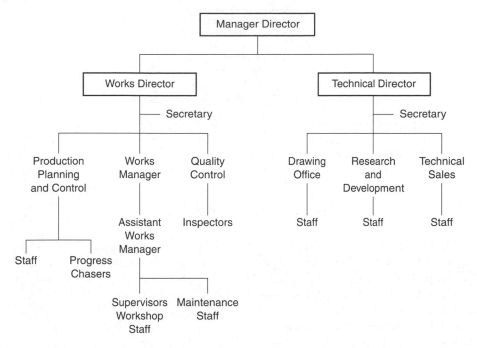

Figure 2.19 Production function: medium-sized engineering firm.

(a) production planning;
(b) production control (including staff who investigate the progress of various orders—'progress chasers');
(c) production departments (machine shops, assembly departments, foundries, heat treatment rooms, etc.);
(d) maintenance (of buildings, plant and machinery, fixtures and fittings);
(e) quality control (usually *not* under the direct supervision of the works manager).

The technical director heads those departments which give a *technical* service to production.

Process manufacturing company

The production function illustrated in Fig. 2.20 is allied to design, maintenance, quality control and stores. The production manager in this case is restricted to the three major production processes: cutting, sewing and finishing.

Small firm (special orders, small runs)

The small firm illustrated in Fig. 2.21 is typical of a great many in the UK, particularly in areas such as the South East of England and the West Midlands. The

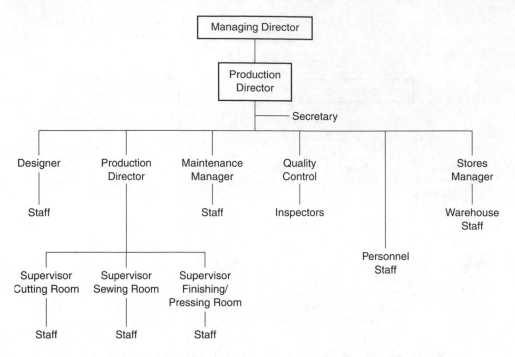

Figure 2.20 Production function: process manufacturing (textile industry).

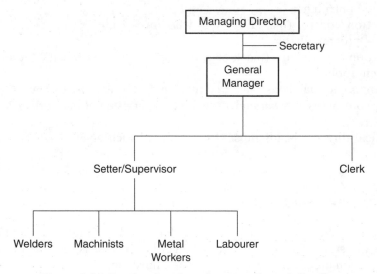

Figure 2.21 Production function: small specialist firm.

general manager not only oversees the workshop but often acts as a sales manager as well.

The workforce of 10–15 employees includes a supervisor/setter who keeps control of the shop floor. There are welders, sheet metal workers and machinists, though it would be expected that all would be able to tackle the others' jobs, as the situation demanded. One general labourer would be needed for cleaning, carrying, etc. The whole emphasis is on flexibility.

2.5.6 The personnel function

The personnel function is covered in detail in Unit III. It is normally headed by a Personnel Manager, or rather more rarely by a Personnel Director. See Fig. 2.22.

Figure 2.22 Personnel function.

In some organizations, the responsibility for industrial relations is placed on the personnel department, but in others, senior managers prefer to set the policy and to participate in the bargaining, using personnel staff in an advisory capacity.

2.6 THE STRUCTURE OF NON-MANUFACTURING ORGANIZATIONS

Basically, the structure of non-manufacturing organizations does not differ from the model we have already examined. The major differences lie in the emphasis given to the *functions*, or to their absence. A wholesale warehouse will have no production function, but a highly-developed stores function. A flying school takes the training function and translates it into a major production-style activity, though it is people (trainees) who are going through the conversion process, rather than, physical products. Even if we take a District Council, we meet the familiar functions of sales (recreational facilities, for example), purchasing, administration, finance/accounts, personnel, as well as specialist ones such as planning, housing and public health. A military base has a basic function such as maintaining aircraft, or training, but again needs supplies, money to run it, an administrative staff, and so on.

Local government provides an interesting contrast to the earlier model. Instead of shareholders, we have electors, who elect councillors instead of directors. The full council corresponds to the board of directors, which in turn delegates responsibility to standing committees. However, in some instances the standing committees will only *recommend* rather than make final decisions. Figure 2.23 shows the committee structure.

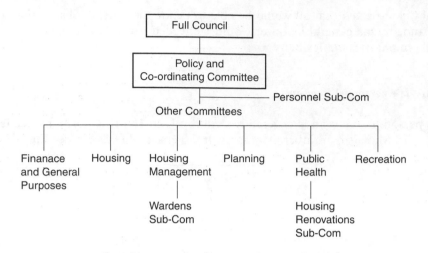

Figure 2.23 District Council committee structure.

These committees are serviced by council employees. Figure 2.24 shows a possible management structure.

Chief Executive

Chief Executive Department	Finance	Technical Services	Planning	Environmental Health	Housing
Legal	Accountancy	Building services	Development control	Pollution	Housing management
Personnel	Council tax	Engineering	Local plan	Food hygiene	Lettings
Information technology	Housing benefit	Leisure facilities	Conservation architect	Health & safety	Administration
Administration	Audit	Building control	Administration	Waste management	
	Administration	Direct labour organization		Administration	
		Administration			

Figure 2.24 District Council office management structure.

These officers are responsible for the day-to-day running of the various services provided. They attend the committee meetings, advise the councillors, and carry out the decisions, plans, and instructions of the committees. The precise structure and duties of the committees are largely dictated by the responsibilities laid upon the Council by an Act of Parliament, and of course County and Town Councils will have differences of function because of this.

A different emphasis again is seen in many private sector service organizations. As in the example (Fig. 2.25) below, it is the service being offered, rather than a production function, which features strongly.

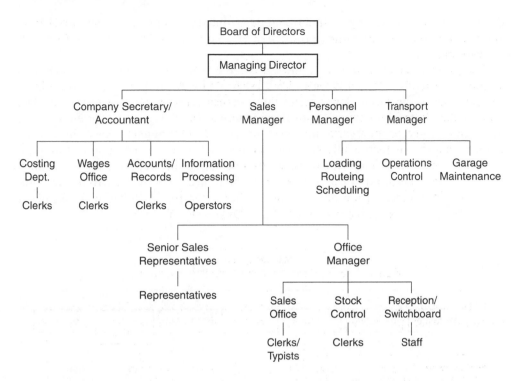

Figure 2.25 Organization chart, road transport and distribution operators.

The Company Secretary and Accountant functions are merged, and in this firm the computerized operations are central under the Accountant. The Sales Manager is responsible not only for seeking new business, but also for administering the internal sales effort. In addition, stock control and some general services (with a high sales content) come under this executive. The transport manager oversees the provision of the haulage and distribution services offered by the firm, both in respect of planning and control. The personnel function is also represented (by just one person in this case).

No special purchasing or technical functions are to be found in this example. (Capital equipment purchases are usually agreed between the executive concerned and the Managing Director in consultation with the Accountant.)

2.7 MATRIX ORGANIZATIONS

The beginnings of (formalized) matrix organization structure can be traced to the aerospace industries, where it was developed for tackling specific projects. Today it can be used for such purposes as new product development; for use in the first year after a take over; or the installation of new plant. The essential idea is the formation of a *team*, sometimes called a 'project team' or 'task force' whose members are drawn from a wide variety of functional departments—technical/design, marketing finance, purchasing, personnel, production etc.—under the leadership of a project, or team manager.

The project manager aims to achieve a specific task within a given time (say two years) and usually within a given budget. He does this by attempting to co-ordinate the activities of functional departments through their representatives on the team. The team make all decisions (except those having implications outside the original remit) and agree to accept the overall authority of the project manager—even though the team manager may technically have less seniority or status in the organization than some members. Team members, however, still 'belong' to the departments from which they were seconded, and at the conclusion of the project may well return to their previous role. A representation of this state of affairs (see Fig. 2.26 below) looks like a mathematical matrix, hence the name 'Matrix Organization'.

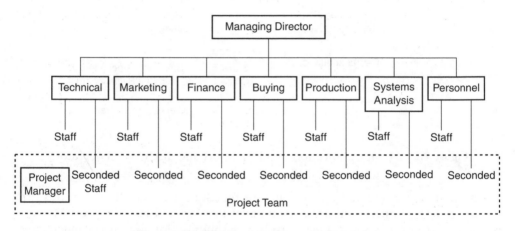

Figure 2.26 Matrix structure—project team.

Many problems can emerge using such a structure (for example two or more 'bosses' for a given employee), especially where there are clear departmental boundaries and rivalries. Experience has shown, however, that for a limited period with a limited task, it enables projects to be completed more quickly and effectively. Staff development is a bonus.

A later development of matrix structures was to have, as it were, long-lasting, almost permanent project teams built into the organization. We can for example imagine a detergent manufacturing organization with *product* (as opposed to *project*) managers responsible for their particular brand from start to finish, from the ordering of the raw materials to the final marketing and distribution. This type of management calls for an even higher set of skills than project team management. Product managers must be able to negotiate with line managers for production capacity share, or advertising finance for example,. and be in competition with other product managers. Some organizations have a regional-based matrix structure.

There are even some colleges of further education who have adopted or are considering some kind of matrix structure to cope with new college-wide courses, where keeping to existing departmental boundaries could possibly be a disadvantage. Changeover periods are likely to be difficult and uncertain but much greater flexibility or resource usage *could* be the result.

SUMMARY

1.   Present day organizations are more complex than earlier ones, resulting in a sharing or delegation, or decentralization of power and authority. The way in which the power is decentralized is reflected in the organization's structure, although external influences will affect the final form.

2.   Models are useful aids to understanding, but often, and deliberately so, are not exact copies of that which they model. They sacrifice complexity (detail) in order to concentrate on particular aspects.

3.   Maps are also models concentrating on particular aspects of the world. Maps of organization structures exist but they are usually called 'organization charts'. These help to throw light on the formal relationship between functions, departments and individuals in the organization.

4.   Various ways of presenting organization structures exist—Fayol's scalar chain, the 'T' chart, wheel and circle, and various modifications of these. A concentric or circular chart shows power at the centre, for example.

5.   Charts are used to show the whole enterprise, individual companies, divisions or departments. However, they should be kept as simple as possible to avoid confusion.

6.   Organization charts are useful when considering the work of an organization: the investigations needed to draw an accurate chart can reveal problems, show areas of overlap and reveal inequalities in staff members.

7.   However, there are drawbacks: such charts are static 'snapshots', and unless constantly updated, quickly become inaccurate. They can be taken too literally, and can be taken to indicate sharp demarcation lines in responsibilities; they can even upset staff if charts show the truth about people's real status. Only job titles and names are given: the full nature of the job is not indicated.

8.   We can, when looking at organization structures distinguish between 'task functions'—basic to the organization—and 'element functions'—those of lesser importance. 'Line' managers are those managers of 'task' functions, in one view.

9.   'Staff' (in our context) means people employed in 'element' functions, such as personnel.

10.   Another viewpoint is that managers with power to act on their own are 'line' managers; those who have to refer for guidance to higher management to go beyond certain limits are 'staff' personnel.

11.   Some specialist personnel have special powers—'functional authority' related to their job—which enables them to exercise authority in departments other than their own; the Safety Officer is one example.

12.   Conflict can occur between 'line' and 'staff' departments where:

   (a) A line manager's authority seems threatened.
   (b) A line manager has an unorthodox approach.
   (c) Questions of departmental status arise.

13.   Delegation is the giving of power and authority to another, to carry out functions or perform work, or give orders to a third party. Delegation is usually *downwards*.

14.   In a company, power originally lies with the owners—the shareholders. It is delegated downwards to supervisors in a series of steps:

   (a) Shareholders to the Board of Directors.
   (b) Directors to the Managing Director.
   (c) Managing Director to the Senior Executives.
   (e) Senior Executives to the Middle/Junior Management.

15.   However, the receipt of power and authority renders the recipient accountable for what he does with that authority. Authority and accountability are inseparable.

16.   The number of people reporting to one superior directly—the 'span of control', as it is called—cannot be laid away down precisely. The limits to any supervisor's 'span of control' are:

   (a) The supervisor's ability.
   (b) The nature of the job.
   (c) Time available for supervision.
   (d) The nature of the employees.
   (e) The nearness of the work group.

17.   Suggestions have however been made for the maximum span of control: four, five, six and eight have been advocated. In practice, much larger spans have been identified, up to 90.

18.   Taking any individual situation, too wide a span leads to a lack of control: too narrow a span to increased cost, and communications problems.

19.   Systems diagrams can be used to help describe organization structures.

20.   The structure of a manufacturing organization normally includes the following functions: secretarial, finance, marketing/sales, purchasing, production, technical, personnel.

21.   The Board elects a Chairman to conduct meetings (who often has prestige or influence rather than power), a Managing Director to manage the day-to-day affairs of the company, and to whom the various functions (both line and staff) report.

22.   By law, every limited company is required to appoint a Company Secretary to deal with legal matters, matters relating to shareholders, company meetings, but in addition, particularly in smaller organizations, the company secretary might well deal with general administration, of office services, reception, transport, etc.

23.   The Accountant (usually professionally qualified) controls the financial/accounting function, which includes 'keeping the books'—an historical record of money transactions; forecasting the future financial position of the company (by preparing appropriate budgets), as well as the general financial management of such activities as wages preparation, credit control, etc.

24.   The marketing function, controlled by a Marketing Manager (or Director), is concerned with sales, contracts or bargains. Making sales, promoting them, ensuring the whole selling and distribution process runs smoothly are the basic activities. They are accomplished with the help of such techniques as market research, sales promotion, and by back-up activities—order processing, quotations, estimating and general sales administration.

25.   Purchasing (or buying), headed by the Chief Buyer/Head Buyer/Purchasing Manager, ensures that raw materials required for production, consumable items used in production, and other purchases are made effectively.

26.   Production—or the manufacturing—function, headed by a Production Director/Production Manager/Works Manager, etc., can often be found divided into a Works sub-function on the one hand, and a Technical sub-function on the other. The Works control the actual manufacturing processes, the machinery and work people: the Technical sub-function furnishes the back-up services such as provision of drawings, the research and

development of new products and services (often including pre-production activities), and the Technical sales force.

27.   The personnel function basically covers the following activities: manpower planning; recruitment and selection; training; health and safety; wages; welfare and statistics.

28.   Other non-manufacturing organizations have the same basic structure: mostly the differences are in emphasis. Common to most such organizations are administrative, purchasing, financial, personnel, and in place of production, some service functions.

29.   An additional organization form is the *matrix* structure, which runs across normal departmental boundaries. Based initially on teams of seconded personnel from existing departments, it furthers the progress of a particular project, deciding what is to be done. A later development is a product (or sometimes regional) based matrix with managers who have across-the-board responsibilities for a particular product or region.

REVIEW QUESTIONS

1.   What is meant by a 'model'? Why do we use models when they are not exact copies of the original?

2.   Why are maps models? What do we call maps of the structure of organizations? What do we use such maps for?

3.   Explain the differences between a 'T' chart, a circular chart, and a wheel chart. Could we use one only, two or all three to represent the sales (outside selling) organization of a company? Explain your answer.

4.   What are the advantages and disadvantages of organization charts?

5.   Distinguish between 'line' and 'staff' personnel. What is functional authority?

6.   Explain the meaning of the following terms:

   (a)   Delegation
   (b)   Span of control
   (c)   Authority and accountability.

7.   Describe the responsibilities of the following functions:

      (a) Secretarial
      (b) Marketing
      (c) Personnel

8.   Describe the relationship between council committees and council officers.

9.   What is a systems diagram of the firm?

10.   What functions are basic to most organizations?

DISCUSSION TOPICS

1.   Discuss the value and the use of the following models:

      (a)   The architect's model of a new office block.
      (b)   A plan of the office block's ground floor.
      (c)   The purchasing function organization chart.

      Does each explain the total situation? Do you agree that taken together they explain more than they do individually?

2.   Is there a justification for distinguishing between 'task' functions and 'element' functions?

3.   Discuss the claim that the maximum number of people one manager can control satisfactorily is four. How many, in fact, do you think any one person *can* be responsible for, given the right set of conditions?
      Would spans of control be narrow or wide in an assembly department; in a clerical section; in a classroom; on a parade ground, or in a data processing (computer) section? Can you come to any conclusions based on your answer?

ASSIGNMENTS

A2.1   (a) Prepare an organization chart of the organization for which you work, setting out the principal functions.
       (b) Prepare an organization chart of the division or department in which you work, setting out the job titles and present occupants. (Full-time students are to carry out the assignment using their college or school as the basis.)

A2.2   Take any function in your organization, and describe its responsibilities, objectives and the type of personnel employed (qualifications required, etc.).

A2.3   Visit, by arrangement beforehand, a local firm, supermarket or department store, for which you do *not* work, endeavour to prepare an organization chart of the various functions.

   Compare the results of this assignment with what you know about your own organization.

   (a) Is the structure different basically?
   (b) What differences are there, if any?
   (c) Account for the differences.

Case studies

A2.4   Tobias Phibber, Technical Director of Truth Drugs Ltd, was very disturbed when I called on him last week. He told me of the problems in the Research and Development Department. 'These boffins are all in the clouds. We've got about forty of them here, all of them doing their own thing I feel, and most of them not working on research directly useful to the company.

   'The Manager, Tom Doddy, was a good pharmaceutical chemist in his day, but he's due to retire in three months and perhaps isn't as active as he was. He doesn't seem to understand what all his staff are doing, I mean from a chemical angle, and when I spoke to him on Wednesday he couldn't even tell me what research at least ten people were supposed to be tackling. When I asked him what he recommended should be done with the department in the future, he told me he didn't have time to worry about that, as he had enough problems at the moment—an extraordinary answer.

   'What do you think is wrong? What do you advise me to do about the department?' he asked.

   (a) What advice do you think I gave Mr. Phibber?
   (b) What is wrong with the department?

A2.5   Things were certainly going wrong at Greyland Electrics. There had been a thunderstorm, water had leaked through the roof, and was dripping slowly but steadily on a junction box. Terry Sparkes was busy replacing a fuse in the box (there had been a surge of the power during the storm, the fuse had blown and work had stopped in the workshop), with a great deal of haste as production needed to restart quickly.

   Paul Pry, the Safety Officer, entered the shop just as Terry pulled the lever over to 'ON', and the machines started. 'Just a minute,' he shouted. 'Switch that thing off again at once!' Terry obliged. 'Now,' continued Pry, 'leave your machines, and organize someone to get into the roof to plug the leak. Come on, you're wasting time!'

   At that moment, Tom Shepherd, the Supervisor, entered the department. 'What are you playing at, Pry?' he shouted, 'These are my men, not yours.'

'They're on safety work, now, and that's my responsibility,' Pry replied.

(a) Was Pry right to intervene when he did? What kind of authority was he exercising?
(b) Did Tom Shepherd have a right to argue with Paul Pry about the safety job he had set them to do?
(c) How could problems like these be avoided?

3
Management Theory

From time to time the members of most major religions in the world receive instruction or teaching from priests, elders, or prophets on the principles behind the rituals, services or observances the believers practise. An understanding of the underlying principles helps people to appreciate the purpose, meaning and form of the rituals. Similarly, it is a very useful exercise for any manager and supervisor to look at the sources of the ideas lying behind present management practice. At the conclusion of this chapter, you will have recognized, no doubt, at least one principle held by your superior, and perhaps one he or she has failed to follow.

3.1 THE MANAGEMENT THEORY TANGLE

We must appreciate, right at the beginning, that there is no single, simple, quick way of explaining organization theories nor, indeed, can we pick upon any particular theory, or group of related theories as being a unified whole. This means we cannot hope to explain the behaviour of organizations, or elicit principles of management in one scheme. As yet there exists no General Theory of Organizations, or of Management, like Einstein's General Theory of Relativity, which attempts to explain a wide range of phenomena.

Now problems of management, and the creation, preservation and modification of organizations have existed since the time man became sufficiently conscious of his environment to want to control it, and, in addition, to control the activities of particular individuals in any particular group. As far as we can see, few human beings have ever lived in complete isolation—if they had, the human race would have died out. So human beings lived in communities—the family, the clan, the tribe, long before recorded time; and by 10 000 BC were organized sufficiently to live in towns and villages, carrying on trade, working in groups on common tasks. All these situations created what we can justifiably call management and organization problems. These problems grew as man became more organized.

Consider, for example, the building of the Pyramids or Stonehenge; the organization of the Carthaginian fleet or the Roman state; or the conquests of Alexander the Great. A wide variety of problems arose from the need to organize and manage people, from the need to set up complex administrative and legal structures to maintain the systems built up, and from the need to modify and adapt these systems to cope with change. Problems of this kind have been a challenge to countless generals, superiors, civil servants and officials for thousands of years.

It is indeed strange that with some notable exceptions—for example Plato's attempt to formalize his Republic on a theoretical basis—little attempt has been made to examine, comment upon, or evaluate organizations one against another. The serious systematic and continuous study of organizations and their management really only goes back for a little less than 100 years; the more important work is less than 50 years old; and the more exciting and possibly the most fruitful advances have been made in the last 25 years.

In the earlier years we had a few reflections of managers of various kinds, but later came the deluge of academic research and writing as well as the continuing statements from practising managers. The authors of the studies included a whole host of sociologists, psychologists, economists, political scientists, and others including even biologists. The number of books on management is still increasing rapidly.

While the interest and concern of some people shows that there is a need for a great deal of work to be done, the student may be forgiven for wondering what the subject is all about. There are a host of varying approaches and 'cult-figures' peddle their own distinct and individual theories, as if their theories alone were valid, downgrading, at least, or denying, at most, everything that everyone else has said or done.

In the following section, we shall try to unravel the tangle, select the more important strands and construct an overall picture of current management ideas.

3.1.1 How the confusion has arisen

We are faced with a varied collection of ideas, theories, propositions, comments, research and investigations approached from a wide variety of standpoints. How has this come about? Let us consider the following reasons.

Newness of the subject

As already indicated, the study of organizations and the art of management is relatively recent, particularly when we compare it with other disciplines. For example, biology, astronomy and mathematics—to name but three—have a long history of study, research and development, as well as the use of enormous resources in terms of people's time and money over the last 2500 years. The impetus in management studies is now enormous, and ideas, theories and different approaches proliferate, but it will take many years for a coherent picture to emerge enabling us to identify common strands, amalgamate what appears now to be separate streams of thought, and to evaluate which ideas are significant, and which are not.

Background of the theorists

Most disciplines in the past have had a history of spectacular contributions, significant advances, momentous discoveries. Who made them? Sometimes brilliant individuals, sometimes fertile partnerships, sometimes a team working long and hard at their research. Common to them all (except those who belonged to the very newest of the disciplines) was the fact that they were life-long professionals, steeped in one subject and totally committed to it. Thus biologists produce biological theories; the 'steady state' theory of the universe was the contribution of Fred Hoyle, an astronomer of many years' standing; and Einstein was certainly no amateur physicist.

It is true that from time to time amateurs and emigrés from other subjects contribute significantly to the development of particular subjects outside their original or main sphere of activity. For example, Herschell moved from music to astronomy, and a music-hall comedian of the inter-war years, Will Hay, discovered a phenomenon on the surface of Saturn, but even here those concerned had studied their interests very seriously and were in total sympathy with the work of others long before they made their contributions.

It is also true that in recent years, in particular, the crossing of boundaries from one discipline to another has occurred on a significant scale; and work on one subject has been used and refined in others, but this has not altered the general picture of professional specialists contributing to their specialisms.

Little of this is true in the case of organization and management theory. As with any new subject there is no long history, no central body of doctrine, no well-documented research upon which to build and advance. Contributions have, as we have seen, come from many different subject areas.

The contributors have included: *practising managers* who have tried to generalize from their own, often rather limited experiences; sociologists (of different schools within their own subject) who have, in the main, concentrated on the factors which they feel shape the structure of organizations; *industrial psychologists* who have been concerned with the problems of the individual in his efforts to adapt to his environment at work, as well as to technical, administrative and social stresses and pressures in order to equate, somehow, efficiency at work with human happiness; *mathematicians* who regard the firm or organization as a complex mathematical model; *biologists* who regard the organization as the human system writ large; and amongst others, formal *organization theorists* who have tried to extract basic rules and principles of alleged practical use to those who have to design and maintain organizations.

Confusion over the definition of the subject

As the contributors to management and organization theory belong to such diverse fields, there is very little consensus of opinion about the precise nature of 'management' and 'organizations'. Not only are the definitions of the individual subjects in question, but also the classification—should management be regarded as a branch of sociology or as a branch of sociology and psychology combined, or even as part of systems theory?

The confusion exists even in the institutes of Higher Education where topics such as O and M, accounting, computer science, etc. are grouped together under the heading of 'management'. These are incidental to the job of a manager and do not actually form part of it unless, of course, he is an O and M practitioner, Accountant or Computer Manager.

Funding of research

Owing to their work experience many of those first involved in inquiries into industrial problems concentrated on what was happening in private enterprise; and, in particular, on what was happening on the shop floor. When increased profits were promised as a result of adopting the new techniques suggested industry was not slow in promoting further study.

Until recently, the broadening of research into *management* problems was still restricted to industry because the problems there were greater and more immediately apparent, especially in larger firms. Considerable sums of money were required for research and study and industry provided that money, either directly to individuals or indirectly to institutions like the Massachusetts Institute of Technology. It was, in fact, only recently that organizations such as hospitals, mines, military units, the civil service and trade unions, etc. have been studied in depth.

Lack of uniformity in study methods

The varied contributions to our field of study came, as we have seen, from many different backgrounds; each contributor brought to bear on his work his own opinions and experience. Some earlier contributors tried to generalize from sometimes limited experiences; others researched in great detail in isolated and haphazardly chosen experimental situations. In the celebrated 'Hawthorne' experiments the starting assumptions were quite wrong and the researchers did not fully understand the significance of the results at the time.

3.2 UNRAVELLING THE TANGLE

The least confusing way of unravelling the tangle involves looking at some aspects of the work of seven selected individuals, with a brief biographical note on the most important to establish their credentials. Beginning with the end of the last century, this historical survey covers 'scientific' management from two related approaches; 'bureaucracy'; the 'human relations' movement, and finally the more recent psychological or 'behaviourist' approach. The seven chosen writers are not only representatives of these different 'schools' of thought, but are felt by many to be important because of the way in which they expressed their ideas, and because they have influenced so many managers and executives in the past, and still do so now.

It is always better to gain first-hand knowledge of research findings, therefore, students are strongly recommended, once they have grasped the material of this chapter, to read the original books by the seven authors. They can set about this by either consulting the bibliography at the end of the chapter, or by obtaining a copy of the appropriate Penguin 'Management Readings' which contain useful *extracts*.

3.3   H . FAYOL (1841-1925)

The first principles of management were set out in 1916 by Henri Fayol, a French industrialist. Unfortunately, a complete translation into English of his major work was not available until 1949, therefore, his contribution was not widely known until comparatively recently; in the intervening time others may have claimed the credit for many of his ideas. It is true to say, however, that many of his ideas are now widely accepted, almost without criticism, in business and management circles.

Biographical note

Henri Fayol was born in 1841. At 15 he entered the Lycée at Lyon, where he spent two years. From there, he passed to the National School of Mines at St. Etienne: at 17 he was the youngest student and graduated as a mining engineer at 19.

He got a job as engineer with the French mining and metal producing firm of Commentary-Fourchamboult-Decazeville, spending most of his working life with this combine. He worked his way through general management to become managing director from 1888 to 1918. The success he brought to the business is one of the romances of French industrial history—the company was in a bad way in 1885; when he retired in 1918 the financial position was excellent, and the quality of staff exceptional.

So committed to his job was he that though he had the intellectual ability to think, write and lecture on his ideas of management, he did very little in this line until his retirement. During his retirement he wrote his book—*General and Industrial Management*—founded a centre of Administrative Studies, which influenced the French army and navy, and undertook a commission from the French Post Office to investigate the working organization. In the course of his work he overhauled the Post Office from top to bottom and at the time of his death, he was engaged in a similar task at the request of the French tobacco industry.

3.3.1   Fayol's approach

Both F. W. Taylor, an American we shall consider later, and Fayol realized that the problem of personnel and its management at all levels was the key to industrial success. Both tried to apply 'scientific method' to this problem. But while Taylor concentrated primarily on the operator or worker level, from the bottom upwards, Fayol concentrated, not unnaturally, on the managing director downwards.

3.3.2 Fayol's doctrine

Fayol examined three aspects of management and attempted to define:

1. The *activities* of the enterprise—what the enterprise *does*.
2. The *elements* of management—what management does.
3. The *principles* of management—series of practical suggestions.

We shall consider the activities and *principles* in this chapter: the elements are discussed in Unit II, Chapter 5.

Activities of the enterprise

Fayol said, 'All activities to which industrial groups give rise can be divided into the following six categories.

1. Technical activities (production, manufacture, adaptation).
2. Commercial activities (buying, selling, exchanging).
3. Financial activities (search for, and best use of capital).
4. Security services (protection of property and persons).
5. Accounting services (stocktaking, balance sheets, costs, statistics).
6. Managerial activities (see Chapter 5).'

These six elements, he said, will be found regardless of whether the undertaking is simple or complex, big or small. Most jobs will encompass the activities in varying measure; the largest managerial element will be present in senior jobs and the least (or even a complete absence) in direct production or lower clerical tasks.

Fayol even went to the lengths of producing charts to show the percentages of each activity to be found in particular jobs. For example, the job activities of a manager of a firm might be broken down into: 40% managerial, 15% technical, 15% commercial, 10% financial, 10% security, 10% accounting. How he arrived at these figures we do not know, but he obviously drew on his experience.

We can see immediately that Fayol made an attempt to define the task functions which were discussed in the previous chapter. (Interestingly, his inclusion of security was somewhat unusual as the Victorian attitude to safety was not impressive.)

3.3.3 General management principles

Fayol set out fourteen principles (although he said they might also be called 'rules' or 'laws') which in his experience had been those he had had most frequently to apply. The list was not exhaustive; nor were the principles to be used rigidly and on single occasions; but as the situation demanded.

Here is a brief statement of the essence of each principle, followed by comments:

Division of work

Economists call this 'specialization'. The theory is that the fewer tasks a person does in his job, the more efficient, skilled and effective he becomes. (The only trouble is that mass production is an overkill of this idea of specialization, and many workers in an industrial country such as ours are unhappy with the dull, boring and repetitive nature of their jobs. Here is the key to our industrial troubles.)

Authority and responsibility (accountability)

Authority is used by Fayol in the legal sense—the power to compel people to do what you want them to do; the right to give orders. It is generally accepted throughout the world that this power should exist, but in systems such as the Chinese one, at least on some levels, authority is a joint power wielded equally by a group and not by one person.

However, even in many non-capitalist countries as well as in capitalist countries the idea of the authority of a leader over a group of people still holds good.

If we accept the idea of authority, then the group leader must be responsible to someone for his actions. In the firm even the managing director is ultimately responsible to the board, the board to the owners—the shareholders or the government, if a nationalized firm.

Fayol said, and this we noted in the previous chapter, that authority and responsibility (and accountability) must go hand in hand. In addition, managers should have a high moral character. Note, Fayol did not consider here or elsewhere the concept of 'delegation' in detail. As we have seen authority can be 'delegated' or handed down to a subordinate, but responsibility or accountability cannot be so. Even though an office manager hands over to a section leader the authority to control a section, the office manager is still responsible for the section's good and efficient working; and is still accountable for it to *his* superiors.

Discipline

'Discipline is, in essence, obedience, application, energy, behaviour and outward marks of respect observed in accordance with the standing agreements between the firm and its employees.'

Fayol saw the necessity for discipline and precise and exact obedience at all levels for the smooth running of a business. He quoted from an army manual 'Discipline constitutes the chief strength of armies', but he added 'discipline is what the leaders make it'.

Discipline is best obtained by *agreement*, and he noted with favour the increase from 1870 onwards in collective bargaining. If workers and management *agree* then discipline is not difficult. Where breaches occur, we should look not only at the offending workers, but at the leadership. However in the last resort penalties must be exacted from the offenders.

To sum up, discipline is best obtained by:

1. Good superiors at all levels.
2. Agreements as clear and as fair as possible.
3. Sanctions (penalties) judiciously applied.

Unity of command

This means each subordinate has one and only one immediate boss. Fayol went to great lengths to substantiate this principle, and claimed 'should it be violated, authority is undermined, discipline is in jeopardy, order disturbed, and stability threatened'.

Not only did he show clearly the results of the practice of workers reporting to two bosses, but also the equally bad effects of what we now call the 'line bypass', that is a top manager giving direct instructions to someone several ranks down. Many managements declare total acceptance of Fayol's rule and then proceed to break it daily with all the predicted conflicts and confusion.

Unity of direction

Where there is a group of activities with the same basic objective there must be one co-ordinated plan to accomplish the co-ordination of the effort, and one person at the head of such co-ordination: one head, one plan, one set of objectives.

Subordination of individual interest to the general interest

The interests of the organization must come before the individual. This principle became popular particularly in the USA, leading to the growth of the 'Organization Man'—someone totally committed to his job, following all the rules and dutifully applying himself to every job however distasteful or even immoral. The ultimate expression of this idea was, I suppose, the Nixon 'plumbers' and the Watergate team.

The modern view is that every attempt should be made to make individual objectives compatible with those of the organization, and vice versa. In this way, instead of the faceless individual losing individuality and freedom, people can operate in more creative ways, 'doing their own thing', within reason, of course. However, it should be stressed that this more contemporary approach is by no means universally adopted; nor where it is adopted is it adopted in its entirety. (Service personnel have to be ready to be sent anywhere at any time, for example.) Means of effecting this principle include firmness and good example by superiors.

Remuneration (payment) of personnel

Pay should be fair. Time rates, piece-work, bonuses, profit-sharing, straight salaries all have a place in the pay structure of the organization. The best and most appropriate schemes should be chosen. Fayol examined various ways of paying people, and even included what we would now call 'fringe benefits'. (See Unit III, Chapter 18 for a full review of the current wages position.) He concluded that there is no such thing as a perfect system.

Centralization

There should be one central point in the organization that exercises control over all the parts. However, Fayol did state that in very large organizations some decentralization was permissible. The real aim was to find the best balance between the two.

Centralization is always a vexed question in any organization. Arguments still rage between the supporters of the large, centrally organized enterprise, and those who feel that even large corporations should be decentralized into small, independently run divisions. A. P. Sloan Jnr, one-time head of the former largest corporation in the world, General Motors of America, spelt out the problems involved in being either too highly centralized, on the one hand, or too loosely controlled, on the other.[1] He argued, rather in the spirit of Fayol, for a 'co-ordinated decentralization' which attempts to get the best of both worlds.

Centralization facilitates consultation and communication between departments, particularly those at the centre: and in these days of electronic and computer control, centralization has its attractions. Decentralization offers more participation in decision-making at lower levels and local decisions can be taken on the spot.

The interesting fact about the centralization/decentralization argument is that it can be applied both to the organization as a whole, and to individual services or departments. We can discuss whether to centralize all word processing in one area, combine all welding activities in one shop, or have a decentralized tool store system to avoid unnecessary walking around a large factory.

Scalar chain

We met the scalar chain in Chapter 2 (see Fig. 2.2). Nowadays we tend to call it the 'chain of command', that is the chain of superiors ranging from the highest (managing director, chief executive, president), to the lowest. Unity of command must be preserved, said Fayol, and this entails all communications from the top moving downwards link by link. Unfortunately, this can be a lengthy process in large organizations.

Problems could arise, for example, where two managers in different departments need to co-operate: to get permission from someone up the chain to work in co-operation might take days, and the matter could be urgent. The sensible thing to do would be to get together, sort things out, and then inform higher authority of the action taken. Fayol called this the 'gangplank' (see Fig. 3.1). The 'gangplank' runs from D to H on this diagram of the scalar chain, removing the need to refer to A, which could be a lengthy process. Nowadays we call the 'gangplank', 'lateral communication'.

---

[1] Sloan Jnr, A.P. (1964) *My Year with General Motors*. New York: Doubleday.

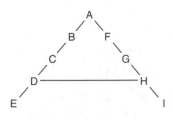

Figure 3.1 Fayol's 'gangplank'.

Order

The formula that Fayol advised for *things* is the proverb, 'A place for everything and everything in its place': similarly for *people* the (amended) proverb is 'A place for everyone, and everyone in his place'. Thus both material and social order is necessary.

Material order in Fayol's eyes has much in common with the 'scientific management' approach we shall look at when we examine the work of F. W. Taylor: social order also demands a precise investigation into the requirements and resources of the concern. Organization charts should be drawn up to aid this process.

Equity

Kindliness and justice on the part of managers will help employees to be loyal and devoted workers.

Stability or tenure of personnel

Efficiency will be promoted by a stable work force, i.e. not too many people leaving and joining at any one time. However, when we come to consider labour turnover, we shall see there are times when a work force can be too stable.

Initiative

A wonderful experience for people is that of working out a successful plan of action: it is a stimulating activity. An essential task of the organization is the encouragement and harnessing of this activity. Initiative is to be encouraged, even if it means the manager has to 'sacrifice some personal vanity' to allow it.

Nowadays, we talk about 'motivating' staff by allowing them to participate in decision-making. This idea is very similar to Fayol's.

Esprit de corps

The morale of employees must be fostered, and a unity of purpose encouraged. The principle of 'divide and rule' is definitely *not* one to be followed: real talent, he said, is required to co-ordinate efforts, promote keenness, use everyone's talents, without causing dissension in the group.

Here Fayol touched on what would now be called 'motivation', that is getting people to work willingly; as well as on the problems of leadership. Although he wrote only a few paragraphs on this topic, it is extremely clear Fayol had a surprisingly modern outlook.

3.3.4 Comment

The first writer to attempt a review of the manager's job would always deserve an honoured place in the history of management ideas: Fayol deserves his place on merit, as well as on the grounds of being first. His principles live on to influence us all in our daily working lives even many years later, perhaps because each one is born out of experience and each one is positive.

Fayol's views on the manager's special role are discussed in Chapter 5.

3.4   M. WEBER (1864-1920)

Weber's principal contribution to the study of organizations was his theory of the structure of authority. This developed from his enquiries into why people did what they were told. His major works and ideas were published in translation after his death, from 1947 onwards.

As far as organizations were concerned, he was primarily interested in the notions of 'power', 'authority', 'leadership', and *'bureaucracy'* . It should be noted, however, that Weber was a sociologist and the greater part of his work was concerned with much wider sociological enquiries into the many forms of social organization in history.

Biographical note

Weber was born in Germany in 1864. He qualified as a lawyer and then became a member of the staff of the University of Berlin. He remained an academic all his life, studying as indicated above, social organization in history. He examined world religions such as Judaism, Christianity and Buddhism; and also the development of capitalism.

3.4.1 Weber's ideas

To appreciate the points Weber makes we shall need to look briefly at his ideas about leadership, authority and obedience. When we come to the section about the three kinds of organization—charismatic, traditional and bureaucratic—we must remember that Weber is presenting us with three *models,* and, as we saw in the previous chapter, models can be an aid to understanding. Each model represents a *type* of organization, and any particular organization we care to take—Whitbread PLC, IBM, the Communist Party of China—can be compared to one of these models. We may find, of course, that any particular model may not fit precisely, and our chosen organization may be partly charismatic, partly traditional; or partly bureaucratic, partly traditional.

Weber was most interested in the bureaucratic organization, and it is very probable that the organization you work for—be it factory or bank, bus company or insurance corporation—is 'bureaucratic' in the way Weber uses the term. If Weber has pin-pointed the basic structure of most formal organizations, we must pay careful atten-tion to the model he presented.

Organization

Weber used the term 'organization' to mean the ordering of social relationships, the maintenance of which certain individuals took upon themselves as a special task. So, the presence of a *leader* and an administrative staff was a characteristic of an organization, in fact, it was they who *preserved* the organization. Basic to Weber's ideas was the notion that human behaviour was regulated by *rules.* The existence of a distinct set of rules was implicit in the concept of organization. The leader and administrative staff had dual relationship to rules. Not only was their own behaviour regulated by them, but they had the task of seeing that the other members of the organization adhered to the rules.

Authority

Weber distinguished between power and authority. Authority was a limited kind of power: authority only covered certain aspects. People accepted the authority of others if and only if they believed that:

1.　The orders were justified.
2.　It was right to obey.

Leadership

There were, however, three different kinds of belief that people had about orders and the givers of orders:

1.　Obedience was justified because of the nature of the persons giving the orders; holy, sacred or charismatic. (The pope, a prophet, a king.)
2.　Obedience was justified because of a reverence for the past—we have always done things this way before.

3. Obedience was justified because the person giving the order was acting in accordance with a set of rules already in existence, and agreed upon.

We can conveniently continue with Weber's ideas of leadership. He identified three categories of leaders, and the organization types which are to be found with such leaders:

Charismatic organizations.   The word 'charismatic' was coined by Weber from the Greek *'charisma'*—the supernatural quality found in some people which not only sets them apart from others, but makes people in general, without knowing why, treat such leaders as possessing superhuman powers, knowledge etc. The prophet, Messiah, and Hitler are examples, as well as Lord Nuffield, or Henry Ford. The basis of the *authority* of the leader is his special powers, and if these powers fail he may lose his leadership powers too.

The organization structure is small: decision-making is concentrated in the leader, delegation is limited to a small select band of intensely loyal staff (disciples) and personal obedience and devotion are the best ways of 'getting on'. Few rules and regulations exist; decisions are arbitrary and irrational. Everyone who considers the decisions they themselves can make in such a system will always measure the alternatives against what the leader would wish, approve of or need.

While the charisma lasts, the organization preserves its original identity but once it has gone or the leader dies, unless a new leader with charisma succeeds, the organization may change. Even a successful charismatic leader eventually has to lay down some rules, have deputies, and these are the beginnings of routinization of charisma!

Traditional organizations.   Here the accent is on what has gone before. Precedent and usage are the basis of authority. The leader usually inherits the top position, and has authority from having status—this status being fixed by custom. When charisma is traditionalized, it becomes part of the role, not of the leader's personality. The average Pharaoh was not a charismatic leader, but by *custom* he was regarded as a man-god.

The organizational form is feudal—the feudal system being the most developed— and can be found in the family firm where managerial positions are handed down from parent to child. Ways of doing things are often justified in terms of precedent as a reason in itself. (Many supervisors will undoubtedly have had experience of situations of this kind !)

Bureaucratic organization.   Weber said less about the bureaucratic leader than about the bureaucratic system itself; in fact, he goes into it in great detail. We must be clear that Weber is *not* using the term in its common, quite critical sense to mean red tape, top-heavy administration, bumbling inefficiency. For Weber it is a type of organization which is *rational* because such organizations have aims or goals they try to achieve—abolition of poverty; a 10% increase in profit next year; or a greater share of the market—either in goods, or maybe even in the number of converts achieved.

It is *legal* because authority is exercised by means of a system of rules and procedures laid down by various officials who occupy a particular office at a particular time. The whole system revolves around the fact that the entire structure including management techniques is largely determined without reference to named leaders or power holders: it is the *office* not the holder of the office which is important. The job of managing director is what we concentrate upon, not upon Mary Brown or Joe Smith who holds the post.

Analysis of bureaucracy.   Weber never precisely defined bureaucracy, but wrote a great deal about the role of the official in modern society. What made the official distinctive was:

1. There were duties to perform.
2. There were facilities and resources provided by someone else with which to carry out the duties (as, indeed, the factory worker is so provided for *but* the official had a major, distinctive advantage—authority).

As all officials had authority, all were involved in administration. Thus a wide variety of people could be 'officials' in this sense: army officers, bishops, the office and factory managers who were spending their time interpreting and transmitting instructions, often in writing. Perhaps the closest we can come to a definition of bureaucracy in Weber's terms is 'an administrative body of appointed officials'.

Weber saw bureaucracy as the dominant form of the institutions of modern life. What intrigued him was the *continuity* of institutions of this kind, 'Men may come and men may go, but I go on forever': well, perhaps not for ever, but for a very long period. People join organizations, leave them, and they still exist. Why?

The basis of legal authority.   According to Weber, legal authority depended upon:

1. The establishment of a legal code claiming the obedience of organization members.
2. The code forming a system of general rules applied to particular cases.
3. The official obeying the law.
4. The obedience being due, not to the person who holds the authority, but to the law, rule, regulation which granted the official his position.

Structure of bureaucratic systems. The basic structure of the bureaucratic system is hierarchical—the typical pyramid we saw in Chapter 2. This means that:

1. In the 'ideal' organization tasks would be organized on a continuous, regulated basis.
2. Tasks would be divided into functionally distinct spheres—specialization and division of work.
3. Offices would be arranged in a hierarchy, with job descriptions.
4. Rules, technical or legal, would exist in a sufficiently complex form to create a need for *trained* men to fill official posts.
5. Officials would not provide the equipment and resources they used in their work. They would have to account for what is used, and for money spent, however.
6. Great use would be made of *written* documents, making the office the hub of the organization.

While authority systems might take many forms, the best, present and most effi-cient is the bureaucratic system. Not only was it important, but it would continue to become more so as time went on: it had

> precision
> continuity
> discipline
> reliability

which made it technically the most satisfactory form of organization.

Characteristics of administrative officials. Seven main characteristics are put forward by Weber:

1. Officials observe impartially the duties of their offices.
2. They are ranked in grades.
3. Job descriptions are clearly formulated.
4. Officials are *appointed* (with a contract).
5. Jobs are filled by full-time, permanent officials, on the basis of professional merit (plus exams and other qualifications).
6. Officials get money salaries and pensions. The higher the grade, the greater the salary.
7. A career structure exists, promotion being either by seniority or merit.

Supplementary points. Other points made by Weber are briefly:

1. *Need for training.* People must be adequately trained to do their jobs properly.
2. *Keeping of files and records.* This ensures continuity and is essential for stability. If information about the organization's business is transmitted orally it is lost when the person with that knowledge leaves.
3. *Separation of personal and business life.* A job is something apart from one's social life. As such the organization must provide space for work to be done, equipment and files etc.; the worker should not be expected to provide anything of his own, e.g. tools, paper.

3.4.2 Comments

Weber pointed to many features of modern organizations—officials, hierarchies, the keeping of files and records, the appointment of experts, the professional manager. He saw all this as a highly effective system. No longer is power dependent upon the whim of one man: instead properly trained people all knowing their precise tasks run the organization along well-defined and understood lines.

Weber concluded that all this adds up to a very efficient system of order and control; and, in fact, he goes on to claim that bureaucracy is technically the most efficient form of organization possible, and superior to all others.

It was obvious that Weber had never considered other forms of arrangement: 'participative management' or the types of specialized groups noted by later investigations—the team set-up, for example. Briefly, this is where a project is conceived, planned, and hopefully brought to fruition by a team of people drawn from all 'ranks' and all sections of an organization. Here control cannot be 'bureaucratic', nor hierarchical.

Weber should also have highlighted the fact that power, authority, call it what you will, in the hierarchy, comes from the possession of information. Those higher up know more about the 'inner secrets' as well as a great deal about what their subordinates are doing. This knowledge alone helps them to be more powerful. A bureaucracy is always ruled by a minority: a minority who have the facts.

You can appreciate that a bureaucratic structure was excellent for the Roman Catholic Church, good for the Civil Service and adequate for many industrial firms. As such it has become as Weber saw, dominant in our society. Because of this, and Weber's assertion it was the best system, it is imposed in areas where it is possibly not, such as education, and professional organizations. Power-sharing and other contemporary ideas of a similar kind are basically in conflict with bureaucracy. If participation occurs on a large scale, it could either destroy or at least severely modify what we now know as bureaucracy.

3.5 OTHER WRITERS' CRITICISMS

Several writers have criticized not only Weber's theoretical analysis of 'bureaucracy' but have also looked at actual organizations and claimed to have found that such organizations are unsatisfactory and that their operation leads to both unexpected, and/or unsatisfactory consequences. J. G. March and H. A. Simon (the latter a consultant to US Government and business organizations as well as a Professor of Administration at Carnegie-Mellon University) have coined the term 'the dysfunction of bureaucracy' to cover such criticism.

We will look at several of these writers in turn.

3.5.1 Alvin W. Gouldner

Gouldner was an American sociologist working at Washington University, St. Louis, researching into industrial organizations, and acting consultant to the Standard Oil Company (now 'Exxon' in the USA, 'Esso' in Europe) of New Jersey.

Gouldner studied the operation of an American gypsum mine—too detailed to recount here, but he found that rules and regulations and the attitude of workers and management were very important. What is significant here is that such rules lay down what is not allowed. They define minimum acceptable behaviour but this tends to become standard behaviour. The effect is to increase supervision, and the number of rules. The effect becomes worse as more and more rules lay down more precisely the minimum behaviour pattern.

3.5.2 R. K. Merton

Merton argues that bureaucracy begins with a demand for control by the top manager. Behaviour must be reliable and consistent. This leads to:

1. A reduction in personal relationships.
2. Rules originally designed as means to an end become ends in themselves.
3. Decisions are taken on the basis of the rules—which are relatively few—this limits the number of choices of action available, and eliminates, on the whole, any search for new ways of tackling problems.
4. A rigidity of behaviour.

3.5.3 J.G. March and H.A. Simon

March and Simon review Merton's and Gouldner's criticisms together with those of some other writers and collectively call the problems the 'dysfunctions' of bureaucracy.

3.5.4 The 'Socio-technical' school

This school argues that a factory, mine, or organization of any kind, particularly if using machines *and* people, is a 'socio-technical' system. In some industries technology changes quickly. Bureaucracies are too slow to adapt to a changing environment. This demolishes Weber's claim that bureaucracy is the most efficient organization system.

3.5.5 C. Northcote Parkinson

This gentleman, well known for 'Parkinson's Laws', had a distinguished career, teaching in Malaya, Liverpool and Illinois. He made the following points:

1. There is no relationship between work done in a bureaucracy and the size of the staff. 'Work expands to fill the time available for its completion.' He quotes the example of the Royal Navy declining in numbers since 1900 but increasing rapidly in administrative size. The Colonial Office was at its largest when the Empire was at its smallest.
2. Bureaucracies are not made up of experts on every subject. Higher managers are likely to know little about what the specialists are doing, with the result that they will then tend to approve and authorize quickly projects which are very expensive and very technical, but spend a great deal of time on the trivial they know all about. 'The time spent on any item of an agenda will be in inverse proportion to the sum involved.'
3. Bureaucracies are prone to spending money on elaborate buildings and offices. Indeed, history has shown that the greatest expenditure often occurs just before

the organization collapses. The Palace of Nations, Geneva, was completed just in time for the Second World War; the Colonial Office was finished just as the Empire began to shrink. He adds 'expenditure rises to meet income'.

3.5.6 Lawrence J. Peter—the 'Peter Principle'

Briefly, Peter states that bureaucratic systems promote people who are good at their jobs until they are finally promoted to jobs they are *not* good at. 'In a hierarchy every employee tends to rise to his level of incompetence.' This leads to the situation in time when 'every post tends to be occupied by an employee who is incompetent to carry out its duties.' This leads to ulcers, colitis, insomnia and sexual impotence—others call this the price of success: Peter claims that it is the price of incompetence.

3.5.7 Final remarks

These are not the only criticisms put forward. Many writers make just odd points in books devoted primarily to other subjects. We may just list three of these as follows:

1. The accent on centralization can be disastrous. Alfred Sloan of General Motors gives an example of an attempt by central authority to impose a special type of engine on all departments for all models. The move eventually was defeated.
2. Informal relationships exist as well as formal links. Many people see Weber's analysis as leaving this out altogether. The human relations school felt this in particular. P. M. Blau and W. R. Scott in *Formal Organizations* (1962) pointed out the two were intermingled.
3. The 'firm' or organization is more than the hierarchy—we must not forget the shareholders, customers, suppliers, lawyers, tax inspectors and the Government. Their interaction generates problems which can only be solved by experts, and each sub-group of experts may see its sub-problem as more important. This acts across the whole Weberian ideal. The Weber bureaucracy is stable perhaps even fairly static: the systems approach shows the organization to be dynamic and changing.

3.6 F. W. TAYLOR (1856–1915)

Another man who had an 'ideal' was F. W. Taylor. However, his ideal was no theoretical model, like bureaucracy: it was the ruthless, restless search for 'the best'. Taylor was obsessed with the idea of maximizing efficiency in an organization in order to maximize profits. He assumed that:

1. Men could be related to their work, rather like machines, and made as efficient as it was theoretically possible to make them.

2. Properly used (money) incentives would get people to work harder to earn more.
3. People would see the need to co-operate with management—the financial rewards from doing so would benefit the firm (more profit) and the men (increased wages).

Many writers on organizations have tended to assume that the strength of the attachment of members is determined by their psychological feelings. Man as an economic animal, responding directly to money (and other similar carrots) is much in the thoughts of people like F. W. Taylor.

Taylor is interesting, not only because he was one of the first in the field, not only because he was a practising manager, but because he is one of the founders of the now well-established management techniques we know as 'O and M' (Organization and Method Study), Work Study, Time Study, and the like. He could be described as the 'father' of Scientific Management.

Biographical note

Frederic Winslow Taylor, born in USA in 1856, was trained as an engineer. He was to have become a lawyer, but studying by candle-light affected his eyesight and he decided to enter industry. However, he decided to start at the bottom, to find out what the problems were at the grass roots, and joined the Midvale Steel Works as a labourer, rising quickly to foreman, then to Chief Engineer. He later moved to the Bethlehem Steel Works, winding up in his latter years as a consultant and propagandist of his ideas.

His earlier publications were on piece-rate systems, shop management and similar topics, expanded into *Principles of Scientific Management* in 1911. But a fascinating series of events at a US Government arsenal resulted in a House of Representatives' Enquiry into his methods; and his address to the Committee plus his earlier work was collected in 1947 and published under the title of *Scientific Management*.

3.6.1 Scientific Management

Taylor's experience in the steel industry led him to believe that all was not well in modern industry. Managers approached their jobs in arbitrary rule-of-thumb ways. Workers were casual and lackadaisical in meeting their work commitments.

He considered that the main obstacle to efficiency was a failure by managers to find ways to co-ordinate and control workers' output, and a failure to work out fair and satisfactory ways of paying the workers to ensure full co-operation and the desired output. In particular, he claimed that managers had not studied workers' methods of working to find better ways of doing jobs but had left the workers to do their jobs as best they could—with disastrous results.

Taylor recommended making management a science, resting on fixed principles instead of more or less hazy ideas. In particular, he set himself the task of devising methods of job study, control of work flow and incentives, and succeeded brilliantly. That is, he did what he set out to do. In hindsight, many of the troubles of the modern mass production industrial scene have origins, or so it seems, in his methods and their application.

In modern jargon, we would say, that Taylor preached the doctrine of 'cost effectiveness'. Cost effectiveness implied *control* and control is really the central pivot of Taylor's message.

3.6.2 The four principles

Taylor felt that 'maximum prosperity' was what every firm and every worker wanted. The necessity for management and workers to work together towards this common aim was self-evident. But there were conflicts, strife, strikes. Why?

Taylor suggests three reasons: the workers feared that more output meant fewer jobs; bad management resulted in workers 'going slow' to protect themselves; and, worst of all, inefficient ways of doing jobs.

Scientific management would overcome these obstacles, and the following four principles were vital:

Development of a true science of work

We do not know what a fair day's work is. The boss does not, so how can we expect the worker to? This is to be remedied by establishing each person's daily task, i.e. the output expected. Workers are to be well paid if they meet the target, fined if they do not.

Scientific selection and training

So that workers can earn this high rate of pay we must ensure those hired are up to the job physically and mentally. Proper training is to be given, so that they become a 'first-class' employee. Promotion opportunities are to be made available.

Bringing together science of work and the trained man

The main obstacles are the managers. The workers would welcome it; would be willing to co-operate in training if they knew much would be gained, e.g. a high rate of pay.

The constant and intimate co-operation of management and workers

Worker and manager divide the work. The manager provides the specification, instructions, estimates the size of job, supervises and pays up afterwards. The worker does the job. With this close personal co-operation conflict is eliminated. Both managers and workers are subject to the same basic philosophy—the scientific study of and approach to work, to find the one best way of doing a job.

3.6.3 The science of shovelling

Perhaps the best known example of Taylor's methods is his experiments in finding the ideal shovel for the job of feeding coke into the blast furnaces at the Bethlehem Steel Works.

In his evidence to the Congress Enquiry, Taylor first made it clear a seemingly simple job like shovelling coke had many steps and stages to it. A great deal of investigation was carried out into that—but he did not trouble his listeners with it—it was too technical, perhaps. He did, however, say one crucial question to be answered was 'What shovel load was the one at which the best shoveller could do his biggest day's work?'

He found that the workers brought (and bought) their own shovels. The smallest could hold 3½ lbs of coke, the largest 38 lbs. Which was right? 'Under scientific management', he said 'the question is not anyone's opinion, it is a question of careful scientific investigation'.

Two men were selected, and carefully controlled tests on different sized shovels were carried out. Starting at 38 lbs, the shovellers moved 25 tons of fuel each; at 34 lbs, 30 tons; and finally at 22 or 21 lbs a much higher output (not stated). Ergo, the best shovel was one carrying 21½ lbs!

Taylor also considered the total yard in which the fuel was kept—2 miles long, a quarter of a mile wide, and the six hundred men who shovelled in that area. To ensure that the right men were in the right place using the right shovels (other types of fuel with differing 'best' shovelling sizes existed in the yard) and so on, meant forward planning, working out the positions and movements of the men in advance. 'It was like playing a game of chess with six hundred men.'

A special paperwork system was evolved, bearing in mind that some shovellers could not read, and careful records were kept of work done so that wages could be calculated. Training and advice would be available to 'poor' shovellers, although the threat of transfer to a lesser-paid job lurked in the background if the 'training' did not produce the required results.

The results were dramatic: in 3½ years the staff working in the yard were reduced from 400-600 to 140 (they handled several million tons of material each year). The cost of each ton handled was approximately halved, even after the expense of a control system, telephones, work study people, trainers and clerical work.

From this type of investigation, and those of others whom he mentions in his book, Frank Gilbreth for example, sprang *method study*, i.e. the study of the best method of doing a job. All this activity involved observation, recording and analysis of the results, and the techniques of observation and timing were the beginnings of *time study*.

Time study led to *work study*, the study of the work itself. In fact, in the USA 'work study' is known as 'time and motion' study, which is perhaps a more precise definition of the actual activity. By analysing work methods and materials used, the aims of work study are to:

1. Establish the most economical way in which the job can be done.
2. Standardize this particular method, type of labour used, and materials/equipment needed.

3. Establish the time needed by a properly-trained and qualified worker to do the job, working normally at a defined level of performance.
4. Instruct that the chosen method be followed as standard practice.

Taylor would have totally approved of this modern definition.

3.6.4 Work group organization

Perhaps lesser known is Taylor's idea of a work group structure. It would, today, be called a 'functional organization'. Taylor was convinced that the military type hierarchy in industry was not appropriate to the shop floor.

The foreman, or group boss, did not have the technical skills of each of his workers—there were often too many different jobs under him. It was impossible, thought Taylor, for the foreman alone to do this job. His solution was to share supervisory responsibilities between a number of foremen each skilled in one job. A worker no longer had one boss, but for different parts of his job different ones. The specialists were: route clerk, instruction card clerk, cost and time clerk, group boss, speed boss, inspector, repair boss and shop disciplinarian.

In Britain little appeal has been found in this idea. It goes against Fayol's unity of command. Nevertheless, Joan Woodward studied firms in south-east Essex and found two, in recent years, where something along Taylor's lines was found. In one, there were 30 supervisors all reporting to five senior executives—programme manager, chief chemist, maintenance engineer, personnel manager, and works accountant. The system appeared to work well.

3.6.5 Comments

Even in his lifetime Taylor's work was bitterly criticized for his inhumanity and people said he had reduced workers to the level of machines. As an engineer, his emphasis on a mechanism, which if set up properly, and paid properly would work along predetermined paths, is not surprising. We must, in Taylor's defence, mention that he did stress the vital necessity of 'getting the right atmosphere', but he never applied a scientific approach to getting the right atmosphere.

If there were conflicts, Taylor condemned them, and said the only reason they occurred was because of unscientific management. His major failings were:

1. Not to realize what motivates individuals to work—he thought that motivation was purely economic.
2. Not to realize that people in *groups* behaved differently than as individuals. He, in fact, did not like groups. Purely social relationships were superfluous and tended to reduce efficiency. Work groups were broken up and operatives separated so they could not distract each other with idle talk.
3. Not to appreciate fully the evils inherent in piece-work systems, such as the sacrifice of quality or the taking of dangerous risks.

4. The assumed existence of a world of perfect competition where maximum output and efficiency were always required.
5. Conviction that he was right every time when in fact he was not infallible. Mistakes, and costly mistakes at that, were caused by adopting his ideas too inflexibly.

Taylor's investigations only covered part of the operation of the firm's production. There was much he omitted. But the main significance of Taylor's work was that it demonstrated the possibility and importance of a systematic analysis of business operations, and of the scope of using 'scientific' methods in a new field.

As we have seen, he was instrumental in creating techniques for increasing efficiency, which, despite the controversy at the time and since, have been progressively developed and are in widespread use in factory and office at the present time.

3.7   E. MAYO (1880-1949) AND THE 'HAWTHORNE' EXPERIMENTS

Earlier writers on organizations followed traditional economists in making the following assumptions about individuals, either as owners of firms or workers:

1. Individuals act in isolation, and without regard for others.
2. Individuals act in pursuit of their own interests so as to maximize their income.
3. Individuals act rationally, logically relating ends and means to ends.

In particular, the school of 'Scientific Management' assumed that:

1. People could be related to their work, rather like machines, to be made as efficient as possible.
2. Properly used incentives would get people to work harder to earn more.
3. People would see the need for management and men to co-operate with each other as the financial rewards from increased efficiency would make both richer.

Mayo and his co-workers eventually came to attack these assumptions—the 'rabble hypothesis', as Mayo called it. Organizations are systems of human beings, dependent on one another. In effect, people are not part of the organization—they *are* the organization. Mayo[2] and his associates' conclusions from their researches are still disputed. The impact of the studies was so great that some textbooks devote a great deal of space to them—they are part of the 'Canonical Books of the Testament of Management'.

Finally, however, we must be clear, before we examine the studies in more detail, that Elton Mayo and his team began by acting on scientific management principles, being hired by the Western Electric's Hawthorne Works in Chicago to test an

---

[2] Some writers, including M. Rose in *Industrial Behaviour* (Penguin, 1978) throw doubt on Mayo's *direct* involvement in the experiments, though others definitely state or imply that Mayo was in charge of operations. Mayo certainly acted as an interpreter of the events at Hawthorne.

assumption of the scientific management school that better lighting would result in increased production.

Biographical note

Elton Mayo, born an Australian, moved as a young man to America, in due course accepting a post at Harvard University as Professor of Industrial Research. A trained psychologist, he was no remote academic figure, but very much involved in the industrial work-a-day world. He was responsible for a great many research projects and, in particular, was associated with the 'Hawthorne' investigations.

Like many other industrial psychologists, Mayo began by being interested in the problems of tiredness at work; accidents, and the turnover—particularly high turnover of staff, and how such problems might be overcome by changing the working environment, or by introducing rest 'breaks' in work.

3.7.1 Before Hawthorne

Mayo was invited to look into the high labour turnover (i.e. frequent resignations and replacements of workers) amongst spinners in a spinning mill in Philadelphia. As astronomically high as 250%, compared with 6% in the rest of the plant, something was obviously wrong. Following F. W. Taylor's methods to the letter, he conducted his investigations, proposed new methods, a bonus scheme, and introduced breaks during the working day. (The workers were involved in helping to determine when the breaks should be.) The results were dramatic: production improved, labour turnover fell to normal factory levels.

At the time it was believed breaks relieved the monotony of the job, and people felt more alert after the rest. Later, Mayo changed his view somewhat.

3.7.2 Hawthorne Plant, Western Electric Co., Chicago

We now move to the Hawthorne Plant of the Western Electric Co., which made telephone switchboards and ancillary equipment, and a series of studies made from 1927 to 1932. To begin with, experiments were conducted with levels of lighting: scientific management-based theories predicted improved lighting would bring increased production. The experiments were inconclusive, no relationship being established between the two. Worse was to come when two groups of workers, a test group and control group, were formed and isolated in different areas. Whatever was done in the control group, either the increase or decrease in the intensity of the level of lighting, production rose; even more startling was the fact that production rose at an equal level in the other, control group, where no changes had been made in the lighting at all!

This was indeed a puzzle, and three further studies were put in hand, over a longish period:

1. A small group of women engaged in assembling telephone relays were segregated in the relay assembly test room to test the effects on morale and production of changes of work.
2. An extensive factory-wide interviewing programme of increasingly unstructured interviews.
3. Observation of a group of men in the bank wiring observation room, for a period of six months.

The relay assembly test room—the effect of changes in conditions

In this test, for five years of the experiment, various changes of working environment were introduced and a continuous record of output was kept.

With the workers' co-operation, conditions of work were changed one at a time: breaks of varying lengths; shorter worker days, shorter working weeks, food, soup or coffee in the morning break: in all 10 changes. Before any change was made, full discussions were held with the six ladies involved. Slowly at first, then quite definitely, production increased with every change. Then came another surprise: the workers were put back to the original conditions of work—six-day 48-hour week, no rest periods, no mid-morning snacks, no concessions in fact. The daily and weekly output rose to a new height, and for three months it remained steady.

'The itemized changes experimentally imposed,' Mayo reported, 'could not be used to explain the major change—continually increased production.' Again, 'There is no evidence in support of the hypothesis that the increased output was due to relief from fatigue.' If it was not this, what was it, then? Years later, Mayo believed it was due to the following factors:

1. The operatives enjoyed an increase in work satisfaction because of their greater freedom and control over the pace of the work; they felt that they were participating freely.
2. The six ladies had become a social group.
3   By being set apart, the social group developed a special set of values, practices, rules and relationships, which gave the group cohesiveness.
4. The researchers took a personal interest in the six ladies and reassured them.
5. The group felt flattered by this personal attention.
6. The improvements were the result of change in the workers' attitude to their work.

The interview programme

At the time of the relay assembly investigations, the continual rise in output could not be explained. As it was such a mystery, an enquiry was instituted into the factory at large. This was accompanied by a change in the methods of the investigators. They began to look at the firm as a social system, unconsciously, perhaps. they began to ask employees about conditions in the factory. Soon they realized that they would learn little about the actual conditions; but a great deal about the attitudes of employees, particularly to their supervisors.

They recommended a programme of confidential interviews to give workers an opportunity to let off steam or to complain. This would enable workers to release pent up emotions and would act as a kind of therapy. In fact, the interviewers noted this in several individual cases (see Mayo's own account and also that of F. J. Roethlisberger and W.T. Dickson—*Management and the Worker*). Mayo felt that workers were affected by their troubles and feelings towards their bosses.

The programme of counselling interviews has been vigorously attacked by J. L. and H. L. Wilensky in 1951 in the *American Journal of Sociology* (pp. 265-80). The Wilenskys claim that 'counselling has helped protect management's freedom to promote, downgrade, transfer, train, discipline, lay off, apply a variety of rewards and sanctions (with a minimum of interference from the relatively co-operative union) in short, has helped the company retain its control over the worker'. Thus one criticism is 'it's just a con'!

The bank wiring observation room

The third stage of the enquiry was the observation of a group at work. It was suspected in another part of the factory that girls were determining the output of individual workers, using as a yardstick a mysterious, unspoken, yet mutually agreed set of output standards. These standards represented what the girls' group felt was a 'fair day's work' which, not unnaturally, was somewhat out of line with the standards set by the work study engineers.

In the bank wiring observation room experiment, the fourteen workers were in fact paid individual hourly rates based on their weekly average output, plus a bonus for group effort. In addition, they were paid for idle time beyond their individual control. The job was to wire telephone switchboards known as 'banks'; this called for both individual work and group co-operation. The management had believed, in line with Taylor's theories on incentives, that each member would work hard on his own to maximize his own pay, and co-operate with the others to boost the group bonus. Detailed records of stoppages would make up 'lost' pay to those unavoidably idle and everyone would he happy.

Mayo's team found, as anticipated, that output was being deliberately restricted, and that the standard that the group fixed bore little relationship to the standards set by the managers, or to the targets (and corresponding rewards) of the bonus system. The attitude of the men (except for the odd 'loner') to the incentive scheme was, in effect, absolute indifference. Output was dictated, not by ability, but by group solidarity. Workers who 'stepped out of line' were criticized.

In addition, group members were under pressure not to reveal to their superiors that they *could* work harder. After all, it was the time of the (last) Great Depression, and many workers felt that greater production would lead to existing orders being too quickly completed. This would entail loss of jobs, or reduced pay. However, to reduce production too much would be 'unfair to management' (although obviously at the back of their minds was the threat of the sack, for slacking).

It was plain from these observations, the sense of 'belonging' to the informal group was much greater than either a worker's wish to earn more, or the company's power to enforce targets.

3.7.3 Conclusions from Mayo's work

The supporters of Mayo's work and ideas are known as the 'Human Relations School', and the basic conclusions of Mayo and later followers, from the Hawthorne experiments are:

1. Work is a group activity.
2. Workers, therefore, do not normally act or react as individuals but as members of groups. The need for security and belonging is more important than the work environment.
3. These groups need not be the formal groups set up by management: informal groups throughout the factory exercise control over the way individual workers think and act.
4. Therefore, levels of work are not set by physical abilities, but by group attitudes.

Later, the human relations approach stressed the importance of the informal group leader in setting the group standards: if the formal leader (supervisor) could also become the informal one, he could get his standards accepted. All this leads to a need for communication between all levels of employees, participation in decision-making (as the relay assembly test ladies had had a chance to do), and a democratic style of leadership.

These conclusions have been trumpeted again and again; tens of thousands of managers of all kinds have been sent on courses to learn about the experiments and the Mayo conclusions. 'Being nice to the workers' is a perhaps facile summary, but in essence this is what managers in the USA, the UK and on the continent have been taught, and some still are, in human relations seminars, and courses on social skills.

3.7.4 Some criticisms of the experiments

Criticisms have centred upon:

1. *Methods used.* Looking back, the methods used were somewhat crude, but the major fault here was to generalize from particular, small, selected groups.
2. *Restricted approach.* The study looked at only one aspect—the work group—and ignored the type of the people (mostly immigrants or first generation Americans out to prove themselves 'good' Americans), the actual work being done (the technology), the union or lack of it, the local labour market, and so on. Nearly all external influences were ignored.
3. *Absence of conflict.* Critics say the researchers were employees of management and were 'on their side', as it were, leading them to say there was no reason for

conflict between men and management, provided of course management were 'nice' and did all the right things. But this is to assume people always see their objectives as those of their employers, which is, of course, nonsense. Often they have to be persuaded to do so by some carrot or stick; and sometimes they will *not* be persuaded and we have conflict. There are those indeed who say conflict is necessary for any organization to grow and be healthy.

3.7.5 Final remarks

The teachings of scientific management and the human relations schools are in opposition to one another; the Taylor view was that what was best for the firm would be also best for the worker, while the human relations view was what was best for the worker would be best for the firm. As Amitai Etzioni points out[3] scientific management assumed the most efficient organization would be the happiest, as it would pay most; the human relations argument was that the happiest firm would be the most efficient.

Once management developed social groups on the job, provided them with democratic, participating and communicative managers, then organizational life would be happy. Thus paternalism was fostered. Human relations experts appeared—and are still with us—the firm's directors talked about 'teams' and 'team work'; or referred to the firm as a 'family' or even 'one, big, happy family'.

The ideal conditions for this had to be created and many attempts have been made to do this, without much success either in the USA or the UK. Industries with an equal emphasis on human relations have had a consistently good or a consistently poor strike record. This is possibly due, I feel, to the lack of examination of the other factors which later investigators have tried to cover.

Finally, we note that the two viewpoints gave rise to two related concepts: scientific management pointed to the importance of the *formal* organization—the hierarchy, the rules and regulations, the bureaucracy; human relations stressed the *informal* group—the attitudes, opinions and ideas of its members.

3.8   THE ORGANIZATIONAL PSYCHOLOGISTS

Industrial psychology is a fairly recent applied science (dating from about 1900), and was concerned originally with matters such as fatigue, accident proneness, and the like—the work of people such as Elton Mayo, for example. Moving into the personnel field, the techniques of selection and training were imposed by the introduction of IQ and various aptitude tests. Later still, the interest shifted to the role of managers and management in the organization; the interaction between managers and the managed, and the amount of conflict that existed between them. We might call those who particularly studied these matters, 'Organizational Psychologists'.

Organizational psychologists start with the view that there is, or can be, a genuine conflict between a human being and his or her work; between the satisfaction of the

---

3 Etzioni, A. (1964) *Modern Organization.* New York: Prentice Hall.

individual, and the needs of an organization. Hence what is good for the individual is by no means always good for the organization and vice versa.

From a large number of writers in the field of organizational psychology, I have arbitrarily selected a few who are either representative or outstanding. Chris Argyris was one who particularly looked at the need to examine and control the conflict we have mentioned; A.H. Maslow has propounded a persuasive and brilliant theory about personality, which despite justified criticism is a very useful model to work from; Douglas McGregor, following on Maslow, rejects all the previous assumptions that managers have made about people and proposes new methods of management based on a more adequate system of motivation. In Chapter 5 we shall also meet Frederick Herzberg, who looks at how human needs can be satisfied in work, under the topic of motivation.

3.8.1 Common ground

We can see some common ground in the diverse ideas they put forward:

1. People are seen as having needs and, consequently, motives for doing things.
2. These needs and motives, therefore, do affect people's behaviour, and this behaviour can be *explained*.
3. There can be conflict between the goals of organizations and the goals of people working for those organizations.
4. The only way to avoid such conflicts is *not* by offering bribes and 'sweets' to the workers, or by offering massive welfare programmes, but by changing the very structure and goals of the organization to accommodate people's goals.
5. The best type of organization is one which succeeds best in (4) by:

    (a) Promoting participation in decision-making.
    (b) Enabling workers to fulfil themselves and use a wide variety of talents.
    (c) Management by objectives, rather than by authority.
    (d) Good communications and expressive supervision.

The foregoing does not mean that all these writers have the same theory: they look at different things, tackle different problems. But they are sympathetic to each other. Most were professional psychologists. They wrote for their own profession. They are very persuasive and we must, therefore, beware of being carried away too much by what they have to say.

3.9 C. ARGYRIS—THE CAUSES OF INDUSTRIAL CONFLICT

This writer looks at the impact of the organization upon the individual. He is a theorist, and he takes for granted a great deal of the past experimental data in constructing what he thinks is a model of the modern organization.

He concentrates primarily on the post Second World War large mass-production type of firm, but in many other jobs conflicts do not arise in the same way. But there is a valid message, a diagnosis perhaps of the troubles which existed as recently as the mid-1980s in, for example, the car industry, and for this reason, his work is worthwhile looking at. His theme throughout is an attack on the formal (business) organization on the grounds that its objectives are in conflict with those of individual employees, particularly those at operator level, and the results of this conflict are examined in some detail.

Biographical note

Argyris, an American, took his first degree in psychology. He was for a long time Professor of Industrial Administration at Yale University. He consistently studies how the personal development of the individual is affected by the kind of situation in which that individual works.

3.9.1 Individual potential

Argyris claims that everyone has potential or undeveloped powers which, given the right environment, can be developed, and fully realized. As we shall see, he (and the other two writers in this section) approved of the development of people's potential, as it not only benefited the individual ('matures him') but all those around including the organization to which he belonged. Regrettably, the majority of industrial and commercial organizations are so organized as to inhibit such personal development.

There are aspects of the situation which must be considered:

1. The development of the individual to 'maturity'.
2. The degree to which people have developed 'social skills', i.e. how well they relate to each other.
3. The character and structure of the organization for which they work.

3.9.2 The process of maturity

To explain the ways in which people behave at work, it is necessary to examine how far they have progressed from the childish ways of their earlier years. Argyris sets out seven different ways people can be imagined to develop in our (Western) culture. (He is careful to use the word 'hypothesis' at this point.)

From childhood	*To maturity*
1. Infant passivity	Increasing adult activity
2. State of dependence on others	Relative independence as adult
3. Limited range of behaviour	Different and varied behaviour patterns

4. Erratic, casual, quickly forgotten interests	Deeper interests: doing things for their own sake
5. Short time perspective (the 'now' dictates behaviour)	Longer time perspective (past, now and future all dictate behaviour)
6. Have an inferior/subordinate position in the family	Aspiring to equal/superior position in respect of fellows
7. Lack self-awareness, control over feelings/behaviour	Has self-awareness, can control behaviour, develops sense of integrity

This development of 'growth' as Argyris calls it to maturity is normal: anything which interferes with it, or stops it, is harmful. But really 'mature' people will not only want to develop themselves, but others as well: 'people are incomplete by themselves, so maturing people help others (and themselves) to maturity.'

3.9.3 The formal, scientifically managed organization

Argyris also considers the organization: who chooses the goals, who sets the strategies it follows? The original shareholders decided the objectives and followed the traditional way of designing the organization structure.

A suitable set of strategies is to be found by drawing up the ideal structure, wit (following Henri Fayol) order everywhere, and a place for everything. There are four other principles of Fayol that he singles out as important to the organization planners:

1. *Specialization of jobs*—e.g. fitting a windscreen wiper to a Ford.
2. *Chain of command*—a hierarchy of officials to control, direct and co-ordinate all the sub-parts of the organization, now split up into separate jobs. More and more power exists as we go upwards.
3. *Unity of direction*—industrial and administrative efficiency increases if each sub-unit has one single activity designed and planned to a specific end.
4. *Span of control*—the number of subordinates controlled by one manager. Argyris quotes the view that five or six subordinates only should report to a superior.

3.9.4 The impact of such an organization on the individual

Obviously, the impact made by any organization upon any individual depends upon the organization and individual. But if, for the sake of argument, we take a relatively 'mature' person (in Argyris's sense) in a formal organization run on scientific management principles, for example, an assembly line plant, then the impact puts him in a situation where:

1. He has little control over his working world.
2. He is expected to be passive, dependent and subordinate.
3. He only uses a few trivial abilities or skills repeatedly.
4. He is expected to produce.

This situation can only lead to trouble for both the individual and the firm. We are asking a mature person to behave in a less than mature way. Although this is a hypothetical situation, it does describe with reasonable accuracy the work lot of a great many people in western society in the recent past.

3.9.5 Social skills

Argyris comments that research has shown in a wide variety of working situations that interpersonal skills are inadequately developed. People do not relate properly to each other with the result that mutual suspicion and mistrust abound. People are less than honest and do not take into account other people's feelings. Job commitment is missing, and the worker concentrates only on his immediate surroundings ignorant of the connection between what he does and the enterprise as a whole.

3.9.6 The process of conflict

Summarized in a series of propositions the process of conflict is analysed. It would seem that Argyris views the organization as a *system* reacting with the employees.

Proposition

1. There is a lack of equivalence ('congruency' in Argyris's language) between the needs of 'healthy' (i.e. mature) individuals and the demands of (initially) a formal organization. There will always be an inherent tendency towards disturbance.
2. There will be as a result: frustration, failure, short-term outlooks, not long term, and conflict. But even if people leave, can they get another job? Will it not bring the same problems?
3. Under certain conditions the degree of frustration, failure, short-term outlooks and conflict will tend to increase:

   (a) As individuals become more mature.
   (b) As you get further down the hierarchy.
   (c) As management controls increase—and they will as soon as conflict and trouble start, making things worse.
   (d) As jobs become more specialized and humdrum.

4. The nature of the (Fayol type) principles causes subordinates to experience competition/rivalry with each other, to focus on their own departments and to lose sight of the whole.
5. Employees react to the situation by creating informal activities, i.e.:

   (a) Leaving.
   (b) Getting promoted.

(c) Daydreaming, aggression, vagueness, etc.
(d) Becoming apathetic and uninterested in the job.
(e) Starting to cheat, slow down, restrict output, make errors.
(f) Creating their own groups—unions etc.
(g) Becoming interested in more money only.

6. The way that employees adapt helps them to cope with the situation and helps them to come to terms with the organization.
7. The changed behaviour has a cumulative and increasing effect on the organization. A feedback process occurs.
8. Management will react to the changed behaviour, and certain reactions will tend to increase the conflict:

(a) Increasing the 'directive' side of leadership.
(b) Increasing the number of conflicts.
(c) Increasing the attempts to 'bribe' the workers with welfare facilities and 'human relations' programmes.

The total effect will be that the firm will find it harder to maintain a given output without spending a lot more money on increased staff, more equipment, bribes etc. What Argyris is saying, then, is:

(a) Formal organization, for historical reasons, is based on reducing tasks to minimal specialized routines.
(b) Its principles include a chain of command by which people working can be directed and controlled, via superiors and managers.
(c) The concern is with spans of control and instructions.
(d) In such an environment the individual cannot progress from infantile behaviours. While he looks forward to the end of the day's work, he cannot see how he fits into the progress of the firm over the year. He comes to accept a dependent, subordinate, passive position without initiative.
(e) To his superiors his behaviour is inexplicable, and faced with it—not only amongst workers, but even in junior management, executives become more autocratic and directive. As more and more controls are imposed, as fewer and fewer opportunities for 'doing your own thing' occur, so less effort goes into the job itself.

3.9.7 The way out

To cope with this it is not the individual but the organization that must change. Management must:

1. Aim at the full development of individual potentialities.
2. Allow a more widespread involvement of subordinates, and let them express their ideas and feelings.

3. See that jobs are 'enlarged', not only to de-specialize them as much as possible, but to use people's abilities more fully. Let people handle their own work problems, participate in making decisions, for thinking ahead. In short, let them have more control over what is done in their own sphere of activities.

3.9.8 Comments

Argyris used the word 'hypothesis' to describe his model of the industrial organization. A great deal depends on the truth of what he says. We cannot be sure whether he is saying people are 'mature' by his definition, *do* want to feel part of the organization, to feel the esteem of others, or whether they *ought* to be like that.

Is it not possible that people may actually desire jobs that offer little opportunity for initiative and responsibility? Admittedly, elsewhere Argyris counters this with the statement that the 'lower class worker is still *capable* of aspiring towards (his full potential), but has *suppressed* his desire'. How you would test that, I don't know! However, it is an interesting theory which does attempt to explain what happened in the car industry for example. I am inclined to think that there is much in what he says about the conflict and the way firms react to workers but there is probably a more convincing explanation.

Maslow, whom we will consider next, and McGregor, are somewhat more convincing. Indeed, people are trying in fact to tackle the problem in the way he and others (Herzberg in particular) suggest. The whole emphasis of the Total Quality Management (TQM) / Total Quality Involvement (TQI) movement looks to involve and empower every individual in the workforce. From the instances I have studied or been involved with personally, the gains in corporate morale, improved problem solving and increased efficiency were real and sustained.

3.10 A. H. MASLOW (1908-1970)—THE HIERARCHY OF NEEDS

Abraham Maslow, a psychologist of Brandeis University, was an important member of both the humanist and existential schools of psychology; the latter being primarily concerned with the individual's attempts to discover who he is, his personal identity, and to give a meaning and purpose to his life.

Many writers have dealt with human needs. Maslow's version is chosen because it is simple, wide in scope, easy to understand, and has a convincing ring about it. It has been widely copied, or included in more elaborate theories more or less unaltered. As such it is important to consider.

3.10.1 Why do people work?

Management, and others, had for years searched for an explanation of why people behave as they do, and more particularly looked for an answer to the question 'Why do people work?' Indeed, to go further, we could ask why people work *at all*, and of those who do work, why some people work more enthusiastically or reliably than others. You can see from any group of people doing the same job, some do it well, others badly, some do it grudgingly and others gladly. This is true of workers whether secretaries or fitters; salesmen or managers.

One set of explanations is, of course, that each person has different levels of ability, skill or expertise, has more or less training than his fellow workers. A poorly trained operator could turn out bad work, for example. Explanations of these kinds cannot cover *every* case however: the answer is that different work performances often reflect different levels of 'motivation', or ambition, energy, drive and commitment to work.

Now the problem of what motivates people to work, or do anything at all is not an easy one to answer. Maslow attempts to solve it with his theory of the 'Hierarchy of Human Needs'.

3.10.2 Needs

Maslow, in common with other contemporary psychologists, starts with the assumption that every human being has needs, the forces that drive him to act, and that these needs can be arranged in some kind of order or hierarchy.

Traditionally, these needs are represented in a diagram in the form of a pyramid, as in Fig. 3.2. This diagram clearly illustrates the point that the physiological needs are the *basic* needs; and the others, as we ascend the pyramid, are *higher-level* needs. We will consider each in turn.

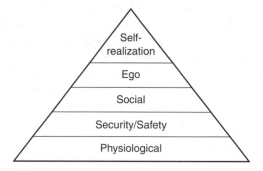

Figure 3.2 Maslow's hierarchy of human needs.

3.10.3 The physiological needs

These are at the lowest level of the hierarchy. We may consider these as including all the basic needs necessary for the support of the human being as an ongoing system: food, water, oxygen; to this we may add more: sex, need for sleep, maternal behaviour. All will be characterized by the fact that we can identify them separately; and by the fact that a need which has to be satisfied is signalled to a particular part of the body.

	Examples:	Hunger	Stomach
		Thirst	Mouth/Throat
		Lack of air	Chest

Undoubtedly, says Maslow, the physiological needs are the most important of all. Survival of the individual and the race are paramount. A soldier lost in the desert during a war would be more concerned about where his next drink, his next meal was coming from, and where to find shade, rather than his impending promotion, or his application for a mortgage.

It is true then, that man lives by bread alone—when there isn't much bread, as one commentator on Maslow, Douglas McGregor (see below) puts it.

3.10.4   Satisfaction of the physiological needs

What happens after these needs are satisfied? After a person drinks a cup of coffee, eats a good meal, goes for a walk in the fresh air? Maslow's answer is that immediately one set of wants is satisfied, *at once other (and 'higher')* needs emerge and these now dominate human behaviour. And once the second lot are more or less satisfied, again newer, and still 'higher' needs emerge and so on. This is what he means by saying basic human needs are organized in a hierarchy. Satisfaction of a need means it is no longer important to us for the time being; and only *unsatisfied* needs motivate people to do things.

3.10.5   The next level—safety needs

If and when the physiological needs are satisfied, then there emerges a new set of needs, the safety, or security needs. People in western society prefer a safe, orderly and predictable world, and even if they may not show it on the surface, have a greater liking for the familiar rather than unfamiliar things.

Safety needs are great motivators: whole societies can be galvanized by danger. So the security of a steady job, home, mortgage protection policy, an income to keep home and family free from eviction or destruction, are important needs.

3.10.6   The social needs

It is a self-evident statement that 'Mankind is a herd animal'. People prefer to live in groups, groups which are often larger than the immediate family. Even in quite primitive societies a person may belong to various, different groups simultaneously. The average individual now may be a member of:

1.   A family (group).
2.   A work group.
3.   A leisure group—a social club, football team, dancing club.
4.   A political group (from an organized political group to something like a Parent/ Teacher Association).
5.   An informal group—people who meet in a pub, a group of friends.

The need to belong is strong: consider what it feels like to be shut out of a group, divorced, sacked, dropped from the team, voted off the local council, ignored in the bar.

Maslow in an early version of his theory describes these social needs as 'love' needs (not to be confused with sex), with the implication of both receiving and giving love.

3.10.7 Ego/esteem needs

Now most people not only want to belong, but to be respected as a person; to achieve status in the group. This does not imply they all want to be leaders. Many are content to work in the background, but they (as we all do) like praise and the approval and esteem of others.

Alfred Adler has stressed our needs for reputation, recognition, attention, importance and appreciation. Satisfaction of these needs gives self-confidence, adequacy, a feeling of being wanted and being useful in the world. Thwarting of these needs leads to inadequacy, feelings of inferiority, weakness and helplessness.

The ego/esteem needs to have, in fact, two dimensions: the one, mentioned above, group respect; the other is the need for *self-respect*, confidence, independence, the need to 'hold one's head high'.

3.10.8 Self-realization/self-actualization needs

Probably (for management) the key need in Maslow's explanation. Even if well-fed, with a secure income and with fellow human beings to relate to and be respected by, a man will become dissatisfied, restless even, if he is not doing all that he is both capable of, and likes doing. 'What a man *can* be, he *must* be' Maslow tells us. While all 'self-actualization' (the term originally used to describe this highest need, later replaced by 'self-realization') activity is not in itself 'creative', much creative work stems from the desire to satisfy this need.

The whole emphasis here is on the need for people to develop their whole personality, to grow and make the best use of their abilities, and to respond to challenges. This message has been brought out by later writers who have stressed the importance of redesigning jobs to make them less repetitive, more challenging; more demanding of skill and endeavour.

3.10.9 Maslow's own comments

Maslow makes the following comments, amongst others:

1. There are creative people who are motivated by the self-actualization need, despite or in spite of the fact other needs are *not* satisfied.
2. People may have very low levels of aspiration, if their life experience has been narrow. A starving peasant may be satisfied for the rest of his life if he suddenly gets food regularly.

3. Satisfied needs lead to new wants, as we have seen. The new wants continue even when the lower needs suddenly become unsatisfied. The unemployed director may still go to expensive concerts or go to the golf club even though he/she has no money coming in and is practising (for him/her) incredible economies in other directions.
4. Further to the last point, some people have high ideals, religious views or values, which they will maintain against public opinion, the state and armed force. With such ideal values, religious views, people will become martyrs. The need to maintain their values outweighs any other need.

So we see there are exceptions to the general theory, which are to be taken into account.

3.10.10   Frustration of needs

Any need not satisfied, at whatever level, leads to problems, one of which is that the next set of needs below the unsatisfied level become even more important, and extraordinary attempts will be made to ensure satisfaction is safeguarded at this lower level. This happens, for example, when a frustrated person at the self-actualization level becomes preoccupied with status, and tries to get others to admire or esteem him; or when, excluded from a group, a person retires into himself and tries to make his world as secure as possible.

3.10.11   Comments on Maslow's theory

Not only applicable to work

The message many wanted to preach, using this analysis, was that work should provide the means for the satisfaction of all these levels of need. The danger was, they preached, that if these needs were not met then trouble would result.

Self-actualization not met	job dissatisfaction
Esteem needs not met	inadequacy and low morale
Social needs not met	severe maladjustment and physiological problems
Security/safety needs not met	obsessive neurosis
Physiological needs not met	starvation and poor work

In a modern western democratic society, organizations would never get away with not meeting the last two; people would leave rather than work for next to nothing.

It is true many of industry's problems in the immediate past could be analysed on the following basis: workers were not 'self-actualized', and became dissatisfied with their jobs; they had no esteem given to them by their bosses; and they were often made to work in virtual isolation. The net result was constant labour troubles, and disruption of production.

However, even if we accept everything Maslow says, in fact many people achieve their self-actualization from activities outside work—the aspiring actor belongs to an amateur dramatic society; the aspiring craftsman has a shed full of tools; the industrial leader becomes a union branch secretary, or president of a working men's club. Work can be of comparative indifference to such a person: a means to an end.

Those, then, who feel that challenge should be built into jobs, that the jobs itself should be the main source of satisfaction of needs, have seriously overstated the situation. Indeed in a future world where many, perhaps the majority of people will not 'work' in today's sense, the importance of fulfilling oneself in leisure activities will dramatically increase.

Satisfaction of needs not the sole motivator

There are other things which motivate people besides their own needs. Group allegiances are very important—remember the Hawthorne experiment—and people do not normally, and this is even more so true at work, act as totally independent persons. What other people feel and think are going to affect (or motivate) what the individual feels and does.

Inability of management to provide for human needs

This point is related to the first two. It is clear from what Maslow says that there are a large number of events which satisfy human needs; and an equally large, if not larger series of events which will not be liked by humans. Only a small number of the possible pleasant or unpleasant alternatives are under managerial control. Some indeed are under the control of the informal, as opposed to the formal organization of the firm.

3.10.12   Conclusion

As an interesting, challenging and fruitful analysis. Maslow's theory is worthy of consideration. It makes some significant points, and his implications are similar to those of other theories, such as Argyris's for example. Maslow's ideas are now widely known in Europe as well as America and have greatly influenced the work of others— Douglas McGregor (see below) drew heavily upon the need hierarchy.

3.11   D. McGREGOR (1901–1964)

Biographical note

For most of his life Douglas McGregor was a social scientist who investigated the behaviour of people in organizations including their motivation and also managerial behaviour. An American, McGregor spent some years as President—or Chief Executive—of Antioch College, a job which gave him plenty of experience and material to draw on when he looked at the management, administration and operation of organizations. In the last ten years of his life, he was Professor of Management at the Massachusetts Institute of Technology.

3.11.1 Theories 'X' and 'Y'

McGregor is undoubtedly best known for his analysis of behaviour of people at work. In Theory 'X', he sets down what he believes managers have felt about the workers of whom they were in charge; the *traditional* views of workers' attitudes to work. In Theory 'Y', he states what *he* feels is a much more realistic explanation of workers' motives, and general behaviour. This new experimentation means managers have been wrong about the way they have viewed and treated their work force, and McGregor recommends managers should change their ways and adapt their management techniques.

He offers certain suggestions as to how the 'new manager' should operate, and also indicates changes that should be made to the organization.

3.11.2 Theory 'X'

Traditional ideas about 'the workers' have been handed down and are not available as a precise, written set of beliefs, so McGregor examines these views and tries to set out those beliefs which underlie what was said and done. Even if certain types of behaviour like punishing people by cutting off their heads or beating them, become unfashionable, the underlying ideas—the need to punish people—can remain without significant change.

The later (and shorter) version of Theory 'X' is as follows:

1. The average human being has an inherent dislike of work, and will avoid it if possible.
2. Because of this human characteristic dislike of work, most people must be coerced, controlled, directed, threatened with punishment to get them to put forth adequate effort toward the achievement of organizational objectives.
3. The average human being prefers to be directed, wishes to avoid responsibility, has relatively little ambition and wants security above all.

He adds: 'Theory "X" is not a straw man (constructed just) for purposes of demolition, but in fact a theory which materially influences managerial strategy in a wide sector of American industry today'.

3.11.3 Comments on Theory 'X'

Theory 'X' is a restatement of the comments of Argyris (and others) on the causes of industrial conflict from a new angle. Theory 'X' is the *management* viewpoint, the opinion of the industrial elite. In this case, we do not have a feudal baron looking down upon a rabble of ignorant peasants, but rather the clever, dynamic, go-ahead manager regarding, even perhaps with some pity, the indolent, indecisive workers, the 'average' human beings. The managers are, of course, *not* the average: as there are only a few managers, the implication is almost that 95% of mankind is subnormal which, by definition, cannot be true. Put another way, 95% of the population is average, and rather a poor average at that, and the brilliant 5% of managers have to do the world's thinking.

We must, of course, ask if McGregor is correct in saying that managers in the past believed workers were lazy, disliked work, had to be led, etc. If we look at the work of Fayol and Taylor the emphasis on control, discipline and order is apparent: conformity, obedience and dependence have been demanded of workers. Such pressures would not have been applied if they had not been thought to have been necessary. Certainly managers prior to, and at the height of the Industrial Revolution, if the stories about them are true, demonstrated they not only believed in Theory 'X', but some even felt they were doing people a favour by imposing work upon them; helping them towards salvation.

One thing is certain: if you treat people *as if* they are dumb, rebellious, easily led, lazy oafs (and feel the need to control them and form them into submission) they may even come to believe they are inferior and, furthermore, they will almost certainly rebel against such treatment.

If they rebel, the manager's beliefs about staff are reinforced: the more they rebel, the more this confirms the manager's notions about them: the reaction is to introduce more control and apply more discipline. We call this a self-fulfilling prophecy—Theory 'X' is just that. Managers who tend to hold views similar to those expressed in Theory 'X', are called 'Theory "X" Managers'.

3.11.4 Theory 'Y'

When setting out his alternative explanation of general human behaviour, McGregor first restates Maslow's Needs Hierarchy, and Argyris's view on industrial conflict, then moves on to a general set of statements:

1. The expenditure of physical and mental effort in work is as natural as play or rest.
2. External control, and the threat of punishment are not the only means for bringing about effort toward organizational objectives . . . people will work, and discipline themselves in the service of objectives to which they are committed.
3. People are committed to objectives in proportion to the rewards associated with achieving the objectives. (These rewards could be the satisfaction of ego and self-actualization needs.)
4. The average human being learns, under proper conditions, not only to accept but to seek responsibility.
5. The capacity to exercise a relatively high degree of imagination, ingenuity, and creativity in the solution of organizational problems is widely, not narrowly, distributed in the population.
6. Under the conditions of modern industrial life, the intellectual potentialities of the average human being are only partially utilized.

He adds: 'These are not framed in the terms of . . . the factory hand, but in terms of a resource which has substantial potentialities'.

3.11.5   McGregor's comments on Theory 'Y'

First, let us consider what McGregor himself said in his critique of his own ideas. Here, a curious echo of F. W. Taylor, he begins by saying that the key to success is the way that the management takes the initiative, and discovers what its human assets are: '. . . the limits on human collaboration in the organizational setting are not limits of human nature, but of the management's ingenuity in discovering how to realize the potential represented by its human resources'.

If management adopts Theory 'X' it can easily explain away poor performance: Theory 'Y' implies that poor performances lies with management's methods of organization and control. The essential task of management is to arrange organizational conditions where opportunities are created for workers, i.e. the removal of obstacles, the encouragement of growth and the provision of guidance. Suggested, specific methods are:

1. *Decentralization and delegation*—particularly with the use of management by objectives.
2. *Job enlargement*—this would provide for the satisfaction of social and egoistic needs, by the acceptance of responsibility at the bottom of the organization.
3. *Participation and consultative management*—with all our present talk of worker participation it is interesting to see the emphasis placed by McGregor on this topic. He says: 'Under proper conditions these results provide encouragement to people to direct their creative energies towards organizational objectives: give them some voice in decisions which affect them; provide significant opportunities for the satisfaction of social and egoistic needs.'
4. *Performance appraisal*—performance appraisal is no new idea; it has been with us for a long time, but in a Theory 'X' manner. Consider the inspection of a product on the assembly line: a sequence of viewings and tests laid down. McGregor says: if you substitute 'subordinates to be appraised' for 'product'; 'executive' for 'inspector'; 'retraining' for 'rework'—putting the fault right—then you have virtually the same thing.

    As his solution to the appraisal problem, McGregor once again advocates 'management by objectives', rather than 'management by directives'. A Theory 'Y' type of appraisal is where people are involved in setting their own targets, and carrying out regular self-evaluation. Management are still left with a job to do in promoting such activities amongst the work force.

3.11.6   Comments on Theory 'Y'—others

In addition to McGregor's own comments, other critics have appraised Theory 'Y'. After all, Theory 'X' is a rather polarized view to take as your model representing the 'executive right' as it were; does not Theory 'Y' belong to the 'extreme left' end of the scale, pushing to the extreme the ideas of autonomy, self-direction, individual freedom and participation in decision-making? Perhaps, and I would tend to agree, the need or desire for freedom is not shared by everyone: some people actively seek to put limitations on their own behaviour; if insufficient rules exist, they quickly invent them.

Even a modified freedom of action is out of place in part of the work of such organizations as hospitals, the police, armed forces and civil aviation. An air traffic controller could find total freedom to act a great burden. Further, the goals of separate organizations conflict with the freedom of action advocated by McGregor, so we are left with 'freedom within limits'. The difficulty with limits is that people want different limits and want freedom to differing degrees. An organization could find it a very awkward task permitting differing degrees of freedom according to the individual needs of workers nominally doing the same job.

Again one of McGregor's assumptions is that people are *capable* of taking on more responsibility than their present jobs demand. Bound up with this assumption is the inference that to give more responsibility upgrades the contribution of most employees. Fine for those individuals who can take it; not so fine for employees who cannot or will not; a mixed blessing for the organization coping with a work force seeking constant upgradings.

A further major criticism of Theory 'Y' is similar to one that is made against Maslow's Needs Hierarchy: it over-emphasizes the role of work in people's lives. Many people get their satisfactions outside work. The vast increase in the leisure industry, DIY, and the like, provides many opportunities for people frustrated at work in 'self-actualization' terms to blossom out as leaders, decision-makers, craftsmen, designers and artists in their spare-time activities.

3.11.7   Final comments

The analysis that McGregor makes of managers' assumptions in the past (that is the past before McGregor, they know now!) that work does not come naturally to people so they must be bribed or punished to work, is clear, sound and useful, though perhaps not the *whole* story by any means. His explanation does throw light on worker/management relationships in the past and could form a basis for new ideas other than those put forward in Theory 'Y'.

Theory 'Y' advocates what we now call 'participative management', the situation where workers join in decision-making under the chairmanship or leadership of their immediate boss. Obviously, there are difficulties here such as managers who cannot or will not swallow the pill, who rebel against such ideas and workers who do not want to join in. But so quickly have we progressed that we are already considering the next step: the situation where management decision-making, or parts of it, are handed over to the work force, or to their elected representatives; 'worker participation', and the logical, final stage of Theory 'Y' is where workers make the decisions—'workers' control'. (These are matters we shall discuss in Chapter 29 in more detail.)

The basic message of the behavioural scientists to supervisors and managers is a simple one: try to understand how human beings 'tick', why they behave in different ways. When you have solved this problem, do not attempt to fight this behaviour. Instead go along with it, try to motivate the work force by harnessing their skill, aptitude, and expertise. The results can only be of benefit of all.

RECOMMENDED FURTHER READING

Argyris, C. (1960) *Understanding Organizational Behaviour.* London: Tavistock.

Fayol, H. (1949) *General and Industrial Management.* London: Sir Isaac Pitman & Sons.

Handy, C. B. (1976) *Understanding Organizations.* Harmondsworth: Penguin.

Maslow, A. H. (1960) A Theory of Human Motivation. *In Management and Motivation.* Eds. Vroom, V, and Deci, E. Modern Management Readings. London: Penguin.

Mayo, E. (1949) *The Social Problems of an Industrial Civilization.* London: Routledge and Kegan Paul.

McGregor, D. (1960) *The Human Side of Enterprise.* New York: McGraw-Hill.

Pugh, D.S. (Ed.) (1970) *Organization Theory (Selected Readings).* Modern Management Readings. London: Penguin.

Roethlisberger, F. J. and Dickson, W. J. (1939) *Management and the Worker.* Cambridge, Mass: Harvard University Press.

Taylor, F.W. (1947) *Scientific Management.* New York: Harper and Row.

Vroom, V. and Deci, E. (Eds.) (1960) *Management and Motivation.* Modern Management Readings. London: Penguin.

Weber, M. (1947) *The Theory of Social and Economic Organization.* New York: Free Press.

SUMMARY

1. There is no unified body of 'management' views or principles.

2. The study of management, as a separate (academic) subject is very new, compared with other branches of knowledge.

3. Writers on management have come from a wide variety of backgrounds— managers, sociologists, industrial psychologists, mathematicians, even biologists have contributed in some way.

4. There are disputes as to what 'management' means, what topics it covers, and to what other branches or knowledge it is related.

5. Most research in the field of management has been restricted in the past to the private sector of industry, who paid directly or indirectly for such

research. Only recently has research moved into other fields—hospitals, mines, military units, etc.

6.   Rather than discuss ideas as 'ideas', it is useful to study them in context of the people who either thought of them in the first place, or developed and popularized them. A representative selection of seven authors was examined.

7.   Henri Fayol, a practising manager, saw the work of management as distinct from the other work carried on in the organization. He thought of managing as an activity; saw the managers themselves arranged in a hierarchy, given responsibility, having power delegated to them, with a subsequent accountability for expected performance.

     Work should be divided up so that workers can concentrate on a few tasks and do them well; discipline was required from all (by agreement, preferably); any worker should have only one recognizable boss, each department should play its co-ordinated part in achieving the general objectives of the organization—these are some of his *fourteen principles.*

     The general interests of the organization come first; the organization should be centrally controlled, though some degree of decentralization could be necessary in large enterprises, but order should prevail everywhere in the organization. Kindly, just managers can help retain a loyal and stable work force, encourage the appropriate amount of initiative, and stimulate a group spirit—*esprit de corps.*

8.   Max Weber, a sociologist, developed some of Fayol's ideas about power and authority, but looked closely at the structure of organizations (and the type of leadership such organizations had). After discussing the notion of charisma, and organizations headed by charismatic leaders, Weber considered the traditional organization where precedent and usage were the guiding lines for decision and action.

     The most important form of organization for Weber was not either of these but *bureaucracy,* the idea of a rational/legal organization. A bureaucracy is identified by its legal rules (which all obey) and a salaried staff of administrators, with specialized functions. The office not the person is important, jobs are not hereditary; written records and files are kept. For Weber the rational bureaucracy was the most efficient type of organization and a major element in the modern world.

9.   Weber has been challenged: his model is not the only possible one; and bureaucratic organizations are not the perfect animals they are alleged to be. *Gouldner* stressed the overemphasis on *rules* and the consequent effect on behaviour, *Merton* adds that rules become ends in themselves, promote rigidity in decision-making and behaviour.

     Where technology changes, and new methods arise, bureaucracies are slow to adapt (socio-technical school). Parkinson's 'laws' attack the amount of work in bureaucracies, the inability of general management to understand the work of specialists, the tendency for bureaucracies to have large buildings erected.

10.   F.W. Taylor, an engineer, coined the term 'scientific management' to describe the techniques he was advocating to increase workers' output. Such increased output would benefit both worker (more money) and firm (more profits). His *four principles* concerned: the 'science of work'— observation and measurement to be used to establish a fair day's work; secondly, the scientific selection and training of workers for the work for which they are best suited; thirdly, the co-ordination of the trained worker and the standardized job so that employee earns high wages while the employer enjoys low production costs; finally, the necessity of a constant and willing co-operation between employees and employer in order to reap the full benefits of all the 'scientific' investigation into methods and procedures.

11.   Maximum specialization was the key; and this idea carried over into the work of management. By improving the resources and instructions given to workers, greater demands were made on supervisors. No supervisor would have *all* the skills required, so by applying the specialization rules, we get 'functional management'. Each specialist function—progress control, maintenance etc. had a specialist supervisor, eight in all. All eight could give orders—so any workman could have eight bosses. Although widely criticized, some companies do use such a structure.

12.   Taylor is best known as the advocate of work study, and although his ideas have been widely criticized and his assumptions challenged, the techniques he advocated are still in wide daily use.

13.   Elton Mayo, a psychologist, was a committed follower of the Taylor 'school', and liked to think that he approached industrial problems 'scientifically'. Success in dealing with problems in one factory using 'breaks' as a part of the work pattern, led him to believe they relieved fatigue and aided productivity. When tried again at the *Hawthorne* Works, Chicago, rest periods introduced did result in increased output, but when withdrawn hardly affected the rate of production, so total output increased!

  Despite other investigations, no single experimental variable (bonus, rest periods, etc.) could be found to be responsible. Later it was concluded that the company consisted of a social system in which informal work groups were of considerable significance, groups which had their own values, practices, rules, relationships; and that participation in decision-making gave increased worker satisfaction.

14.   At the time, the results were puzzling: in an attempt to get more information, an interview programme was instituted with the hope that it might

provide clues to workers' attitudes to their work environment. Very quickly, the interviewers found they would learn little about these matters; but a great deal was revealed about workers' attitudes to work, supervision and the company. Morale improved because employees appreciated being treated as individuals.

15. The final stage of the Hawthorne experiments consisted of an investigation into the work practices of a team of fourteen workers. It was found that the group restricted output, there was a 'code of conduct' which set a balance between producing too much and producing too little. Group solidarity took preference over a desire for greater earnings.

16. Basic conclusions from these investigations were that work is a group activity and as people act as group members rather than as individuals levels of work are dictated by group attitudes.

17. More contemporary work is focused on psychological interpretations of behaviour: the analysis of industrial conflict, the basis of motivation. Three writers were selected as representative.

18. Chris Argyris, first a psychologist, later a social scientist, develops as his central theme the idea that the formal (Fayol/Taylor influenced) organization and the individuals who work for it come into conflict because basically they have different goals. The behaviour required of them tends to create frustration, particularly if they are 'mature' individuals, i.e. showing 'adult' behaviour patterns—independence, varied behaviour, self-awareness—and the organization demands compliance, 'doing as they are told', doing work which hardly demands more than trivial skills and abilities.

19. He traces the process as the conflict increases: employees react by doing things which do not meet with the approval of the organization (daydreaming, cheating, slowing down, etc.) which then reacts by imposing tighter controls; this repressive action creates a vicious circle: the more repressive the reaction, the more evasive action is taken by the workers.

   The way out is to encourage 'job enlargement' at a low level in the organization: to allow people's potential to develop, to give the individual more control over his own activities.

20. Abraham Maslow, a psychologist, began by analysing people's needs. He arranged these needs into an order, a hierarchy, beginning with the physical ones necessary for life. When these *physiological* needs are satisfied, *safety* or security needs assert themselves; these needs ensure that material needs will be satisfied in the future. On the next level, group acceptance, the need to belong, to give and receive affection, is followed by the need to gain the respect of the group and also self-respect. Finally, self-realization or self-development is the 'highest' need of all.

21.   Maslow's ideas can be criticized on the grounds that they are not totally applicable to the work situation, other things beside needs motivate people, and that often organizations just cannot or will not satisfy *all* the needs in the hierarchy.

22.   Douglas McGregor, a social scientist, distinguished between two explanations of behaviour at work. Traditional theories and views (even if not written down in a formal manner) assume that the average worker is lazy, work-shy, devoid of ambition and prefers to have everything done for him. The only way, therefore, to get work out of him is to bribe him and/or control him, coerce or punish him. This set of views he calls Theory 'X'.
        In contrast, we are given Theory 'Y', McGregor's attempt to set out what he feels is the true state of affairs, namely that work is as natural as play or rest; people can learn to accept responsibility. A great reservoir of talent exists amongst the work force which is untapped, and people could contribute more to problem-solving. If the organization is so structured, people can follow both organizational objectives *and* realize their own potential. Management's task is to remove obstacles to growth, encourage decentralization, delegation and participation.

23.   The criticisms are that some workers may indeed want to be led; not everyone wants to 'participate'. There are people who like guidelines and rules. Some organizations, by their nature, cannot allow freedom of action and precise procedures have to be followed. However, Theory 'Y' *is* important and points the way to perhaps another future approach to the problem.

REVIEW QUESTIONS

1.   Why, do you think, is there not at present a set of Universal Management Principles?

2.   Why is the study of management and management practices a comparatively recent development? Why has there been such a concentration on research in the private sector?

3.   Outline what Fayol meant by:

        (a) Specialization.
        (b) Unity of command.
        (c) Decentralization.
        (d) Order.

4.   Give three examples of charismatic leaders. What kind of leader would be the son of the founder (succeeding to the post of managing director), if he felt he had to 'follow in his father's footsteps'?

5. Are bureaucracies only found in the civil service and local government? Explain your answer.

6. What advantages does an employee who works for a bureaucracy have over, say an employee in a 'charismatic' organization?

7. What do critics of bureaucracy mean when they say rules proliferate in such organizations, and these rules, instead of merely preventing people from doing things, e.g. smoking, actually lay down the *minimum accepted behaviour?*

8. What is meant by the term (as used by F. W. Taylor) 'Scientific Management'?

9. Outline the 'four principles' on which Scientific Management was based.

10. How did Taylor apply the notion of *specialization* to the supervisory grades in his functional foreman theory?

11. Distinguish between *time* study, and *method* study.

12. Why was Taylor criticized for 'being inhuman'?

13. Outline the three Hawthorne experiments. The relay assembly test room, the factory-wide interview programme, and the bank wiring observation room. What conclusions eventually emerged from this research?

14. Why does Argyris feel conflict is inevitable in a typical (Fayol/ Taylor/Weber) bureaucracy? Describe the 'feedback' effect. (Refer to the 'Propositions'.)

15. How does an individual 'mature', according to Argyris?

16. What is job enlargement?

17. Describe Maslow's Needs Hierarchy (with diagram). What distinguishes a high-level need (for example, *ego/esteem*) from a low level one (say *physiological*)?

18. Distinguish carefully between Theory 'X' and Theory 'Y'. What were each meant to describe?

20. Why cannot organizations such as the ambulance service, the police, air traffic controllers, etc. allow total freedom of action for workers to make their own decisions about how to tackle problems?

DISCUSSION TOPICS

1.   Discuss how the organization with which you are associated (i.e. as an employee, or as a student) uses or might use the following principles: discipline; subordination of individual interests to the general interest; order.

2.   Do principles governing our understanding of human behaviour change with the times? Discuss this question in relation to Fayol's fourteen principles. Are they still relevant today?

3.   Are most formal organizations bureaucracies? Is the local army base, the town hall administrative machine, ICI, the golf club? Discuss the view that bureaucracy is *superior* (to other kinds of organization).

4.   'Bureaucracy often develops into a sort of closed society where the loyal and faithful are promoted regardless of how well they do.' Discuss this statement. Is it true, in the experience of any class member? Why? Would Weber be pleased or upset if he had found that the state of affairs mentioned in the quotation occurred frequently?

5.   Review Taylor's work and discuss the following statements:

    (a)   'Taylor was deceiving himself when he claimed to be scientific: where was his laboratory?'

    (b)   'Time and motion study has caused more trouble and suspicion amongst workers, than the good it has done.'

    (c)   'Taylor was sensitive to the criticism that scientific management destroys the worker's initiative, and transforms him into a "wooden man".'

6.   Discuss the concept of the 'functional foreman'. Would it work in your place of employment?

7.   Do work groups in your place of employment behave in a similar way to that described in the final experiment of the Hawthorne Experiments (bank wiring observation room)?

8.   How significant are informal groups at work? Relate the discussion to such groups that are to be found at your place of employment.

9.   'Argyris seems to feel that conflict will occur in any bureaucratic, Taylor-ridden firm.' How can you account for the fact that there are thousands of firms which are efficient and well structured, and which have never had a strike, go-slow or work-to-rule?

10.   What do you feel about 'job enlargement', a method of making originally low-level jobs more demanding, needing the use of technical skill, and interpersonal skills?

11.   How true an account of people's needs and behaviour is Maslow's Needs Hierarchy? Can you use the theory to account for behaviour (a) at work; (b) outside work?

12.   How important to you are the self-realization needs? Discuss the reasons.

13.   'McGregor develops an analysis of how the acceptance of Theory "Y" as a basis for actually running organizations, would work out. He is particularly concerned with the effects on performance appraisal, salaries and promotions, participation.' Take any one of the last, plus 'participation' and discuss how far organizations are becoming closer to the Theory 'Y' model.

14.   'Under a Theory "X" regime, workers rarely, if ever, can achieve their potential.' Do you agree? Why?

ASSIGNMENTS

Case studies

A3.1   TO: Branch Manager, Extown Branch   10 March 199X
             FROM: B. Snoop, Accountant, Regional Office
                              ACCOUNTING SYSTEMS
         On 1 February this year two members of my staff paid a surprise visit to your branch while you were at the annual conference. Some serious inaccuracies in entries were noted when your books of account were examined prior to the auditor's visit. All the inaccuracies were taken up with the clerks concerned, and they were also told to introduce some new accounting procedures that I, personally, laid down last December.
         I happened to be in Extown on Monday, and popped in just after you had left for lunch. I was disturbed to find that only two clerks were on duty at 1.15 pm, and to note that the errors pointed out had not been attended to.
         Unless you take immediate action to punish these recalcitrant clerks, I will report the matter to the managing director. Your reply is expected by return.

(a)   Using Fayol's principles, and what you learnt in Chapter 2 of organization charts, state what has gone wrong in this instance.
(b)   What action, if any, would you take if you were the Extown Branch Manager?

A3.2   Thomas Blacklook, the enthusiastic, newly-appointed production manager at Individual Potteries Ltd, looked somewhat disturbed as he went for lunch last Friday. 'I can't understand it', he told Sylvia Caprice, his secretary, 'three people gave in their notice this morning.'

'What's it about then?' asked Sylvia anxiously—her future depended on Thomas's success. 'You remember, Sylvia, that we saw those management consultants last week, they told me on Monday that all this "hand-made" work was a load of rubbish, really. We could turn out a great many more pots at lower cost—they might look mightily alike, but that's a risk I'm prepared to take.

'Well, we got this O and M chap to time the staff when they weren't looking and he thinks we can halve the times. I sent him down on Tuesday to show the workers exactly how to do the job, so they don't make a mistake, we must keep up the quality as well as quantity. Tim Brand, who's been here donkey's years, gave his notice in first. I rather thought he would—the "craftsman" type, but what shook me was Bob Wright and Sid Broome, both young lads!'

'You'd better have a stiff drink now,' advised Sylvia.

(a)   What type of management approach has Thomas Blacklook, Theory 'X' or 'Y'? Is this a suitable approach for this factory?

(b)   How was the visit of the consultants, and the O and M staff handled? Give reasons for your answer.

(c)   If you were Sylvia what advice would you give Thomas to save the situation?

4

The Supervisor and the Organization

So far we have been considering the *background* to management and supervision: we have looked at what is meant by 'an organization' as a whole, reviewed the different kinds of organization, examined the ideas of a wide range of people concerned with management and administration. We shall now need to look more closely at management and supervision, and, in particular, at the activities of the people who manage and supervise.

Before, however, looking in detail at the jobs that managers/supervisors do, the functions they perform, we might well consider what sort of person a supervisor is, and indeed whether we can define the term 'supervisor', and point to any differences between the job of a manager or supervisor.

4.1 THE SUPERVISOR—SUPERIOR OPERATIVE, LINK PERSON OR MANAGER?

There is a considerable divergence of views as to what a supervisor is, or a manager for that matter. We shall see in the next Unit that we can identify fairly precisely the basic day-to-day functions of management, functions shared by all managers from the highest to the lowest level. More difficult to establish are the differences between various grades of management; and the lower we go in the hierarchy, the more particular and specialized the 'technical' aspects of the supervisor's job become. The result is that we find a very large number of different supervisory jobs even within one organization. A machine shop supervisor in factory A could control nine machinists and a collection of sturdy but old equipment; in factory B the machine shop supervisor could control 25 operatives and a great deal of new highly specialized equipment, and perhaps two clerical staff as well. Bearing these points in mind, any definition must cater for this wide variety of job, responsibility and status. At this stage all we could reasonably accept as part of our definition is that a 'supervisor' is a member of the most junior level of management in the organization.[1]

---

1 Note, however, I point out later the managers have a supervisory function too.

A related problem immediately arises, however, with the use of words other than 'supervisor' to describe a member of the first level of management. 'Foreman' or 'assistant foreman' is well known; but a whole host of other titles such as: 'field sales manager', 'overseer' (or 'overlooker' in some industries), 'office supervisor' 'charge-hand', 'leading ambulance-man', indicate supervisory-type positions. More recently, terms such as 'first-line manager', or 'front-line manager' have been used. For convenience's sake throughout the rest of this book we will use the term 'supervisor' to include them all.

4.1.1 Superior operative

As business grew in size during and after the Industrial Revolution, it became necessary to appoint supervisors to help cope with the growing numbers of people being employed. It seemed an obvious thing to do to promote the 'best' operative, whether this was in terms of the quality of his work, his output, speed, dedication, skill or some other desirable (to management) characteristic. Such a tradition, established so early on, has not left us. I have come across cases such as the best toolmaker being appointed toolroom foreman; the salesman with the highest turnover being appointed to a field sales manager's post, and the accounts clerk with the greatest aptitude for 'doing sums' being promoted as accounts office supervisor. It is amazing to think that management had faith that good performance in one area would automatically imply the promotee would do equally well in another, and overnight a thousand new skills would descend upon the new supervisor.

Many would argue that because of their previous position in the organization they have a better appreciation of the problems, outlooks and attitudes of the people they supervise. My view is clear: there are specific reasons for appointing (or promoting) supervisors or managers; the major one being the ability to supervise/manage (i.e. do the job described in subsequent chapters), and if this means we promote an average workman, a run-of-the-mill salesman, so be it. If the person we choose, using the right criteria, also turns out to be the 'pick of the bunch', that is a happy bonus.

4.1.2 Link person

A great many definitions seen in learned journals or textbooks like to stress that the supervisor is a 'link person' between what is consciously or unconsciously seen as two opposing forces—management on the one hand, and the work force on the other. Supervising is often defined as the overseeing of a process, a worker or workers plus the linking of these employees with the top levels of management. Some would go on to say that this is the 'unique challenge' of supervision, coping with these two opposing forces, and to do this the supervisor has to be a 'master of double talk', conversing with the workers in their language and the management in theirs.

Others, using 'system-type' language, describe the situation that the supervisor occupies as a 'boundary position' in a non-managerial sub-system, acting consistently as an intermediary between that sub-system and the managerial sub-system, interpreting one to the other.

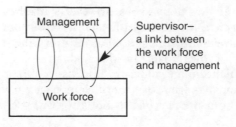

Figure 4.1 The supervisor as link person.

A view of this kind has an implicit assumption: that in some way or other the supervisor is different from both the run-of-the-mill workers, *and* the managers. I shall argue in the next Unit that the functions of managers and supervisors are indistinguishable, that it is differences in *emphasis* which perhaps distinguish managers from supervisors. In fact, what the 'link person' supporters say is that between two different groups there is a third which links them; but, in fact, as we see in Fig. 4.2 management has a series of levels, and you can argue similarly that any level between two others—such as senior executives, for example, is a link between the level above, and that below. Supervisors are link people, then, but no more or no less than any other level of management.

4.1.3 Manager

When we analyse the job of a manager in the following Unit we find the major functions to be creating, planning, organizing, communicating, motivating and

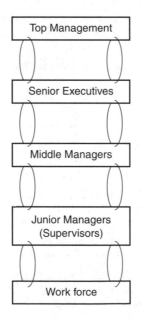

Figure 4.2 The levels of management seen as links.

controlling. We shall see that these six words describe reasonably well what most managers and most supervisors do most of the time.

An interesting definition, from an unknown source, of the manager's job is as follows:

> A possible definition of a managerial role is 'any role in an organization where the occupant is authorized to get part of his work done through employed subordinates for whose work he remains wholly accountable'.

Such a definition is equally applicable to supervisors as it is to managers.

Other definitions stress differences between supervision and management in terms of the closeness of supervision: the supervisor 'operates at close range', whereas management 'controls remotely'. There is again an error of interpretation in such views. Yes, the supervisor *does* closely control the activities of his work group, who happen to be clerks and operatives, yes, the manager only controls such people remotely; *but,* when the manager is dealing with *his* work group, i.e. the supervisors, surely he is not expecting to control *them* remotely.

Even the managing director is a supervisor of his work group which could be, as we have seen, senior executives such as production manager, accountant, sales manager, and so on. Equally, these senior executives will supervise the work of their immediate subordinates.

I would therefore argue that every manager is a supervisor, and every supervisor is a manager. It is interesting to note that the supervisors' professional association has solved the problem by incorporating both words in its name—'The Institute for

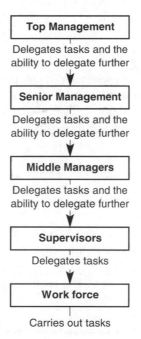

Figure 4.3 Management delegation pattern.

Supervision and Management'. However, there *is* a distinction between other managers and those of the first level which is quite clear and well defined.

The supervisor is part of the management team, but is special in the sense that his subordinates are not managers, but operatives, clerks, fitters, etc. He is a person given authority for planning and controlling the work of his group, but all he can delegate to the group is the work itself.

4.2   THE SUPERVISOR'S VARYING ROLE

As we have already seen, supervisors come in all shapes and sizes, and it would be an impossible task to review every possible different role. We will, however, begin by considering what aspects of the supervisor's role could be common to the majority of, if not all, supervisors; and then look at the major types of industrial processes, and examine supervisors' more specific roles in these areas.

4.2.1   Basic roles

As a first-line manager

The supervisor is the official manager of the work group. Like a manager the supervisor is responsible for determining objectives, planning/organizing, communicating, controlling, motivating, etc.

Defining the work roles of subordinates

By studying the nature of the job, selecting the methods to be used in performing the job and laying down specifications and tolerances, etc., the supervisor defines the work role of that job. Then comes the decision of to whom to allocate the job. Usually at operator level people have to be fitted to jobs: it is difficult to make jobs to suit the individual.

Role in job relations

The supervisor must deal with:

Subordinates. The supervisor has to handle their moods and difficult attitudes, secure their co-operation and motivate them; resolve individual problems and counsel them. A good understanding of human nature is required together with an appreciation of the fact that a little praise goes a long way.

Own immediate supervisor. This is no easy task. This individual may be domineering, weak, approachable, distant, good at the job, incompetent, or somewhere in between.

The supervisor has to receive instructions and orders, and pass them on and see that they are carried out. In return, to pass up the line information on what is going on either verbally or in written form—reports, returns, etc. Supervisors should try to visualize what it is like to be someone more senior within the organization and try to imagine their problems and difficulties. Supervisors will make better guides or assistants if they can see others' points of view.

The supervisor as a boss in one sphere—his or her work group—and subordinate in another—the staff of his boss—will find all his or her actions viewed from two angles. You will not please everyone at the same time. (The 'link person' role.)

Subordinates think in terms of wages, working conditions and benefits they can wring from the firm: higher management think in terms of cost-savings, economies, increased productivity.

Colleagues. Again compromise and conciliation are the order of the day. As an equal, a supervisor cannot enforce orders, but must use persuasion and justify requests—not a bad exercise in itself.

The trade union representatives (shop stewards). The increase in the influence and status of shop stewards has made a considerable difference in their relationships with supervisors. We have conflict here between the *official* leader of the work group, and the *elected* leader.

4.2.2 Production systems

Following the scheme adopted by Joan Woodward,[2] based upon the research carried out amongst firms in south Essex, production systems can be broadly divided into three major categories. Little dispute exists about the categories themselves, although there could be some argument about what you actually call them. The categories are:

Job/small batch production. These would be 'one-offs', specials, prototypes, technically complex units. Also under this heading we could include repairs, modifications of a non-routine kind; runs of two or three only, or a number sufficiently small for hand-made work, evidence of craftsmanship or unusual methods of production.

Large batch/mass production. Here we have larger runs of standard products, to meet actual orders, or for stock. Assembly-line methods, machinery with automatic control systems are in evidence.

Flow or process production. Such processes would be similar to that of, for example, the manufacture of chemicals or industrial gases; brewing, milk pasteurization, etc. virtually continuous manufacture of products in a strict controlled sequence. The end products are measured, not in units of output—number of cars produced, or say packets of tea, but rather by cubic area, or weight.

---

[2] *Management and Technology*. (1958) London: HMSO

Now, not every firm's activities can always be fitted neatly into one of these categories: a large batch producer may devote say 10% of productive capacity to job or small batch production, or the repair of customer's items originally produced in an assembly line. However, usually one or other can be identified as being 'typical' of the firm in question, and the organization and administrative structure will tend to be dictated by the major activity. Such environments and production methods will inevitably affect the kind of supervision required.

Whilst this classification was originally used to apply to manufacturing organizations, and with production systems in mind, it can equally well be used (with some minor modifications) with a service organization such as a hospital, or a garage.

4.2.3 The implications for supervision

Different styles of supervision, levels of technical skill and knowledge are required to deal with the special problems arising from each of these major categories.

Job/small batch production

This 'one-off' type of production varying as it does from building a factory to supplying purpose-built equipment is usually to order and rarely for stock. The essential requirements for this kind of production include:

1. Versatile machinery.
2. A skilled and versatile work force.
3. Sound purchasing skills.

Supervisors for this type of production should be technically competent to understand the problems which could be encountered, fully aware of the capabilities of the equipment in their charge, imaginative, good at problem-solving, able to take calculated risks, but, above all, they should be *advisers* to their already competent work force. Very personal relationships will exist with a comparatively small labour force; communication is predominantly oral, administrative controls are not highly developed.

Thus the supervisor (and indeed to a certain extent the work force as well) has considerable freedom of action and decision-making in the job.

Large batch/mass production

This, in some ways, is a half-way house between the 'one-off' and flow production. The machinery used is often still multipurpose, but frequently grouped to function together, such as capstans, looms, milling machines. Some specialist machinery will be found, more so in the predominantly 'mass production' environment.

Quantities produced are either to fulfil customers' orders, or to build up stocks in anticipation of orders: this has an important consequence: the need to control stocks and schedule orders correctly so optimum quantities are produced. Changeovers of a line can be extremely expensive, so machine loading planning can be crucial. Production control is even more important where a basic product is sold with a variety of small differences, for example, thread sizes, varying dimensions of some parts, or different grades of finish.

The essential requirements of this type of production include:

1. Versatile machinery, grouped to function.
2. Less-skilled labour,[3] with some degree of adaptability.
3. Sound purchasing back-up, material ordered to schedule.
4. Sound stores control and accurate sales forecasting.

Supervisors do not need to know every job precisely or to be an expert on all the equipment used. They should, however, be able to spot trouble, and know which specialist person or department to contact to help sort out the problem.

Supervisors must be able to schedule work, make immediate decisions to alter production priorities to meet rush orders and emergencies, and deploy the labour force to best advantage. The span of control is likely to be far larger than that of job/batch department supervisors.

Their contact with the labour force will be predominantly verbal, and interpersonal skills will be required. They must not forget the influence of group identity (remember the 'Hawthorne' findings) on the work situation.

Supervisors will be faced with more specialization at this level of duties, as well as coping with demarcation lines between functions and, regrettably, an increase in paperwork (or computer entries), with the recording and submission of statistics.

Flow/process production

A major characteristic is the ordering of the various operations in a fixed, predetermined sequence. As each operation depends upon its predecessor and affects its successor, the speed of production is governed by the slowest operation. There can be thus no rescheduling of work once a job has started, but the batch sequences (i.e. the weekly 'brew', the daily 'clean out' of milk pasteurization equipment), stopping and restarting the flow, must be scheduled.

While production control is less complicated, the whole sequence needs careful monitoring as breakdowns or inefficiencies make an immediate impact both on quality and output levels. The essential requirements for this kind of production include:

1. Fairly specialized or purpose-built machinery, arranged in a careful, logical flow sequence.
2. Semi-skilled or unskilled labour willing to do relatively repetitive jobs for long periods.

---

[3] The amount of skill required will vary enormously even within this category from quite highly-skilled at the smaller end of batch production, to semi- or even unskilled personnel in mass production. On the whole, however, there will be less evidence of skill than in the first category considered.

3. The monitoring process may need highly trained, technical staff, probably few in number.
4. Carefully planned production sequences, based on sound sales/marketing forecasts.
5. A 'standard' product with relatively few 'options' with a standardized set of production methods.
6. Almost continuous production.

Supervisors in this situation must be 'process' experts and must be able to monitor the performance of both the equipment and staff of their section. They must be able to act quickly if malfunctions are spotted; and know how to get the right kind of help without delay. Serious problems can arise if any part of a continuous flow process is interrupted.

4.3   AUTOMATION

Automation is, in a sense, an extension of flow/process production, although the day of the fully-automated factory has hardly dawned. However, the trend is well established, in the office as well as on the factory floor. More and more offices are looking like a factory workshop with 'trimmings' with rows of machines, tended by machine operators. Organization and methods staff often call the individual desks 'work stations'.

The role of supervisors with a small, or even very small, and highly specialized labour force to control is very different. In this situation they are a technocrats with in-depth training in the actual process, the application of computers and the most up-to-date information on data presentation. They may be on a different intellectual level, but this situation is not unlike that of the staff-supervisor in job/small batch production. Contact between supervisor and staff will be close and personal, and while instructions will often be verbal, there will be a much greater emphasis on precise, detailed written documentation.

4.4   THE SUPERVISOR IN THE 2000s

There is evidence that the supervisor's role has been changing significantly in recent years, especially since the end of the last recession. An American definition of a supervisor (dating back to 1975) includes having the authority to hire, fire, transfer, suspend, fine, reward and discipline employees. Few supervisors in Britain today could claim to have such powers; and a similar trend is apparent in America where a disciplinary system rather like ours has emerged, in terms of counselling, and oral and written warnings before a final dismissal.

Supervisors are coming more and more under a series of constraints to action which can lead to ineffective supervision. Points made to me by supervisors include:

1. *Lack of management support*—demonstrated by failures to delegate to supervisory level, not being given sufficient authority, not being consulted;
2. *Lack of training* in supervisory skills leading to poor decision making, lower staff morale;
3. *Changes in technology*—demonstrated by lack of confidence through ignorance of the technology, its implications for the work group, and feelings of insecurity if some of the work group have more information or knowledge of techniques than the supervisor;
4. *Role confusion*—mostly demonstrated by the failure of organizations to define each supervisor's role clearly to all, and a lack of proper job descriptions. The position becomes worse where the organization is expanding or contracting, or introducing new technology;
5. *Role overload*—demonstrated by the failure of organizations to establish the capacity of those occupying supervisory roles to carry out what management want them to achieve. Made worse where conflicts occur between supervisors and subordinates, where workers question authority or even the protestant work ethic.
6. *Role conflict*—demonstrated by inconsistencies in management's attitude to supervisors, on the one hand stating the supervisor is part of management, making decisions and controlling work, and on the other 'by-passing' the supervisor (union representatives dealing direct with higher management). Again supervisors may be treated as 'link persons' (see Section 4.1.2) with management and workers having different expectations.

Some of these constraints arose from the problems stemming from the undoubtedly under-resourced, over-manned, uncompetitive state of British industry and commerce, particularly in the early 1980s. The inevitable consequences were shake-outs and the significant de-manning of what had been very labour-intensive organizations. The service sector, too, has experienced considerable restructuring: for example, both retail and banking have shed many full-time staff, in favour of a greater emphasis on a more flexible, increasingly part-time workforce.

Two recessions, denationalization (for example in the power and telecommunications industries), and the arrival of foreign companies (particularly Japanese ones) bringing with them new work cultures and their emphasis on quality, and customer service, have caused further, major changes.

The consequences for supervisors (especially in organizations where whole layers of management had been dispensed with; and/or massive decentralization had occurred in what were once large, highly centralized hierarchial entities) have included the complete restructuring of their jobs. No longer merely concerned with allocating work, and 'keeping an eye' on the workforce, supervisors have increasingly found themselves involved with the more technical aspects of their jobs, and accordingly needing to become more qualified; and assuming the roles of supportive facilitators to work groups who are more or less autonomous. (This trend I have observed personally within both the car components and food industries.) Where firms have needed to introduce fundamental changes, they have tended to turn to supervisors to assist the process—by becoming 'change-agents' (discussed further in Chapter 9).

These trends have been augmented by increasing automation and investment in computer-driven systems (as with banking); more emphasis on mental rather than physical work; and smaller work groups. The growth of participative practices ('empowerment', as it is often called), discussed in Chapter 28, implies the need for supervisors to enhance their team-building and team-leading skills. The development by the National Forum for Management Education and Development, and the Department of Employment Training Agency of their *Personal Competence Model* in 1990 and the subsequent enlargement of the skills/knowledge profile in the current version of the current level 3 management NVQ, demonstrate clearly that the successful supervisor of the twenty-first century will need to be a very professional, competent (but undergoing continuous development), highly-trained, and well-motivated individual.

Flexibility, too, will be an essential supervisory ingredient. Organizations are becoming more diverse, perhaps even unique; each has its own very special combination of resources, products, services and workforce. This implies patterns of supervision could be unique to each organization. The view that no one leadership style or supervisory attitude will do for all organizations is called 'contingency management'. The very nature of such an idea—that each and every organization could develop its own specific style of management—underlines the difficulties facing the contemporary supervisor.

SUMMARY

1. It is a useful exercise to try to define what a supervisor is.
2. Many definitions and views exist. The basic functions can be identified, but it is much more difficult to establish what the differences between levels of management are.
3. A statement which can be made with confidence is that the supervisor is a member of the most junior level of management in the organization.
4. Supervisors are given many names: foreman, charge-hand, ward sister, etc.
5. Some people maintain, and many have acted *as if* the obvious choice for promotion to supervisor is the 'superior' operative: in other words, the best worker. There is no justifiable reason for this, unless the chosen person does have (or is being trained in) supervisory skills.
6. Many people maintain that the supervisor is 'special' in the sense of being a 'link person' between management on the one hand and the work force on the other. This view is incorrect, because while supervisors *do* link the work force with the next level of management, that manager is a 'link person' between the supervisor and yet more senior management. The 'link person' label is common to many grades of management and is not unique to supervisors.
7. Every supervisor is a manager and every manager a supervisor. A major difference is that while other, higher levels of management can delegate delegation, the supervisor can only delegate the actual performance of tasks to his or her subordinates.

8.   The basic roles of the supervisor as a first-line manager of the work group are: defining the work roles and dealing with the problems of subordinates, liaising with colleagues, dealing with his or her immediate superior, and liaising with the trade union representatives.

9.   Production systems can be classified into:

  (a) Job/Small Batch Production—'one-offs', specials, calling for technically competent, imaginative, risk-taking, problem-solving supervisors who will have close relationships with their work force and who may enjoy freedom to make task-oriented decisions themselves.

  (b) Large Batch/Mass Production—larger runs of standard products, calling for supervisors who are less machine-orientated and more concerned with people; who have the ability to schedule, deploy and control staff; who possess good verbal communication skills and are able to cope with the group as well as the individual. The supervisor's own job is likely to be more 'specialized', and will involve a great deal of paperwork.

  (c) Flow Process Production—a precisely ordered sequence of production operations requiring a high degree of control, calling for supervisors who are 'process' experts, able to monitor and control the process and the technical staff.

10. Automation, an extension of flow/process production, is entering the office as well as the factory floor. The supervisor in a highly automated section will have a small and highly specialized labour force to control, and will need to be technically competent.

11. The supervisor's role is changing: particularly noticeable is the loss of powers of dismissal, transfer and discipline held unchallenged in the past but now considerably modified.

12. Supervisors are apparently coming more and more under a series of constraints: lack of management support, lack of training, technology changes, role confusion, role overload and role conflict. Other problems include flatter organizational hierarchies, an increased technical content in supervisory jobs; increasing automation. The need for continuous personal development to cope with fresh roles such as being a support service to more autonomous work groups; or acting as 'change-agents'. Supervising implies being flexible.

13. The latest view on supervision is that there is no one style of management which suits all organizations on all occasions. Each work situation calls for its own type of supervision—'contingency management'.

REVIEW QUESTIONS

1.   Is there any justification for promoting the 'best' worker in the group if there is a vacancy at supervisory level?

2.   What is meant by supervisor as a 'link person'? Even if this statement is true, does it mean that the supervisor is somehow 'special' in any respect?

3.   Make a list of at least six names given in different work situations to first-line managers.

4.   Can it be said that the supervisor is any way different, or that his powers differ from that of a manager?

5.   What are the basic roles of a supervisor?

6.   Describe three categories into which production methods fall. What different demands are made on supervisors of the three different categories?

7.   What is 'automation', and how does it affect the supervisors?

8.   What is meant by 'contingency management'?

DISCUSSION TOPICS

1.   Discuss the following definitions, and assess how close they are in defining what a supervisor (or supervision) is.

(a)   '. . . the supervisory function is concerned with the day-to-day running of a (work) group, which will entail a certain amount of attention to details depending on the size of the section' '. . . management implies controlling remotely by using administrative means . . . the management function should be concerned with thinking well ahead on questions of policy, programmes of expansion, new products and new markets'.

(b)   'Supervisors directly control the operatives for whom they are responsible: the supervisors link the operatives with the levels of management above them.'

2.   Mention has been made of the four important resources available to the supervisor: money, men, machines, materials. In your job which is the most and which the least important? Why?

3.   Is Joan Woodward's division of different kinds of production into three major categories realistic? (Before discussing the question, make sure you have all read and grasped the detail of the *original* text, which shows a rather more sophisticated situation than the summary in this chapter.) If not, discuss a better scheme.

4.   Will automation increase? Besides such effects as a possible growth in unemployment, what problems could such an increase in automation bring to a supervisor previously working in large batch production?

5.   Do you agree that a supervisor's job is essentially the same irrespective of the type of organization for which he or she works?

6.   Consider the problems outlined in Section 4.4. Then

   (a) discuss each 'constraint' in turn. Do you agree that any or all of these operate at your place of work? Are there any roles not listed that you have experienced?
   (b) examine the other 'factors' listed. Discuss whether any or all of these operate now or could operate in the foreseeable future. What problems do they bring for supervisors?

ASSIGNMENTS

A4.1   Construct a definition of a supervisor from the material in this chapter. By researching into other texts on supervision assemble at least four other definitions and compare them critically.

A4.2   (a) Course members as a group assignment are to evaluate each manufacturing organization represented on the course, and to attempt to place it in one of Miss Woodward's categories. Are there any 'misfits' or organizations difficult to place? Account for them in your group report to the course tutor.
   (b) Could this three-part category scheme be extended to non-manufacturing organizations?[4]
   Attempt to classify the following:

   (i)   Any service or public sector organization represented by course members.
   (ii)   Fire brigades, hospitals (noting there are many different kinds of hospitals), banks and 'pop' groups.

   Prepare a group report to your course tutor on your findings.

---

[4] That is to say could you draw a parallel between say job production and a unique treatment for a medical case in a private nursing home, etc?

Case studies

A4.3   Tom Boreham had been a senior fitter for sixteen years at Denbridge Manu-
facturing, but it came as a surprise to him three months ago when Percy
Small, the personnel manager, called him to an interview at which the
Works Manager was present.

Percy praised Tom for his long, loyal, devoted service. 'We all know', he
said, 'what a good job you have done as a fitter; I cannot recall our ever
having had a complaint which could be traced to any work of yours. As a
result, now that Sid Old is retiring as foreman fitter, we are proposing to
promote you to his job.'

At first Tom was thrilled, and flattered, and his wife bought a new dress for
the staff party to which they were now invited. Lately, however, he had confided to me that he was finding it difficult to cope with the discipline aspect.
'After all,' he said, 'I'm a fitter, just like them. I'm not different even if I've
got an office and a posh chair to sit on. Anyway I still give the lads a help on
the jobs from time to time: it's nice to have an appreciative audience.'

(a)   What do you feel about the decision to appoint Tom as foreman? Was
he a good choice?

(b)   In a way Tom has a feeling he is not part of management. Can you
suggest any ideas why he feels this way?

A4.4   The lunch crowd in the Black Heart was always overflowing into the 'snug',
and Bill Cousins was more depressed than usual.

'Terry,' he told his opposite number in No. 2 Machine Shop, 'I don't know
what's happening in my department. Only two years ago, I knew every worker—
well there were only six in all, then, and every job was different. Remember that
water tank we built for the narrow gauge railway, and that prototype container
for carrying those top secret explosives? Well, it's all different now.'

Terry was told as if he didn't know, that after the take-over Bill's department had been reviewed, expanded considerably and a lot of new,
specialized machinery purchased. At first Bill had been enthusiastic about
the situation. He felt that with all the new machinery a whole new host of
jobs could be tackled.

'Yes,' he continued, 'there's thirty-five of them now, and we've been running that control valve for six weeks now. It's all right but Mr Pringle the
Works Manager is in here every day, asking questions about production
levels, what my plans are for next month and so on. Had a row with him
this morning I did. I told him I was too busy with the present problems to
start looking for ones in the future.'

(a)   What problems is Bill facing at the present time?

(b)   What changes of attitude must he make to come to terms with his
new situation, or do you think he should never have taken the job?

(c)   Contrast Bill's job two years ago with the one he has now.

UNIT II

The Functions of the Supervisor

Organizations need managers just as a car needs a driver. Whether formal or informal, organizations deprived of managers would quickly cease to function effectively.

In this unit we attempt to identify those functions that all managers perform to a greater or lesser degree, and examine in more detail the actual work done under these functions.

Every job brings its own peculiar responsibilities, and after discussing the functions of supervisors, we conclude the unit by considering the supervisor as leader of a work group.

5
The Basic Functions of Managers

5.1 FAYOL'S FIVE MANAGERIAL ACTIVITIES

Henri Fayol, whom we met in Chapter 3, besides setting out his fourteen principles of management was very concerned with the *process of management*, that is what the job of a manager was. Drawing upon his years of experience as the managing director of a large company he suggested that there are *Five Elements of Management* that are universal to all managers of all organizations. They are, in his words: 'to manage is to forecast and plan, to organize, to command, to co-ordinate and to control'.

5.1.1 To forecast and plan

The French word *'prévoyance'* means 'foresight' or 'forethought'. Managing, then, details looking ahead, assessing the future and planning for it. Most contemporary organizations have taken this idea to heart (even though some may be rather less successful in the practical application of it), and have both long- and short-term plans on a company basis, expecting individual managers and supervisors to do their own local planning to fit in with the overall planning.

5.1.2 To organize

By this Fayol meant the division of the material and human resources of the organization. Not only does this include the purchasing process for material and the recruitment procedure for personnel, but also the task of dividing up the work (specialization) amongst the employees, determining the sphere of action of each person or group, and giving the appropriate training—all these activities lead to the best use of resources.

The unities of command and direction (discussed in Chapter 3) must be present, and responsibilities clearly defined.

5.1.3 To command

Fayol was conscious of the need to keep everyone on his toes, to keep the organization in an active, rather than passive state.

Commanding implies knowing the staff well and the business thoroughly, and issuing instructions in such a way that a high level of activity by the staff is maintained. By using leadership skills the manager gets the best possible performance from his subordinates.

5.1.4 To co-ordinate

The underlying theme here is *harmony*. Each manager's efforts must dovetail with those of others, and he must keep his department in line with the total, overall objectives of the organization. Regular exchange of information (including meetings) is necessary for the 'binding together, unifying, and harmonizing (of) all activity and effort'.

5.1.5 To control

When all the activity has been put into motion, we must be certain that what is being done is in conformity with the plan: to use modern terminology we want a control system, an inspection organization to set standards, monitor performance, and take corrective action if it is needed. (We noted this idea first in Chapter I when we looked at the notion of *feedback*.) Inspection must be impartial therefore departments responsible for checking, inspection or quality control must be independent of production departments.

5.2 MODERN VIEWS OF MANAGEMENT FUNCTIONS

Various ideas have been put forward as to what the manager's job is, but they can all be traced back to Fayol's ideas.

It is true that when someone is promoted to a supervisory or management position, they *could* continue to do some of the things they did before promotion: the garage manager may take his turn in serving petrol, the cricket captain still bats and bowls, the foreman roundsman at the dairy may have to deliver milk from time to time, but everyone would agree that these managers take on new duties that are entirely managerial: working out duty rotas, setting the field, checking roundsmen's accounts.

Table 5.1 lists suggested aspects of a manager's job. Fayol's list is on the left.

There can be no *complete* agreement as to what precisely the supervisor's job is, but it could be said that different jobs call for all of these activities, but with vastly different emphases. The drill instructor will command, direct, control and measure performance most of the time, but at other times will need to plan his work, report

Table 5.1 Five summaries of the manager's role

To:	To:	To:	To:	To:
Forecast and plan	Plan	Plan	Set objectives	Create
Organize	Organize (including staffing)	Organize staff	Organize	Plan
Command	Direct	Direct	Motivate	Organize
Co-ordinate	Control (including co-ordinating)	Co-ordinate	Communicate	Motivate
Control		Report	Measure performance	Communicate
		Budget	Develop subordinates	Control

back to superiors and motivate his staff; the technical foreman would probably be more concerned with organizing, setting objectives, measuring performance and communicating, but he will need to plan ahead, be creative and motivate at particular times.

However, there is a degree of overlap between the terms. Of all the lists, the final one seems closest to a complete survey: creating, planning, organizing, motivating, communicating and controlling.

5.2.1 Creating

It used to be thought that most people were not 'creative'. We even use the term 'creative people' to describe artists, authors, advertising staff; we have 'ideas people' in large organizations; and the governments have had 'think-tanks'. The notion that creativity only belonged to a small, special group was dispelled by, amongst others, Douglas McGregor (see Chapter 3 for a fuller account) who concluded that . . . 'the capacity to exercise a relative high degree of imagination, ingenuity and creativity in the solution of organizational problems is widely, not narrowly, distributed in the population.'

Creativity can include innovation, synthesis and development. Innovation is where we find an absolutely new way of thinking about, or doing something: the hovercraft principle; or prefabricating buildings—innovations at the time they were revealed to the world. It is one thing, however, to have plenty of time to think about something new, another to improvise quickly at work: but when a supervisor makes 'bricks at work without straw', uses an alternative material for a job in an emergency, finds a quicker way round a job, works out a new procedure, then that *too* is being innovative or creative.

Synthesis is where we take ideas from different sources and combine them: anyone doing a project at work or for an examination such as the NEBS Management Certificate is usually engaged in this type of problem-solving exercise.

No-one has a monopoly of the truth, or of good ideas: advice from half-a-dozen people in the organization, a dash of help from a course tutor, the essential contribution from you, and the whole can be put together providing a useful and satisfactory solution.

Development occurs when we take a basic idea and extend it. The original idea of the car has been altered out of all recognition, its use extended to freight carriage (lorries), warfare (motorized guns, half-tracks), medical use (ambulances) and so on.

5.2.2 Planning and forecasting

Forecasting means looking into the future, while *planning* means making decisions on what course of action should be adopted to meet the challenge of the future.

No-one can plan in the abstract. Planning implies having precise aims or objectives, and working out how to achieve them. This planning is involved in:

(a) Setting goals.
(b) Deciding on the means by which the goals will be achieved.

At the company level this could mean:

(a) Setting a target-line: a £7 million turnover next year.
(b) Deciding to sell abroad, as well as to the home market, as a way of achieving this (higher) target than present progress.

Forecasting is an art, not a science, and no-one can predict the state of the economy, or an organization's probable situation in ten years' time with a great degree of accuracy, but the better the forecasting, the better the plans can be.

Planning at different levels

All levels of management are involved in planning; but as the plans of lower levels depend on the higher, higher level plans:

(a) Must be developed first.
(b) Must be more long term.
(c) Must be more flexible.

Top management.   Top managers should therefore concentrate on overall *strategies* and long-term plans; what the organization's goals should be in two, four, five, even ten years ahead.

Middle management.   Middle management should concentrate on *tactics,* that is how the overall strategies are to be achieved. This often entails devising and operating short-term plans, say from six months to two years ahead.

Supervisors.   Supervisors should plan work activities such as how to meet this month's production quota, for example, and decide what each of their work force will be doing at any given time. Plan time-scales can vary from a few minutes ahead to a year, or even longer.

5.2.3 Organizing

In *organizing* we carry out the next stage after planning. Organizing can be broken down into:

(a) Working out the actual jobs needed to be done to fulfil the plans agreed upon.
(b) Grouping activities into a pattern or structure.
(c) Giving specific people in the organization specific jobs to achieve the objectives the plans agreed upon.

Thus if a test team is selected to tour Australia, a plan is worked out to win the series: it might be to use fast bowlers in spells of eight overs each, with spinners held back until later in the match, in which case *organizing* would involve drawing up details of the actual bowlers to be used, and on the type of field to be used. In the light of the way play develops decisions can be taken on the order of the bowlers, and the setting of appropriate fields. (The hallmark of good sports teams is the way in which they function, apparently without orders (obviously planned and organized in advance).)

The organization chart (which we have already looked at in Chapter 2) is a picture of the formal organizational relations within the organization.

Co-ordination. If we have a series of plans covering not only all departments in the organization, but each individual in each department, we must ensure that all their efforts move together, in the same direction. Co-ordination is, then, an essential part of organizing, rather than a function in itself.

Bureaucracy. The organization's role and purpose was explained by Max Weber (see Chapter 3), and you will remember in his *Theory of Bureaucracy* organizing had a central position: specialization, hierarchy of authority, rules, and trained managers in precisely defined jobs—all these are facets of organizing.

Summary. Organization is a method of ensuring that:

(a) The work required to fulfil plans is broken into parts and given out to various individuals in the organization.
(b) There is no duplication, nor underlap of work.
(c) All efforts are harnessed to a common goal.

5.2.4 Motivating

In fact, in Chapter 3, we looked at various contributions—Argyris, Maslow, McGregor—to the literature on this topic. Here we will not only examine and summarize their approaches, but also look at other contributors to the topic, such as Herzberg, Vroom, Porter and Lawler.

Why motivation is necessary

D. Katz[1] said that there are three basic types of behaviour essential for an organization to function properly and effectively:

1. People must be induced to enter and remain within the system—labour turnover and absenteeism can be costly and dysfunctional if allowed to get out of control, *but* physical attendance is not enough.
2. People must do their appointed jobs in a dependable fashion—organizations if they are to function at all, have to rely on a continuous, fairly stable pattern of relationships over time.
3. People must, on occasion (and depending on the job), be innovative, and exhibit spontaneous activity in achieving organizational objectives which go beyond that which is laid down for them to do.

Any motivation enquiry must try to find the factors which will influence an individual to devote time and energy on any or all of these types of behaviour.

Basic models of motivation

Equilibrium. Various explanations of this concept spring to mind immediately, but an important meaning is linked with the idea of *homeostasis,* a term used in physiology, which describes the drives and mechanisms which come into play when the *balance* of the human being is disturbed, *balance,* here, being used to describe the *normal, optimal* conditions.

If the body temperature is 37°C normally, and it rises because of, say, violent exercise, sweating processes automatically try to restore the original, normal body temperature. If this example is extended to behaviour: people have needs and drives arising at different times, the existence of an unsatisfied need leads to disequilibrium, disequilibrium leads to activities and behaviour likely to restore the situation.

Human needs. Any attempt to codify human needs is subjective, and such a list, anyway, may vary from age to age, culture to culture. Maslow's Hierarchy of Needs: physiological, safety, social, esteem and self-realization, is a theory. For Maslow the significance is that the behaviour of any one individual is dominated by the lowest group of needs remaining unsatisfied. The highest need, however, is different (in later revisions of the theory); increased satisfaction leads to increased need strength. This theory, largely untested in any organizational setting, has influenced management thinkers and managers ever since.

Money. Earlier theories depended on the notion that the need for money, i.e. economic need, was uppermost, and on the 'carrot and stick' approach of F. W. Taylor (Scientific Management).

---

[1] The Motivational Basis of Organizational Behaviour', in *Behavioural Science* (1964), Vol. 9, pp. 131–46.

'What the workmen want from their employers more than anything else is high wages, and what employers want from the workers is low labour cost'. Such a type of view is called Theory 'X' by Douglas McGregor, and is based on the assumptions that people have an inherent dislike of work, avoiding it where possible, with the result that they must be coerced and threatened with punishment to make them work; and that people prefer to be directed, have little ambition and want security above all.

The implications of such a view were close supervision, making tasks simple and easy to learn; the working out of complex organization and production structures to cater for the reluctant ignoramus who worked in the system, and for maximum productivity for the benefit of the management, owners and shareholders.

Relationships. After the 'Hawthorne' Experiments the emphasis shifted to the need for human relationships at work. Initially, the studies sought to examine effects on production of changes in the physical environment. Later the results seemed to indicate work held little or no meaning, and what emerged was an emphasis on man as a social animal; relations with supervisors and peer groups were all important. The result was the emphasis on keeping up morale, group incentive (as opposed to individual incentive) schemes, company journals, social clubs, football teams and the like.

But, all these strategies did not really work: R. M. Steers and L. W. Porter[2] state:

> The basic ingredient of (the situation) that typically was not changed was the nature of the required tasks on the job.

'Self-realization' man (neo-human relations). This school, rejecting the Theory 'X', 'Scientific Management' approach, and the Human Relations scheme share the common view that the task of management is to make full use of the potential of the workers by providing as far as possible for their self-fulfilment at work. We have looked at McGregor, Argyris and Maslow (by implication); and we need to consider R. Likert and F. Herzberg briefly.

McGregor's Theory 'Y' pointed out that management's task was to organize work to enable workers to achieve their own goals best by working to further the company's interests. This means that by organizing tasks so that people can fulfil themselves in their work, they will work without coercion, in other words, management by objectives and not management by control. Argyris showed the incompatibility of the organization's goal and the workers' goals. The enforcement of limited organizational objectives, i.e. maximum profits, may well conflict with the development of a healthy individual's psyche: technical organizational efficiency is gained at severe human cost.

Likert shares these general views and says that to motivate people we must explore the various management styles listed below (dealt with in more detail in Chapter 8):

System 1 = Exploitive authoritative
System 2 = Benevolent authoritative
System 3 = Consultative
System 4 = Participative

---

[2] *Motivation and Work Behaviour*. New York: McGraw-Hill, 1975.

He prefers system 4, advocating group involvement in setting goals of expected performance (the higher the better), an:i widespread participation in decision-making.

All this assumes that *all* workers will react in the same way to particular management initiatives. A now famous study in Britain by J.H. Goldthorpe and D. Lockwood (Luton—Vauxhall Motors, Laporte Chemicals and Skefco Ball Bearings, 1960[3]) favours the idea that workers do select (with a real choice to be made) higher-paid more boring jobs with little participation in preference to more interesting jobs with lower rates of pay. In fact, they showed a tendency (in this study) to want to be left alone rather than be invited to relate to management in either formal or informal ways. 90% of those questioned claimed to get on well with supervision, most relating *infrequency of contact* as their reason.

Herzberg's ideas. Finally we will look at the ideas of Herzberg, the Motivation-Hygiene Theory.

A study of 200 Pittsburgh engineers and accountants made in 1959 seemed to find that:

1. When people were asked about what they felt to be good about their jobs they talked about achievement, promotion, recognition, responsibility and the job itself.
2. When people were asked about what they felt to be bad about their jobs they talked about company policies, administration supervision, salary, interpersonal relations and working conditions.

These findings clearly seemed to indicate that job satisfaction and job dissatisfaction are not two sides of the same coin, but are dissimilar and reflect different aspects of human nature.

Satisfaction, according to Herzberg, will be sought in those aspects of *job content* such as achievement, advancement, etc., that *provide growth* of the personality. These he called *motivators.* The absence of motivators does *not* lead to job dissatisfaction, but merely to the lack of job satisfaction. This can be avoided by the continual monitoring and maintenance of working conditions—using a medical analogy—hygiene factors.

While it is necessary to get the hygiene factors right, if we want to motivate employees then we must focus our attention on their jobs, and provide a programme of 'job enrichment' (not 'enlargement' which is a horizontal broadening) which entails a vertical enlargement demanding a wider range of skills, and by inference, greater opportunity for growth e.g.

1. Remove some controls while retaining accountability.
2. Increase the accountability of individuals for own work.
3. Give a person a rational unit of work.
4. Give a person as much freedom as possible in his job.

---

[3] *The Affluent Worker, Industrial Attitudes and Behaviour*. Cambridge: Cambridge University Press, 1968.

5.   Make periodic reports directly available to the worker.
6.   Introduce more and difficult tasks not previously handled.
7.   Assign individuals a range of specialized tasks enabling them to become experts.

The research evidence available suggests that job enrichment leads to lower turnover and absenteeism and increased job satisfaction; there is little evidence of increased productivity. Unfortunately, there are criticisms of the methods of the researchers. These include:

1.   Anecdotal approach.
2.   Unstructured interviews.
3.   Responses interpreted by researchers reflecting preconceptions.
4.   No real identification of what 'job satisfaction' is.

Also, others, for example, R. J. House and L. A. Wigdor[4] comment:

1.   A given factor can cause job satisfaction for one person, and not for another e.g. age, sex, job.
2.   A given factor can be a source of both satisfaction and dissatisfaction in the same group.
3.   Herzberg has twisted his own evidence: achievement and recognition (or their absence) are just as much causes of dissatisfaction as satisfaction, therefore the division between job satisfaction and job dissatisfaction does not really exist.

Despite their criticisms, there is no doubt that Herzberg has persuaded many managements to look at job design and worker participation just as carefully as at wages, bonus and incentive schemes.

Achievement motivation. This focuses on the needs for achievement, power and belonging (application). We need not dwell on it here: it explains the motives of people like managers, salesmen, and those jockeying for position in a bureaucratic or similar organization, but it is not applicable to all levels of employees.

Expectancy theory. The basic assumption of many of the previous theories is that people will *willingly* direct their efforts to goals they value. But as C. Cooper[5] points out, 'People will only act when they have a *reasonable expectation* [my italics] their actions will lead to desirable goals.' Thus *needs alone* are not enough: the possibility that goals can be fulfiled is also necessary for motivation.
   As developed by Victor Vroom (1964), and Edward Lawler III and Lymen Porter (1967), and subsequently by others, this idea can be illustrated diagrammatically as in Fig. 5.1 below.

---

[4] Herzberg's dual-factor theory of job satisfaction and motivation, and review of the evidence. In *Personnel Psychology*, No. 20 (1967). Richmond, Virginia: William Byrd Press.
[5] *Job Motivation and Job Design*. London: IPM, 1974.

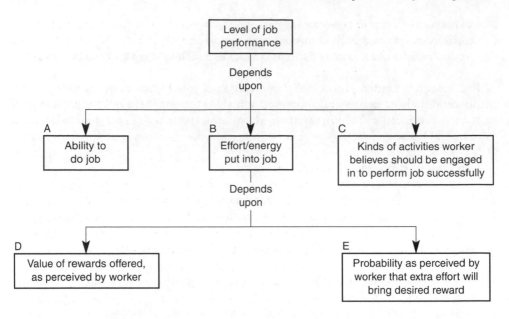

Figure 5.1 The 'Expectancy' model of motivation.

In this version of the model, it will be clearly seen that job performance depends on much more than B, motivation. Both the *ability* to do the job (A), and the worker's *perception* of the behaviour/activities required for him to complete the job success fully (C), are equally important.

Assuming that both ability and a correct interpretation of what has to be done to complete the job successfully are present, then job performance will depend primarily on. the effort put into the job (B). The model suggests there are two factors determining B:

1. The *value of the rewards* to the worker—that is to what extent the rewards offered appear to satisfy the worker's needs (e.g. more money, promotion/increased status, public approval); and
2. *The degree of probability* (as perceived by the worker—not the actual probability) that the desired rewards will actually be achievable by effort (or extra effort, enthusiasm etc.) put into the job. These are in fact the worker's *expectations*. (The degree of perceived probability will be greatly affected by past experience—did the money actually materialize last time?)

Thus, a worker wanting a high income who is given job X to carry out with a promise that a substantial bonus is payable at the conclusion of the job, will work hard at the job to the extent that (a) the worker believes hard work will actually lead to the bonus being paid, and (b) the bonus in question will be big enough to help satisfy his need for a high income.

A general conclusion of expectancy theory is that in any given situation the greater the number and variety of rewards available to a worker, the greater is the probability that extra effort will be expended in attaining targets set, in the hope or expectation of gaining the rewards desired. Indeed studies associated with the development of the theory do tend to show that money payments (if tied to performance) can assist in increasing output or production.

There is of course the problem that this increased motivation or extra effort is only of use if properly channelled. Of itself increased motivation does not necessarily lead to increased performance. (A student, for example, who works very hard revising irrelevant material, or works at the wrong syllabus may perform poorly in an examination.) Further, some people can become *over-motivate*d and over-anxious to do well, leading to stress, indecision and error.

It is clear that what motivates worker A may not motivate other workers, B, C, D etc. If they all work in the same team, a whole range of different motivations/ rewards should be available to suit each of them—which could be difficult, or even impossible.

Whatever rewards are offered for effort expended/performance achieved, workers will always be tempted to compare such rewards with those offered elsewhere—inside or outside the organization. This notion of fairness or 'equity' could result in a reward which management might feel is good—even generous—being perceived as poor or mean in comparison with another reward for the same job offered in the offices down the road.

Conclusions

What are we to make of all this? My own view is as human beings are so diverse, what attracts one does not another. To try to obtain universal motivations leads one on a fool's errand. However, we might take the following propositions as being worthy of consideration:

1. Human beings like working in groups, and many of them prefer to identify with a group.
2. Many people like to be consulted about the work they are to do; and to feel they have a say in how their work is to be carried out.
3. Certain people are underemployed (i.e. not sufficient use is made of their talents), and this is a cause of dissatisfaction.
4. Repetitive assembly work is likely to be less attractive in the long run (and more conflict is likely to be generated in such surroundings) than work demanding the use of skills and decision-making. Playing about with the job surroundings and not the job is likely to have little or no effect.
5. Money is not the only motivation, but it can be regarded as a levy exacted on the society which asks some workers to work at repetitive tasks.
6. People want status and a superior position *vis-à-vis* others; and very often the need for a certain status is a strong motivator. (For example, in pay claims, workers often talk about 'relativities'.)
7. It is up to the supervisor to try to find what motivates the group most, and to convince each subordinate to want to do what has been assigned, or asked to do.

8. Performance depends upon ability as well as motivation.
9. High motivation does not always result in high productivity.
10. Motivation can be increased by

   (a) effective training
   (b) clearer job descriptions, and increased understanding of roles and tasks to be done
   (c) clearer standards of performance being laid down.
   (d) an ever-increasing involvement and empowerment of team-members.

5.2.5 Communicating

This is the most difficult of the six functions to review, as we are using the very function to study itself!

By 'communicating' we mean the transfer of an idea in my mind, to yours such that it is understood. Good communication occurs when a useful or appropriate idea is transferred efficiently. Bad communication has many causes, but it entails either the non-arrival of a message or the arrival of a distorted or inappropriate message. A useful analogy of the communication process is the transmission of a message by radio from the source to the receiver. See Fig. 5.2.

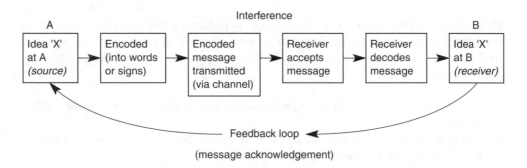

Figure 5.2 The communication process.

Note that in this model the journey of idea 'X' from A to B faces *interference* (distraction, such as noise, movement; or distance fading the message; or anything which *prevents* the message from getting through). In radio transmission this is usually 'crackling' or 'static'. In actual communication, the noise of machinery, the worries on the receiver's mind, the inability of the receiver to decode the message accurately— all these are *interference*.

Secondly, we see the need for the sender to *encode* the message: in radio terms this means to convert sound into a 'signal', or series of electrical impulses. For communicators, this means converting ideas into a recognizable set of symbols, written or spoken, or into the form of gestures.

Encoding-decoding problems

The point about the code is that it should be understood by both sender and receiver. If we both use the same code book, the message is understood, if we *think* we use the same code book, but in fact we use somewhat different books, then messages will get muddled.

Ask a class of supervisors, 'What is the name of the meal normally eaten between noon and 2 pm?' and you will get at least three answers—'lunch', 'luncheon', 'dinner'; or the name of the space between two houses, and you will get a long (and some words are virtually unknown) list: 'path', 'pathway', 'entry', 'alley', 'alleyway', 'jennel', 'jinnel', 'straiker' and so on. So much for the notion we all speak the same language in the same country!

If we look at the differences between 'British' English and 'American' English, the position becomes marginally more confusing: until recently British 'billions' were ten times greater than American ones; Americans hearing the word 'bonnet' would normally think of a woman's head covering, Britons, the cover over a car engine; a Briton would naturally regard the time of year from September onwards as 'autumn', an American would normally use 'fall'.

The supervisor's communication problems are greater than most at work: he or she may have to use no fewer than three 'code books'. The language normally used may well have to be varied when dealing with his or her own staff, or when speaking with superiors or technical staff.

Attitudes

Another serious problem occurs at the 'decoding' part of the process. The way that people see or view the world, in other words their established prejudices, assumptions and expectations, will affect how they receive messages. (Psychologists have coined the term 'mind set' to cover this state of mind.) This way of interpretation can affect the message, or even the message-sender. The staunch supporter of a political party may well receive an unpleasant message (e.g. a tax increase) favourably because *his* party and *his* leader are responsible for the message: the same message issued by the opposition party, if they came to power, might be criticized strongly or even resisted. So the supervisor must be prepared in some circumstances for perfectly good and reasonable ideas to be resisted by the work force simply because the ideas come from 'them', the management.

Basis of good communication

A subject like 'communication' is so large and complex that it requires a fuller treatment as a separate subject—which it receives in syllabuses such as the NEBSM Certificate in Supervisory Management. However we may establish a few general rules for good communication:

1. A source-sender of a message should ensure that the facts in it are accurate; and that the language is clear, concise and readily understood by receivers.
2. Unless it is appropriate, a source-sender should keep prejudices, emotions or attitudes out of messages, the more so if such messages are *supposed* to be factual.
3. The source-sender should introduce a feedback system into all communications: not only does it give the receiver a chance to become a sender, but it helps the original sender to check that his/her communication was received, understood and acted upon.
4. A source-sender should therefore become a *listener/receiver* when the feedback response arrives. There is a need to pay as much attention to the return message as the sender would expect from someone receiving the original message.
5. In a formal situation communications should be sent up or down the chain of command. (Remember the 'line bypass'—people tend to get upset if they are left out.)
6. A source-sender should choose the most appropriate channel for each communication—verbal[6] for interviews, meetings, order giving; written for order giving, messages over a long distance, very important matters and matters of great detail.

Informal communications

Besides the formal network of the chain of command, there can be, as we saw in Chapter 1, an informal (or more than one informal) network of relations between members of an organization.

Fayol's 'gangplank', as we have seen, allows two departmental heads to communicate directly, as indeed such managers do frequently, rather than following protocol, and referring matters upwards. The formal network may be far too slow, particularly in an emergency.

Again a very senior executive may communicate directly with experts in the organization on their particular specialist subjects, as to go through their departmental head may even be counter-productive if the head does not specialize in that particular area. Thus an accountant specializing in overseas investments could be consulted in his own right by the board of a company with overseas interests.

Grapevine. However the most significant, and the most often distrusted by management, network of informal communication is the *grapevine*, that mysterious mixture of rumour and truth, surmise and gossip, which circulates at all levels within the organization.

It only needs one member of an informal group within the organization to receive an interesting piece of information—an extra day's holiday at Christmas, for example,

---

6 'Verbal' is used here and subsequently in the commonly accepted sense of 'spoken'. The Oxford English Dictionary defines 'verbal' as 'expressed or conveyed by speech instead of writing; stated or delivered by word of mouth; oral'.

and for him to circulate the message quickly round his group; most of the group members will inevitably belong to other small informal groups of people, and in turn they will pass the message on to them. If a message is interesting enough it will be passed on very quickly—it is estimated 95% of the citizens of the United States living in towns knew of President Kennedy's assassination within 90 minutes of the event.

Thus the grapevine is not 'special' to business firms and formal organizations devoted to profit-making: every week we seem to read about minutely detailed discussions occurring at 'secret' parliamentary party committee meetings; or reports of what happened at cabinet meetings; or rumours about political manoeuvrings.

Management tends to dislike, and possibly fear, the grapevine, because information management would like to keep to itself becomes common knowledge, and often in distorted form. The possibility of a temporary cut-back in production becomes (in the grapevine) threatened redundancies; the possibility of some redundancies becomes a plant shut-down, and so on.

The only way to counter the grapevine, and help it to wither, is for management at all times to keep the work force as fully informed as possible about the organization's present fortunes and future prospects. In any event legislation encouraging the publication of this type of information is already in existence, and will without doubt be reinforced in the future.

Non-verbal communication[7]

Before we leave the topic of communication we must remind ourselves that we also communicate, sometimes consciously, sometimes unconsciously, by the use of facial expressions (yawns, smiles, the delicately raised eyebrow), gestures (the Churchillian 'V' sign means one thing, the reverse something else), or the use of the eyes ('looking at' implies interest, 'turning away' implies disinterest, or even dismissal). All these methods of communication do not use words so we call them 'non-verbal communication'.

A whole subject area has grown up rapidly in the last two decades, Desmond Morris's 'Man Watching' was a popular exhibition of this topic, and while we shall not wish to examine the subject in detail we should note that the way we present ourselves to our work force is very important—dress, grooming, positive speech, pleasant acceptable gestures and facial expression all tell the world about us. These factors can affect the way a message is received. A pay rise or promotion given with a scowl and an unwilling sounding voice is not worth much to the recipient; whereas a sincere statement of approval or praise could work wonders.

5.2.6 Controlling

Controlling is the essential process of seeing that what was planned to happen actually *does* happen. Thus we can set objectives for the whole organization; or particular

---

[7] Non-verbal communication is used here in the commonly accepted sense of body language.

departments. What we must do (if we want to succeed in achieving our objectives) is to check before things have gone too far that we are 'on track'; and if we have fallen short or wandered off course to see by how much.

Controlling involves the following activities:

1. Setting objectives, or standards of work.
2. Devising ways of measuring actual performance.
3. Measuring actual performance against the objectives, or standards.
4. Evaluating what deviations from the planned results exist, and why they occurred.
5. Taking corrective action where this is possible, to restore the position.

In essence, control is a 'feedback system' (the idea we first met in Chapter 1, when we discussed Systems Theory), the 'checking-up' part of a supervisor's or manager's job. Of course it implies planning; the setting of the original targets, objectives and standards is absolutely essential, as well as the planning of the checking, or inspection process.

Other parts of your course deal with control systems in great detail—budgeting, accounting, costing and auditing in Managing Financial Resources; network analysis, production control, work study in Managing Products and Services—but we shall take two illustrations from budgetary control to explore the idea of control further.

Budgets

A budget is a statement (usually in *financial* terms, but sometimes in *volume* terms) of what is planned, or of what we expect to happen. The Chancellor of the Exchequer is responsible each year (at least!) for reviewing the state of economy publicly, and estimating government income and expenditure over the next twelve-month tax period.

Such a budget is made up of many, smaller items, and it is the same with the firm, or organization. A company, called Winnits Ltd, making parts for the motor industry will start by working out total income and expenditure budgets for the year. Included in the expenditure is an item: oil for heating the offices. If we consider this in detail, we will get a clearer picture of the process.

Constructing a budget. Budgeting requires careful record keeping: if we have not done this in the past, the first time we prepare a budget may be somewhat difficult. In the case of our oil heating budget, we will, however, have last year's total consumption figures (from the oil company, even if we have not recorded this total) of, for example, 5500 litres. Now it is obvious we cannot simply divide the yearly total by 12 and say our monthly consumption is about 450 litres: consumption will be high in mid-winter and very low in the summer, probably just enough heat to warm the water for washing purposes. We must also take into account considerations such as lengths of the months, February being shorter than the others, holidays, including perhaps complete shutdowns in July or August, or a whole week at Christmas and New Year. We could eventually come up with a budget on the lines of Table 5.2. We would then compare the *actual* consumption measured through an appropriate flow meter month by month.

Table 5.2 Winnits Ltd—office block (volume) heating (plan)

					Budget-litres						
Jan	*Feb*	*Mar*	*Apr*	*May*	*Jun*	*Jul*	*Aug*	*Sep*	*Oct*	*Nov*	*Dec*
1000	900	850	500	250	100	50	50	200	250	500	750

Variances. Any differences recorded between what was originally budgeted and what was actually consumed are called *variances.* In any control system we must be able to spot variances; and try to find explanations for them. The results of our investigations can then result in corrective action to bring us back on course (or sometimes to reset the objectives or standards, though this should not be done without careful thought).

Suppose we obtained the actual results during a given year as shown in Table 5.3. Now during the year we have consumed exactly what we anticipated, but in any good control system we should want explanations for each of the monthly variances, perhaps there was a very cold spell during January and the thermostat was turned up too high, a warm spell in March which reduced consumption, boiler trouble in November and December, resulting in a not very efficient oil/energy ratio, and so on. The point is we need to pinpoint every variance[8] and explain it.

Table 5.3 Winnits Ltd—office block (volume) heating (actual)

	Jan	*Feb*	*Mar*	*Apr*	*May*	*Jun*	*Jul*	*Aug*	*Sep*	*Oct*	*Nov*	*Dec*	*Total*
Budget	1000	900	850	500	250	100	50	50	200	350	500	750	5500
Actual	1100	950	750	400	300	50	50	50	200	250	600	800	5500
Variance	+100	+50	–100	–100	+50	–50	–	–	–	–100	+100	+50	

Production budgets. We can now take the idea a stage further by considering a production budget. Here, we have not only a budgeted volume output for a period (say a month) but budgets for material used up in manufacture, and a budgeted cost per item (usually called a *standard* cost). We must then look for variances in each of these (and any other factors we consider).

Let us imagine that Winnits Ltd are in business to make winnits, devices which when fitted to a motor car will decrease petrol consumption significantly. The manager of the assembly department has been given a budget of £30 000 for production in January, and is pleased to note he has underspent by £750, when the results are circulated in February. The works superintendent is not so pleased. Look at Table 5.4. Can you see why?

Analysing the variances. The superintendent would look at:

1. *Output*—why were only 4500 units started? Was it lack of orders? Shortage of operatives? Industrial relations problems? Lack of usable machines?

---

[8] That is a very *significant* variance. A very small one – such as five or ten litres – could be ignored. We do not want to waste valuable management time on trivia.

Table 5.4 Winnit Assembly Department – performance January 19XX

	Output	Sets of components used	£ Cost per winnit	£ Total winnit costs
Budget	5000	5000	6.00	30 000
Actual (at budget cost)	4250	4500	6.00	27 000
Actual (at actual cost)	4250	4500	6.50	29 250

Why were only 4250 units completed? The scrap rate was about 5½%. Is it in line with normal scrap rates? If not, was it the fault of poor workmanship? Over zealous inspection? Mistakes in previous departments? Inadequate machinery?

2. *Costs*—why did the actual cost rise 50p above the budget (standard) figure? Was it material price increases, labour cost increases, or inefficiency in the department (here he would want to look at overtime figures)?

3. *Remedies*—depending upon the findings, remedies would have to be sought. Inadequate machinery repaired or replaced; workers recruited, or trained; consideration given to making the job cheaper by using alternative materials or reappraising the assembly forces.

So we see plenty of avenues of investigation present themselves in a small set of figures. With experience in the business solutions to many of the questions would soon be forthcoming and appropriate action would be taken to correct imbalances. Of course, variances cannot always be corrected, material price increases or wage awards cannot be reversed, cold spells avoided, or economic recessions ignored.

Variances do show where to direct the scarcest of management resources, time, in maintaining a dynamic steady-state, or equilibrium in the organization.

5.2.7 Supplementary points

Finally we will look at some general points.

Universality of the six functions. Whenever we look at an organization; at the work of the chief executive on the one hand and at the first-line manager on the other, we note that the tasks of creating, planning, organizing, motivating, communicating and controlling are both the essence and the content of the job in both formal and informal organizations.

Importance of each function. Each function has its own importance, but we cannot say one is *more* important than another. However, in a particular job there may be considerably more *emphasis* on one aspect. Thus an army NCO might spend more time on communicating to and motivating a platoon, while the platoon commander may be concentrating on planning and organizing the next stage in an exercise.

Order of performance. Although in this review we have placed the functions in a *logical* order, this order is not chronological, that is there is no specific sequence a manager or supervisor would follow in a day's work—all of the functions would be done, all the time.

5.3   THE TRANSFERABILITY OF MANAGEMENT

We have seen that the functions of management—creating, planning, organizing, motivating, communicating and controlling—are universal and belong to all managers. We can say then that there is a job called 'managing', or 'supervising', and there are definite similarities between one manager's job and another.

In principle it would seem possible to remove an office manager in a textile company, and place him in a supervisor's job in a garage. *In practice,* this would be an unsatisfactory move as the manager's job has two elements: the *management* aspect and the *technical* aspect. This particular example emphasizes the importance of the technical aspects, particularly in the supervisor's position.

However, it would be an easier transition from being the company secretary of the garage to the company secretary of the textile company. The technical aspects of the job are very much more alike in this case.

An example of management transition is provided by British Rail. At different times Britain's railways have been managed at the top by an army general (Sir Brian Robertson), a one-time director of ICI (Lord Beeching) and an ex-Cabinet Minister (Richard Marsh). Politics also lends itself to this type of managerial move; for example, the late Ernest Marples became first a Housing Minister and later the most remembered (and the most decisive) Minister of Transport since the war.

Thus, we can say:

1.   The more technical a managerial type job, the more difficult it is to transfer (unless the technical aspects of both jobs are similar).
2.   The greater the managerial aspects in the job, the easier it is to transfer.

SUMMARY

In this chapter we have noted:

1.   Henri Fayol suggested there were *Five Elements of Management* namely:

   (a)   To forecast and plan.
   (b)   To organize.
   (c)   To command.
   (d)   To co-ordinate.
   (e)   To control.

2.   Modern views, though different from Fayol's list, are still based upon it.

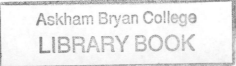

3.   Various lists exist, but the one which seems to provide the best general pic-
          ture of a manager's role includes the following functions: creating,
          planning, organizing, motivating, communicating, and controlling. These
          functions are carried out by managers in all organizations—both formal
          and informal.

4.   Because of the universality of these functions it is possible, provided the
          technical aspects of the job are not so specialized nor so large a part of the
          total job as to overshadow the 'managing' aspects, for a manager to move
          from one organization to another, and be successful in his new job.

REVIEW QUESTIONS

1.   What did Fayol say were the Five Elements of Management?

2.   What are the six functions (discussed in detail in the chapter) that summa-
          rize a modern view of the manager's job? How do these functions differ
          from Fayol's list?

3.   Suggest (by taking particular aspects of the job in question, and relating
          them to particular functions of management) how the six functions would
          be performed by:

          (a)   A headteacher of a comprehensive school.
          (b)   The manager of a local supermarket.
          (c)   A football team manager.
          (d)   The chief executive of a local bus company.

4.   Take all the lists of managerial functions mentioned in the early part of this
          chapter, compare them, and decide which list *you* think is the best summary.

5.   Why do you think planning is necessary? What would happen to an organi-
          zation without any future plans?

6.   What do you understand by the objectives of an organization?

7.   What is the purpose of organizing?

8.   What is meant by *motivators*, according to Herzberg?

9.   Why is motivation necessary?

10.   Outline some of the problems of communication.

11.   What is meant by 'non-verbal communication'? Why is this concept important to supervisors?

12.   What are the basic principles of any control system?

13.   Explain the purpose and importance of budgeting.

DISCUSSION TOPICS

1.   What would happen to an organization, if next Monday morning, all the managers ceased to perform the six functions?

2.   'Information is power.' Discuss this statement with particular reference to the relationship between senior executives and supervisors; supervisors and the work force.

3.   If you were the chief executive of an organization, and discovered topics discussed at board meetings were being circulated through the grapevine, would you:

    (a) Take no action.
    (b) Track down the culprit and discipline him or her.
    (c) Deny the truth of the stories.
    (d) Make a full statement to the staff about the meetings.
    (e) Use a different approach. If so, what?

4.   The majority of the organizational psychologists would say *needs* were the causes of human behaviour. Is this true?

5.   Could you ever satisfy *all* an individual's needs? Why?

6.   Discuss the methods by which a teacher can control the work of a class: how can individuals' performances be checked? Which is better—continuous assessment or periodic tests?

ASSIGNMENTS

A5.1   Each student already practising a supervisory or managerial role can make a list of the functions he or she performs, allocating particular jobs to each function and suggesting the total time spent each week on each separate function. Students who are not yet supervisors or managers could ask a practising manager for this information. Results should be discussed in class, and compared.

A5.2 Imagine your course is to hold a residential weekend in two months time, and you are the course tutor. Plan the weekend, paying attention to:

(a) Selection of reasonable accommodation and facilities required.
(b) Cost of the accommodation.
(c) A balance of activities throughout the weekend, including 'free' time.

Work out a budget, to include speakers at £40 per hour (including expenses), which will give a cost per student for the weekend.

A5.3 Breakdowns in communication take many forms. Select an instance from your own work/college/school experience, state what happened, and attempt to find out, as far as is practically possible, why this mistake occurred.

A5.4 Part of the process of organizing entails ensuring that there is no duplication of effort, overlap of functions or jobs. Take an example from an organization with which you are familiar, work organization or college, where such duplication has occurred, and suggest how improvements could be made.

CASE STUDIES

A5.5 Burntin Limited, whose main business activity is tinning and exporting Scottish stream water, has a problem on its hands. A relatively recently formed company, the majority of the 60 or so office staff are under 30, single and 20 are recent graduates. They live in a well-run, well-equipped hostel; facilities exist for salmon fishing, sailing, climbing, football and cricket. Salaries are well above average, and particularly in high summer, working hours are reduced to 32, to take advantage of the long, warm days.

A few days ago, a notice was posted up in the mess-hall, calling for two volunteers to help in the opening of a small office in London. Hours would be long, especially in the beginning, with no paid overtime; salaries would be no higher than in Scotland, and the successful candidates would have to find (and pay for) their own lodgings.

Mr Plod, the personnel manager, is disturbed because no less than 50 people have applied for the jobs, and everyone is talking about the situation.

Bearing in mind behaviour explanations such as Maslow's:

How do you account for this (present) state of affairs? What advice would you give to Mr Plod, who is fearful many staff will leave soon?

A5.6 After completing her teacher training, Mary Flaske spent many years as a Chemistry mistress in secondary schools. She earned a reputation as being an efficient organizer of laboratory work and the courses that she taught; and was well respected by her pupils.

During her late 30s, she was encouraged to seek promotion, and within the space of five years she held in succession the post of Senior Chemistry Mistress, Head of Science, and in her previous school she became a Deputy Headmistress. Recently she applied for, and was appointed to the Headship of a new comprehensive at Trumpton.

In her latest job, Mary seems to spend a great deal of her time interviewing staff who either have grievances or teaching (and personal) problems; dealing with parents, and 'problem' pupils; setting up new courses and timetabling across the school; and spending time at numerous meetings with staff, the governors, and the local education authority.

Last Saturday, Mary met John Standfast, a friend from her teacher training days, who was now a Senior Physics Master at a nearby school. 'I don't know whether this is really the job for me, John' said Mary, over a dry sherry. 'I spend all my time in my office, dealing with mounds of paper, coping with a stream of callers, and organizing people, and coping with their problems. I never have time to solve my own; I just never seem to get anything done these days.

'I wish I were back in the schoolroom again, John, doing a *real* job of work, like you.'

(a) Why do you think Mary appeared to think her teaching job was somehow more real or important than her present job? Do you agree with Mary?

(b) Mary had teacher training, but seemingly never attended a supervisory or management course. How would you go about explaining to Mary what the functions of management are?

A5.7   After the revolution in Ruritania Commissioner Brown issued Industrial Proclamation No. 1. This read as follows:

RURITANIAN GOVERNMENT PROCLAMATION
WORKERS' CONTROL

With immediate effect workers will assume control of the factories they work in. The jobs of all directors, managers and supervisors are hereby abolished; ex-managers will join the work force as producers forthwith. In future, factory policy decisions will be taken by mass meetings of workers, and shop production problems will be handled by the individual work groups concerned.

(a) What do you think would be the immediate consequences of such an order, including production?
(b) What are likely to be the longer term consequences?

6
The Supervisor and the Functions of Management: Creating, Planning and Organizing

In the previous chapter, it was argued that six functions of management (creating, planning, organizing, motivating, communicating and controlling) were the most important, and that the jobs of managers could be analysed under these six headings. We must now look more closely at the *application* of these functions to the job of the supervisor. Obviously every application cannot be covered but examples discussed in the text should indicate how the principles could and should be applied. Creating, planning and organizing are dealt with in this chapter; Chapter 7 covers the remainder.

6.1 CREATIVITY

The word 'create' is usually associated with the depiction or invention of something new; we call painters, artists, poets, and indeed scientists 'creative', when they produce a new masterpiece, design a unique building or announce an elegant, yet simple theory which simultaneously solves a myriad scientific problems. The pity is that by emphasizing that such people are creative, the implication is the rest of us are not. McGregor, as we have seen, rejected this idea and claimed that most of us had the capacity to exercise a high degree of imagination, ingenuity and creativity in the solution of problems.

Unfortunately, at school we learn the need to get the 'right' answers. F.W. Taylor spent his life looking for right answers in a logical way, and so do most of us who have received any further training in scientific or technical subjects. Such training helps us to identify weaknesses in proposals and makes our criticism devastating but it is not conducive to innovation. Logic on its own helps to maintain the status quo. In fact, the veneration of logic leads to the feeling that if a problem is solved in an illogical way, such a solution is fraudulent, and in some way untrustworthy.

The amazing point about the really outstanding creative ideas is that at the time they were announced there was no logical justification for them, although later on we have established the logical links: Marconi was not aware of the ionized reflective layers of the upper atmosphere which 'bounced' his radio transmission back earthward, Velcro fasteners were based on a simple observation of the way seed burrs cling to cloth or clothes with which they come into contact.

If logic cannot solve a problem, and there is no answer available in a suitable textbook, people may conclude that the problem is insoluble. All that has happened, however, is that all *known* attempts at solution have failed and new ones are needed. How do we find ways of providing new solutions, how do we train ourselves to use the untapped capacity that McGregor talks about? There are two main ways of stimulating the creative process—group work, and an individual approach.

6.1.1 Group creativity

The commonly used group creative activities are all versions of brainstorming. While this technique is *usually* best implemented by a group, once a supervisor has grasped the idea, it can be operated by individuals. An American, A. F. Osborne, developed the idea in 1941, and it was envisaged as a general procedure for a *group* to tackle a problem, such as, for example, what name to call a new motor car. The rules are as follows:

1. Ideas are to be offered without criticism of any kind, every idea is acceptable at this stage.
2. Evaluation of ideas only takes place when the ideas have been produced, that is, all critical judgement is suspended.
3. People are encouraged to enlarge on ideas of others.
4. There is a certain formality about the setting with a group leader, and someone is designated to write all the ideas emerging on a flipchart. People usually find the 'one-ness' of the group stimulating and ideas flow fast after the first few minutes. The main emphasis at this stage is to generate alternatives *for their own sake,* no matter how illegal, absurd, anti-social or impractical they may seem. In fact a 'competition' feeling quickly becomes apparent, with participants vying with each other to produce stimulating or unusual ideas, and even if solutions offered are quite ordinary, there may be an odd remark which will start some on to a new track.

After about fifteen minutes, the output of new ideas will tend to ease off, and the group leader should always close a session before participants get bored. The best of the ideas put forward are then debated and analysed one by one—a process which can lead to yet more ideas, until an acceptable solution is seen to emerge. (Some authorities feel the evaluation session should not take place on the same day as the 'idea generating' process; the intervening period may result in fresh ideas emerging 'subconsciously'.)

Other forms of brainstorming include one where the problem (which in reality is very specific, such as getting highly finished and expensive cloth from one factory to another in the open air exposed to the weather) is put to the group in very general terms under a heading such as 'problems of movement', 'carrying things about'. The 'buzz' session is more competitive with parallel groups of 'brainstormers' who pool the best ideas at the end in a joint session.

6.1.2 Individual creativity

To become creative or more creative needs application, some training (or some would say re-orientation) and plenty of experience in trying out various techniques. Much interesting work has been done on 'lateral thinking', and supervisors (and others) are recommended to obtain Edward de Bono's *Lateral Thinking*,[1] a concise, clear and very readable textbook on individual creativity.

De Bono contrasts 'vertical' (or logical) thinking with lateral thinking: what is 'right' is the safe vertical way of viewing things; lateral thinking looks for the revolutionary, possibly unsafe, risky (on the face of it), provocative, least likely kind of answer.

To become a lateral thinker involves removing blinkers from the mind: realizing that there is an infinite number of ways of looking at the world Thus, the search for alternatives for their own sake, as in brainstorming, is an essential part of the process, and something the individual can train himself to do quite quickly. Less easy is the ability to reorganize existing patterns of information into new ones; quite hard for entirely different, and this time emotional reasons, to throw overboard treasured attitudes and assumptions. In a sense the work study questioning of a process did this: the first question 'Is it necessary?' was such a challenge to accepted ideas. Any process and way of doing things can be questioned, not just from the point of view of whether it is being done in the quickest, cheapest, simplest way, but whether it should be done at all.

De Bono goes further, and points out that many of the assumptions we adopt, are in fact self-imposed. The supervisor with the problem of a succession of minor but irritating breakdowns in his department may assume from past experience that his supervisor will not sanction further expenditure to modify or replace the machinery involved. In fact, a programme of replacement could be the most suitable solution, but the supervisor rules it out before properly considering it.

A dramatic lateral thinking technique is the 'reversal' method of looking at a situation. Let us suppose that a male lecturer is having problems with his students. They are late, miss some classes, are noisy, inattentive, are slow in giving in assignments. He writes down the sentence 'lecturer instructs the class'. Now if he turns this around, we get 'the class instructs the lecturer'. Immediately this suggests that an answer to the problem may be for our unlucky lecturer to get his students to instruct him as to where *he* might have gone wrong: poor material, bad presentation, or failure to establish good relationships with the students perhaps.

Finally (although De Bono mentions several other techniques) we could consider the use of analogies to help solve problems. There is a natural reluctance to use this technique because people are taught not to use analogies in arguments: just because the boy next door has a new bike because he has passed an exam, does not mean you can claim one too. But we are not *arguing* from analogy in this technique: we are using analogy to help generate new ideas, to stimulate possible solutions. For example, we might have as our *problem*, getting tickets for the men's finals at Wimbledon: the *analogy,* trying to start a car with a flat battery on a bitterly cold morning. The starting

---

[1] Published by Penguin.

problem would have to be worked out in detail, perhaps by a brainstorming technique, even if the problem solver is on his own he can get people who know about cars to help; using 'jump' leads; getting a tow and so on. Of these perhaps 'getting expert help' gives a clue to possible further action.

We are now in a position to set the problem-solving and decision-making process in a more formalized way.

Problem-solving and decision-making

Problem-solving and decision-making are so interrelated they are really part of the same process: most decisions are made to solve (or forestall impending) problems and most problems have a host of possible solutions, a decision has to be taken as to which solution to adopt.

We can describe problem-solving in terms now quite familiar to us, as a system. See Fig. 6.1. However, we must be clear from the start that there are two distinct types of decisions you will be called upon to make, routine and non-routine.

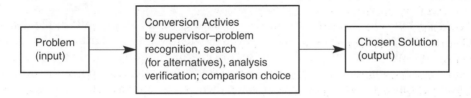

Figure 6.1 Problem-solving in system terms.

Routine decisions are ones which have to be made frequently—so frequently that a definite procedure has been worked out for everyone to follow. In a sense, there is no choice about routine decisions, covered as they are by company rules, Queen's Regulations, college regulations and so on. Many examples of routine decisions will undoubtedly occur to you—re-ordering of goods out of stock, the granting of discounts to particular classes of customers, the use of particular tools to do particular jobs.

It is important for the supervisor to abide by the chosen solutions to problems, especially if they are laid down in written rules and procedures, but the more challenging problems are those which are not covered adequately by existing practice or specific rules. Here is the supervisor's chance to be creative, perhaps using the ideas we considered above such as lateral thinking.

Here we shall concentrate on the novel, non-routine problems, and start with the threefold question:

What is the problem?
What are the possible alternatives?
Which alternative is the best as far as can be ascertained?

Identifying the problem

A stage in problem-solving that is often neglected. Consider the problem which often
occurs at exhibitions, zoos or fairs—children get lost, or separated from their parents.
When people are asked to define what the problem is in this type of situation, many
respond by saying that the problem lies in children getting lost; and possible (some
ingenious) solutions all lie in the area of reuniting those separated as quickly as possible. Others take a different view: they see the problem as one of *prevention,* that is
solutions lie in the area of preventing parents and children from being separated in the
first place.

It is always a good idea, if you have a non-routine problem to sit back a minute and
try to identify the *real* problem. If a worker suddenly changes his or her behaviour,
becomes casual, works badly, the situation is more complex than saying, 'I've got a
problem with Joe'. The problem could be in Joe's personal life, or in his relationship
with co-workers, or even in something you have done.

Setting standards and gathering information

It is important for the supervisor to set standards of work for *all* jobs in the department. The supervisor is faced with a problem whenever a standard is violated. If a
failure to look into a variance can make it likely that a problem will arise sooner or
later, a certain amount of control will be lost. One unfortunate factor in the situation
is that operators set different standards for themselves: one may stop a machine if it
runs badly; another might let it carry on until it breaks down, another might try and
adjust it, and a fourth may report the failure, plus the fact that he smelt burning first.
The use of standards for gathering information cannot be overstressed.

Six-step problem-solving

Supervisors will find this *six-step* problem-solving technique useful; it should be
learnt by heart.

Step 1: *clearly identify the problem.* As we have already seen, this is a vital preliminary. Try to isolate the real problem.

Step 2: *gather all the relevant facts.* This may be a tedious, time-consuming business,
but to avoid drawing hasty conclusions every possible care must be taken in obtaining
information. If there are two witnesses to an accident it is best to interview both: hear
all sides of an argument and check people's records before taking a disciplinary step.
Obviously, some *assumptions* will have to be made, particularly about people's behaviour and past history, but never forget to find out all you possibly can.

Step 3: *establish the cause of the problem.* It is very difficult to solve any problem until
its cause is identified. What is a 'cause' is so often difficult to establish as a whole

sequence of events may have to take place before a problem emerges. For example, a product may have a design fault which has been responsible for many failures in the past; when asked to comment on the failure of a particular customer's component it would be natural to give the standard answer without much investigation. From personal experience I have come across cases where in fact it was not the obvious, known fault that had caused the failure.

Technical failures can usually be more easily traced than human problems, which can be more complex. The operator who hurts his hand in a machine may have a 'don't care' attitude to work today because his wife left him over the weekend; but the apparent and immediate cause is a faulty component jammed in the machine. Underlying this could be the reason that your predecessor was lazy, and overlooked occasional lapses of this sort, provided nobody was hurt.

Step 4: *search for and develop a variety of solutions.* One of the curious aspects of our upbringing is the accent on 'right answers', or correct solutions. At school you learn what earns ticks and marks, and what does not; the accent is on problems with one and one solution only. Mathematical problems often are of this kind: 4 is the only answer to 'what is 2 + 2?'

Sadly, over the years we have tended to discard the ability to be imaginative with which we were born in an effort to 'get things right' and to conform. But when, as supervisors, we face human and work problems suddenly we realize that there are no right or wrong solutions, just a range of alternative courses of action of which one or two are better or more acceptable than the others. To cope with problems of this more complex kind we need to be creative as well as logical.

So, the imaginative supervisor will develop several different, alternative solutions to problems, the technique of brainstorming is one way of doing this, for their own sake. Ideally *every* possibility should be explained.

Let us take the operator who has tried to free a jammed component, and hurt his hand. We could, amongst other courses of action:

1. Dismiss him.
2. Transfer him (to another machine, another department).
3. Suspend him until he sorts out his domestic problems.
4. Give him (paid) compassionate leave.
5. Reprimand him.
6. Send him to the welfare officer, company's solicitors etc.
7. Have the machine repaired, faulty components replaced.
8. Promote him.

More than one solution could be adopted at one time.

Step 5: *evaluate alternatives, choose the most practical.* Any solution considered must be both practical and practicable. If dismissals are the prerogative of higher management, then (l) above is a solution you could not implement; in addition you must evaluate every alternative in the light of constraints:

1. Acts of Parliament and other statutory requirements.
2. Relationships with the union.
3. Established rules and practices.
4. Urgency of action.
5. Cost of implementation.

All these things would have to be considered. Probably, a compromise would result.

Step 6: evaluate results of solution adopted.   This is a step often neglected. Particularly where a change in behaviour is involved, it is important to follow up the results. A constant check has to be kept against operators 'relapsing' into bad habits.

Improvising.   Even the most methodical, well-in-control supervisor has to improvise from time to time. Often there is time for careful thought about the problem, but improvisation is *synthesis or development* (see Chapter 5). The ability, developed from techniques like brainstorming, to be able quickly to use a different tool, a different material, to do a job a different way—all these single out the imaginative and creative supervisor.

Intuition, 'hunches', 'off the cuff' solutions.   As opposed to the methods outlined above some supervisors adopt an 'intuitive' approach. A careful analysis of this approach has shown that often the mind is taking a mental 'short cut' and is making decisions based on subconsciously remembered, real and valuable experience—like we do when driving a car in a tricky situation.

'Automatic' problem-solving can run into trouble in the situation already mentioned of a 'regular' or frequent cause of trouble turning out not to be the specific cause in a particular case. But this method is useful when time is short.

My advice is to think out your decisions properly when you can—a second look at a problem pays dividends.

6.2   THE TASKS OF PLANNING AND FORECASTING

As we have already seen, planning is:

1. The process of ascertaining the facts of situation.
2. Determining a line of action to be taken in the light of all the facts.
3. Detailing the steps to be taken in keeping with the chosen line of action.
4. The provision of appropriate resources to carry the plan through.
5. The establishment of standards and checks on progress to keep the performance as close as possible to the original plan.

If planning is essential in the large aspects of the enterprise, it is just as important in the smaller unit of which the supervisor is the head. The ability to plan is an essential part of the supervisor's armoury, even if we have a production planning and control department, or some central organizing body (e.g. a control room in a county ambulance service) to co-ordinate the work of different sections.

Since planning requires 'pre-vision' (Fayol's *'prévoyance'*), the supervisor should try to cultivate the following approach to planning work:

1. Try to see every situation as a whole.
2. Break down each problem into its elements.
3. Exercise imagination and creativity to develop new methods.
4. Be as impersonal and analytical as possible (leaving out personal prejudices, for example).
5. Be able to evaluate the way things are going, and detect variances quickly.
6. Keep spare time for planning, whatever else happens. If planning is put off, the chances are it will never be done.

6.2.1 Making time for planning

Some people criticize planning as a waste of time, especially when plans have to be altered, modified or even scrapped frequently. By prodigious efforts of improvisation some supervisors do indeed cope without planning, often with the resulting waste of:

1. Equipment capacity, because the best use is not made of it.
2. Manpower, because some people are either idle, or doing jobs below their capacity.
3. Materials, because of late arrival more expensive substitutes are used.
4. Money—the first three all cost money.

6.2.2 The four M's

The objectives of the supervisor are therefore the four M's, to make the best use of:

1. Machine capacity* (including proper servicing and maintenance of machinery).
2. Manpower (including training staff properly in the use of equipment).
3. Materials (including ordering in time).
4. Money—a scarce resource in any organization (including cost reduction plans).

(*In a service industry for machine capacity we would substitute the prime resource—vehicles in the case of a taxi firm, for example.)

6.2.3 The planning process

We can set this out in a seven step plan.

Step 1: clarify the objectives

In a *production* situation this would entail setting production targets over a period of a day, week, month, in terms of:

1.   Quantity.
2.   Quality.
3.   Delivery date.

In a *service* situation this would entail setting targets over a period for:

1.   Jobs to be done.
2.   Mileage to be covered.
3.   Invoices to be raised etc.

Step 2: break down the targets

Here the overall objectives, for example 10 000 car heaters per month, are assessed in terms of the individual tasks—pressing, forming, drilling, tapping, polishing, etc.—and facts are gathered about the resources available—machines, manpower, materials and money.

Step 3: analyse the tasks

This entails taking each individual task, e.g. polishing, and asking a series of simple questions:

What materials, equipment and supplies will I need?
Where is the best place in the shop to site the machinery used?
When in the sequence will the job be done? (Obviously near the end in this case, but in
     other instances the sequence is by no means self-evident.)
How is the job to be done?
Who will be used for the job?

The same basic approach would be used in planning office work, special routines in the armed forces (often worked out in minute detail in the form of checklist), or in organizations such as the ambulance service, police (planning an in-depth investigation into a well-organized crime ring such as 'Operation Julie') or in work such as farming.

Step 4: work out several different plans

These would be based on the first three steps. There could be various combinations of machines and men available: or the choice might be of materials, bought to size, or cut up in our own shop. Here we would have to weigh the extra cost of the ready-made items against the inconvenience of using men and machinery on the preparatory work. As with any problem-solving situation, the generation of a fair number of alternatives is essential.

The plans would need to take into account:

1. The original objectives.
2. Maximizing standardization of quantities, quality, materials and components.
3. The need to be flexible—the plans must be capable of modification.
4. Economy—using resources to the optimum.
5. Balance—using the most appropriate machine (i.e. not using sledge hammers to crack nuts).
6. Constraints—company policies, etc.

Step 5: select the most suitable plan

This means evaluating the alternative proposals (asking advice from others if necessary), and choosing the most suitable one. What is the most suitable one may not be apparent if you are new to supervision, and it will pay you to ask the advice of others, until you have had enough experience.

Step 6: put the chosen plan into effect

Here we implement our plan. Part of the pre-planning stage should, of course, be consultation with the staff concerned, particularly where change is involved, and once the decision to 'go' is taken your staff should be told as quickly as possible. You need their co-operation.

Others might need to be told too: other supervisors or managers involved in the job at the preceding or subsequent stages; maintenance and servicing staff (especially if machines are to be re-sited, for example) and personnel department or wages office, if your plans involve such items as overtime or special working.

Step 7: review and modify

The supervisor should review every plan after a definite period, to find out what went right and what went wrong, so that he or she can learn from any mistakes. The supervisor who is ready to admit to an error of judgement, and redresses the situation is sure to get more co-operation than one who rarely reviews or modifies a decision. (A similarity with the problem-solving process will be noted.)

General review process

Following on the idea of Step 7, it is advisable for every supervisor to review the work of the group regularly: in cases where job cards are used the contribution of each worker, or the time spent on particular jobs can soon be ascertained.

With clerical or administrative staff this may be less easy, but the use of activity logging or similar techniques (which you will study under Managing Products and Services) would help you keep a track on everyone's performance.

You are now able to look more carefully at the work going on in your section: of each activity we can ask (by now a familiar list) our six questions.

1. *Why* is the job necessary?
2. *What* does it achieve?
3. *Where* else could it be done?
4. *Who* else could do it? (Would they do better at the job, or would it be useful training someone?)
5. *When* could it be done (other than its present time, helping perhaps to smooth out peaks and troughs)?
6. *How* much time is spent on the job, relative to other jobs, is the balance right?

Finally a general review of the work force.

1. Is the most appropriate person doing the job?
2. Is it the monotonous, can a greater interest be added to it (see under Motivation)?
3. Should work be shared out more?
4. Who has too much work?
5. Who has too little work?

6.2.4   Diaries and wall charts

Forward planning can be considerably helped by the use of diaries (large with plenty of space to record meetings, target dates for orders, reports etc.), periodic reviews can be entered at the beginning of the year, maintenance programmes can be listed, and so on. Larger still, are 'Year to View' charts: a wall diary, in fact. These can contain information such as staff holidays, target dates for completion of orders, and highlights times of peak activity, etc.

6.2.5   Gantt charts

Gantt charts, so named after Henry Gantt, are a special version of the bar chart. Bar charts should be familiar to most students, a typical example of the kind of chart used in school is shown as Fig 6.2—a rainfall chart. In industry, bar charts can be used to show monthly stock levels, sales by volume or production/output levels.

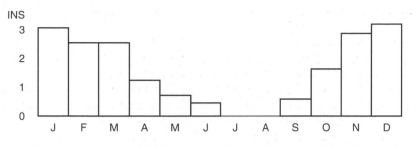

Figure 6.2 Bar chart. Typical Mediterranean climate monthly rainfall chart.

The Gantt chart—which can appear in a multitude of forms—is a bar chart 'turned on its side'. The basic principle is that a line (or more than one line) moving from left to right represents the amount of work done, or time used up. In Fig. 6.3 the 'time used up' is the time that Bill, Mary, etc. are on holiday. Students will quickly realize that a chart of this kind highlights at a glance simultaneous activities: the departmental manager in this case will have a problem in late July with three members of staff away at the same time.

Figure 6.4, record of orders received, is a useful indicator of orders on hand, with the delivery dates promised. Such a chart was used in the branch offices of a well-known fork lift truck manufacturers some years ago, and was very useful to the sales staff for checking the progress of orders: fourteen days before the promised delivery date a routine request for confirmation of completion date would be sent. Given the right kind of peg-board, different colours of lines, etc., can be used to indicate extended delivery information, revised promises, how often customers have pressed for delivery, etc.

Taking matters a stage further, in Fig. 6.5, by having a 'thin' line to represent the promised or target delivery date, and a thicker line beneath, to represent the percentage towards completion, we can see what stage a job has reached. A 50% completed order would have a 'thick' line half-way along the length of the 'thin' line.

The major advantages of this type of chart for the supervisor are that such charts are:

1. Easily understood as they have a simple visual impact.
2. Can be easily constructed to *show progress* towards some target.
3. All on one piece of paper, or cardboard.

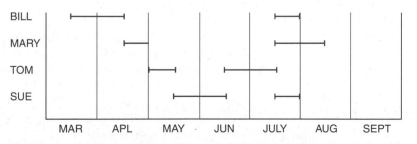

Figure 6.3 Gantt chart, showing holiday periods March–September for four members of staff in a department.

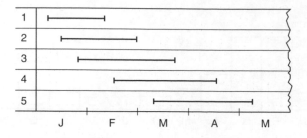

Figure 6.4 Gantt chart, showing record of orders received, with promised delivery dates.

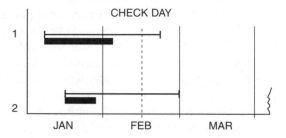

Figure 6.5 Gantt chart. An expanded and revised version of Fig. 6.4 showing degree of completion on orders 1 and 2.

4. A constant reminder to the supervisor that action is required on lack of progress noted on the chart.

Obviously, like anything well-presented and easy to read a great deal of work may have to go into obtaining the appropriate information; charts are quite useless, indeed misleading, if allowed to get out of date.

Special planning techniques

Typical aids to planning are those under the heading of Managing Products and Services, and full details of them will be found in textbooks on Work Study and associated subject areas. Among the more important are:

Network analysis. This term covers several slightly different techniques. CPA (Critical Path Analysis—sometimes called CPM: Critical Path Method), and PERT (Programme Evaluation and Review Techniques). Later, a bewildering collection of initials representing variations on the basic theme emerged (CPPS, RAMPS, SCANS, SPERT, etc.) and those students interested in pursuing this topic further will be pleased to find there is a wide range of textbooks covering not only the basic principles but many of the subtler refinements (generally under the library, Dewey reference 658.5). Both CPA and PERT methods date back to the late 1950s, and in particular PERT was developed to help build the US Navy's Polaris missiles.

If we take a large project (such as erecting a large building) and find we are using say 250 major suppliers of components and 9000 subcontractors, it is obvious that we need a method of planning what is to happen at any time well in advance, so that the right components arrive at the required time; and the staff trained to fit them are available to do the job. So we are concerned with:

1. Scheduling the sequence of jobs.
2. Estimating the time each job takes.
3. Calculating the resources needed to do the job and supervising it.

We shall find that a delay in certain jobs will delay the completion of the *whole* project—this sequence of jobs is the *critical path*. Other parts of the project can be completed within a more flexible framework, and it is possible to reallocate workers from such jobs, if required, to assist in the urgent work.

Work study. Work study is an extremely widely known technique used in production management, and in service work, for example, in refuse collection, developed from the ideas of F.W. Taylor, his disciples and colleagues, Gantt, Gilbreth, Halsey and Rowan. As there are many, comprehensive textbooks covering the various subdivisions of work study, we will confine the detail to aids to planning and flow process charts. The supervisor is a key person in the application of work study, therefore, it is vital that he has a good grasp of the various principles and techniques as he will be responsible for putting any planned changes into effect.

Work study is traditionally divided into two parts: method study and work measurement. Method *study* implies method *improvement*; and any planning must take into account proposed new or improved methods. It should be noted, particularly by those supervisors not normally involved in production or manufacturing processes, that method study can be applied to service industries. As O and M (Organization and Method) departments grow and extend, method study is being more extensively applied to the work of offices and administrative departments. All this work has the primary aim of producing the same result with less effort.

Method study can be thought of as a fivefold process:[2]

1. *Preparation*—doing the initial groundwork.
2. *Collection*—gathering information, observing, monitoring existing methods, practices, procedures.
3. *Collation*—sorting out, arranging or rearranging the facts revealed by the collection process, into a coherent picture.
4. *Appraisal*—a critical examination of the collated information, and the establishment of alternative methods.
5. *Implementation*—putting the new methods/procedures into effect; consolidating them, and reviewing subsequently; and ensuring that staff are trained in the new procedures.

---

[2] It is important to ensure that consultation with all interested parties (including workers' representatives) takes place at every stage.

Method study procedures—collections. There are many ways of gathering and analysing information, of which one of the most widely used is the Flow Process Chart. Before looking at the flow process chart, we shall need to consider the five *basic*[3] symbols used widely in the western world. See Fig. 6.6.

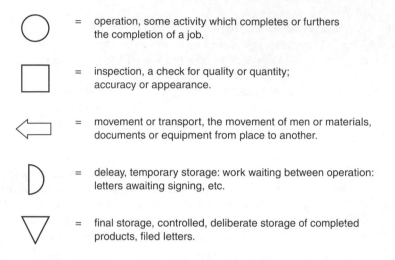

| = operation, some activity which completes or furthers the completion of a job. |
| = inspection, a check for quality or quantity; accuracy or appearance. |
| = movement or transport, the movement of men or materials, documents or equipment from place to another. |
| = deleay, temporary storage: work waiting between operation: letters awaiting signing, etc. |
| = final storage, controlled, deliberate storage of completed products, filed letters. |

Figure 6.6 Conventional flow process chart symbols.

Using the operation symbol we can consider the job of putting diaries into a presentation box. To do the survey properly it will be necessary to observe the job several times before then drawing up a properly titled and ordered chart. Conventionally, we must indicate where the job starts and finishes; whether we are observing the worker's actions (*person* chart) or the progress (via several workers) of a component or document. The survey is an observation, so we term this the *observed* method: if we revise the method, and put forward a new, fresh way of doing the job, we say we have a *proposed* method. It is usual to indicate the number of operations, delays, etc. at the foot of the chart. See Fig. 6.7.

Normally, the methods study staff would carry out investigations of this sort, but every supervisor should have a working knowledge of this technique, and could review individual jobs himself. During such studies, the supervisor should note which elements are obviously inefficient and could be improved. Particular care should be taken when reviewing:

1. Hazardous activities.
2. Awkward jobs.
3. Unpleasant or difficult jobs.
4. Wasteful use of machines, men, materials, money.

Work measurement (time study). The second major division of work study is *work measurement*, which is the application of techniques which establish the *standard*

---

[3] In recent years several variations of the five basic symbols have been used.

```
┌─────────────────────────────────────────────────────────────┐
│                     Flow Process Chart                       │
│                                                              │
│   Observed Method                        Date 11.11.–        │
│   Person Chart                           Sheet 1 of 1.       │
│                                          Analyst             │
│                                                              │
│           Job: Placing a diary in a presentation box         │
│           Chart begins: Pick up box                          │
│           Chart ends: Places boxed diary on conveyor         │
│                                                              │
│    ①   Picks up box                                          │
│                                                              │
│    ②   Opens lid, places aside                               │
│                                                              │
│    ③   Picks up diary                                        │
│                                                              │
│    ④   Places diary in box                                   │
│                                                              │
│    ⑤   Picks up lid                                          │
│                                                              │
│    ⑥   Lid on box                                            │
│                                                              │
│    ⑦   Places on conveyor                                    │
│                                                              │
│      Summary: Operations 7                                   │
└─────────────────────────────────────────────────────────────┘
```

Figure 6.7 Flow process chart.

times that it would take a qualified manual worker to do specific jobs. Time study is that aspect of work measurement concerned with establishing the times of jobs by the use of a stop-watch, photographic or even electronic means. Sometimes *activity sampling* is employed: we might observe a clerk 100 times in a given period, and record on each occasion exactly what he or she is doing (typing, writing, answering the telephone, reading correspondence, filing—or even doing nothing). We can then estimate what *percentage* of the clerk's time is occupied by the various activities listed.

Other techniques. These include:

1. *Multiple activity charts* (showing various activities affecting machines, men, materials over the same period of time—shows up particularly the *idle time* of men or machines).
2. *String diagrams* (charting the routes taken by components or documents through a department).

Managing time

This important topic is now dealt with in Unit VI, Chapter 31, pp. 568–579.

6.3   THE SUPERVISOR'S ORGANIZING ROLE

As we have seen in the previous chapter, in the organizing role, the supervisor will be:

1.   Working out the actual jobs needed to be done to fulfil the plans agreed upon.
2.   Allocating them to members of staff.
3.   Making sure that there is no duplication or underlap of work.

Organizing for the supervisor entails such activities as:

1.   Ordering materials required for production, or for the provision of the service the department performs.
2.   Ordering equipment (large, expensive items might need authorization at a higher level, but spares, components, loose tools, etc., are certainly his or her responsibility).
3.   Making sure all jobs are allocated in accordance with the overall plan, with his or her own plan, and with forced, last minute changes being taken into account, e.g. absen-teeism, etc. At lower levels in the organization, individuals are normally allocated to jobs—rarely can such jobs be tailored to the individual's abilities.

Note: The implications of these points are: the supervisor knows the technical aspects of the materials used; the potentialities of his or her equipment; the skills, abilities (and weak points) of his or her staff.

6.3.1   Organizing in practice

A typical example of organizing in practice (and which many of us will have experienced) is giving a small party at home. We have decided in advance (planned) when and where it should be held, whom to invite, what food will be provided, what music will be played. Organizing will entail seeing that the invitations go out, the food is ordered, supplied and prepared; the room re-arranged suitably, records and tapes are available, or a disco hired, that various people will take on tasks like serving food and drinks, washing up and so on.

   Similarly, in a work situation, an adjutant in the services will organize orderly officers, and orderly sergeants, parades, and similar activities; the garage manager of a company will organize deliveries of petrol and oil, a maintenance schedule for the company cars and vehicles, as well as special jobs such as resprays or major repairs.

   In short, organizing is making all the arrangements.

6.3.2   A supervisor's organizing checklist

A conscientious supervisor will want to use checklists as they are a great help in organizing. Here is a list to help you with organizing itself.

1.   Do you always order materials correctly so that the items you need arrive at the most appropriate time?

2. Do you communicate your requirements clearly to all employees, so that they know exactly what is wanted?
3. Do you allocate jobs fairly, balancing the skills required against the labour available?
4. Do you ensure that every employee is doing a fair share of the work?
5. Do you organize the work so that machinery is not idle, materials are not lying around unused, and workers are not without jobs to do?
6. Do you know the capabilities of all employees in your section, so that you can make best use of them helping them to develop at the same time?

SUMMARY

1. In this chapter we examine the application of the principles of management to the supervisor's job.

2. Creativity is not confined to a few favoured intellectuals, most of us are perhaps unaware of our own potential. This is the result of schooling and other training aimed at finding 'right' answers.

3. There are two ways of tapping this talent, group and individual creative activities.

4. Group activity is some form of brainstorming, where a group can discuss a problem in an uninhibited manner with the aim of generating as many solutions as possible within a given time. No attempt is made at this stage to criticize, comment upon or evaluate any suggestion: this activity comes some time later.

5. Individual creativity has to be striven for, and the lateral thinking approach is to be recommended. To be able to use such a technique, the lateralist has to undergo a significant change in mental attitudes and outlook before practising this art consistently. Many times when we look at problems, we hedge ourselves around with self-imposed limits, boundaries and assumptions.

6. An example of the lateralist technique is the 'reversal' method where we turn an idea on its head. For example, to solve traffic problems, we consider how vehicles can control traffic lights *not* how the traffic lights can control the vehicles.

7. The exploration of analogies is another useful idea, once the natural reluctance to employ the technique has been overcome. Consideration is given to talking around the analogy, which is itself a problem, and the possible

solutions to the analogy problem could provide at least one pointer to a possible solution to the original problem.

8.   Problem-solving can be organized into a scheme split into separate steps:

(a) Identifying the problem itself.
(b) Gathering all the relevant information.
(c) Establishing the cause of the problem.
(d) Searching for and developing a variety of solutions.
(e) Evaluating the results of how the chosen solution works in practice.

9.   Intuitive solutions may be useful in an emergency, however, decisions arrived at after much thought are usually much better.

10.   Planning on a localized, departmental scale is a vital as company, corporate planning.

11.   Planning needs supervisors who:

(a) See situations as a whole.
(b) Can then break down problems into elements.
(c) Are innovative, creative, yet impersonal and analytical when evaluating their ideas.
(d) Are quick to spot variances.
(e) Have planned time for planning.

12.   In planning the supervisor should aim to make the best use of the four M's—machinery, manpower, materials, money.

13.   Planning is a seven-step process:

(a) Clarifying the objectives.
(b) Breaking down the targets.
(c) Analysing the tasks.
(d) Working out several different plans.
(e) Selecting the most suitable plan.
(f) Putting the chosen plan into effect.
(g) Reviewing and modifying.

14.   Use can be made of charts and diagrams to help the planning process. Modifications of the Gantt chart have been of considerable benefit as a great deal of information can be seen at a glance; progress towards targets can be shown; under or overloading of resources at particular times can be noted.

15.   Other planning techniques include critical path analysis (and its many variations), and work study, which implies method improvement.

16.   Method study involves: preparation, collection, collation, appraisal and implementation.

17.   There are five basic concepts used in the flow process chart, a popular way to present information:

Work moving to complete a task = operation
Evaluation of quality/quantity = inspection/check
Movement of men, materials   = transport
Temporary hold up   = delay
Permanent storage   = final storage

(Each concept has its own symbol.)

18.   Certain conventions must be obeyed in preparing a chart: it must be title properly; the start and finish of a job must be clearly indicated; a statement must be made as to whether the chart is *observed or proposed.*

19.   The management of time is vital to the supervisor as it is a costly resource, and scarce too. Time should be used to the best advantage, i.e. jobs done in priority order, proper use of delegation, restriction of interruptions, etc.

20.   The supervisor is an organizer, and this means ensuring the four M's are available as required.

REVIEW QUESTIONS

1.   Why have many of us *apparently* lost the ability to be creative?

2.   What is meant by 'group creativity'? What advantages does it have over individuals trying to be creative on their own?

3.   What is meant by saying that many assumptions (which are restrictions on action) are self-imposed?

4.   Describe the 'reversal' method of dealing with problems.

5.   Outline the 'six-step' problem-solving technique.

6.   What is a Gantt chart? Could you use one in your work? How?

7.   Why is it important for the supervisor to plan and manage his or her own time?

8.   Briefly describe the purpose of method study.

9.   What is the supervisor's organizing role?

DISCUSSION TOPICS

1.   Discuss the view of McGregor that the ability to be imaginative and creative
          is widely distributed amongst the population. Is it true or false? How would
          you prove or disprove it? How creative is the group discussing this question?

2.   Should organizations make use of their members' creative talents? Does
          not the discovering that one's subordinates are cleverer, have more ideas
          and are better at problem solving pose a threat to managers?

3.   Using the six-step sequence, how would you go about solving the problem
          of getting a twenty ton load of material from the docks 100 miles away,
          your own transport fully committed elsewhere, and a strike in the road-
          haulage industry? (You are not asked to *solve* the problem, but to discuss
          what investigations you would make, information you would need, etc., to
          arrive at a decision. We are concentrating on the *method,* rather than the
          actual solution.)

ASSIGNMENTS

A6.1   Arrange the class in a single group for a brainstorming session.

          (a) Discuss the following topics using the brainstorming technique.
                   uses of the paper clip;
                   the ideal learning situation;
                   saving energy in industry;
                   revising the tax system.
          (b) Criticize the brainstorming technique.

A6.2   Arrange the class in two groups to discuss a topic agreed by all before the
          start. After the brainstorming session compare the answers of the two groups.

A6.3   Each class member is to attempt to estimate how he or she spends each
          working day in percentage terms, under headings such as direct super-
          vision, counselling, answering the telephone, writing letters/reports,
          seeing supervisors, attending meetings, verbal discussions with colleagues,
          doing nothing. Honesty is important. Answers can be reviewed anony-
          mously, if necessary.

Case studies

A6.4   Bill Shepherd, works manager of Marinecraft Ltd, summoned all his supervisors to an emergency meeting last week. 'It's amazing,' he told them, 'the Boat Show was many times more successful than we could have possibly imagined—the Velocity class was in great demand. The plain fact is, with new orders coming in every day, we must start increasing production now; the target being at least 50% up this time next week. I'll leave it up to each of you to decide how to cope.'

Shepherd dismissed the supervisors, and Tim Newman, the recently promoted supervisor in the marine engine shop, was keen to show his mettle. Within minutes he was in Personnel: 'I'll be needing another ten fitters at once,' he said eagerly, 'there should be plenty around now Johnson's are closing down.' Within three days Tim's section was augmented, but he was having problems finding everyone work to do, as parts were slow in coming from other departments.

Percy Hull, on the other hand, opted to get his staff to work overtime and for several days his targets were easily met and passed. At the end of the week, however, he was surprised to find that there was a slight increase in absenteeism, and that Harry had cut his hand again. Monday lunch time, Percy confided to Tim Newman that he wondered how he was going to cope. Tim shifted uneasily in his seat 'I've a problem too,' he said. 'My men are jealous of all the overtime your people are getting.'

(a)   What problems are there at Marinecraft Ltd? How did they arise?
(b)   What should be done to put matters right, and who should do it? What solutions can you offer for the problems of the supervisors? (You can use a brainstorming session.)

A6.5   Philip Jones mumbled his apologies as he entered the staff meeting ten minutes late (as usual). Abraham Wise, the managing director, was a tolerant man, but he did comment that punctuality was vital for a meeting so important as this was. Jones replied tartly:

'It's all very well for you office people, I've a hundred problems on the shop floor. I called a meeting of all the charge-hands and assistant foremen for 7.30 am today, over half of them couldn't make it till about ten to eight—some stories about urgent work problems—and of course I had to go over everything all over again; the meeting dragged on till nearly nine. Then there's the post to go through; I can't trust my secretary to deal with it. Then there was Joe—I'm glad he's not here—who came to discuss his problems with me for at least twenty minutes. I've just had time to get a coffee before coming here.'

Mr Wise peered over his spectacles, and proceeded with the meeting.

(a)   What are Philip Jones' problems?
(b)   If you were Mr Wise, and decided to have a word with Philip after the meeting, what would you say to him?

7

The Supervisor and the Functions of Management: Motivating, Communicating and Controlling

7.1 MOTIVATION

We have already looked at theories of motivation in some detail, those of Maslow, Argyris and McGregor, for example; and we have attempted to arrive at some general conclusions in Chapter 5. Now we must try to relate these general principles to the work place.

Motivating is not a question—as we have already seen in our discussion of the human relations school in Chapter 3—of 'being nice' to your staff; indeed there are times when a firm approach is better. It is a question of creating a total environment at work where employees work willingly to further the organization's interests because they feel at the same time they are furthering their own interests. Remember McGregor's point that people will exercise self-direction and self-control in the service of objectives to which they are committed. In other words, given the right environment, there is no need *actively* to motivate people; they will motivate themselves. A well-motivated subordinate does not need close attention except when asking for technical help or advice. If the subordinate understands the needs of the job well, works well without being told (or even asked), he or she may indeed 'do a bit extra'.

7.1.1 The supervisor's role

The supervisor has a key role to play in motivation. Before we look at two checklists, one for individuals, one for the group, there are some general guidelines we should consider first which supervisors are advised to follow.

Recognize and base rewards on performance

Naturally, high performance can bring financial rewards for some workers: those on incentive or piece-work schemes. Not all employees, for example, office workers, can be immediately financially rewarded for improved work or extra effort. Recognition by the supervisor, the quiet word of praise or thanks, an extra half-day off, if related to performance, can help to encourage and motivate.

Practise loyalty towards subordinates

Supervisors are often heard grumbling about the loyalty, or lack of it, of their staff. Certainly supervisors look for loyalty from subordinates, but how often are supervisors loyal *towards* subordinates? There are times when as leader of the group, the supervisor may have to take the part of individual workers or the group as a whole. Perhaps someone has been unjustly treated by a superior, or perhaps the supervisor has to fight to get some working conditions changed.

Even more important, is the need to accept responsibility for the mistakes of subordinates when reporting to higher management. Following this principle the supervisor should discuss with a subordinate the seriousness of a particular error, advise him, even let him know in no uncertain terms of his displeasure, but should be reluctant to 'name' him to higher management. By being seen to 'carry the can' and to stand by my staff, I soon found that I was gaining loyalty from them.

Be employee-centred, not task-centred

Be an employee supervisor rather than a process or function overseer: human relations are not a question of being 'nice' to people, rather being interested in them. In Chapters 14 and 19, we shall consider the supervisor's role in appraisal and counselling, but in addition we should note the need to speak to *every* subordinate *every* day; to be as friendly as the occasion demands, and always to be polite; to recognize the need to address people by the name they like best, whether it be Bill, Mary, or Mrs. Jones.

Be concerned about employees' safety and welfare

Much is said about health and safety in Unit IV. We can say here, however, that a genuine concern in the safety and welfare of employees is not only a general motivator, but may also help to improve employees' safety awareness.

Meet individual needs

We have seen (Maslow and others) that each member of a group needs:

1. To continue to live and express him/herself as an individual.
2. To provide for any dependents.
3. To find satisfaction in life—in both work and recreation.
4. To win the acceptance of the members of the groups of which *he or she* feels he or she is a member.

If the degree of motivation is to be sufficient to give satisfaction at work the worker:

1. Should feel a sense of personal achievement in the job being done; that he/she is making a worthwhile contribution to the overall objectives of the group, section or organization.
2. Should feel that the job itself is worth doing, is challenging, is demanding the best and is giving responsibility to match the worker's capacity.
3. Should be given adequate recognition by you (and other managers) for the effort expended (reflected also in the pay packet).
4. Should have control over those aspects of the job which have been definitely delegated to him or her.
5. Should feel he/she, as an individual, is developing (or 'maturing' in Argyris's language), is advancing in experience and ability.

It should be noted that research undertaken by Rensis, Likert, Michael Argyle[1] and others tends to show that a successful supervisor is one who:

1. Gives subordinates feedback on their performance.
2. Looks after the needs and welfare of the work group.
3. Disciplines by persuasion rather than punishment.
4. Allows participation, group discussion and decision-making (about tasks in hand).

7.1.2 Checklists

The two checklists which follow are not intended to be exhaustive, students should try to extend them.

Supervisor's checklist for each member of the group

1. Have you agreed with each of your staff the scope of the job and standards of performance expected?
2. In positions where improvements in performance can be expected in time, have you agreed targets for continuous improvement?
3. Have you made adequate training and (where necessary) retraining provision? If after opportunities for training and development employees still do not measure up to the needs of the job, do you try to give them jobs nearer to their capacity, or pass them on to other departments which might have a suitable vacancy?
4. When subordinates are successful, do you recognize it and encourage further effort: conversely, in case of failure, do you give constructive advice (*not* destructive criticism), and guidance on improving future effort? (Staff often look for feedback in their performance.)

---

[1] Argyle, M. (1974) *The Psychology of Interpersonal Behaviour*. London: Penguin.

5. Does each individual have or see some career pattern?
6. Can you remove some controls: cutting down on the amount of checking you do; making people more responsible for their work? Can you put more challenge into the job or enrich it in some way, perhaps by allowing staff to set their own goals, or helping them to find their own solutions to problems?
7. Do you review the overall performance of each member of staff at least once a year?
8. Do you know enough about the character and life outside work of all of your staff, to enable you to have an accurate picture of their needs, attitudes and behaviour generally within the working situation? Do you really know how they will react to a particular idea, order, suggestion?

Dealing with the group as a whole

Although people are engaged on the basis of individual contracts, it is in groups, teams, departments, offices, shifts and classes or sections that most of our work is done. Many groups are *contrived* or artificially created—by the technology or by management decision. However within these larger groups, smaller or *informal* groups arise.

Why do individuals form themselves into groups? (Note: This is a different question from that posed in Chapter 1 where we considered why people joined *organizations*; here we are considering why people already belonging to (formal) organizations might form themselves into smaller, more informal groups.) The simplest explanation put forward is that it is due to *proximity*, that is people who are geographically or physically close to each other tend to form groups. Thus individuals working together (i.e. sitting at the same table, working in the same area, stationed in close proximity) will be more likely than not to form a single group. There is some evidence to support this explanation.

A more sophisticated view is that the *sharing* of experiences is fundamental in group formation. The more activities people *share*, it is argued, the more they will *interact*. The more they interact, the more they will develop *sentiments* or feelings for one another. These functions build upon each other, so having sentiments will lead to further sharing and interaction, and so on. It is further argued that this interaction will lead to increased participation in problem solving, and co-ordination of the group's efforts. The more the process develops the more powerful the group becomes, for good or ill.

A further school of thought holds that people are attracted to each other as they discover they have similar attitudes to their surroundings, and/or share similar norms or values (i.e. religion, political views, feelings about sport, work, etc.). Undoubtedly all three views mentioned here help to explain why people join informal groups.

Members of informal groups do however tend to subordinate *some* of their individual needs and values to those of the group as a whole. In return individual members look to the group as a source of protection and support. Thus informal groups help to reinforce the commonly held attitudes and rules. As we have seen from the *Hawthorne experiments* (Chapter 3), a group can set its own standards of behaviour, make its own rules, agree on its own targets, and impose them even when such rules or targets could be contrary to the interests of individual group members, or of the organization for which the group works. They can, of course, have other negative virtues as far as the supervisor is concerned—they could fuel conflict, generate and circulate rumours, and add to resistance to change (see Chapter 9).

Informal groups tend to choose informal leaders—those individuals who speak up more than others, or who form opinions, or demonstrate leadership by achievement or example. Even if not 'voted upon' or formally chosen, the informal group will usually heed the views of its informal leader, and by so doing weaken the hold of the formal leader (supervisor) on the group. As we will see in Chapter 8, there are two basic roles for a manager to fulfil: first, to get the job done (to be *task* orientated); and second, to show concern for the work force (be *people* orientated). Some people feel the second role should be more aptly described as *'group building and maintenance*—that is, concern for the group in addition to individual members.

Ideally the supervisor or manager should attempt to play both roles, and if possible become a '9.9 manager' (see Chapter 8, Section 8.6). Then the supervisor will be able to help the group perform with a high degree of commitment and effectiveness. (If the supervisor/manager will not, or cannot, cover both roles, then it is inevitable that the informal leader will move in to try and take over the role which has been abandoned.)

Thus the successful supervisor realizes that a group has its own personality, standards and needs. In the context of the group the key functions are:

1. To set and maintain group objectives and group standards.
2. To involve the group as a whole in the achievement of objectives.
3. To maintain group unity; and to see that morale is kept at a high level.

Supervisor's checklist for the group as a whole

1. Do you set group objectives, and make sure that everyone understands them?
2. Is every member of the group clear about the standards that you set with regard to the quantity or quality of work, safety or attendance? Are you fair and impartial in rewarding those who succeed?
3. Is your working group of the optimum size? Are you under or overstaffed? What are you doing about it, if the answer to the latter is 'yes'? Do you need to split up a large group into small groups?
4. Are the right people working together?
5. Do you ensure, as far as is practicably possible, that work loads are evenly distributed and that overtime is allocated fairly?
6. Do you have a fair procedure for dealing with grievances? Do you deal with them promptly?
7. Do you use opportunities, as they arise, of genuine consultation with the work team about work matters, methods, overtime, etc? Do you accept the ideas and suggestions of the group?
8. Do you regularly brief the group on present progress and achievement as well as plans for the future?
9. Do you accord to the shop steward (or equivalent trade union representative)   not only the legal minimum of facilities to carry out his or her work, but also respect?

Do you give him or her assistance (where you can) in being an effective spokesperson of the group?

7.1.3 Establishing a satisfactory climate of work

As a summary of many of the ideas discussed in this section we might finally consider what we hope to receive from work.

Money. Money *is* one of the things people want from work, but wages without in-built incentives tend to be maintenance/hygiene factors. However, money *as the only* incentive is not very satisfactory.

Activity. The majority of people have a basic urge to be active and active to *some purpose*; aimless activity does not fulfil the basic urge.

Social needs. Most people need to belong to a group, a group which has a degree of permanence, and has a centre of purpose.

Good working conditions. The definition of good working conditions will vary from person to person: some journalists, for example, still like to work in small, smoke-filled, untidy offices; but in general people will want not only a reasonable physical environment, but also good relationships with fellow-workers and supervisors.

Recognition (esteem needs). All workers (including, of course, supervisors and managers) need to have their efforts recognized by their superiors.

Involvement. In recent years, writers have stressed the need to get everyone in a group involved in helping, planning, organizing and completing the work of that group.

Success. People like to be attached to successful groups, whether a football team, or a record-breaking relay team: in the same way, employees like to work for a successful enterprise (public or private, making goods or providing services).

To sum up, there are human needs to be satisfied: the satisfaction of these needs is a motivating force which can be harnessed to work activity. A successful supervisor will find out what his subordinates' needs are and will attempt to structure or allocate the work so that *some* of them are satisfied.

7.2 THE SUPERVISOR AS COMMUNICATOR

In the previous chapter we looked at the basic theory of communication, here we shall look at common situations faced by the supervisor/manager, where communication plays a vital part. We shall look at the advantages and disadvantages of verbal and written communication, and proceed to the techniques of presenting a case verbally and in writing, giving orders and instructions, interviewing and handling grievances. As meetings are intruding more and more on the supervisor's time we shall also need to consider this aspect of communication. Report (and project) writing is covered separately in Unit V.

7.2.1 Verbal and written communication

For many (although not *all*) supervisors and indeed managers, verbal communication is by far the most frequently used medium. Face-to-face communication has many advantages:

1. We can alter our presentation to suit the receiver, i.e. use his or her language.
2. We can produce very subtle shades of meaning by the use of *stress* or emphasis on a word as in the example: 'I would like you to do this job tomorrow afternoon'.
   —stress on I   = I, as opposed to anyone else, would like the job done.
   —stress on you   = I would like you, as opposed to anyone else, to do the job.
   —stress on this   = the job in question, as opposed to any other job.
   —stress on tomorrow = tomorrow afternoon, as opposed to any other time.
   (If you want to convey emphasis *in writing,* you cannot do it subtly; you may have to use many more words, or a host of typographical tricks, some of which may be lost on the reader.)
3. We can express shades of meaning, emphasis, hints of our own attitude to the message by our gestures or facial expressions.
4. We do not have to worry about layout, spelling, full stops, paragraphs and the like.
5. It is also possible to get a two-way communication, and we can check instantly to see that our message has been received—a 'feedback loop'.

However, there are times when *written* communication is in fact preferable.

1. Instructions to manufacture goods or provide services; specifications, part numbers, or any *complex* or *complicated* mass of information.
2. Where sender and receiver are far apart, or on different shifts (night staff may have to rely heavily on written communication).
3. When a message applies to large numbers of employees: 'All personnel will report for work at 8.00 am on 2 January 2001.'
4. *Copies* of a message (such as in 3 above) can be handed to a number of receivers at the same time; such messages, and copies can be *filed*, for future reference.
5. Where legal relationships (contracts between firms, etc.) are involved and there is a possibility of future legal action.
6. Where it is *vital* that there is no misunderstanding; where the written communication stands undisturbed in cases of emergency, e.g. fire notices, first aid notices, etc.

7.2.2 Presenting a case verbally

Occasions which may necessitate the verbal presentation of a case may include the following: a change in staffing levels, request for new equipment, new tools, variations in working methods. As we will see in Report Preparation later, the way the case is made out is very important and many requests fail to win acceptance because of the lack of preparation.

There are three stages in presenting a case verbally: preparation, presentation, and question handling.

Preparation

1. Make sure that any facts you propose to use are correct and, if possible, that you have evidence to support them.
2. Make sure that you consider *all* possible objections to your idea, and that you have arguments to refute them.
3. Make sure that you have supporting material available (such as production figures, costs, diagrams, absence figures, duty rotas, outworkers' expenses, etc.).
4. Make sure that you have considered *all* possible aspects of your plan and questions that might be asked on them.
5. Consider carefully the selling aspect of your presentation: what benefits would your proposals give to your organization, to other workers and to yourself.
6. Make notes of what you intend to say.

Presentation

1. Get to the point as quickly as possible.
2. Explain *why* you have made your proposal.
3. List the alternatives that you have ruled out, and why.
4. Point out advantages *and* disadvantages, but stress how the former outweigh the latter (by means of cost savings, reduced waste, better use of time, etc.).
5. Finally, summarize what your proposal is, what it will cost to carry out, and what the benefits will be.

Questions

1. Be prepared for questions—these should not be taken as criticisms: in fact, the more questions that are asked, the more interested your listeners are, and the better chance you have of succeeding.
2. Objections also show interest. Do not violently disagree; in fact, compliment the objection, but show how your proposal overcomes the objection.
3. Keep a few arguments, and the odd fact, in reserve.
4. Answer all questions politely. Never lose your temper, or appear to show irritation at criticism.

7.2.3 Presenting a case in writing

Unit VI covers report writing in greater detail but here we consider the short, straight-forward, relatively simple matter. Examples of situations requiring a written case would include justifying a day off to attend a special supervisor's course, extra overtime in the department, or a recommendation for promotion or transfer of a member of your staff.

The normal format, or layout, is that of the 'memo' (short for *'memorandum'*—something to be remembered), see Fig. 7.1 for an example.

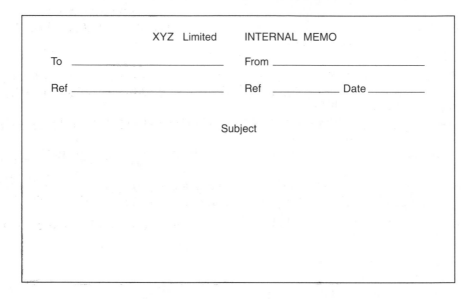

Figure 7.1 Internal memorandum.

You can see at once that the memo has little room for flowery beginnings or end-ings: memos should be short and to the point. To help the memo writer memos are often standardized on pre-printed forms like the example above, although the layout may be varied in some organizations.

A memo should deal with one topic and one topic only. If you want to write to the works manager to ask for the day off or for a new notice board in your department or for another filing cabinet for your office, you must write three, separate memos.

The preparation of your case will be generally similar to that of the verbal version; the memo, however, will need to be organized in the following order:

1. An *introductory* paragraph, explaining what the problem is, or outlining the basic request.
2. A series of *explanatory* paragraphs (four or five at the most), setting out the facts, an evaluation of the facts, and possible alternative solutions (where applicable).
3. A final paragraph with the *request or recommendation* for the course of action.

Example of presenting a case in writing

Assume your course tutor has arranged a visit to the personnel department of your local firm as an extension of your studies of recruitment, selection, induction, and training. Make out a case, in memo form, for a whole day off for the visit—that is, you would need two days off in the same week.

Example:

XYZ limited   INTERNAL MEMO

To: I.M. Wise, Works manager.   *From:* K. Foreman, No. 1 m/c
shop supervisor

Ref: *Ref:* KF/ABC *Date:* 30.6.9X
Subject: Request for absence

As you are aware every Thursday I attend the Certificate in Supervisory Management (NEBSM) course at South Loamshire Technical College. Next week, however, I shall need to be absent on Wednesday as well.

Mr. V. Keen, our course tutor, has arranged for the course to visit the Personnel Department of ABC Ltd, starting at 9.00 am next Wednesday.

Not only does the visit tie in with our present pattern of studies, but ABC's Personnel Department is large and has many services we do not as yet have. Mr. E. N. Gage, our Personnel Officer, has heard about the visit and has asked me to give him a report on their training programmes.

Bill Norman can deputize for me, as he has done successfully for the last ten Thursdays.

Will you officially approve this request?

(signed) K. Foreman.

7.2.4 Orders and instructions

The distinction between an order and an instruction is rather fine: there are many occasions where the two words are virtually interchangeable in everyday use. The *order* can be regarded as a *simple direction* to do something; whereas the *instruction* is an order, *plus* an *explanation* of *how* the job is to be done. For example:

Order: 'Report to the Managing Director at Head Office, at 10.30 am on Monday 21st . . .'

Instruction: 'You are to report to the Managing Director on Monday 21st . . . Take the 8.00 am train from Weatherfield and you will be met at New St. Station by the company chauffeur.

'On arrival at Head Office, take the lift in the main foyer to the 4th floor. Leaving the lift turn left: the MD's secretary's office is at the end of corridor. Report there, and await further instructions.'

Note: we often (as in the last example) use 'instruction' in the plural, which underlines the use of the word in a 'how to do it' sense. For the rest of this section, however, I shall use the word 'order' to cover both orders and instructions.

7.2.5 Written orders

Many, far too many, written orders are used. An obvious, very suitable use, is the 'works' order', a document authorizing production of goods in a particular shop or factory or authorizing a service visit to repair a customer's equipment—e.g. a television set. These are so common, routine, well-understood and standardized that everyone understands that they should be in writing (in theory to avoid any possible error), and the people who get them know exactly what is expected of them.

The vital point for supervisors is, if they have to use written orders, such orders should be short, clear, complete, and capable of being obeyed without further explanation. 'All personnel in this department must wear goggles when welding', is such an order.

7.2.6 Oral orders

As we have seen, oral communications have a great flexibility than written ones: a coaxing, persuading, friendly or urgent tone can impart further meaning to the words. It is also possible to get two-way communication, and we can check to see if orders have been understood.

We will consider the various kinds of oral orders separately.

The direct order

Written orders tend to be of this type: 'Keep Out!—Radiation Hazard'. 'Parade, open order, march!', is a verbal equivalent. It is one-way communication to get something done quickly, *when the receiver knows exactly what to do*. 'Open order, march!' is a shortened expression for a sequence of precise movements, which must be learnt and practised beforehand, for the order to be carried out successfully. (This underlines the necessity of rehearsing safety drills, etc. regularly.)

Supervisors should be cautious of using commands as they not only assume knowledge on the part of the worker (which may not be there), but may antagonize a sensitive person. A person who is always giving direct orders or commands runs the risk of creating both uncertainty and ill-will, and may make a fool of himself if he has to give a worker detailed instructions after a command.

In the work environment commands are best left to emergency situations: 'Look out!', 'Abandon ship!', 'Ring the Fire Brigade!' are all commands likely to be obeyed without question, whoever gives them.

The appeal

This type of order is softer, a request rather than a command and it helps to reduce the receiver's resistance to a minimum by arousing an air of co-operation. Examples of this type of order are:

'Bill, will you look into this one for me?'
'Do you think you can finish the job by Thursday afternoon?'
'How about having a go at the polishing bit after dinner, Fred?'

With this approach we can treat people in a courteous, friendly way, we can play down the superior/subordinate relationship, and treat the worker as a human being.

The appeal is useful for dealing with those who have failed in some way, committed the 'clerical error', or slipped up on the job, and who may be upset with themselves. 'Perhaps we can have another try at this?', 'How about if next time, you pull the lever forward first?', or 'Shall we go over the figures again, together?' are examples.

However, like the command, it assumes the recipient of the order knows quite a lot about the job and detailed instructions are not required.

The hint

The mildest type of order. Here, we just mention the subject, sometimes in a very oblique way, to an experienced and reliable worker who knows what is wanted without instructions. 'There seems to be a large number of empty boxes in that corner, Jack'; or 'The sooner I get your report, the sooner we can get that machine moved'; or 'Didn't see you draw your goggles today, Bill'—all these avoid giving direct orders, commands or even requests. We sometimes call this type of order an *implied order*.

The open order

This is where we announce a piece of information: 'We've just had the Johnson order in', 'Can we hope for 50 this week, then?', 'I'm afraid it looks like we have to complete the stock check by the weekend'. Usually this information, like the examples above, sets a target, but again no instructions on *how* the job is to be done. It leaves the subordinate free to use his own initiative in carrying out (or delegating) the task.

Signing or taking the initiative

These are non-verbal methods of giving orders: the cricket captain who waves a fielder to a new position, or the supervisor who says, 'We'd better clear this lot', and starts to do the job himself. This method is useful, where there are:

1. Areas of noise and speech is difficult.

2. Workers whose command of English is limited.
3. People in the vicinity you do not want to disturb.
4. People who are reluctant to a job in a certain way, or feel the job cannot be done in that particular way.

The detailed order (instructions)

Giving people job instructions is very like training people: the only difference being that untrained people need a more careful and longer instruction period. So the giving of instructions is, in effect, a modified form of learning. The implication is, therefore, that we shall use a strategy similar to a training approach.

The famous 'Training Within Industry' cards, developed in the USA during the Second World War divide the training process as follows:

Step 1—prepare the worker. Put the worker at ease, state the job, and find out what he or she already knows about it. See that the worker is in the correct working position.

Step 2—present the operation. Describe and illustrate the job, stress each key point. Choose a pace with which the worker can cope.

Step 3—try out performance. Ask the worker to do the job alone, explaining to you each key point throughout. Continue until you are sure the employee knows exactly what to do.

Step 4—follow up. Now leave the employee alone, to get on with the job, but check back on progress from time to time and encourage questions.

Step 3, with the exception of the feedback check, can probably be omitted in the case of trained and experienced workers, but in general, if you carry the four-step training process in your mind, every time you give an instruction, you will have a greater chance of success.

7.2.7 Interviewing

An interview is essentially an exchange of ideas or opinions between two or more persons. In *that* sense it is no different from thousands of other instances of communication which occur in a day. However, an interview is different for the following reasons:

1. It is communication for a particular purpose (see below).
2. It is conducted with a greater or lesser amount of privacy.
3. One participant—the *interviewer*—takes the lead and (in theory) controls the course the interview takes.

7.2.8 Types of interview

There are many different types of interview. The most important include: recruitment, coaching, induction, instruction, appraisal (a discussion of the employee's progress), correction or disciplinary, explanation of company rules, regulations or procedures ('putting an employee right'), and also interviews dealing with grievances, requests or suggestions coming from the employee.

Employment and appraisal interviews are dealt with in Unit III: here we restrict ourselves to a few general remarks on interviews, and an examination of disciplinary interviews and handling grievances.

7.2.9 Conducting an interview

As we have seen interviews take many different forms, and it is difficult to produce a universal guide to interviewing. However, the following points are worth noting:

1. Keep interviews as private as circumstances allow. *Complete* privacy is the aim.
2. Choose surroundings which are free of noise and distraction.
3. Whatever the reason for the interview, show normal politeness and courtesy. Allow the interviewee to sit down.
4. Try to ensure that both of you sit on the same level.
5. Plan the interview, as far as possible in advance. Make a note of all the points you want to cover.
6. Listen as well as talk. Show your interviewee that you do take him or her seriously.
7. Sum up both during the interview and at the end, and make sure that the other person understands what (if anything) has been agreed upon, and what he or she has agreed to do.

7.2.10 Disciplinary interviews

These are usually equally hated by both supervisors and workers, and for that reason, often avoided. Failure to act can only lead to increasing trouble as time passes and a steady erosion of the control a supervisor should have in a department.

The Employment Protection Act requires that a statement of the stages in disciplinary proceedings must be included in the contract of employment—thus all employers must have a definite procedure, which the supervisor *must* be fully aware of. Very important are the limits to his powers to discipline.

Before the interview starts

We need to plan the interview in advance whenever possible. Of course, there will be situations where immediate action will be required, but even a short time to prepare for the interview will help us make a better job of it.

In the time available:

1. Obtain as much of the background as possible. If you have a file on the employee, read it.
2. While it is vital that the supervisor should communicate disapproval of a subordinate's act as quickly as possible after the event, at the same time the supervisor should wait until he is in a calm frame of mind before acting.
3. Be sure of the organization's policy with regard to the steps you are contemplating taking, and be sure that you do not need to refer the matter to others first. Remember the law is complex, and you do not want to find yourself in the wrong at an Industrial Tribunal.

At the disciplinary interview

The points to note, especially, are:

1. Cultivate an impartial manner, and stick to it throughout the interview—the interview is no place for carrying on personal feuds.
2. Know the employee's name in advance and use it.
3. It may be useful to start with something else—perhaps even something you could give some praise about.
4. Try to get the employee to admit any errors committed, or any unacceptable behaviour.
5. If appropriate, point out the consequences of the employee's action in terms of lost production, morale, effects on the feelings of others.
6. Tell the employee clearly the consequences of the act in question: the present punishment (if any), and the consequences of any future similar acts. If an ultimatum has to be given, give it in a calm, firm way, without apologizing for what you are doing.
7. Unless the punishment is dismissal (a situation unlikely without prior consultation with superiors, in any event) provide hope for the disciplined person. Try to find an encouraging, hopeful note on which to end.
8. Remember disciplinary interviews could well include the presence of a witness, e.g. trade union representative or a fellow-employee.

After the interview

The process does not end with the end of the interview. After it is over:

1. Make notes of the interview in the employee's file. Record any promises or agreements made; or warnings whether verbal or 'official'.
2. Check as often as required to see if the expected results or standards are being maintained.
3. Be sure to notice and praise any improvements noticed.

7.2.11 Handling grievances

A grievance is a feeling in the back of an employee's mind that there is something in the work situation which is felt to be wrong, unjust, unfair or unreasonable. It follows, therefore, that while some grievances are genuine and well-founded, others are less well-founded, or even imaginary. They must *all* be treated seriously. As with disciplinary matters, the law (in this case the Contracts of Employment Act) lays down that information on grievance making is to be given to employees at the time of their engagement by the organization.

Such procedures are usually negotiated between management and union, and consist of a series of agreed steps. The aim is to prevent an individual grievance being left unresolved and gradually growing until it becomes a grievance of all workers and a subject of a dispute. This is why all grievances must be treated seriously.

7.2.12 The supervisor's role in grievance handling

Following on the last point, it is now obvious that the supervisor cannot wait for grievances to be raised officially. Supervisors must know their workers sufficiently well to appreciate when something seems to be 'bugging them'—a change from normal behaviour is a possible indicator: the willing worker who virtually 'works to rule', the employee who normally takes care (and pride) in work, and who now does what has to be done in an indifferent or even careless way. At this stage it is important to *act quickly*.

Types of grievances

Some grievances are individual: dislike of something you have done or said, or some other manager's approach. Others are really group grievances, and one person volunteers to represent others. Many grievances are about pay in its various forms, e.g. a bonus scheme or a seemingly unfair situation where one person feels he is getting less pay than another for doing the same job, incorrect deductions (some workers always feel they have been overtaxed), or some inequity in a piece-work system. Others, particularly in times of economic uncertainty, will be worried about job security and will express this in 'territory defending' behaviour, complaining that others are doing what is a particular worker's job.

7.2.13 The grievance interview

As well as the general interview comments we have already noted, the following points are important:

1. Be sure *exactly* how far you can resolve the problem. *If in doubt ask*. Take as much advice as you can beforehand, especially if you have not dealt with this kind or problem previously.

2. Listen carefully to the grievance, perhaps all the employee wants is to get things off his or her chest (rather like the open interviews of the Hawthorne experiments).
3. If you are asked to act, and you can do so without taking the matter higher, then act as quickly as possible. Do not promise anything you cannot fulfil.
4. If there is the slightest suggestion that what is wanted is beyond your capability to provide, or beyond your authority, tell the complainant you will take the matter higher. Do so as quickly as possible and as objectively as possible.
5. Remember at all times the company's attitude to grievances.

7.2.14 Meetings

The word 'meeting' has changed somewhat in meaning over the years: 'an assembly of a number of people for entertainment or discussion' (OED), has been modified to something more precise such as 'an assembly of people for a lawful purpose' by the case *Sharp v. Dawes,* 1876 and a host of other legal decisions as to what constitutes a meeting.

From definitions such as these we learn that meetings:

1. Involve two or more persons (except in very special circumstances).
2. Are called for specific purposes.
3. Are publicized beforehand (including the agenda).
4. Can be formal or informal in character.

If a meeting is an assembly of people for a purpose, then clearly it is a particular kind of organization, therefore, what we said about organizations in general in Chapter 1 can apply to meetings.

Meetings are generally not popular, for reasons we will look at later, but they are growing in size, frequency and length. It is clear we pay considerable attention to meetings these days. Supervisors cannot escape attending meetings called by others, and indeed may themselves have to call meetings. It is important that all supervisors know what is expected of them, both as members and leaders of meetings.

7.2.15 Classifying meetings

As with organizations in general, we can classify meetings as *formal* and *informal;* as with organizations *formal* and *informal* are not two, mutually exclusive categories, but rather extreme ends of a continuous spectrum. Indeed, strangely, it does make sense to talk about 'informal, formal meetings' or even 'formal informal meetings'!

However, we can make some broad generalizations which distinguish one type from another, here are some in no particular order:

Formal	*Informal*
Notice of meeting given well in advance, in writing	Advance notice of meeting, if given at all, may only be verbal
Written agenda (order of business) in formal terms	Often no written agenda—if written, often in informal terms
Has officials—chairman, secretary	Has discussion leader, rather than chairman
Rigid procedures often in accordance with written (even printed) rules or constitution. Difficult to vary	Flexible procedures, reference rarely made to rules or conventions of discussion
Minutes of record	If minutes taken, minutes of narration
Matters discussed usually of policy, or general application to whole organization	Matters discussed usually recent, current, particular, specific, reviews, problems, emergencies, or reports—to do with the day-to-day running of the organization, or sub-systems

The structure of a meeting

Notice of meeting. This document if formal would read:

EXPLODING CHEMICAL COMPANY LTD

NOTICE IS HEREBY given that the 60th Annual General Meeting of the above named company will be held at the Westlake Hotel, Westlake on Wednesday 24 June 200X—at 2.30 pm.

BY ORDER OF THE BOARD

DATED I June 200X—

S. CRIBBLER, Secretary.

Its informal counterpart could be the sales manager writing to the sales team:

Dear ....

Monthly Representatives' Meeting

We are holding our next meeting for Sales Representatives in the Sales Manager's office at Head Office next Tuesday afternoon at 5 pm.
You are especially requested to attend this important meeting, where new ideas will be discussed.
Light refreshment will be available.
D. Jones, Sales Manager.

Agenda. (This word comes from the Latin meaning 'things to be done'.) It is a list or programme of the topics to be discussed at the meeting, in the order in which they will occur. It helps people to know in advance what a meeting is about.

Formal meetings, such as the company AGM or directors' meetings, have long agendas in the form specified by the Companies Acts or written statements of procedures such as the company's Articles. We need not consider these here, those who are interested should consult a book on secretarial practice. Those attending would be shareholders or directors. The informal formal meeting such as a Works Management Committee Meeting however could be attended by supervisors as well as other levels of management.

A typical agenda for a Works Management Committee could be:

1. Apologies for absence.
2. Minutes of the last meeting (agreed and signed).
3. Matters arising from last minutes.
4. Sales prospects—next six months.
5. Production reports:

   (a) Machine shop.
   (b) Press shop.
   (c) General assembly.

6. Stores and purchase reports.
7. Research and development.
8. Personnel situation.
9. Any other business. (A useful item: it leaves the meeting open for discussion on a topic not previously taken into account.)

Procedures.   Formal meetings have very rigid procedures usually laid down in writing by the company's Articles, a club's constitution or a council's Standing Orders. Many of these procedures are based on those used in Parliament. More detailed explanations of these can be found in a book on Secretarial Practice or Meetings, but discussion is usually centred round a form of words commencing with 'that' and with the verb in the subjunctive, for example, 'that the Chairman's Report and 16th Annual Accounts of the company be adopted'. Such a form of words is called a 'motion', before it is put to a vote, and a 'resolution' when it has been voted upon and passed. Amendments are allowed, if proposed in a formal way. Voting procedures are laid down. The agenda stands almost unaltered year after year.

However, in industry or commerce, it is not practical to run meetings according to formal procedures. If anything is to be achieved, ideas, positive thinking and purposeful problem solving must be encouraged at meetings. At our less formal, industrial meetings we should let the needs of the situation dictate the form of the meeting and the rules, customs and practices that we follow.

Chairman or discussion leader.   The duties of the formal chairman are: to keep order, follow the agenda, conduct the meeting according to the laid down procedure (or interpret the rules), and to see that the opinion of the majority is clearly recorded. He may have to resolve a deadlock.

On the other hand, a chairman of a less formal meeting may have a more difficult task: to get people who may not normally concentrate on one idea for more than a few minutes, to concentrate on a topic for ten or fifteen minutes; and then make balanced and careful judgements.

Minutes. Minutes are a record of what happened at a meeting. *Minutes of record* report the topic discussed, who proposed and seconded a motion, the wording of the motion; and the result of the vote on the motion taken by the meeting. *Minutes of narration* are more likely to be seen by supervisors. These minutes are a (shortened) record of what everyone said on each topic at the meeting, including arguments for and against, promises made, undertakings given. These are invaluable later as a reference to see who agreed to do what.

7.2.16   The supervisor as a meeting member

If meetings are to be effective, every member, including the supervisors should be:

1. *On time.* Being late can waste everyone else's time, even if it saves yours.
2. *Adequately prepared.* This means reading the Agenda, if there is one, making notes of what you propose to say; bringing your departmental statistics, records and other appropriate documents and returns.
3. *Able to keep to the point.* Only talk about the topic under discussion, not your department's current hobby-horse.
4. *Able to concentrate first on solving problems.* Rather than winning arguments.
5. *On guard against talking too much.*
6. *Willing to compromise.*
7. *Objective.* Try not to be dogmatic, or put forward arguments unsupported by facts.

7.2.17   The supervisor as chairman (discussion leader)

To get the best out of a meeting, and its members, the supervisor should:

1. *Be adequately prepared.* Know the objective of the meeting, have as many facts available as possible; see agendas are issued (if this is the procedure) to members plus any supporting information. If necessary, see people beforehand to go over with them the particular contributions that they are to make.
2. *Make clear what is being discussed.* This will help to eliminate *some* irrelevant discussion. Work through agenda items in turn.
3. *Steer the discussion.* Help members to continue with the discussion by adding questions and making points where you think others are reluctant to intervene.
4. *Try to get everyone to take part.* It may be necessary to ask a member a question or encourage him or her to reply to a point.
5. *Summarize the discussion at intervals.* This is useful because it reminds members of what has been said, or agreed upon, already. A final summary should be made at the end of the discussion before the vote, if one is to be taken. (In this case *both* sides' views must be set out.)
6. *Make sure members understand what they have promised to do.* Clearly indicate such promises in the summing up, and see they are clearly shown in subsequent minutes.

7. *Get as much agreement on each topic as you can.* It is poor chairmanship to let a discussion wander on without coming to a definite conclusion.
8. *Avoid being autocratic.* This can be seen in chairmen who are full of their own ideas, give too many opinions of their own, cut short any opposing ideas, treat members in a rude or peremptory fashion.
9. *Avoid time-wasting.* A finishing, as well as a starting time, helps.
10. *Minutes.* Make sure these are written up and circulated promptly.

If a meeting is a failure or does not achieve the desired results, the chairman should always ask the question: what did *I* do wrong? Was it my fault?

7.3   THE CONTROL FUNCTION

In Chapter 5, we saw that controlling was the essential process of seeing that what was planned to happen does happen (or as nearly as possible), that targets are set, standards laid down, and budgets prepared. However, it must be admitted that in many organizations many of the plans, and indeed the control systems that go with them, are neither formulated, introduced nor even monitored by first- or second-line management. The supervisor may feel 'left out' of the situation.

We must, therefore, clearly see that with or without plans or control of such plans, the supervisor *does* have areas of work where he can control events and eliminate the purposeless use of the four M's—men, materials, machines, money. In the end most adverse variances can be translated into money as nearly everything that happens in the firm results in *expenditure*. It follows that the supervisor's department (and staff) starts to cost money the minute the shop starts work, the office opens or the drivers clock on. The control of *costs* is therefore of paramount importance.

7.3.1 Waste

While it is not the exact equivalent of 'unfavourable variances', *waste* is a good word for the supervisor to remember. *Waste* has many meanings:[2] a piece of uncultivated land (i.e. not put to use); useless expenditure or squandering of money, time, etc.; useless by-products of an industrial process; material or products so damaged as to be unsaleable; material surplus to requirements; not applied to any purpose; rejected as defective, or produced in excess of that which can be used—these and other meanings all carry the same message that waste is undesirable, expensive and an expression of the misuse of resources and mismanagement of manpower.

In fact, waste arises from the improper use of or failure to use men, machines, materials or money.

---

[2] All the meanings given here are taken from the Shorter Oxford English Dictionary.

7.3.2 Records

Any control system, and therefore any attempt to combat waste, needs information. How can we tell how big the problem is without precise information? It is one thing to be vaguely aware of the fact that there was a lot of scrap last month; quite another to realize that 7.37% of the shop production was in fact quite worthless. To be useful records should be:

1. Easy to keep and maintain.
2. Clear and simple to read.
3. Available quickly for inspection.
4. *Always* up to date.

   Many non-clerical supervisors dislike paperwork, but records (for example, of output against standard or of weekly scrap percentages) are a *tool* just like a spanner or screwdriver.

7.3.3 Waste control

Using records, a supervisor (whether service, clerical or production) can control waste (or adverse variances) in many of the following areas:

1. Scrap from the production process.
2. Stock 'going off' whether soft fruit, or other items with a shelf-life.
3. Idle machines (lack of material or people to operate them, or no work).
4. Reworking.
5. Overtime.
6. Excessive use of consumables—coolant, rags, cleaning materials, etc.
7. Over- or under-maintenance.
8. Duplication of effort.

7.3.4 Cost reduction

Remember '£1 saved is £1 made'; to make a £1 profit on sales after tax may involve a considerable amount of work and effort. Here are some ideas and questions which supervisors would do well to put up in the office:

1. What about fitting time-switches to heat sources?
2. Do you use the wrong labour on jobs: highly-skilled people on routine work?
3. Do you use *all* the talents of your workers (remember McGregor)?
4. Do you try to minimize waiting time?
5. Do you have proper maintenance rotas for equipment, saving expensive repairs?
6. Do you give your staff precise and clear instructions (which will help to minimize unnecessary work, or mistakes)?
7. Do you cut corners, sacrificing quality for quantity?

8. Do you use the cheapest material (consistent with specification and safety) for the job?
9. Do you order materials, consumables, etc. in economic quantities, well in advance of need?
10. Do you encourage your staff to be quality minded?
11. Do you report faulty materials, components, etc. *immediately* to stores or purchasing dept? (This of course would not apply if you are following instructions to use and rectify faulty items.)
12. Do you re-use whatever you can?
13. Do you insist on good housekeeping at all times?
14. Do you keep a watch on 'foreigners'[3]?
15. Are the limits you work to more precise than they need be?

7.3.5 Safety

It is obvious that accidents, in addition to causing human suffering, and embarrassment to the firm and supervisor if the Health and Safety Inspector intervenes or prosecutes, cost money through unmanned machines, damaged equipment, overtime worked by others or loss of sales.

7.3.6 Training

Accidents can be reduced, mistakes limited, quality of work improved and overtime restricted by training. The supervisor must ensure appropriate training is given—this is an essential part of the control function.

7.3.7 Inspection

In many production environments inspection is carried out officially by a special class of employee called 'inspectors', whose particular job it is to check the quantity, quality and acceptability of production. However, this does *not* mean that the supervisor is absolved from checking his subordinates' work, even if he does not have the sophisticated tools, gauges and electronic test equipment of the inspectors.

In a clerical or service situation checking is either carried out by a fellow worker or by the supervisor himself.

7.3.8 Need for inspection

However well-planned and organized a company and its departments are, faulty parts do get manufactured, mistakes are made in invoicing, accounting and recording,

---

[3] An expression which means work carried out in any organization for the benefit of the worker, or a friend or friends of the worker.

errors creep into drawings, specifications and orders. The control aspect of inspection cannot be overemphasized: the efficiency of inspection can make or break the good name of the organization, enhance or jeopardize future orders, influence the number of complaints, cause costs to be held steady or to rise.

7.3.9 Maintenance

Finally we should examine the idea of maintenance, an important aspect of the control function. Maintenance has the following purposes:

1. To help safeguard the assets of the organization.
2. To prolong the use of the assets of the organization and minimize the waste.
3. To maximize the efficiency of the assets of the organization.
4. To help reduce accidents which could cause damage to life, limb or property.

Many people recognize these points but fail to plan and control maintenance. It is, however, very clear that failure to carry out any maintenance increases cost, causes breakdowns possibly at the most inconvenient times, and could cause accidents and generally leads to a loss of control of the work environment.

The extent of maintenance

The fixed assets of the organization which need maintenance:

Buildings (including window cleaning).
Plants (for large processes).
Machines (including office equipment).
Vehicles (commercial and private, including fork lift trucks, etc.)
Service facilities (telephones, heating systems, compressed air pumps, electrical wiring, etc.).

Planned maintenance

It is obvious that capricious or impulsive decisions to overhaul a particular lorry or piece of equipment, or leaving things to the very last possible moment do not give the best results. Planned, or periodic maintenance is carried out to reduce, as far as possible, the number of sudden breakdowns of machinery or equipment, and to make the best use of maintenance staff. While there are bound to be times when there is less work to do, it is desirable to spread the work load as evenly as possible.

This can in part be achieved by having spare sub-assemblies ready (e.g. in a garage a wheel already fitted with a fully inflated new tyre), so that the actual time taken to maintain equipment is cut to a minimum; and the maintenance staff can use a slack period to examine, and repair the defective sub-assembly (e.g. a punctured tyre).

Preventive maintenance

Under a preventive maintenance scheme, specific time intervals or mileage intervals, etc. between inspections and servicing are laid down. The regularity of inspection varies according to the asset: the factory building perhaps requiring inspection two or three times a year; a moving piston driving a heavy load, several times a month.

Some maintenance such as window cleaning is carried out regardless of the state of the asset and, for example, electric light bulbs may be replaced every 1000 hours, or a machine not in use may still be regularly oiled and inspected.

The use of records

To develop an effective programme of maintenance appropriate records should be kept showing:

1. The name of the individual asset or part of an asset.
2. How often the asset should be inspected.
3. How often the asset is actually inspected.
4. Nature of condition at each inspection.
5. Repairs carried out.
6. Cost of parts, amount of time (and cost of this time) involved on each repair.

By keeping records of individual machines or vehicles, important information can be obtained for determining its ability to stand up to the job required of it. When the repair costs climb past a certain point, usually the level of the first year's depreciation, on a new machine, consideration can be made to replace it.

Records will also show, if experiments are carried out, what the optimum periods are for each piece of equipment. Cost savings must be a target of planned maintenance. If you maintain equipment *every day*, so that it never breaks down, you may spend many times more than the cost of three monthly maintenance inspections plus two or three sudden breakdowns a year.

The supervisor's role

While it is usual for the maintenance department to see that plant and equipment are kept in good order (a functional activity) line supervisors should see that equipment is kept clean and not abused. 'Good Housekeeping' is not only the name of a magazine, it is part of a supervisor's job. Supervisors are responsible for seeing that employees clean up after using machines or equipment, thus reducing maintenance charges. In addition they may have much to give to the maintenance department in the way of advice in planning the maintenance scheme for the department. They may even press for a PM scheme on the grounds of cost reduction if one does not already exist.

Where supervisors are normally responsible for their own maintenance (i.e. transport/garage managers) they will find that the time spent on planning periodic maintenance will be beneficial in the long run.

Finally, maintenance is closely related to safety and supervisors whose motto is 'safety first' will want to encourage all their operatives to co-operate in planned maintenance in order to avoid carelessness or deliberate negligence by failing to report short-comings or defects in machinery or equipment until it is too late. This particularly applies in the case of road vehicles, were legal as well as moral requirements have to be met.

SUMMARY

1.   Motivation is creating a total work environment where employees will work willingly to further the objectives of the organization, because they feel they are simultaneously achieving their own objectives.

2.   Supervisors are advised to:

    (a) Recognize and base rewards on performance.
    (b) Practise loyalty towards subordinates.
    (c) Be employee centred.
    (d) Be concerned with employees' safety and welfare.
    (e) Meet individual needs.

3.   To provide conditions for a sufficient degree of motivation, the worker should:

    (a) Feel personal achievement in the job.
    (b) Feel the job is worth doing.
    (c) Be given adequate recognition.
    (d) Have control over certain aspects of the job.
    (e) Feel he/she is developing as a human being.

4.   For every individual worker, the supervisor should:

    (a) Agree standards and targets.
    (b) Provide adequate training.
    (c) Recognize success and counsel failure.
    (d) Remove unnecessary controls.
    (e) Review performance regularly.
    (f) Take trouble to get to know them.

5.   Dealing with groups, the supervisor sets and maintains group objectives; involves the group, and maintains its unity, and should:

(a) Make sure that everyone understands the objectives and standards.
(b) Ensure that the group is of optimum size.
(c) Ensure that people agreeable to one another work together.
(d) Ensure that work is fairly distributed.
(e) Ensure that grievances are dealt with.
(f) Consult and brief the group.
(g) Accord the shop steward respect.

6. People want various things from work, including:

    (a) Money.
    (b) Activity.
    (c) Satisfaction of social needs.
    (d) Good working conditions.
    (e) Recognition and success.

7. Verbal communication is the most frequently used medium for most managers/supervisors. Advantages include:

    (a) Ability to alter presentation to suit receiver.
    (b) Subtleties of tone and stress.
    (c) Facial expressions which can help convey meaning.
    (d) Availability of feedback (a check on whether the message has been received).

8. Written communication has, however, advantages when:

    (a) Used to give precise orders or instructions, where information is complex/complicated.
    (b) Sender and receiver are far apart.
    (c) There is a multitude of receivers.
    (d) Records (files) are needed of communication, especially for legal reasons.
    (e) Faced with emergencies.

9. Presenting a case verbally entails:

    (a) Preparation including all facts, supporting material and notes.
    (b) Presentation—getting to the point quickly, giving reasons and advantages, summarizing points.
    (c) Forestalling questions and objections.

10. A case in writing needs similar presentation to a verbal case but will need:

    (a) Introductory paragraph.
    (b) Explanatory paragraphs.
    (c) Request or recommendation.

11.   An order is a simple direction to do something; an instruction is an order *plus* an explanation of how the job is done.

12.   The various types of order/instruction are:

(a)   The direct order (implies knowledge on how to carry out the order on the part of the subordinate).
(b)   The appeal (still implies some previous knowledge).
(c)   The hint or implied order.
(d)   The open order (usually a statement of fact that a particular job has to be done).
(e)   Taking the initiative.
(f)   Detailed order/instruction.

13.   Giving instructions is similar to training: preparing the worker, presenting the operation, trying out performance (omitted with skilled workers), checking progress.

14.   Interviews are:

(a)   Communication with a purpose.
(b)   Conducted in privacy, without distraction preferably.
(c)   Situations where one person takes the lead.

15.   Interviews should be:

(a)   Conducted politely, with courtesy.
(b)   Planned in advance.
(c)   A two-way flow of communication.
(d)   Summed up at the end by the interviewer.

16.   These points in general apply to many types of interview. Special considerations apply to disciplinary interviews:

(a)   Study employee's background carefully.
(b)   Be sure about organization's disciplinary policy.
(c)   Attempt to obtain admission of error.
(d)   Warn of consequences of actions.
(e)   Record *carefully* the result of interview, warnings given, etc.
(f)   Remember a witness may be present (e.g. trade union representative).

17.   Grievance interviews have special considerations too:

(a)   Take advice beforehand.
(b)   Make sure how far you can act alone, but only promise what you can fulfil.
(c)   Be prepared to refer the matter upwards.

18.   Meetings can be formal or informal. Formal meetings have written notice in advance, agendas, formal procedures, minutes of record and are called usually to discuss policy matters. Informal meetings may not have advance notice, nor agendas, may have very flexible procedures, have a discussion leader, rather than a chairman, and may discuss recent, current specific issues.

       The distinction between formal and informal is not precise as there are degrees of formality.

19.   An agenda is a list of the topics to be discussed at a meeting.

20.   Meeting procedures in general are greatly influenced by Parliamentary procedures.

21.   Minutes are a record of a meeting: minutes of record set down the *minimum* of information; minutes of narration cover the arguments for and against and are a *précis* of the discussion.

22.   The supervisor as a meeting member should be:

       (a)   On time.
       (b)   Adequately prepared.
       (c)   Able to keep to the point.
       (d)   Able to concentrate on problem-solving.
       (e)   On guard against talking too much.
       (f) Willing to compromise.
       (g)   Always objective.

23.   The supervisor as meeting chairman (discussion leader), should:

       (a)   Be adequately prepared.
       (b)   Make clear what is being discussed.
       (c)   Steer the discussion, encouraging participation.
       (d)   Summarize at intervals.
       (e)   Make clear action to be taken, and by whom.
       (f)   Get agreement, as far as possible.
       (g)   Avoid becoming autocratic.

24.   The supervisor's control function includes controlling *costs,* and *waste.*

25.   Records, if properly kept, are the basis for any control system.

26.   A proper attitude to safety, training, inspection and maintenance can aid the control function.

REVIEW QUESTIONS

1. What *general* guidelines should a supervisor follow in motivating the work group?

2. What is meant by saying a supervisor should be 'employee centred'?

3. How can a supervisor aid the motivation of:

   (a) Individuals?
   (b) Groups?

4. Consider what people want from work, and make a list of *five* possibilities other than money.

5. Distinguish between written and verbal communication: list the appropriate circumstances for each method of communication.

6. How would you go about preparing a case verbally? In writing?

7. Give examples from your own work situation of direct orders, hints, open orders, detailed orders.

8. What preparations would you make before conducting *any* interview? What special preparations would you make for grievance interviews?

9. Define a meeting. (You should try to find as many definitions as possible from a variety of sources.)

10. Make a list of the characteristics of:

    (a) Formal meetings.
    (b) Informal meetings.

11. What is the difference (if any) between a chairman, and a discussion leader; minutes of record, and minutes of narration?

12. How can a supervisor who becomes the chairman or discussion leader of a meeting get the best out of it and its members?

13. Make a list of *ten* ways a supervisor can help to control costs and/or waste.

14. Why is the maintenance of equipment an important factor in the supervisor's control function?

DISCUSSION TOPICS

1. Discuss how best to motivate:

    (a) Assembly-line workers.
    (b) Word processing staff.
    (c) Shop assistants.
    (d) Students on supervisory courses.

2. Is it a good idea to get to know your staff, and their problems? Discuss the view that this approach is merely prying into personal matters (and therefore possibly private and confidential), which have nothing to do with work.

3. Discuss the view held by many supervisors (and others) that there is too much paperwork and that verbal communication is to be preferred. Is there really a place for written orders?

4. As a group or groups discuss how you would represent Bill Smith's case for two days' compassionate leave because of his mother's illness to your immediate superior. You know Bill is a long service (15 years) employee; good time keeper; usually tells the truth; has had all his holiday entitlement. What other kind of information would you need in preparing the case?

5. Discuss the view that there is no need for a supervisor to control the quality of the work of the department if there is an inspection team or quality control department.

6. Many people think that there is far *too much* maintenance of equipment and that it is probably cheaper to repair when the need arises. Apply this viewpoint to the plant/equipment used in your department or office.

ASSIGNMENTS

A7.1 Make a list of the ways in which your organization attempts to motivate its employees. Evaluate how effective such methods are; and suggest improvements. (Results could be discussed and compared in class.)

A7.2 Prepare a case in writing for someone known to you, in the organization in which you work, to be sent *next year*, on the course of which you are at present a member.

A7.3 Review the department in which you work. How could quality, output levels, use of materials be better controlled? Investigate at least one area of waste, and suggest how savings might be made.

Case studies

A7.4   'Thug' Smithson pushed back his helmet, and stared at Dr Seeker with some disbelief. 'I'm sure you and I are not on the same wavelength,' he said. 'It's all very well for those big shots at head office to commission surveys into motivation, and all that rubbish, but I'm at the sharp end where it all happens!'

Smithson pointed round the building site: everywhere piles of bricks, machinery, and men working under the hot sun. 'Look at this lot,' he said, 'not a single one of them gives a damn about working conditions, how the job is organized, and as for recognition....' Smithson seemed at a loss for words.

'Look, I'm very busy now. There's always a moving population here, and I've another three people to hire within the hour. I'll tell you one thing: I can only get people because we pay the highest wages around here. The only thing this lot is interested in is money, money and more money. They get their hundreds of pounds a week and are quite satisfied until they've got enough to move on somewhere else. What more can anyone want?'

'Thug' returned to his office: the interview was at an end.

(a) Do you agree that 'Thug' is right about his men? Why?
(b) Is 'Thug' ignoring anything in the work situation? What might he consider doing?

A7.5   'I don't know what this meeting is about, do you?' asked Terry, the Sales Office Manager, as he met Charlie, the Cost Accountant, in the corridor. 'No, I haven't a clue, but I bet it'll be another fiasco,' Charlie replied.

Ten managers sat round the table in the board room and waited for a quarter of an hour, then Tony Billboard, the Advertising Director, breezed in. 'Good morning,' he announced, 'I'm just checking on the progress of the autumn sales promotion campaign which we discussed last month. Now Terry, what have you done about extracting those statistics on customer preferences that I asked you for?'

Terry blushed: 'I know we talked about it, but I don't remember our having *decided* to get that information. It'll take my staff hours and hours to get it—anyway haven't the market research people any figures?' It was Sydney Pollit's turn to wriggle—'It's not my responsibility to prepare these kinds of figures—Dave Hakey's in charge of the Stats section, and he's not here.'

Tony Billboard banged on the table: 'Something must be done about this soon. Now let's consider the budget for this promotion. How much will it cost, Charlie?' Charlie took a deep breath. 'As I remember it, Tony, last time we talked about three schemes, and I wasn't really sure at the end of the meeting which idea we were going for!' Billboard was getting angry. 'What the devil do we have meetings for?' he asked. 'Of course we must do the retail outlets in the south-west first as a pilot scheme; surely everyone sees the logic of it?'

Just then the telephone rang and Billboard was called away. 'Now gentlemen,' he said, 'we'll meet again same time next Thursday, and I want *all* the answers then.'

(a) What kind of chairman/discussion leader is Tony Billboard? Why do you think the other managers did not contribute much to the meeting?

(b) Decide what the particular *shortcomings* are in Tony's approach, and try to estimate how you would feel if you were a member of this meeting.

(c) Prepare a list of suggestions which Tony might consider, which could probably help him run more successful meetings in future.

8
The Supervisor as a Leader

8.1 INTRODUCTION AND DEFINITIONS

We have already noted difficulties in defining some ideas and terms used in management. Leadership is no exception. Various alternative theories are discussed in this chapter, some quite different, others variations on a theme. However, we may find an acceptable definition by defining leadership in terms of the *results* it can give.

Leadership has often been described as influence, or the art, skill or process of influencing people to work towards the achievement of group, or larger organizational goals. Whilst this should not be taken as implying leadership is the same as management, we can see that it is *part* of the job of managing—particularly that of motivating and controlling. There can be no leaders without followers, and such followers need to be influenced, persuaded or inspired to follow the leader. However, leadership as we shall see, need not be mere domination, but could be effective through supportive or co-ordinative behaviour, as with, for example, the conductor of an orchestra.

Theories of leadership can be classified under the following headings:

1. Activity based.
2. Trait (or quality) based.
3. Contingency based.
4. Style based.
5. Continuum based.

(There is a certain amount of overlap between 4 and 5.)

Before we attempt to explore these ideas, we must note three further points, the first being the important distinction between *formal* and *informal* leaders. The formal leader is the *appointed* leader, the one holding a particular rank or position to which he has been elected, or for which he or she has been selected by some process in a typical bureaucratic organization. (There are, of course, some formal leaders who get their posts by other means, say, by inheritance or seizing power.) The formal, appointed, *official* leader has the power and authority about which Weber wrote. The informal leader, on the other hand, is the natural leader chosen or selected by the group to which he or she belongs. Such natural leaders *could* be shop stewards, but, in my experience, by no means necessarily so. Having an unofficial leader in his work group is a real problem for any supervisor. The aim should be, therefore, to win the group's allegiance so that only one leader remains—the supervisor, who becomes both formal and informal leader.

The second point that we should continually bear in mind when evaluating the various ideas and suggestions connected with leadership is that it is dangerous to isolate leaders from the situation, i.e. the environment, structure and composition of the group concerned. Different circumstances will bring forth different leaders.

Finally, we shall find that leadership and motivation are bound up with each other; indeed C. S. Deverell[1] thinks of them as two sides of the same coin. So we shall not be surprised to find 'good' leadership equated with highly motivated workers and vice versa.

8.2 LEADERSHIP AS AN ACTIVITY

Some people regard leadership as an *activity*. On this basis practising leadership means doing things: issuing orders, persuading, motivating people, getting tasks completed. Lt. Colonel L. Urwick[2] (a British Management Consultant of pre- and post-Second World War influence) approved of definitions which for example described leaders as people to whom others would go for advice and get it, and whose influence guided others. Leadership was demonstrated by example.

Unfortunately he seemed to confine his considerations of leadership to the 'leader of the business', who was, by inference, the managing director. The activities he described as characteristic of such leaders were *representing* the company to the outside world; *initiating* innovation, seeking new ideas; *administering* the undertaking, and above all imposing *order*, and finally interpreting the reasons for everything decided to the workforce and winning support for changes. This seems a rather restricted view of leadership and certainly not one which covers all leaders.

Another military man, John Adair,[3] whilst at Sandhurst, developed an *activity based* view of leadership, 'Action-Centred Leadership'. Training based on this theory has been widely implemented in the Army and was later adopted by the Industrial Society. Usually considered in terms of 'overlapping circles' or of a juggler attempting to keep three balls in the air all at the same time to keep performing, we could perhaps re-interpret the idea as a 'three-pronged attack'.

The basic idea behind the theory is that the leader of any group or team has constantly to strive to achieve three major goals while at the same time maintaining a position as an effective or successful leader (see Fig. 8.1).

The first goal is to consider the *needs of the tasks* or missions which the leader is required by the organization to achieve: these are the objectives upon which he must

---

[1] *Acquiring Management Skills*. London: Gee. 1973. p. 83.
[2] *Leadership in the 20th Century*. London: Pitman, 1957.
[3] *Action Centred Leadership*. London: Gower, 1979.

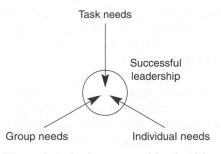

Figure 8.1 Action-centred leadership.

focus the efforts both of the team and himself. The second goal is to consider the *needs of the group* as a whole, and to show by his or her actions that the leader is concerned with their well being and morale. If the leader does not do this, then the team might not perform as effectively as it should. The leader needs to concentrate on team building, developing inter-dependence and keeping the group briefed and informed. Finally concern for the team as a whole is not enough: it is necessary to consider *individual needs* as and when they arise. The leader needs to motivate by supporting and developing each individual. The target—overall effectiveness—is achieved by all three goals being reached: a shortfall in any one of them would damage the chances of achieving the target. (The theory does allow for changes in emphasis temporarily to meet some emergency, but any 'imbalance' such as spending a great deal of time over one individual's needs, must be corrected as soon as possible.)

8.3   LEADERSHIP QUALITIES

Early studies of leadership were largely based on the assumption that leaders were born and not made. The search was therefore for a set of qualities, attributes or physical characteristics that leaders actually possessed. Even after the Second World War, whole lists were being compiled of leadership qualities: *physical* traits (such as drive, energy, appearance and height); *personality* traits (adaptability, enthusiasm, self-confidence); *social* traits (co-operation, interpersonal skills such as tact, courtesy, and administrative ability) and so on.

Unfortunately as leaders in history have come in every shape, size and sex, it is not surprising that not much came out of such endeavours. A major stumbling block is that not all leaders possess all the traits or qualities which can be found in the lists: worse, many non-leaders possess a great many of them. In fact there is some evidence that characteristics such as initiative, dependability, feelings of responsibility, respect for others, are more the kinds of behaviour that go with the *role* of being leader, which can be assumed or learned on taking up the position.

Another version of the trait/quality theories is the *situational approach*. The idea here is that leaders are products of particular situations—Hitler in Germany of the '30s, Churchill in England of the early '40s, Mao's rise after 1946. A given set of factors exist in a situation—economic depression, high unemployment, weak government, disenchantment with traditional politics, say, and a leader emerges who recognizes the problems and has characteristics or traits which fit the needs of the situation. Here we are not saying the 'born leader' will become a leader independent of his or her life chances, but only in a given set of circumstances. In another related sense such leadership qualities could arise from special knowledge possessed by a member of a group uniquely, and essential for that group's survival. American studies seem to give some evidence to this theory, and its implication for managers in successful leadership can depend, at least in part, on a correct interpretation of, and response to, the values, feelings and personalities of the group they lead, as well as the economic environment.

8.4   THE CONTINGENCY APPROACH

An interesting extension of trait/situational theories is the so-called 'contingency' approach of F. Fiedler.[4] He states the ability of a leader to exercise influence depends upon the *situation* facing the group led. A wide volume of research among military personnel, steelworkers, senior executives, church leaders and others in the USA, lead him to three 'critical dimensions' of the situation that affect a leader's ability to lead:

1.   *Position power*. The actual power that the organization has given the leader.
2.   *Task structure*. The extent to which tasks can be clearly defined and spelt out to people who have to carry them out, in contrast to conditions where tasks are only vaguely defined.
3.   *Leader-group member relations*. The extent to which a work group like and trust a leader and are willing to follow that person.

Fiedler's conclusions were:

1.   A leader faced a 'favourable' situation (one which was easy to control) if the leader had been assigned power and authority; the tasks the work group had to tackle were clearly laid down and structured; and the leader was well-liked and trusted by the group.
2.   A leader faced an 'unfavourable' situation (one less easy to control) where formal authority was not clearly defined, where there was ambiguity in the tasks to be performed, and where there was not a high degree of trust or liking for the leader.
3.   The best strategy for the leader in highly favourable or highly unfavourable conditions was to be directive, task orientated, or hard-nosed.
4.   The best strategy for the leader in moderately favourable/moderately unfavourable conditions was to be a more supportive or lenient leader.

The organization itself can do a great deal to help leaders by making sure authority and power is clear and certain; and tasks are clearly defined. Leadership performance will then depend as much on the organization as on the leader.

---

[4] F. Fiedler, 'Engineer the Job to Fit the Manager', *Harvard Business Review* (1965) No. 51, pp. 115–122.

8.5 LEADERSHIP STYLES

As can be seen, it is difficult to separate the theories of what leadership is from what leaders do—that is their behaviour or leadership styles. Fiedler spoke of only two— task orientated and people orientated. Other purely style based theories have many more categories.

Rensis Likert reviews four types of management:[5]

System 1: exploitive authoritative where decisions are all made at the top; communication is all one way—downwards; fears, threats are constant weapons.

System 2: benevolent authoritative where there is some delegation with close policy control; the accent is more on reward than punishment and some upward communication is allowed.

System 3: consultative where attempts are made to allow constructive use of subordinates' ideas and opinions; where there is some involvement in decision making, particularly at lower levels.

System 4: participative (group management) where there are economic rewards, full use is made of group participation in setting performance goals; communication flows upwards, downwards, sideways. There is a 'supportive' atmosphere with a leader who helps and advises rather than dictates and commands.

Likert asserts, in general, successful supervisors are those whose work groups have high co-operative attitudes, and a high level of job satisfaction from *System 4* management. In effect he plumps for people-centred supervision.

Other writers using slightly different terminology have differentiated between *autocratic* managers (job centred, relies on power, likes conformists, keeps information, rarely delegates); *semi-autocratic* (more a father figure, likes a finger in every pie, loves to praise particularly 'team people' or those totally loyal to the firm); *democratic* (unsure of himself and his relations with the group; all policies are up for group discussion, with majority verdict endorsed by the 'leader'. Discipline is noticeable by its absence—a *laissez-faire* leadership); and finally *consultative/participative* (the Theory 'Y' manager) where the leader *consults then decides*; delegates, encourages, counsels.

The latter version has many of the virtues of democratic leadership involving other people without the work group feeling insecure. The leader backs the group up and therefore gives it basic security, indicating what he wants from them.

8.6 THE MANAGERIAL GRID AND THE '3D' MODEL

A difficulty with the style analysis is we just have two, four or perhaps five or six slots into which to fit particular managers/supervisors/leaders. A more dramatic approach

---

[5] R. Likert, *New Patterns of Management.* New York: McGraw-Hill, 1961.

is to have a grid with potentially 81 (i.e. 9×9) points of reference to describe the balance between the two extremes: concern for production, and concern for people. (In practice only five major points are precisely identified and described.) Known as the *Managerial Grid*, it was devised some 30 years ago by Robert Blake and Jane Mouton and widely used in consultancy and training. 'Concern for production' includes the attitudes of supervisors towards procedures, processes, work efficiency and volume of output: 'concern for people' includes personal commitment, maintaining trust and esteem of the work group, and good working conditions, and having satisfying interpersonal relations.

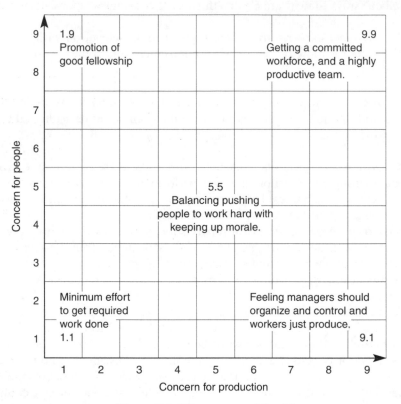

Figure 8.2 The managerial grid.

The leadership styles obtained by combining the two dimensions range from 1.1 (described as 'impoverished') to 5.5 (described as 'middle of the road'—a leader who feels concern for people and concern for production as two entirely separate goals, and leading is an uneasy compromise between the two), to 9.1 (described as 'task management' because of its lack of concern for people), to 1.9 (called 'country club management' because whilst people's needs are well catered for there is lack of concern for the job) and finally to 9.9 (called 'team management', thought to be ideal). Once a leader's position on the scale is established, the objective of further training is to change the management style to the 9.9 approach where there is equally high concern for people and for task accomplishment.

W. Reddin has developed the grid into a third dimension: the '3D Theory of Managerial Effectiveness'. Both higher and lower levels of effectiveness exist in this model. At the lower level is the Deserter, the minimum achiever, almost 'opting out' (1.1 position on the managerial grid), the Autocrat (near 9.1), Missionary and Compromiser (near 5.5). At the higher level the same four basic styles appear a second time in a more effective guise, the Executive being the 9.9 equivalent.

When used with a battery of questionnaires and tests, a *leadership style profile* is obtained, which can show several styles existing at the same time in the same individual, though often one is clearly dominant. Reddin does not believe in pushing managers to adopt the Executive Style—he believes the appropriate style of management should fit the actual situation the manager is in.

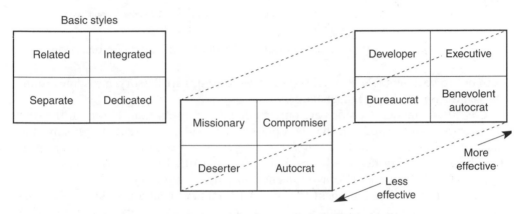

Figure 8.3 3D model of managerial effectiveness.

8.7 A CONTINUUM THEORY

Some of the leadership theories previously considered present two basic choices: a task-centred leader on the one hand and an employee-centred one on the other hand. It is agreed that more choices are available in Likert (4), and with the managerial grid (5). R. Tannenbaum and W. H. Schmidt have proposed there is a whole range of styles between the two extremes, each shading into the next, like colours in a spectrum. However, they do mark some basic points in the 'continuum' (or range of qualities). A leader's position on the continuum depend upon his personality; the nature of the individuals in the work group; the nature of the traditions and values of the organization, and the pressures of time on decision-making.

Additionally the leadership style can be affected by forces *outside* the organization: unions, consumer movements, political climates, the state of the economy. There are, in this model, no judgements made about which style is 'best', or even 'better than'. However commentators have said that *telling* alone can result in lack of commitment, poor morale and high labour turnover. *Selling* will only work if the 'goods' or rewards

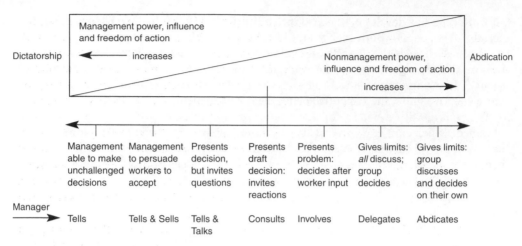

Figure 8.4 Tannenbaum and Schmidt's 'continuum' of leadership behaviour.

turn out to be acceptable: if benefits (to the work group) are illusory, next time around the selling job will be that much harder.

Consulting implies decisions are only made after consultation. However, the final decision may not include all the ideas put forward: subordinates may feel somehow cheated and not truly involved. *Involving, delegating* and *abdicating* will enable group members in varying degrees to reach and be committed to solutions. Thus, once again, the conclusion is that involvement and participation in decision making will bring the effort and commitment to work which management are seeking. The 'stick and carrot' methods of leadership are now seen as inadequate and inappropriate in contemporary society.

8.8   LEADERSHIP AND EMPOWERMENT

As we noted in section 4.4, the functions of the supervisor, team or group leader have been, in the recent past, undergoing changes of emphasis. There is an increasing tendency for work groups to become more independent, more self-reliant. Indeed, the group may take upon itself some of the functions traditionally associated with supervision, as well as handling technical problems: for example, the maintenance of quality standards.

Even the innovations in working methods, quality systems and the like may be products of a group or groups of employees, who in a sense 'own' the innovations. The current, fashionable term for this is 'empowerment'. Some people may feel that the existence of partly or wholly autonomous work groups (or even individual employees) undermine, or even make redundant, the position of supervisor, group or team leader.

In fact, there need be no conflict between the two ideas of leadership and empowerment. Sales people 'on the road' have for decades worked on their own, planning and sorting out their own calls and patterns of work, but still reporting to a field sales manager. The latter's job was to *encourage and support* the team; to act as a facilitator, as well as to monitor performance.

In those production-based organizations of which I have had personal knowledge, where empowerment has been successfully promoted, the success has depended greatly upon the total commitment of management at all levels to the planning for, and implementation of, the idea in the first place; and the personal involvement of managers and the work group leaders in the training activities prior to the setting up of the 'empowered' groups. (How change can be brought about is discussed in the following chapter.)

It is interesting to note that in the original MCI NVQ (Supervisory) level 3 standards, in Unit 5, (Element 5.3, *Provide feedback on work performance to teams and individuals*), specific reference was made about the need to encourage team members to make suggestions on how systems/procedures could be improved; and again in Unit 6, (Element 6.1), the need to encourage team members to put forward their ideas and views.

The latest level 3 NVQ is clearly the model for the future: rather than 'telling', or 'telling and selling', the supervisor/team leader of the twenty-first century will be an 'involving/delegating/facilitating person'.

8.9 CONCLUSIONS AND SUMMARY

While it is difficult to come to a final, precise, definitive set of conclusions about leadership (the whole subject is still rather speculative) there are some general conclusions which emerge. These are listed below, and will serve as a summary for this chapter, although some new points are made.

1. Different situations demand different leadership styles. Could we consider consultative or participative management on the battlefield; when an emergency threatens the group, time is short and immediate action is essential? Conversely, would it not be equally unsuitable to propose radical changes in pay structures, working conditions, job procedures without some kind of prior consultation?

2. Following on the first point the implication is that the same leader should and would use different styles at different times; changing his approach to suit the environment of the group, its members' attitudes and the current work needs. We might call this approach *pragmatic* (or *adaptive*) management.

3. However, in a stable, run-of-the mill industrial or commercial situation, given no special outside pressures, a policy of communicating with, consulting or involving the work force is likely to result in greater effort and output, than any policy which excludes these activities. In a phrase, consultation counts, participation pays.

   (This view, while expressed with many different variations and emphases by different writers, is very commonly advanced at the present time; and indeed many managements are experimenting with consultation or participation schemes.)

4.   Some researchers, however, feel that attention has to be paid to the *type* of decision to be put forward for participative debate. Workers would, it is felt, want to be very much involved in proposed changes in work practices, or in what service the canteen provides, but very much less in the routine purchases of materials, deciding which contractor should clean the windows. Participation, in accordance with this view should be *selective*.

5.   Research (in the USA) has shown employee-centred supervisors have been more successful than task- or job-centred supervisors.

6.   Successful leaders are those who (amongst other abilities) can identify problems and find ways of solving them (even if this means getting the help of others); and communicate clearly what needs to be done to the group members.

7.   Successful leaders are likely to be more intelligent than the group average; to have drive and enthusiasm for the job; to be sociable and adaptable to both individual and group needs.

8.   Supervisors who set (challenging, but attainable) targets for their subordinates to meet, are likely to get a higher performance from their work group, than supervisors who do *not* set such targets.

9.   Hand-in-hand with employee involvement and participation is *delegation:* simultaneously subordinates are involved, feel more important and feel that they are being trusted. Delegation is a spur to commitment, uses more of the pool of talents available in the work group, and is a step towards employee development or self-realization.

10.   It is very difficult to prepare a list of characteristics which are common to all, or even many leaders. All we can do is perhaps say that successful leaders do exhibit a fair proportion of the characteristics such as self-confidence, dependability, honesty and integrity, etc., though others such as the possession of communication skills, and problem-solving abilities seem perhaps much more common characteristics of successful leaders.

REVIEW QUESTIONS

1.   Distinguish between leadership as an activity, as a personal characteristic, and as a concept of leadership style.

2.   What is the difference between a 'formal' and an 'informal' leader?

3.   What is meant by 'action-centred leadership'?

4.   Explain the ideas behind the search for leadership qualities. Why have such searches not really been successful?

5.   Describe 'contingency' approach of F. Fiedler. To what conclusions does he come?

6.   List and comment upon Likert's four 'systems of management'.

7   Draw the managerial grid. What leadership style occupies co-ordinates 1.1? Where would you place an enthusiastic, driving manager whose aim is to increase productivity considerably?

8.   Set out in your own words the analysis of leadership styles at the seven points indicated on the Tannenbaum and Schmidt continuum (i.e. under the headings 'tells', 'tells and sells', etc.).

9.   Why do you think that difference circumstances demand different management styles? Would 'abdication', for example, be appropriate in an emergency?

DISCUSSION TOPICS

1.   What are the virtues of delegation (a) from the leader's point of view and (b) that of members of a work group/subordinates?

2.   Discuss the view leaders are 'born and not made'.

3.   Who makes the better leader: a man or a woman?

4.   Discuss the virtues (if any) and disadvantages of allowing work groups to participate in decision-making. Why is this style most frequently advocated nowadays?

ASSIGNMENTS

A8.1   Take two managers known to you (you need not name them, nor their jobs) and compare and contrast their leadership styles. Do, in fact, either of them fall into any category discussed in this chapter? Give examples of behaviour, decisions or actions to illustrate your answer.

A8.2   Taking yourself as the subject try to assess what leadership qualities and/or style you possess. Discuss your findings with someone who knows you on the course, or at work, and see how near your friend's views are to yours.

A8.3   Consider each of the ideas/theories on leadership discussed in this chapter. Select the one you think is the most useful, and express the reasons for your choice.

Case studies

A8.4   Brian Sharpe was a little surprised when Tom Fathers, the Chief Draughtsman of the company, sent for him. Brian was a quiet, hard working rather self-effacing young man, but he had had an idea about a problem that had been worrying the designers of the new centrifugal pump for some time. 'Sit down, Brian,' said Fathers in a kindly fashion, 'take the weight off your feet lad.'

Fathers shuffled the papers in front of him. 'First, I'd like to say how pleased I was to read that piece about you in the Gazette last week. Anyone who could swim thirty lengths for charity deserves a real pat on the back, and I'm glad the company's name got mentioned as well. Reflects great credit on you.' Brian blushed and got up to go. 'Just a moment, Brian,' Fathers added, 'there's just this matter of this piston ring. I hear you have been over to Design about this one.'

'We're a happy team in this department Brian, all working together, but there's one rule I like my team to follow: we all pull together, and everything we do I want to know about—after all you wouldn't like me to talk about you behind your back. It's something I'd never do. If changes are needed to that piston, Design will come to us, and I will decide who'll tackle the job. Naturally, in view of your interest, I think I'd get you to look at it, and then talk it over with me, and we'll put it up as a departmental idea, under my signature, to give a stamp of authority as it were. How's that?'

Brian was upset, although he did not show it. After all, he thought, this idea of his could save the company money, and it was *his* idea.

(a) Comment on Tom Fathers' management style.
(b) How could Brian resolve this problem? If he put his idea up through the company suggestion scheme, what would Fathers' reaction be?

A8.5   Tim Sellars and Bob Pullen usually met at the 'Three Pigeons' after a day on the road. Tim sold office equipment and Bob was a representative for a local bacon processing factory. 'I've had a rotten day,' said Tim, 'my boss met me, by accident, he said, at nine o'clock, just when I was starting out. He stayed with me all day. The worst moment was when I was just about to sell Jones and Jones two new duplicators—the really expensive model. Harry Smart—he's the boss—jumped in with both feet, offered a discount I couldn't have given, and took the order, yes I'll get the commission on it, but it *was* my sale after all.' Tim ordered another round.

Bob looked happier. 'Well Tim,' he smiled 'my boss came out with me too, today. He asked if he could last week, and he spent all morning with me. Every call we made, he stayed well in the background until I introduced him. We had a tricky problem when we got to that big supermarket chain's Central Purchasing Office. I didn't quite know what the position was about discounts and deliveries if they doubled their order next month. Harold suggested we all went to lunch, and while the buyer was in the cloakroom, he passed me some suggested figures and delivery dates on the back of an envelope. For some reason, he said he couldn't stay any longer and excused himself. I got the sale, and had a good lunch into the bargain!'

(a) Compare the two management styles of Harry Smart, and Bob's boss, Harold. If you were a salesman, which of the two sales managers would you prefer to have as a boss?
(b) Why?

9
Planning, Introducing and Managing Change

9.1 INTRODUCTION

The problem of change and its effect on supervision was noted in Chapter 4, Section 4.4. Chapter 8 dealt with leadership in a generalized way. But implicit in any consideration of leadership is the management of change, when high degrees of leadership skills are usually required.

Most organizations have been undergoing rapid changes during the last decade (some hardly realizing it), and not all this change is immediately related to current economic problems. Prophets of change have talked about the 'Space Age', the 'Post Industrial Society' or the 'Information Revolution'. Already we are moving towards a society in which many repetitious jobs such as adding up or typing endless columns of figures, or endlessly feeding highly specialized one-task machines are being phased out, and are being replaced by jobs requiring more skill, resourcefulness and increasing discretion. Many possibilities and visions of the future are discussed by Alvin Toffler in his books *Future Shock* and *The Third Wave,* but the basic message is change and increasing amounts of it. The *rate* of change is accelerating too.

Thus, coping with change, introducing changes in work patterns, technology and work methods is a real, contemporary and continuing one for management and supervision alike. Where real problems emerge is where change stops occurring at a steady gentle rate and becomes rapid, fundamental and significant. This in turn can bring about bewilderment, personal stress, lack of motivation and commitment in the work force.

A great deal can be done to plan for and anticipate change which would have the major objectives of maximizing the benefits of change, minimizing any adverse consequences, and gaining the acceptance and co-operation of the work force in the proposed changes. All this involves a concerted effort by management as a whole, and supervision in particular.

9.2 DEFINITION AND CLASSIFICATION

'Change' is defined in the OED as the 'substitution or succession of one thing in place of another; substitution of other conditions; variety'. All the elements in this definition point to possible danger areas—'newness' which is often distrusted because it *is* new; 'substitution' or replacement which could lead to fears of the unknown; and 'variety', which again takes us away from simple, familiar things.

Change, for our purposes, can be classified into two categories: unplanned, and planned. *Unplanned changes* are those which the organization has thrust upon it by environmental functions beyond its control: variations in bank base rates, sudden changes in the value of currency, or unexpected scarcities in raw materials, a serious fire, changes of political control. In system terms (see Chapter 1) unplanned change brings *disequilibrium* to the organization as a sudden variation (addition, modification or curtailment) in inputs to the organization/system. Usually the system needs to act quickly to restore equilibrium—even if it is at a new level.

Planned change has significant differences. It is deliberate, conscious, eyes-open effort which can be designed to meet forthcoming input changes that can be foreseen or predicted: changes in buying patterns or customer requirements; the effects of new legislation such as the Data Protection Act, or the need to conform to a new industry-wide code of practice. Alternatively, planned change could be to prepare for some desirable improvement in the organization itself: the upgrading of accommodation, introduction of word processors, opening new retail outlets etc.

Any successfully planned change requires three main elements:

1. A carefully worked-out, preconceived plan.
2. A person in charge, a 'change-agent' committed to the change who carefully monitors every stage.
3. An organized co-operative effort from the work force involved (including management).

9.3 FACTORS INFLUENCING CHANGE

All the factors operating on the organization shown in Fig. 1.2 (Chapter 1) can and do influence change. Here we will consider briefly some of the significant factors.

Economic

The general economic environment could affect an organization: a depression could reduce, say, the amount of public sector spending which would have consequences for institutions as diverse as hospitals, colleges or research establishments. On a more immediate level, any resource shortage—*people* (attracted, say, by better conditions elsewhere); *money* (lack of new capital to renew assets); or *materials* (due perhaps to a crop failure, a war, or the drying up of non-renewable resources)—is usually the trigger for a series of changes within an organization.

Market

Changes in demand (both increases and decreases) for products or services; and increase in supply (new competition arising); changes in public taste or fashion—are all significant factors.

Technological

At the present time this is possibly the most important of the headings. New or substitute materials (all the plastics, synthetic fibres etc.) are both less labour intensive to produce than older materials and also cheaper/less labour intensive to use in production. Similarly the mechanization of physical processes from writing by hand to word processors, or from Hargreaves' Spinning Jenny of 1770 to the 1990-style robot production line often means less labour intensive activity: certainly new working methods and practices.

Sociological

Besides the effects of organized unions in industrial bargaining, a new and increasingly powerful factor has been the rise of 'consumerism', and the ecology/conservationist movements. No longer can organizations take certain points of decisions unchallenged: they may even need to change processes or even close down enterprises felt to be dangerous.

Legislative

Changes introduced by government—reorganization of various aspects of the NHS, privatization of previously nationalized industries; health and safety, environmental health regulations—all these involve significant changes for those involved in affected organizations.

9.4   INDIVIDUAL RESPONSES TO CHANGE

Not every individual reacts adversely to change. Some lucky people actually thrive on change—even at a moment's notice—and relish the challenge. If such people can be identified within the workforce or a particular work group they can be used in the change process.

However, where change is concerned, most people will react adversely in one way or another. Such reactions must be taken into account, particularly to unplanned or poorly planned change. (Poorly planned change introduced without warning will look like unplanned change to the workforce, and they will react accordingly.)

Typical responses include:

1. Surprise, shock, grief, even disbelief. (People suffer from a feeling of disequilibrium, feel insecure and bewildered.)
2. Depression. (Especially if the future looks bleaker than the past.)
3. Guilt. (People look into themselves and might even blame themselves for being responsible for conditions bringing about change.)
4. Blaming others. (Rather than blame themselves, some would put the blame on colleagues or other departments.)
5. Resistance. (Discussed in the next section.)
6. Integration. (Some try to slot change into their work, and turn the change into some advantage.)
7. Acceptance. (The individual accepts change willingly, with enthusiasm, or with an air of resignation.)

9.5   RESISTANCE TO CHANGE

Many different reasons have been identified for resistance to change. They can be grouped under two main headings:

1. *Feeling of insecurity*. This feeling is derived from uncertainty, possibly about the causes, and almost certainly the perceived effects of the change. Insecurity feelings are most likely to arise when:

    (a) Uncertainty remains about future job security.
    (b) The purpose of the change is unclear.
    (c) The details of the change are not clearly communicated.
    (d) Those affected have not been involved in any way in planning the change.
    (e) Demands could be made on work force for increased production/productivity.
    (f) Existing work patterns seem not to have been considered.
    (g) There is great job satisfaction with present jobs, present career opportunities.
    (h) There is awareness of serious deficiencies or weaknesses in the proposals for change.
    (i) Perceived rewards are inadequate.
    (j) The rate of change is viewed as too rapid.

2. *Fears*. Commonest fears are fears of:

(a) Loss of skills, coupled with the need to learn new skills.
(b) Hard supervisors.
(c) Loss of 'work mates' (e.g. being transferred to another department/work group).
(d) Increase of controls on work methods.
(e) Loss of power, status, prestige, promotion.
(f) Reduction in income, differentials, bonuses.
(g) Less interesting work or having to work much harder.
(h) Redundancy and unemployment.

(There may also be *resentment* based on a feeling that the proposed change is a criticism of present methods of working or that the change benefits the organization and not the work force.)

9.6   INTRODUCING AND IMPLEMENTING CHANGE

Planning for change has two distinct elements: logistics of the *mechanical change* (the redesign, say, of new forms for revised office procedures), and of the *people* aspect. The remainder of this chapter concentrates on the latter.

Senior management will usually deal with overall arrangements, the long term strategies and objectives (in conjunction perhaps with specialist help). Individual supervisors will however be involved in selling change, introducing and implementing it within their own work groups; and on a smaller, departmental scale could even be responsible for initiating change in the first place.

9.6.1   Organizational development

The term *organizational development* (OD) is usually taken to mean the *process of introducing change* to an organization. As we have already noted, people tend to cling to objectives, ideals and practices when the situation in which they are in requires change. What is needed then is some *dynamic process* to bring about a shift in objectives, attitudes and practices of the workforce; and to refashion their whole approach to the job.

The process of OD is often called *Force Field Analysis*. This useful concept, theory and method was originally developed by Kurt Lewin, a social scientist. He argued, basically, managers should consider ANY change situation in terms of (a) the factors encouraging and facilitating the change (*the driving forces*); and (b) the factors against change (*the restraining factors*). Some examples of these forces are shown in Fig. 9.1. These forces can act both on individual workers, and the work group as a whole.

The change process. This consists of:

1. Identifying the restraining forces and overcoming/removing/getting round them.

Figure 9.1 Restraining and driving forces in a change situation.

2.   Carrying out the change.
3.   Stabilizing the new situation by reinforcing the (now changed) behaviour of individuals and work groups with praise and encouragement.

Problems with change. A common experience in organizations is that a change is followed, after an interval, by a return to an older or previous way of doing things—once the pressures for change have been relaxed. It could be those affected by the change may not have been involved enough to have been completely committed to it. They are only too ready to 'slip back'. To minimize the possibility of this type of problem, we will need to devise a planned programme for introducing and implementing change.

9.6.2   Types of change

In section 9.3 we looked at *factors influencing* change. It is also useful to classify the *kinds* of change found in *organizations.* Briefly, these are:

Types of change	*Example*
environmental	changes in customer needs and requirements; interest and tax rates; government legislation; planning rules
organizational	changes in the aims/objectives of the whole or part of the organization; in the categories of jobs within it; the numbers employed
job-related	changes in working methods; kinds of customers serviced; hours of work (e.g. Sunday trading); job sharing
equipment/technological	changes in type and sophistication of equipment (e.g. introducing EPOS tills in a retail outlet), or a new range of delivery vehicles

employee-related   changes in recruitment/selection/induction procedures; training
                    opportunities; reward systems

(Note: a change in one area may have a knock-on effect in others: a change in a customer's delivery requirements could have effects on the numbers (and kinds) of staff
employed; the purchase of entirely new delivery vehicles; engagement of specialist
staff, and retraining of existing staff.)

9.6.3 Managing change

The ability to manage change is becoming increasingly part of the on-going role of
managers and supervisors. However *before* any kind of change—however big, however
small—is embarked upon, vital questions must be asked; and honest answers sought.
These include:

— Has the need for change been clearly identified?
— Have all the potential risks in making the changes envisaged been carefully
  analysed and evaluated (including the possibility of failure-adverse consequences)?
— When is the right/most appropriate time to make the change?
— Has the change-plan been researched, evaluated and put out to consultation as
  necessary?
— Does the plan include an employee-awareness programme?
— Will all work groups involved be encouraged to make their views on the proposals
  known?
— Have any training implications for staff been catered for in the plan?
— Is the need for extra resources (such as new equipment, extra services, or tempo-
  rary staff) allowed for in the plan?

9.6.4 Implementing change

To ensure the highest probability of successfully implementing a change, or set of
changes, we need to make sure the workforce (or individual group) will accept it willingly. Any intended change or innovation will have a much better chance of
acceptance and implementation where the organization can demonstrate to the
employees concerned:

– the relevance of the proposed change to an accepted objective or set of objectives
  (e.g. more customers, increased turnover, lower costs)
– the proposed change is achievable
– the positive short, medium and long-term advantages to the organization in general; and to them, in particular.

Summing up, we can say that change is more likely to be implemented successfully
if there is:

— consultation with all parties likely to be affected
— careful planning in advance by management (including supervision), and possibly involving work groups (these two points will help promote feelings of 'ownership' of the change)
— commitment of the workforce affected to the changes (hopefully as a result of the kinds of involvement mentioned above)
— guidance given or available to all concerned, during the change period, as to how possible problems that might be encountered could be overcome
— a carefully prepared 'change timetable'; with clear target dates for each stage of the proposed change, including any pre-change 'training' stages
— an on-going system of monitoring and review, both during and after the change is complete.

9.6.5 Introducing change to the work group

The following eleven suggested lines of action are recommended to supervisors and others introducing and implementing change within work groups. The aim is to maximize the advantages, and minimize the disadvantages.

1. Give all workers concerned the maximum possible warning of impending change (this will give them time to get accustomed to the idea of change).
2. Explain as far as possible, the reasons for change (the provision of both adequate and accurate information scotches rumours before they can be circulated; let people known where they stand).
3. Involve as far as possible employees/work groups in the planning for and implementation of change. (Employees will be more likely to become committed to change if they feel they can have some influence on the change and its outcome. It is also of considerable advantage to be able to make use of any valuable suggestions. It makes the communication two-way.)
4. Keep the lines of communication going. Monitor progress, and communicate results. (Once established regular feedback on the progress of the changes should be given, and should only cease when the end result has been reached.)
5. Try to introduce changes gradually. (Many workers will accept a change package provided it does not contain a large number of simultaneous changes. Phased change stands a better chance of acceptance.)
6. Offer and provide appropriate training. (Training in new skills, new methods, new equipment creates interest, and helps to remove some of the feelings of future insecurity.)
7. Ensure the work force are aware of the benefits (to them) of the proposed change. (Things like increased responsibility, job enrichment, up-grading better conditions need to be stressed. It is important to provide as many incentives as possible. Some monetary incentive is often useful.)
8. Minimize interference with hygiene factors. (Take, for example, existing work patterns into account. Avoid breaking up happy and effective work groups, putting together incompatibles, disrupting individual shift patterns, upsetting holiday arrangements.)

9. Consider the effects of change on individuals. (Besides considering groups of workers, the worries of individuals need taking into account—their fears and objectives. Individual counselling may be necessary.)
10. Follow up regularly. (See how people are coping with the changes. Be somewhat tolerant to begin with, always be supportive.)
11. As a result of the successful introduction of change, it is important to develop a favourable climate for the acceptance of the next and subsequent changes envisaged.

SUMMARY

1.   Change is now an ever-present part of everyday life, and the rate of change accelerating. Change is to be found at work, too, and planning, introducing and managing change a continuous and containing job for management and supervision together.

2.   Change can be *unplanned,* that is thrust upon the organization (possibly without warning), or *planned*, that is carefully prepared, introduced and implemented.

3.   Factors influencing change include economic (resource shortages), market (demand changes, competition), technological (changes in materials, machines, processes), sociological (industrial relations, consumerism, conservationism), and legislative (government-inspired).

4.   Individuals react to change by either accepting (or even welcoming it) or reacting against it. Typical responses include surprise, shock, grief; disbelief, depression, guilt, blaming others or resistance.

5.   Resistance is mainly caused by a feeling of insecurity or uncertainty about the change (due to lack of knowledge, being uninvolved, weaknesses in the proposals etc.), fears about loss of skills, workmates, power, income or the job itself, or resentment that there is implied criticism of work methods.

6.   Supervisors and managers, in introducing and implementing change, should:

    (a)   Give maximum warning;
    (b)   Explain the reasons for change;
    (c)   Involve workers/work groups at all stages;
    (d)   Continually brief and explain;
    (e)   Introduce change gradually;
    (f)   Offer training;

(g) Ensure benefits/rewards available from change are understood;
(h) Minimize interference with work patterns;
(i) Consider individuals as well as groups;
(j) Monitor and follow up regularly;
(k) Develop a climate of 'change acceptability'.

REVIEW QUESTIONS

1. Explain what is meant by change. What is the difference between planned and unplanned change?

2. List the three main elements for successfully planned change.

3. (a) List three resource shortages which could be factors affecting change.
    (b) Why are technological factors so important?
    (c) What is meant by 'consumerism', and the 'ecology/conservationist movement'?

4. Describe three typical responses to change.

5. Describe in your own words:

    (a) Why change should create feelings of insecurity in people at work;
    (b) What fears people at work can have about change.

6. List the eleven steps supervisors and others can take to minimize the disadvantages and maximize the advantages of planned change.

DISCUSSION TOPICS

1. 'Every organization has to prepare for the abandonment of everything it does.' (Peter Drucker, *Harvard Business Review*, Sept/Oct 1992.) What does Drucker mean by this? What implications does this have for the organization you work for; what activities or ways of doing things might have to change in the short, medium or long-term?

2. 'Employees will resist any change which would require them to learn new skills or procedures.' Discuss.

3. Discuss the view that a supervisor should have some private discussions with the more intelligent workers, before introducing a change in work practices.

4.   Some people say the best ways to get workers to accept change are:

(a) Presenting them with a *fait accompli* (i.e. a fully-worked out scheme) and;
(b) Offering them more money.

Do you agree? Why?

5.   In this chapter the emphasis has been on how managers might reduce resistance to change in the work force. Do you think managers might resist change too? If so, what reasons might they have for such resistance? Discuss.

6.   Are there some people who *like* change? What kind of people are they?

ASSIGNMENTS

A9.1   Write two reports dealing with the following topics:

(a) Analyse in your first report your reactions to two examples you have experienced recently of *unplanned* change in either your personal life, or that at work/college. Did your reactions relate to any of the ideas discussed in this chapter? Explain.
(b) Analyse in your second report your reactions to two examples you have experienced recently of *planned* change in either your personal life, or that at work/college. Indicate in this report your reactions to the changes, and whether your reactions could be related to the amount you were involved in making the changes.
(c) List any resistance you can remember to a planned change discussed in (b) above, by others. Explain, as far as you can, the reasons for such resistance.

A9.2   Suggest, in report form, how you would go about changing the payment of wages to a largely weekly-paid in cash work force to monthly payments into workers' bank accounts. Besides the purely practical aspects, how would you deal with selling the idea to the employees and how would you attempt to overcome their undoubted resistance?

Case study

A9.3   The Board of Ambridge Electronics decided Quality Circles[1] must be introduced throughout the whole organization quickly. The directors proposed to

---

[1] Chapter 29 contains information about Quality Circles.

ask for 100% co-operation from the work force at a mass meeting, when all the details and implications would be spelt out to the 250 strong work force.

'Communication is important,' Julia Asher (a joint managing director) emphasized. (She had just returned from a management training session on introducing change.) 'People must be given *all* the facts: no-one must be left in the dark. Doubt breeds insecurity. We must avoid any doubts or feelings of insecurity which may arise from ignorance. The company cannot therefore afford to waste time fiddle-faddling about over minor details, leaving major decisions hanging in the air.' Julia's view prevailed.

The mass meeting was duly held and the details of the scheme announced. A quality circle was to be set up in every department, and circle leaders' names were read out. Meetings would start immediately and be held weekly, on Monday mornings. It was stressed that this was the chance for every employee to be involved in coping with the changes envisaged in the near future, as well as with quality control.

The news was heard quietly and Julia was surprised that there was little reaction to the idea, only a few questions being asked, about meeting times and no comments.

Julian, Julia's brother and co-managing director, decided to visit the inaugural meetings the following Monday. He found it a disturbing experience; confusion reigned in most, arguments raged in some, and many workers just sat and watched the proceedings. Worst of all, not all workers were present. By the end of the second week, Julian was totally disillusioned: morale was lower than before, production down and circle leaders had resigned. 'It was a silly idea, Julia,' he said, 'I'm afraid all your wonderful theories don't work out in practice!'

(a) Explain what went wrong at Ambridge Electronics.
(b) How could the introduction of quality circles have been launched with a reasonable chance of success?

UNIT III

The Supervisor and the Personnel Function

Personnel management is part of the job of every manager, whatever his or her particular task. However, to advise and support managers modern organizations have developed a complex set of services and activities commonly called the 'personnel' or 'human resources' department.

In this unit we will examine the workings of the personnel function, and how the supervisor's job relates to it. In many organizations supervisors still can and do involve themselves in various aspects of personnel work—manpower planning, selection, training or appraisal—and there are few oganizations now where there is no interplay between the personnel function and other developments. Even more important is the supervisor's role in very small organizations where no separate personnel function exists. In such cases it is not uncommon to find the owner/manager and the supervisor share personnel work between them.

A working knowledge of personnel practice and procedures is therefore not only desirable for all supervisors, but may be a necessity.

10
Introduction to the Personnel Function

10.1 DEFINITION

Dozens of definitions of personnel management are to be found: 'getting and keeping employees' is the simplest I know of, but other, longer and more elaborate versions exist.[1] In essence, however, personnel management means exactly what it says: personnel management = managing people.

The task of managing people is given a great many names. Here are some of them:

The Management of Human Resources
Employee Relations Management
Human Relations
Employee Resource Management.

However, whatever such a task is *called*, what is being said is that managers or supervisors are managers of *people*, never mind what else they manage (money, machinery, stores); and when they manage people, they are carrying out the functions of personnel management.

The Institute of Personnel Management recognized this point in the '60s when it stated, 'Personnel Management is a responsibility of all those who manage people, as well as being the work of specialists'. It further explained that, 'Personnel Management is that part of management concerned with people rather than finished goods'.

Since then, ideas have become more specific, and personnel management would now see its objectives as:

1. Recruiting, motivating and developing the work force required by the organization.
2. Helping in creating a working climate and appropriate organizational structure to promote maximum commitment and effort from the workforce.
3. Ensuring that the abilities and skills of the workforce are used to the optimum in pursuance of organization objectives.

---

[1] For example, the Institute of Personnel Management 1963 definition which included phrases such as 'personnel management aims to achieve efficiency and justice,' . . . 'enabling each (worker) to make his own best contribution to its (the enterprise's) success.'

4. Ensuring the organization complies with its legal, social and moral obligations both to employees and to others (including the general public) affected by the organization's activities.

10.2 GENERAL OBJECTIVES

There are at least two schools of thought on the general objectives of personnel management. One view is that the primary aim is the accomplishment of productive work, with less accent on the needs of individuals or groups: the 'profit-minded' or 'profit-centred' approach. Another, contrasting view is that of having as the number one priority the individual worker and of recognizing his or her worth, helping him or her to work effectively: the 'human relations' approach.

The major problem is of reconciling two sets of goals and objectives: those of the organization (or firm) and the employees. In addition, outside influences such as Government legislation, public opinion (not only in the form of pressure groups) now have to be taken into account. Moral questions like 'What are the firm's responsibilities towards workers made redundant (through no fault of their own) after the legal 'pay-out' has been made?' or 'Should management go beyond its legal responsibilities in areas such as safety, health and welfare?' are posed to management daily, but whatever their personal views, managers must take into account these outside influences and opinions.

It is not surprising, therefore, to see in objectives, policies and responsibilities of personnel departments, as well as their formal structures, aspects of all three elements:

1. Workforce efficiency.
2. Welfare and well-being of employees.
3. Implementation of legal obligations.

Plus a certain amount of public relations, in terms of 'trips round the works' and the like.

10.3 HISTORICAL DEVELOPMENT

Institutions change and develop over time. We have seen that personnel management is the function of every manager, but nowadays we find large personnel *departments* in every organization over, for example, 2000 workers; even in much smaller firms we may find a personnel manager, and various staff including a training officer and perhaps a welfare officer, besides clerks and secretaries. If we went back a hundred years, the idea of transferring what was then part of the job of every manager—hiring and firing, training and counselling, deciding on rewards and punishments—to a separate department would have hardly been considered at all; even if considered, it would have been strongly opposed by both owners and managers.

Now things have changed, but the extent to which the personnel department has taken over line managers' functions does vary from organization to organization and the duties such departments perform are not always the same. (Students who visit factories or plants other than their own during courses are often surprised to find what is an every day personnel practice in their organization is not to be found in other enterprises. At your place of work training may well be the job of the line manager; at the firm next door a highly organized training office will carry out most of the work of training within the firm.)

But let us be quite clear: any differences between the personnel department's duties and those of supervisors in respect of:

1. Engaging and dismissing staff;
2. Training and counselling;
3. Preparing job descriptions;
4. Taking disciplinary action;
5. Fixing wages/conditions of work;
6. Drawing up rules and regulations;
7. Dealing with grievances;

merely reflect the degree to which the duties have shifted from the initial position where all these functions were carried out by the owners of firms, their managers and supervisors. Even in large firms, with well-developed personnel departments, the personnel staff would have little or no influence in some very important areas, for example:

1. Recruitment of directors and managing directors.
2. Appointment of chairman and company secretary.
3. Deciding upon overall policy (usually decided at board level) in personnel matters.
4. Industrial relations formal negotiations on non-routine matters (line management often retains such a role).

How did this change, this shift of emphasis come about; how was the personnel department born? Why indeed, did managers and supervisors cease to hire and fire, promote or discipline as they had for the greater part of the period we call the Industrial Revolution (1740 onwards)?

Five major influences can now be seen to have been at work, at first separate and distinct, but later becoming increasingly intertwined; taken together they form the basis of personnel work. They can be seen in Fig. 10.1.

In addition to these, we have had the effects of two World Wars.

10.3.1 Increasing size of organizations

By 1900, the trend towards increasingly large enterprises had become well established. Individual firms, which had done well, expanded, needing more factory space to meet the demand for their products. Smaller organizations merged or amalgamated with

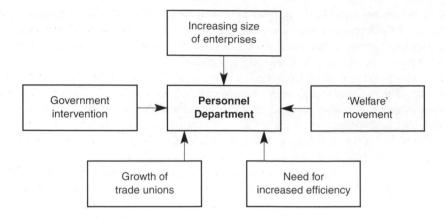

Figure 10.1 Factors important in the development of the personnel function.

other firms or were taken over and naturally became larger. Railways, for example, began to show this trend back in the 1840s. The Great Western Railway was the result of the amalgamation and take-over of many smaller lines.

In such an enterprise a works manager or foreman recruiting 20 or 30 people a year could easily cope with such a task within his work load. When this figure is increased to 200, the task becomes more time consuming. If it is doubled or trebled (especially if the hiring and firing is on a very temporary basis), managers begin to feel they are not doing their 'real' job.

Delegation to someone else became a necessity, and gradually more senior managers (though not first-line supervisors) began to lose touch with individual workers and to listen to people like F. W. Taylor (see Chapter 3) who had advocated 'labour offices' for the 'scientific' selection of personnel, and the need for trainers (remember the 'professors of shovelling').

Finally, increasing specialization in other areas—sales and purchasing, accountancy, drawing offices—was well established by 1900. Thus there was no special innovation in appointing 'employment officers' whose job was purchasing not goods but labour.

10.3.2 Drive for increased efficiency

Part of the basic philosophy of the earlier pioneers of the Industrial Revolution had been based on a stern, mostly non-conformist version of Christianity: 'idleness is a sin' was just one of many beliefs which formed part of the justification for employing people for long, wearing hours. But people had not just to work for work's sake, but to help make profits for the firm's owners. The parable of the talents was a favourite one for such entrepreneurs. Gradually the old 'master-servant' relationship disappeared and gave way to a more depersonalized system. Fixed hours were a tremendous change for those used to a more 'leisurely' rural life.

As the Industrial Revolution developed, workers gradually became excluded from decision-making even at the lowest levels. They began to explore ways of increasing participation through joining unions and similar organizations. This growing effort on the part of workers to influence employers to improve working conditions (as well as pay) meant employers naturally tried to retain as much control over the situation as they could.

By the end of the 19th century the ideas of F.W. Taylor (and his disciples, see Chapter 3) spread in respect of increased efficiency and the search for the 'one best way' of doing jobs. The 'scientific management' movement led to the setting up in many firms of 'Work Study' sections or departments, but in addition arose the need to study total *job contents*, to select the right people for the jobs available, to *train* those engaged so that workers became more efficient more quickly.

Inevitably, these functions became separated from line managers (often with little formal training of their own) and the purchasers of labour—employment or labour officers—extended their activities further from selection to training and, indeed, to record-keeping on all staff, particularly in respect of time-keeping. In larger firms, records were also kept of personnel matters which had been matters of dispute and subsequently settled.

In fact, firms and similar organizations were becoming 'bureaucratic' in Weber's sense (see Chapter 3), with defined jobs and duties, and administrative work as a full-time occupation. Specialization in personnel management is essentially a consequence of the development of bureaucratic organizations.

Concerning the need for efficiency, there have been, and still are, those who view this aspect of personnel management as the most important: the 'one simple and basic' objective of personnel administration is to get the best possible return for the money invested in the labour force of an organization.[2]

10.3.3 The 'welfare' movement

The conditions in which large numbers of people lived and worked during the early and middle periods of the Industrial Revolution were appalling by today's standards. Factories were damp, dark, noisy and dirty; by turns hot and stuffy, cold and draughty; and work dangerous and hard. Hours were long, the pay low. Workers were very much at the mercy of the employers who often exploited workers and their families out of working hours (for example, paying wages in tokens only acceptable in the company shop).

Strangely, the 'welfare' movement which emerged towards the end of the middle period was motivated by the same Christian principles as the 'efficiency' movement. Philanthropic factory owners who were strongly non-conformist in belief, appeared concerned about individuals' physical and moral welfare, yet, at the same time, were strong disciplinarians and tough masters.

One of the first enlightened employers was Robert Owen (1771–1850) a friend of Dalton (the chemist) and James Watt (of steam engine fame). He became, in 1800, the managing director of a woollen mill in New Lanark, Scotland. He soon came to the conclusion (even if for reasons of labour scarcity or economic gain in the long run)

---

2 See K. C. Laurence, *Personnel Management*. London: Hutchinson Educational, 1972. p. 7.

that it was necessary to look after his men, as much as his machines. He introduced shorter working hours, provided housing facilities, education in hygiene and education for workers' children. Although his political and union activities were not so successful, such an example was not entirely lost.

On any list of outstanding benevolent employers of this period we can find several Quaker families. Religious motives impelled them to be concerned about the lot of their workers and their conditions of work—the social facilities (including housing) provided at Bournville by Cadbury's was such an example. This was real, practical help for the poor: less so was the provision of flowers in workrooms, which had a much more charitable flavour about it.

This more personal, charitable welfare work was sometimes carried out by the female relatives of the owners, but as early as 1896 people, mostly women, began to be appointed as 'welfare officers' in large firms. Indeed, my grandfather was holding such a post about 1909 in a Sheffield engineering company. Not only did he look after apprentices and their training, but visited employees in hospital. However, there was no clear view as to the precise job welfare officers should do, and in 1913 an association of industrial welfare workers was formed. Eventually, after several changes of name, this became the Institute of Personnel Management.

From such beginnings a whole complex set of duties and functions grew up (see Fig. 10.2 which shows the present stage of development of the personnel department). The repercussions of the Hawthorne experiments meant a greater emphasis on certain welfare and counselling aspects of personnel work and the growth of the 'human relations' movement. The welfare approach originated at a time when it was considered that improvements in physical conditions of work, uplifting surroundings and opportunities for leading moral and rewarding lives outside working hours would lead to contented, happy and productive work forces.

10.3.4 Growth of unionism

The growth of unionism is described in Unit VI but it is clear that a significant change occurred in the late 1880s with the arrival of the 'New Unionism'. The matchgirls' strike of 1888 and dock strike of 1889 were a watershed; combinations of *unskilled* workers (as opposed to the earlier Craft Unions) displayed a more political, militant approach. Tom Mann, President of the Dockers' Union, wrote in 1886—'The true unionist's policy of *aggression* seems entirely lost sight of'.[3] He, and others to follow did *not* lose sight of aggression.

The growing and more active trade unions looked on the welfare workers with grave suspicion. Active union leaders like to be seen to lead: if management handed out costly welfare facilities as gifts, whether houses or sports fields, canteens, or restrooms, without being asked to, then such advances would not be credited to the unions or their leaders. Secondly, the spirit of 'lord of the manor' paternalism in which such 'gifts' were offered placed the giver in a superior position and the recipients in an inferior one.

---

[3] Tom Mann: *What a compulsory Eight Hours' Working Day means to the Workers* (From a pamphlet by Tom Mann and James Burns).

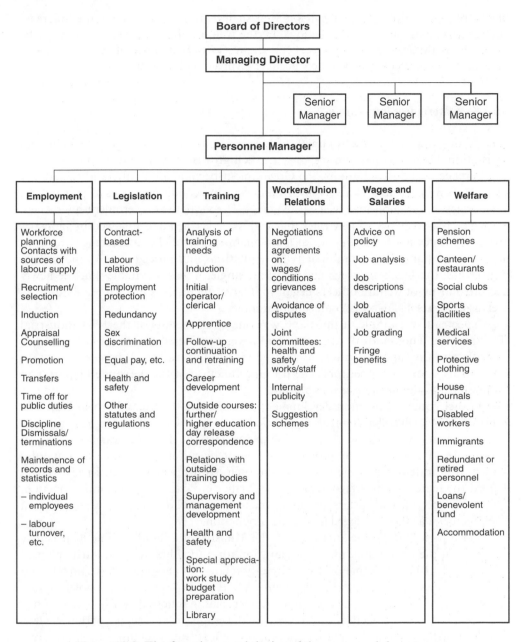

Figure 10.2 The functions and duties of the personnel department.

It is not surprising that the trade union leaders worked hard to get an independent, equal status role for themselves in negotiations with employers, became more aggressive, began to learn negotiating skills, took up not only national issues, but the cases of individual workers with grievances. In turn, management had to accommodate to the changing climate of strikes, workings to rule, overtime bans, and the cut and thrust of negotiation. It was inevitable that such matters would be handled increasingly, particularly in routine situations, by the welfare officers who indeed might be quite sympathetic to individual workers' claims, as well as those of the more senior staff involved in such work who now became involved with negotiations.

10.3.5 Government intervention

Unit V describes the rise and growth of the trade unions and Unit IV the industrial legislation which was partly a response to such growth. From a position of seeming indifference to industrial affairs, the Government became gradually (and reluctantly at first) then increasingly actively involved in working conditions, rates of pay and the regularization of union-management relations. The more the Government intervened, the greater the number of new rules that had to be learned and followed by industry, the more necessary it became for at least one member of the management team to become familiar with the multiplicity of regulations and procedures. As the earliest legislation, the Factories Acts, had a welfare angle, it was inevitable that the newly recruited army of welfare officers began to interest themselves in such regulations, as well as other related aspects—safety, for example.

A spectacular example of this trend was one of the results of the 1964 Industrial Training Act. Thousands of firms who had never considered having a full-time training officer either appointed one or entered into group training schemes with other local firms or even competitors. The training function of the personnel department increased considerably in status as a result.

Another equally important development came during the Second World War. The crisis of June 1940 called immediate attention to the problems of maximizing production, particularly for the war effort. The prime need, at the time, was for increased production. Focusing on the problems of labour recruitment, training and maintenance of morale in war-time factories, the then Minister of Labour, Ernest Bevin, helped to create a climate favourable to the further growth of the personnel function. Under his and other Ministers' encouragement, personnel departments were set up in such factories as those engaged in aircraft production.

After a period of decline after the war, the Ministry of Labour became increasingly involved in the contemplation of, preparation for and submission to Parliament of industrial legislation. Some of it was directly related to personnel departments and their functions: the Redundancy Payments Act 1965 and the Contracts of Employment Act 1963 are examples. Other industrial legislation followed swiftly; much of it is discussed in Unit V. The effect was to increase the emphasis of 'keeping within the law' and part of the personnel department's time and effort was taken up with interpreting new laws for the management (and sometimes even the unions) of their organization. So complex has the situation become that a new trend towards the employment of legally-trained graduates in personnel departments has emerged in the last decade.

10.4   THE MODERN PERSONNEL DEPARTMENT

The work of the modern personnel department is thus wide-ranging and complex. This, in turn, has led to an increasing number of qualified members of the Institute of Personnel Management (IPM) being recruited to lead and staff personnel departments. However, vast differences in training, power and status exist between personnel managers in different organizations. Few (probably too few) personnel managers are directors of the companies for which they work.

But the job of personnel managers is an exacting one, coping with all the many different functions, the various different strands—welfare, efficiency, industrial relations, legal aspects—which go up to make the whole. Not only do they have to cope with the competing and differing needs and approaches of these sections, but they must also face the conflicting aims of trying to get the maximum effort from the work force at the least cost, on the one hand, and on the other, trying to create the best possible environment for the work force as a whole and career and personal development for individual workers.

In addition, they have the main responsibility for discharging the legal duties imposed on employers by existing industrial legislation. Thus, a personnel manager is a specialist who is capable of creating and administering a suitable working environment in an organization, which will attract and keep a work force of useful, effective and reasonably contented employees. Above all, personnel managers must be good communicators and understand human beings; they should also know exactly how they fit into their organization.

If any of the qualities described here are not possessed by particular personnel managers, their jobs will become more difficult and their departments less successful than they might have been.

Figure 10.2 shows the personnel function in the form of an organization chart. It should be appreciated that in *particular* firms the duties and functions may be somewhat different (or even absent), but every major function can be found in large enterprises. Most of these functions will be covered in the following chapters of the unit.

SUMMARY

In this chapter we have noted:

1.   There are many definitions of personnel management. Whichever one we choose, must include the two important (but conflicting) aims: the need to maximize the effort of the human resources employed in the organization and to create the best possible working environment for the work force.

2.   Such a definition must stress that every manager who manages people (even if he manages other things as well) is engaged in personnel management.

3.   The job of managing people has, however, become so complex that certain parts of it—recruitment and selection, welfare, etc., have now been centred in a special department of the organization—the personnel department.

4.   The origins of personnel management (or 'personnel administration' as the Americans call it) can be traced back to:

   (a) Increasing size of organizations and the growth of bureaucracy.
   (b) A drive towards increased efficiency.
   (c) The 'welfare' movement.
   (d) Increasing unionism.
   (e) The gradual increase in the intervention of government in industrial affairs.

5.   The job of the present day personnel department still contains these elements from the historical past but is becoming more complex and specialized. Thus both personnel managers and their staffs are becoming more highly qualified.

6.   However, as yet, few personnel managers have director status.

REVIEW QUESTIONS

1.   Is the job of personnel management the job of every manager or supervisor? Why?

2.   What are the major objectives of personnel management?

3.   Who performed the functions (i.e. those now taken over by the personnel department) of personnel management for the first and middle periods of the Industrial Revolution (e.g. 1740–1890)?

4.   What were the major influences at work during the Industrial Revolution which led to the birth of the personnel function?

5.   Why was there a drive for increased efficiency by the end of the 19th century?

6.   Why do you think the 'welfare' movement started? Was there a need for it?

7.   Why did trade unions and their leaders look upon welfare movements, or the setting up of social facilities for workers, with suspicion?

8.   Why are the staff of modern personnel departments more specialized and highly trained than they used to be?

DISCUSSION TOPICS

1.　　Discuss the view that the 'one simple and basic' objective of the personnel department is to get the maximum return from the money spent on the work force employed.

2.　　Can such a view as expressed in (1) above be reconciled with the aim of creating the best possible environment for the work force and for the personal and career developments of individual workers?

3.　　What is the position of a personnel manager in a dispute between the company and its workers (i.e. their union)? Should the manager try to be a neutral arbitrator, acting independently, or act as a representative of management?

4.　　Concerning the functions and duties of the personnel department (as shown in Fig. 10.2), should the personnel manager report directly to the board, or the managing director, or to another executive, say the company secretary?

5.　　Why are so few personnel managers directors of the companies for which they work?

ASSIGNMENTS

A10.1　Collect at least three different definitions of personnel management from textbooks in your local library (reference 658.315). Compare the definitions and decide which is the closest description of the way your organization's personnel department works.

A10.2　Take the functions and duties of the personnel department (as shown in Fig. 10.2) and compare them with those of your personnel department, or, if a full-time student, with that of a local organization with which your college or school is in contact.

　　Try to account for any differences.

Case study

A10.3　Johnson Valves Ltd is an engineering company situated close to a small market town. About 300 workers are employed on various production lines making different kinds of valves. The remaining staff (about 100) are made up of directors, senior executives, middle management, supervisors and clerks, plus some outside sales staff.

George Johnson, founder Chairman and Managing Director, is also Sales Manager. Selling is his total preoccupation. Before starting the firm 12 years ago, he was the salesman of the year in his previous company. The Works' Director is James Tappit, his life-long friend, who was in the venture at the start. He drew up the plans of the works, supervised the building and has monitored every development thoroughly since.

Tappit believes in letting managers make their own decisions, subject of course to his right to intervene if it is in the company's interests. He encouraged all line managers to attend to such matters as recruiting their own staff, but was always willing to carry out or help with interviews if supervisors were busy. Lately, however, George Johnson has become a little concerned about the large numbers of staff who were leaving and the quality of the people taken on. He lost an important repeat order from a large customer last year and the buyer of the firm concerned told George, in confidence, that delays in deliveries, as well as a significant increase in faulty valves were the major cause of the lost order.

George's daughter, Joy, graduated in Business Studies at a university in the summer and George spoke to her about the problem. 'You need a personnel manager, and a proper department to handle all these things, Dad,' she said. 'Look at all the notes I took about personnel administration.' George felt his daughter should get involved with the firm as soon as possible and told James Tappit of his plan. James was shocked but after all George was the boss and some of his doubts were removed when George told him that Joy would be responsible to James for all aspects of personnel work.

Joy began briskly and within a month had engaged a personnel officer, a training officer and a welfare supervisor, each with a secretary. Joy also sent a memo, under her father's signature, to all line managers to tell them in future she (Joy) would be dealing with *all* personnel matters, including grievances, personal problems, disciplinary action, as she had a fully qualified staff to carry out these duties. In addition she instructed all line managers to prepare lists of workers and staff who needed training, as the company would be carrying out a comprehensive training programme both at work and on outside courses. The managers and supervisors were all surprised at the memo; some were amused, others sceptical, others angry.

Within a fortnight Tappit began to get complaints from all levels of management about the latest recruits to the work force. 'A load of punks!' exclaimed Sid Reamer; 'A rabble!' said Joe Green. Both Sid and Joe saw Tappit. 'How can you get the output you need and the quality standards you insist on if you can't even tell a worker off. These lads are laughing at us, I can tell you !' Tappit managed to calm the foremen, but George could not be contacted for a week as he was away on another trip to France.

By the time George Johnson returned, he faced a revolt led by Tappit who recommended that the company returned to its previous practices and disband this expensive, ineffective personnel department. 'Once bitten, twice shy!' he told George.

   (a) Comment on Johnson Valves' policy towards personnel administration *before* Joy's appointment.

   (b) Do you think George was right to decide to form a personnel department and to engage a qualified person to become personnel manager? Give reasons for your answers.

   (c) Analyse Joy's approach to the job. Why do you think she did not get the whole hearted co-operation of the managers? Why are poor quality workers being recruited?

   (d) If George asked you for advice, what would you suggest he should do now?

      (i) Agree to scrap the personnel department?

     (ii) Retain it?

    (iii) Some other course of action—if so, what?

11
Workforce Planning

Workforce planning[1] is one of those techniques which are sometimes dismissed as 'trendy nonsense' or 'optional extras'—and expensive extras at that. Certainly, many successful businesses have not practised workforce or manpower) planning in the past. Recent experience has shown that such an attitude is sadly mistaken, even dangerous. The maintenance of a large labour force in a declining industry, with gradually decreasing sales, only leads to increasing costs and a mounting wage bill. Sooner or later dramatic and costly redundancies are announced, with accompanying social and political repercussions.

The Code of Industrial Practice, first issued with the (now repealed) Industrial Relations Act 1971, stressed that manpower planning should be operated in firms, and that such planning should be backed by the authority of management 'at the highest level'. This does not mean supervisors and line managers have no interest in the matter, in fact, they are vitally concerned (see Chapter 20).

11.1 DEFINITION

In essence, workforce planning is planning directed specifically to the size and composition of the workforce of an organization. It is concerned with:

1. *Predicting*. Estimating (as precisely as possible) the staffing needs of the organization at some specific date in the future (e.g. 1 January next year), in terms of *numbers*, the various job *categories*, and *skills required*—that is identifying staffing needs. Simultaneously, estimating staffing *supply* at the future date based on present trends. Identifying possible labour surpluses (overmanning) or labour shortages (vacancies), well in advance.

---

[1] Sometimes called 'Human resource planning'.

2. *Evaluating*. Working out the implications of the predictions in terms of *action to be taken* and the *possible expense*, as not only may more staff be needed, but buildings to house them.
3. *Controlling*. Making sure that the most effective use is made of *available resources,* and implementation of the plan proceeds in an *orderly fashion.*

11.2   FORECASTING AND PREDICTING

As workforce planning is an attempt to forecast how many and what kinds of employees will be needed (in 1, 2 or 5 years ahead) in the future, estimates will have to take into account a great many factors. Amongst the more important, the following points will have to be given considerable thought:

1. *National economy*. How will the economy perform in general—boom, steady state, slump, more inflation, etc.?
2. *State of the industry.* How will the changes forecast in the economy affect the industry or sector to which the organization belongs? Will there be an increase or decrease in demand for a product? Will the market change? Will competition from home or abroad increase or lessen? Will there be an increase or decrease in unemployment? Will the interest rates rise or fall?
3. *Technological advances* in both production and administration. What effects will these have on the quantity and quality of the workforce?
4. *New products, new materials, new company objectives.* How will these affect the quality and quantity of the workforce?
5. *Future management structure.* What will the future 'succession training' or 'grooming' requirements be? What mergers or take-overs are under consideration?
6. *Local population trends.* Will the local population provide a sufficiently large workforce?
7. *Political decisions.* What employment legislation is under consideration? Will the Government provide support in the shape of grants towards equipment and training, etc.? Will there be changes in the world power balance which could affect (our particular) industry or area of commerce?

In addition to other factors such as the amount of capital available for expansion, the union–management relationships and the time taken to train people to take on jobs in the organization will have to be considered. Surveys of the existing use of staff will reveal present effectiveness in the use of the workforce. Shortcomings can be remedied by incorporating the necessary changes in the current workforce plan.

11.3   DRAWING UP THE PLAN

Workforce planning is not easy. It can be costly when a firm starts to look into this technique. Problems abound in making the type of forecasts mentioned above. How indeed can anyone forecast accurately the state of the economy one year ahead, never mind five years! If government departments have not been very successful in preparing such forecasts in the past, will your firm or organization be much better?

Even more difficult to estimate are possible changes in demand for your company's products or services, even if the national economy changes as predicted. The high price of energy hardly stops people from consuming vast quantities of it in houses and cars, but put up the cost of postage, and there is an immediate pronounced drop in mail traffic.

Organizations must try to become as efficient as possible in forecasting (experience helps), they can then embark on the preparation of the staffing plan, in the following stages:

Step 1: identify future needs

Based on the predictions gathered from the analysis of *all* the forecasts, we can quantify the objectives/targets for the organization for a given period (e.g. 5 years) ahead. Suppose our firm makes fork lift trucks, and we forecast:

(a) An expanding economy;
(b) A considerable increase in stockpiling prior to increased demand;
(c) The need for an expansion in the nation's warehouse/stores space, etc;

then we might conclude that we need to expand current model production by 25% at the end of a five year period, to take advantage of demand increases for fork lift trucks, plus the addition of a middle range of trucks, we do not at present make.

Step 2: assess the implications

The implications of such a decision could include for example:

(a) Recruitment of more design engineers.
(b) Building of a new factory and/or extensions to existing premises.
(c) Increase in labour force of 15% after normal wastage.
(d) The introduction of remote/computer-controlled fork lifts—new designs, materials, control systems (need for more technical staff trained in electronics, computer-controlled equipment).
(e) Increase in number of apprentices taken on.

(In effect, this would be a list of precise requirements.)

Step 3: assess the present resources against future needs

Before subtracting the present resources from future resource needs, and planning how to make up the difference, we must examine the present resources. Can we make them more effective by, for example, retraining, by using other equipment, methods, etc., rather than increasing their numbers?

Work study, method study and organization and methods departments could be called in to help this present resource inventory check of the workforce.

Division into various categories of age, skill and ability will considerably aid our task.

Step 4: ensure that the target labour supply will be available

Labour must be recruited and trained, or shed and made redundant, as required at the most appropriate time. If we build a new factory, the works manager will be appointed long before the first turf is cut; supervisory staff will be engaged or transferred before initial production commences and training courses for the new operators/clerks put in hand before full production gets under way. A precise plan, job by job is required. Decisions have to be taken about:

(a) Those workers surplus to requirements (retrain, redeploy, make redundant, etc.).
(b) Those workers to be upgraded (training, etc.).
(c) Those jobs needing to be filled (internal/external recruitment, plus training).

Step 5: monitor and update regularly

This is the *control* element. As we have seen, any control system needs to set standards or objectives, measure performance, note deviations from the pre-set standards, and finally to take action to eliminate the deviations.

We shall need to alter our plan if any one of the factors (economic, technological, market, etc.) changes in an unpredicted way, or we fail to recruit sufficient staff of a certain kind. Perhaps against the national trend unemployment locally drops significantly, we shall need perhaps to recruit from much further afield.

11.4   BENEFITS OF WORKFORCE PLANNING

The major benefits are:

1. The review of present staffing levels can reveal inefficiencies, overmanning, understaffing.
2. Personnel can be recruited in good time.
3. Redundancies can be anticipated or even avoided by redeployment or natural wastage.
4. Training programmes can be prepared well in advance.
5. Succession planning can be worked out in advance.
6. The implications of changes such as new resources required (canteens, rest rooms, etc.) can be assessed, costed and provision made.

Predictions may not always be accurate, and plans sometimes turn out to be inadequate, but this does not invalidate the whole technique. At worst you will know where you went wrong.

SUMMARY

1.   Workforce planning is one which attempts to forecast the future demand for labour in an organization, and formulates policies to ensure that as far as possible the right number of each grade of staff is available when needed. It is usual to forecast for five years ahead.

2.   Such forecasting has to take into account:

(a) Changes in the economy, and the effects of such changes on the organization.
(b) Changes in technology.
(c) Changes in production methods.
(d) Changes in product range.
(e) Changes in materials used.
(f) Changes in company objectives.
(g) Needs for succession training.
(h) Future management structure.
(i) Population trends.
(j) Political decisions.
(k) Amount of capital available, union-management relations.

3.   The workforce plan needs effort, skill and imagination in drawing up. Few people would claim to predict with certainty what the future holds but the job must be attempted.

4.   The planning sequence is:

Step 1. Quantify the objectives, targets of the organization (based on the forecast).
Step 2. Assess the implications of each and every objective in material as well as manpower terms.
Step 3. Assess present resources, and compare against future requirements. Note the differences, shortfalls and surpluses.
Step 4. Ensure as far as possible the planned labour force is available when it is needed. Appropriate training, recruitment, redeployment or redundancy/retirement action taken as required.
Step 5. Monitor and update regularly.

5.   The major benefits include:

(a) Knowledge can be gained about present inefficiencies in the workforce.
(b) Recruitment and training programmes can be properly phased.
(c) Implications of changes—redundancies/natural wastage, provision
of fresh resources, etc., can be assessed.

6.   Workforce planning is worth the effort. A 'near-miss' is better than no plan
at all.

REVIEW QUESTIONS

1.   What kind of planning is workforce planning?

2.   Suppose you were asked to form a staff planning section (and one had not
existed previously) in the organization of which you are member—firm,
public sector, services, college, school—what would be your very first task?
Would you regard the task difficult—why?

3.   What are the essential steps in the planning process?

4.   Outline the major benefits of workforce planning.

DISCUSSION TOPICS

1.   Discuss the view that the future will take care of itself; that even if you make
plans, they have to be altered, anyway; that workforce planning is just a
paper exercise.

2.   Tiptop Products Ltd proposes to open a new factory in five years' time. It is
estimated that the buildings and services will take two years to be completed
from start to finish.
    You are to assume that you are made responsible for recruitment of staff
at the new factory and that you are to make a list of how soon before 'O'
Day (the day the new factory is opened and starts production) various
grades of staff will need to be recruited.
    Spend about ten minutes on your own considering your estimates, then
(under a chairman or discussion leader) compare lists. You should be prepared to justify your solutions.

Jobs

Works Manager	Design Engineer
Lavatory Cleaners	Security Manager
Industrial Nursing Sister	Car Park Attendant
Site Safety Officer	Canteen Staff
Assembly Shop Workers (semi-skilled)	Machine Shop Foreman
Toolroom Staff	Training Officer
Production Planning Officer	Personnel Manager

ASSIGNMENTS

A11.1   From your own experience and from:

(a) Any published sources—library, statistical reference section, news-
     papers, etc.;
(b) Company, organization records;
(c) Superiors, colleagues, subordinates;

try to assess (for your own organization) what increases or decreases there
might be *next* year in the demand for the products and/or services of your
organization.
        (Full-time students at college or school should estimate increases/
decreases in *total* student population, split up as far as possible between
departments and/or courses.)

Case study

A11.2   Robert Bailey, Sales Administration Manager of Alpha Pipes, had just
returned from a management development course, where he had learned
about workforce planning. He was determined to try to introduce the
technique into his own department, then to persuade other managers to
follow suit.
        Robert decided to try to estimate the position for next year, and was
studying two documents. Alpha PDI (Personnel Document No. I) (Table
11.1) contained, in effect, details of the present labour situation, and Alpha
PD2 contained in the predictions of various departments including his own.

Alpha PD2 Summary of Forecasts: All Departments

The results currently have been very encouraging. The contract for Betabend pipes from the
local authorities was just what we needed to get the order book filled, but now we have decided
to call on small builders merchants and even the larger individual builder direct. The increase
in sales could be over 50%, though obviously spread over perhaps three to three and a half the
number of customers at present on the books.
        As an act of faith, realizing the potential sales previously missed, the board had decided to
increase sales promotion and selling activities in the hope of securing a large section of the

Table 11.1 Alpha PD1 Sales Administration Dpt. manning statistics

Category	Last year	This year Budget	This year Actual
Sales Admin Manager	1	1	1
Asst Sales Admin Mgr	—	1	1
Secretaries	1	2	1
Departmental Heads	3	3	2
Shorthand Typists	3	3	3
Clerks—Invoice	4	5	4
Clerks—Order	8	7	9
Clerks—Admin	5	6	3
Area Sales Managers	7	8	7
Sales Representatives	28	32	35
Showroom Manager	1	1	1
Showroom Staff	2	2	2
Advertising Controller	1	1	1
Shorthand Typists	1	1	—
Clerks	2	2	2

pipework market. They recommend doubling the advertising budget next year; and as we only call on 3000 customers now, there is plenty of potential. Omega Pipes, our largest competitor, has decided that the local authority is the most lucrative source of business, and is to drop retail-type sales soon. However, public sector business may be affected by further expenditure cuts.

Salesmen will be encouraged to persuade potential customers (and their staffs) to visit the works to familiarize themselves with our products; extensive alterations to the showroom are envisaged next year, with provision for at least double the previous space.

Another keynote decision by the board is the 'personalization' of correspondence; replacing printed, duplicated letters. All letters will be individually prepared and signed.

The Assistant Sales Administration Manager reported that an experimental small order has been received from Pipe et Cie, based in Paris, and the chairman has met a number of foreign buyers at the National Exhibition Centre from EU Countries who were interested in Betabend pipes. The chairman wants the Assistant Sales Administration Manager to go on an extended exploration trip abroad, his place being temporarily taken by an Area Sales Manager.

Personnel advise that Williams and Smith, two ASMs are due for retirement next year, and ask for your suggestions for suitable retirement presents.

Other than cuts in local government expenditure, economic prospects are good, both at home and abroad.

(a) Assuming you were Robert Bailey, draw up Alpha's Sales Administration Department manpower budget next year, based on this year's figures, and the assumptions in the case.

(b) What do you think about the forecasts summarized in Alpha PD2? As Robert Bailey would you be satisfied with the information given? Give reasons for your answer.

12

The Recruitment and Selection Process

As we have seen, the aim of most organizations is to produce goods or provide services at a profit, or at least to break even. If the goods are to sell and the services to be demanded, then the people working in those organizations will need to be efficient in their jobs. True, people can be *trained* to do jobs, but it is obviously better from the start—and makes the training easier and simpler—if people are placed in jobs to which their natural abilities and interests are reasonably suited.

From the point of view of managers and supervisors the process of filling vacancies is of great importance. After all, they will be responsible for newly recruited staff in his section; and not only for the initial, training period, but perhaps for years afterwards. Many supervisors have the good fortune to have a say in choosing their staff, and even those who do not will benefit from understanding some of the problems recruitment brings.

A with so many other customs, practices and procedures in industry and commerce there is no 'master plan' for recruitment and selection, no ultimate model to be followed. First, perhaps, because there is no agreement as to what is the 'ideal' method of selection; and secondly, how could such an 'ideal' be enforced? What *is* important is to be aware of what has proved useful and successful in the past, and to try to ensure that whatever system is chosen is well designed and systematically applied.

We shall be looking at such a set of tried and tested methods and procedures in this chapter.

12.1 DEFINITIONS

The terms 'recruitment' and 'selection' are often misused. Many people believe they are similar in meaning, and cover the whole process of engaging staff.

Recruitment is properly used to cover the first stages of engaging staff, namely:

1. The clarification of the exact nature of the job to be filled.
2. The sorting out of the skills, aptitudes and abilities required to do the job in question.

3.   The drawing up of a profile or 'pen portrait' of the 'ideal' candidate.
4.   The attracting of a field of candidates by advertising or other means.

Selection is properly used to cover the later stages of engaging staff, namely:

1.   The sorting out of the total field of applicants into a sufficiently small 'short-list' for interview (and possibly intelligence/personality tests).
2.   The selection interview stage, which leads to the ultimate decision to engage a particular candidate.
3.   The induction process which turns a successful candidate into a useful and co-operative worker.

   (See Fig. 12.1, which shows the distinction between these terms in diagrammatic form.)

   The recruitment and selection of individual employees should, of course, fit in with the overall staffing plan.

12.2   AGREEING THE VACANCY

A necessary preliminary assessment is needed when an existing employee leaves. We should ask:

1.   Do we need to replace the employee who is leaving?
2.   Do we need to change the job, upgrade it, downgrade it, etc.?

   In local and national government, as well as in the private sector, there can be periods when staffing economies are being made. In such cases agreeing the vacancy is no mere formality. Each proposed replacement will have to be justified in terms of the current and immediate future workload.

   For an entirely new post, the process is if anything even more difficult than replacement, and the new post is usually approved at a high level in the organization.

12.3   JOB ANALYSIS

The ideal starting point in the process of recruitment and selection—once the vacancy has been agreed—is *Job Analysis*. Indeed it plays a fundamental part in the whole procedure (see Fig. 12.2).

   Any job can be seen as a series of tasks: some may be important, such as deciding how to spend thousands of pounds; others less so, such as stapling two sheets of paper together, but all are part of the total job. Very few jobs have just one single task: such jobs would be highly repetitive and probably very boring.

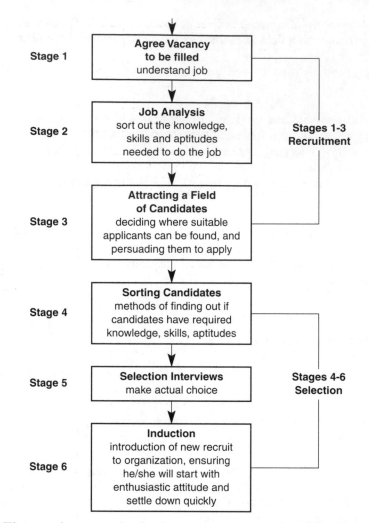

Figure 12.1 The recruitment and selection process—general outline. Note that the vacancy would arise either because an employee left or because it was created as part of the manpower plan.

Job Analysis is the total process of investigating and evaluating jobs, during which the facts concerning each job are systematically recorded, including:

1. Tasks (individual work activities).
2. Procedures.
3. Responsibilities (of the job holder).
4. Personal attributes, qualities and qualifications required of the job holder.

From such information we can see how jobs may resemble or differ from each other, and get some indication of the status and rewards of the job as well as the content of the

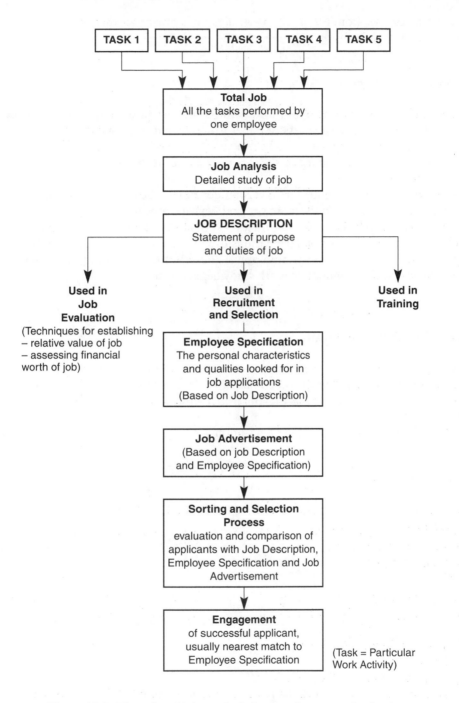

Figure 12.2 The role of job analysis in recruitment and selection.

job. (As we can see from Fig. 12.2, Job Analysis has other uses than in recruitment and selection, e.g. training.)

Collecting the information

Collecting the information about jobs is difficult, complicated and time consuming. Try to write down on two sheets of paper *exactly* what your own job is! Even if you could do this reasonably quickly, and to your satisfaction, do you feel your boss (if given the task to write what he or she sees your job to be) would come up with a list of tasks similar to your list?

Probably the best method is to have an independent fact-collector to question both the present job holder and the manager, and perhaps others with whom the job holder comes into contact. Ideally, the information should be collected and available before a vacancy arises, and fairly regular revisions of information are required as jobs change over a period of time. Information about the job may be held by other specialist departments, such as training or work study departments.

12.4   JOB DESCRIPTION

This is a formal document, based on the information obtained during the Job Analysis, and defines the job that needs to be filled. Usually the Job Description states the purpose, duties and relationships of the job; lists the physical, social and economic factors that affect it.

The information given in a Job Description is often given under a series of headings:

Identification of job

This includes current job title, the department concerned, the number of people doing the job.

Purpose of job

A brief, general statement of the major objectives of the job (for example, the purpose of a works manager could be: 'To manage the manufacturing unit of the company making valves and pistons').

Duties

A list of all the tasks and duties involved in the job. Ideally one of two methods is used:

1. Where each duty is preceded by an *active* verb (for example: 'Lists totals of debtors', 'Prepares and word-processes letters to customers'); and
2. Where each duty is preceded by an infinitive (for example: 'To prepare budgets for expenditure on loose tools', or 'To suggest improvements in security').

It is important that methods are standardized and that *one* is used consistently throughout.

Responsibilities

A statement of responsibilities for resources, i.e. men, money, machines. Particularly important for supervisory staff and above, but could also apply to operator/clerk level.

Relationships

A statement of the relationships involved in the job, with other people inside and outside the organization; including the job title of the person to whom the employee is accountable.

Physical conditions

Here we would include not only details of noisy, dirty, dangerous conditions (or the reverse if pleasant office conditions apply) but hours of work, overtime, unsocial hours, too.

Social conditions

An indication of the work group or groups the employee will be concerned with.

Salary/wages and fringe benefits

A clear statement of salary/wage rates, increments, piece-work, bonuses, commission, plus details of such 'extras' as pension schemes, sickness benefits, car, etc.

Promotion prospects

A clear statement of the prospects of promotion or transfer, if applicable.
See Appendix A for a typical Job Description.

12.5 EMPLOYEE SPECIFICATION

The Employee Specification[1] is another formal document, and is a profile or 'pen portrait' of the kind of person who would be suitable for the job vacancy. In building up the picture of the ideal applicant, we start to place limits on the person we have in mind.

In recruiting a commissionaire for the front of our head office we could well feel we must fix:

1. Upper and lower age limits.
2. Lower height limit.
3. The amount of relevant previous experience required.

It is helpful to quantify these limitations under two main headings—'essential' and 'desirable'. For example, part of the specification for an invoice clerk could read as follows:

Quality	*Essential*	*Desirable*
Skill with figures	Reasonable ability with simple calculations and use of calculators	GCSE Maths Grade C/D

12.5.1 Checklists

A convenient way to prepare an Employee Specification is to produce a checklist under a number of main headings. Two commonly used lists are those of J. Munro Fraser (the Five-Point Plan) and Professor Alec Rodger for the National Institute of Industrial Psychology.

The five-point plan

The main headings are:

1. *Impact on other people*: relations with co-workers, subordinates, customers, etc.
2. *Qualifications*: formal education qualifications gained, training or experience.
3. *Brains and abilities:* intelligence, alertness.
4. *Motivation*: drive, enthusiasm, the ability to set and achieve personal objectives.
5. *Adjustment*: the ability to slot into groups, cope with work pressures and the unexpected.

---

[1] Some personnel staff would want to call this document a 'Job Specification'. As the document describes the *person* envisaged to *do* the job, rather than the job, I prefer to use the term 'Employee' Specification.

The seven-point plan

The main headings, with typical supplementary points added by means of such lists:

1. *Physical make-up.* What are the requirements for:

   (a) Height;
   (b) Weight;
   (c) Physical characteristics such as *hearing, vision, bearing,* as well as *general appearance* and *health?*

2. *Attainments.* What do we expect of the candidate in terms of *education, job-related training* and *experience?*
3. *General intelligence.* Here we consider what *level of intelligence*—possibly measured by intelligence or similar tests—and *reasoning ability* we need in the job holder: the degree of quickness and accuracy of comprehension required.
4. *Special aptitudes.* Are there any *special* skills or abilities the successful applicant should have, for example, *mechanical;* those connected with *communication both written and verbal; manual dexterity?*
5. *Interests.* Here we should consider how far any leisure interests, activities or hobbies are relevant to job success, under such headings as *social, physically active, practical constructional, intellectual.*
       Such interests could reveal qualities useful for the job holder to have: social interests could suggest an ability to influence or persuade others.
6. *Disposition.* Under this major heading we should consider the character and disposition of the ideal applicant: how important is it that the job holder should be *acceptable* to other people; do we require him/her to *work on his/her own;* what importance is attached to *stability* (i.e. steadiness) and *self-reliance* (independence of thought and action).
7. *Circumstances.* What requirements does the job demand in terms of the job holder's personal circumstances? We should consider here such questions as the *age limits* of the job; whether we need a *married,* or a *single person* (or either); the requirements to work irregular hours, be away from home (mobility). Are there children (*dependents*) whose education could be affected by a move?

In each section you would need to identify the 'essential' and 'desirable' characteristics.

12.6 ATTRACTING SUITABLE CANDIDATES

Attracting a sufficient number of applicants is essentially the process of:

1. Bringing the vacancy to the attention of suitably qualified people.
2. Stimulating them to apply.

Such an activity is an art in itself: if badly done the organization could have hundreds of totally unsuitable applicants; or, just as unsatisfactory, very few candidates, with no real choice available.

Ideally, then, this stage of recruitment aims to deter those who do not meet the requirements for the job in a variety of ways from applying at all, without discouraging those who have much to offer, even if they do not match up with the Employee Specification on every count.

We can divide the process into two separate considerations:

1. Identifying the most suitable source of applicants for the particular vacancy.
2. Deciding upon the best method of contact, if the most suitable source does not perform this task for us.

12.6.1 Some possible sources of applicants

Internal

Promotion of existing staff.   This is cheap and can aid morale. Internal promotion may even be demanded by the union. The advantages of this method of recruitment are that an employee's abilities are known and the employee is already thoroughly familiar with the organization.

Searches or trawls.   This means going through the records of existing staff and trying to match qualifications and experience against the job requirements. Used mostly in large organizations, this could result in some existing employees at least reaching a short list.

Internal advertisements.   Advertising jobs available internally at least allows employees to feel they can apply for more senior posts, and saves the organization a lot of expense (see also *Advertising* below).

Recruitment of relatives and friends of staff.   This also constitutes a cheap method of recruitment, particularly of people more likely to be loyal to the organization.

External

College/schools connections.   Few people are recruited directly from this source.

Colleges/schools direct careers' service.   Again a cheap source of applicants often already appropriately trained or qualified. However, as a rule this service is only useful at Easter or in the summer.

Job Centres.   These provide wide coverage and free service for the recruitment of staff with a wide range of skills, manual and clerical.

PER (Professional and Executive Register).   This can help with the recruitment of administrative, specialist and management personnel. However, the charges for the service could be considerable.

Private, commercial employment agencies.   These are covering an increasingly wider range of jobs, though mainly clerical. Their services are relatively expensive, but the employer only pays for results.

Management consultants.   These can be used for very senior appointments, but they are very expensive.

Advertising

National, daily, Sunday newspapers.   These provide wide coverage but are expensive. They produce quick results for senior posts.

Local, daily, weekly newspapers.   All posts can be advertised in a newspaper with wide local coverage. Advertising in local papers is cheaper than the nationals and can produce reasonably quick results.

Trade, professional magazines.   These cover a particular market. However, the magazine may only be published monthly therefore there may be some delay in the recruitment process.

Factory notice boards, notices in shops, on trees, etc.   These are cheap *but* cannot give much information.

In addition it should be noted that in recent years the Government (through the Training Agency) has run various schemes involving (in some cases) temporary subsidized employment and work experience placements. The current situation can be checked by contacting the local Job Centre.

Regretfully, many firms neglect to consider existing staff when making appointments. It is a sound policy to look inside a company or organization to see if there is an existing employee who could already do the job now vacant, or could easily be trained to do it.

Internal appointments or promotions can:

1. Make it easier to assess the candidate's potential from past knowledge of both character and performance.
2. Stimulate morale and help to ensure that trained and qualified people stay with the organization, rather than seek better jobs elsewhere.
3. Make it easier for the person appointed to settle down in the new job.

12.6.2 Newspaper advertising

Although many organizations have very good and useful relationships with colleges, schools, and both public and private recruitment agencies, newspaper advertising is still a very popular way of recruitment. Economy is important in these days of rising costs, but newspaper and magazine advertising can be a very effective method of attracting candidates; it follows that it is really a waste of money to 'skimp' on the space for the sake of a few pounds.

The aims of the job advertisement, then, are to obtain an effective response, at a reasonable cost. Factors affecting this are:

1. The content of the advertisement.
2. The timing of its appearance.

12.6.3 Advertisement content

The information that the advertisement contains is taken largely from the Job Description and Employee Specification, namely:

1. The name of the company, location, nature of its business.
2. The Job Title (in terms familiar to potential applicants) bearing in mind the requirements of the Sex Discrimination Act 1975 and the Race Relations Act 1976. Careful attention to the precise wording of the whole advertisement, and the job title in particular, is essential (see also Section 23.7). Additionally, the information given should include the purpose of the job, its aims and responsibilities (Job Description).
3. Some of the more important tasks and activities (Job Description).
4. Qualifications, age limit, job experience expected; plus required personal qualities of significance (Employee Specification).
5. Salary (range), allowances, fringe benefits, opportunities for training and promotion (Job Description).
6. Procedure for applying.*

See Fig. 12.3 for a typical advertisement.

12.6.4 Timing and position of advertisement

Attention will have to be given to:

1. Category of advertisement. Should it be a display—an advertisement surrounded by a rectangular 'frame' of black lines—or should it be included under a 'classi-

---

Note: It would be rather expensive to include in print *all* the Job Description. The most convenient way would be to request those interested to send for further details (see below) and an application form. Alternatively, the applicants can be requested to write in about themselves, or telephone for an appointment (this latter being quite suitable for junior clerical and most manual positions).

DRILL, REAMER AND TAPPIT, LTD
require a
WORKSHOP SUPERINTENDENT

Salary £22K

Applicants should be capable of supervising the work of the largest section of the plant producing precision-turned parts for the aircraft industry.
The successful candidate will help to establish production programmes to meet sales requirements, plan and organize the arrival of raw materials into the workshop, and oversee the work of 4 foremen, 60 operatives, 6 office staff and 2 inspectors.
Preferred age 30-45 with at least three years' production supervisory or management experience. Knowledge of stock control procedures and work study a definite advantage. Applicants with the NEBSM Certificate in Supervisory Management especially welcomed.
The post carries a car user allowance, pension, and a company mortgage scheme, Removal and relocation expenses met.

Application forms and further particulars are available from:

Personnel Manager, Drill, Reamer and Tappit, Ltd,
16 The Ridings, Stablebridge, Middleshire.
Closing date: 26th May.

Figure 12.3 Example of a job advertisement.

fied' section where advertisements are listed under headings such as 'Office Vacancies', 'Drivers', 'Engineers' or 'Part-time'?
2. Which day of the week is best to advertise? Many people feel that Friday evening is a suitable time, but as with the category problem, experience and experiment will provide the answer.

12.7 REPLIES TO INITIAL ENQUIRIES

If the increasingly popular practice of promising further details to applicants is followed, we shall need to forward along with the application form:

1. Information about the organization, including an outline of its history and development and present structure.
2. Information about the job, including perhaps a copy of the Job Description.
3. Details of local facilities; e.g. housing available, shops, schools, local attractions.

12.8 THE APPLICATION FORM

The organization also needs information about the candidate. The purposes of the Application Form are:

1. To obtain all the essential information about the applicant.
2. To organize this information in the most suitable way for the selection process.
3. To act as a basis for the personnel records of the engaged applicant.

The design of application forms is crucial; so often we find forms with not enough space to enter the appropriate information. It may also pay to have different forms for different jobs; one for senior staff, one for supervisors, another for shop floor personnel, and so on. (A typical Application Form for shop floor personnel is shown in Appendix B.)

Other considerations are:

1. A standard A4 is preferred.
2. Headings should follow the order of Employee Specification as far as is convenient to do so.
3. Questions too difficult to answer should be excluded—'How many days off have you had for illness in the last five years?', for example. (Can you remember this—exactly?)

12.9 SORTING THE APPLICATIONS

The first stage of the *Recruitment* process begins when applications received are assessed to see how the details on the forms match up with the 'essential' and 'desirable' characteristics listed in the Employee Specification. We can categorize the applications as 'probable', 'possible', 'rejected', or use some similar set of headings. The aim is to find *about six* candidates who meet at least most of the 'essential' requirements and some of the 'desirable' ones.

Six is considered an 'ideal' to aim for, as all six candidates can be interviewed during a single working day; and compared with one another whilst impressions are still clear in interviewers' minds. More than six 'probables', and we can set more stringent standards to reduce the numbers; less than six, and we will need to sort through the 'possibles' to select enough to make the number up.

We now place the selected applications on a 'short-list'. Short-listed candidates are invited to interviews.

12.10 THE FINAL SELECTION

The final selection can be done by:

1. Interview only.

2. Interview, plus tests of varying kinds.
3. As above, plus a medical examination.

12.11 THE INTERVIEW

An interview process can be:

1. Carried out by one interviewer once.
2. A succession of interviews by different people.
3. A panel of people sitting in judgement on the candidates.

We shall concentrate on the first kind, the individual face-to-face interview, as it is probably the kind that the supervisor will be called upon to conduct. However, when a supervisor seeks another job, he or she may be faced with a panel of interviewers. In any event, the aims are the same:

1. To confirm the information given in the application form, or other documents, or on the telephone.
2. To provide the candidate with further information about the organization.
3. To evaluate the suitability of each candidate for the job.
4. To decide upon the most suitable candidate.
5. To encourage the most suitable candidate to take the job.

Let us be quite clear at the start; interviewing is *very* subjective. The selection interview tends to be a very brief affair—thirty minutes to three-quarters of an hour is not very long to get to know someone, give that person information and come to a conclusion. Inevitably personal prejudices emerge: 'he's got a shifty look' (the candidate is nervous), or 'she looks efficient' (the candidate looks attractive) are familiar responses. Added to this, is the fact that interviews are highly artificial situations: the candidate is on his or her 'best behaviour', and wearing his or her best clothes. The interviewer may be nervous, and in reaction becomes overbearing and over-talkative. (There does not seem, however, any suitable alternative which is any better, though attempts are being made to try to use computers to replace the interview.)

12.12 PLANNING THE INTERVIEW

The first requirement for making interviews as effective as possible is proper preparation. Assuming that the details of the interview timings, confirmation of attendances are handled in a competent routine manner, the interviewer should:

1. Read through the Job Description and Employee Specification.
2. Read each Application Form carefully. Make out a list of *specific* questions to ask each candidate ('Why did you leave your last job?'), as well as a list of questions to ask *every* candidate ('What do you see as the most important task in the job?').

3. Check that the room is comfortable. Try to remove barriers; i.e. come out from behind the desk and sit down with the interviewee at a table if possible.
4. See that there are no interruptions—no callers, no telephone calls.

In fact the totally prepared interviewer will ensure that both he or she and the candidate feel confident and at ease.

12.13   CONDUCTING THE INTERVIEW

Much advice is available on interview procedure. Provided that the interviewer is adequately prepared, and is prepared to take advice from others who have had training and experience, conducting the interview can be a satisfying as well as productive activity.
Supervisors will find the following suggestions useful:

1. The interviewer starts with a *welcome,* settles the candidate down, explains the procedure. (We often say that the interviewer *'establishes rapport'*.)
2. As a beginning to the interview, to get discussion moving the interviewer asks an *'open'* question, a question which cannot be just answered in a word, or by 'yes' or 'no'. (e.g. 'I see that your last job was with a supermarket—tell me about your job there?')
3. The interviewer should follow up the candidate's replies with 'probe' or 'prospect' questions, which force the candidate to go more deeply into the answers. (e.g. 'How effective was the check-out system you introduced?')
4. The interviewer should keep to a *logical sequence* of questions (following perhaps the order of information on the application form), and avoid jumping from subject to subject. The pre-interview preparation should help considerably in maintaining a steady flow of questions.
5. The interviewer should be *prepared to listen* to the candidate's replies: an interview is a *two-way* communication. At least half the time should belong to the candidate. While the interviewer should pay great attention to what is said, at the same time there is a need to observe the candidate carefully: hesitations, gestures, facial expressions, tones of voice, are signals which the interviewer can use to assist the final evaluation of the candidate.
6. From time to time the interviewer should *summarize* the discussion. It helps to clarify particular points, attitudes, opinions expressed by the candidate, and helps to create a generally structured, and well-ordered atmosphere.
7. After each summary, 'link' questions should be used to move on to the next topic. (e.g. 'Talking about your experiences in the Army, did you ever have to train soldiers in basic engineering skills?')

All these suggestions, if followed, will help the interviewer to proceed in an orderly manner, but at the same time the interviewer should not lose sight of the essential task of the *evaluation* of each candidate interviewed. Here one might well make full use of the

Employee Specification—has, for example, the candidate lied about his or her health? Perhaps he has exaggerated his qualifications, or the status of his last job, perhaps he has not really made good use of his talents. Indeed, some organizations produce checklists based on the Employee Specification which can assist interviewers greatly.

12.13.1 What to avoid when interviewing

Interviewing faults are probably far too numerous to be able to cover every single one, but the following faults should be particularly noted:

1. Asking 'YES/NO' questions. The interviewer who does this sounds rather like a quiz master. Unfortunately, after much hard work relatively little information is obtained, and little to go on to *evaluate* the candidate as an individual is extracted.
2. Questions expecting the answer 'YES' (or agreement seeking questions). Here the interviewer virtually tells the candidate what answer to give (e.g. 'You do feel that you are competent enough to do this job, don't you?', must get the answer 'YES' almost *every* time).
3. Interrupting the candidate in mid-answer because the interviewer wants to go on to the next question.
4. Using excessive gestures or mannerisms.
5. Staring out of the window.
6. Criticizing the candidate.

12.14 CONCLUDING THE INTERVIEW

Before bringing the interview to a close, the interviewer should be sure:

1. To have answered all the candidate's questions fully.
2. To find out when the candidate would be available, if the job were offered.
3. To tell the candidate when the result of the interview will be advised. (It is at this stage that interviewers may suddenly find out that the candidate is going to other interviews/waiting to hear about the result of other interviews.)
4. The candidate leaves in as pleasant a frame of mind as possible. Today's candidates may be tomorrow's customers.

12.15 PANEL INTERVIEWS AND SELECTION BOARDS

These can reduce the effect of individual prejudice, or may even be a statutory requirement (in the public sector, for example). Panel interviews do inhibit candidates, are more formal, and cause people to behave in uncharacteristic ways.

Unless panel members agree on what they do beforehand, the management of the situation may be difficult, and the interview less than successful.

12.16   GROUP SELECTION

The technique of group selection (which has been used in various forms by the military, civil service and at management/trainee management levels in larger organizations) involves putting a number of candidates (between five to eight through a number of tests/exercises. Performance of candidates is carefully monitored by a number of observers: leadership skills are usually tested. Participants are ranked by observers using a set of criteria, such as:

1. Ability to think quickly in an innovative/logical way about the problems set;
2. Ability to put forward his/her opinions;
3. Powers of persuasion;
4. Willingness to accept/seek responsibility;
5. Degree of willingness to accept and react positively to criticism.

This proves to be an expensive and time-consuming method of selection. However, it is often combined with other techniques such as personality testing, or panel interviews and depends significantly on the skills and abilities of the observers in assessing the various performances impartially.

12.17   ASSESSMENT

At the end of each interview the interviewer must make an assessment, writing down thoughts and feelings, consulting any checklists or pre-prepared formats. It is important such recording is complete before the next candidate is seen.

12.18   SELECTION TESTS

The use of intelligence, psychological and other tests in selection is increasing in Britain every year. The design, use and interpretation of such tests is a specialized subject, and beyond the scope of this book. However, we may mention a few, briefly.

1. *Work tests*. Here we give the candidate a test to check if a claimed skill really has been mastered. A secretarial candidate may be given dictation and be asked to type the material in a given time; drivers to drive a lorry round a yard, or salesmen to 'make a sale'.
2. *Aptitude tests*. Here we give the candidate simple tasks to do which test nimbleness of the fingers (manual dexterity).

3. *Intelligence tests.* Primarily these are tests of reasoning ability, of seeing relation-ships between things. Such tests should only be administered by qualified people.
4. *Personality tests.* These are tests which, it is claimed, can identify in people such characteristics as stability, confidence, or adverse ones such as anxiety states, frus-trations and the like. Again a matter for experts.

The major problem with tests is they need to meet two requirements. That is they must be *valid* and *reliable.*

To avoid problems of validity and reliability, many organizations using tests, use a number of different ones, and make assessments based on the total results plus the selection interview.

12.19 REFERENCES

Applicants are often asked for either written references, or the names of persons who could provide references. Regrettably, references should always be treated with cau-tion. Star students can turn out to be less than star employees and, conversely, sacked employees could turn out to be real winners in your organization.

Again, employers wishing to rid themselves of an unsatisfactory employee could well write a glowing reference, or at best one which leaves a lot unsaid. Conversely, a poor reference may be submitted on a worker an employer does not wish to lose. While past performance could be a guide to future behaviour, people dissatisfied or frus-trated in their present jobs could come out badly in a reference.

References and reports do obviously have some value, but should be considered as supplementary information to that gained in other parts of the selection process.

As a guide to the form a reference request from a potential employer might take, it is suggested that the following questions should be asked of the referees:

1. Period of employment, or time spent at school/college etc.
2. Job title and nature of duties.
3. Salary grade/level of earnings.
4. Absence/sickness record: general health.
5. Would present/previous employer be willing to re-employ in the future?
6. Any further comments.

12.20 COMPLETION OF THE SELECTION PROCESS

At the end of the day the interviewer, or panel of interviewers, has to make a choice. This will be easy if one candidate stands out, is obviously better qualified, more experienced than the other candidates. Where two or three candidates seem equally good even after we have carefully matched them with the Employee Specification, then the key question to ask is 'Which candidate will best fit in with the work group he or she will be with?' After all, acceptability in the work group is a consideration which should never be far from an interviewer's mind (particularly as a supervisor choosing, or helping to choose, the team).

The next step is to:

1. Inform the successful candidate in writing of the appointment, the starting date, and the person to whom the new recruit will report.[2]
2. Inform all other candidates (as soon as the successful candidate accepts the offer of the job) that they have been unsuccessful and thanking them for their time and courtesy in attending the interview. Applicants not on the short-list should also be advised the position has been filled.

The final step, introducing the new recruit to the organization, *induction*, is deal with in the following chapter.

SUMMARY

1.   An understanding of the process of Recruitment and Selection is vital to every manager and supervisor, whether or not involved personally in the process.

2.   Practice in Recruitment and Selection methods varies from organization to organization. However, whatever system is chosen should be common and systematically used throughout the organization.

3.   *Recruitment* is the process of understanding the job, the knowledge, skills and abilities required to do it, and attracting a number of applicants for the job. *Selection* is the process of compiling a short-list of candidates from the applicants; interviewing (and perhaps testing) them, making the actual choice, and ensuring that the chosen candidate starts the new job enthusiastically. The Recruitment and Selection process is linked to the manpower plan, especially when employees are to be engaged in accordance with the overall plan.

4.   The stages of the process of recruitment and selection are:

(a)   *Agreeing the vacancy*. Deciding that the job should be filled.
(b)   *Job Analysis*. Preparing and writing the Job Description and Employee Specification; the process by which the facts about each job are systematically identified and recorded, and information is

---

[2] The Contracts of Employment Act 1963 (as amended 1972, 1975), also lays down a long list of written particulars of terms and conditions to be given to employees within 13 weeks of appointment. (Details are given in Chapter 13.) These written particulars may accompany the letter of appointment.

obtained concerning the tasks, responsibilities and personal attributes required to do the job.

(c) *Basis for Employee Specification.* The Employee Specification is based on the requirements that an individual would need to meet in order to do the job. It is helpful to list such requirements under 'essential' and 'desirable'.

The Seven-Point Plan, one method of classification of these requirements, lists the main headings as:

> Physical Make-up
> Attainments
> General Intelligence
> Special Aptitudes
> Interests
> Disposition
> Circumstances

(d) *Attracting suitable candidates.* The process of bringing the vacancy to the attention of suitably qualified people and encouraging them to reply.

Considerations to be made include:

(i) identifying the most suitable source of applicants;
(ii) deciding on method of contact.

(e) *Sources of candidates.* Candidates can often be found within the organization (internal recruitment); or by contacting state and private agencies. Newspaper and magazine advertising is a popular method of external recruitment.

An advertisement should contain:

Name of organization.

Job title, overall purpose of job, some of the more important activities.

Qualifications, experience and other required attributes.

Salary allowances, fringe benefits.

Procedure for applying.

(f) *Application Forms.* Properly designed Application Forms provide relevant information in an easily obtainable form, when completed. This speeds up the handling of applications and ensures all the information needed is supplied by the applicants.

It may be useful to have different forms for different categories of job.

(g) *Sorting the applications.* Received, completed Application Forms are compared with the Employee Specification, and graded into:

Probable
Possible
Reject

The aim is to have about six candidates to interview.

(h)   *Interviews*. Can be single face-to-face; a series of interviews; a panel interview; or interviews where candidates are left on their own to interact with each other and the 'selectors' observe them. (This latter method while used by some larger companies and organizations is in my view underhand, and should be avoided.)

The purpose of interviews is to gain information from the candidates to help in evaluating them; to provide candidates with information about the organization; to choose one candidate and motivate him to accept the job.

Each interview should be well planned in advance, and appropriate questions prepared. Interviewers should master Job Description, Employee Specification, candidates' Application Forms.

The setting for the interview is important, and comfortable informal surroundings are preferred. Privacy is essential.

After an initial welcome to establish rapport, the interview should proceed with a logical sequence of open, prompt and link questions, interspersed with summaries. The candidate must be allowed to speak at least half the time.

To be avoided: 'YES/NO' questions, agreement-seeking questions, interruptions, excessive mannerisms, criticism of candidates.

Finally, the interview should be concluded pleasantly, all the interviewee's questions should be answered, and an indication should be given as to when the result of the interview will be made known.

(i)   *Assessment*. This should be made at the conclusion of each interview.

(j)   *Selection tests*. Various tests exist including work tests, tests of aptitude, intelligence and personality. These are not to be used on their own, but as supplements to the interview.

(k)   *References*. All references should be treated with caution.

(l)   *Appointment*. Official letters should be sent—one to appoint the successful candidate, the remainder to inform unsuccessful candidates of the filling of the vacancy.

REVIEW QUESTIONS

1.   What is the difference between *Recruitment* and *Selection*?

2.   Why do we need to agree the vacancy before starting the recruitment process?

3. Why is it necessary to write a Job Description before we can even begin to write an advertisement?

4. What kinds of information about a job would be included in a Job Description?

5. Define what is meant by the term 'Employee Specification'. To what use is this specification put in the recruitment process?

6. What is the 'Seven-Point Plan?

7. Increasingly organizations are requiring job applicants to fill in printed Application Forms, for *all* levels of jobs. Why do organizations feel the use of such forms is preferable to asking applicants to write a letter of application?

8. What is the purpose of job interviews? Why does the intending interviewer need to plan the interview in advance?

9. Who should do the greater part of the talking during the job interview—the interviewer or the applicant? Why?

10. Why should references be treated with caution?

DISCUSSION TOPICS

1. 'Given three candidates who have equal qualifications, experience and ability, the decision to appoint rests on whether the interviewer feels that the successful applicant is the most likely to get on with his colleagues.' Discuss.

2. It has been pointed out by Professor Eysenck that interviewing as a method of selection is very unreliable. Do you agree? Can you think of a better way of selecting people (e.g. by computer, by lottery, etc.)?

   How much should a supervisor (either on the shop floor, or in the office) be involved in the selection process.

   (a) All the way through?
   (b) Just going through applications, helping to work out a short-list and helping to interview?
   (c) Just interviewing only?
   (d) Not at all?

ASSIGNMENTS

A12.1   Write your own Job Description, if you are in employment. (If still at college or school, write a Job Description of a friend, relative or college/school official such as head caretaker or librarian.)

A12.2   Trying to be as objective as possible, prepare an Employee Specification for the Job Description in A12.1. Compare the Specification with the actual job holder. Do they match reasonably well?

A12.3   If you had to advertise your job, or that of someone you know, how would you lay out the advertisement? Prepare the advertisement, and suggest where the job should be advertised. Find out how much the advertisement would cost.

A12.4   Obtain a copy of your organization's Application Form, analyse it against the requirements of Application Forms set out in the chapter, and against the sample form (Appendix B) make a series of lists showing:

(a) The strong points of the form.
(b) Weaknesses (questions missing, not enough space for answers).
(c) Where improvements could be made.

A12.5   Using either a Job Description based on A12.1, or any other Job Description available, in groups of four or five,

(a) Prepare an Employee Specification.
(b) Prepare a series of questions to be asked of all candidates at an interview for the job described in the Job Description.
(c) Appoint a chairman to report back.

A12.6   Using an existing Application Form, select an appropriate number of students to complete copies to apply for a job chosen by the course tutor/class lecturer. One member of each group of four or five to interview the 'applicants', the remainder of the group to observe the interview and make notes on the progress of the interview. (Interviews could be videotaped, or sound taped if appropriate equipment is available, to be played back and analysed later.)

Case Study

A12.7   Robert Williams met his girl friend Gillian last Friday evening to tell her about his search for a new job. Robert had left school three years before with six GCSEs including Maths and English, and had joined a local engineering company in the accounts department as a junior. His job was mainly dealing with suppliers' invoices and subsequent payments, very routine work for a boy with ambition.

Robert told Gillian that he had had two interviews during the week—he had taken the whole week off as a holiday so as not to be away without good reason. His first interview was with the Exploding Chemical Company[3] as a senior accounts clerk. 'I'd heard a lot about the firm,' he said to Gillian, 'and thought it would suit my abilities and my experience.'

An application form had been completed by Robert and sent in a week before the interview, fixed for Tuesday at 10.00 a.m. When Robert arrived at the entrance, the receptionist was unsure about his visit, but quickly sorted matters out with the personnel department. About quarter past ten, Robert was summoned to see Mr Frazer, the personnel manager. Mr Frazer was apparently busy with some important papers, and it was at least two or three minutes before he glanced up and saw Robert. 'Well, lad,' he asked, 'what do you want?' Robert hesitated, then sat down uninvited and explained he'd come about the accounts job. 'Oh! yes, I've got the papers here.' Mr Frazer alternately read through the application form and stared at Robert in silence.

After a few minutes Mr Frazer began to question Robert about where he lived, what his job was, how much he earned. Robert was just explaining why he wanted to move when Miss Smythe, the personnel secretary, burst in to tell Mr Frazer that the managing director wanted to see him in ten minutes. Glancing quickly at his watch, Mr Frazer rapidly ran through the rest of the form then laid down his spectacles. 'We are really looking for someone older than you,' he said, 'someone with more experience and some progress with an accountancy qualification. You will hear from us in the next few days. Good morning.' With that he left in a hurry leaving Miss Smythe to escort Richard to the reception area. 'This is the third time this year this job has been advertised,' she confided to Richard as he left.

Later that day, he had been interviewed for a similar position at the Acme Engineering Company. Although it had a much less pretentious reception area, the receptionist smiled as he entered. 'Mr Williams?' she enquired. 'Will you please come with me.' Two minutes later Richard was met by an undistinguished, quietly-spoken man who introduced himself as Mr Parker, the company accountant. 'I'm sorry,' said Mr Parker, 'we don't go in for frills like personnel departments, and I'm not the world's best interviewer. However, Mr Williams, please make yourself comfortable.'

Throughout the next hour, Mr Parker seemed to take a great interest in Robert. At the beginning of the interview, Mr Parker said he had been impressed by Robert's qualifications, and sympathized with his (Robert's) desire to make progress. They discussed at length the requirements of the job, and it seemed that Robert had plenty of potential, but needed further training. Robert was asked his opinion on this, and Mr Parker mentioned

---

[3] A copy of this (fictitious) firm's Application Form is shown in Appendix B.

day-release opportunities to study for an appropriate accountancy qualification.

Robert was given time to ask his own questions, and taken round the accounts department, a small but pleasant area. Before Robert left he was given a copy of the firm's balance sheet, and a firm promise he would hear the result of the interview by Friday.

Robert told Gillian he had had offers of employment from both companies, although the Exploding Chemical Co. would pay slightly more to start with. 'Which offer would you accept?' enquired Gillian.

(a) What answer do you think Robert should give? Why?
(b) Contrast the two interview styles of Mr Frazer and Mr Parker. Make a list of the good and bad points of each.
(c) Why do you think there is such a turnover of accounts staff at the Exploding Chemical Co.?

13
The Induction Process

13.1 DEFINITION

Induction is that process by which a newcomer to an organization is introduced to his job and integrated into the work group to which he or she will belong, in such a way that the newcomer settles down into a productive, efficient and satisfied employee. At the same time, the newcomer's new colleagues have to accept him into the group—a fact often forgotten in induction procedures.

Anxiety and apprehension are common to all new employees—especially to the young, and those starting their first job. Any good induction scheme will aim to minimize these twin fears. However, such a scheme should go on to build confidence and a 'feeling of belonging'. Induction cannot, therefore, be completed in a moment, a minute or even perhaps in a month. It is a gradual process which begins at the interview —particularly if the candidate is shown round, meets possible new colleagues, gets the feel of the job—and it does not end until the newcomer is totally accepted by the work group, and is working to the expected standards.

A clear distinction has to be made, however, between *induction* training and *job* training. *Induction* training is primarily a familiarizing process with the total work environment: *job* training is directed at giving the worker the necessary knowledge and skills to carry out the various tasks that are part of his job. Agreed, both kinds of training may go on simultaneously, but they are different and have different aims.

13.2 LEGAL ASPECTS

The Contracts of Employment Act 1972, as amended by the Employment Protection Act 1975,[1] requires that written statements of the main terms of employment should be given to employees not later than two months after an employee begins work. It has, of course, long been the practice of many employers to write letters of appoint-

---

[1] Subsequently incorporated in the Employment Protection (Consolidation) Act 1978, and further amended by the Trade Union Reform and Employment Rights Act 1993.

ment to successful candidates setting out some of the terms of the appointment; and some employees with a specific written contract may have indeed received (and signed) a long bulky legal document embodying the contract. Contracts of apprenticeship are examples.

The contract of employment, however, usually consists of rather more than written documents and letters. Verbal agreements made at the time of appointment, the common law duties of an employee (such as giving 'careful service' and 'obedience' to his employers), the common law duties of the employer (such as paying 'the agreed remuneration or what is reasonable'), all these could be included in a contract of service. Indeed, totally binding contracts can be made wholly by word of mouth.

Thus it is then clear that the written statement given to employees not later than two months after starting work is NOT a contract of service, but merely a statement of the important particulars, or main terms that Parliament felt should be drawn to every employee's attention.

The principal terms (set out below) must be set out within a single document; and this is a strict requirement.

1. *Identification of the parties,* legal language to mean the names of the employee and employer.
2. *The starting date of employment*, stating, if applicable, whether employment with a previous employer forms part of the total employment with the present employer; and when such earlier employment began. This is important if after a take-over or merger people receive fresh appointments and are later made redundant.
3. *The scale of remuneration,* rates of pay, salary, etc., or methods of calculating remuneration, e.g. overtime, piece-work rates.
4. *The intervals at which remuneration is paid*, that is weekly, monthly, or at some other interval.
5. *The terms relating to hours of work*, e.g. 8.30 am–4.45 pm with three-quarters of an hour for lunch Monday to Friday. (Whatever hours are stipulated they must conform to the legislation current at the time of appointment based on the European Working Time Directive.)
6. The terms and conditions relating to:

   (a) *Holidays and holiday pay*, in the case of holiday pay, sufficient information to enable the employee to calculate the amount of holiday pay due if leaving during a 'holiday year'.
   (b) *Incapacity for work* due to sickness or injury, including provision for sick pay.
   (c) *Pensions and pension schemes.*

7. The terms relating to the *length of notice* that the employee is obliged to give and entitled to receive when the contract is terminated by either employer or employee. If the contract is for a fixed term, the date of the expiry of the contract.
8. *The title of the job* the employee has been engaged to do, but not the duties involved.

In addition, the written statement must also specify the following:

1. *The disciplinary rules of the organization,* or refer to a document containing the rules, which should be reasonably accessible.
2. *The person to whom the employee can apply* in respect of any grievance, or dissatisfaction with any disciplinary decision, and who can explain in each case the way application is to be made.
3. *The subsequent steps* which can be taken in any grievance procedure, which may be available.
4. *If the employment is 'contracted out'* under the terms of the Social Security Pensions Act 1975 (the implication here is that the employee will be in a company pension scheme and will not need to pay into part of the state scheme and thus National Insurance deductions will be somewhat less than a worker not covered by a company scheme).

Many larger organizations add further information to employees, as appropriate. This extra information is over and above that legally required, and can include the following:

(a) A clear statement of the duties to be undertaken (this need NOT be the complete, formal job description);
(b) Specific requirements laid down by the organization in respect of the self-certification of sickness;
(c) Special regulations in respect of ideas and suggestions put forward by employees;
(d) Particular conditions applying to the possession and use of confidential information.
(e) The place where work is to be carried out (including the possibility of transfer or relocation).

13.2.1 Exemptions

Employers are *not* required to provide a written statement of the kind mentioned above for:

1. An employee who works less than eight hours per week.
2. Registered dock workers, Merchant Navy employees, workers in fishery fleets.
3. Situations where employees are crown servants.
4. A situation where an employee is a close relative—father, mother, husband, wife, son, daughter—of the employer.
5. A situation where all the details required on the written statement are in fact already contained in a full written contract of employment.
6. Employees working abroad.

(*Note:* It is in fact not necessary to spell out in full detail every aspect, e.g. the company disciplinary rules, as long as the written statement refers the employee to some document readily available.)

13.2.2   Changes

If any change is agreed in any of the terms that have already been advised in the written set of particulars, then the employer must notify the employee of such changes within one month of the changes taking place.

13.2.3   A note of caution

A book such as this can only set out the broad provisions of industrial law current at the time of going to print, with special emphasis on areas of greater interest to managers or supervisors. However, if faced with particular workplace problems which have a legal aspect every manager or supervisor should, as appropriate:

1.   Check with the complete text of all the Acts or Regulations concerned, including any subsequent amendments of changes to these.
2.   Take advice from supervisors, and/or the personnel department.
3.   Contact the local office of the Department of Employment for help and advice.
4.   Take the advice of a solicitor.

13.3   INDUCTION PROCEDURES

In a great many organizations induction consists of two separate activities:

Primary induction.   To give the newcomer an 'overview' or overall appreciation of the organization.

Secondary induction.   To concentrate on the immediate surroundings of the actual job the newcomer will be doing.

Of course, in the smallest of organizations, the work group that the newcomer joins may be the complement of the total pay roll in which case such a distinction is irrelevant. However, most firms do see the need to distinguish between the two, leaving the personnel department or at least a senior manager, to deal with the organization as a whole, and the newcomer's immediate manager or supervisor to deal with 'local' aspects.

Regrettably, the amount of induction training, its length and detail, even its efficacy varies widely from organization to organization. In some firms a newcomer would be fortunate to receive a quarter of an hour's induction in total: other establishments run long (and expensive) training courses, lasting perhaps for more than a week. It is indeed strange that some organizations fail to see the value of proper induction procedures. Poor induction can lead to people leaving quickly, extra recruitment costs, constant misunderstandings and unnecessary queries and grievances, as well as a decrease in productivity generally.

13.3.1 Code of industrial practice and induction

This code was originally brought out soon after the Industrial Relations Act 1971, and is still in being. It lists the following information to be given to an employee (by implication, during the induction period):

1. The requirements of the job, and to whom he is responsible.
2. Disciplinary rules and procedures: circumstances which would lead to suspension/ dismissal.
3. Trade union arrangements.
4. Opportunities for promotion/training for promotion.
5. Social and welfare facilities.
6. Fire prevention, safety and health rules.
7. Suggestion schemes.

Obviously such information should be included in any induction procedures. Attention is also drawn to the advice given in the ACAS Advisory Booklet No. 7—'Induction of New Employees' (1982)—free from Job Centres.

13.3.2 The role of the personnel department—primary induction

The importance of the personnel department (or in the smaller organization the manager who carries out the personnel function) in induction cannot be overemphasized. For many new employees, particularly workers on the shop floor, the selection process has taken place within the personnel office, and newcomers are not totally unacquainted with its staff. Thus, to be met on the first morning by a recognized, friendly face in a place previously unexperienced is a tremendous help in winning the battle against anxiety and apprehension.

At this stage the general, overall induction can take place, covering aspects applicable to *all* employees, and could include some or all of the following:

1. History of the firm or organization.
2. Description of the present organizational structure.
3. Details of the company products and/or services; methods of manufacture.
4. General conditions of service; important disciplinary rules (with the issue perhaps of an employee handbook with such information).
5. Information on trade unions recognized by the company or organization.
6. Suggestion schemes.
7. Health and safety training (see below).
8. A tour of the *complete* site, and a general appreciation of all the departments and what they do; as well as the facilities in use such as canteens, toilets, car parks, sports and social facilities.

During the tour—a vital part of induction—special attention can be drawn to points needing emphasis such as safety hazards, fire points, emergency phones, exits, etc. A matter of concern to many employees (and as a consequence to managers, supervisors and shop stewards) is how gross and net pay is calculated and how pay slips are laid out. Specific 'classroom' training can be backed up by calling in at the wages department where queries can be answered and misconceptions removed at the start.

13.3.3   Health and safety training

One of the duties of employers under the Health and Safety at Work etc. Act 1974 is to provide such information, instruction, training and supervision, as far as is reasonably practicable, to ensure the health and safety at work of employees. Such instruction, training and supervision ideally should be provided the moment the newcomer sets foot in the organization.

Basic health and safety training should therefore commence on the first day; postponing this training until there are enough people to run a course is not good enough as someone could be in hospital with injuries caused by ignorance by the time the course begins. It will be necessary for both general safety rules and the duties of employees under the Act to be clearly laid out at the start; in addition, employees should be made aware of safety problems and hazards at the work point.

13.3.4   Content, timing and length of primary induction

The precise content, timing and length of primary induction will depend upon local conditions, but it should certainly be worked out with the fullest consultation with managers and supervisors, who are indeed able to 'feed back' information about problems and queries arising during the first weeks of work.

Two major difficulties arise, however, for the organizers of primary induction. One is the pressure to compromise between needs and costs—running a full-scale course for one person, for example; and the other is the amount that you can teach a newcomer in a given period.

Perhaps the ideal solution is to spread out induction over a period—for example, a fortnight—with several half day sessions, so that information is supplied at a steady rate and is for that reason more successfully acquired by newcomers.

13.3.5   The role of the supervisor—secondary induction

The supervisor's role in induction is complementary to that of the personnel specialists. The task is to relate the general, overall aspects of knowledge already acquired to the individual work bench, desk or laboratory. The supervisor, therefore, carries a heavy responsibility to reinforce the primary induction. Where the primary induction is in any way defective, the task becomes even more difficult and important.

A simple, nine-stage checklist, such as that shown below is something that every supervisor should have. Preferably, a jointly agreed company form should be adopted but the following guidelines could be used, if necessary, in drawing up your own list.

1. Welcome the new employee to your section *yourself*. Be sure that he or she:

    (a) Knows your name.
    (b) Knows how to contact you.

2. Check that the newcomer knows the company regulations in respect of hours of work, etc., and confirm any special departmental rules—tea-breaks, timing of lunch hour, privileges, etc.

3. Explain the function of the department. Show the newcomer around—not too quickly. He or she has much to learn. See that the employee knows:

    (a) Entrances.
    (b) Exits.
    (c) Location of fire appliances.
    (d) Fire evacuation procedure.
    (e) Departmental safety rules.
    (f) Location of toilets, cloakroom.
    (g) Where to find overalls, safety clothing: ear defenders, goggles, etc.
    (h) Own locker location.

4. Explain the part that the newcomer will play in the department.

5. Induct the newcomer into the group—with introductions to future co-workers. (Use both first names and surnames in all introductions.)

6. Explain at the work place what the duties will be; ask for questions.

7. Introduce the newcomer to the sponsor allocated.[2]

8. Introduce the newcomer to the union representative.

9. At the end of:

    (a) *the first day*—check that the newcomer knows the way around, can clock in/out, has no major problems;
    (b) *the first week*—check that there are no problems, advise the newcomer how he or she is getting along;
    (c) *the satisfactory probation period*—advise the newcomer that he or she is now officially an established member of the team.

Using such a list, mark each aspect as it is covered. This helps the supervisor to keep in touch with the newcomer without seeming to spend too much time with him or her.

---

[2] The 'sponsor' or 'buddy' system entails putting the newcomer in the charge of an experienced worker who will help to teach the job and help the newcomer in every possible way. Provided the chosen 'sponsor' knows what is expected, this system helps considerably in integrating the newcomer into the work group.

Following up by the supervisor not only builds a relationship between supervisor and newcomer, but will frequently bring minor problems and grievances to light before they get too large.

13.3.6   Special categories of newcomers

Newcomers come in all shapes and sizes, but some categories present specific problems.

Immigrant workers

The supervisor must take special care to ensure that the immigrant worker fully understands all the rules, particularly those relating to safety.

School leavers and government-sponsored trainees

Many school leavers find the transition from school to work a difficult one to make. Longer hours, noise, bustle, movement, application to one task, the company of much older people—all these can present problems. There are no 'golden rules' for the supervisor to follow in dealing with school leavers, but he should keep a special watch on them in the first few weeks, and give them as much encouragement as possible. As with immigrant workers, a major emphasis should be placed on safety rules. A general 'safety-consciousness' needs encouraging from the start.

Men and women returning to work

All people returning to work after a break are faced with problems associated with readapting to paid employment. Those unemployed for a period may find it difficult to come to terms with the disciplines and constraints of shift work, or laid down hours. Women who return after a break of some years in bringing up a young family may not only encounter the basic difficulties of general readaptation, but also changes in technological processes: machinery is more sophisticated; computers and word processors have replaced typewriters. Both reassurance and re-training may be required.

Disabled people

A characteristic of most disabled people is their fierce independence. The supervisor (and indeed the workforce) may have, from time to time, to restrain their natural impulses to rush to the aid of disabled people. The one thing above all others is that the disabled person wants to be treated 'just like everyone else'. In general, show sympathy but never pity.

SUMMARY

1.   Induction is the process by which a newcomer to an organization is introduced to a job and integrated into a new work group.

2.   Induction—primarily a process of familiarization with the total work environment—must not be confused with job training, equipping the newcomer with the new skills required to do the job.

3.   Contracts, including contracts of employment do not have to be in writing. A binding contract can be made by word of mouth. However, the Contracts of Employment Act 1972, as amended, lays down that within two months of starting work every employee should receive a written statement of certain basic particulars of his or her employment. This statement records:

     (a)   The names of employer and employee.
     (b)   The date employment began.
     (c)   The title of the job.

     It must explain how a dissatisfied employee can appeal against a disciplinary decision, or ask for a grievance to be redressed and must contain details of:

     (a)   Pay, hours of work, holidays, holiday pay.
     (b)   Sickness and sick pay arrangements.
     (c)   Pension rights, length of notice.
     (d)   Company rules.
     (e)   The pension scheme provisions for the employee being 'contracted out'.

4.   Certain categories of employees are exempt—part-timers (less than 8 hours per week), dock workers, seamen, crown servants, close relatives, employees working abroad, and where a complete contract of service has been drawn up and signed.

5.   Induction often takes the form of two separate processes: *primary induction*, to give the newcomer a total impression or overview of the organization and its functions and rules; and *secondary* induction which aims to integrate the newcomer into the 'local' environment of his individual job. (In the smallest organizations these two processes are usually amalgamated.)

6.   Primary induction is normally carried out by the personnel department.

7.   Primary induction should cover:

     (a)   Organization history.
     (b)   Organization structure.

(c)   Products/services.
(d)   Conditions of service.
(e)   Disciplinary rules.
(f)   Trade union information.
(g)   Suggestion schemes.
(h)   Health and safety training.
(i)   Tour of the site/plant/offices.

8.   Special attention should be paid to health and safety training from the first day of employment.

9.   Too much information in a short period is to be avoided; primary induction should be spread over a period if at all possible.

10.   The supervisor has a *complementary* role to the personnel function in induction integrating the newcomer into the 'local situation'.

11.   A simple checklist for the supervisor to use should be drawn up and agreed.

Example
(a)   Welcome employee.
(b)   Check knowledge of company regulations.
(c)   Explain the function of the department. Show employee around, not too quickly.
(d)   Explain the role of the newcomer to him or her.
(e)   Induct newcomer into work group.
(f)   Explain the duties to him or her.
(g)   Introduce newcomer to a sponsor.
(h)   Introduce newcomer to union representative.
(i)   Follow up at end of:
      (i)   First day.
      (ii)   First week.
      (iii) Probationary period.

12.   Immigrant workers, school leavers, trainees, those returning to work after a break, disabled workers, all present special induction problems.

REVIEW QUESTIONS

1.   Define the induction process.

2.   State one *purpose* of induction.

3.   Distinguish between primary and secondary induction.

4.   What are the main items of information which should be contained in the 'written particulars' of employment (i.e. the document handed to new employees within 13 weeks of starting employment)?

5.   What are the main points the primary induction period should aim to cover?

6.   What is the supervisor's role in induction?

7.   Outline a possible induction procedure checklist for supervisors.

8.   What is the 'sponsor' system? Why is it useful?

9.   What categories of starters need special attention? Why?

DISCUSSION TOPICS

1.   'Induction is a waste of time: whilst the new employee is wandering round the firm and sitting in classrooms, he could be doing real, productive work.' Discuss this statement.

2.   What are the advantages and disadvantages of involving *all* line managers and supervisors in the planning of both primary and secondary induction procedures?

3.   Once you have an induction procedure introduced and working, how can you be *sure* it is really effective? What built-in checks could it have?

ASSIGNMENTS

A13.1   Each student in employment should research into his or her organization's induction procedures, both primary and secondary, and produce a report for presentation to the class. (It is very important to get clearance from personnel departments.) Schemes could be discussed by the class and constructive comments as well as criticisms obtained.

A13.2   Looking at your own department, find out what each newcomer to it would need to know (apart from the *actual skills* of doing the job):

(a) By the end of the first day.
(b) By the end of the first week.
(c) By the end of the first month.

Suggest who might give the information you have listed under each heading.

A13.3   Write a letter to yourself setting out a written statement of particulars applicable to your present job. (For students still at college/school, they could either take a job known to them, or a post at the college—head caretaker, registrar, secretary, etc.)

Case study

A13.4   Robert Williams arrived home exhausted on Monday evening. His first day at the Acme Engineering Company had evidently been a very busy one. His mother looked at him with some concern. 'Golly,' he told her, 'the place is bigger than I thought. I seemed to have walked miles today!'

Robert went on to explain that when he had arrived at nine o'clock, the Managing Director's secretary had made him a cup of tea until Mr Wise, the Managing Director, had arrived. He had invited Robert to go round the works with him. Mr Wise seemed to know everything that was going on, and spoke at length to nearly every employee. Robert had felt rather awkward whilst Mr Wise discussed important policy matters with his staff, but was flattered when Mr Wise asked him what he thought of the works. Mr Wise was very enthusiastic and answered every one of Robert's questions at length.

Finally just before lunch they arrived in the accounts office, and within minutes, Mr Wise, Mr Parker and Robert set off on foot for lunch in a local public house. A great deal of shop was talked and lunch dragged on until after two. Eventually Robert found himself back in Mr Parker's office. Mr Parker was as pleasant and efficient as he had been at the interview. He went to great lengths to explain to Robert how the department functioned, discussed the job descriptions of the three junior clerks for whom Robert would be responsible. Finally he went in detail through Robert's duties, both routine and supervisory.

At last, at half past three, Mr Parker stood up and shook Robert's hand. 'I've got to go to the tax office now,' he announced, 'but you know enough to carry on on your own for a while.'

Robert walked into the accounts office and immediately the room went quiet, and in silence he walked over to an empty desk which he assumed was his, and sat down. Six pairs of eyes watched him as he picked a memo out of his 'IN' tray. Just then a cheery face peered round the door. 'Hello! Mr Williams? I'm John Webster, the buyer. Can you spare a minute?' Gratefully Robert followed John Webster across the yard to the works offices.

When John Webster had finished talking about a query he had, Robert explained there was an atmosphere in the office. Webster expressed surprise. 'There's quite a jolly lot in that office—Susan is always bubbling over with fun.' 'Which one's Susan?' asked Robert, 'The one who sits over by the corner?' Webster stared at Robert. 'Come on you old son,' he said , 'I'll get you acquainted!' With that they returned to the accounts office, and within five minutes a more relaxed atmosphere prevailed although Robert felt the others still regarded him with a certain distance.

At twenty to five the girls left the office and the male clerks began to tidy their own desks, and so Robert decided it was time to go. He was just putting his car key in the driver's door when he saw Mr Wise. 'Decided to go home early, Williams? Ah, well, I suppose it *is* your first day.' Robert blushed. 'I'm sorry,' he stammered, 'I thought we finished at quarter to five.' 'Five o'clock Mr Williams, except on Fridays,' was the firm reply.

Robert drove home in a thoughtful frame of mind.

(a) Analyse Robert's first day. Do you think he had a good introduction to his job? Why?
(b) What do you think of Mr Parker's approach to introduction?
(c) Why did the accounts office go quiet when Robert entered? How could this situation have been avoided?
(d) Why did Robert go home early? Was he to blame?
(e) If you were Mr Wise what changes would you want to make to the induction of staff?

14
Performance Appraisal

14.1 DEFINITION

Appraisal (often called 'performance appraisal') is that process during which the progress, performance, results (and sometimes personality) of an employee are reviewed and assessed by his immediate superior; and, in many instances by other, senior managers.

Such appraisals or reviews can be carried out:

1. To meet a specific purpose such as aiding an internal selection process. This would entail appraising competing candidates from one standpoint only, for example, promotion prospects. Similar reviews could be carried out in respect of proposed transfers, reassignments, or even demotions or dismissals.
2. On a regular, structured basis (at three, six or twelve monthly intervals). Sometimes only specific categories of staff would be appraised—supervisors, technical and managerial staff; and sometimes every member of the workforce. This entails reviewing staff from various standpoints, for example, the need for training or relationships with others, as well as promotion.

14.2 PURPOSE

There is no single *general* purpose in appraisal, unless appraisal is regarded, as indeed it often can be, as part of the 'controlling' job of management. It will be recalled in any control system we need:

1. A standard, or yardstick with which to judge.
2. A careful measuring of performance.
3. An assessment of variances (both favourable and unfavourable) from the pre-set standards.
4. Action to be taken to eliminate, as necessary, unfavourable variances.

Appraisal is, as far as staff is concerned, in part a control system, except that the standards or yardsticks are in effect presented ready-made to the person carrying out the appraisal.

Particular purposes of appraisal include the following (many are interrelated):

1. To determine whether an employee is in a job where proper use is being made of that person's skills and talents.
2. To identify hidden potential in employees.
3. To determine the future employment of an employee (for example, to remain in present job, be transferred, promoted, retired early, etc.).
4. To identify work of particular merit done during the review period.
5. To identify work or task areas where performance is below the required standard, but where improvements could reasonably be expected if appropriate training were given.
6. To identify individual training needs (which added together would help formulate the company training plan).
7. To encourage and motivate the employee to improve job performance.
8. To identify and provide a record of any special difficulties/hazards surrounding the job, perhaps not previously realized.
9. To improve communication between managers and the managed (only true of appraisal systems which adopt the 'joint problem-solving' approach described below).
10. To help a manager or supervisor decide what increase of pay should be given or recommended on *merit* grounds (as opposed to pay for work done, or to meet inflation, etc.).
11. To help to create a more effective organization where staff not only know what jobs they have to do, but also the reasons for doing the jobs, and how good they are at their work; and where management are fully aware of what their staff are supposed to be doing, and how they are actually performing.

Thus, in appraisal, we are seeking to review and change; to inform and monitor; to examine and evaluate employees. Such activities cannot be done at a distance. It should be obvious that the supervisor is placed in an excellent position to make such assessments, and the methods and systems described in the next section are well within the abilities of the average supervisor or manager. Even where an interview system is used, the interview is one between superior and subordinate about work performance; the interviewer is required to exercise only those skills, including communication skills, which should already be in daily use at work.

14.3 METHODS OF APPRAISAL

There are several, quite different methods of appraisal. All have disadvantages, not least that supervisors or managers are reluctant to commit themselves on paper abut their own staff. This reluctance can arise because they are not sure *how* to assess people; or because they feel that more senior managers will judge their (the supervisors') total evaluation skills on the way that they appraise staff; or even perhaps because they may have to justify their ratings either to higher management or to the workers themselves. It is important to select the best possible methods of appraisal and train supervisory staff how to use them, to create a really effective system.

The principal methods are shown below. In addition, it is possible to combine two or even more in one appraisal system.

14.3.1 Essay report

Here the supervisor/manager is invited to write a free-ranging, unstructured portrait of each member of staff and is left to decide what to put in and what to stress.

The major problems with this method are:

1. Supervisors will be reluctant to complete portraits if they feel their abilities to write such reports are not adequate.
2. The report will be entirely subjective. Appraisers may leave out facts damaging to employees, if they are disposed to them (or the reverse).
3. Reports throughout the organization will not be consistent.

14.3.2 Ranking/grading systems

In these methods the supervisor/manager ranks employees in order of 'merit'. In the simplest form it means making a list with the best employee, say Jean, at the top, and Joan, the worst, at the bottom. This could be used for deciding who is to receive a rise, for example. The more sophisticated version, or 'forced grading' system consists of first ranking employees in order, then breaking them into grades as follows:

Top 10% (Exceptional)	Grade I
Next 20% (Above Average)	Grade II
Middle 40% (Average)	Grade III
Next 20% (Poor/Below Average)	Grade IV
Bottom 10% (Very Poor)	Grade V

The disadvantages of this method are:

1. Although it is a simple method, it is very subjective.
2. It is difficult to define 'better than'.
3. It cannot be undertaken with a small number of employees. 'Forced grading' needs a large enough workforce, probably at least fifty people.
4. It has very limited application and could not be used for the majority of 'purposes' listed in Section 14.1.

14.3.3 Rating systems

As with ranking and grading, there are various degrees of complexity in rating systems. The aim is to bring out employees' strengths and weaknesses, giving some indication of training requirements. This is achieved by asking the supervisor or manager to review the subordinates work in specific areas such as:

1. Quantity of work produced.
2. Quality of work produced.
3. General level of technical knowledge.
4. Knowledge of the job (now being done).
5. Relationships with:

   (a) Subordinates.
   (b) Fellow workers.
   (c) Superiors.

6. Degree of co-operation with others.
7. Enthusiasm.
8. Dependability.
9. Adaptability.
10. Initiative displayed.
11. Organizing ability.
12. Willingness to take responsibility.
13. Leadership qualities.
14. Attitude to safety.
15. Oral and written communication.
16. Suitability for promotion.

(In addition the appraiser might be asked to give an overall report on the employee, plus any training needs.)

We then assess each of the headings in our rating system under a 'scale'. The simplest scale is:

1	2	3
GOOD	SATISFACTORY	POOR

or

ABOVE AVERAGE	AVERAGE	BELOW AVERAGE

We call these 'three-point' scales.

Other scales include The 'four-point':

1	2	3	4
OUTSTANDING	USUALLY GOOD	COULD DO BETTER	NEEDS CONSIDERABLE IMPROVEMENT

The 'five-point' scale is very popular, and here are four variations of it.

1	2	3	4	5
EXCELLENT	GOOD	SATISFACTORY	POOR	VERY POOR
EXCELLENT	VERY GOOD	GOOD	FAIR	INDIFFERENT
VERY HIGH STANDARD	ABOVE STANDARD	MEETS REQUIRED STANDARD	BELOW STANDARD	UNSATISFACTORY
MUCH ABOVE AVERAGE	ABOVE AVERAGE	AVERAGE	BELOW AVERAGE	MUCH BELOW AVERAGE

A sixth point is sometimes added signifying that the appraiser has not known the employee long enough to be assessed properly; or the employee has only been in the post a short time. Below is an example of a five-point scheme for a worker with this additional point:

1	2	3	4	5	6
SUPERLATIVE	SUPERIOR	EXPERIENCED	QUALIFIED	STARTER	NOT ENOUGH KNOWLEDGE TO ASSESS

14.3.4 Problems with rating systems

A mere description of some 'excellent, good, average, etc.' rating system for a given number of qualities does not present a clear, significant and useful picture of employee appraisal. In addition a further problem is that without adequate training and guidance, supervisors and managers may mis-assess employees in one of the following ways.

Averaging.   This is where the appraiser rates too many employees in the 'average' or middle category. True, there *could* be forces composed of workers all of whom are average, but in reality virtually every work group has workers 'above average', or better; 'below average' or worse.

Over-rating.   This is where the appraiser rates all employees in *higher* grades than they should be (while differentiating between different employees).

Under-rating.   This is the opposite of over-rating. Under-rating is where the supervisor consistently marks all employees in lower grades than they should be.

Prejudice/bias.   The appraiser may be prejudiced, or biased, for or against particular employees. Perhaps the appraiser went to the same school or was in the same sports team. He or she *must* therefore be good. This situation is often called the 'halo effect'.

Other problems include:

Scales not universal.   It would probably not be possible to use the same set of qualities for operators and clerks; for junior and senior staff, etc.

Misinterpretation of terms.   Terms such as 'initiative' and 'enthusiasm' need clearly defining so that all appraisers interpret them consistently.

Recent behaviour. The *recent* behaviour of an employee might well be in the appraiser's mind when the assessment is made.

14.3.5 Forced choice rating systems

One way of trying to overcome some of the problems outlined above is to expand the 'excellent, very good, good', etc. categories into a series of statements, one of which the appraiser must tick. For example, under the heading 'Relationship with fellow workers' the appraiser could be asked to select one of the following.

(a) Exceptionally good team worker; always gains respect of others.
(b) A good team worker; gets on well with others.
(c) Fair team worker; does not stand out from average.
(d) Slow to mix, indifferent; sometimes the odd person out; not able to get on with others too well.
(e) Thinks only of him/herself; causes friction and difficulties in the group.

As must be obvious, this is a five-point scale in disguise. The 'forced choice' element is there to encourage the appraiser to think more carefully about the person being assessed, before being committed to any particular assessment point.

14.3.6 Appraisal review forms

To get away from this 'scientific' or quasi-statistical approach, some organizations prefer to prepare appraisal review forms which can be a mixture of ratings, essay, free-ranging views. The format can vary widely. Many forms are divided into sections, with guidelines to aid thought, with adequate space for comments. Stress is usually laid on:

1. Strengths and weaknesses.
2. Performance in appraisal period.
3. Notable successes and failures.
4. Career development suggestions including training or transfer.
5. Potential for promotion.

It should be noted that, in compliance with the Data Protection Act 1984, any personnel records held in a computerized system must be available for inspection by the individual who is the subject of that data.

14.4 APPRAISAL INTERVIEWS

It would seem very odd, perhaps even absurd, if students took examinations and were never told the results;[1] did homework or projects which, though carefully marked by

---

[1] However, there are some examinations where students are told merely that they have passed or failed with no precise indication of how they have done. Students often remark on this.

the lecturer, were never returned, nor discussed with the student. Similarly it would seem odd to carry out appraisals in secret, never to reveal how people were doing to themselves. Most people in fact clearly like to know exactly what there superiors think of them.

Re-reading the purposes of appraisal in Section 14.1 of this chapter should reveal the fact that many of the purposes listed there could not be achieved without some discussion of the appraisal findings. Nevertheless there are organizations which do carry out appraisals and either keep the results completely secret, or only reveal them in the barest outline, or discuss them in very general terms.

To make the best use of the appraisal system, management will want to find out what is wrong with say induction training, or administrative procedures, as well as how Mr Robinson needs developing, or retraining. This can only be done with a well thought out and prepared appraisal interview system.

14.4.1   Who interviews?

An interesting question is: who should conduct the appraisal interview? There are organizations that believe in the 'grandfather' system. Here, the actual interview is carried out by the employee's superior's immediate superior. Thus if an operator's appraisal form is completed by a foreman, the operator would be interviewed by the departmental manager; if a clerk is appraised by the office manager, the interview carried out by the chief executive officer, or company secretary.

There are occasions when this could be highly desirable—a new supervisor faced with appraisals for the first time soon after promotion, for example. Appraisals by 'grandfathers' may also result in an improvement in communications between different grades. However, in other organizations the immediate superior not only appraises, but carries out the appraisal interview (though in consultation with others before the interview takes place).

14.4.2   Interview strategies

There are only three interview strategies which have any relevance to appraisal interviewing, and of these only the last is the most appropriate for nearly every occasion.

Tell and sell

As the name implies the interviewer adopts the strategy of a salesperson and tries by *persuasion* to convince the employee that the appraisal is fair; that the employee can and must change in various ways; and to agree to the training/retraining/transfer, etc., that are recommended. It implies that the initiative is taken by the interviewer, not only at the outset, but virtually throughout. In effect, we have just one-way commnication, which we have seen is far less effective than two-way communication. Tell and sell would only be acceptable as a strategy, if—and only if—the joint problem solving method—mentioned below—fails because the interviewee is unwilling or incapable of responding and playing a full part in the interview (for example, people with a low IQ or low-comprehension level).

Tell and listen

Here again, the interviewer takes the initiative, lays down the objectives of the interview, goes through the ratings, then invites comment. But is it better to tell someone they have a particular problem, or help them to identify their own problem? Is it better to suggest a training course to an employee and await a (possibly tentative or half-hearted) reaction, or encourage a suggestion from the interviewee? (Reminiscent of a mother spoon-feeding a child now well able to eat its own meals.)

Joint problem-solving

This represents a considerable shift in emphasis from the first two methods. Here the interviewer does everything possible to encourage employees to assess themselves, admit their own problems, suggest their own solutions, set their own goals for future work performance, commit themselves to changes in work practice.

A major problem is that such interviews take time, need preparation, and the supervisor or manager interviewing needs some prior training. But, after all, we are considering an interaction between superiors and subordinates using the social skills supervisors and managers should have, or be developing. Joint appraisal reviews should therefore be within the capability of every supervisor.

14.4.3 Preparing for the interview

The appraiser will need to be prepared for the interview. The interviewer will need:

1. A copy of the job *description*[2] (and to read it).
2. A statement of performance, *appraisal form or rating sheet.*
3. The employee's file with general background notes (home background, etc.). Details of personality/temperament, etc.

With this information, the interviewer can prepare an 'agenda' for the interview, which will be a list of points to be discussed at some time during the proceedings. (A rigid order of items would be against the spirit of the more 'free-wheeling' joint appraisal/problem-solving interview.)

---

[2] The implication here is that having a job description is an essential ingredient of a really efficient appraisal system. Even if a carefully researched and written description has not been prepared, an appraiser should have a clear idea of what the appraisee's job is.

14.4.4 Aims of the appraisal interview

The aims of the appraisal interview are mainly those expressed in paragraph 14.1 applicable to the whole process of appraisal, but specifically the interviewer should:

1. Discuss the employee's job performance in the last period (3, 6 or 12 months).
2. Obtain acceptance from the employee that the assessment is correct and fair. (If necessary to revise the assessment if the interview reveals mistakes made at the time of appraisal.)
3. Attempt to get an understanding of the employee's problems, and difficulties in the work environment.
4. Motivate the employee to co-operate in helping to highlight strengths—which can be built upon—and weaknesses—which need correcting.
5. Reach agreement on action to be taken by the employee to improve job performance, and action to be taken by the interviewer to assist the employee in meeting his/her side of the bargain.

Note here, especially, that the end result of the interview could well be a 'deal', bargain or contract between the interviewer and employee. In return for an employee undertaking to undergo a training course at a local college, he/she may be offered:

1. Time off for study prior to exams.
2. A promise of a merit increment on passing.
3. A promise of transfer to other work.

14.4.5 Interview tactics

Whatever preparations the interviewer makes, whatever plans he formulates, he must be prepared to be infinitely flexible, to explore some side paths, not be tied down to a rigid format. This said, a few important points should be borne in mind.

Introduction

After putting the employee at ease, explain the purpose of the interview—to *discuss* the employee's progress—a good way to start is to go over the job description with the employee. (The interviewer might even find the job has changed since the job description was drawn up!)

A discussion on the nature of the job, the tasks, duties and responsibilities will naturally give opportunities to slide over into talking about the present level of success the employee is achieving in the job. A few questions should help:

'I see you are now responsible for machine maintenance in your section. What problems has that brought you?'

And later:

'In what way, then, do you think you've improved the general standard of maintenance?'

The body of the interview

When the interviewer has succeeded in starting a useful dialogue with the employee, every encouragement should be given to self-criticism on the part of the employee. Self-criticism is always more acceptable, and can lead to changes in attitudes and behaviour, than criticism from someone else.

The emphasis now shifts to self-help: the interviewer helps the employee to formulate his or her *own* solutions to his or her shortcomings, and to make positive suggestions. The ideal situation to aim for is the arrival at a mutually acceptable solution. The person interviewed must feel (after the interview was over) that there had been adequate opportunities to put forward any points in mind; that the views expressed would be considered, and, if appropriate, acted upon.

Frequent summaries of what the employee has said serve to clarify the position in the interviewer's mind, and make the interviewee feel a real, two-way communication system is in operation.

Conclusion

At the end of the interview, the interviewer should sum up the whole discussion, and restate any decisions, commitments, agreements or recommendations that have been made, so that there is *full* understanding about the future action or plans of both parties.

After the interview

After the appraisal interview is over, *without delay* (while all is fresh in the interviewer's mind), notes on the following points should be written up:

1. Changes of view on the original assessment after the interview, by the interviewer.
2. What shortcomings or weaknesses were discussed; and with what result.
3. What plans for the future were agreed.
4. What help the employee needs; and what was promised at the interview.

14.4.6 General comments on appraisal interviews

We have seen, in general, that the role of the interviewer is to encourage the employee to talk, to be self-critical and to propose solutions to overcoming weaknesses. It is fairly clear that just to do this exercise, once a year and no more, is not going to be very successful. Really successful and useful appraisals—even if they are annual—will be made much easier by frequent contact, a stable, long-term relationship between managers and managed.

Such a relationship can be cemented and maintained if the supervisor/manager regularly 'counsels' staff (see Chapter 19). We should not forget that counselling and formal appraisal are close relatives, and have much in common with each other. Subordinates who are in regular contact with their superiors, are being regularly counselled and will accept the joint problem-solving appraisal review quite naturally.

As well as revealing weaknesses in the employee, the appraisal interview may bring into the open problems connected with the supervision, or organization not previously recognized.

It should be noted that an appraisal system and interviews carried out under such a system are covered by the Sex Discrimination Act 1975 and the Race Relations Act 1976. Performance appraisal schemes should be reviewed periodically, to confirm they conform to equal opportunity criteria.

Finally, appraisal interview reports must be *used*, that is, not just filed away for posterity. Action to be taken; and information from them can be immediately retrieved and considered when considering promotions or transfer.

14.5   MANAGEMENT BY OBJECTIVES

A rather different approach (and one which became very popular in the early '70s) is the 'management by objectives' approach. The essence of management by objectives (generally called MBO, sometimes M by O, and occasionally even MbO[3]) is simple.

It will be recalled that in McGregor's Theory 'Y', he points out that people will exercise self-direction and self-control in the service of objectives to which they are committed: and commitment to objectives is a result of the rewards associated with their achievement. The advocates of management by objectives/results would support this view.

The essence of MBO, as we will call it from now on, is that instead of telling people exactly how to do their work—they have plenty of freedom in that—all managers do is to give their subordinates definite tasks or assignments, and targets, goals or objectives to reach. In fact, in more refined versions of the idea, the subordinate is involved with fixing the goals in the first place, the idea being (following McGregor) that people involved with fixing goals will have a greater motivation in trying to achieve them.

The supervisor now has a clear-cut model or set of standards with which to judge employees: employees' progress and accomplishments are measured by what they achieve, not by what they are, or by their ability to carry out instructions to the letter.

---

[3] At least one writer, Herbert Hicks, uses the term 'management by results', which throws emphasis on the end product rather than the starting point.

14.5.1 Aims of MBO

The major aims of MBO seem to be:

1. To identify the goals, aims, objectives of the organization.
2. To attempt to achieve the defined goals by giving individuals, managers, supervisors and others sub-goals or targets related to the major goals.
3. To make assessments (continuously rather then on comparatively rare occasions, e.g. annually) of the degree of achievement of goals or targets set. Thus the accent is on performance not personality.
4. To give advice, if requested or it seems necessary, to subordinates to help keep them on the right track. A fair degree of security should be given and subordinates should not be left in ignorance of their performance.

Of course, to encourage and to motivate managers and others to accept the targets they are set, the need for participation in fixing targets is stressed by some MBO enthusiasts. On the whole, though, the feeling is that such goals/targets are more or less fixed in advance by top management. There might be room to modify the *detail*, but not the basic policy, objectives, goals. Peter Drucker in *The Practice of Management*[4] goes so far to say that in deciding upon objectives, higher management should have the power to approve or disapprove of them (the implications being: what is not approved of, will not be adopted).

14.5.2 The MBO programme and the individual

The MBO programme has then, for the individual, several elements:

1. Target setting in consultation with/under the control of superiors.
2. Being left to work out his or her own salvation, but with help and assistance (ideally) being available. Frequent information is given on how commitments, targets and goals are being met.
3. Being given the opportunity at fairly frequent, periodic reviews or appraisals to discuss progress. Being assessed on performance, not personality.

14.5.3 Some problems of MBO

There is no doubt that MBO has achieved its successes. In fact, sales staff have been working to targets for a very long time. Many very large organizations have implemented MBO, if not in its 'pure' form, widely and with presumably satisfactory results. Some managers have reported to me that they feel more secure in knowing what is expected of them and, therefore, they can operate more effectively, but others have drawn attention to problems associated with MBO.

---

[4] Mercury Books, 1961.

1. MBO is time consuming to implement and needs the whole management's involvement from the top downward.
2. Considerable training is required (with expensive consultants hired from outside the organization) in teaching staff an appreciation of MBO and its implementation.
3. Considerable and costly and monitoring systems need to be introduced to collect all the facts and data required. (In one instance, a departmental manager claimed he spent over two-thirds of his working month in preparing, reviewing and commenting on statistics and other control information.)
4. There is a possibility that an individual may accept targets too difficult to achieve, because he does not want to lose face at a meeting, or maybe just for a quiet life.
5. The wrong targets may be selected.
6. Managers/supervisors may ignore anything not on their 'MBO lists', and give less attention to valuable parts of the manager's job such as counselling or some safety requirements.
7. People may feel 'guilty' if they fail to reach targets, even if there are valid and acceptable reasons why the targets were not attained.
8. The whole process can become ritualized and so bound up with administrative procedures that the flexibility needed to cope with emergencies might be lacking: changing objectives quickly could be difficult.

There is much to be said for MBO, an appraisal system which is simple to appreciate. If a total system is used, all major parts of the organization will be regularly scrutinized. On the other hand, if we have just another control system in disguise, then the chances of long-term success must be questioned.

14.6   RESEARCH INTO PERFORMANCE APPRAISAL

Considerable research has been done into whether or not performance appraisal and specific schemes of appraisal are effective. Whilst it is not within the scope of this book to examine such research in detail, it is interesting to note that many writers have questioned the value of performance appraisal—particularly when conducted once a year. Some American conclusions are of interest.[5]

1. Coaching (i.e. giving feedback to employees on their progress and performance) should be an on-going, not an annual, activity.
2. Criticism of past performance can have a negative effect on future effort.
3. Praise for good past performance has little effect one way or the other.
4. Performance is best when specific goals are established, and employees are involved in the setting of such goals.

---

[5] H.H. Meyer, E. Kay and J.R.P. French, 'Split Roles in Performance Appraisal', *Harvard Business Review* Jan/Feb. 1965, Vol. 43, No. 1, pp. 123–9.

The message here is to think of the annual appraisal as the day in the year when objectives and strategies for the coming twelve months are set; to think of coaching as what the supervisor does during the other 220 or so days in the year to help each of his team meet those objectives.

SUMMARY

1.   Appraisal (or performance appraisal) is that process during which the progress, performance and sometimes personality of an employee is assessed.

2.   Appraisal can be for a specific purpose—when considering promotion, etc.—or can be used to monitor performance on a regular, structured basis.

3.   Appraisal is part of the 'control' system of the organization.

4.   Appraisal assists in:

   (a) Determining if employees are properly employed.
   (b) Identifying potential.
   (c) Determining future employment.
   (d) Identifying outstandingly good or bad pieces of work over a given period.
   (e) Encouraging employees.
   (f) Record keeping.
   (g) Determining merit (pay) increases.

5.   There are different methods of appraising:

   (a) Descriptive essays (subjective, not consistent).
   (b) Ranking/grading systems.
   (c) Rating systems (three-five-seven-point scales).

   The major problems with the last, very popular system include:

   (i)   Averaging (scoring towards the average too often).
   (ii) Over- or under-rating (scoring too high/low).
   (iii) Prejudice or bias for or against the employee being assessed.
   (iv) Scales not applicable to all employees.
   (v)   Misinterpretation of terms.
   (vi) Recent behaviour may influence assessment.

6.   An alternative possibility is forced choice rating systems where the brief categories are expanded into longer statements, so precise that a definite choice has to be made.

7.   A further variation is to use a prepared appraisal review form, a mixture of the formal and informal, structured and unstructured. Such forms concentrate on a review of performance, strengths and weaknesses, notable performances, career development and promotion potential.

8.   As a back-up to the written assessment, it is of great advantage to interview the employee being assessed. Advantages are:

    (a) The employee learns how he or she has done.
    (b) Training needs are identified.
    (c) Organizational inadequacies are revealed.

9.   In many organizations the immediate boss or supervisor interviews: in others the 'grandfather' system prevails where the employee is interviewed by the boss's boss.

10.   Three interview strategies can be adopted:

    (a) *Tell and sell.* Here the interviewer persuades the employee to accept the assessment, and to take what action to improve himself is necessary. (This is not two-way communication and is not likely to be acceptable to most employees.)
    (b) *Tell and listen.* The interviewer takes the initiative, reports the assessment and with suggestions, then invites a response from the employee. (This strategy has an element of two-way communication but does not help materially in getting the employee to be self-reliant and self-motivated.)
    (c) *Joint problem-solving.* A total attempt throughout to maintain a two-way flow of ideas and suggestions. The emphasis is on the employee appreciating his or her own shortcomings and providing his or her own answers to problems.

11.   Before carrying out a joint problem-solving appraisal interview, preparation should include reading the job description, all the written assessments, and the employee's personal file.

12.   The interviewer then prepares an 'agenda' for the interview, bearing in mind the need to be infinitely flexible during the interview.

13.   The aims of the interview include discussing the employee's job performance, and the accuracy of the assessment; trying to motivate the employee to improve or change attitudes, and agreeing on any action to be taken by either side to aid such improvement.

14.   The beginning of the interview concentrates on building support, perhaps by going through the job description. Detailed discussion of the tasks can

        lead to self-evaluation on the employee's part, plus, with encouragement from the interviewer, positive suggestions for improvement.

15.   Frequent summaries of what the employee has said aid clarification, and a final summary of all that has been agreed is important and vital.

16.   After the interview, the interviewer should make detailed notes of all aspects of the proceedings.

17.   A follow up after a suitable time is important.

18.   Management by objectives (MBO) is a variation of the appraisal system. Here standards of performance are laid down in advance (usually agreed upon by the employee as being reasonable and attainable), the actual performance is recorded, so that the appraisal is made on the basis of the *results* rather than on the personality of the employee.

19.   MBO aims to see the individual tasks, objectives and goals of individual employees fit in with the total, overall objectives of the organization.

20.   In practice, it has been found considerable training is needed; monitoring systems are considerable and costly; the administrative work is large and time consuming. Other problems involve employees accepting the unattainable, the wrong targets being selected, and MBO becoming so important that other vital aspects of supervision and management are overlooked.

REVIEW QUESTIONS

1.   Define 'appraisal'.

2.   Besides dealing with performance over a period, what other aspects of the employee's work are assisted by appraisal?

3.   Describe the different methods of appraisal, noting advantages and disadvantages.

4.   Why is it important that employees should learn about any assessment made of them?

5.   There are three strategies that an interviewer might adopt in an appraisal. What are they? Which kind is to be preferred, and why?

6.   What preparations does an interviewer need to make before the interview?

7.   What is the purpose of *summaries* during the appraisal interview?

8.   What is management by objectives? How does appraisal fit into such a system?

9.   Do you think appraisal systems are necessary at all? Give reasons for your answer.

DISCUSSION TOPICS

1.   Discuss the view that 'everyone has a right to know how he's getting on at work'.

2.   There is some evidence to suggest that supervisors are reluctant to appraise others because they do not like playing God. Discuss.

3.   Discuss what it would feel like to have to explain to someone who believed he was doing well, that in fact his performance was far from satisfactory. Contrast this with explaining to someone how well he has done.

4.   Ascertain the different appraisal systems used by the employers of the students in the class. Take two of them and discuss them from the point of view of:

(a) What *type* of appraisal system is it.
(b) How difficult—or otherwise—is it to run.
(c) How effective the scheme is.

For full-time students, discuss the appraisal systems used in school/college, such as assignments, homework, tutorial, etc.

ASSIGNMENTS

A14.1   For course members whose firms run appraisal schemes: research into the schemes; produce folders with examples of forms, rating sheets, etc., plus a factual description of how the scheme operates.

A14.2   For course members whose firms do not (as far as is known) run appraisal schemes, devise a suitable scheme for their department (or the whole organization if this is not too large task), and draft a suitable appraisal form.

A14.3   Based on the previous work, prepare a report, addressed to your training officer, *either* commenting on your organization's present scheme, with recommendations for improvements, *or* recommending the introduction of an appraisal system, putting forward your suggestions.

Case studies

A14.4   Mr Wesley Hound, Managing Director of Volatile Oils Ltd, called a meeting of his senior sales executives. At the end of a long, inspiring address on the progress of the company which had just 'struck it rich' in the North Sea, he pointed out that production would be trebled over the next five years.

'As a start,' he told the assembled managers, 'we've got to increase our sales next year by 25%. I want every executive here to go away determined that his division is going to hit the new quota.

'As you know, my policy is to delegate, and I shall leave you to work out how you sort things out in your areas, and I want you all back here next Wednesday when you can tell me exactly what your propose to do. By the way, you can tell your sales representatives that we are considering revising sales commission rates upwards, and you can mention possible redundancies in the sales force if sales don't go up.

'Have you any questions?'

Not a single question was forthcoming and in silence the managers trooped out to the car park.

(a)   Does Mr Hound believe in management by objectives?
(b)   Evaluate the way he went about setting the objectives.
(c)   If you had been one of the managers at the meeting how would you deal with the matter when you called a meeting of your own sales staff?

A14.5   Robert Williams had much to tell Gillian when he returned home. 'I've had a queer sort of interview, today,' he said, 'with old Parker. He said it was an "appraisal" interview, and I wasn't sure what he meant at the time. I'm still not all that sure now,' he added.

In response to Gillian's questioning Robert related how he had seen Mr Parker that morning. Mr Parker smiled at Robert and said as he had been at Acme now for six months it was time for an 'appraisal' chat. Parker looked at a large form on his desk and began to tell Robert his overall progress had been good, he seemed to be on top of his job; but there were some problems which seemed to have come to light.

It seemed that there had been some queries from the auditors on the accounts which Robert had controlled, minor discrepancies on the whole including many arithmetical errors. While his enthusiasm for the work could not be faulted, the report had pointed out Robert had not yet had complete success in motivating his own small section, and his personal relationship with them could be improved.

'I think you need more accountancy training,' Parker had told him, 'we did talk about this at the interview, so I'm having you enrolled—paid for by the company, mind—on the Advanced Accounts course starting at the local university in October. In the meantime, this communication business with your staff needs dealing with: I've seen just the course for you, it is taking place in Devon over the Easter weekend. Do you a world of good, lad!'

Mr Parker returned to the form. 'You've done well in "willingness to take responsibility". I liked the way you coped last week with that emergency when Mr Figgures was taken ill. Now, how would you feel about taking on more staff?'

Robert had replied by pointing out that he had just been criticized about his handling of staff, agreed he'd been somewhat distant and aloof with his section. Parker had smiled again. 'Glad to hear you're aware of it, lad. However, I see you'd like a challenge. Good. I can't promise anything at the moment, but later we'll see about it.'

'Well now,' Parker had concluded, 'We've had our little chat, and you know where you stand. I shall be seeing you again in six months time to see how you are progressing then.'

Gillian leaned forward anxiously and stared at Robert. 'I thought we were going to Yorkshire for Easter,' she said.

(a) How did Mr Parker handle the appraisal interview? How successful was he, and why?
(b) What kind of strategy did Mr Parker adopt? What other approach might have been more effective?
(c) Did Mr Parker resolve the problems he identified with Robert's performance, relating to accounts and the handling of staff?
(d) Did Mr Parker use the interview constructively to identify future objectives, and build on Robert's strengths?
(e) Did the interview achieve anything for Robert?

15
Training

15.1 DEFINITION

In discussing what training is, some writers try to draw a distinction between 'education' and 'training'. The Oxford English Dictionary's definition of 'education' includes the words: 'systematic instruction, schooling or *training*'; and conversely, in defining 'training', includes: 'to *educate,* rear, bring up'! Perhaps the distinction is a class one—such as the distinction between 'wages' and 'salaries': managers are perhaps 'educated'[1] and workers 'trained'! It would seem one way to settle the matter is to look at how people use the two terms in an industrial or commercial context.

Often we find that education is used to describe what goes on in schools and colleges of a formal, theoretical or academic nature (though even here we do talk about industrial training at a technical college), or where the learning is directed to wider aspects of study, than the work of the organization to which the employee belongs. On the other hand, training is very often used to describe the imparting of specific, practical skills, often manual, to employees, which will be relevant to the employee's present or next immediate job. Regrettably, there are organizations whose view of training is even more restricted than this last definition. Despite remarkable training resources, they limit training to impart the minimum amount of knowledge and skill to cover just their present needs. Such training can be said to be 'job-centred'.

Precise distinctions are not important for us, and in this section we shall give a wide interpretation to the word training. Certainly we do not want to view it in the light of the narrow, immediate situation. True, we need to impart to employees the knowledge and skills they need in order to do their jobs effectively now, but it would be an unusual organization that did not change in some way sooner or later. We, indeed, live in a world of accelerating change. Hardly has one marvel passed into everyday use, before two other ones (both, 'new, improved' versions) arrive to challenge it. In our grandfather's time a machine might last 50 years: nowadays a computer and (particularly) its associated programmes can well become obsolete in less than five years.

---

[1] Sometimes 'developed'!

Employees must be trained, therefore, to acquire new skills to cope with new technology, and probably even more important how to cope with change itself, be more adaptable, acquire attitudes sympathetic to change. Such training could be part theoretical as well as practical, deal with the implications and potential of new equipment, be more 'education' than training. Such training can be said to be 'future-centred'.

Finally, as we have seen, a way of tackling the problem of motivation is to try to cater for people's needs and to ensure that their goals equate as far as possible with those of the organization. Individuals in general, and our work force will not be any different, have aims and needs to develop abilities and talents, will want to satisfy their needs for self-realization. If we can help them to develop whatever potential they may have, we shall hopefully make them more contented on the one hand; and have a use for their newly acquired skills in the future. Such training can be said to be 'individual-centred'.

15.2 HISTORICAL BACKGROUND

Training is not a modern invention; the handing down of important skills like the use of tools and implements such as knives, ropes and nets has been necessary for the survival of the family, tribe and ultimately the human race. The accent, then, right from the distant past has been on the handing down of manual-based skills, and the apprenticeship idea is far older than the recent, formal western system.

The general pattern was then a simple one: young boys (not girls) were taken on by master craftsmen, were taught the use of equipment and other techniques. In Josiah Wedgwood's time (1744), for example, the master was required to teach him the 'art, mistery, occupation or employment of throwing and handling'. This talk of 'art' and 'misteries' dates back to the Middle Ages and even earlier. Additionally, there were other less manual-skill based areas of training: in religion (particularly for those becoming priests), in the service of the law or the stable bureaucracies. (Indeed in ancient China to be able to write beautiful poems was a good recommendation for high public office.)

However, it was easy (and common) for apprentices (and other trainees) to be used as cheap labour, being exploited, and used as a general runabout for his master, not always being taught the 'arts' and 'misteries' very well. We can say about this training activity that:

1. It was not organized nor consistent from trainee to trainee; nor were there any usual or national standards of attainment agreed upon or recognized by groups of masters.
2. Such training was specific to a trade or profession (job-orientated).
3. Very few people in the whole population actually received such training.

A significant impetus for change came with the Industrial Revolution. There was a need for an ever increasing number of skilled people to undertake the complex tasks of running and maintaining machinery. Engineering, as opposed to construction or coopering, became the prime industry for apprenticeships. To help in their training

'Mechanics Institutes', or 'Night Schools' were founded, the forerunners of today's Technical Colleges and Polytechnics.

Further very significant changes in training took place as a result of the two world wars. In each war, large numbers of men were taken from factories to serve in the armed forces; and the vacant jobs in the factories were filled by other people, some men but mostly women. Lessons were learned in the training of large numbers of people to reach certain minimum standards in a short time. An example can be seen by the emergence of the 'Training Within Industry' movement in the USA during the Second World War, based on lessons expounded by Charles Allan in his book *The Instructor, the Man, and the Job*, published in 1919, and based on First World War training experience.

Additionally, the Second World War provided opportunities for psychologists to research into training theories and methods (as well as into selection) used in the armed services, particularly in the USA.

After the Second World War interest in training did not cease, and government working parties on Technical and Higher Education looked at providing what we know as polytechnics. However, concern about the numbers of qualified engineers needed annually and the urgency for change was lacking, until the government and industry realized that other countries were overtaking us economically, at the end of the '50s.

15.3 DEVELOPMENTS IN TRAINING SINCE 1960

At the beginning of the 1960s, the view gained ground in political and some industrial circles that one of the factors contributing to our comparatively poor economic performance *vis-à-vis* other advanced nations was inadequate training. A White Paper identified the need to strengthen links between industry, government and education services; to establish minimum training standards; and to share the cost of training broadly across different industrial sectors.

The initial result was the Industrial Training Act of 1964. This set up some 30 Industrial Training Boards (ITBs), each comprising of equal numbers of employers and trade unionists, plus an independent chairman, and a few academics. Each ITB had an advisory role; as well as checking standards of training given, and awarding certificates. They also placed levies on employers, creating funds to carry out the advisory role, and make grants available to firms carrying out training approved of (in advance) by the boards.

By 1970 it had become apparent that the Act was not achieving all its objectives; and many problems had emerged. There were too many boards, each with different and seemingly random methods of establishing levy rates; and levels of grant. Many boards had spent disproportional sums on administration. A lot of training had occurred, but too often in a random manner.

On the positive side, there had ben a vast increase in training, and the appointment of a considerable number of training officers. Training had now become a significant part of the work of personnel departments; and there were now some really well researched training programmes.

15.3.1 More recent developments

A further White Paper in 1972, and the Employment and Training Act 1973 made some alterations to the original scheme, but it was not until 1981 that government decided major changes were needed. The annual cost of the ITBs had reached £48m. The consequence was all but seven boards (plus one for Agriculture) were abolished. The ones that were left were to be run by the industries concerned on a voluntary basis.

Instead the accent was put on the Manpower Services Commission, later the Training Agency. The Agency has considerable involvement in work-related non-advanced further education. In addition there was to be a restructuring of adult training, with the offering of training in skills needed by employers; and skills needed in growth business areas.

Recessions led to labour-shedding; and further training/retraining programmes, the former for the unemployed, and the latter more aimed at those made redundant.

Supervisors and managers at all levels are increasingly being involved nowadays with 'work experience' training for school and college-based students, as well as assisting those on government schemes who are work-based during their training. There is no doubt that in a formal way through one or other of these schemes, or as a result of informal contacts between schools, colleges and employers, more and more young people are being given a much better appreciation of the world of work before taking up permanent employment. (See also the remarks below on GNVQs.)

Changes still more recent in the training scene have included the establishment of regional Training and Enterprise Councils (TECs)—also known as Local Enterprise Councils in Scotland. These are mostly composed of local industrialists with the remit to promote (with government funding) the developments of vocational education and training.

In addition the National Council for Vocational Qualifications (NCVQ) has been set up to simplify the vocational qualification system; and to ensure its relevance at work. For example, the Management Charter Initiative issued a series of standards in 1992 at both (NVQ) levels 3 and 4. Awarding bodies such as NEBSM and ISM then used these standards as a basis for their NVQ programmes for supervisors and managers. (Revised standards have now been issued: see Chapter 29).

A further development has been the introduction of GNVQs (General National Vocational Qualifications) aimed primarily at those still in full-time education, covering programmes in a wide variety of employment areas (e.g. business studies, art and design, agriculture, engineering and the built environment). Work experience is widely used as a means of providing candidates with assessment opportunities.

More details of the Council's Work, and NVQ management standards, are given in Unit VI (see pages 545–643), but we might note here two aims of NCVQ. The first was by the end of 1992 to establish equivalence between academic and vocational qualifications (e.g. a GNVQ at level 3 is now equivalent to two 'A' levels); and the second to ensure that by the end of 1995, at least half the employed workforce were to be aiming for new or updated qualifications within the NVQ framework.

NVQs are normally assessed in the workplace, and this has already had profound implications for training departments (as those assessing NVQs have themselves to be qualified to do so); and to those managers and supervisors involved in such assessments.

15.3.2 Employers' training duties

Despite this legislation, an employee generally has no legal right to demand to be trained for a particular job, unless his contract so specifies (e.g. apprentices). However, we shall see training in health and safety and associated regulations is mandatory, and this could imply job training.

As regards day-release, off-the-job training, this is not generally obligatory on employers, compared with other European countries where all workers under 18 are entitled to day release. (*All* employees can claim day release in Sweden.)

Obviously, it should not require legislation to encourage organizations to train. Most jobs are skilled, and the job holder needs training so that he can efficiently fulfil the tasks assigned to him. It is part of good management that such training is provided and is as effective as possible, to the benefit both of the employee and the organization for which he works.

15.4   AN ORGANIZATION'S TRAINING PLAN

A whole series of different activities must be completed before an organization's training policy and plans can be carried out. We will consider the activities in turn. (Fig. 15.1 sets out these steps in diagrammatic form, showing both the inputs and outputs of the training plans.)

Stage 1: identification of knowledge and skills required

Identification of the knowledge and skills required in each job is a vital first step. Without it, training (while not necessarily inefficient) will be haphazard and incomplete.

Although a laborious exercise, job analysis (which we encountered in Chapter 12) has a bonus, as once done, it can be used in training. If we take a job description, and add to it columns which enable us to list the knowledge and skills required for each task, then we shall have a document which we can further use in Stage 2.

Stage 2: identification of present levels of knowledge and skill

In this stage, we identify the present levels of knowledge and skills possessed by each job holder. With newly recruited staff, we should have a good idea of their abilities and skills, but those staff in employment for some time need further

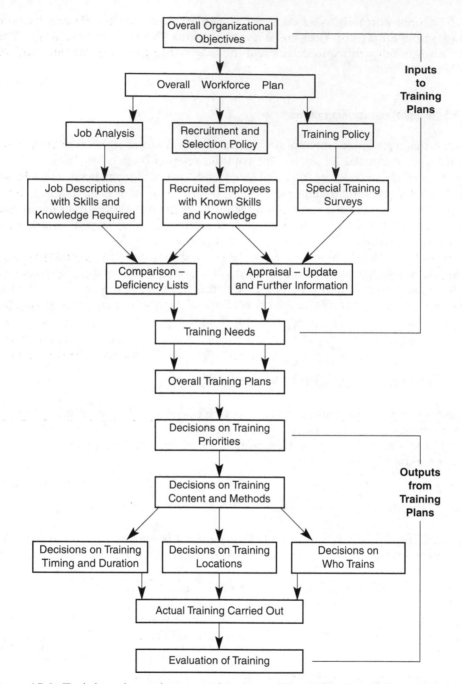

Figure 15.1 Training plans—inputs and outputs. The evaluation of the training will almost certainly affect training policy; training survey objectives; decisions on training content and methods, timing, duration and selection of trainee. The complex set of feedback loops which would signify this monitoring effect is omitted from the diagram. to avoid making it unwieldy.

investigation. This could be done, if we have failed to operate an appraisal system in the past, as a crash programme of special training surveys, for example. Where appraisal systems exist, there will be a useful guide to present levels of knowledge and skill .

Stage 3: identification of training needs

We must now compare the original job descriptions with the information we now have on the present levels of knowledge and skills possessed by each job holder.

For each individual we shall obtain from this comparison a deficiency list. The total of all the deficiency lists, i.e. for the whole workforce, represents the immediate 'job-centred' training required. (See Fig. 15.2 for an extract of a composite form, incorporating the job description, knowledge and skills required, and training needs for a particular job holder.)

Requests for training (particularly for training not specifically related to the present job) from managers, supervisors or from other staff can reveal 'individual-centred' training needs.

Finally the overall manpower plan is used to help estimate what vacancies could arise in the future; appraisals give information about transferable or promotable employees. Such information can be used to plan for training to be undertaken *in advance* of moving to the next job. This covers 'future-centred' training needs.

EXPLODING CHEMICAL COMPANY
TRAINING NEEDS ANALYSIS BY TASKS

JOB: Security Manager
JOB HOLDER: A Marks

Sheet 6 of 12

Task No.	Task	Knowledge Required	Has Yes/No	Skill Required	Has Yes/No	Training Need
16	To prepare annual estimates of all expenditures on security, staff wages, installations, vehicles and equipment	Budgeting to company requirements	YES	Ability to calculate	YES	
17	To investigate and report on all fires on company premises	Fire-fighting procedures Basic knowledge of causes of fires Insurance procedures	YES	Ability to observe record and analyse information	YES	
				Ability to liaise with Fire Brigade personnel and insurance assessors	YES	
			NOT ADEQUATE	Ability to write clear, concise and accurate reports	NOT ADEQUATE	Insurance law and procedures Report writing
18	To keep maintained all fire-fighting apparatus on the company inventory	Familiarity with all types of fire-fighting apparatus and the testing thereof	YES	Ability to check and test fire-fighting apparatus	YES	

Figure 15.2 Training needs analysis (extract).

Stage 4: preparing the overall plan

All the different training needs are collated from the sources described above, and priorities established in relation to the urgency of the training—e.g. safety training in places with radiation hazards might be a 'top' priority—and the training funds available.

Stage 5: making training decisions

Decisions will need to be taken on syllabuses and training methods, length and duration of training, training locations and who actually carries out the training.

Stage 6: evaluation

After training is complete, we need a system of evaluation. Lessons learned about the training methods, improvements needed in a course, or content will then be fed back into the training plan.

15.4.1   Location of training

There are three possibilities:

1.   All training done within the organization.
2.   Some training internal, some external.
3.   All training external (to include courses run by outside bodies, even if on company's premises).

15.4.2   Internal organization

If any training at all is done by the organization, decisions will have to be made about location and equipping of classrooms, training workshops, training record system and the selection and training of training officers and instructors.

15.5   TRAINING METHODS

At this point it will be necessary to define the difference between on-the-job and off-the-job training. Training methods chosen in any particular instance do partly depend upon training location.

15.5.1   On-the-job training

This is training which takes place in the normal work place of the job holder, using the equipment, tools, etc., which the employee would normally use. Where a job consists of a variety of tasks, the trainee is given instruction in a simple task, then as this is mastered, increasingly challenging assignments until he is capable of carrying out the job unsupervised.

15.5.2   Off-the-job training

Off-the-job training (or 'vestibule' training as it is called in the USA) takes place away from the normal work place. Typical locations on the firm's premises are: special training areas for operatives equipped with basic workshop equipment; an office, training department classrooms; the boardroom. Sometimes such training takes place away from the company in hotels, colleges, residential training establishments.

15.5.3   Methods available

A wide variety of training methods is in current use, but of these the ones the supervisor or manager is likely to encounter most are:

Demonstrations

Here the demonstrator/trainer lifts the veil on the 'mysteries' of some skill: shows exactly *how* to tie a knot, use a tool, kick a football. This is very suitable for helping to teach manual skills, and sports coaches have successfully used this method for teaching games skills for well over 100 years, drill instruction in the armed services for much longer.

Skill practice

Under the supervision of the trainer, the employee attempts to perform a skill which has been described or shown to him. The footballer attempts the kick he has been shown; the recruit tries to perform the drill movement just demonstrated.

Simulation

This can be very similar to skill practice. A pilot can train in a flight simulator, reproducing an aircraft cockpit, or a trainee in a department store put into a mock department. It is important that the essential aspects (key points) of the task being learned are reproduced as accurately as possible in the simulated environment. (Some of the later methods mentioned are less precise stimulations, but do not attempt as 'pure' simulation does to prepare a trainee for a total situation.)

Lectures and talks

The trainer delivers a prepared address on a given topic—e.g. the Health and Safety at Work etc. Act. Where a group of trainees need precise information on a new topic which is capable of a reasonably simple presentation, the lecture or talk is very suitable. But, and there is a *big* 'but', the lecture needs careful planning, must follow a simple logical sequence, should be delivered in terms readily understood by the trainees and be backed up by visual aids (see below), and ideally last half an hour at the most. Particularly with trainees not used to note-taking, prepared hand-outs summarizing the key points of the lecture should be circulated. (See also Unit VI, 'Briefing a Work Group'; 'Making a Presentation'.)

Discussions

To be effective, discussions need an informal chairman or leader, and as well as meetings called to discuss a topic. Many lectures provide either for discussion periods at pre-set times, or even in some cases lecturers are prepared to discuss any point made, at any time. Discussions help people to feel involved, and motivating people to learn is as important as motivating them to work.

Tutorials

A method used frequently in colleges and other institutes of further and higher education. The student/trainee produces work which is discussed, often on a one-to-one basis, with the tutor/trainer.

Audio-visual aids

Covers a wide variety of aids—films, film-strips, audio cassettes, video recordings (of TV programmes), and live TV programmes.

Case studies

As will be seen from the shorter case studies at the end of chapters, the aim of this method is to provide trainees with a varying amount of background information (financial, organizational, personal, etc.) and to ask trainees to evaluate the general situation and/or to decide how they would tackle the problems outlined.

An ideal training method for teaching trainees the skills of analysing, and decision-making. All trainees can be involved. If in teams, chairman training, note-taking practice, reporting experience are useful by-products.

Role-playing exercises

These are both extensions of the case study method, and skill practice. Besides analysing a situation, participants are required to act out an attempt at a solution— interviewing for selection, negotiating with union representatives etc. A problem here is that setting up exercises can be administratively time consuming, and not all trainees may have a chance to participate as actors.

'In-tray' exercises

As well as background information about the organization and the supposed personality that the trainees assume, a large number of letters, memos, documents have to be assimilated and evaluated in a short time. Trainees may also have to make decisions, reply to letters or draw up reports. Very useful for teaching skills such as delegating or assessing priorities.

Business games

Probably the most ambitious training method. An attempt is made to stimulate a whole business, and trainees given large amounts of information on financial, production, marketing, industrial relations and legal aspects of the organization. Both broad policy decisions and detailed decisions on particular problems (how much material to order next week from which supplier) are required from trainees, who can play parts such as managing director, purchasing manager, sales director, etc. If a game can be computer based and details of decisions fed into a pre-programmed computer, the implications of the decisions can be reported quickly to the participants. Different groups operating simultaneously can lend a competitive flavour to the proceedings; and two years' trading decisions made in a few hours.

Projects

As will be seen from Unit Vl, projects involve investigation, evaluation and problem solving. For a supervisory or management course, projects can be seen as a valuable back-up to training, providing trainees with a challenge, the need to use newly acquired skills, facts, attitudes or concepts, the motivation to consolidate learning.

There will be times when several different methods are used together, or in succession, and trainers will want to take as much care in preparing a suitable sequence of methods as a good cook would in preparing a suitable balanced menu for a memorable meal.

15.6   THE TRAINING OFFICER

From what we have seen, the work of the training officer is managerial in content; planning, organizing, creating motivating, communicating and controlling. Whatever training officers used to do, the modern training officer is an organizer, initiator and controller of training, rather than a mere instructor. The administration of training is now extremely complex, and, in addition, more and more of the training of officer's time is being taken up with liaison with outside bodies—colleges, trade associations, TECs, other trainers, plus the vast quantity of paperwork. So, while the responsibility for organizing and providing expert advice on training, administrative support and general help is clearly included in the duties of the training officer, the carrying out of the actual training is being delegated increasingly to line managers, supervisors, technical staff or to outside trainers in colleges, institutes of higher education, universities; or to consultants.

15.7   THE SUPERVISOR'S ROLE IN TRAINING

The supervisor has, it is now quite clear, a very important training role. We can identify two, separate elements in such a role.

The training plan

Supervisors will contribute to the overall training plan. The appraisals made, the training needs identified, the recommendations put forward on particular individuals, all will be of considerable use. In addition, supervisors may be entirely responsible for the on-the-job training in their department. They will then need to do on a smaller scale, all the initial work we have already considered on an organization-wide scale: analysing the work done in their section, assessing the knowledge and abilities of their work force to do the work, and creating a deficiency list as a basis for training. They will also have, as does the overall plan, to consider future-centred training which could involve training charge-hands for permanent supervision, or junior staff to move on to more complicated work. The supervisors' more intimate knowledge of their own work force can ensure that they will be aware of training needs, and of its timing. In addition, supervisors may be called up to do some, or all of the training in their departments.

The supervisor as instructor

Before starting on any training or instructing, the supervisor must consider what learning, as opposed to teaching, is. Many books on the principles of learning exist, but for our purpose we may define learning rather generally as a 'change in behaviour made as a result of some past experiences'. This allows for a very wide interpretation: the motorist who ignores a 'give way' sign, is summoned and fined, learns the hard way not to repeat his error; the housewife learns where the best shopping bargains are to be found and shops there.

But this is an unreliable way of learning: the motorist who ignores road signs may never be caught and punished, but precisely directed training by a driving instructor could eliminate the driver's faults quite quickly. It is the same with on-the-job training: if we leave it to someone—perhaps the supervisor or perhaps an experienced worker—to show the new entrant what to do when the trainee can be fitted in (or even leave the new entrant to cope unsupervised to pick up the job), then this training period will lead to less than satisfactory results, and:

1. Could be lengthy.
2. Could lead to a high rate of initial errors.
3. Could lead to learning unsafe, less efficient ways of doing jobs.
4. Could even discourage the new entrant, lower his enthusiasm and motivation generally.

Precisely directed training is obviously needed. The major elements of such training are set out in the next section.

15.7.1 Teaching a skill

The teaching of a skill can be best considered in a series of steps. *AT ALL TIMES DURING THE PROCESS THE INSTRUCTOR SHOULD BE PREPARED TO ANSWER QUESTIONS.*

Step 1: self-preparation

The instructor must be thoroughly prepared, and will need to know:

1.1 Who is to be trained.
1.2 What the training objectives are (i.e. what is to be achieved during the training period).
1.3 What time is available for training.

The instructor will need to analyse and break down the job into separate elements by:

1.4 Listing each distinct operation, or movement.
1.5 Highlighting key points, i.e. anything special at any stage: checking that a nut is tightened, before going on to the next stage. (For example, safety checks are always key points.)

(The Work Study Department could help with such an analysis.)
There will be a need to have ready:

1.6   Tools, safety equipment and clothing, training manuals, materials, etc.
1.7   A training prompt sheet (a list of the points to cover in correct, logical order).

Step 2: prepare the trainee

The instructor is now prepared. Next he or she must ensure the trainee is ready to start learning by:

2.1   Putting the trainee in a relaxed frame of mind and adopting a friendly, confidence-building approach.
2.2   Stating very clearly exactly what the trainee is to learn.
2.3   Finding out how much (if any) knowledge of the task to be taught the trainee already has.

Step 3: demonstrate the skill

The instructor now demonstrates the task or skill to be taught:

3.1   Going through the task at normal speed, once.
3.2   Going through the task, stage by stage, slowly, making sure that the trainee knows exactly what is being done and why.
3.3   Repeating 3.2 as often as the situation demands.
3.4   The instructor could finish the demonstration by performing the task at normal speed several times.

Step 4: putting the trainee to practise the skill

The instructor now gets the trainee to try the task for himself, ensuring that:

4.1   The task is done slowly.
4.2   The trainee explains what is done verbally as the task is performed.
4.3   Any errors are picked up, pointed out to the trainee, and corrected.
4.4   Subsequent tries are done close to normal speed.

Step 5: putting the trainee to the normal task

The instructor, when satisfied that Step 4 is complete, puts the trainee to start the normal task. The instructor must ensure that:

5.1   The trainee is not set too high a target to start with.
5.2   There is someone (if the instructor is not available) around to advise and assist the trainee, at all times.

5.3   The work is checked frequently, at the start, and followed up at subsequent intervals.

5.4   Praise is given when a satisfactory standard is attained.

15.7.2   Learning curves

Experience has shown that learning does not take place at a steady rate. Initially progress might be very slow, with sudden improvements, perhaps at totally unexpected times, followed by little further progress for some considerable period. There will be a final levelling off when without enormous effort little further progress will be achieved. (Consider the Olympic athlete who trains and improves performance largely in relation to the effort put into training. However, when having reached a certain level, to clip a further tenth of a second off the record may need a considerably greater effort than the clipping of the previous tenth of a second did.)

If we are able to plot learning progress on a graph, we obtain what is called a learning curve, an example of which is shown as Fig. 15.3.

15.8   EVALUATION

Training itself needs to be reviewed from time to time, just as any other procedure. Some organizations have continuous assessment of training in general, others prefer to look at specific training—e.g. induction, or supervisory, at regular intervals. Whatever else evaluation takes into account, there are two basic questions to ask:

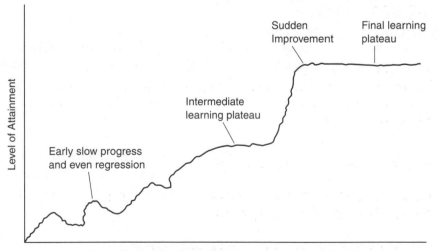

Figure 15.3 Imaginary learning curve.

1. Is the training cost effective, that is, does the organization get value for the money spent? If the organization is more efficient, more profitable, safer, at the end of the day, the answer is probably 'yes'. However, this is a question for the training specialists and the accountants to decide upon.
2. Has it done what was required? If it can be shown that training objectives have been attained, and appropriate numbers of trained workers made available when required, then it has passed this test. The supervisor will be able to judge from the section's point of view the skill levels achieved by the trainees, against the needs of the work; and the time taken to carry out the training.

Admittedly some training is difficult to evaluate precisely—because the changes in behaviour noticed *could* perhaps have had causes other than the specific training course. Some training may not be immediately relevant, as we have seen. The benefits of a long-term external management course may be difficult to quantify in the short run.

We can, however, finally try to establish after training:

1. The extra knowledge and skills gained by trainees.
2. How relevant to the immediate job, next immediate job or personal development the training was.
3. How efficient and relevant were the training methods and techniques used by instructors.

For such methods and techniques to be effective, long experience on both the Youth Training Scheme and skills associated with NVQ/GNVQ programmes has shown that:

1. Trainees must be motivated to learn. Not only must they understand why the training is necessary, but what benefits accrue for them.
2. Training must give personal satisfaction, and this will happen more often when the training meets the trainee's needs.
3. Clearly defined objectives and targets must be set for trainees.
4. Trainees will succeed more often where they are involved with the training (i.e. 'action centred' or 'discovery learning') than if they are merely passive spectators.

SUMMARY

1.   It is difficult sometimes to distinguish between education and training, and a way of dealing with this problem is to use the term training to cover all aspects of instruction at work, and in outside, educational establishments.

2.   Training can be of three kinds:

   (a) Relevant to the immediate job—job centred.
   (b) Relevant to next immediate (or subsequent) job or jobs—i.e. future centred.

      (c) Relevant to the individual employee's general, personal development —individual centred.

3.   Training in skills, and the imparting of knowledge has a long history, and apprenticeship schemes have played a significant role in the history of training. However, until more recent developments, training was:

      (a) Not organized and inconsistent.
      (b) Not governed by universal/national standards of attainment.
      (c) Specific to certain trades.
      (d) Restricted to a few.

4.   The two world wars, with the need for large number of workers/members of the armed forces to learn new skills quickly, heightened interest in training and training methods.

5.   The government felt by the '60s that a nationwide review of training was required. This review stressed the need for relating training to actual needs; for the establishment of minimum training standards; for the cost of training to be more fairly distributed.

6.   The Industrial Training Act 1964 attempted to provide for these needs by setting up the Industrial Training Boards to provide courses, make recommendations on training and training methods, set training standards and place training levies on firms, paying grants for training done.

7.   In some ways the work of the boards initially attracted criticism but many good results were achieved, notably a large increase in the number of training officers appointed, and amounts of training done, good training research and a definite improvement in the quality of training.

8.   Amendments were made to the levy-grant scheme in 1973, with firms considered to be providing adequate training excused from the levy.

9.   Employers' (legal) training duties are almost non-existent, except for the provisions of the Health and Safety at Work etc. Act. However it would be foolish and self-defeating for an organization not to train.

10.   An organization's training plan is constructed from a systemized investigation into training needs and includes the identification of the skills and knowledge required to the labour force, the identification of the skills and knowledge already possessed, the difference between the two providing a picture of the job-centred training needs. Future-centred and individual-centred needs also have to be established (through appraisal and other methods).

11. Training needs now identified are incorporated into the training plan, and decisions taken on priorities, location, duration, timing and content of training.

12. All training needs to be evaluated.

13. Training methods include: demonstrations, skill practice, simulation, lectures and talks, lecture/discussions, tutorials, audio-visual aids, case studies, role-playing exercises, 'in-tray' exercises, business games and projects.

14. The work of the training officer is becoming more administrative, advisory, and as a back-up to training, rather than being mostly instruction. The actual training is increasingly being delegated to outside agencies, lecturers, technical staff, line managers and supervisors.

15. The supervisor's role in training is to help prepare the organizational training programme by providing the information on training needs of all kinds in the department. The supervisor may have to prepare a departmental training plan; and almost certainly will have to give on-the-job training.

16. Instruction should be systematic, not haphazard, directed not casual. The supervisor as instructor should:

    (a) Carry out self-preparation.
    (b) Prepare the trainee.
    (c) Demonstrate the skill.
    (d) Put the trainee to practise the skill.
    (e) Put the trainee to the normal task, following up as required.

17. Learning does not always proceed at a steady rate, but rather in a series of improvements followed by little further progress (and in early stages even a falling back). Plotting progress of this nature on a graph produces what is called a learning curve.

18. Training needs to be evaluated to check if it is cost effective; relevant and adequate.

REVIEW QUESTIONS

1. Distinguish between 'job-centred' training and 'individual-centred' training.

2. What are the reasons why training in earlier centuries was not always relevant or effective?

3.   Explain in detail the various stages leading up to the preparation of a company overall training plan.

4.   Describe what decisions have to be taken when the training plan is translated into actual training. Could you envisage not all the plan being put into effect? Why?

5.   Why does training need to be evaluated?

6.   Which training methods would be suitable for (and give reasons for your choice) the following situations:

   (a) On-the-job training of a newly joined school leaver in wiring a three-pin plug to an electric drill.
   (b) Training supervisors to give five-minute talks.
   (c) Training staff generally in health and safety at work.

7.   Why is the supervisor's role in training important?

8.   Outline the basic steps in on-the-job training of skills.

9.   What is a learning curve?

DISCUSSION TOPICS

1.   'Training is an unnecessary luxury. All you need to do is to engage properly qualified people to fill the jobs in your organization, and the need to train disappears.' Discuss, and try and estimate the short-term and long-term consequences of putting such a view into practice.

2.   'Only trained instructors should be allowed to instruct, therefore supervisors should not attempt to instruct, but leave it to training officers and the like.' Examine the implications of this statement.

3.   Comment on the view that to put a newcomer with an experienced worker, as a sort of assistant for a week or two is as good a way of training as any other.

4.   Which training methods do you find most useful/least useful on your present course, why?

ASSIGNMENTS

Case studies

A15.1   Peter Smart, training officer of DISCO CDs, walked into the personnel manager's office with a confident step. Smart was a go-ahead young man, newly qualified and anxious to make his mark in the world quickly. His first major task on joining the company was to look at various aspects of training.

Firstly, he had tackled induction training. He had read a great many books on personnel matters during his degree course, and had selected a wide variety of ideas from them—tours of the factory, visits to retail record outlets, a report on the organization. Smart had built up what he considered to be the 'perfect' course, lasting a week.

Secondly, a close look at supervisory training showed that too many supervisors were sent on rather general courses, such as the Diploma in Management Studies, or the NEBSM Certificate in Supervisory Management. Such courses covered far too many irrelevant 'background' topics like work study and costing, and not enough training on specific relevant matters like the maintenance of fire-extinguishers, or acquiring up-to-date technical information, in leadership, communication and production control. Peter picked out the outstanding supervisors and arranged for them to go on special short courses run by a training firm who advertised regularly in a training journal.

Mr Stone, the personnel manager, stared at Peter disapprovingly: 'I've been getting complaints about you from Webster, the works manager,' he said, 'about your training schemes. That last batch of new entrants were mostly cleaners and labourers, and having to write reports on the factory site so annoyed three of them, they've already left. Another thing, Webster says the supervisors coming back from your special courses are filled with enthusiasm but within a few weeks, they're jogging along again, just as they were before. Goodness knows how much all this is costing us!'

Stone told Peter he was reconsidering the whole training programme.

(a)   With regard to Peter Smart, describe and comment on his attitude to training.
(b)   Where did Peter go wrong in his training programmes?
(c)   If you were Mr Stone, how would you go about trying to put things right?

A15.2   Mary Merrit was sobbing in Mrs Gentle's office and was obviously distressed. Mrs Gentle had only recently interviewed and appointed Mary to the knitwear department of the store, and felt she had a good future with the company. Determined to get to the bottom of the matter, eventually she persuaded Mary to explain what happened.

'It was ever so nice yesterday when you showed us in your office how to fill in the sales tickets, and do all the paperwork, and I think I got hold of it all so quickly. But today's been so dreadful. When I got here this morning your assistant took me to see the floor manager, who took me over to the men's jumpers. The woman there was very old, and didn't like it when the man told her to show me what to do.'

Mary continued with her explanation. 'I didn't mind the customers, they're nice, but she kept looking at me, and never told me much. Eventually at half-past twelve she went away, and another girl told me I should go and get my lunch. I got back at two and a man I didn't know came over to me and told me I was half an hour late, and if I wanted to stay I'd better pull my socks up. He said I wasn't wrapping up the jumpers properly and snatched one off me just as I was serving a customer. He wrapped it up, handed it to the customer and said, "Now, that's how I want the job doing in future".'

'Ten minutes later, he came back and said I wasn't doing the job properly and I'd better report to personnel as I was no use to him.'

(a) Why did the departmental manager get cross with Mary? What is his attitude to training?
(b) Comment on the general training system at the store.
(c) What steps have to be taken to sort out the training problems at the store? If you were the general manager what would you do?

16
Parting Company with the Employee

Very great attention has been paid in recent years to recruitment and selection, sadly less (except when the law steps in) to the other end of an employee's association with the organization for which he or she has worked, be it resignation, retirement, redundancy, or dismissal. It is, of course, inevitable that a work organization that lasts any length of time will not only need to recruit people, but will lose them in one way or other. The 'in-out' situation over a period is what is called 'labour turnover' or LTO for short, and while Chapter 17 looks at LTO more from a statistical viewpoint, here attention is paid to the 'human' aspects of such problems.

16.1   RESIGNATION

By resignation we mean the *voluntary* termination of the contract of employment by the employee: the employee makes the decision to leave.

Normally this would be done by the employee giving notice, that by handing in a written letter addressed to the company (or a particular executive) stating the wish to leave by a certain date. (The amount of notice to be given is usually known from the company-employee agreement, but normally is a *minimum* of one week.) Often, but not always, the supervisor is the first to learn of the impending resignation, but whatever the order of things a major problem is what should be done by the company in general, and indeed by the supervisor in particular with resignations.

16.1.1   Exit interviews

Organizations may well have an established practice of exit interviews, undertaken by personnel or senior executive staff. The aims of such interviews are to find out the *real* reason why the employee is leaving, and to leave as good an impression of the organization as possible with the future ex-employee. Now, such interviews are not only worth while but absolutely essential. Surely, if something *is* wrong with the organization, wrong enough to cause people to leave, we should:

1. Want to know about it.
2. Want to see if we can do something about it.

It is indeed possible that a resignation is a 'cry for help', and not really intended to be pursued through to the end (rather like that of 'attempted suicides' who carefully arrange to be rescued before it is too late), but rather to draw attention to some major problem or grievance. An exit interview could result in a withdrawn resignation, a happier employee and a better organization.

Where such exit interviews are *not* company practice, supervisors should consider conducting their own. Whoever does interview will find that resignations fall into two categories: avoidable and unavoidable.

16.1.2   Avoidable resignations

These are resignations which could possibly have been avoided if the conditions of employment in some particular aspect were different. It also implies that the organization has the ability to modify the condition complained of. Pay, or lack of it, could be an example, as most organizations have *some* control over their pay policies but, of course, in times of incomes restraint, or rigid incomes policy resignations over pay become *unavoidable* if nothing can be done within the given government ground rules.

Avoidable resignations are usually due to dissatisfaction or problems with one of the following:

1. Pay.
2. Hours of work.
3. Physical working conditions (heat, smell, noise, posture).
4. Job dissatisfaction.
5. Relationship with:

   (a) Fellow workers.
   (b) Supervisors/managers.

6. Personal advancement.
7. Failure to achieve the same work standards as others (i.e. criticism, spoken or implied from work group about job performance).

Exit interviews can reveal one or more of these reasons, and if possible remedial action of some kind should be taken. In a sense, exit interviews are appraisal interviews of the organization by the individual worker. Perhaps with exit interviews, they can be turned to everyone's advantage by making them joint problem-solving appraisals.

Supervisors should in any event report any information, opinions and comments made either at exit interviews or informally, by employees leaving for what could be considered as avoidable reasons.

16.1.3 Unavoidable resignations

Unavoidable resignations are those where the reason for resignation lies outside the organization's present ability to modify the situation. Typical resignations under this category are those due to:

1. Public (or personal) transport difficulties. (Especially where there has been a reduction in bus services in some country districts.)
2. Housing difficulties, particularly if rented accommodation is not suitable.
3. Illness, accident, general health.
4. Marriage, and the spouse's job is elsewhere.
5. Pregnancy, and the woman does not intend to return to work.
6. Intended move of spouse to job elsewhere.
7. Death.

(Note: to combat transport difficulties some organizations are now providing free or subsidized transport to outlying areas.)

With unavoidable resignations, again, details of the reasons of leaving should be made known to personnel, or senior management.

16.2 RETIREMENT

Retirement is when an employee leaves the organization because he or she reaches a certain age; and not because of resignation, redundancy or dismissal. State retirement pensions are (at the time of going to press) paid to men reaching 65, and women reaching 60, provided they give up working. Additionally, company pension schemes often come into operation at these minimum age limits, although there are some organizations with earlier retirement provisions—the armed services, for example.

Behind the notion of retirement are two common assumptions: first, that the older a person becomes, the less able and efficient he or she is likely to be as an employee; and second, a person reaching the appropriate age should no longer work (giving way to a younger person to take the vacant job) but spend the rest of what years of life remain, in an environment where no work is expected of the former employee. Both assumptions are challengeable: there are employees perfectly capable, and able to carry on working well into their 70s (as there are others who would be better retired in their 50s), and who want to work; there are those to whom work, and all its social relationships are preferable to retirement. To be 'put out to grass' with a reduced income is to them a frightening prospect.

Retirement, if not properly planned and prepared for, can be a fundamental shock to the system. Consider an active, experienced worker, perhaps with a company for 40 years, who suddenly one Friday afternoon receives his parting gifts with no more requirement for his services the following week, services which could be useful to the organization. Even worse perhaps is the supervisor or manager with no more decisions to make or people to manage. It is not surprising that retirement without preparation has been a great disappointment to many.

16.2.1 Counselling for retirement

Certainly employees would benefit from pre-retirement counselling. Advice on such matters as leisure opportunities, retirement finances, and voluntary activities can be very valuable. Additionally, a knowledge of all the help available from the social services, and possibly a meeting with the officials concerned would be a positive contribution from the company.

Such detailed knowledge is unlikely to be available to the supervisor and this aspect of welfare is probably best dealt with by the personnel department.

16.2.2 Phased retirement

An interesting development in recent years has been 'phased' retirement. An organization adopting such a policy might have a scheme such as in Table 16.1.

Table 16.1 A suggested scheme for phased retirement

Age reached	Days worked per week	Comments
60	5	Pre-retirement counselling during the year
61	4 ⎫	Still paid full wage, attends company sponsored courses
62	3 ⎬	
63	2 ⎫	Successor begins to take over most of the decisions
64	1 ⎬	
65	Retires	Final counselling

As the free time slowly increases, opportunities are provided to undertake leisure activities and acquire new interests. Successors can see the 'light in the tunnel', get practice in taking over, but are able to refer to the job holder during the long handover period.

(Some schemes reduce hours worked rather than days and others reduce over much shorter periods than five years.)

16.2.3 Flexible retirement

Some organizations allow employment to continue after normal retiring age, either for a series of fixed, renewable periods, or indefinitely. It is true problems can arise from this method even when it is in everyone's interests including the employee's. As an alternative, employees can be retained on a 'consultancy basis', if at supervisory/managerial level, or as a 'relief'; or some firms even have special workshops reserved for employees past normal retiring age, with flexible hours and light work.

16.2.4 Keeping in contact

Many retired employees will want to keep in contact with their previous employers. Some supervisors do not welcome ex-employees wandering in and spending time talking to their former colleagues, but it is important for both past and present employees to keep in touch, and morale can be improved by keeping friendly contacts. In any event, the usual trend is for fairly frequent visits at first, but after a while new interests will take over, and visits become rarer.

Many firms put on special, formal activities for their pensioners: lunches, visits to see new buildings, machinery, social facilities. Supervisors would do well to support them, and be seen to be involved.

16.2.5 House visits

House visits to retired employees are usually welcome. While the supervisor does this in his spare time, and receives no pay for his time, there are hidden benefits, and the respect of his work team may well be one of them.

16.3 REDUNDANCY

Coldly stated in legal language redundancy is defined as occurring when an employee is dismissed and when the whole or main reason for his dismissal is that his employer's needs for employees to do work of a particular kind have diminished or ceased. For those (including myself) who have at some time or other been made redundant, behind such legal language lies a whole area of emotional and psychological problems; and may involve financial difficulties as well.

There is little that the average manager or supervisor can do about the circumstances leading to redundancy—economic decline, changes in demand, strikes at suppliers, mergers, amalgamations or take-overs, 're-organization', closing down of a factory in one area, perhaps to move elsewhere; or even the dramatic, total failure of a company—but if there are employees who are being made redundant they should be treated with special consideration. It is *this* aspect which is considered in this chapter: the legal aspects (including the company's *legal* obligations) are discussed in Chapter 23.

16.3.1 Telling the employee

Nothing could be worse than an official letter delivered at home through the post, or a typed note in a wage packet on a Friday afternoon baldly stating out of the blue that an employee's services are no longer required: he or she is redundant. Of course, in many cases there can be advance warning. In the case of multiple redundancy (ten or more employees in, or covered by, recognized unions) notice to the unions, Department of Employment (and by implication to the employees) must be given well in advance of the effective date of redundancy. But here a cliff-hanging, nerve-wracking period will elapse while negotiations and a certain amount of bargaining go on until the details are finalized.

Whatever the formal arrangements, it is important wherever possible that the line manager or supervisor should tell the employees concerned individually. Personally, I found this duty the most difficult to perform and I was grateful for the support of my immediate superior.

Firstly, the *reasons* for the need for redundancy have to be explained: a fall in orders, change in product and so on. Secondly, why this particular employee is one of those being made redundant. Try and salvage the employee's pride by expressing your sincere regret at losing someone who has given valuable service. Stress that it is the situation not the *work record* which is responsible.

The news will be shattering,[1] whether expected or not, and it is best to allow the employee to cease work, and go home immediately if the employee so wishes, but not to banish him or her from the premises forthwith. Further counselling on his position will be necessary, and an offer made to discuss any problems at an early (fixed) date before notice expires. Try to make him feel that he has some support, something to hang on to, for the immediate future.

16.3.2   The work group

Even if only one or two of the work group are made redundant, morale can suffer alarmingly. 'Who's next for the chop?' will be a question in everyone's mind. Workers may leave for more secure employment elsewhere, or try to preserve the situation by going slow and spinning the work out, so a backlog builds up. Besides official union reaction, workers may hold unofficial meetings or discussions during work time.

The supervisor (and his superiors) must realize that such behaviour is natural and attempts to prevent it with threats, or disciplinary action will in the main be counter productive. The situation will have to be lived with until the period has passed.

16.3.3   Further help to redundant employees

After the initial shock, the employee will probably welcome all the help available. The company might ease any contacts with the Department of Employment, and the social services; and even arrange for interviews on company premises. The supervisor should re-check the provisions of the Employment Protection Act 1975, which gives

---

[1] It is appreciated that in some redundancy situations voluntary redundancies are called for, or employees are invited to opt for 'premature voluntary retirement' (PVR). Some employees may welcome (or even seek) such a course of action, and in those cases, of course, the news is not 'shattering'; there will, however, be some uncertainty and anxiety.

an employee under notice of redundancy the right to time off, with pay, for a reasonable, limited period during working hours to seek employment, or to arrange for appropriate training.

Whatever the legal provisions, the company and the supervisor would be well advised to give the employee as much positive help and encouragement in job seeking as they can, and allow every facility—including enough time off. Simple things, such as help in filling in application forms or drafting letters will assist in alleviating real problems for some.

16.3.4 Procedure agreements

Many organizations have planned in advance, during periods of prosperity, for redundancy by negotiating and signing redundancy agreements with unions, setting out procedures to be followed. Much more can be done in a calm, unhurried and unpressurized environment, rather than in an atmosphere of fear, tension and undoubted aggression when redundancies arise.

Such agreements would cover matters such as length of notice to be given of impending redundancies and methods of selection. While in a sudden, unplanned situation unions would tend to stick by the 'last in/first out' formula, agreements have managed to cope with 'hardship' exceptions, and voluntary redundancy schemes, where employees are invited to make themselves redundant. Other matters covered would be appeals procedures, the level of proposed payments (that is, how much *more* than the legal minimum the company would pay).

16.4 DISMISSAL

Even less than 20 years ago, many managers, foremen and supervisors had the power to dismiss employees who were unsatisfactory in one way or another. Merely to argue with a foreman could result in dismissal, but now the whole question of dismissal is full of pitfalls for the impatient, ill-advised or improvident supervisor—as well as the rest of the management.

An employee is treated as dismissed[2] if the employer:

1. Terminates the employment with notice (dismissal with notice), or without notice (summary dismissal).
2. Does not renew a fixed term contract—that is the kind of contract a football manager might have—after it has expired.
3. Behaves in such a way towards the employee (i.e. virtually forces the employee to resign) so that the employee terminates the contract, with or without notice (constructive dismissal).

[2] Trade Union and Labour Relations Acts 1974–6, see Chapter 23.

The advent of industrial legislation, as the result of changes in government policy, has entailed dismissal being an expensive proposition for an employer, if badly handled. Such considerations have accelerated the shift of power to dismiss from the supervisor or line manager, to the personnel department; to the extent that from merely recording (or later vetting) decisions, the personnel staff now tend to be very much involved in dismissal decisions. Also senior management often wish to be involved.

Supervisors should be fully aware of their company disciplinary rules, which in turn should take account of the ACAS code on disciplinary action, and should ensure that their subordinates are also clear about such rules and procedures. Provision should be made for appeals to a high level against dismissal.

In addition, many more records than previously kept by supervisors or the personnel department are now necessary, and they need to contain details of oral and written warnings which could be used as evidence if a dismissal is taken to a tribunal.

SUMMARY

1. Resignation is when the *employee* decides to terminate the contract. All resignations should be taken seriously and intending leavers should be interviewed (to establish the reasons for leaving) so that in appropriate cases action may be taken to try and persuade the worker to remain.

2. Resignations can be either unavoidable—where the employer can have no effect on the situation—or avoidable.

3. Avoidable resignations (and the reasons for them) should be carefully studied to see if company policies need modification.

4. Retirement is when an employee leaves because of having reached a particular age. Pre-retirement counselling is important, and best left to the personnel department. Keeping in contact with the retired employee serves a valuable function.

5. Redundancy occurs when there is no work for a particular person or group of persons. It is a very dramatic event in a worker's life, and should be handled carefully from the start. Explaining the redundancy *individually* is vital; and later, as much help and encouragement as possible should be given to the redundant employee.

6. Procedure agreements often exist to cover possible redundancies, and also dismissals (where the employer wishes to terminate the contract, with or without notice), and supervisors need to be aware of the details of such agreements.

7.   The power of dismissal (particularly instant dismissal) has tended to shift away from the supervisor or line manager to the personnel department and/or senior management.

REVIEW QUESTIONS

1.   Distinguish between resignation, retirement and redundancy.

2.   What are exit interviews? Why are they necessary?

3.   What points should the supervisor have in mind if any workers are made redundant?

4.   Why has the power to dismiss shifted away from the first-line manager in recent years?

5.   What is a 'procedure agreement' in respect of redundancy or dismissal?

DISCUSSION TOPICS

1.   Is the best person to decide on the dismissal of an unsatisfactory employee: the employee's immediate superior, or a senior manager in the same section, or the personnel manager? Prepare a list of pros and cons for each suggestion.

2.   Who is best suited to conduct an exit interview? The immediate supervisor, another manager or someone from the personnel department? (Prepare a similar set of lists as for the previous question.)

3.   Is 'pre-retirement' provision a benefit:

      (a) To the individual?
      (b) To the organization?

ASSIGNMENTS

A16.1   Students should obtain copies of a procedure agreement *either* to cover dismissal *or* redundancy, and prepare a summary of the agreement in simple language, which would be suitable for issue to the workforce.

Case study

A16.2   Alice Bairstowe is in her 50s. Working on a computer, mostly inputting data in your section of 20 staff, she was once the previous Chairman's secretary. Many years ago she had a nervous breakdown and, when she eventually returned to work, was allocated to you.

    Her work generally is of a poor standard, and her mistakes not only cause you embarrassment, but annoy the rest of the staff, who constantly complain about her. Yesterday, you were told by the Managing Director that business was falling off and four redundancies were being considered, one immediately.

    You walked into the office, announced redundancies were in the pipeline, and that Alice would be the first to go. Amazingly within ten minutes there were protests from members of staff who reported that Alice had gone home in tears.

(a)   What, if anything, have you done wrong? How should you have handled the situation?

(b)   Can you account for the staff's changed attitude to Alice?

(c)   What do you imagine will be the effect on work output in the immediate future?

17
The Rate of Change in the Workforce—
Labour Turnover

17.1 INTRODUCTION AND DEFINITION

This chapter looks at the problem of labour turnover (often shortened to LTO), how different statistical ratios can be calculated, and some idea of the sort of costs which a high labour turnover can attract.

Research into LTO can be traced back to the start of the century, and most of the early work was American. Labour turnover—LTO—is the term most often used to describe the total movement of employees in and out of an organization, during a given period—usually a year. Obviously, as we saw in Chapter 16, some LTO is unavoidable—ill health or death, for example, but the greater proportion is avoidable; for example employees leaving voluntarily. No employer can afford to ignore LTO if he wishes to retain a stable, productive and efficient organization.

Until the oil crises of the '70s, the prevailing unemployment figures since the Second World War were very low and caused high rates of LTO, and even since that time a high mobility of labour has continued in many industries. A high LTO increases the costs of running an organization, and *such costs are normally wholly hidden in any published figures*. It will be useful to see where such costs might be incurred.

To study LTO statistics *is* a useful activity: a figure which is too high or too low is an indicator that something is wrong with an organization; it does not tell us *what* is wrong, but other information (from appraisal or exit interviews, attitude surveys, analysis of other statistics, for example) can help us. So LTO is an extra monitoring device we cannot ignore.

A well-known company with a rubber-producing plant discovered in 1969 that its annual LTO was 2%. This might seem a matter for extreme congratulation, but a moment's reflection reveals the labour force would only turn over *once* in 50 years! Coupled with this, the company discovered that the average age of the 76 operatives and 40 staff was 40 years. The warning signals were there: true there was a stable secure workforce, but one which was ageing, and younger blood was needed before the generation gap and forthcoming retirements became too great a problem.

17.2   LABOUR TURNOVER STATISTICS

An employer's interest in LTO statistics is the separation or wastage rate, i.e. those leaving the firm over a period of time. A standard formula was developed as follows:

FORMULA 1

$$\text{Separation rate} = \frac{\text{Total number of leavers in period}}{\text{Average number of persons employed in this period}} \times 100$$

(This gives a percentage figure)

However, this early, standard form is rather unreliable and misleading—in fact it is now called the '*Crude* LTO Rate', so a second more refined version—called by Americans the 'quit rate', takes into account the unavoidable separations and concentrates *only* on the avoidable ones, thus:

FORMULA 2

$$\text{Quit rate} = \frac{\text{Total number of voluntary leavers in period}}{\text{Average number of persons employed in period (usually 1 year)}} \times 100$$

(This again, gives a percentage figure)

Even so, this second formula is not reliable and still does not tell us much. Neither formula distinguishes between the loss of *newly engaged* workers, and *long-service* workers. Investigations over many years have revealed that the new entrant is more likely to leave than one with a long service. An attempt to improve the statistics further is the stability index:

FORMULA 3

Long-service stability index

$$= \frac{\text{Total number of employees with 1 year's service or more}}{\text{Average number of persons employed at start of period}} \times 100$$

(This is also a percentage figure. We could have indices prepared
for 1, 2, 3 or 5 years, as required)

We can see from this last formula that even if we have a high turnover of short-service employees, we could yet have a relatively stable workforce. Formula 2 might reveal a 20% LTO on 1000 workers: Formula 3 might reveal 950 workers had over one year's service. (The implication is that a few, probably nasty, jobs were filled four times during the year.)

If we wanted to look more closely at this rapid turnover of a few jobs, we would use the following:

FORMULA 4

Fringe turnover rate

$$= \frac{\text{Number of employees joining and leaving within 1 year}}{\text{Average number of employees in one year}} \times 100$$

(If the percentage figure is high, then attention needs to be given to recruitment, selection, induction and training procedures; or possibly working conditions. These are certainly where we would start looking.)

17.2.1 Other statistics

There are other LTO statistics which lay less emphasis on percentage statistics which in any event are only significant if:

1. Several years are available for comparison.
2. The persons doing the comparison know what the averages are for the local area as a whole, the trade or business in the local area, and in other areas.

An interesting one uses a concept from physics, the half-life. (A radio-active element is said to have a half-life of 50 000 years, if after that time half the atoms of a particular lump of it have lost their radioactivity and been changed into another element.)

FORMULA 5

'Half-life' survival index = Time elapsed before a bunch of entrants is reduced by resignation, retirement, redundancy or dismissal to one half its original size.

Thus, if on 1 March, 1990, a total of 50 people started, and we discovered that 25 were still with the organization on 1 March, 2000, then the half-life survival index would be (at least) ten years. This statistic emphasizes the *survival time* rather than the numbers surviving.

We contrast this with a statistical method emphasizing numbers:

FORMULA 6

New starter survival index = Percentage of new employees taken on in a given year still with the firm after 1, 2, 3, etc., years.

17.2.2 Analyses

In addition analyses can be prepared of length of service (by sex, department, age, travelling time, wages, etc.).

Note: All these formulae assume a reasonable (e.g. over 50) number of employees: very small numbers distort the figures.

17.2.3 Records

In order to calculate any or all of these LTO statistics records have to be kept, and the supervisor or manager may well be asked to make various returns to the personnel department, who consolidate the figures and produce the statistics. It will be seen that this figure can be extremely useful, and supervisors should endeavour to see that the information they compile is as accurate as possible.

17.3 CAUSES OF LTO

The causes of LTO are shown below. Many of them were discussed in Chapter 16.

Group A: Discharge

Unsuitable
Result of disciplinary action
Redundant

Group B: Unavoidable

Transport difficulties
Housing difficulties
Illness, accident, general health
Marriage
Pregnancy
Moving house
Death

Group C: Avoidable

Pay
Hours of work
Working conditions poor
Job dissatisfaction
Relationships with others
Better job (lack of promotion opportunities)
Failure to meet standards set
Poor supervision

17.4   GENERAL PATTERNS OF LTO

Research undertaken in 1957[1] showed some general patterns of LTO, which seems to support what common sense would suggest. There are five propositions:

1.   LTO differs for the sexes. In all the factories surveyed, it was higher for *women* of the same age, and length of service.

2.   LTO differs for different age groups. It tends to decrease with age, especially after 30.

3.   LTO differs for workers with different lengths of service. The longer a worker has stayed, the longer the worker is likely to stay. Turnover is therefore highest amongst new comers.

4.   LTO differs with type of work. It tends to be lower for skilled than for unskilled work.

5.   LTO is affected by the number of jobs in the local labour market.

17.5   EFFECTS OF LTO

17.5.1   Costs

The costs of filling the vacancies are large. From our review of recruitment and selection procedures we can see that recruitment is expensive in itself, but there are other major, and hidden costs of employee resignation that the supervisor should be aware of. (Indeed some costs may be virtually impossible to quantify at all.) It is worth remembering that any reduction in LTO can help to reduce costs (or minimize cost increases). A lower LTO may also increase production totals, and more sales could result.

The major cost headings are:

1.   Wages cost of learning. (That is wages not really earned, while the employee is under training.)
2.   Costs of recovering lost productive time:

   (a)   While the job is vacant.
   (b)   While the new employee learns. (Such costs would be incurred in the working of overtime by other employees; redeployment of workers in same or other departments; using 'temps' or sub-contracted workers.)

---

[1] By Dr Hilde Behrend

3. Costs of using people redeployed (under 2) instead of doing own jobs ('opportunity cost').
4. Extra scrap (or office equivalents) produced by learners; and refurbishing checking/repeating required.
5. Extra supervision required:

   (a) To cope with the time that the job is vacant.
   (b) To train the new employee.
   (c) To watch over the new employee, help, assist.

6. Recruitment and selection (as already noted).
7. Training (induction, on and off the job—extra to 5(b)).

17.5.2 Other effects

Once a firm is known to have a high LTO, workers will be less likely to apply for jobs, thus making a serious problem worse. Long-service employees tend to lose heart if they have to train new people continually, only to see them leave again after a while. Production is bound to suffer, tempers rise; there is an atmosphere of frustration. In short: general morale declines.

17.6 POSSIBLE WAYS OF REDUCING LTO

Now we know what LTO is; next, the problem is to try to reduce it, keep it to acceptable levels, bearing in mind (as we have seen) that to eliminate it *entirely* is equally as dangerous as having a high LTO. The essential step is to try to identify the primary cause or causes of LTO in the organization, where LTO is greatest and in which age group, department or trade it constitutes a problem.

17.6.1 Exit interviews

Exit interviews are those interviews which take place when an employee is about to leave an organization. Many organizations—if they ever conduct exit interviews at all—view such interviews as 'fire-fighting' activities, trying to persuade intending leavers to change their minds, sometimes even offering the odd bribe or extra inducement to stay. Alternatively, exit interviews are times when employers make some formal, ritual, goodwill gesture to the departing employee, particularly in cases of long service or retirement.

However, if conducted properly, the exit interview should reveal information about *why* the employee is leaving. Such interviewing is a time when the employer has a unique opportunity of learning a great deal about how employees see the organization. Sadly the chance is often missed. A major difficulty is that people can be reluctant to discuss why they want to go, or the reasons for leaving are so complex and involved that employees are perhaps not really sure themselves *exactly* why they want to leave.

So the exit interview is as much a fact-finding activity as perhaps a persuading or thanking activity. When the facts are established, they need recording and collating in a way which will quickly reveal *trends*. Three employees (even if in different departments) leaving in one week over a bonus scheme, the withdrawal of a local bus service leading to several resignations highlight general trends, rather than just a collection of individual reasons for giving notice. Unique individual reasons can be important, but general trends should act as alarm signals, and attempts at remedial action made.

17.6.2   Avoidable LTO

Where exit interviews reveal avoidable LTO, the next question is what could be done if the organization (or the individual supervisor or manager) is prepared to review the particular problem. Young married women leaving to start families *might* be persuaded to return later if nursery facilities for young children were provided, and those with somewhat older children *might* be encouraged to remain if a 'flexitime' system were introduced. What has to be considered is the size of the problem, the cost of LTO weighed against the cost of any remedial scheme.

Other possibilities are:

1. Pay review—examine the wages to see if they are out of line with local and competing firms. Such a review should include fringe benefits. Is *merit* catered for?
2. Review of working conditions—can improvements be made to the environment: are workplaces unnecessarily dreary, rules too rigid, etc?
3. Job rotation—can work life be made less boring, by giving people regular changes in routine?
4. Job enrichment—can workers be given more responsibility for what they do, make more decisions about their own work?
5. Review welfare services—could an introduction or increase in counselling services help with personal problems and tackle such matters at source, averting an emotional resignation' (which is sometimes a cry for help or of frustration)?
6. Review transport provision—could a free or subsidized service for employees to get to and from work pay for itself in reduced LTO costs?
7. More information—joint consultation—about the organization, its future plans, its present progress.

17.6.3   The supervisor and LTO

The supervisor and line manager both have a special responsibility to keep LTO under review. Not only do they have to minimize its size, by providing the best possible working environment for their staff, but they must also try to identify causes of dissatisfaction.

A considerable debate exists as to which person should carry out exit interviews. Some feel that the personnel department is more neutral, and its staff will get more from a leaver, particularly if his grudge or complaint is against a supervisor or manager. Frank talk will, it is felt, be encouraged. Others, however, feel that the 'man for the job' of exit interviewing is the immediate supervisor or line manager, who will know the leaver more intimately than any other executive; be able to assess the truth of the leaver's assertions.

On balance, the supervisor is the better placed person: if doubt exists, then a *further* interview with personnel could act as a check. The personnel department would however receive information on *every* leaver.

SUMMARY

1.   No employer can ignore the LTO of his organization. It is one (of many) indicators of the health (or otherwise) of the enterprise. In itself, it can be costly.

2.   Either a high or a low LTO figure could be a warning signal.

3.   Useful statistics are:

Formula 1:

Crude LTO
Separation rate
$$= \frac{\text{Total numbers of leavers in period}}{\text{Average number of persons employed in period}} \times 100$$

Formula 2:

Quit Rate
$$= \frac{\text{Total numbers of voluntary leavers in period}}{\text{Average number of persons employed in period}} \times 100$$

Formula 3:

Long-Service Stability Index
$$= \frac{\text{Total number of employees with 1 year's service or more}}{\text{Average number of persons employed at start of period}} \times 100$$

Formula 4:

Fringe Turnover Rate
$$= \frac{\text{Total number of employees joining and leaving within 1 year}}{\text{Average number of employees in one year}} \times 100$$

(All these statistics take different views of the situation. Consult the appropriate part of the text for detailed explanations.)

4.   Further statistics include the 'half-life' survival index—the time elapsed before a group of starters is reduced to half its original number; the 'new starter' survival index—the percentage of new employees remaining after a given time; and detailed analyses of lengths of service.

5.   The *causes* of LTO can be broken down into the major categories of:

    (a) Discharge
    (b) Unavoidable
    (c) Avoidable

    (The latter includes pay and conditions; job dissatisfaction; lack of training/promotion opportunities; poor supervision.)

6.   LTO differs:

    (a) For sexes. Higher for women.
    (b) For age groups. Decreases with age.
    (c) For workers with different lengths of service. Decreases with length of service.
    (d) With type of work. Lower for skilled workers.
    (e) With employment levels.

7.   The *effects* of LTO are increases in the costs of both productive and non-productive areas:

    (a) Learning and training.
    (b) Lost production, or less useful work.
    (c) Increased scrap, refurbishing.
    (d) Redeployment.
    (e) Recruitment/selection.
    (f) Extra supervision required.
    (g) Lowering of morale.

8.   Every effort should be made to contain LTO. Careful monitoring of each separation should be carried out to identify underlying causes, and those causes common to more than one leaver. Exit interviews are a vital part of the monitoring process.

9.   Exit interviews are not just methods of persuading leavers to stay on, or ritual gestures of farewell, but are part of the LTO fact-finding process.

10.   Once the reasons for each-leaver are collated, trends may be revealed (particularly in the 'avoidable' category) to be immediately investigated. Appropriate steps can then be taken (if justified on 'cost-effective' analysis grounds), to improve matters, by general management.

Reviews of pay and conditions, welfare and transport provision; job enrichment and possibly schemes of joint consultation may be ways of overcoming the problem.

11.   The supervisor has special responsibilities in this area: keeping LTO under review, trying to remove, as far as possible, likely causes of dissatisfaction, and conducting exit interviews. The personnel department may carry out supplementary interviews, and will need to collate information on all exit interviews carried out by supervisors and line managers throughout the organization.

REVIEW QUESTIONS

1.   What is meant by 'labour turnover' (LTO)?

2.   If the personnel department reports labour turnover is 1%, and has been around this figure for the last *three* years, would you as Managing Director be:

(a) Very pleased?
(b) Neither pleased nor concerned?
(c) Be concerned?

Give your reasons.

3.   What is the 'Crude LTO' statistical formula? Why is it 'crude'? What is an 'improved' version?

4.   Could you use the formulae given in this chapter with a firm of:

(a) 2000 employees?
(b) 500 employees?
(c) 50 employees?
(d) 5 employees?

(What does the answer tell you about the use of statistics?)

5.   What is needed to calculate any or all of the formulae?

6.   Distinguish between avoidable and unavoidable LTO. List the causes of avoidable LTO.

7.   What are the *effects* of a high LTO in an organization?

8.   What is the first step that might be taken in trying to investigate the problem of a high LTO in an organization?

9.   Suggest *five* ways in which LTO might be reduced.

10.   What are the supervisor's responsibilities in dealing with the whole question of LTO? How does his role in the matter tie in with the responsibilities of the personnel department, and general management?

DISCUSSION TOPICS

1.   'People who leave, are best left to leave. It's no use persuading people to stay, they'll only go later. Thus it's a waste of time interviewing them before they go, except for those who are retiring.' Discuss this point of view. Is it a valid argument? Is it true? What are the implications of holding this view?

2.   Discuss the best way to approach an exit interview. Should you:

   (a) Lecture the employee because he or she wants to leave?
   (b) Plead with him or her to stay?
   (c) Offer an inducement to stay?
   (d) Find out the reasons for wanting to leave?
   (e) Encourage the employee to gossip about workmates?
   (f) Ask for suggestions to improve matters?
   (g) Suggest he or she goes to the personnel department?
   (h) Get the employee to comment on your own complaints against the company?

3.   'Labour turnover remains one of the more important indices of morale available to an organization.'
        Discuss this statement. Besides LTO, what other indications of morale are there?

ASSIGNMENTS

A17.1   Students at work should:

   (a) Estimate the level of LTO in their department (or company as a whole).
   (b) Suggest reasons why it is what it is, high, low or in between.
   (c) Suggest any improvements to the company's employment policies which would improve LTO figures. (Sensible suggestions not 100% wage increases!)

A17.2   Students at college/school should visit the local Job Centre (preferably by appointment with the manager) to discuss the types of jobs which from the Job Centre's point of view have the greatest turnover. Then:

(a)   List the jobs studied in rank order (jobs with the greatest turnover at the top; with the least at the bottom).
(b)   Try to establish the reasons for the findings established under (a).

A17.3   The class should divide into two groups. Group A will decide on a member to play the part of a student who wishes to leave the course. The group will discuss and agree on the reasons (which could be both related and unrelated to the course).

Group B will elect an interviewer to represent the course tutor and plan the form of the interview to try to elicit the reasons for leaving.

The two chosen students then act out the interview, the remaining students should act as observers and comment on the way the interview is held. (Were the real reasons discovered?)

Case study

A17.4   Royal Air Force Jetham is a small but vital link in the country's defence, and is stationed near the borders of Loamshire and Glebe County. About two miles from Jetham, a thriving market town, the RAF station's main task is to service, maintain and promote a home base for their new jet fighter—the Flying Fox.

Squadron Leader Swann took over command of the Base Hangar five months ago. Until this time the staff of 60 in the hangar had been in the control of Wing Commander 'Buster' Smith, DFC and Bar, a Falklands fighter ace, who was greatly admired (even worshipped) by all ranks: now in retirement he lives in Jetham village, and frequently visits the station and the Officers' Mess.

Before Swann took over command, he was interviewed by Smith, and was told how lucky he was to have got this posting. The work was challenging, the aircraft the very latest in technological gadgetry, and the servicing team in Base Hangar were absolutely top-line. Smith had used his (considerable) influence with war-time friends in high places to get together a group of highly qualified, experienced and hard-working NCOs and tradesmen, who worked well with each other, taking a considerable pride in their work. While Swann could, of course, make any changes in working patterns and practices as were appropriate, the Wing Commander suggested that the tried and tested methods of working and duty rotas should be retained. Finally, Smith suggested Swann would do well to have dinner with him the first Friday in each month to talk over any problems he might have; and very often this was the time the Station Commander (Group Captain Ivor Kyte) dropped in for drinks.

On the day he took over Swann ordered all work to cease at noon, assembled the men and addressed them. He told them that he expected them to work as a team, and that he would not tolerate any dissension. He expected the turn-round time for aircraft servicings to be improved on the already quite reasonable figures. This would be done by introducing fundamental changes in working methods. In particular, the regular shift-work patterns would be abolished, and replaced by a much more flexible system which would mean more men working at times of peak demand, and fewer when say only one aircraft was in for servicing. NCOs and tradesmen could be working long hours in bursts, followed by days off. Additionally, to obtain maximum flexibility, the membership of the work groups and servicing teams would be changed periodically. Swann pointed out the change was also necessary to accustom everyone to coping with an emergency or war situation, so that all Hangar staff could readily work with anyone else, not just a regular 'mate'. He concluded by saying although the changes might be a bit inconvenient to some, the requirements of the Service were paramount. In any event they would be on top of their work at all times.

Swann asked for questions, and there were none. At one o'clock he dismissed them. As he left for lunch the Hangar Warrant Officer, Mr O'Mallet, suggested to Swann that Sergeants Gates and Davies would not approve of the new arrangements at all, because of their commitments. Swann discovered that Gates was heavily involved in promoting sporting fixtures such as cricket, football, snooker and darts between Base Hangar and teams from surrounding villages. Sergeant Davies had been the moving force in starting the Jetham Hospital Kidney Machine Fund, and was involved in a local Scout Troop.

The following month the revised rota systems were put into effect, and the flexible hours arrangements were used on three occasions in the first fortnight. Tradesmen in work teams were changed over on a random basis every three days. Swann was annoyed to find the turn-round times increased rather than decreased even though more manpower was used to accelerate the work. He was even more upset to find Sergeant Davies had submitted a request for posting 'to anywhere'. Swann interviewed Davies and persuaded him to think the matter over. With great reluctance, Davies agreed to withdraw his application.

Early the next month Swann met 'Buster' Smith in the Mess, and Smith said it was a great pity that valuable local contact was being lost now the Base Hangar team had withdrawn from the Jetham and District Football League, and the darts final at the 'Jetham Arms', and the Scout Group was languishing. Swann expressed surprise, as even when peak working occurred more than 11 people were available for matches. Discussing the situation with O'Mallet, he advised the Squadron Leader that the appeal for harmony and team work had fallen on deaf ears, and both Gates and Davies were being obstructive.

Today, five months have elapsed, and the Group Captain, Ivor Kyte, is about to interview Swann. Kyte has just learned from 'Buster' Smith that Sergeants Gates and Davies (17 years' service each) actually want to resign from the RAF at the earliest opportunity; and three corporals and 20 airmen have put in applications for transfer, posting, or premature retirement. The Ministry of Defence has just telephoned to warn him that the local press have had a tip-off that there were problems at RAF Jetham.

(a) What, if anything, has gone wrong?
(b) Could today's events have been foreseen?
(c) What advice should Kyte give Swann?
(d) What will be the effects on:
    (i) The work output in the short and long term;
    (ii) The morale of the work group;

if the resignations, transfers and postings go through?

18
Wages and Salary Structures

Probably never before the latter half of the 20th century has the question of wages and salaries been so much in everyone's mind. Frequent wage claims, incomes policies, Prices and Incomes Boards, strikes in both the public and private sectors were often in the news. The arguments are varied: sometimes relating to whether certain groups should or should not have particular wage levels, sometimes it is the *difference* between particular rates of pay that is the discussion point. Many aspects of the problem are economic, ethical, or political and therefore beyond our scope, but what is obvious is that one of the most difficult things to achieve, particularly in times of inflation, is a wage and salary structure which is, and is accepted to be, fair by most people.

18.1 DEFINITION

Popularly, 'wages' is the term used to describe the money payments made to manual (and some other) workers. Historically, wages were normally based on piece-work or hourly rates, as at one time many workers were hired on a short-term basis, sometimes measured in hours. Later the payment of wages was formalized to a single, weekly payment made at, or towards the end of the week. On the other hand, managerial and clerical workers were hired for longer periods. In times when reading, writing and numerical skills were less readily available, such people having these skills were in demand; received various privileges, and were often called 'staff', rather than 'workers'. Gradually their wages tended to be set out as a yearly rate, and they began to be paid at longer intervals (monthly-paid staff). 'Salary' was the name given to managerial and staff wages.

Nowadays, these distinctions tend to be blurred: shop-floor workers are given staff status, executives can (and some do) demand to be paid weekly, for example. For convenience, and to simplify matters, the term wages will normally be taken to include salaries, during the rest of this chapter.

18.1.1 Wages and the economy

Imagine a country with a completely free enterprise economy: without a single state-run business or enterprise, full and open competition, little restriction on business and commerce, without unions, the only public employees being administrative. In such a country the level of wages in an industry would depend upon:

1. How many workers were available (the supply).
2. How many workers were required (the demand).

If labour of a particular kind was in short supply (compared with demand), e.g. people willing to and capable of working on a dangerously sited, off-shore oil-rig, then the oil company would offer (and pay) high amounts to attract the workers needed. Conversely, where the supply of workers exceeded demand, to get jobs some workers might offer to take or keep jobs at a lower rate of pay, and wages would tend to fall.

The real world is of course quite different. This is not to say supply and demand for labour has no effect: North Sea oil workers *are* attracted to work in dangerous and difficult conditions by high wages, but other factors are at work. Trade unions, while welcoming wage rises, oppose most strongly any possibility of an attempt to reduce them. Governments have tried since the Second World War to influence wage levels and wage settlements either by exhortation or legislation affecting the nation as a whole; and in particular by its control over the 'purse strings', by acting to hold down wages in the public sector (including nationalized industries). Again, inflation over a period, provided that it is not too severe, can create a situation where people actually *expect* prices to rise, or are less resistant to rises. Thus some companies find it less difficult to pass on extra wage rises to their customers, and such companies will be more likely to concede wage claims without much argument to avoid loss of production.

18.1.2 Differentials and relativities

Another very significant element in this complex, intricate national wages picture, is that for various historical or economic reasons, different kinds or grades of workers earn different rates of pay. We find that generals earn more than privates, senior executives more than shop-floor workers. So, besides the market rate for labour *now*, other and less clear assumptions are made by many people that certain kinds of labour should receive higher wages than others: that, for example, skilled workers should be better rewarded (because they contribute as individuals more to the wealth-creating activity of the enterprise) than the unskilled; or underground workers should earn more than surface workers (because underground work is harder, more dangerous, and in less pleasant surroundings). Other differences might be defended on the grounds of amount of responsibility for plant or people; or that of status.

Other related ideas, held by some, are that office work is superior to manual jobs and clean, safe jobs are better than dirty, dangerous ones; additionally, jobs which demand that the employee has some recognized qualification—a degree, City and Guilds Final, GCSEs, etc., are superior to those who do not. Indeed it has been argued that if we really put our minds to it, we could grade every job into a gigantic league table so that we can end once and for all the problems of differentials (the amounts in cash/privileges that one job earns compared with another, usually in the same industry or firm), and relativities (the relative position of a job, compared with others) usually based on the size of the wage paid.

Regrettably, this idea is impracticable because, quite apart from the problem of how to decide whose job is the top one of all and who gets paid least (the latter a decision worthy of Solomon), such a system would need to be flexible to meet change. New jobs (in computers/electronics, for example) would have to be slotted in as they arose and changes in working conditions might lead to a need to revalue jobs.

Another solution advanced is to pay everyone, irrespective of job, the same wage. This is very much favoured by some radicals and on the face of it there are attractions, but it could only be imposed by force or complete consensus. People would soon find reasons to get some extras—doctors could demonstrate the need for a car to do their job, which might be used on non-medical occasions, and before long differentials would creep in. This all leads back to our present, rather confused system. Within individual firms there have been successful attempts to grade workers, establish differentials, and relativities. Such schemes have worked, primarily because the grades are fairly sharply defined, the work done by each grade very different, the numbers of people and grades relatively few. The extension of such systems to a wider, national context would lead to difficulties of the scale of the job. The comparison between two jobs in different industries would probably be too difficult to make. It should be noted, however, that comparability studies, and other investigations of this nature are viewed by some as the first, faltering steps to a national scheme.

18.1.3 Power

Yet another important element in wage determination is the power possessed by particular employers or groups of workers. The balance can be tipped towards employers in times of high unemployment, or workers when the economy is booming, but there are certain groups who consistently have enormous power. These include:

1. Workers, highly trained, in short supply.
2. Workers, highly trained, whose continued presence is essential for the provision of basic services—water, electricity, transport, banking, etc.
3. Very large unions, where sheer numbers of members have an effect (threat of a total stoppage).
4. Well-organized, well-led groups.

18.2 PAYMENT SYSTEMS

We have already identified some of the major influences in wages and wage rates nationally. The resulting interplay of these and other factors is to produce a system which is complex, inconsistent, unequal (and some might add, unfair). It is no surprise, therefore, to find *payment systems* (i.e. the *methods* of calculating the pay of different kinds of workers) are legion. Some are simple to calculate and operate; others are so illogical and complicated that they virtually defy description. A comprehensive survey here is impossible: the payment systems described, do however, represent those likely to be encountered by most managers and supervisors.

18.2.1 Payment for fulfilling a function

Many payment systems are in effect payments for doing a particular job, with a particular, perhaps even individual title. No account is usually taken in a formal recorded sense, of attendance 'at work', indeed being 'at work' might mean travelling, entertaining, speaking at conferences. Overtime is not paid for, and people may be on call at any time. Such systems include:

Fixed wage (calculated on annual basis)

This type of payment is paid to those whose 'rate for the job' is laid down by Act of Parliament or some legal document. Once the annual wage level—say £30 000 per year—is fixed it is not changed automatically with inflation, open to negotiation, or reviewed for long periods (perhaps even for five years). Such wages are usually very high in relation to the average wage, many times that amount. People in this category include Cabinet Ministers, MPs, judges, employees on 'fixed term, fixed salary' contracts.

Fixed wage (calculated on annual basis) with irregular reviews

A large number of senior staff in industry (and sometimes more junior clerical or administrative staff) come into this category. Such staff start at an agreed annual salary, and as they get older and more experienced, or get promoted, this salary increases. Often the onus is on the job holder to apply for (and justify) an increase. While overtime or extra work is not paid for at the time, it may be rewarded by a future increase.

Fixed wage (calculated on annual basis) with regular (annual) reviews

This category is similar to the previous one but the reviews are regular, and usually annual. Increases usually have two elements—cost of living (i.e. to cover inflation) and merit (i.e. reward for exceptional service). This category contains a larger number than the previous one, composed of employees from the most senior down to junior clerical positions.

Incremental system (calculated on annual basis) with regular (annual) reviews of system

A series of job grades are established and each grade has a series of levels or increments. Where an individual might find himself on the grading system will depend upon the *job* he is doing, where he might find himself on the incremental scale will depend upon his qualifications partly, but mostly upon the *length of service* in his job. An example of such a system is shown in Fig. 18.1. Each incremental point will be given a money value (say zero on Scale A is £10000, increment No. 1 £11000, No. 2 £12000 and so on).

It will be seen that the scales overlap. It is simple to transfer people by promotion, and some merit element can be added by extra increments at this time. However, with this exception (i.e. promotion), the accent is on rewarding long service rather than merit or outstanding performance. This type of payment system is useful to an employer who can readily calculate what the wage bill is likely to be over a coming period; and the employee (not yet at the top of his scale) can see more gain tomorrow, and the day after as well.

With an annual review (or wage negotiation) the incremental scales as a whole are revised upwards, so the employee can expect a cost of living increase as well as an increment.

Civil servants, local government employees, teachers and lecturers, as well as many junior clerical employees in the private sector are paid on various kinds of incremental scales. A major problem is that all employees of a certain age/length of service, in a given grade are all paid the same, even though their jobs may differ in content and their performance of the job vary considerably.

18.2.2 Payment for attendance

A considerable percentage of workers are paid, not for performing a particular function, but rather for the *time* spent either doing a job, or sometimes just being available to do it. A basic week is agreed by negotiation, and a basic hourly rate, or a weekly wage based on the hourly rate is fixed. In such systems, timeworked in excess of the basic week is called overtime. Overtime is paid for in one of the following ways:

1. At the same basic rate as before.
2. At a fixed hourly rate in excess of the basic rate for job.
3. At different hourly rates in excess of basic rate, the rate *increasing* with the amount of overtime worked.

There are many subtleties or extra benefits, such as guaranteed payments when work is not immediately available, unsocial hours payments, or other rules, such as overtime being payable for all hours worked after a 'basic day', that is after say eight hours.

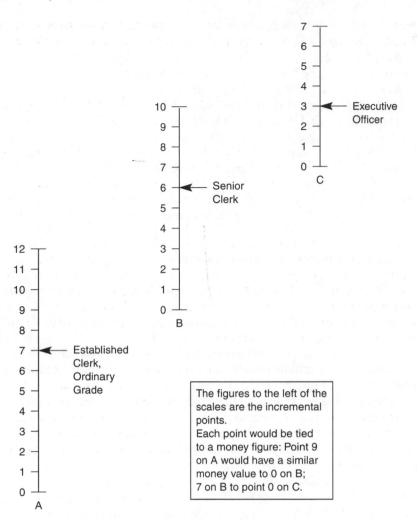

Figure 18.1 An incremental system. Note (1) The position on the scale at which a clerk joins could depend upon his or her age, qualifications, or experience. Note (2) Rules could apply for transfer between scales—an ordinary grade clerk at point 10 on scale A, on promotion to senior clerk, might receive an extra increment and start at point 2 on scale B.

(This could indeed result in an employee not working a complete basic week—ill for a whole day, for example, and yet receiving payment at overtime rates for overtime on other days.)

Like the incremental systems, attendance payments systems ignore merit or extra effort, and indeed, if there is a slack part to the day, workers may be paid for doing little, if any work.

Flexitime. More recent developments of attendance schemes include flexitime. Wide variations of detail exist, but basically employees contract to serve so many hours per month, e.g. 140, and attend during the 'core-time'—the central part of the day, say

11.00 am to 3.00 pm. In return, employees can (within the limits set) choose their own starting and finishing times. Some schemes even allow whole days to be taken off work, in return for longer hours worked before and after the holiday. Others allow surplus hours worked to be carried over to the next month. Supporters of such schemes claim absenteeism is reduced; workers finish jobs begun before leaving at night; they like the ability to be able to control their attendance; they are able to cope more easily with domestic emergencies; and they can avoid the 'rush-hour' and its attendant frustrations.

All attendance payment systems presuppose carefully monitored attendance. Checking attendance and hours worked can vary from signing attendance registers, 'clocking-in' (still very common in factory environments), or the more recent 'employee key' idea. Each employee has his own plastic key inserted into a keyhole connected to a computer, which updates the attendance throughout the month, and the information can be used to calculate wages without the necessity of further computation.

18.2.3   Payment by results—non-manual workers

A broad category, which needs further division as the concept applies to quite different types of workers.

First, in the non-manual classification managers can be paid partly by salary and partly on the production levels, the amount of sales made or the amount of profit made. Salesmen are often on commission, that is a payment related to the amount of orders secured, and sales managers get an 'overriding commission', a payment related to the total amount of orders secured by the salesmen under their charge. This is obviously 'payment by results' or, using current jargon, 'performance related pay'. As many aspects of the jobs where performance related pay has been introduced (or intended to be introduced) are not all specifically ones where 'output' can be readily measured, emphasis has shifted to batches of 'performance indicators', or targets to be attained. These targets could be *qualitative*, as well as *quantitative*. For example the *way* in which a shop assistant dealt with customers could be appraised (amongst many other qualities), and graded. Pay levels could be affected by the gradings achieved.

Less obvious at first sight are those in service-giving occupations—outworkers, self-employed people hired at particular times to do particular jobs, such as solicitors, window cleaners or plumbers. The more wills prepared, windows cleaned, taps mended, the more the service-giver gets paid.

18.2.4   Payment by results—manual workers

There are several methods, and we will consider the most common:

Simple piece-work

Piece-work has had a long history. Under this system workers are paid a fixed amount for each item produced in an industrial or manufacturing situation, regardless of the time taken to do the work. For many years miners were paid so much per ton for coal at the pithead; 'navvies' so much per ton for earth moved, weavers in accordance with the length of cloth woven, and so on. Piece-work prices were fixed by bargain between workers and employers. When the job went well and workers worked hard they earned good money: when work was scarce, or difficult, earnings suffered.

The one great advantage was that the system was easily understood, and payments easily computed. Employers could estimate labour costs in advance.

Standard time systems

As time went on, the influence of Taylor's scientific management school meant that management began to look for 'more efficient' methods of working, and offered to pay, not what had been agreed upon as the price for the job, but what was a 'fair' price based on some technique such as work study or time measurement. Bargaining did not disappear from the scene, but rather was relegated to the querying of rates fixed as the result of time study, or attempting to modify upwards the figures put forward.

The introduction of such methods as work study and time measurement had other implications: first and foremost we can now not only fix a rate per piece, but an acceptable rate of production also. This 'acceptable rate' is called the 'standard time', and attracts a 'base rate' payment. Workers who produce more (or take less time than the 'standard time' to produce a given output) earn more than the base rate payment.

Differential piece-work

Basically, differential piece-work systems are those which normally have various *steps* of piece-work prices for different levels of production. The straight proportion system is one where earnings are *directly proportional* to the results achieved (subject to meeting a bonus starting performance as in Fig. 18.2). Thus, this straight proportional system is the same as simple piece-work when based on output only.

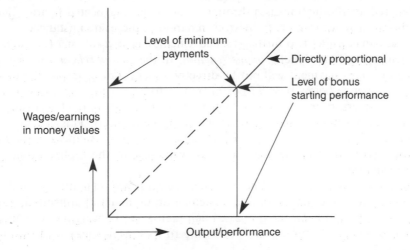

Figure 18.2 Straight proportional system.

This scheme can be based, however, on the standard time system, and any increase in worker performance over an agreed base performance results in workers receiving an increased payment *directly proportional* to production output, up to an agreed ceiling—say 130 performance.[1]

We can compare this type of system to 'progressive' or 'regressive' differential systems, in which the payments made are not proportional to production (i.e. price per unit of output is *variable*). Figure 18.3 illustrates this situation.

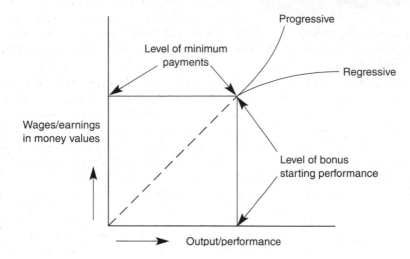

Figure 18.3 Progressive differential system.

Once a minimum level of performance is reached, the steps may be 'progressive' (to encourage more production); or 'regressive' (to discourage production over a certain level). The regressive schemes are obviously favoured by management as they can recoup some money if the time rates fixed were inaccurate (in the workers' favour) when calculated; or production rises through some other unexpected factor. Clearly, there is a disincentive for workers to strive even harder in these circumstances.

Finally, we can consider two further, related schemes: *geared schemes* (or 'premium bonus' schemes); and *multi-factor bonus schemes*. In the *geared schemes* worker performance and bonus payment will not be directly related. For example, bonus payment may commence below base 75 performance, to give some encouragement to lower output workers, or we could have higher bonus payments in the lower range 60-90 performance, but bonus payments over 90 would be reduced. This gearing could also be applied vice versa, to give a *reduced* payment for performances in the lower range, with a (considerable) increase for performances in the higher ranges, say 90–130 performance.

Multi-factor schemes are those schemes where rewards are related to a number of (agreed) factors: typical examples of factors being output, material utilization, quality of the product, or yield from the process. Each factor can be weighted (i.e. given a greater or lesser degree of emphasis, according to its importance); and should be

---

[1] The base performance is often set at 75 performance (equivalent to the guaranteed hourly base rate).

within the control of the worker *and* measurable. Normally the number of factors is limited, and not more than three.

Implications of piece-work systems

The use of strict methods of observation, i.e. checking before, during and after a scheme is introduced, plus a strict inspection of work to monitor quality, now becomes a necessity. Some workers may not only skimp on quality to earn more, but disregard safety regulations. Absenteeism may increase if workers feel they are 'earning enough' in four days' attendance; or output may be restricted for fear of lack of work in the future.

It should also be noted that calculation of standard times would take into account *both* the performance rating of the worker and additional allowances which would include *personal needs*,[2] and *relaxation allowances* to cover increasing fatigue (depending on the nature of the job). The standard time could also include a contingency allowance to meet legitimate delays which might occur during the work cycle, and which may be inconvenient or uneconomical to measure due to their infrequency of happening (e.g. adjusting a cutting tool).

Certain *waiting time* which may be incurred (e.g. waiting for fresh material supply, machine breakdown, waiting for further instructions) and which is beyond the control of the worker would *not* be included in the standard time, but would be calculated independently, and paid for at some agreed rate (e.g. basic hourly rate, or at a figure based on a percentage *above* this).

Group piece-work/bonus schemes

To overcome the problems of individual workers who are put together in a team or gang where the flow of the work is such that D depends upon the work of C, C of B, and B of A and so on, group piece-work systems have been evolved. It is said that such schemes encourage team spirit and co-operation, but experience has shown that the success of group schemes does depend partly on the size of the group. Sub-groups tend to form with groups of over 15, for example; and some feel that a group of eight people is as large a group as you can get without fragmentation.

It is necessary with this type of scheme to consider also the compatibility of the working group in terms of skill, experience, age, physical ability and background.

Indirect labour bonuses

The argument is advanced that as indirect labour (i.e. labour not totally involved in producing, such as supervisors, tool setters, labourers) can make or break incentive schemes, they too should be offered incentives to work harder. Schemes exist where a

---

[2] E.g. visits to the toilet, etc.

total department's production performance can be measured, and whatever bonus is due is divided between the productive and non-productive workers—typically 75% to production staff, 25% to indirect labour.

Schemes of this kind are not always popular: it is argued that some indirect labour cannot become more productive, does not have to work harder even when production workers do (cleaners, for example), and there is a reluctance to share the bonus payment.

Total factory bonuses

In total factory bonus schemes typically most workers are on basic wage or piece-work system, but increased production (on a factory basis) over a certain pre-determined level is converted into a percentage figure, which is added to the basic figure to arrive at the gross wage for the period concerned. All employees can benefit from managing director downwards, but a major criticism is that the higher paid workers get more in actual cash than the average employee.

Bonus schemes—general considerations

Whatever bonus scheme is chosen, its two major aims should be to act as an incentive to increased effort (i.e. a motivator), and as a reward for the amount of work done. It is not surprising therefore to find such incentive schemes are usually:

(a) *Financial* (rewards are paid in money, not in any other form).
(b) *Payment by results* (earnings are related to output or work done).
(c) *Direct* (the money earned is related to the workers' own efforts).
(d) Related mainly to *manual* workers (though there is an increasing tendency for such schemes to be applied to office work, where output is measurable).

In general, therefore, successful bonus schemes are those which:

(a) Are likely to add a figure of at least 10% to the basic wage, and possibly around 25%.
(b) Are easily understood by the workforce affected, and where *formulae* are used to calculate payments such *formulae* are relatively clear and simple as well as being acceptable to the workforce.
(c) Relate to measured effort.
(d) Take into account any special skills required, or unusual working conditions.
(e) Ensure money due is paid as soon as conveniently possible.

Measured day work

Payments by results schemes can become complicated to design and administer. The work involved in the recording of standards, the logging and checking of actual results, the sophisticated calculations to work out exactly what an individual worker would receive is non-productive, and some firms have felt that there is something to be said for getting rid of it, provided an incentive element could be retained. Such considerations led to the introduction of measured day work, which offers a fixed rate of pay for a defined and agreed standard of daily performance.

The high time rate is usually set so that earnings are at least as high as under any previous system, and work measurement is used to establish the time standards for each job, and to define a given level of performance expected. Provided that the operator meets the targets set, he is guaranteed a regular weekly wage; if he fails consistently to reach the required standard, the worker is transferred to a less demanding job at a lower rate of pay.

Unfortunately (unless we add other incentive elements, thus defeating the objective of making the scheme simpler) there is no incentive to exceed the predetermined level of output. Thus workers on measured day work can either 'spin the work out', as the day wears on, or cease work altogether when they have done their quota for day. Such (legitimate) behaviour can be frustrating to a hard-pressed supervisor.

One way out is to introduce a 'banded' or *stepped* measured day work scheme (see Fig. 18.4). While such a scheme is similar to the one described above, it has (agreed) bands or steps of payment related to various predetermined output performance standards. Thus a worker may move into a *lower* payment band if he consistently returns a lower output than the preferred norm; or into a *higher* band if his output is higher than the preferred norm. Certain time limits would have to be agreed for reviewing payment band changes.

Productivity bargaining

Increased productivity does not necessarily mean more production, but rather more efficient, cost-effective production. The same output with lower costs is just as much increased productivity as greater output without increasing the previous costs. Productivity bargaining is the union-management discussion of plans proposed by

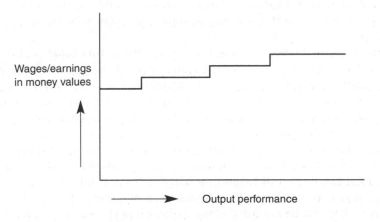

Figure 18.4 A 'stepped' measured daywork scheme.

management for new and more effective methods of operation for the whole plant or company. It is then possible to examine proposed changes in working practices, new wage structures, interchangeability of labour, control of overtime, and consolidation of premium payments into higher basic rates.

The incentive here is to offer a complete package of benefits in exchange for workers giving up certain restrictive practices, being willing to be more flexible in working hours. Part of the growth of productivity bargaining since 1960 has been due to management trying to regain control over methods of work, lost through general overmanning and labour hoarding, and maintaining staff rendered redundant through changes in technology, i.e. retaining mates no longer necessary, keeping old gang sizes when these were no longer appropriate.

Successive governments' prices and incomes policies drew attention to the need for increased productivity; and productivity bargains were exempted from some 'wage freezes'. This led both unions and management to explore such schemes as ways round incomes policies. What often happened was that overtime was cut down, the same work done in shorter time, but wages kept up to (or even above) previous levels. All that had happened was that workers had a reserve of idle time, which they 'sold' to management, and the earlier pretences were done away with.

The claimed advantages of well-known schemes negotiated in the '60s (Esso, BOC, Alcan, ICI, etc.) centred round removal of excessive overtime, relaxation of demarcation lines; increased flexibility in the use of labour, elimination of some restrictive practices; introduction of work study, job evaluation, and staggered work patterns. However, a close analysis of the actual savings in cost shows rather a mixed set of results, and when there is inflation, this obviously distorted the picture further.

Profit sharing

The kinds of schemes we have considered so far fulfil one of the usually highlighted objectives of incentive systems—the payments for extra effort are passed over to the employee very quickly (within a week or two) after the event. Profit-sharing schemes, however, tend to defer payment for much longer periods, but one of the objectives is to encourage employees both to stay for long periods; and to consider the company's long-term prospects.

Various profit-sharing schemes are found: some involve setting aside part of the profits to be shared amongst the workforce (an annual payment); some involve issuing shares (free) to qualifying employees (subject to certain status and/or service conditions), which become the sole property of the employee either immediately or after a period. In any event, dividends are paid on the shares: the employee is now a shareholder, and has a stake in the company's future.

Some schemes concentrate on *cost-savings*, on the premise that reduced costs can lead to increased profits. Indeed, it is often easier to save £1 than to make £1 profit. Schemes of this kind can be tied to suggestion schemes, so not only can continuous cost-saving programmes be mounted with rewards to *all* employees, but specific proposals for further savings can be rewarded either with cash payments, or a share in the first year's savings.

18.3 JOB EVALUATION

Job evaluation is a collection of techniques of differing methods and approaches. However, all have the same end in view—they attempt to find the 'money's worth' of jobs.

Job evaluation is basically a process of comparing jobs, one with another, in an endeavour to establish an acceptable ranking system within an organization and to establish pay rates for each job. (However, there could still be, within a job-evaluated pay structure, exceptions for workers in short supply or with very special skills.)

Although we noted in the introduction that it would be a difficult task to carry out a nation-wide job evaluation exercise, it is possible to do this on the smaller scale of a firm or organization where:

(a) The jobs can be easily identified.
(b) There are sufficient differences between jobs.
(c) Agreements on the relative importance of various jobs can be made between workers (unions) and management.

An essential part of job evaluation is job analysis, though different systems require different levels of sophistication in analysis. Unless the relevant facts about a job have been revealed, and the similarities and differences with other jobs investigated, we cannot compare one job with another. Job evaluation essentially implies comparing jobs to determine differentials and relativities. Job evaluation is a set of methods designed to help produce a structure of wages and salaries in an organization.

The first and most important point to grasp in understanding job evaluation is that we are not concerned with the individual worker doing the job—this is a matter for assessment and appraisal by the supervisor or manager. If any rewards are to be made for merit, such rewards would be superimposed on job evaluation gradings (see Section 18.4). So job evaluation is concerned *only* with the qualifications, training, experience, expertise, strength, intellectual abilities and demands of a job.

18.3.1 The place of job evaluation

The wages and salaries policy of an organization (if the organization has a deliberate policy) usually attempts to cope with the following objectives:

1. To determine the wage levels applicable to basic grades.
2. To determine the differentials to be established for different grades, and jobs within grades.
3. To negotiate and agree the resultant structure with the workers concerned, or their representatives (unions).
4. To reconsider the structure from time to time to determine what changes might be necessary to cope with economic or technological changes; or local conditions.

It is quite apparent that none of these four objectives necessarily implies the need for job evaluation, indeed many firms get along without it, but more and more organizations are coming round to the idea that the second objective can be more easily achieved with job evaluation. If, however, job evaluation is adopted, it must be capable of fulfilling the other objectives: it must not be disapproved of by the work force; it must not be so expensive that it bankrupts the firm, or so rigid that it cannot cope with change.

18.3.2 Job evaluation methods

There is no single method of job evaluation. Three common methods are listed below:

Job ranking. This treats each job as a whole and ranks the whole job in relation to other jobs in the organization.

Job classification. A similar method insofar as it treats each job as a whole, but with different sets of procedures.

Factor comparison. A method which is in effect an extension of points evaluation, and is claimed by its supporters to eliminate some of the disadvantages of points evaluation.

18.3.3 Job ranking

The simplest of the three methods. We merely take the jobs in the organization, and rank them from highest to lowest in terms of duties, difficulty, value to the organization, responsibilities for men, money or materials. We do not need a detailed, complete job analysis for this system: the preparation of a general job description will do. By this process we can group together various jobs with roughly the same amount of difficulty, value, etc., and can then allocate a grade to such a group of jobs and an appropriate pay scale.

It is a reasonable choice in the small firm, where the types of jobs done are few and executive levels are clearly distinct. In fact, the organization chart could well present the job-ranker with a ready-made, rank-order system. In the large organization, the many subtleties of distinctions between jobs cannot be catered for, as the system does not *measure* differences between jobs; merely indicates that certain jobs are different. Experience such as that of the Clegg investigations into comparabilities of teachers' and others' pay has shown how difficult it is to rank different kinds of jobs.

While job ranking assessments can be carried out quickly, with little cost, a serious disadvantage is that the person who does the ranking must know the organization intimately; and because of this may rank the people (whom he knows well) rather than the jobs they do; or end up by ranking in terms of existing wage levels—that is the highest paid are assumed to be the most valuable to the organization.

18.3.4 Job classification

Job classification (as already mentioned) has some similarities to the job ranking system. While jobs are still treated as complete entities, there are differences. In job classification the first task is to determine the number of grades and the appropriate salary scale/wage rate for each grade.

In one version of the method, the next step is to allocate *one* job (usually called a 'key' or 'benchmark' job) to each grade. Each job in the organization is then examined to see which 'key' job it is closest to, and then allocated to the same grade as the key job it relates to. Thus we may have a system:

Key Job

Grade 1 Labourer (No. 2 machine shop)

Grade 2 Semi-skilled machine operator, assembly

Grade 3 Skilled machinist (No. 1 machine shop)

Grade 4 Toolroom worker

Grade 5 Supervisor welding shop

Reviewing various jobs, we may consider that the labourer in the foundry has a similar job to that of the No. 2 machine shop labourer, and should also be in Grade 1; and the supervisor in No. 1 machine shop has similar duties, problems and responsibilities to the welding shop supervisors, and should also go into Grade 5.

Alternatively, the work can concentrate on compiling the detailed characteristics of the grades, stressing the factors such as skill, responsibilities, training/experience required and job difficulty.

As with job ranking, job grading can be carried out quickly; and the system is easy to operate. *But* the grading system can be subjective—even arbitrary, especially if a job straddles two grades; e.g. a charge hand/tool setter. Differences in *ability* are not catered for, nor rewards for extra effort. A limited number of grades can lead to a reduction in chances of promotion. In fact, we can say for both job grading and job ranking *quantitative* differences between jobs are not established—all that is being said is that one job is of more value than another, but we do not know by how much.

18.3.5 Factor comparison

A third method attempts simultaneously to rank jobs, and calculate appropriate money values. Usually five factors only are used:

1. Mental effort.
2. Skill required.
3. Physical effort.
4. Responsibilities.
5. Working conditions.

Like the job classification system, we use the 'benchmark' job technique. Key jobs (i.e. jobs for which a known or correct market rate already exists or can be established), which can be clearly defined in terms of the five factors are chosen for each level of jobs needed to be evaluated. We then examine the total wage at present paid for the job in question, and endeavour to identify how much of the total wage is applicable to each factor. For example, we might take a pattern maker paid £3.09 per hour:[3]

Factor	*Job—Pattern Maker* *Money Value*	
Mental effort	90	
Skill required	111	
Physical effort	30	
Responsibilities	54	
Working conditions	24	
Total	£3.09	—this amount known in advance

Using the 'benchmark' approach—not to the whole job as job classification does, but to each factor in turn—we examine other jobs in the light of the established job. Suppose that we wanted to compare the job of a machinist with that of the pattern maker. We might estimate the machinist:

Uses less mental effort (say 72 as opposed to 90).
Uses about the same amount of skill (108 compared with 111).
Uses more physical effort (39–30).
Has fewer responsibilities (48–54).
Has slightly adverse working conditions (30–24).

From this survey we would calculate the machinist's pay at £2.97 per hour.

In its favour, we can see the system works with money values from the start, and there is no overlap between the factors. However, if the wage rate paid to a 'benchmark' job is raised as a result of wage bargaining (or possibly more because of shortage of that particular skill), then the wages of all jobs dependent on the 'benchmark' job are affected. In addition, this method of job evaluation is not easy to explain to employees.

18.4   OTHER SYSTEMS

Various other systems for evaluating jobs, or providing a basis for calculating wages or salaries abound, and those interested in pursuing the matter further should consult a specialist textbook.[4] However, we can briefly summarize the more significant:

---

[3] Continuing inflation makes nonsense of any quoted wage figures. This amount is used to illustrate a principle, not to indicate that pattern makers necessarily earn this amount.
[4] Such as Thomason, G. F., *Personnel Manager's Guide to Job Evaluation*. London: Institute of Personnel Management, 1968.

Time span method

Here the evaluation concentrates on one factor only: the maximum period of time during which an employee can exercise his own unchecked discretion in doing his job, i.e. remains unsupervised. The longer the time span, the higher the level of work. The age of the employee is also taken into account. (This concept is the work of Professor Elliott Jacques of the Tavistock Institute of Human Relations.)

Decision-making based methods

Here the evaluation concentrates on the problem-solving or decision-making aspects of jobs. An extremely complicated (and highly personal to the company or organization concerned) system is the 'Grade Chart Profile Method', developed by Hay MSC Ltd. (This system also takes into account 'know-how' and amount of accountability of the job holder.) A variant of this idea is the 'Decision Band' system which classifies decision-making into six levels, namely:

1.E	Policy making	Top management
2.D	Programming	Senior manager (within limits set by group)
3.C	Interpretive	Middle managers (within the limits set by D group)
4.B	Routine	Skilled worker (within limits set by prior training)
5.A	Automatic	Semi-skilled worker (follows laid down instructions; makes decisions in accordance with set rules and procedures)
6.O	Defined	Unskilled worker (with very limited decision-making scope, except perhaps in speed of working)

(Grades 1–5 are each subdivided into two sub-grades.)

18.4.1 Miscellaneous methods

Merit rating

Very much related to appraisal systems (see Chapter 14). Basically it is a method of rewarding employees for good behaviour—long service, quality of work, 100% attendance, a year's driving accident-free, the successful completion of a training course, or willingness to take on other jobs, etc. This means we pay not only the rate for the job, but add on an extra payment to a particular individual, which for simplicity's sake is called a 'merit' award.

Age scales

This system is particularly found in clerical jobs, and shop work, and applies to younger workers, from 16 years upwards, usually terminating at 21 (but in at least one case continues to 24).

18.5 FRINGE BENEFITS

Besides payments in money, many employees receive benefits either of a more indirect monetary value, e.g. subsidized mortgages or interest-free loans, or in a totally non-monetary form (free car). From the employee's point of view a payment in kind is very valuable in times of inflation. He does not need to put in for a wage claim for the car that is free, or for a subscription to BUPA. Indeed the increase in such benefits was spurred on by incomes policies.

However, criticism has come from two areas: unions who resent the differentials that fringe benefits represent, and successive Governments who have attempted to tax such benefits and suggest their removal.

The commonest are:

Company cars. Most companies provide cars for executives. They can be awarded for status, e.g. the Managing Director, or by virtue of the job itself—salesman or technical staff. In either event use is permitted out of working hours, holidays, week-ends. Tax has to be paid as laid down in the Budget, whether or not the car is used for private purposes. It can sometimes be cheaper to give the use of a car to employees than raise their salaries by the amount involved. (Sometimes firms lease cars rather than buy them.)

Expenses. Not all expenses are tax deductible but additional financial benefits in the form of entertainment or meals can be a pleasant addition to one's life. Besides travelling, meals, etc., some organizations even meet such expenses as the payment of subscriptions to professional organizations.

Private medical services. Many employees are given free membership of a private medical service (e.g. BUPA); or the services of a company doctor.

'Catalogue' items. As a reward for good service, or for an outstanding sales effort employees (and sometimes their wives) are allowed to order goods/holidays from catalogues from firms specializing in supplying items for incentive fringe benefit schemes.

Subsidized meals. Most firms run either canteen services on a subsidized basis, or even free; or offer luncheon vouchers or similar methods of obtaining cheaper meals than the true cost.

Pension schemes. Both contributory (where the employer and employee *both* contribute towards the final pension) and non-contributory schemes (where only the employer contributes) are very common for managerial and office/administrative staff although less common amongst shop floor workers.

Sick pay/leave. The majority of staff in both public and private sector organizations are paid for time off caused by illness. Such benefits are constantly being extended to shop floor workers. The actual amount of entitlement varies widely: some firms guarantee twelve months' payment at full rates, for serious illness; others six months' full pay and six months' half pay. Other organizations actually permit employees to take so many days' sick leave during the year, the entitlement based on length of service.[5]

Length of notice. Many employees are on much longer periods of notice than the legal maximum.

Holidays. Three to four weeks' holiday is now becoming increasingly the norm; with more senior staff ranging from four to six weeks. While some holidays may be fixed, that is taken during shut-down weeks, the rest is by choice.

Housing assistance. This is a wide-ranging term which covers allowances paid to existing staff who are 'posted' by an organization to another location (moving expenses, disturbance allowances—even solicitors' and estate agents' fees); similar assistance given to new employees on joining an organization; or the provision of cheap house loans/mortgages. An extension of this is 'equity funding' where the employer purchases 50% of the property, the employee the balance. On resale, the profits, if any, are shared between employer and employee. Very useful in attracting staff to areas of high house values.

Low interest loans. Given often to purchase cars where these are not provided by the organization, but where the use of a car is essential in carrying out a job.

School fees. Some organizations pay the school fees and other expenses incurred in educating children. In some cases this is a *status* benefit, but where employees are asked to work abroad, accompanied by their spouses, there is a *practical* reason for it (Civil Service or armed forces' families for example).

Time off. Besides time off for trade union or public duties, staff may be allowed the 'odd day' for social or personal reasons, and may be almost universally allowed a day off for serious illness of near kin, or family bereavement.

Discount purchases. Where organization either makes or handles consumer goods, such goods are often made available to employees at a special rate.

---

[5] The author has actually encountered an organization where sick leave could, in extreme cases, extend virtually throughout the year.

Christmas presents. Instead of (or even as well as) a Christmas bonus, many organizations give staff presents at Christmas time. This can vary from turkeys, beer, wines, spirits, or gifts such as handbags. (Particularly where the type of present reflects the *status* of the recipient resentment may be caused amongst some employees.)

(Note: *Welfare* benefits are considered in Chapter 19.)

18.6 CONCLUSION

A wage and salary structure must always be consistent with the nature of the work, the surroundings, and the objectives of the organization. The total package offered to any particular employee could be unique and will need to be carefully worked out. At the same time, the distinction between staff and manual workers is constantly being questioned.

Whatever structure is chosen must be acceptable to employees and be capable of modification in response to technological, local and social and economic conditions.

SUMMARY

1. The term 'wages' is usually taken to mean weekly payments made to manual workers.

2. The term 'salaries' is usually taken to mean payments made to non-manual workers, and paid at longer intervals (normally monthly).

3. For convenience 'wages' is taken in the present chapter to include 'salaries'.

4. Wages are just another factor of production, like materials. In a totally free-enterprise, total competition economy, the level of wages would depend upon the supply and demand for workers of particular kinds.

5. However, the position in modern societies is complicated by the following:

   (a) The power of trade unions (strike threats, etc.).
   (b) Complex technology needing highly skilled people to control it.
   (c) Notions of status, and worth (translated into money income aspirations).
   (d) Notion of responsibility.
   (e) Specific labour shortages.

6. Payment systems fall under broad headings:

   (a) Payment for fulfilling a function—where job holders are paid for carrying out a total job, without specific conditions such as hours of work or place of work. Such employees can be on a fixed annual wage (static for some years); fixed annual wage, subject to review on a regular, or irregular basis; incremental system (nine-position scale dependent upon length of service).

(b) Payment for attendance—where job holders are paid for attendance at the work place (and may in fact not always work during such attendance). Hourly-paid employees come under this heading. Attendance beyond a certain set time is paid at overtime rates, usually in excess of the normal hourly rate.

Where flexible hours schemes are in use the control and measurement of attendance is as equally important as for the hourly-paid workers.

(c) Payment by results—non-manual or service-giving workers—where job holders are paid for achieving a goal or target, such as a certain level of sales, or for *all* sales made; or performing a service, i.e. self-employed, professional workers for example.

(d) Payments by results—manual workers:

   (i)   Simple piece-work—payments are directly related to the amount produced by the worker.

   (ii)   Standard times systems—payments are not only related to the amount of work done, but the *speed* at which it is done.

   (iii)   Differential piece-work—piece-work systems which normally have various *steps* or piece-work prices for different levels of production.

   (iv)   Group piece-work/bonus schemes—payments schemes where the members of a work gang participate in a shared scheme.

   (v)   Indirect labour bonuses—payments schemes where non-productive (i.e. those not directly involved in the productive process) workers participate in bonus schemes, often receiving a lower level of bonus than production workers.

   (vi)   Total factory bonuses—payments schemes where all workers participate in a bonus based usually on output/sales.

   (vii)   Measured day work—payments schemes which offer a fixed rate of pay for a defined and agreed standard of daily performance.

   (viii)   Productivity bargaining—payments schemes introduced to attempt to increase productivity. Can include the purchase of restrictive practices, the removal of (excessive) overtime while increasing basic rates. Much favoured in times of incomes restraint as a method of getting pay increases.

   (ix)   Profit sharing—the sharing of profits with workers, as well as paying dividends to shareholders. Can be done by cash, or shares. Some schemes are based on *cost* saving.

7.   Job evaluation is a collection of techniques, which, while differing in method and approach, all attempt to rank the relative worth of jobs or groups of jobs (often in money terms).

8.   While in present circumstances unlikely to be agreed *nationally*, within an organization some or all of the jobs can be analysed by one or more of the methods of job evaluation.

9.   The objectives of any wages structure are:

(a)   To determine wage rates in basic grades.
(b)   To determine differentials.
(c)   To negotiate proposals with the unions/workers.
(d)   To reappraise the system at regular intervals.

Job evaluation can help with the achieving of all these objectives.

10.   (a) Job ranking treats each job as a whole, and ranks the whole job in relation to other jobs in the organization. This exercise needs only general job descriptions.
       (b) Job classification achieves the same result as job ranking using the 'benchmark' procedure. Each grade is allotted a 'benchmark' job: jobs are examined and allocated to the grade containing the nearest 'benchmark' job.
       (c) Factor comparison attempts to evaluate jobs and calculate monetary values at the same time. Using the five factors—*mental* effort, *skill*, *physical* effort, *responsibility*, and *working* conditions—the total wage paid to 'benchmark' jobs is split between the five factors.
           Jobs similar to 'benchmark' jobs are examined to establish where (if any) the *differences* lie in the emphasis given to the five factors. Once established, differences can be translated quickly into money values and the total 'worth' of the job calculated.

11.   Other systems include:

(a)   Time span method—a price is put upon the unchecked, discretion period of a job.
(b)   Decision-making based methods—an estimate is made of the quality of the decision-making involved in a job; either converting this directly to some money value, or to a job grade.

12.   In addition to wages, some employees receive payments in kind—fringe benefits; These include:

(a)   Company cars.
(b)   Expenses.
(c)   Private medial services.
(d)   Catalogue items.
(e)   Subsidized meals.
(f)   Pension schemes.

(g) Sick pay/leave.
(h) Extra notice.
(i) Extra holidays.
(j) Cheap house loans/mortgages.
(k) Time off.
(l) Discount purchases.
(m) Christmas presents.
(n) Welfare benefits.

13. Any total organization wage structure should be tailor-made for the institution; and this could also apply to individual workers. Any scheme chosen must be acceptable to employees.

REVIEW QUESTIONS

1. What is the difference (if any) between wages and salaries?

2. Ruritania is a free-enterprise country: unions are forbidden by law. A free market exists for all products, including labour. In such a situation what would you expect to happen to:

   (a) The wages of mathematics teachers, if there was an acute shortage of such teachers?
   (b) The wages and employment levels of sugar-cane cutters, if the world demand for sugar fell dramatically?

3. How does the power of the trade unions affect wage levels in this country?

4. What is meant by saying that some employees are paid for fulfilling a function?

5. Are hourly-paid employees normally rewarded for working longer hours than the normal (say eight hour) day? Explain your answer.

6. What is meant by saying that some non-manual or service-giving workers are paid by results? Which of the following workers come under this heading:

   (a) Accountant in business with one partner?
   (b) Window cleaner?
   (c) Insurance salesman?
   (d) Police constable?
   (e) Author of a book?

7.   Distinguish between simple piece-work and standard time systems.

8.   What is meant by an indirect labour bonus? Why, do you think, there is often opposition to such schemes from production workers?

9.   (a) 'Productivity means more production.' Is this statement true? Justify your answer.
         (b) What is the basis of the productivity bargain? What sort of deal is usually made?

10.   (a) What is the main objective of any job evaluation scheme?
         (b) What are three common methods? Explain them briefly.

11.   List the main fringe benefits that employees of British companies and other organizations might enjoy.

DISCUSSION TOPICS

1.   Discuss the view that every worker, whatever his job, should earn the same wage. (The class might divide into two groups, Group 1 prepare arguments in favour; Group 2 the case against.)

2.   'Piece-work is an evil system; it encourages greed and selfishness, makes men slaves to their machines, and discourages safety; favours the strong at the expense of the weak.' Discuss the view.

3.   Do we need fringe benefits as part of the total wage package? Would it not be simpler to pay everyone solely on a cash basis?

4.   Discuss together, in class, the most appropriate way of paying the following types of employee:

         (a) Managing Director (excluding any fees he or she might earn in legal capacity as a director).
         (b) Warehouse supervisor.
         (c) Technical representative.
         (d) Wages clerk.
         (e) Assembly-line worker.
         (f) Premier division football team manager.

ASSIGNMENTS

A18.1   Prepare a list of all the different methods of payment in use in the company or organization for which you work. (You may need to talk to the accountant and wages office, as well as the personnel department.) By the side of each, list the types of job covered by that method.

Note any unusual methods, or apparent anomalies. Do the workers *understand* the schemes by which they are paid? If not, why do you think this is so?

A18.2   Students not in employment should ascertain (in groups to avoid undue pestering) the way in which their lecturers or teachers are paid; the structure of Further Education salary agreements, and the relative differentials.

Results of these investigations to be presented in report form with charts or diagrams.

If time permits, students should be asked to comment on the scales: are the differentials justified in terms of extra duties and responsibilities?

A18.3   One student is to volunteer as the 'benchmark' job holder. He or she should provide the groups into which the class is split with a job description and be willing to answer questions.

Each group should carry out a factor comparison on the job, analysing the total salary under the headings:

(a)   Mental effort.
(b)   Skill required.
(c)   Physical effort.
(d)   Responsibilities
(e)   Working conditions.

In a reporting session, the class groups should compare and justify the findings, the job holder being called upon to judge what he considers to be the most appropriate analysis.

Case study

A18.4   Pottem Ltd were engaged in wholesale horticulture. They purchased potting compost, plastic plant pots in two sizes and large quantities of flowers suitable for potting, for resale to garden shops as potted house plants.

Workers had to carry bags of compost, plant pots and flowers from the end of the work shed to various benches set out in the work space available. At any time twenty-five (monthly casual) workers could be employed, and they received 10p for each complete potted plant, or 12p for the larger pots. Mr Blossom, the owner, discussed his business recently with his friend John Figgures, a time-study engineer at a local engineering company.

'I know, John,' Blossom conceded, 'you would immediately say I should divide the work up. Even I'm sure we could be more productive if the workers remained at their benches, and supplies of materials and plants were brought to the work station; and completed plants removed, by one or two "utility men".

'My problem is how to pay these people. I can't pay them so much a pot, as they won't be filling any. And, worse, the other workers will have less to do now, and if I keep the price the same—10p or 12p according to size— they'll be getting more for doing less.'

(a) What do you feel about the present organization of the workforce at Pottem Ltd and its pay structure?

(b) If John Figgures visited the firm and agreed that the work methods *should* be changed as Blossom indicated, how can the pay problem be overcome?

19
Looking after the Workforce

As we saw in Chapter 10, welfare was one of the five major strands in the development of the personnel function. Further examinations of this strand revealed that, in fact, it has two constituents. The first was seen to be the duty or need to protect or watch over the employee; the second to offer some extra stimulus outside the work environment, e.g. recreation, although the original motive for such provision was probably to encourage highly moral behaviour in leisure time.

So under the broad heading 'welfare' can be found rather a hotch-potch of provisions from what nowadays might be termed 'necessaries' such as canteens; to optional extras like social clubs, company magazines or libraries.

No hard and fast rules about *how much* welfare provision an organization should make, exist. Each firm, each public sector organization has its own way of dealing with the situation. However, we live in a welfare state (which, even though its role is being re-examined, is still pervasive) which provides so much for many of its citizens. In less developed countries firms may well have to provide homes, medical care, education or a social life as well as a job, for its employees: a special case in the UK is the armed services whose welfare function has become highly developed over the years.

While the 'welfare' idea has been attacked over the years as being 'paternalistic', or something done by 'do gooders' (of whom workers should be very suspicious), the plain facts are that welfare services are not only *provided* but (mostly) are also *used*. There must be a need for them.

The rest of this chapter deals first with the type of welfare services normally found in companies; and finally with counselling, a fast developing activity in which the supervisor plays a vital direct role.

19.1   WELFARE FACILITIES

Some of the welfare facilities mentioned have also been included in Chapter 18 under 'Fringe Benefits'. Such duplication is unavoidable as it is often difficult to distinguish between them.

19.1.1   Canteens, restaurants, refreshment facilities

The provision of canteen facilities, often subsidized by the organization, has been common for many years. While the original need for providing workers with a good meal in times of widespread poverty has gone, the cost of 'eating out' is high and a canteen is therefore a real benefit, especially where the meals are subsidized, i.e. the worker does not pay the full cost of the meal.

A vexed question is the status element with some employees enjoying a high level of service and choice, compared with others, e.g. production employees. Some organizations have endeavoured to eliminate this situation, all employees sharing a common dining hall. Japanese firms set up in England have introduced this practice, apparently very successfully.

Rather than have tea-breaks some firms have installed vending machines, employees being allowed to purchase a drink when they need one.

19.1.2   Sports and social clubs

The development of the sports and social club before and after the last war was a significant feature of the welfare scene. However, as people began to live further and further away from their place of work, and as television and more local entertainment have proved attractions for workers' leisure hours, there has been an inevitable decline. Cricket and football pitches have been sold off or leased to local authorities, club buildings are less than fully used.

In the past one of the aims of establishing firms' sports teams and other similar facilities was to promote company loyalty: it will be seen that such an aim is increasingly unlikely to be fulfilled as far as the majority of employees are concerned.

19.1.3   Rest rooms, common rooms

Whatever name such areas are called the provision of a room or rooms without a work atmosphere where employees can relax in non-working periods can only be beneficial.

19.1.4   Medical services

Many organizations go further than the law demands: they provide a trained nurse in a properly equipped medical room, and may employ (either on a part-time or full-time basis) a company doctor. While there could be problems of conflict between the local GP and the company practitioner, there is no doubt that the cause of absenteeism and sickness amongst employees may be more precisely identified by having a medical back-up. Accident reporting is also encouraged.

Other firms prefer to hive off this aspect by providing some or all of their employees with private medical cover.

19.1.5 General welfare services

Under this umbrella heading comes a wide variety of provision such as:

Washrooms, cloakrooms (of a high standard).
Creches and nurseries for the young children of employees (a recent development).
Loans, grants, benevolent funds to meet specific financial problems employees may have and which merit the company's help.
Housing—particularly for employees of a specialist kind recruited from other parts of the country.
Visiting of pensioners; sick visiting of current employees (particularly those in hospital); helping bereaved employees get over the immediate shock, and putting them in touch with outside (welfare) services as appropriate.

19.1.6 Transport

A welfare provision, though some would argue that particularly if public transport is inadequate, without company subsidized transport retaining an appropriate labour force would be difficult, if not impossible. Often the transport is, if not free, partly subsidized by the company—a heavy and ever increasing expense for those companies who do offer transport facilities to employees.

19.1.7 Pre-retirement provision

More and more organizations are seeing the need to prepare employees for retirement, and the details of such schemes are discussed fully in Chapter 16.

19.1.8 House journals

These may take several forms—a newspaper presentation, a glossy magazine or type-written sheets. Regrettably the high cost of production of the former means that such newspapers or magazines often double as disguised sales promotion material and are distributed to customers and suppliers as well as employees. Having been a House Journal Editor for some years, I have never been totally convinced of their value.

19.1.9 Community welfare

Organizations may take an interest in the wider welfare of the surrounding community, sponsoring local events and providing facilities, prizes, etc. In some cases where local facilities are lacking (swimming pools, sports pitches etc.) organizations may offer to share their facilities with the surrounding community. Such involvement is often criticized as being merely a public relations gimmick.

However, behind the scenes much laudable work is being done. Students requiring work experience in their courses are helped to gain valuable knowledge; in the case of the unemployed school leavers this is doubly valuable as when they eventually apply for jobs, they will have not only some experience to show, but may even receive references.

19.2   COUNSELLING

Counselling has become a very important personnel function in recent years, but a clear distinction should be made between the role of the supervisor, and that of the personnel specialist in counselling. In fact counselling, the talking over of problems and what has to be done about them often relates either to *work-related* problems, or to problems of a more personal kind, not related to work. An example of the first would be dealing with a series of errors made by an employee, or a general lack of efficiency in a typist; an example of the second, a woman employee deserted by her husband.

Clearly, the supervisor is very much involved with the work-related problem; and indeed may be the first person to encounter the personal problem, but he will undoubtedly refer such problems to others, particularly a personnel specialist. Admittedly a more difficult situation exists where the two kinds of problem overlap: poor performance at work is related to a personal problem. In such cases the supervisor and the personnel specialist may well have to work as a team to tackle the situation satisfactorily.

Counselling is communication. Communication, as we have seen is *two-way*, so counselling implies a joint problem-solving approach and does *not* imply telling, ordering or demanding.

19.2.1   Counselling objectives

The objectives of counselling are to improve performance, efficiency and effectiveness, the methods of achieving such objectives vary, but almost always involve problem solving.

19.2.2   Opportunities for counselling

Sometimes the necessity to counsel is thrust upon the supervisor by the facts of the immediate situation, or where the employee requests counselling, however, the supervisor does have a chance to manage the interview, identify the problem in advance and do some preliminary pre-planning. Opportunities for counselling can occur when:

1. Giving employees information, instructions.
2. Giving out work.
3. Reviewing reports and progress of work.

4. Checking completed jobs.
5. Dealing with grievances.

(In fact, any occasion where there is normal communication between a supervisor and employee is an opportunity for counselling.)

19.2.3 Counselling methods

Basically counselling is one way of dealing with unsatisfactory attitudes or performance. As there can be so great a variance between one 'problem' and the next, there is no set, uniform method for handling all counselling situations. Sometimes counselling is in effect an unscheduled appraisal interview and appraisal methods would be appropriate; but more often the problem itself is not always clear, or there is little initial information to go on. Flexibility of approach is therefore important, but the essential ingredients are:

1. *Breaking the ice*: where the supervisor initiates discussion by leading the conversation around gently, and introducing points for consideration.
2. *Directing the discussion*: although counselling is often 'non-directive' interviewing, a gentle touch on the reins at intervals is essential.
3. *Summarizing*: it is as important (as with other kinds of interviewing) to summarize at intervals.
4. *Questioning*: 'open ended' questions are essential.
5. *Listening*: to listen attentively and politely helps convince the other party that his point of view does matter.
6. *Watching*: particularly to look for the underlying causes of the problem, which may be revealed by hesitations or nervousness. Typical causes include:

    (a) Feeling of insecurity.
    (b) Feeling unwanted, unrecognized.
    (c) Fear of losing face.
    (d) Inadequate information.
    (e) Lack of training.
    (f) Inability to predict the consequences of acts or omissions.
    (g) Inability to cope with change.
    (h) False impressions of abilities.

19.2.4 Concluding the session

After discussing the problem, an attempt should be made to arrive at a mutually acceptable solution. As with the appraisal interview a 'bargain' may be struck with obligations on both sides. The nature of the bargain must be totally clear to the employee, and the counsellor should ensure that the employee knows what is expected of him or her in future.

19.2.5 The supervisor as counsellor

To fulfil the role as a counsellor to a work group, the supervisor would do well to establish a climate of mutual confidence in the section; and in addition should:

1. Frequently consult staff on decisions affecting them.
2. Be impartial and as objective as possible, eliminating personal prejudice as far as he is able.
3. Recognize the 'differences' between employees.
4. Set a good example to the rest of the staff.
5. Before passing judgement on an employee make quite sure the instructions were clear, the work load realistic and within that person's capabilities; and that the supervisor has as many of the facts as possible.
6. Display a sincere interest in his subordinates, and show an awareness of their hopes, fears and feelings.

The outcome of counselling is, hopefully, changed behaviour at work; counselling therefore looks to the future rather than dwells on the past. The supervisor should accordingly focus on future hopes and prospects for success.

Finally, it is only too easy to concentrate on the problem workers, the backsliders and the inadequate, and fail to notice the good steady workers. In particular, those who will never become star workers, or gain promotion need encouragement and counsel from time to time, they may well, after receiving it, do their job even better.

SUMMARY

1. 'Welfare' is a wide term covering a wide variety of provision based partly on the need to 'look after' employees at work; and partly on the need to offer facilities for out of work activities.

2. The amount of welfare provision varies greatly from organization to organization. The UK welfare state indeed fulfils needs which in other countries firms may have to provide.

3. Welfare facilities cover, amongst others:

    (a) Canteens, restaurants, refreshment facilities.
    (b) Sports and social clubs.
    (c) Rest, common rooms.
    (d) Medical services.
    (e) Nurseries, loans, housing, transport, sick visiting.
    (f) House journals.

4. A recent development has been 'pre-retirement' provision.

5. Organizations realize the obligation to be involved in the wider community; including helping students and the younger employees.

6. Counselling is an important welfare provision: it relates to work-related problems (in which the supervisor plays an important role), and personal problems (dealt with initially by the supervisor, perhaps, but usually passed on to a more expert adviser).

7. Counselling aims to improve performance, efficiency and effectiveness by a joint problem-solving method, often similar to the appraisal interview. Opportunities for counselling exist whenever the supervisor and subordinate are in contact during the working day.

8. Methods of counselling vary: these must be flexible in approach as no two counselling situations are alike. However, essential ingredients are:

    (a) Breaking the ice.
    (b) Directing the discussion (gently).
    (c) Summarizing (at intervals).
    (d) Questioning (open-ended).
    (e) Listening (promotes rapport).
    (f) Watching (for clues to causes of the problem).

9. As with the appraisal interview, the counselling session should end with definite decisions and arrangements on future action, about which both parties are clear.

10. The ideal counsellor consults staff, is impartial, displays an interest in staff, always attempts to check the facts first; sets an example to others. He or she should aim to create a climate of mutual confidence.

REVIEW QUESTIONS

1. In view of the many benefits and help available from the welfare state, is there a justification for the welfare provision by organizations for their employees?

2. Why do firms provide:

    (a) Canteens;
    (b) Transport;
    (c) Sports and social clubs;

    for their employees? What benefits (if any) does the firm obtain in return for providing these services?

3.   What is 'pre-retirement' provision? Why may it become more important in the future?

4.   What is counselling? Why is it important for the supervisor to be a counsellor to subordinates?

5.   Outline the main requirements of a counsellor.

DISCUSSION TOPICS

1.   'What distinguishes the various welfare service provisions is, at least in the opinion of some, that none of them is absolutely vital to the daily running of the organization.' Discuss this statement:

   (a)   In general.
   (b)   With particular reference to counselling.

2.   Discuss the view that the supervisor should leave welfare matters to the personnel department, or outside specialists (e.g. social workers).

ASSIGNMENTS

A19.1   Students should prepare lists of the welfare services provided by the organizations for which they work, dividing each list into three categories:

   (a)   Supervisor's main responsibility.
   (b)   Personnel department's main responsibility.
   (c)   Joint responsibility.

   Lists should be compared and discussed in class.

A19.2   Alternatively, students to prepare lists of the welfare services NOT provided for the organizations for which they work, which students feel could be offered to the advantage of employees, supervisors, managers or the organization as a whole.

Case study

A19.3   André Pascal, a member of the assembly department of Precision Parts, has been one of your workers for five years, ever since he came from France. He has always kept himself to himself, speaks little to his fellow workers, but his work has been outstanding, and his appearance (always clad in an immaculately white coat) an asset to a department often on view to the many visitors to the firm.

You have been disturbed to find André has been frequently coming in late in the last three weeks, and today was no exception. When interviewed he was bleary-eyed and unshaven, hardly the smart worker he had been. Counselling him, you find his wife has been taken ill (she is French, too) and there are two young children to take to school as well as a young baby. André has been trying to cope with his domestic problems, as well as taking on more intricate work.

André has no relatives in Britain, has no friends locally to turn to.

(a)   As André's supervisor what can you do about the situation yourself?

(b)   Will you need to contact the personnel department? What do you think they could do to help André? (Make a list of possible suggestions.)

20

The Supervisor and the Personnel Function

It should be quite clear from the survey in this unit of the functions of the personnel department, that the responsibilities of personnel management are shared in a complex way between personnel specialists and individual managers and supervisors. In some areas—welfare, for example, the specialists provide most of the services. In others—recruitment interviewing, induction, training—the load is shared: the personnel department provides the framework or support, the manager or supervisor is involved in making the decision or carrying out part of the function. Direct assistance may also be given on request, e.g. help with a discipline problem, hints on training methods or help over audio-visual aids.

The following summary indicates the division of responsibilities in the average organization. It should be emphasized that individual organizations may differ in some respects from the review below, and all managers and supervisors should compare the review with their own situation. Every member of the management team needs to have an accurate idea of how the distribution of responsibilities is effected in his organization.

It is appreciated that *some* supervisors will actually be employed in the personnel function. They will be, by the very nature of their work, providers of the services offered by this function to those other supervisors—obviously in the majority—who are not personnel specialists. However, even specialist personnel supervisors may need to draw upon the expertise and advice of other personnel employees; and may need to be reminded of the other aspects of personnel work other than their own particular spheres of activity.

20.1 OVERALL REVIEW

The chart overleaf is an outline of the individual functions, and the normal division of responsibilities.

Function	Personnel Specialists	Individual Manager/ Supervisor
Employment		
Workforce Planning	Quantify objectives from top management information and policy decisions. Assess resources against implications of objectives. Pinpoint variances (short falls, surpluses).	Provides information about own section as requested.
Recruitment/Selection	Devise recruitment/selection routines, forms, test problems; make interview arrangements.	Is involved with interview and has say in final selection.
Induction	Devise induction routines, carry out initial stage, plus health and safety training.	Carries out departmental induction, and initial training.
Appraisal	Devise appraisal procedure routines forms, records.	Carries out initial assessment and possibly interviews.
Counselling	Provide counselling training for managers/supervisors. Provide specialist advice for personal problems.	Counsels employees on work problems/initial counselling of personal problems.
Promotion, discipline, dismissal	Arrange for promotion. Consider and initiate disciplinary action (in conjunction with senior management).	Gives advice on promotion. Gives minor warnings and reprimands. Refers more serious breaches to personnel specialists.
Records	Keep records on all employees.	May keep records on own subordinates.
Statistics	Provide management with personnel statistics—LTO, etc.	Sends returns on own department.
Training	Analyse training needs. Formulate general policy. Supervise apprentice training. Arrange for outside training (college, etc.). Train supervisors to train on the job. Arrange for supervisory and management development. Negotiate with training boards and TECs.	Submits information on department training needs. Looks after apprentices. Sees that employees are released. Gives on-the-job training, attends courses.
Legislation (relating to employment)		
	Keep an eye on all new and proposed legislation: assess its implications for organization and management/supervision, and advise accordingly.	Reads personnel briefing documents.
	Devise routines and procedures to cover the various contract-based and other employment legislation. Advise of special points to note; provide training if necessary.	Reads, understands routines and procedures. Asks advice if in doubt.

Function	Personnel Specialists	Individual Manager/ Supervisor
Wages/Salaries	Advise management on general wages policy. Job analysis, job evaluation, job grading procedures, established and monitored.	Provides a foundation for job descriptions and job evaluation.
	Record individual wage rates. Advise on fringe benefits.	Provides information on special pay claims. Investigates queries on pay.
Welfare	Advise management on general welfare policy. Provide the organization with information to run: Canteens Social facilities Medical facilities Protective clothing Care of disabled Transport Housing, etc. Counselling (see above).	Should be aware of company welfare policy, exactly what services can be offered, so he can advise his subordinates accordingly.
Industrial Relations[1]	Advise management on industrial relations policy, which should define action to be taken by managers/supervisors when handling everyday matters. Policy to include strategy for achieving objectives.	Makes appropriate suggestions about industrial relations policy. Follows as best he can laid down policy.
	In conjunction with senior management decide on industrial relations policy and prepare the final document.	Monitors operation of policy, draws attention to problems, anomalies.

DISCUSSION TOPICS

1.   'The personnel department is merely a support service for managers and supervisors.' How far do you think this statement is true?

2.   Discuss whether in the experience of students the personnel department exceeds (what students feel is) the boundary of its authority. What can the supervisor do about it?

---

[1] Industrial relations aspects covered in Unit IV.

ASSIGNMENT

Case study

A20.1 'I'm not letting Thompson go on that course,' Curzon Page (foreman in the maintenance section) said firmly to the training officer. 'He's totally unsuitable for such training. What's that? Very well, if the works director wants to see me, I suppose I'll come over to your office.'

It was a five minute drive to the training section, and Curzon mulled over the problem of Phil Thompson. Originally an apprentice destined for the toolroom, Phil had withdrawn from the scheme after the second year, for reasons of illness, and had spent the last six months with Curzon's maintenance group. Phil was a keen worker, was picking up the job well, but to think of him as a potential foreman was ridiculous. Fancy wanting to send him on a three day course on junior industrial management! Phil was too young—hardly nineteen and looked like all the other youngsters these days in the works, a 'punk' one minute, 'mod' the next.

Now, a course in engineering, particularly mechanical, would be ideal for Phil, I could really use him then, Curzon mused as he parked outside the training office.

William Bliss, the works director, waved Curzon to a chair in the training officer's room. 'What's all this about Thompson; I've heard you don't like the idea of him going on this management course.'

'No, I don't,' replied Curzon, 'He's very good as a fitter and could become a good all-rounder in my section, but he'll never make supervision or management, I know your course will waste his time, which could be better spent working for me, waste the company's time and give him false hopes.'

Bliss quickly advised Curzon that Thompson was obviously management material. He had five good GCSEs, had been a Queen's Scout and school football captain and must go on the course.

'Just a minute, sir,' intervened George Bluff, the training officer, 'don't I get a say in this?'

(a) Is Curzon Page right in opposing Phil's training course? Should he be allowed to oppose Phil going on it?
(b) Is William Bliss right to champion Phil's case?
(c) What is the training officer's complaint?
(d) How should the position be resolved?

The Supervisor and the Law

In the modern industrial environment no manager or supervisor can afford to ignore the law, especially in the fields of employment and industrial relations. This unit sketches the background to the law, highlights the essential aspects, including recent legislation, and discusses some of the implications for managers and supervisors.

SPECIAL NOTE This unit does not attempt to cover completely what is a very wide and complex subject; merely to highlight some important ideas and concepts, which directly affect that part of the law which supervisors and managers are likely to encounter at work. This law is constantly changing, and you are strongly recommended to keep up to date with all the changes.

21
The Background to the Law

Of all the terms we need to define probably the most difficult to tackle is 'law'. It certainly is not, for example, related to the 'laws of science' which are really summaries or generalizations of what is observed in nature, from which predictions can be made. Nor indeed, is the law morality, or a code of morals. What is unfair or immoral may be perfectly legal, and much industrial legislation is seen as fair or unfair depending upon which viewpoint you take—employer or employee.

However, it is probably true to say the 'law' of any country is made up of many rules and regulations which reflect to a certain extent current public views and also the views of those who can exert considerable influence in society. For a country or state we can say that the law is 'that body of rules for the guidance and regulation of human conduct, and enforced upon the members of that state or country'. In other words 'the law' is a collection of rules which citizens are obliged to obey in the interest of peace and good order.

Of course, people have to obey the law but we must ask what do they do if the law itself seems to be immoral, illegal or unfair? This and similar questions have arisen in the past on several occasions with respect to industrial legislation, and it would seem that no new industrial laws can last long in the future unless a considerable consensus in their favour exists in society.

The law, or set of laws, in which we are interested is *English law*: and by this we mean that body of legal rules enforced in England and Wales.[1] Both Scotland and Northern Ireland have different legal systems.

21.1   THE ORIGINS OF ENGLISH LAW

The origins of English law are various.

---

[1] Many of the ideas of English law have, however, spread abroad, particularly to countries once part of the British Empire.

Customs

These are general rules which evolved over time without being *formally* set out and agreed. Many of them, particularly those practices with regard to dealings between merchants, were eventually officially codified in Acts of Parliament.

Acts of Parliament (statute law)

Most people are aware that Parliament discusses proposals to change the law, and the final, agreed form of words is called an 'Act of Parliament'. Acts can be short, but are often long, contain several sections, and sometimes well over one hundred sections.

The language used is not always as clear as it might be, particularly to the layman. Every Act has to be *interpreted* to be applied, and the courts of the land are recognized as the bodies competent to do the interpretation. Very often the exact meaning of the words used is in doubt: what does 'reasonable' really mean? Judges adopt the policy of saying that the words should be given their ordinary, plain meanings.

Despite the need for interpretation, the ultimate legislatory body in England *is* Parliament and the courts realize that they have to accept statute law. So it would appear Parliament is the supreme law maker. (There are many doubts about this question in relation to the powers of the European Union and the European Court of Justice, but these are too complex to be discussed here. However we might note that, for example, some of the changes in maternity rights and tribunal compensation limits are due to rulings of this court.)

Before we leave this topic, we should note that an Act of Parliament obviously cannot cover every situation and circumstance. A useful addition to legislation has been the 'statutory instrument'—rules made by Ministers using powers given to them under an Act. Decisions to change compensation payments, speed limits or certain regulations can be made quickly. Secondly, Codes of Practice can be issued with Acts of Parliament, or under clauses permitting such Codes (see Chapter 25).

Common law (judges' rulings)

It makes sense if someone is faced with a problem and solves it reasonably satisfactorily, to use the same solution again or to pass the information on to another individual with a similar problem. The greater part of English law, therefore, consists of rules and principles set out in judicial decisions throughout the centuries. Each time a judge gave an important ruling, his decision was followed by other judges: the first judge was said to have 'set a precedent'.

In instances where judges are faced with cases unlike any previous one, the decision is an 'original' precedent, and some people say that judges (as well as Parliament) make laws. However, a precedent is nothing more than a statement of a legal principle: whether it applies in a particular case depends upon the facts of the case.

Most of the law that we shall consider in this unit is statute law, but some aspects of the contract of employment are common law. Additionally, the judgements made by industrial tribunals, on the interpretation of Acts of Parliament, do create new rules.

Finally, we should note that industrial tribunals, once having set a precedent, have tended to follow it, but the Employment Appeal Tribunal has power to overrule industrial tribunals' decisions, and the precedents it sets on tribunals are *binding*, that is tribunals are bound to follow them for the future.

21.2 CASES

We shall consider the difference between civil, criminal (and industrial) law in the subsequent section, but we should note that every legal dispute whether a criminal trial, a civil action or complaint brought to an industrial tribunal is a 'case'.[2] Normally there are two parties to a case. When we wish to give examples of a judge's rulings we talk about the cases that he decided, and in legal textbooks many cases are discussed (or 'cited' in the legal jargon), and the names of the parties are given. For example, in talking about 'fair' dismissal, we might quote the case of *McQuade v. Scotbeef (1975)*, where an industrial tribunal agreed that a convenor of shop stewards was fairly dismissed because he had repeatedly failed to see that proper procedures were carried out before strikes were called.

However, in an attempt to present information as simply as possible, mention of individual cases is omitted generally in the chapters dealing with particular legislation, although brief mention is made of some of the principal decisions (without naming the cases).

21.3 CIVIL AND CRIMINAL LAW

The law, as we have seen, can be divided into two main branches: statute based and common law. An entirely different division can be made between civil and criminal law.

21.3.1 Criminal law

Already noted is the fact that legal proceedings are disputes between two parties, normally one opposing the other. Crimes involve (except on rare occasions) all legal proceedings being instituted by, or on behalf of the state. (In fact, in England, we use the term 'the crown' to signify that the prosecution is being carried out in the name of the sovereign of the day.)

We can say, then, that a crime is an offence against the state (or community in general), which renders the offender, if the case is proved against him (found guilty), liable to be punished, e.g. by being fined or imprisoned. (In consequence when recording criminal cases we would see say *R. v. Jones*, where '*R*' is the initial letter of the Latin words for king or queen, and Jones (or whatever else the accused person's name is) being the 'accused' or 'defendant'.)

---

[2] Sometimes called an 'action'.

As far as the law is concerned, not only can *people* commit crimes but a company or other organization can even though in reality the crimes might have been committed by directors or other employees. Thus firms can be prosecuted for breaches of the law, such as failing to observe the Health and Safety at Work etc. Act, for example.

21.3.2   Civil law

In civil law, there are again usually two parties in dispute, but in this situation the state does not constitute one of the parties: civil law is concerned with the rights and duties of people not to the crown, the state, or society, but to one another. If I borrow money from Mr A, and fail to pay my debt, I owe the money to Mr A and not to society. Thus civil proceedings are brought normally by individuals (although as companies *are* legal persons, companies can and do bring proceedings), who can at any time decide to discontinue the proceedings, whether or not a settlement is reached.

In most civil cases the person who proceeds against another is called the 'plaintiff'. The plaintiff is said to 'sue' the other party, the 'defendant', in an effort to obtain judgment. A person bringing proceedings against companies or organizations before an industrial tribunal is often called the 'complainant'.

Criminal proceedings have as a major objective, once an accused is found guilty, the punishment of the wrongdoer, or some other similar action, to deter him from repeating the offence. In civil proceedings, the objective is to try to satisfy the claim of the plaintiff by perhaps restoring what was his to him (e.g. property, or in a case of someone being unfairly dismissed his own job back). A second objective could be to stop someone from doing something hurtful to the plaintiff, by means of an 'injunction'—an order of the court stipulating that a person (i.e. the defendant) should not do a particular act. More usually, however, the remedy most sought after is monetary compensation, or 'damages'.

Thus the civil law in general is not concerned with the punishment of wrongdoers but with ensuing that the plaintiff (or complainant) is compensated for losses caused by the defendant (provided, of course, the plaintiff/complainant wins the case).

21.3.3   Torts

A 'tort' is a private or civil wrong (derived from the French *tort* or 'wrong'), with some special characteristics. Thus torts are *one part* of the civil law. Persons who suffer as a result of someone's torts usually claim damages as recompense for their suffering. As we will see later, an employer could be liable for torts committed by his employees in the course of their employment even if the employer had forbidden the employee to do what he did. This is called 'vicarious liability', and will be discussed in Chapter 22.

Typical torts include: negligence, false imprisonment, nuisance, trespass, defamation (i.e. slander or libel), and intimidation. We shall consider negligence below.

Finally, we should note that the Trade Union and Labour Relations Acts gave unions legal *immunity* from being sued for their torts, provided that the alleged actions were done in furtherance of a trade dispute. This will be further discussed in Unit V.

21.3.4 Negligence

Negligence is carelessness, although in particular circumstances it is said that a person can owe another a *specific* duty of care. Judgments have made it clear that people must take reasonable care to avoid acts or omissions which could have been foreseen to be injurious to their neighbours.

Employers have a duty of care towards their employees, and cases have shown that they have duties to provide competent staff, adequate plant and a safe system of work. Many situations which were covered by negligence are now under the umbrella of the Health and Safety at Work etc. Act, but the common law duty remains.

In assessing whether an employer has taken 'reasonable' care to see that his employees are not subjected to unnecessary risks, courts would take into account whether the risks were reasonably foreseeable, that is could the employer have done something to reduce or remove them? Other considerations would be the obviousness and seriousness of the risks.

21.4   THE COURTS

The system of courts is complex and it is not important for a supervisor to study it in detail; it will be sufficient to note that *criminal* matters are normally either dealt with by Magistrates Courts and/or Crown Courts (with a jury). Appeals from the latter can be made to the Court of Appeal (Criminal Division), and ultimately to the House of Lords.

Civil cases are normally heard in County Courts, and comprise mainly 'tort' actions and claims for damages for breach of contract. Appeals can be made to the Court of Appeal (Civil Division) subject to certain conditions. Some cases can go on further appeal to the House of Lords.

Of much greater interest are industrial tribunals.

21.4.1   Industrial tribunals

These tribunals were set up originally by the Industrial Training Act 1964—an Act we met when considering training as a part of the personnel function. Their purpose then was to hear and decide upon appeals made by employers against assessments of training levies made upon them.

Their workload has greatly increased and they now cover complaints and appeals under a whole series of Acts, including matters relating to equal pay, sex discrimination, maternity rights, time off work, unfair dismissal, redundancy, and employment contracts. They also consider appeals from improvement and prohibition notices usually under the Health and Safety at Work etc. Act 1974.

The composition of industrial tribunals is as follows:

England and Wales

There is a President of Industrial Tribunals, a barrister or solicitor of at least seven years' standing, who decides how many tribunals there should be and when and where they should meet.

Each individual tribunal has a chairman—the President or his nominee (selected from a panel of barristers or solicitors appointed by the Lord Chancellor)—and two other members representing management and labour. These lay members are nominated by the Employment Secretary.

Proceedings are relatively informal compared with other courts, because some complainants (and defendants for that matter) may be unaccustomed to proceedings of this kind and may have little legal knowledge. Legal representatives or union officials may act for the parties.

Tribunals are a cheap form of justice: each side pays its own expenses but there is no charge for the tribunals' services. Certain changes have been made to tribunal procedure rules. These, combined with other effects of the Employment Act 1980, could have the result of reducing the work of industrial tribunals. The provisions of the Act now make it harder for a worker to prove that he was unfairly dismissed, and in those sections relating to small firms with 20 employees or less and those modifying maternity rights, new procedure rules were introduced in October 1980 designed to discourage 'unreasonable' claims. Significantly, there is now an implication that a complainant may have costs awarded against him. As a safeguard, the new regulations provide for an initial vetting of applications by the Secretary of Tribunals.

This procedure may result in an application failing to be officially recognized unless the applicant so requests in writing. Further, tribunals now have the power to set up a 'pre-hearing assessment', at which a potential complainant/applicant can be told of the possibility that he could have costs awarded against him if the hearing proper proceeds. (Costs can now be awarded against a party who brings or conducts a case 'unreasonably'.) An example of this was *Colin Bradley v. Sandwell District Council* (June 1982). Bradley proceeded with an 'unfair dismissal' claim, 'vexatiously' after being warned not to. Bradley lost, and the Council awarded costs of £500.

The Trade Union Reform and Employment Rights Act 1993 (TURERA) contains provisions which permit the Secretary of State for Employment to extend the jurisdiction of industrial tribunals to deal with claims arising from an employer's failure to give an employee adequate notice. This was welcomed as a change from the practice of hearing such claims in the High Court—with a delay of up to two years before a hearing. However, despite increasing the numbers of tribunal chairmen and lay members, a 'Times' report in mid-1993 found average delays of a year in dealing with claims. Worse still is the increasing amount of precedent and European law to be considered. This has changed the original idea where disputes were intended to be settled without too much law, or too many lawyers. Nowadays many employers are legally represented (by barristers, even): complainants without such advice could be disadvantaged.

Scotland

A similar situation obtains in Scotland, except that the President, an advocate of seven years' standing, is appointed by the Lord President of the Court of Session.

Role of ACAS

While individuals who believe their rights under industrial legislation to be infringed can complain to an industrial tribunal, it should be noted that ACAS (the Advisory, Conciliation and Arbitration Service) conciliation officers have a legal (statutory) duty to try to get the complaint settled *before* it reaches the hearing stage. As ACAS point out, the resolution of a problem without a hearing saves both parties time and money, and saves the public expense of the hearing. The success rate has been encouraging.

21.4.2 Employment appeal tribunal (EAT)

The Employment Protection Act (1975) established the Employment Appeal Tribunal. A panel of persons to be drawn upon to constitute a sitting was appointed. Members of the panel consist of judges of the High Court and Court of Appeal, and at least one judge of the (Scottish) Court of Session. Other persons, representing employers and workers, who have special knowledge or experience of industrial relations are also included.

As with the industrial tribunals the Chairman (a judge) sits with two lay members. The Appeal Tribunal normally sits in London, with a divisional office in Glasgow, but it can and does go 'on circuit' from time to time.

Appeals can only be made to the EAT on questions of law, and the EAT decision can be appealed against (on questions of law) to the Court of Appeal (or Court of Session, in Scotland). It is interesting to note EATs have other roles: in January 1983 (*Grundy's/Teddington v. Plummer and Another*) it was ruled it was a useful part of an EAT's function to give general guidance to employees on certain matters, including those relating to what was 'reasonable' conduct by an employer when dismissing an employee.

SUMMARY

1. The law of any country is a set of rules and regulations for the guidance of the conduct of its citizens, which are enforced upon the citizens.

2. English law operates in England and Wales, though many countries abroad (particularly those which once belonged to the British Empire) have legal systems based on English law.

3. Scotland and Northern Ireland have their own legal systems.

4. English law is derived from custom, Acts of Parliament (statute law), and the common law, or judges' rulings. A rule or principle once established becomes a 'precedent' to be followed (normally) when future cases of a similar nature arise.

5. Each dispute in law, whether criminal or civil, is a case. A criminal case involves the state taking action against an individual (or sometimes individ-

uals), with a view to convicting and punishing the wrongdoer. A civil case involves an individual taking action against another, with a view to righting a private wrong (rather than a public one), usually to obtain compensation.

6.   In a criminal case, the initiator of the action is the 'crown'; the other party the 'accused' or 'defendant'. In a civil case the initiator is the 'plaintiff', the party sued the 'defendant'.

7.   Torts are a particular kind of civil wrong, with damages as the usual remedy. Torts include *negligence*, which played an important role in the past in industrial litigation as it involves the duty of care an employer has towards his employees.

8.   Criminal cases are normally heard by Magistrates and/or Crown Courts; civil cases by County Courts, each having their own Appeal Courts.

9.   Industrial Tribunals (set up originally to determine employers' appeals against training levies), now cover a wide variety of complaints, brought under industrial legislation, equal pay, sex discrimination, unfair dismissal, redundancy and employment contracts.

10.   Industrial Tribunals consist of a chairman, a lawyer, and two lay members representing management and workers' interests. Appeals on points of law are made to the Employment Appeal Tribunal, whose chairman is a judge, and he is also assisted by two lay members (with special knowledge of, or interest in, industrial relations).

REVIEW QUESTIONS

1.   What is meant by the 'law' of a country?

2.   What are the sources of English law?

3.   Judges are said to set precedents. What does this mean?

4.   Distinguish between criminal and civil law.

5.   What do the following terms mean:

        (a) Accused.
        (b) Plaintiff.
        (c) Complainant.
        (d) Industrial Tribunal.
        (e) Negligence.

DISCUSSION TOPICS

1.   Do countries need laws? Could you have a country (or any organization) without rules or laws?

2.   Should every citizen obey the law? Are there laws which could (or should) be broken? Would a trade unionist or an employer be justified in breaking a law that he felt was unjust?

3.   Do you feel that Parliament was right to create industrial tribunals to deal with strictly industrial problems? What advantages do you think tribunals have?

ASSIGNMENT

A21.1   Either as a class, or in groups, visit one of the following:

(a) Magistrates Court.
(b) County Court.
(c) Industrial Tribunal.

Notes should be taken on procedure, and students should evaluate and comment on the proceedings.

22
Contracts of Employment

SPECIAL NOTE   As students must already be aware, the law is a complex subject, and it is not intended to go in great detail into the 'theoretical' aspects of the law of contract. This means that some statements made are subject to qualifications; sometimes very subtle ones. In the interest of presenting essential information as clearly as possible, simplification and subsequent loss of detail are inevitable.

This chapter is concerned with the legal rights and duties of employers and employees. The concept of a *contract* of employment is fundamental to this legal relationship between the two parties. A contract is a legally binding agreement between two (sometimes more) parties, and denotes a 'consensus' between them, that is to say both sides are, as it were, 'on the same wavelength', both desire the same results from the agreement. Well, perhaps this is the *ideal* situation, but as far as the contract of employment is concerned, regrettably, there are many occasions where one (or even both) parties are unsure, or are indeed unaware, of all the terms.

Fig. 22.1 illustrates at a glance the complexity of the situation, and we shall need to consider the six main groupings of the possible sources of the terms of a contract of employment.

22.1   WHEN THE CONTRACT STARTS

A contract is said to come into existence when one party makes an 'offer', and that offer is communicated to the other party; and the accepting party—'acceptors' in legal terminology—knowing of the terms of the offer, accept them. It may be relevant to fix the *exact* time an offer was accepted and the contract came into existence, perhaps in the case of calculating pensions, redundancy pay or eligibility for extra holidays due to seniority of service. We can say that there is a contract of employment between an employer and an employee the moment the employee has agreed to work for the employer, and the employer has agreed to pay wages (salary and/or other benefits) for that work.

SELECTION ELEMENTS	COMMON LAW DUTIES	CUSTOMS AND PRACTICE
Job Advertisement Job Description, Interview Letter, or spoken offer of employment; any spoken or written acceptance	(including implied terms) Employer's duties (e.g. to pay agreed wages) Employee's duties (e.g. not to accept bribes, to obey lawful orders)	*of* Trade Industry Firm *and* **Internal Works' Notices** **Company Rules: Employees'** **Handbooks**
ACTS OF PARLIAMENT (embodying various employee/ employer rights e.g. Contracts of Employment Act 1972) *plus* WRITTEN TERMS (as laid down in Employment Protection (Consolidation) Act 1978)	INDIVIDUAL NEGOTIATION WITH EMPLOYER AFTER APPOINTMENT Individual bargaining for wage rises etc. Employer offering rises, transfers, promotions, etc. which are accepted (often verbally)	COLLECTIVE AGREEMENTS Negotiations either at plant, company level, or nationally arranged agreements, between unions and employers

Figure 22.1 Possible sources of the terms of a contract of employment.

The last point is important: basic to a contract is the concept of 'consideration', i.e. each party confers or promises to confer a benefit upon the other party. In the case of employment the employee promises to give up his time and energies to serve the employer, the employer in return promises to confer the benefit of money (wages).

(Note: from the point of view of current legislation, a contract of employment is defined as being a contract of service (see section 22.3.1) or apprenticeship, whether it be 'express' (i.e. verbal, or written down) or 'implied' (terms that are understood to be there but are not actually stated or mentioned); and if it is express, whether oral or in writing.)

22.2 THE TERMS OF THE CONTRACT

As most employees' contracts are a complex mixture of spoken, written and 'implied' terms, we shall have to look carefully at the sources. Only by knowing *exactly* how any employee's contract is made up can we answer questions such as: 'Can I make Tom work overtime?' or 'Can I insist on Tom cleaning out the sludge tank?'

22.2.1 Selection elements

Certain information is usually contained in job advertisements: 'six weeks holiday a year for successful applicant', for example. Provided that no other arrangements were subsequently made, such a statement *could* be an element in the contract. Similarly, and much more significantly, the job description sent to an applicant is an important element in a subsequent contract as it is an indication of the specific duties expected of that employee.

The interview can contain a great deal which could be relevant: agreements to modify the job description in some way, agreements over rates of pay, fringe benefits, special concessions such as being allowed to take holidays already arranged, agreements to allow the employee to get day release—the possible list is endless. A problem here is that what is said, agreed at a selection interview is rarely *all* recorded, nor included in any letter of appointment.

A successful candidate normally expects a letter of appointment sometime after the interview, which *could* contain confirmation of some of the verbal agreements made at the interview.

22.2.2   Common law duties—employers

In this section, we are concerned with duties which, unless a contract covers the points expressly, are *implied* (assumed) of the employer. Thus, if no mention is made of 'indemnity' in a contract, it is assumed that the common law duty applies.

Work

A common question asked is whether an employer is *bound* to provide work for employees: the short answer is—no. There are, however, certain exceptions; and people in similar categories to those mentioned below could be in a position to expect work. For example, in contracts of *apprenticeship*, or contracts made where employees are paid by commission, the employer would be failing in his or her obligations by not providing such work as was envisaged at the time of the employee being taken on.

Indemnity

Sometimes it can happen that an employee, while acting on behalf of an employer, could incur financial liabilities (expenses). The employer is required to refund such expenses, provided that they were properly made while being 'on duty'. (An exception to this duty is where the employee knowingly did something unlawful, e.g. drove carelessly and then had an accident.)

Pay[1]

An employer is required to pay the 'agreed remuneration'—the wage or salary agreed either at the interview, or the rate agreed by some subsequent individual or by collective bargaining, or in accordance with 'recognized terms and conditions' in a particular industry.

There appears to be no clear rule that all work done is to be paid for; all that can be said is that an employer is only bound to pay for such work or services carried out for the employer, done in situations where payment would normally be made—not very precise.

---

[1] See also Section 23.9, Wages Act 1986.

Indeed, it has been decided further that an employee cannot claim as of right any payment 'within management's discretion', no matter how many times it has been paid in the past.

Payment when no work is available is also not straightforward. It seems to be clear that if the reasons why no work is available are, in fact, circumstances beyond the employer's control, such as a mine becoming unsafe to work in, then the employer has no obligations to pay employees. If such constraints do not operate, then the employer *does* have an obligation to pay workers paid by time (hourly, daily) who turn up, and also piece-workers who are 'ready, willing, and able'—it is for the employer to find them work.

Overtime is payable when it is customary, otherwise the employer only has to pay for overtime if it is actually indicated in the contract, or if, of course, overtime payment forms part of a collective agreement.

Finally, the question of sick pay often arises: if an organization can do without someone who is sick, that is get without much difficulty or cost someone else to do his job, for some length of time, the organization may find it hard to dismiss the sick person. Until and unless they dismiss the sick employee, the contract of employment remains in force and he is entitled to payment. (His contract, under the Employees Protection (Consolidation) Act 1978 should have written details about the method of calculation, or amounts due.)

Education and training

There is no obligation on the part of the employer to provide training other than:

1. For apprentices and others who have specific contracts or agreements for such provision.
2. For Health and Safety training (under Health and Safety at Work etc. Act 1974) for all employees.

References and testimonials

Despite a common belief to the contrary, there is in fact no *legal* obligation on an employer to give references to (or on behalf of) an employee or ex-employee. Employers are often reluctant to give references, because what they feel that they would truthfully like to say is less than complimentary to the employee (or ex-employee). In making adverse criticisms of people, there is always the added fear that what is said might be regarded as libellous. However, it should be noted that employers issuing references operate under what is known as 'qualified privilege'. This phrase is used to describe situations where, as with the issuing of references, a statement is made 'in good faith' by someone who has a 'legal, social or moral' duty to make it to others with a similar interest or duty.

There is, however, no doubt that such protection as 'qualified privilege' does not cover statements made with malice. To write deliberately a reference to harm someone's reputation could result in a successful action for defamation of character. The implication of all this, is that if you are called upon to give a reference, it must be made carefully, honestly and without malice.

A recommendation made in the Law Society Gazette (18.3.81) was that when drafting contracts of service, consideration should be given to include a clause entitling employees to ask for a reference which is either (a) a basic testimonial setting out the dates of the start and finish of employment, and details of the work done by the employee, or (b) a qualified testimonial in which the employer would state an opinion on the employee's skill/ability at work; and on general conduct. (Not an unreasonable suggestion.)

Trust

(Mentioned in *Woods v. W. M. Car Services Peterborough*, EAT Times Law Report 24.6.81.) Employers should not without reasonable and proper cause conduct themselves in such a manner calculated to or likely to destroy or seriously damage the relationship of trust and confidence between employer and employee (case mentioned related to the employer who persistently attempted to vary an employer's conditions of service and was declared acting in a fundamental breach of *Trust*).

Legislation

A considerable body of legislation affecting employment contracts exists. Rather than extracting those items which directly affect the contract by adding implied terms or duties, the various Acts will be covered in Chapter 23 in appropriate detail.

22.2.3   Common law duties—employees

In this section we are concerned with duties which, unless a contract covers the point expressly, are *implied* or assumed of the employee. Thus, if no mention is made of obedience in a contract, it is assumed the common law duty applies.

It should be noted that contravention of *any* of these duties *might* provide a sufficient reason for an employer to dismiss an employee; but as students should be aware, dismissal is not a step to be taken without a great deal of thought. However, various recent legislation still accepts failure to comply with some duties—obedience, competence, etc., as among the grounds justifying dismissal.

Misconduct

Employees must not misconduct themselves. Unfortunately the word 'misconduct' covers a wide range of possible sins: frequent, or long and/or unexpected absence, insolence and rudeness (although the *degree* of insolence or rudeness is important when considering whether dismissal is merited), immorality, dishonesty, drunkenness have all been held to be misconduct. The test whether any case *could* justify dismissal is really to ask: does the misconduct directly interfere with the employer's business; or alternatively does it interfere with the ability of employees to perform their duties?

Personal service

The employee undertakes to do the job personally: to ask (or pay) someone else to do the job, someone who is not under the control of the employer is a failure to give personal service.

Loyalty and good faith

Employees are expected to show honesty and loyalty to their employer's interests. This notion again has wide-ranging implications. We could start by considering the taking of bribes, or the earning of secret commissions—a buyer, for example, who placed large orders, getting 'sweeteners', 'kick backs', or presents would *not* be showing loyalty to his employer.

Employees often learn a great deal of confidential information, or trade (business) secrets during their stay with an employer. Certainly during the period of employment there is an implied duty to keep the secrets of the employer; and this duty carries on even after employment has ended. However, if an employer wants to be really sure of keeping his ex-employees from revealing secrets, he would be well advised to have express (written) terms in the contract to cover the point. Revealing trade secrets to others—particularly to competitors—could be harmful to a business, so it would be possible, for example, to take legal action against an employee who made lists of customers to hand over to his next employer. In 1981 in the case of *General Nutrition v. Yates*, it was remarkably held that even when an employee was not a director of a company (but did have control over its affairs), if that employee received information useful to the company from a private source, then there was a duty to give such information to the employer, and having done so, *NOT* to use it in the employee's own interest.

On a practical point, supervisors and others should beware of potential new employees bearing interesting gifts of these kinds. Reflect that those who would willingly tell you about competitors' plans, designs and products could easily do the same with yours no matter how many secrecy clauses were in *your* contract.

Employees often have spare time activities; and not unnaturally a skilled car mechanic might well want to use engineering skills on friends' vehicles, perhaps in some way reducing potential business for an employer. This idea has even been extended to the instance of an editor of a trade publication who contributed articles to other competitive journals. Spare time activities—such as athletics training, which left the employee drained of energy or application—could be as harmful to the employer as 'moonlighting' or the misuse of resources on 'foreigners'.

This leads us on to inventions. Obviously if you engage a design engineer who will 'invent' or draw up patentable designs, you will make a contract with him which clearly states that the whole benefit of any invention belongs to you; or some division of profits or 'royalties' could be agreed. It is true that recent patent law does give employees some monetary stake in inventions, but it is still clear that it is the duty of an employee to disclose to an employer any invention that he or she makes; and provided that the invention was in the employer's 'line of business', the employer could claim the patent rights, particularly if the employer's time and/or resources had been used to perfect the invention.

Obedience

People in the armed services or in the police are quite used to the idea that those in command are entitled to give orders, and those in lower ranks are obliged to obey them. It may be a surprise to supervisors to learn that the *legal* position in industry is very similar: there is an implied duty of any employee to obey all lawful and justifiable orders. Wilful refusal to obey an order *could* be grounds for dismissal; it is certainly a breach of contract, but note the order *must* be lawful, and must not come outside the terms of his job which he has agreed to do. We could not instruct the sales manager to clean a delivery vehicle, and take a refusal as disobedience. In fact, there could be occasions when refusal to do a task as *laid down in the contract* could be justified: a bank employee, for example, who had agreed in her contract to go where the bank sent her, could refuse to go to a country where she felt her life would be in danger.

Supervisors are often faced with the problem of refusals to do particular tasks: careful examination of the contract, including a job description, might be necessary in order to resolve whether such a refusal was justified or not, lawful or not.

Careful service

Employees are required to do their work carefully, to exercise due care and skill in their duties. Where they have skills, not only must they exercise the skills, but do the work carefully and efficiently. There does appear to be, however, a greater degree of care required in the special area of skill, than in other, more incidental areas of work. We would expect an architect to display a great deal of care and skill in designing a bridge, but it would hardly be a breach of contract if the same architect drove a car negligently while on business.

Money, property and gain

An employee who in the course of duty is called upon to look after money or property belonging to the employer, must account for it, and any gains made thereon. This is almost like the parable of the talents.

A large number of people such as sales staff, bus drivers, doorstep milk deliverers and car park attendants collect money from customers, and will have to account for it to their employers.

22.2.4 Customs and practice

Many supervisors are familiar with the term 'customs and practice'. In effect this term is often invoked, usually by the workforce (or more particularly by the union representative) whenever an attempt is made to change methods of procedures. For example, some years ago a particular workshop was dirty; therefore the workers were allowed to finish five minutes early to clean themselves up before they went home. A new workshop was built, surroundings improved dramatically and workers wore spotless overalls, but the five minute concession had now become 'customs and practice', and continued to be allowed.

Customs and practices may extend throughout a trade or industry, e.g. taking holidays at particular times, or (in the absence of an express term to the contrary) workmen providing their own tools.

Works' rules and employee handbooks may also be included under this heading: once published, the rules become added to the customs and practice, though some of the items may have little relevance to the employment contract. Notices, such as 'Entry forbidden to unauthorized personnel', 'No smoking'—especially if there is a safety implication, could be said to be part of the contract. More detailed notices, too, could be involved, such as those pinned to notice boards about proposed changes in shift systems, clocking-in procedures, and wage payment arrangements.

Such notices point to the *changing* nature of an employment contract over a period of time. The man who retired last week after 50 years with one firm was obviously on a different contract of employment on his last day at work than that on which he started as a boy.

22.2.5 Individual negotiation

Despite the growth of collective bargaining in recent years—particularly in the clerical, technical and administrative grades—a great deal of individual contract bargaining goes on. The granting of a day-release request, the taking on of a new job, extra responsibilities, transfer, promotion—all these things can be as a result of individual negotiation. Many of the agreements are purely verbal, but none the less valid for that.

22.2.6 Collective agreements

Here we are not concerned with the bargaining *process* but what happens *after* a bargain has been struck with a workforce. Such a bargain can be at departmental, plant, company, or even at national level. And here we meet a problem. Traditionally agreements arrived at between unions and management, at whatever level, have never been regarded as legally binding! The Conservative Heath Government attempted in the Industrial Relations Act to regularize the situation by laying down that collective agreements would be assumed to be legally binding, unless there were express statements in the agreement to the contrary. The immediate reaction, even before the ink was dry on the Bill, was for negotiators to start making sure *their* negotiations would *not* be legally binding. In the end result, the provision was never really effective.

The Labour Government which replaced the Heath Administration, by repealing the Industrial Relations Act immediately turned the clock back and left the position (legally) as it was before: collective agreements are only legally binding, if the two parties agree that this should be so and as we have seen, such a situation would be a rarity. The implication for supervisors and all levels of management is clear—a union can at any *time* go back on any agreement made with management.

22.3   SUPPLEMENTARY POINTS

In addition to the sources of the contract as discussed above and in the next chapter, there are supplementary points to consider. We have talked about employees, without defining who they are; we also need to consider 'vicarious liability', and 'restraint of trade' briefly.

22.3.1   The employee identified

A contract of employment, as we have seen, is one made between an employer and an employee, and while a contract is in existence, certain duties and implied terms apply on both sides. But, unfortunately, it is sometimes *not* obvious whether a worker working for a particular employer, is or is not an employee. (If he is *not*, then a very different relationship exists, and could affect claims for injury, etc.) For example, in October 1983, the Court of Appeal ruled that a Methodist Minister *was not* an employee of his church. However, in May 1984, that same court ruled that part-time 'home workers', working on machines supplied by a firm but working as and when the workers pleased, *were* employees—for the purpose of the 1978 Employee Protection (Consolidation) Act.

To clarify the situation, we must distinguish between:

1.   A contract *of* service—a contract of employment.
2.   A contract *for* services—a contract between a firm and an independent contractor.

In years gone by, the test used to decide in any particular case whether a worker was an employee or not was the control test. Applying the test, if an employer had *full* control over the worker, then that worker was an employee. This test implies the more control an employer has, the more likely it is that a contract *of* service exists. On the other hand, if all the employer A does is to say 'Clean these windows', and B cleans them in *his or her* own way, then we would be likely to say a contract *for* services exists.

However, there are at least two major problems with this test:

1. Some workers are highly skilled, and it would be unusual for employers to supervise directly all that they do (e.g. skilled craftsmen, lawyers, managing directors, etc.).
2. On the other hand, there has been a considerable increase in 'loaned' employees, i.e. temporary secretaries and the like, who *are* under the *direct* control of an employer, but not employed by the employer.

It is obvious that the control test is not sufficient, and we need to ask further questions:

1. Who deducts income tax from payments?
2. Who pays the N.I. contribution (employers' element)? (This is not a sufficient test on its own.)
3. What does the contract look like? Does it read like a contract *for* services, or a contract *of* service?

In any individual case we shall need to view the total circumstances before we can decide whether or not a worker is an employee, and as we approach the central area of Fig. 22.2, we discover a grey area. Judges' decisions in particular cases may or may not be helpful and may, to the non-legal person, make the situation more obscure.

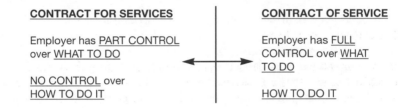

Figure 22.2 The control test.

Supervisors will see, therefore, that if it is intended to *employ* someone, then the contract should clearly state that it is a contract *of* service: if it is intended to have someone's services for a specific purpose, then the contract should clearly state that it is a contract *for* services; the workman concerned being classed as an independent contractor.

22.3.2 Vicarious liability

'Vicarious liability' is to do with an employer's liability to someone who has suffered an injury; therefore, it could be argued that this topic should not be included under a discussion of the contract of employment. However, as there exists this special liability on the part of an employer towards persons injured by the wrongful acts of his employees, provided that they are at work at the time the injury occurs, then part of the implied terms of the employment contract includes taking on the liabilities incurred by his workers for their wrongful acts.

When one person is injured by another, the injured person may sue the other party. If, for example, a pedestrian is knocked down by a bus driver, he may, if seeking some recompense for his injuries, get little in the way of damages from the bus driver. However, 'vicarious' (substituted) liability means that the injured party can also sue the employer, i.e. the bus company. Thus the liability is *transferred* from worker to employer; the employer becomes the 'substituted' wrongdoer. No injured party, of course, is going to miss the opportunity to sue the employer, if for no other reason than that he should be in a financial position to meet the claim because of the legal requirement to be well insured against such an eventuality. Given the choice, we would expect the pedestrian to sue the bus company.

Vicarious liability may be regarded as unfair; it is certainly both a severe and extensive liability on employers. It covers injuries arising from:

1. Tasks that *were* authorized, but done in a wrongful way.
2. Acts that were both wrong and expressly forbidden—e.g. bus drivers racing.
3. Criminal acts[2]—e.g. a delivery driver who drives recklessly is in a sense still doing the job!
4. Incompetence, even to the extent of failure by a company doctor to give correct advice to an employee.
5. Financial loss either from advice negligently given to a third party, or swindling of clients' accounts.

As has probably been realized there are two basic principles here.

1. The injury must be a legal wrong.
2. The injury must have been caused by an employee during the course of employment. (Deciding whether a person is within the terms of employment at the time an alleged injury occurred can be a complex matter, too complex to consider here.)

Finally, we should be clear that vicarious liability can be incurred towards employees who are injured by a fellow employee and 'outsiders', i.e. non-employees like the pedestrian mentioned earlier.

22.3.3 Restraint of trade

Under the sub-section 'loyalty and good faith', we considered the problem of employees and confidential information. As a further protection, an employer could add a clause or clauses to an employment contract putting some restriction on an employee's future employment. The employer can only protect his special 'proprietory' interests: information acquired or derived in the course of business (trade secrets, lists of customers, etc.).

Normally a restraint would specify an area (e.g. a radius of five miles) and/or a time (e.g. three years) where the ex-employee would be forbidden to work or start up

---

[2] In fact, the vicarious liability principle might even extend to prosecution of the employer if say safety were involved; and (*Wigg* v. *British Railway Board 1986*) could also lead to damages awarded to one employee shocked at the consequences of a negligent act of another employee.

on his own. However, in the past judges have shown a dislike for restraints which are unnecessarily wide in time or area, but in special cases areas such as the whole of the UK, or even the world have been allowed.

SUMMARY

1.   A contract is a legally binding agreement between two or more parties. It implies a consensus of ideas on both sides. A contract of employment is such a contract.

2.   A contract of employment starts when an *offer* of employment (with an agreement to pay wages) has been made; and *accepted* (with an agreement for the prospective employee to start work).

3.   The terms of the contract of employment come from six sources.

   (a) *Selection elements*. Job advertisements, job descriptions, agreements made at the interview, the letter of appointment—all contain possible terms of the employment contract.
   (b) *Common law duties—employers*. While, except in certain circumstances, an employer is not bound to provide work, the employer must indemnify employees for expenses incurred, pay the agreed remuneration and provide health and safety training.
   (c) *Common law duties—employees*. An employee must not misconduct him or herself; give personal service, loyalty and good faith; obedience, careful service; account for money, property and gain.
   (d) *Customs and practice*. Customs and practice include the many ways of doing things which have become standard in an organization over the years. Further terms come from works' rules, employees' hand-books, notices and memoranda.
   (e) *Individual negotiation*. Also forming part of the terms of the contract are the individual bargains made by employees with management.
   (f) *Collective agreements*. Agreements made between unions and management. However, it should be noted that collective agreements are, generally, not legally binding.

4.   There is a distinction between a contract of service (an undertaking to work as an employee) and a contract for services (i.e. services provided by an independent contractor).

5.   A 'control test' was the main method of distinguishing between the two at one time. This, with reference to a particular worker, asked the question: Did the employer have direct control over both *what* the worker did at work, and *how* he or she did it?

6.   Changing circumstances have thrown the accuracy of the control test into doubt, it is now also relevant to ask what the contract 'looks like'; who deducts tax and pays National Insurance. However, the basic notion is the more an employer exercises direct control over a worker's work, the more likely that worker is to be the employer's employee.

7.   The implication of the doubts about the tests is that great care should be taken in the preparation of contracts of employment.

8.   Vicarious liability is the liability which an employer could incur from the wrongful or negligent acts of employees. An injured person can always sue the person injuring him; but if the principle of vicarious (or transferred) liability operates on an employer for the misdeeds of one of the employees, then the injured party will almost inevitably sue the employer. The latter usually has greater financial resources.

9.   In an effort to minimize the effects of employees leaving and taking away business or trade secrets and/or setting up in opposition locally, employers often add clauses to employment contracts putting restraints on an ex-employee. Normally, judges have been disinclined to uphold terms which were too wide in application.

REVIEW QUESTIONS

1.   Define a contract briefly. What is meant by saying both parties to a contract must have consensus?

2.   When does a contract of employment normally come into existence?

3.   What are the six main sources of the terms of a contract of employment?

(a) Distinguish between a contract of service and a contract for services.
(b) What kind of contract will the following workers have with a given employer A:
        Sales assistant in the showroom
        Company lawyer (who practises in the town)
        Machine shop supervisor
        Fred Bloggs, window cleaner?

4.   What is meant by the 'control test'? Why is it not 100% accurate?

(a) Explain the principle of vicarious liability.
(b) Eric Fagg, a petrol delivery driver for Mogul Oil, is transferring petrol to tanks in the forecourt of a garage. He lights a cigarette, and there is a fire. Who is liable?

5.   How could problems about whether contracts are for employment or for
         services be avoided?

DISCUSSION TOPICS

1.   Do you think that there is a need to 'tidy up' contracts of employment? Is
         there too much left to chance, even in well-run firms?

2.   Discuss the view that if *everything* is written down in the original contract of
         employment, it will be more difficult to make changes later.

3.   Do you think that it would be useful for supervisors to be more aware of the
         terms of the contracts by which their workforce are bound? Would it help in
         job allocation and discipline?

ASSIGNMENTS

A22. 1   Divide into three groups. Each group should choose one member to provide
         as much information as possible about his or her contract of employment—
         letters, job descriptions, memos, works rules, etc. The remainder of the
         group should write a report (perhaps taking a section each) detailing the
         contract under the six headings in this chapter (and the next).

Case studies

A22.2   Thomas Stubbs was the supervisor who looked after the paint section and
         dipping tanks. He believed in keeping a tidy shop, and was keen on 'spring
         cleaning' at least twice a year. Last week he had a problem with Terry
         Scamp, one of the apprentices who were 'going the rounds' of the factory.
             Thomas sent for Terry just before noon on Tuesday and said, 'Look here
         Terry, you're young and energetic—you've done well here, and I'm going to
         give you a good report at the end of the month—now I want you to dig the
         sludge out of this tank this afternoon.'
             Terry was taken aback. 'I'm an apprentice, and I'm certainly not doing
         that sort of work. Anyway, anyone who did such a filthy job as that would
         need "dirty money" as an extra payment. Heaven knows what the union
         would say about apprentices doing this job, Mr Stubbs.'
             Stubbs shouted at Terry for a minute but Terry held firm. Furious,
         Stubbs made for the executive dining room to find the works manager.

         (a) What is the problem here?
         (b) How could it have been avoided?

A22.3   'Speedy' Plowright ran the best known lorry freight delivery service in the area. Business had been expanding due to a rail strike, and 'Speedy' had decided on a bold plan. He telephoned three independent truckers who each owned one lorry (similar to his) and suggested that they should work for him for the immediate future.

They would each be issued with a 'Plowright' uniform, and stickers with the Plowright name would be put on the lorries. He arranged to pay them so much a mile for any delivery work he gave them.

All went well until the telephone rang: 'Cobweb Warehouses here,' shouted an angry voice, 'one of your lorries has just skidded in my yard, smashed into an outbuilding and severely shaken Mrs Grout. You'll pay for this.'

Plowright checked quickly. 'Golly!' he said to himself, 'that lorry's Carter Blanche's, one of three new drivers I've taken on. What *have* I let myself in for?'

(a)   What has Plowright let himself in for? Need he worry about this accident? Explain your answer.

(b)   Why do you think Plowright was worried: how might the principle of vicarious liability have affected him?

23
Contract-based Legislation

This chapter is concerned with setting out the *essential* points of a number of Acts of Parliament, which, directly or indirectly, affect the contracts of employment between employers and employees. It will be appreciated that Acts of Parliament are not always easy documents to read, and can be phrased in unusual language. The intention here is to make what is relevant to the supervisor as plain as possible, and the effect is that much detail is omitted, but comments and guidance are added.

As this chapter is very selective, it cannot be stressed too strongly that every supervisor (and manager at *any* level) should be able to refer easily to actual copies of the Acts mentioned in the text: if copies do not exist in your organization it is recommended that you arrange for them to be put on order. There is no substitute for the original text. In addition to the comments in this chapter, you will also find the series of booklets on current legislation available at Job Centres useful.

Although less new industrial legislation is going through Parliament at present, supervisors (and others) should be aware that minor changes to the *detail* of existing legislation are constantly being made—the redundancy payment maximum level, for example. Additionally (as you will note in several places), rulings of the European Court can affect existing British legislation quite significantly.

Alert supervisors will, of course, see that they keep up to date with changes in the law; and by so doing will be much better able to evaluate the legal implications of problems, disputes, proposed changes in working arrangements, or disciplinary action, in their departments. At the same time, it should be clear to supervisors that before they take *any* action which might have legal implications for them (or their organization) they should take advice from colleagues, superiors, specialists or personnel staff as appropriate.

The basic implication is that the contemporary supervisor does not need to be an *expert* in the law, but does need to recognize possible legal problems and know from where to seek advice.

23.1 INTRODUCTORY NOTES TO LEGISLATION

It will be noted that each Act of Parliament mentioned in the text is used as a main heading, but that other legislation is mentioned underneath in brackets. This arrangement is necessary because besides passing Acts of Parliament aimed at a particular topic, e.g. contracts of employment, legislators have a habit of 'tacking on' single clauses (or complete sections) in Acts referring to different topics, which relate to or modify earlier legislation. The Acts in brackets thus contain relevant sections or modifications.

This chapter is restricted to contract-based parts of legislation: items orientated toward industrial relations, e.g. picketing, are dealt with in Unit V.

Finally, although several Acts are discussed here as though they have been unaltered, in fact the Employment Protection (Consolidation) Act 1978 which came in force in November 1978, brings together *in one Act*, the provisions on individual employment rights (for example, rights applicable to notice, time off, sick pay, etc.) contained in the following Acts:

> Redundancy Payments Act 1965
> Contracts of Employment Act 1972
> Trade Union and Labour Relations Acts 1974-6
> Employment Protection Act 1975

This 'consolidation', as it were, *extracts* certain items from the above Acts, and repeats them under one heading. Rather than confuse the issue, in the treatment in this chapter, each Act is considered in its original form, and the consolidation mentioned is omitted. Where appropriate, the changes made by the Employment Act 1980 are incorporated in the topic area to which they apply. Later, there was a further extension of union legislation by the government—the Trade Union Reform and Employment Rights Act 1993. Everyone in employment is likely to be affected by it; and references to it in the text will be by the 'short name', TURERA.

23.2   CONTRACTS OF EMPLOYMENT ACTS 1963–90

(Reference also: Trade Union and Labour Relations Act 1974; Employment Protection (Consolidation) Act 1978; TURERA.)

The basic objective of this legislation was to ensure that every employee was at least aware of many significant terms of his contract of employment in writing in a form that he could take away and retain. In the main it prescribes minimum periods of notice of termination of employment; specifies rights of employees under notice; requires written statements of the main terms to be given to employees. Most workers who work more than 16 hours per week (registered dock workers engaged on dock work, crown servants, certain seamen and other miscellaneous categories are excluded) come under the provisions of the Act, including domestic workers.

23.2.1   Minimum periods of notice

The Act gives to both employer and employee the right to expect from the other party a minimum period of notice of the termination of the contract of employment. (Where a particular contract gives rights to *longer* periods of notice than those specified, obviously the longer periods apply.)

The notice that an *employer* must give to terminate the contract of employment of an employee continuously employed for four weeks or more is *not less than*:

1. One week, if continuously employed for up to, but not, including, two years.
2. One week for each year of continuous service, if employed for two years or more, up to but not including twelve years.
3. Twelve weeks for continuous service of twelve years or more.

(Note: an interesting *exclusion* to these provisions relates to employees engaged for *twelve weeks or less* on a specific task, who have been in continuous service for no more than twelve weeks.)

Employment must be continuous: but periods on strike are *not* counted.

The notice that an *employee* must give is *not less than one week*, provided that he has been continuously employed for four weeks or more by his present employer. This minimum period is *not* affected in any way by longer service, though many contracts require employees to give much longer periods of notice: one, three or even six months.

In the absence of any terms in the contract to the contrary, notice can be given on any day.

The contract can be terminated *without notice*, by either employer or employee if the conduct of the other party justifies it. (This right relates to an essential aspect of the law of contract: it would be said that unjustifiable conduct of one party had in fact already broken the contract; once broken, the other party can walk away, as it were.) Of course, whether or not any particular conduct of either party justifies termination without notice is something which could well have to be settled by the courts.

23.2.2 Written particulars of terms of contract of employment

TURERA extended the employer's original obligation to provide employees working more than 16 hours a week, with a full, written statement of the terms and conditions of employment after 13 weeks of employment; to that of requiring the employer to provide the written statement *within two months* to any employee engaged after 30 November 1993, and who worked more than *8 hours* a week.

23.2.3 Changes

There are provisions for changing the terms, once issued: but the employer must notify the employee of changes within one month, in writing, or put the changes in a document accessible to the employee.

23.2.4 Exceptions/exemptions

These include:

1. Situations where the employee normally works less than 16 hours per week, the written statement is not necessary, *but* where a contract for 8 hours per week, or

more, up to 16 hours per week has lasted for *five years*, or more, then the requirement for written particulars applies.
2. Close relatives, e.g. if the employer is the father, mother, husband, wife, etc., of the
    employee.
3. The details listed are already in a written contract of employment.

23.2.5 Failure to provide a written statement

If an employee does not receive the written statement within two months after starting
employment, or is dissatisfied with the accuracy of the information included, he can
have the matter referred to an industrial tribunal. The tribunal in its wisdom may lay
down a set of terms which should have been included to comply with the Act, if no
terms were issued; or, if it feels the terms are not satisfactory, may substitute or amend
the terms.

23.2.6 Note to managers/supervisors

The implication of this legislation is quite clear: the written statements and supporting
documents have to be kept *up to date*. It is surprising to find even now some employees who do *not* receive any written statement as specified under the Act.

23.3 TRADE UNION AND LABOUR RELATIONS ACT 1974-6

(Reference also: Employment Protection (Consolidation) Act 1992; Employment Acts
1980–88; Trade Union Reform and Employment Rights Act 1993 [TURERA].)
    The Trade Union and Labour Relations Act, known generally as 'TULRA', was
widely extended by the Employment Protection Act, EPA for short (both were
passed when the Government had a secure majority). The main purpose of this body
of legislation was to repeal, modify or re-enact various parts of the ill-fated
Industrial Relations Act (IRA) of the Heath Administration. However, some key
ideas, such as that of 'unfair' dismissal, from the IRA, re-appear, with some amendments. There has been much recent legislation as well as court decisions concerning
unfair dismissal.
    The reference to unfair dismissal, is of great concern to supervisors; and indeed of
all levels of management. Not surprisingly, therefore, rather more space is devoted to
this topic, than others.

23.3.1 Codes of practice

The Code of Practice (see general remarks about codes of practice in Chapter 25) on
Industrial Relations issued with the Industrial Relations Act was re-enacted by

TULRA, but was repealed by EPA. The onus to issue such codes was then placed on ACAS (see Chapter 25). We shall look at the 1971 code, as amended by ACAS, in some detail in Chapter 25.

23.3.2 Unfair dismissal

The concept of the wrong of 'unfair dismissal' introduced by the IRA is continued with important amendments. The question of whether the dismissal of an employee is fair or unfair has been for many years of great significance: taking 1987 and 1988, in neither year did ACAS receive less than 34 000 complaints alleging unfair dismissal. Of the 36 340 cases in 1988, only 6479 cases actually went all the way to an industrial tribunal, 23 582 being settled 'out of tribunal' though ACAS's conciliation. What reports of this kind cannot quantify are the *hidden* costs of such claims: where cases are contested, firms may hire lawyers, executives spend time helping prepare the case, or actually attend to give evidence. Out of court settlements, too, can cost money, possibly not as much as contested ones, but several hundred pounds is not exceptional. When considering the term 'unfair dismissal', we will first consider *dismissal*.

Dismissal

An employee is treated as being dismissed under the Act if, while under a contract of employment with an employer:

1. The employer terminates the contract with or without notice.
2. The employer does not renew a fixed-term contract of one year[1] or more, when it expires.
3. The employee terminates the contract, with or without notice, in circumstances entitling him or her to do so without notice, because of the employer's conduct. (This latter situation is called 'constructive' dismissal. It should be noted that it can happen in a variety of ways, but usually involves the employer having broken or proposing to break the contract by attempting fundamentally to change the nature, place or important terms of the contract of employment. A significant or fundamental breach *is* required: the employer's conduct must be sufficiently serious to sustain a claim for constructive dismissal.)
    Cases where employees have been successful in claiming unfair dismissal have included:
    (a) Employee told he was incompetent.
    (b) Senior employee 'treated like an office boy'.
    (c) Employee given a series of unjustified warnings about his conduct.
    (d) 'Resign, or I'll sack you!'
    (e) Changing an employee's shift (and in another case his rates of commission) without prior agreement.

---

[1] This was amended from the two years by the Employment Act 1980.

The main reason why constructive dismissal is so important is that if an employer loses such a claim, the employer is then also liable to a finding of unfair dismissal (and, under certain circumstances, of redundancy as well). (However, the Employment Act 1980 does effect unfair dismissal cases in that it makes the burden of proof *neutral* between the employer and employee, in other words, the claimant now has to prove the unfairness of employer's actions.)

Having now clarified in our minds what 'dismissal' means, we can now look at 'unfair' dismissal under three headings:

General presumption

There is a general presumption that *all* dismissals with or without notice are unfair *unless the employer can prove otherwise*. What the employer must prove to overcome the general presumption is discussed under *fair dismissal* below.

Specifically listed in the legislation

A number of reasons for dismissal are listed in the legislation, all of which are unacceptable as fair reasons and which are in fact *legally* regarded as unfair. All that would have to be shown is that dismissal took place for one of these reasons, for a case of unfair dismissals to be established. The list covers where an employee was dismissed:

1. Because the employee was or proposed to become a member of an independent trade union (i.e. a union which conducted its own affairs, with its own money).
2. Because the employee had taken or proposed to take part in the activities of an independent trade union.
3. Because the employee had refused or proposed to refuse to become or remain a member of a trade union which was not independent (say a staff association, which while running its own affairs had company contributions to its funds).
4. Because the employee genuinely objected to becoming a member of *any* trade union, on grounds of religious belief.

Note 1. Any employee regardless of age or length of service can complain to an industrial tribunal on the above grounds.

Note 2. Dismissal of an employee who refuses to join a union, and who works with a group of workers covered by a 'closed shop' agreement—the restrictions of employment in a workplace to persons who are members of a particular union or unions—can be regarded as *fair*. All the employer needs to show is that a valid closed shop arrangement exists, and the reason for an employee's dismissal was the employee's refusal to join the union in question.

The genuine objection on *religious* grounds still operates even here, though; and even despite a closed shop agreement, a person who declines to join a specific union in a closed shop, on religious grounds, and who is dismissed, would be regarded as *unfairly* dismissed.

Note 3. The Employment Act 1980 carries this a stage further by stating that a dismissal on religious grounds *and* 'on grounds of conscience or deeply held conviction to being a member of any trade union whatsoever, or a particular trade union' would be *unfair*.

Note 4. The Employment Act 1980 also adds that a dismissal would be *unfair* in a closed shop situation, if an employee had worked in a group of employees (who *now* operate a closed shop) before the closed shop agreement came into effect; and the employee concerned had not at any time actually been a member of a union operating the closed shop agreement.

Note 5. The Employment Acts of 1980 and 1982 further affected the circumstances in which dismissal for non-membership of a trade union, in a closed shop situation, is to be regarded as unfair.

1. Where a closed shop agreement has not in the five years preceding the dismissal been supported in a secret ballot by 80% of the employees covered by it, or by 85% of those voting, or
2. Even if so agreed and supported, the employee had at no time since the ballot been a member of a trade union which was a party to the agreement.
3. Where the employee at the time of dismissal has obtained or is seeking a declaration from an industrial tribunal that he has been unreasonably excluded from the trade union he has to belong to, under the closed shop agreement, and
4. Where the employee is bound because of his qualifications to observe a written code of conduct, and has left (or been expelled from) his union (or refused to join a union) because of a conflict between that code of conduct, and a requirement to take industrial action.
5. Finally, an employee who cannot be *fairly* dismissed for non-membership of a trade union in a closed shop, cannot be fairly dismissed either for refusing to make payments to that trade union/some other body/some other person in lieu of union membership.

Other categories of unfair dismissal

A basic principle to be discerned in the unfairness rules is unequal treatment; and this will be evident in the following situations where dismissal would also be unfair:

1. If the reason for dismissal were redundancy, which could have been applied to others who were *not* dismissed, and selection for redundancy related to the employee's exercise or intending exercise of his or her rights to belong to a trade union or take part in its activities.
2. If the reason for dismissal were redundancy, and the employer was in breach of a customary or agreed redundancy procedure. (In fact one recorded case took this idea further, and it was ruled that to make people redundant on the basis of seniority amounted to *unfair* dismissal.) In another case, it was stated employees made redundant without prior warning or consultation were likely to succeed in complaints of unfair dismissal.

3. Where unfair dismissal is alleged as a result of a lock-out by employer (i.e. employer shuts down his place of business), or the employee's involvement with a strike or industrial action, an industrial tribunal will not determine (i.e. not consider) whether such dismissals are or are not unfair. The tribunal will, however, do so if other employees similarly involved are either not dismissed; or if dismissed they are subsequently re-engaged.

    (The implication here is clear. Dismissals after a strike cannot be selective; we cannot just sack the 'trouble makers'. It is either all, or none at all. Grunwicks sacked every striker, and were found to be within the law.)
4. Where constructive dismissal has been proved (see above).
5. Any dismissal of employees trying to assert one of their statutory rights is unfair; as is any attempt to dismiss an employee who, concerned about health and safety matters, attempts to prevent or reduce risks to health and safety at work. (This could include a worker's safety representative, for example, properly performing functions appropriate to such an appointment; or any employee in what could be reasonably felt to be imminent and serious danger who left/proposed to leave or refused to return to his place of work.)
6. Dismissal on maternity-related grounds (for whatever reason) is now considered unfair. The previous two-year qualifying period needed to make a claim no longer applies. (See also Section 23.4.4 Maternity.)
7. Where an employer has failed to show that a dismissal was *fair* and reasonable, the general presumption all dismissals are unfair operates.

23.3.3   Fair dismissals

In attempting to combat a claim for unfair dismissal, an employer has to satisfy the tribunal that the reason for dismissal related either to the capability or qualifications of the employee for the work concerned; or to his conduct, or redundancy; his inability to carry on in his present job without breaking the law, or some other 'substantial' reason—which need not be the same kind of reason as the others mentioned. Until the passing of the Employment Act 1980, it was also up to an employer to satisfy the tribunal that he had 'acted reasonably' in deciding that the circumstances surrounding the case were adequate justification for dismissing an employee. Section 6 of the new Act removes from the employer the onus of demonstrating to the tribunal that he 'acted reasonably', in such circumstances that decision now rests with the tribunal. (In addition, the same section also provides that in deciding whether or not an employer has carried out a dismissal fairly, an industrial tribunal should take in account the 'size and administrative resources' of that employer.)

   In the following sections the individual grounds for dismissal which would normally be regarded as *fair* are laid out.

Lack of capability or qualifications

A very wide category which covers:

1. Incompetence—few cases have been brought, and it would seem to be difficult to establish, especially if it has been condoned over a period or warnings were not given. Even where a tribunal found an employee had contributed to his dismissal by his actions (or lack of them), they still found an 'unfair dismissal' had occurred (*Beck v. West Oxfordshire District Council; Guard v. Wimbledon Conservative Club*).
2. Performance—again adequate warnings would be required, and if the job changes an employee must be given a chance to retrain to cope with new machines, methods, etc.
3. Qualifications—apart from the obvious situation where the employee can be dismissed fairly for pretending to have qualifications he does not possess, there are other situations such as where an employee has to pass an exam in a given time as a condition of employment.
4. Ill-health—obviously a great deal will depend on individual circumstances—how important is the job, can it be done by others, for how long? What is clear from guidance given by the Employment Appeal Tribunal is that medical evidence, the employee's own views, the possibility of alternative employment need to be considered before dismissal takes place.
5. Employees on trial—what is important under the previous heading is the need to identify problems quickly. There is an even more pressing need in the case of employees on *trial periods*. It is true that employees of less than one year's continuous service are not protected by the Act, but some trial periods last a year (teachers/lecturers for example), and the performance of probationary employees should be most carefully reviewed throughout.

Conduct

Another all-inclusive category which covers some ideas that we considered as implied terms of the contract in the previous chapter, but what is quite clear is that the employer's position is strengthened if agreed codes of conduct have been established in the organization. If it is laid down that theft, drunkenness or fighting qualify for instant dismissal, then in a disputed case the employer is in a better position than one who has not spelt out offences and their consequences.

1. Disobedience—a refusal to obey a lawful order can be a serious matter, but again we return to the need for clear contracts, and job descriptions. If overtime is needed then the contract should say so, but not in some vague statement like 'to work such other hours as may be necessary'. Provided that a clear statement is made then a refusal to work overtime breaches the terms of the contract: it would usually be fair to dismiss an employee for refusing to carry out a contract that he had agreed to.

    However, equally certain is the need for any major change in conditions to be discussed with the employees concerned (and unions if appropriate) and their views would have to be considered. Provided that there is evidence of such prior warning and consultation and there is a refusal by an employee to comply with the new arrangements, then the employer has a greater chance of sustaining his justification for dismissal.

2. Absence—cases of absence need careful review. Usually one absence on its own would hardly justify dismissal. In any event the message is clear once again, all employees should know exactly how they stand over absences, and the appropriate procedures like sending in sick notes; and the implications of unexplained absence or failure to forward medical certificates. An adequate warning system should be in operation, so if and when a case is brought, the organization can demonstrate its attempts to be fair.
3. Drunkenness—here we are on somewhat tricky ground. Many employees (including supervisors) might take an alcoholic drink at lunch time, for example, so to accuse an employee of having 'beer on his breath' and dismiss him would almost certainly be regarded as *unfair*.

    The view of tribunals seems to run along the lines that drinking *as a first offence* would normally not merit dismissal, unless of course, the employee was very drunk and attacked someone; or where to be drunk on duty could endanger the safety of others, including the public. (Train or bus drivers are examples of jobs where to be drunk could pose considerable dangers.)
4. Stealing—it seems quite clear that thefts from both customers/public and fellow employees could justify dismissal without prior warning. Obviously where employees are caught 'in the act' the matter is reasonably straightforward, but surprisingly enough tribunals have followed the view that provided adequate grounds for believing an employee is a thief exist, then he can be dismissed *fairly*, even though the employee is later acquitted!

    It goes almost without saying that a wise employer would carefully investigate any alleged case of theft, have appropriate investigations made (perhaps involving the police) and give the employee a chance to put his side of the case. (There is nothing of course to prevent an employer from suspending an employee, normally on full pay, during the investigations.)

    Included, besides money or valuables, under this heading would be theft of ideas, inventions, or trade secrets. We have seen the common law duty of loyalty to the employer, and employees in a position to misconduct themselves in this way are usually fairly senior in the organization, which in itself would increase the seriousness of their actions. An employer who could demonstrate the leaking of confidential documents to a competitor (or to a local newspaper) would have little difficulty in sustaining even an instant dismissal without notice. However, the employer would be wise to have a soundly based case; and the employee given a chance to explain.

Redundancy

The definition of redundancy and the implications of compensation payable are discussed later under the Redundancy Payments Act 1965; however, the Employment Protection Act (EPA) also deals with the organization of group or large number redundancies. Here, where we are considering the dismissal aspect, we shall concentrate on the fairness principle. Employees being made redundant should be consulted or warned in advance if possible; alternatives to redundancy should be explored unless the situation is hopeless.

The *way* redundancies are chosen is important; we have seen already that where someone is made redundant because of being a trade unionist, such dismissal is *unfair*, but leaving this apart, redundancy is generally regarded as *a fair* dismissal, and unless there are agreed procedures for such cases, management are generally free to choose whom they wish to make redundant based on a whole range of criteria—length of service, poor work record, and so on. However, employers would be well advised to have redundancy procedure agreements, on industrial relations grounds. Many of these agreements are on the 'last-in, first-out' principle. It was held by the Employment Appeal Tribunal in 1982 that as much warning of impending redundancy as possible should be given; consultation with unions should endeavour to limit hardship, and the criteria for redundancy selection should not depend solely upon the opinion of the person making the selection. Employers should make every effort to see whether alternative employment was available.

Firms not complying with this current industrial practice could well find themselves on the losing side if their employees who were made redundant claimed unfair dismissal.

Past retirement age

The Court of Appeal ruled in 1983 that once an employee had reached his/her normal retiring age (that is, the earliest age at which he/she could be required to retire), he or she had no right not to be unfairly dismissed.

Breaking the law

This covers cases where an employee, if he continued to do the job he was engaged to do, would be breaking the law. An example would be a long-distance lorry driver who was convicted of drunken driving and lost his licence. However, even if continued employment in that job were illegal, the employer needs to check whether other relevant employment is available (e.g. testing vehicles on private property) before he would be justified in dismissal.

Here again is exemplified the need to make clear in an employment contract and/or on company notice boards, what the penalties are likely to be for breaking the law as far as continued employment is concerned.

Other substantial reasons

On the face of it, the usual umbrella clause to include almost everything, but in practice its use has been to cover instances where the continuance of the contract of employment, or business relationship would be harmful, unsuitable, or intolerable. For example, imagine a wife working for a building firm, and her husband setting up a firm of his own in opposition. A situation would arise which would be awkward to say the least. Her dismissal would be *fair*.

Other examples envisaged as 'substantial' reasons have included personality clashes between senior managers, staff unacceptable to customers, staff refusing to live near the job when it was important they should.

23.3.4   Proper procedures for dismissal

It will have become quite obvious from the repetition in section by section, of the need for the employer to make the contract clear, spell out carefully what penalties would be incurred in particular circumstances, prepare job descriptions, etc., that in the interests of efficiency, fairness and common sense, proper procedures appropriate to each situation need to be drawn up, agreed and implemented. So it is with dismissal procedures: a properly documented warning system, with degrees of seriousness indicated; oral warnings followed by written ones, clearly indicating the reasons for the warnings, and stating the penalty (including dismissal) applicable for future breaches of discipline, or cases of unsatisfactory performance.

A typical procedure would also list the level of management authorized to take the action required, as the following (fictional) example illustrates:

DAYBREAK LTD—DISCIPLINARY PROCEDURES

1. All employees are advised that disciplinary procedures will be taken where an employee's conduct or work performance falls below the required standard; or where an employee fails to abide by the items of his/her contract of employment.
2. The overriding aim is to assist those employees whose conduct or work performance has fallen below standard, or who are failing to keep contract terms, to make the required improvements.

ACTION	MANAGEMENT LEVEL
A. *Suspension with Pay* (Precautionary) Where an investigation needs to be made into an alleged offence, and it could be prejudicial either to company or employee for the employee to remain at work.	Any, including immediate supervisor (but it would be usual for senior line management to be involved in the decision, in consultation with union representatives).
B. *Admonishment* An oral rebuke or warning recorded in employee file, and copies circulated to employee, personnel department, and immediate managers, union representative.	Any, including immediate supervisor. Union representative present.
C. *Formal Warning* An oral and written reprimand or warning stressing consequences of further failure to	Head of dept. or deputy.

ACTION	MANAGEMENT LEVEL
comply, recorded in employee file, confirmed in writing to employee and circulated with copies as above.	Immediate supervisor, union representative present.

D. *Final Warning*

An oral and written reprimand or warning: the most severe, stating that if the employee fails to comply with his contract, meet the required standard, within a set time limit, he will be suspended without pay or dismissed; confirmed in writing to employee and circulated with copies as above.

Works manager or deputy.

Immediate supervisor, head of dept., union representative present.

E. *Dismissal*

With notice, as contract.

Works manager or deputy.

F. *Summary Dismissal*

With appropriate investigation/hearing. Employee present, with friend and/or union representative. Contract ended immediately, no notice. (Reserved for gross misconduct, serious breaches of discipline or gross negligence or where the continual presence of the employee would be inappropriate.)

Works manager or deputy or most senior manager available at the time.

G . *Appeals*

Appeals against any disciplinary action must be made in writing within 72 hours.

All appeals other than against summary dismissal will be held by:

Next highest manager to that initiating disciplinary action.

Appeals against summary dismissal will be held by:

Directors of company.

3. Before any disciplinary action is taken (with the exception of suspension with pay) there will be a thorough investigation, and an examination of all the circumstances. The employee will be able to reply to any allegations made, and may be accompanied by a friend and/or union representative.

23.3.5   Remedies against unfair dismissal

An employee can go to an industrial tribunal to complain about unfair dismissal. (Normally ACAS would review and attempt to conciliate first.) Once a case is upheld, the tribunal must explain to the successful complainant what orders for reinstatement (i.e. employee getting his own job back), or re-engagement (i.e. employee getting another job with his old firm) can be made, and ask what the complainant's wishes are.

An order for reinstatement requires that the employer treat the complainant as if he were not dismissed. The tribunal must specify what arrears of pay, seniority rights, pension rights must be restored, and set a time limit on the reinstatement.

An order for re-engagement requires the employer to employ the complainant in employment *comparable* to his previous, pre-dismissal work, with back pay, etc.

The tribunal must consider the complainant's wishes, and whether it is practicable to make either order—it would obviously not be a sensible thing to do if employer and complainant are incompatible. If the tribunal *does* make an order, and the employer fails in some way to meet it, or refuses to comply at all, the tribunal will assess penalties. The maximum total was originally fixed at £5200, but all figures such as this are increased at irregular intervals (to take account of inflation).

Where the tribunal does not decide to make an order, it can demand straight compensation, based on the redundancy payment rules, plus compensation, for the dismissal and subsequent loss of earnings. For example, in 1978 Vauxhall Motors were ordered to pay a total of £7319 compensation to a worker dismissed for sleeping on the nightshift, made up of £525 redundancy pay, £4984 to cover loss of earnings, and a 'penal' award of £1900 to cover the fact the firm had stated that in no way would they re-engage or reinstate the complainant.

Note 1. The Employment Act 1980, Section 9, makes several changes to the provisions on the *basic award* of compensation for unfair dismissal. It provides, in particular, for this calculation to be on the same basis as redundancy payments.

Further, this section also empowers tribunals to *reduce* the basic award in instances where the employee 'unreasonably' refuses an offer of reinstatement from the employer. It also gives tribunals discretion to reduce the award in the light of an employee's conduct before the dismissal (even where such conduct would *not* come under the heading of 'fault' which contributed to the dismissal). Additionally, the minimum entitlement to two weeks' pay is abolished.

Note 2. More recent changes affect the rights of part-time workers—those working between 8 and 16 hours per week—who now have both the rights of claiming they have been unfairly dismissed, and an entitlement to whatever is the current statutory redundancy payment. (The House of Lords [March 1994] held that certain provisions of the Employment Protection (Consolidation) Act 1978 were incompatible with European Community Law.)

Note 3. During the 1980s, although tribunals has occasionally awarded large sums, more than half were of £1000 or less. However, more recently very large sums have been awarded in dismissal cases related to pregnancy; and it became necessary for the Employment Appeal Tribunal to lay down guidelines to govern any future cases of this kind.

23.3.6 Excluded categories of workers

Certain categories of worker are excluded from the provisions of the legislation:

1. Persons employed by close relatives.
2. Persons working less than 8 hours per week.
3. Persons on a fixed term contract of one year or more who have agreed in the contract to forgo unfair dismissal rights.
4. Persons having reached the normal age of retirement.

Supplementary Notes: The last category is not excluded, if the reason for dismissal is related to an employee's rights to be involved in union affairs.

The Employment Act 1980 brings in a new provision to cope with certain situations where it would seem an employer has been pressurized into dismissing an employee who subsequently claims he has been unfairly dismissed, and who takes his case to a tribunal. Section 10 of the Act enables such an employer to 'join' (i.e. have made a party to the proceedings) a person or trade union whom he claims induced him by industrial action (or a threat of such action) to dismiss the employee for *not* being a member of a trade union. If a tribunal finds such a claim by an employer is proved, then the person (or union) 'joined' in this action may be ordered to pay the employee part or all of any compensation awarded.

Under TURERA, employers are now free to negotiate 'severance packages' (i.e. financial and other inducements to sweeten dismissal or redundancy) directly with employees, which packages can contain terms which exclude those employees concerned from exercising their rights to start proceedings before an industrial tribunal. To be totally effective, employers should ensure those employees involved have had legal advice. Careful attention must also be taken to ensure any written document relating to such an agreement uses a form of words which complies with the requirements of TURERA.

23.3.7 Final comments

In summing up a complicated topic, we can discern several themes which stand out:

1. The onus is on the employer to prove that he was acting reasonably (under one of the headings, misconduct, incompetence, etc.) when dismissing an employee; and he has to convince an industrial tribunal that the principal reason for dismissal was *fair*.
2. The employer does not have to prove that the employee had actually committed misconduct, only that he had reasonable grounds for believing he had.

3. Where proper, agreed disciplinary procedures exist; where the principal reason for dismissal comes under those allowed as *fair*; where the procedures have been carefully followed, and a dismissal results, then it is very unlikely a tribunal will rule against the employer.
4. These procedures should, of course, include the opportunity for the employee concerned to put his case, and be represented by a union representative.
5. If you feel that an employee 'on trial' is not going to 'make the grade' you have just one year in which to make up your mind, before the unfair dismissal clauses begin to affect the situation except where an organization has less than 21 employees, where the operative period is *two* years.
6. Employers should be careful not to treat employees in such a way as to leave room for a claim for constructive dismissal.
7. Employers should negotiate redundancy procedures well in advance of any need to use them.
8. The normal resolution of *successful* claims for unfair dismissal is compensation (and/or damages). In fact, there is nothing in the Act which compels an employer to take a worker back. Indeed in some cases firms who are determined to dismiss a man because they feel they must, willingly either settle out of court or pay whatever is ordered by the tribunal; in effect they purchase the dismissal of the employee.

23.4   EMPLOYMENT PROTECTION ACT 1975

Reference also: Employment Protection (Consolidation) Act 1978; Employment Act 1980; TURERA.

Omitted from the following sections are the items relating to trade union recognition, remedies for unfair dismissal (considered in the previous section), the setting up of the Employment Appeal Tribunal, and various miscellaneous provisions.

23.4.1   The Advisory, Conciliation and Arbitration Service—ACAS

The Act set up ACAS and defined its terms of reference, and added that ACAS was to be responsible for issuing 'codes of practice' giving guidance for improving industrial relations. A fuller consideration of the work of this body is to be found in Unit V, but we should note here that ACAS has had a considerable impact on industrial relations despite criticism from each side, particularly on contract-based matters, including unfair dismissal.

23.4.2   Disclosure of information

We have already noted the saying 'information is power'. When two parties bargain, one in possession of all the facts and background information, and the other not, the advantage obviously lies with the party with the information. This section of the Act attempts to remedy the situation by requiring employers to disclose, at the request of union representatives (for the purpose of collective bargaining), any information about their undertaking without which the representatives would be impeded in their task. Additionally, the disclosure should be made if it accords with good industrial practice—including any code of practice.

Obviously information provided could help clarify what is being discussed, and perhaps remove any (mistaken) preconceptions. A high wage claim made without the knowledge that the firm will only just break even this year in a difficult economic climate is bound to lead to conflict and, whatever the outcome, a dissatisfied work force. ACAS recommended that information should be given on (amongst many items):

Pay. Details of principles and structure of payment systems; earnings and hours analysed under headings such as grade and sex; details of fringe benefits.

Conditions of service. Besides the conditions of service of employees' contracts, details of recruitment training and redundancy plans; job evaluation appraisal systems.

Employment. Here the labour statistics, including LTO, where people are employed, manning.

Productivity. Appropriate statistics, details of savings made from productivity, market share. An important item—the state of the order book.

Financial situation. Costing information, details of profits both gross and net; assets and liabilities, and financial assistance received from the Government.

ACAS stress their recommendations that an agreement should be drawn up between management and unions on:

1. What information should be provided.
2. How it should be submitted—layout, format.
3. How problems and disputes on giving information are to be resolved.

Confidentiality is bound to be a problem, and a company could refuse to disclose information on the grounds that disclosure could cause 'substantial injury' to the company. (Examples could be information on new products; or perhaps financial details which might show an unhealthy cash position which might cause suppliers to refuse to supply raw materials.)

Under the Act, additionally, employers need not disclose information which would be against national security; if it is against the law to do so, or the information was obtained for the conduct of legal proceedings. Employers need not produce, or allow inspection of documents except those conveying information. They can decline to compile or gather information where the work involved would be out of reasonable proportion to its value.

Complaints that information has not been provided, on request, are to be made to the Central Arbitration Service, who attempt to conciliate first. ACAS comments that in the cases dealt with in 1978, a considerable number referred to requests for information in a much narrower context than the Act envisaged unions requiring to deal with grading disputes, for example.

23.4.3 Guarantee payments

After having been employed continuously for four weeks, an employee losing pay on any day in the following weeks because the employer was unable to provide work, is entitled to a 'guarantee' payment for the workless day. (Inability to provide work due to a trade dispute does not so entitle an employee; nor cases where alternative work is offered.)

The method of calculating the amount due is fairly complex, but the daily maximum rate in 1988 was £11.30 per day. However, only 20 days' payments are allowed in a year—five each in any period of three months.[2]

23.4.4 Maternity

This section acknowledges the large number of women at work; and the need to safeguard them and their jobs, if they become pregnant. The expectant mother has three rights:

To keep her job

An expectant mother who has been a full-time employee has the right not to be dismissed because of her pregnancy. To combat a case of unfair dismissal an employer would have to show she would have been dismissed for another substantial reason. In any event an employer should look around for any suitable vacancy, on conditions no less favourable than her earlier job, and must prove that an offer *was* made, or that no such vacancy existed. Dismissal may be unfair, on the grounds of sex discrimination.

TURERA laid down dismissal on maternity related grounds (for whatever reason) is unfair. (The Court of Justice of the European Communities also ruled in July 1994 dismissal of a pregnant woman, who had been recruited for an indefinite period, could not be justified because she was temporarily unable to perform the work for which she had been engaged.)

The European Court also ruled (August 1993) that employees of both sexes who suffer from discrimination must be compensated in full for the loss and damage they might have suffered; and this led to the award ceiling of £11 000 being abolished. Women who had been forced to resign from the Services on becoming pregnant some years previously then began to bring proceedings; and tribunals made awards well in excess of £100 000. Eventually, in July 1994, the Employment Appeal Tribunal advised tribunals 'to keep a due sense of proportion in assessing compensation'.

---

[2] As amended by the Employment Act 1980.

To receive maternity pay

New maternity rights for women were introduced during October 1994. The main points were:

1. Where previously a woman had to work in a job continuously for two years to qualify for any maternity leave, the new regulations give a woman a statutory right to *at least* 14 weeks' maternity leave regardless of her length of service or hours of work. (But see point 3, below.)
2. Where, however, a woman has worked either full-time for two or more years continuously *or* for five years, continuously, for less than 16 hours per week (but for more than 8 hours) she will have an entitlement to a total of 40 weeks' leave: 11 weeks before the birth; and 29 weeks afterwards.
3. The new regulations give a woman employee up to 18 weeks' Statutory Maternity Pay (SMP) whilst on maternity leave, provided that she had worked for at least 26 weeks prior to the 12 weeks before the baby's birth.
4. Statutory Maternity Pay (SMP) entitlement is 90% of her average earnings for the first 6 weeks, and £52.50 per week (October 1994 figure) for the remaining 12 weeks. Women who only qualify for 14 weeks' maternity leave (see point 1, above) do not receive the last 4 weeks of SMP.
5. It should be noted that those women earning *less than* £57 per week, or those who have been in continuous service for less than 26 weeks, will still be excluded from the new rights to statutory maternity leave.
    (At the time the regulations were introduced it was, however, estimated that one in four of employers in the UK provided more than these statutory minimum entitlements. Some, indeed, offer up to 12 months' leave. Others, such as Marks and Spencer pay more than the statutory minimum SMP.)
6. All women who are on maternity leave continue to enjoy all the other elements of their contract of employment (e.g. holiday entitlements, pension rights), excepting of course their normal pay.
    Whilst employers would have 92% of the costs of SMP reimbursed by the government (by deduction from NI contributions), we might still consider the costs to a generous employer with a large number of female staff on the payroll to be significant.

To have leave and to return to work

The employee is able to leave her job (subject to the conditions outlined in the previous section) and return within 29 weeks after the actual date of confinement, in her original job, on terms and conditions as good as if she had not been absent. To take advantage of this right, the notification of intention to return must be made *in writing*, but with the addition that she intends to return to work, 21 days in advance (at least) of the absence. The employer (under the Employment Act 1980) may now himself write to an employee not earlier than 7 weeks from the beginning of her expected week of confinement (or the date of confinement) asking her to *confirm* her intention of returning, and to inform her that failure to reply will lead to the loss of her right to return. The employee must reply within 14 days, or if this is not reasonably practicable, as soon as is reasonably practicable (this provision is not a strong one despite the 'must' in the beginning).

To take advantage of her rights the employee must follow a similar procedure to that for the maternity pay claim. (The return may, however, be postponed by the employer for four weeks; and similarly by the employee if she produces a medical certificate of incapacity to return.)

The implications here are that an employer must try to give the employee her old job back; or try to find similar work in the same or associated company. Failure to do either could result in a claim for unfair dismissal, or redundancy.

23.4.5 Time off work

The Act recognizes that certain activities of employees should take priority over actually doing the job for which they were employed: trade union activities are, however, very much job-related, and some may merit pay during the time spent on such activities; public duties, while important, are not job-related, and do not merit *automatic* payment by the employer. We will deal with these separately.

Trade union duties (with pay)

An employer must allow an employee to take time off with pay (in other words the sum he would have received had he continued working—in a piece-work situation this could be the 'average' earnings of the shop) to carry out duties as an official of an independent trade union; or to take part in union activities which concern the employer, or associated employers; or finally, to undergo industrial relations training (approved either by TUC or his union).

ACAS has advised that such duties would include collective bargaining; reporting to union members about discussions with management; meetings with other union representatives or full-time officers of the union relevant to industrial relations with the employer and employees; hearing grievances from the workforce, and taking them up with the management; and advising new entrants about the union during induction. Additionally, in April 1982, the Court of Appeal ruled that where a union advisory committee for a particular company group existed, discussions on union policies could justifiably come under the term union duties. Thus it is clear union duties are not just limited to activities connected with the bargaining process.

Trade union duties (without pay)

This heading would really include any union member attending a meeting at work in connection with industrial relations matters, and possibly even meetings outside the actual work premises.

Public duties (without pay)

A limited range of public duties are specified in the Act—Justice of the Peace, member of a local authority, statutory tribunal, or health or water authority, or governor of a publicly maintained school or college.

(Note that an employer could—and many do—pay for time off under both the second and third categories. A purely practical matter is how much time off to allow; the Act says 'that which is reasonable in all the circumstances', taking into account the effect of absence on the employer's business.)

Redundancy (with pay)

An employee under notice of redundancy has entitlement to a limited time off with pay to seek employment or arrange training for future employment.

Maternity (with pay[3])

An employee who is pregnant and has an ante-natal appointment has a right not to be unreasonably refused time off to keep the appointment. This right does not depend on the number of hours the woman works for her employer, nor upon the length of her service.

23.4.6 Written statement of dismissal

An employee whose contract is terminated with or without notice (or, if for a fixed term, is not reviewed under the same contract at the end of that term) may require his employer to provide a written statement of the reasons for dismissal within 14 days of receiving the request for it.

The section complements the previous discussion on unfair dismissal: obviously such a letter could be used in evidence at an industrial tribunal.

23.4.7 Itemized pay statement

Every employee is entitled to a written, itemized pay statement, when (or before) wages are paid to him. The details to be shown are gross pay, various deductions (income tax, National Insurance, etc.); and the net amount payable.

23.4.8 Redundancies

Having already considered the redundancy of *individuals,* and the 'fairness' requirement of giving warning of impending redundancy in advance (unless this is not

---

[3] A new provision made in the Employment Act 1980.

practicable) in the previous Act, we are here dealing with the procedures for *group* redundancies, where those to be made redundant are members of recognized, independent trade unions. (By implication single redundancies are included, but the main discussion centres around larger numbers.)

An employer cannot make an employee redundant if that employee is covered by a recognized independent trade union without first consulting union representatives. Consultation must start as early as possible, and fixed times are laid down in cases of larger numbers as follows:

— 100 or more employees: not less than 90 days before first dismissal becomes effective.
— 10 or more employees: not less than 30 days if 10 or more employees are to become redundant within 30 days or less.

As part of the consultations, the employer must make a written submission to the union representatives personally (or sent by post to them or the main union office) which is to include:

1. The reasons for the proposals.
2. The total number and descriptions of employees involved in the proposed redundancies.
3. The total number of employees of each description (mentioned in (2)) employed at the establishment where the proposed redundancies could occur. (This would indicate the percentage of those involved.)
4. The proposed methods of selecting those to be made redundant.
5. The overall procedure, e.g. the phasing of the redundancies.

The employer is required to take account of any representations made by the trade union representatives, and reply to them, giving reasons for his rejection of any proposals made to him. Additionally, he has (in cases of 10 or more redundancies) to advise the Secretary of State for Employment of the situation and of consultations with unions which have taken place.

If a union complains to a tribunal that an employer has or intends to dismiss employees without following the prescribed procedure, and the complaint is upheld, the tribunal can make what is called a 'protective award', that is declare the employer must pay remuneration for a 'protected' period (90 days where 100 or more workers are affected; 30 days if 10 or more workers are affected; and less than 10-28 days). TURERA broadens further the need to consult with unions: the definition of redundancy has been widened now. Organizations undergoing restructuring or reorganization could well come under TURERA's umbrella: employers wishing to implement significant changes (especially with the intent of using the threat of ultimate dismissal against those not falling into line) would be well advised to enter into a prolonged dialogue with the unions involved. ('Protective awards' claims could well increase in such circumstances; such payments can no longer be offset—as in the past—by payments in lieu of notice.) There are a number of complicated clauses covering other aspects of these payments too specialized to consider here.

23.5 REDUNDANCY PAYMENTS ACTS 1965–9

For many years senior staff working for firms in the private sector had received what were described as 'golden handshakes' if and when they lost their jobs due to a merger, take-over or reorganization. It was a matter of individual bargaining, but when such payments were made they were considerable.

These Acts extend the idea of lump-sum payments (now called 'redundancy payments') at most employees dismissed as redundant, provided that certain conditions are met by the employees concerned. The thinking behind the Act includes the following ideas:

1. The older an employee is, the harder it will be to find another job: compensation scales increase with age.
2. The longer an employee works for one firm, the more obligation the employer has to provide compensation: compensation increases with length of service.
3. A minimum qualifying period is needed; and no compensation should be required when normal retirement is reached.
4. The more highly paid an employee has been, the more effect the lack of a job will have on his life-style: compensation increases (partly) with wage levels.

23.5.1 Definition of redundancy

An employee is redundant where the whole or main reason for his dismissal is that his employer's need for employees to do work of a particular kind has diminished or ceased; or where the employer has stopped or is about to stop business in the place (or for the purpose) for which the employees in question were employed.

23.5.2 Employees covered

All employees are covered (excepting those categories mentioned below) between the ages of 18 and 64 (59 for women) who have been continuously in service with the same employer for at least two years. Service before 18 does not count; and the 65th year of age for men and the 60th for women are treated under slightly different rules. Redundancy payments can only be made to workers who normally work 16 hours per week or more.

23.5.3 Employees not covered

The exceptions are shore fishermen, registered dock workers, Crown servants, National Health Service employees; certain long-term contract employees, employees who are spouses of their employers, and domestic servants whose employers are close relations.

23.5.4 Payment scales

The scales are:

1. For each year of service while aged 18 and up to but not including 22—½ week's pay.
2. For each year of service while aged 22 and up to but not including 41—1 week's pay.
3. For each year of service while aged 41 and up to but not including 64 (59 for women)—1½ weeks' pay.

(For men 64–65, and women 59–60, the amount payable is reduced by one twelfth for each complete month the employee exceeds 64 or 59.)

23.5.5 Supplementary points

It should be noted that:

1. Service over 20 years is ignored.
2. The actual current weekly pay level is used in the calculation (ignoring amounts over the current ceiling which needs to be checked at the time the calculation is made).
3. The employer is required to give the employee in writing a statement showing how the redundancy payment is calculated.

23.6 EQUAL PAY ACT 1970 (Reference also to Equal Pay (Amendment) Regulations (SI 1983 No. 1794))

This Act, which came into effect at the end of 1975, attempted to deal with a generally admitted situation that women did not always receive the same pay for 'like work' (as the Act calls it), as that earned by men. (The Act, of course, could work the other way if a women were more highly paid doing 'like work' than a man.) Inevitably, because of the concentration on the 'equal work/equal pay' theme, the Act does nothing to enhance the situation of women working in traditionally 'female only' occupations.

23.6.1 Employees' rights to equal pay

There is a right to equal pay and conditions where employees:

1. Do work which is the same, like, or of broadly similar character, including work equally rated under a job evaluation investigation.
2. All work at the same establishment or some other place controlled by the same organization. (A woman packer in company A cannot claim equal pay with a packer in company B—a completely unrelated company, for example.)

23.6.2 Like work

A woman is regarded as doing 'like work' if her work is similar to that of a man and if the differences that may exist between them are not of practical importance in relation to the contract of employment. Indeed, experience has shown that industrial courts have seen the need to interpret these words widely: differences in *hours worked* were not too important as longer hours were rewarded with more pay; working on a night-shift or 'unsocial hours' could also be rewarded differentially. Job titles, too, have come into the argument; recently a personnel manager claimed a company car on the grounds that all other managers in the company had one. She lost her case because it is not the job title, but the responsibilities that are taken on compared with others that matter. If a female employee takes over a job which was previously held by a male but the job now has a reduced volume of work, then it has been held 'less work is a *material difference*', and the employer could pay the newly promoted female employee less than her male predecessor.

Work of equal value

The Equal Pay (Amendment) Regulations 1983—Statutory Instrument No. 1794 of 1983—allow a man or woman to claim equal pay for *work of equal value*. This means an employee doing job A might feel his or her job was of *equal* value to the firm, or to society as job B, despite the latter currently being more highly paid, and that job A should be paid at the same rate as job B. Under this Amendment such a claim could be taken to an Industrial Tribunal.

The Amendment was initially brought in to comply with a 1982 ruling by the European Court that the 1970 Equal Pay Act did not enable employees to obtain equal pay for work of equal value where there was no system of job evaluation (i.e. job classification). However, now the Amendment goes further in that it is possible for an employee to claim equal pay (for equal value) even if both jobs compared were already covered by a job classification system—*provided* it could be shown that the job (classification) system discriminated on grounds of sex. In May 1988, the House of Lords held that a woman can point to *any* term of her contract which is less favourable than a comparable man's contract and claim equal treatment of that term, irrespective of her total package.

23.6.3 Other considerations

Also to be considered are circumstances other than the job itself; an interesting case, for example, could relate to women workers in a department, into which a man was introduced to do the same work. Suppose that the man was nearing retirement age and that his employers had given him lighter work, but kept paying him his previous (higher) wage. The women might object that they should receive the same pay as the man. In a particular case of this kind—a rather more complex situation—it was ruled the women were *not* entitled to the same basic rate.

The Employment Appeal Tribunal ruled in 1993 that where, in error, an employer had paid (a man) more than the going rate for the job, a woman doing the same job could not claim equality of pay. 'There was no evidence of intention to discriminate, or actual discrimination.'

23.6.4 Who qualifies?

The Act applies to all persons with a contract of employment, except those employees wholly or mostly outside Great Britain, but although generally servants of the Crown *are* covered, it does not apply to service personnel (i.e. Army, Navy, RAF).

23.6.5 Claims

Claims can be made to an industrial tribunal during employment or within six months of termination but awards of arrears of pay are limited to a period of two years before the date proceedings were started. The tribunal could also make an order that the complainant should be given equal pay and conditions.

23.7 SEX DISCRIMINATION ACTS 1975–86

Under the Sex Discrimination Act (SDA) an employer may not discriminate against a woman (or indeed a man) with regard to recruitment, terms of service or dismissal. It is also unlawful to discriminate against a woman because she is married. All employees, except those working wholly or mostly outside Great Britain, come under the scope of the Act. Organized religions are also exempt.

23.7. 1 Recruitment

Job advertisements must be non-discriminating. No longer can employers advertise for a 'waiter', 'sales lady' or 'barman'—unless the establishment employs less than six people. We have, therefore, seen the mushrooming of whole new crop of descriptions such as 'bar persons', 'sales persons', etc.

In the arrangements for selection, both the employer and his (personnel) staff have to be careful that they do not unnecessarily add to a job unjustifiable conditions or requirements which no or very few women could comply with. Where several candidates are interviewed care must be taken not to be biased against a person because of their sex.

The conditions and terms of service offered must be equal for both sexes.

23.7.2 Existing employees

Discrimination is unlawful in matters such as transfers, demotion, promotion, dismissal, training, holiday entitlements. Pay provisions relating to retirement must not be discriminatory (SDA 1986).

23.7.3 Lawful discrimination

Discrimination is lawful (on sex grounds, but *not* on grounds that a person is married) where there is a genuine occupational qualification—female models, prison warders, actors (Hamlet is a male part); or for considerations of decency—airport 'friskers'; or the location cannot provide for proper accommodation for two sexes.

23.7.4 Complaints

Complaints can be made to the Equal Opportunities Commission; or by individuals to industrial tribunals. A tribunal can declare the rights of the complainant, and award damages.

Typical decisions by industrial tribunals have been:

1. It was unlawful for an employer to have a *general* rule excluding mothers from being considered for jobs, because they were thought to be unreliable.
2. It was unlawful for an employer to decide that 'part-time' work was synonymous with 'temporary' work. (A very high award was given in one case as the dismissal was considered unfair as well as discriminatory.)
3. A woman judo referee was discriminated against when told she could not referee male bouts.

23.7.5 Sexual harassment at work

Whilst no law exists specifically covering sexual harassment at work, this topic has become more openly discussed, and industrial tribunals have used the Sex Discrimination Act to cover some acts of sexual harassment—that is tribunals ruled that the women concerned were treated less favourably because of their sex. Not only because of possible legal consequences, but also because of moral implications and the interests of good management, supervisors should be prepared to deal quickly and decisively in all cases of alleged sexual harassment. The assistance of higher management and/or personnel, is advisable at the earliest possible stage.

23.8   RACE RELATIONS ACT 1976

In many ways the Race Relations Act (RRA) is akin to the Sex Discrimination Act, in that discrimination is the major theme; in the case of this Act, it is made unlawful to discriminate in employment (and other areas) on the grounds of colour, race or ethnic origin. The RRA of 1976 brought up to date earlier legislation, and now includes the right of a complainant to decide to take his complaint to a tribunal, if it relates to employment.

Claims can be made in connection with recruitment, promotion, dismissal, as with the Sex Discrimination Act. Some cases are obvious ('primary' discrimination), where coloured applicants for a job are told 'it is filled', while white applicants are interviewed. Others are less obvious ('secondary' or indirect discrimination). They could relate to the special conditions a potential employee might have to meet in a job selection process, conditions which though perhaps very *convenient* for the employer, were not necessary, and which excluded a minority. If, for example, a requirement for a job was listed as 'a British biology degree', when neither was a degree strictly necessary, nor a British one essential, then because there could be a number of potential applicants from abroad (or even already living here) disbarred from applying secondary discrimination would have occurred.

There is no limit to the numbers employed before a claim can be made: an establishment with only one employee could have a complaint made against it.

It should also be noted that an employer is vicariously liable for racial discrimination by an employee done in the course of his employment.

23.9   WAGES ACT 1986

This Act reformed the law from January 1987 onwards on the payment of wages, and removed outdated restrictions contained in the *Truck Acts* (1831–1940). Employees, for example, no longer have the statutory right to be paid in cash, except those in employment in January 1987, and who were then paid in cash.

23.9.1   Deductions from wages and salaries

The basic rule is that deductions from an employee's pay will be unlawful *unless* they are statutory ones (e.g. income tax, National Insurance contributions), or as the result of *earnings attachments* made by a court; or are agreed to by the employee in writing, in advance.

The new provisions do not apply where:

1. Wages or expenses are overpaid—overpayments can be claimed back.
2. Trade union subscriptions are deducted under 'check-off' agreements though TURERA *does* affect such arrangements, and employers now need an employee's written consent before either deducting or increasing an existing deduction of trade union subscriptions from wages. Such consent must be renewed every three years.

3. Employees take part in a strike or other industrial action.
    (Note: *Miles v. Wakefield Metropolitan District Council 1987*—if a worker declines to work, the employer need not pay.)

23.9.2 Retail employment (cash/stock responsibilities)

Where anyone works in retail employment (shop assistants, cashiers, ticket clerks, fare collectors—anyone accepting payment in a retail transaction) who is liable (from the agreed contract of employment) for deductions for cash shortages or stock deficiencies, such deductions are limited to 10% of the gross wage payable in any given pay day. (An employee feeling an unlawful deduction has been made may apply to an industrial tribunal for remedy.)

23.10 WORKING HOURS REGULATIONS

Based upon the European Working Hours Directive, the UK regulations impose a maximum working time on any employee of 48 hours. A standard reference period of 17 weeks (i.e. about four months) is used to 'average out' the hours where an employee works different hours in successive weeks. An employee *can* agree to work in excess of this limit, providing (a) the agreement is in writing and (b) it is always possible for the employee, unilaterally, to terminate such an agreement. (Details of all the hours so worked by employees are to be kept available for inspection by the HSE or local authority.)

From 23 November 1999, all workers were eligible for 4 weeks' paid holiday annually.

23.11 NATIONAL MINIMUM WAGE ACT 1998

This Act brought in a minimum wage of £3.60 per hour, except for those under 18; and apprentices in their first year of apprenticeship (provided they were not 26 years old). Between 18–21 a minimum rate of £3.00 per hour was applicable.

SUMMARY

In view of the complex nature of the subjects covered it is inappropriate to attempt to summarize what in effect is already a summary.

REVIEW QUESTIONS

1.   What periods of *notice* must an employer give to an employee with sixteen years' continuous service?

2.   What items should be included in the list of terms to be supplied to new employees within the first two months of employment? What can an employee do if he does not receive this list of terms?

3.   Explain the term 'unfair' dismissal.

4.   What is meant by 'constructive' dismissal?

5.   What types of dismissal could be considered 'fair'?

6.   What remedies does an employee have against unfair dismissal?

7.   Can an employee who has been employed for five months make a claim for unfair dismissal?

8.   What is meant by 'disclosure of information'? Why is it an important aid to collective bargaining?

9.   Outline the maternity rights enjoyed by a lady employee of four years' continuous service.

10.   When are employees entitled to have time off work (a) with, (b) without pay?

11.   What should be included on an itemized pay statement?

12.   What procedure should be followed if an employer wants to make 150 employees (all union members) redundant?

13.   What is the maximum redundancy payment an employee could possibly receive under the Redundancy Payments Act? What is meant by redundancy under the Act?

14.   When is a woman entitled to equal pay?

15.   Outline the legislation referring to sex and racial discrimination.

DISCUSSION TOPICS

1. Discuss the view that there is too much industrial legislation now. Could not matters be resolved between management and unions without all the legal rules?

2. If you were a personnel manager in a large organization what action would you take to ensure that your 'contract letters' (written particulars of employment) were always up to date?

3. Discuss the following case of a claim for 'unfair' dismissal:

    Tim Stewart became the union representative of a group of workers in an hotel. He was anxious to get them all together as soon as possible to explain his proposals to negotiate with the management for better conditions. He made no bones about his mission in life: he told Mr Mariner, the hotel manager, that he would stop at nothing to get what he felt were the just demands of his workers.

    A week later he went to see the manager and gave notice of his intention to call a meeting of his workers the following day at 6 pm. Mr Mariner protested saying that he had absolutely no objection whatsoever to union meetings, but that 6 pm was a crucial time for the hotel, dinners were being prepared for guests, and a special banquet had been arranged that evening. Tim laughed at this, and replied that he still intended to call the meeting, come what may. Mariner countered by banging the table, and said, 'Call that meeting, Tim, and you've lost your job!'

    At 6 pm the following evening the meeting was held as arranged. Soon after 7 pm Tim went to Mariner's office to present a list of agreed demands to do with pay, working hours and holidays. Before Tim could explain Mariner told him he had been dismissed. Tim made a claim for unfair dismissal, saying he was obviously victimized for his union activities.

    (a) What would you decide imagining you were members of an industrial tribunal?
       (The class could split into various smaller groups, to compare findings and reasons.)
    (b) What reasons would you give for your decision?

4. Discuss the Daybreak Ltd disciplinary procedures. Do they in any way resemble procedures followed in organizations represented in the class? What amendments or improvements could be made?

5. Discuss the following case:

    Charlie Smart knocked on the supervisor's door confidently. A leading trade unionist in the firm, Charlie was a constant 'clocker-off' in the department, and Joe Glum, the supervisor, wondered if Charlie shouldn't be paid by the union, he did so much work for them. 'Joe,' Charlie beamed, 'I've just got elected to the council, and it's the first meeting this afternoon. I'm just off, and I'll book the usual average earnings for the time—I don't think I'll be back today!'

Joe answered, 'Just a minute, Charlie. I think you've had enough time off already. You can't go. I forbid it. Anyway, even if you'd gone, you couldn't claim your wages for gabbling away in that council chamber!'

(a)   Was Joe right to forbid Charlie to go? Did Charlie have an entitlement?
(b)   Was Joe correct in saying Charlie could not be paid for attending council meetings?

ASSIGNMENTS

One or more of the following reviews could be undertaken by individual groups or the whole class. The aim is to try to understand more clearly how individual organizations interpret legislation. Each review should be an evaluation and comparison of at least two organizations represented on the course.

A23.1   A review of methods used to provide written particulars.

A23.2   A review of methods used to monitor the progress of 'on trial' employees. Are any probationary employees dismissed?

A23.3   A review of any redundancy agreements obtained between management and unions.

24
Health and Safety Legislation

Laws designed to protect workers date back to the beginning of the 19th century. The first to benefit were textile workers, and in particular children, starting with the Health and Morals of Apprentices Act 1802, but it was not until a reformed Parliament had considered the problem that the first Factories Act was passed in 1833. The ten hour (daily) limit on the employment of children in the textile industry looks shocking to us, but was hotly resisted then by some employers. In addition the Act was ineffective in practice, the reason being the lack of people, i.e. factory inspectors, to enforce the laws. Four, later ten, covering the whole country could hardly scratch the surface of the situation.

Legislation was also passed in a haphazard fashion to meet public concern, for example, about dust or fumes causing death from industrial lung disease, and at intervals it was necessary to consolidate all that had gone before in all-embracing Acts. It also became apparent that Acts of Parliament were too cumbersome to deal with precise matters. Acts of 1891–5 gave the Home Secretary powers to draw up Regulations to deal with particular processes, or limit hours of employment, or prohibit young people from doing certain duties. These Regulations could be varied quickly to meet changing needs and conditions, thus involving less Parliamentary time. We call Acts which give Ministers powers to issue regulations *enabling legislation*, and the actual regulations are called *statutory instruments*.

As time progressed, mines and quarries, farms, factories, nuclear installations and other agricultural and industrial premises were covered by various Acts, and there were groups of inspectors to enforce them. Finally, in 1963, the Offices, Shops and Railway Premises Act provided protective legislation for a large group of people who had had no cover (other than the employer's common law duties) until then.

24.1 EVALUATION OF PAST LEGISLATION

Except in the case of the mining industry, legislation had the following characteristics:

1. A basic statutory code, supplemented by regulations relating to technical matters, leaving out work systems.
2. Enforcement by special groups of inspectors with only limited powers to enter premises, ask questions, or prosecute offenders.
3. Reliance on petty fines and punishments usually after accidents had occurred.
4. Legal responsibilities usually imposed on organizations, and *not* on managers or officials as such.
5. An emphasis on what went on *inside* the firm or organization's premises (relating to the protection of employees with a failure to protect 'visiting' workers, visitors and neighbours (excepting of course, the common law duties).

24.2   THE ROBENS REPORT

In 1970 Barbara Castle asked Lord Robens to chair a commission to investigate the situation. The 'Robens Report', as it became known, was issued in 1972. It could be said that this commission's work was remarkable for its grasp of the situation and for the recommendations that it made, which provided the basis for the Health and Safety at Work etc. Act 1974.

In particular the report concluded:

1. There was too much specialized legislation. It should be replaced by a single, general law.
2. The present law was too complex: the mass of detail should be replaced by precepts or guidelines of general application.
3. Enforcement procedures were unrealistic. Prevention is better than punishment after the event. Prosecution should no longer be the first and final resort.
4. Previous legislation concentrated on the workplace: visitors and the public should be protected.
5. Instead of undue emphasis on technical standards there should be stress on *management*'s responsibilities for providing and maintaining safe systems of working.
6. A failure to involve the workforce in the safety effort: nothing but good could come from involving workers in accident precautions.

24.3   ATTITUDES TO SAFETY

Attitudes to safety in the earlier part of the Industrial Revolution were in part influenced by the prevailing 'laissez-faire' philosophy adopted by governments towards the affairs of industry and trade; a policy of non-intervention. Life in those days tended to be 'nasty, brutish and short', with large numbers of town-dwellers living in insanitary and squalid conditions. That conditions at work were similar did not occasion surprise, and in any event many enterprises were run on a tight budget with money for safety a very low priority.

The history of the railway accidents in Britain is well documented, and throws interesting light on official attitudes to safety. Railway boards refused to adopt safer signalling methods despite terrible accidents and, at operating level, permitted important tasks to be delegated, sometimes with fatal results, to young, inexperienced, ill-educated and overworked staff. [1]

While we might condemn the Victorian attitudes to safety, the position in 1973 left little room for complacency: 600 000 people were *officially* reported as injured, though the real figure could well have approached 1 million; 1000 deaths occurred and 23 million working days were lost through absences due to injury; 250 000 people received disability benefits. (The American figures were equally disturbing with a yearly average of 6 million work-related injuries or illnesses.) Undoubtedly attitudes *have* changed, but despite the Health and Safety at Work legislation much remains to be done. Hopefully, supervisors will consider their responsibilities carefully and press for improvements where they are needed.

24.4 HEALTH AND SAFETY AT WORK ETC. ACT 1974

Following the findings of the Robens Report, this Act (HASAWA) attempted to jolt both management and workers into action by setting out a series of principles with a wide application, rather than a specific, rigid set of rules. Also needing to be tidied up were the seven different inspectorates, the powers they should have, and the speed with which they could act.

The duties of care (originally found in the common law) are now virtually all included in the Act's provisions, but instead of employees having to take civil action, inspectors can move in and prosecute if necessary.

The Act did not immediately replace or repeal all the earlier legislation (nine major Acts and 500 subsidiary pieces of law), and most of the existing laws and regulations will remain current until officially revoked and replaced by regulations or Codes of Practice issued under the Act. This means that we shall need to look at some salient features of the Factories Act 1961, and the Shops, Offices and Railway Premises Act 1963.

24.4.1 The basic principles

There are four basic principles or objectives of the Act:

To maintain and improve standards of health, safety and welfare of people at work

We should note here that all workers (except domestic servants) are covered by the Act, including the self-employed.

---

[1] L. C. Rolt's interesting book *Red for Danger* (Pan Books, 1986) provides many illustrations on this theme.

Note, too, that welfare is mentioned: in the past much greater emphasis has been placed on health and safety, than welfare.

To protect persons other than persons at work

The protection is to cover people who live near or pass through areas adjacent to workplaces, against the adverse consequences of what goes on in the workplace.

To control the keeping and use of explosive or highly flammable or otherwise dangerous substances

This includes the prevention of the unlawful acquisition, possession or use of such substances. A very important objective. Since 1974 a number of explosions in chemical works have occurred; and this type of accident becomes more likely as more complex substances are discovered and manufactured.

To control the emission into the atmosphere of noxious or offensive substances

This covers not only nasty smells but the far worse hazards (related to the third objective) of poisonous gas, or radio-active substances escaping into the atmosphere.

24.4.2 Duties of employers to employees

In the past, prosecutions could only normally take place where an inspector could point to a specific part of an Act or Regulation covering the alleged offence. Under this Act, an inspector would only need to test his view that in some way an employer has failed to meet either the first, all-embracing duty, or the subsequent ones set out below:

1. To ensure, so far as is reasonably practicable, the health, safety and welfare of his employees at work. (The general duty.)
2. To maintain plant and systems of work that are, so far as is reasonably practicable, safe and without risks to health. (The implication here for line managers (as representing the employer) is that they should keep under review the age, reliability, layout and maintenance of equipment, and work methods. They may wish to consider whether operators should be trained in fault detection, and either how to rectify them, or what to do to get someone else to carry out repairs.)
3. To make arrangements for ensuring, so far as is reasonably practicable, safety and absence of risks to health in connection with the use, handling, storage and transport of articles and substances. (This means that supervisors should keep under review, for example: systems for loading/unloading; the use of fork-lift trucks; the clearness of gangways and exits; the way that goods are stacked in the workplace.)

4. To provide such information, instruction, training and supervision, so far as is reasonably practicable, to ensure the health and safety at work of his employees. (Every line manager, in fact, *every* person with managerial or supervisory responsibility under this duty should ensure that he is equipped to provide not only for his own safety, but for that of all those over whom he has responsibility; to exercise constant vigilance to see that his men are properly trained to operate safely. The personnel function also needs to be directly involved.) Additionally, the European Directive of 1990, on the Management of Health and Safety at Work, makes a specific legal requirement that training for safety specialists, workers, and management be provided.
5. As regards any place of work, so far as is reasonably practicable, to maintain it in a condition that is safe and without risks to health. Further to provide and maintain entrances to, and exits from it that are safe and without risks.
6. To provide and maintain a working environment which is, so far is reasonably practicable, safe and without risks to health, and with adequate facilities and arrangements for welfare.

These are the (comprehensive) duties towards employees at work. There are others of a more administrative kind, but which still have a direct bearing on safety: employers must:

1. Provide a written statement of the organization's safety policy, and how the policy is to be carried out (i.e. spell out procedures).
2. Consult on safety matters with the safety representatives of independent unions (who are entitled to paid time off from work for safety training).
3. Form a safety committee if two or more safety representatives so require.
4. Not charge employees for anything done for their health and safety.

24.4.3 Duties of employers to persons other than employees

Here we shall distinguish between a general duty applicable to everyone other than employees and a particular duty towards contractor's men, or persons not employed by the employer who happen to be working there.

1. There is a duty of every employer to conduct his undertaking in such a way to ensure that persons whom he does not employ are not exposed to risk. (This would include visitors; and in addition the general public and those *outside* the premises who might be affected in some way by the activities inside the employer's premises. Warnings are to be given to the public about potential hazards by both employers and the self-employed.)
2. There is a duty of persons responsible for places of work to ensure so far as is reasonably practicable that the premises, plant and machinery do not endanger persons other than their own employees who use them. (This is the duty affecting visiting workers or contractor's men, and the aim is to secure their health, safety and welfare—safe buildings, properly maintained and heated, safe entrances and exits, etc. Of course, the contractor himself will have his duties to see that the surroundings his men work in are safe.)
3. In addition, in 1981, the Court of Appeal ruled that in order to satisfy this general duty of employers towards non-employees, not only must employers provide for

their general health and welfare, as above, but must also provide appropriate information and instruction to them. (The actual case covered a failure by an employer to distribute copies of practical rules for the safety of the users of oxygen equipment to sub-contractors engaged in constructing a ship. Ignorance of the rules led to a serious fire.)

24.4.4 Duties of manufacturers and suppliers

Novel duties are placed by the Act on both manufacturers and suppliers (including importers of raw materials and finished products). They have to ensure that what they supply will be safe when properly used *before* it is delivered to the place of work. Proper information and instructions for use are to be provided. Inspection and testing is to be carried out as necessary, particularly when an article is erected or installed by the supplier. (It should be noted that the employer, or user of the equipment, is still liable to ensure new, or newly installed equipment is safe, see duties 1 and 2 above.)

Designers also have the same duty and an interesting situation could arise where a manufacturer follows a design presented to him: the designer could take on the safety responsibilities and to that extent release the manufacturer who merely produces an article 'as per specification'.

There are specific duties (Consumer Protection Act 1987) laid on suppliers, manufacturers, importers and installers of fairground equipment.

24.4.5 Users of bought-in items

As we have seen, despite suppliers' responsibilities, the user (employer) retains ultimate responsibility; and indeed after a while will take on the total responsibility for new equipment, and for ensuring both machinery and materials used are safe.

A similar situation exists with chemicals and other substances. Suppliers must test and examine substances for toxicity and other safety risks before marketing them, and should specify what steps should be taken to ensure that substances are used safely. Users, on their part, need to see that their workforce are properly trained and instructed in use, and adhere to all known safety standards. Users would also have to be alert to complaints or reports about instability, etc.

An effect of the Act has been that suppliers and manufacturers often specify precise and limited uses for equipment and substances. The burden then shifts to the user/employer to ensure that what is bought fits the needs of the moment; and that it is used in accordance with the instructions supplied. Stores personnel need to take care to pass on appropriate instructions or warnings when supplying small quantities of items to other sections.

24.4.6 Duties of employees

The Robens Report drew attention to the fact that safety at work needed the involvement of the workforce. Besides the provisions already noted in respect of safety representatives, general duties are laid down for all employees.

1. Every employee must take reasonable care for the health and safety of *himself*, and of other persons who may be affected by his acts or omissions at work.
2. He must co-operate with his employer so far as is necessary to perform any duty or comply with any requirement imposed as a result of any law which may be in force. (Note *all* personnel, including managers and supervisors, come under the heading of employees. This section of the Act therefore *could* be used against any manager or supervisor who failed to institute safe systems of work, and someone became endangered as a result. At operator level, these duties would apply, for example, to a fork-lift truck driver who must control his vehicle with regard to the safety of others.)
3. He has a duty not to interfere with, or misuse things provided in the interests of health, safety and welfare—playing about, for example, with a fire extinguisher would be a criminal offence.

24.4.7 National safety administration

The Health and Safety Commission was established by the Act to deal with research, provide information and advisory services, and develop policies in the health and safety fields. The Commission is made up of members from employers' associations, trade unions, and other appointees. The current Chairman is Dr John Cullen with a wide experience of safety in chemicals, atomic energy and engineering.

The Health and Safety Executive operates under the general direction of the Commission. In particular it has absorbed the inspectorates covering factories, mines and quarries, explosives, nuclear installations and alkali works, plus the Safety in Mines Research Establishment, and the Employment Medical Advisory Service.

24.4.8 Codes of Practice, Regulations

As previously mentioned, existing legislation is to be phased out and replaced by Regulations, which are submitted to the Secretary of State by the Commission. The Commission is also empowered to issue Codes of Practice containing guidance on safety matters. A code dealing with time off with pay for safety representatives came into effect in October 1978. Training was considered desirable in safety law, nature and extent of work plan hazards, and how to carry out safety inspections.

24.4.9 Inspectors and their powers

Some inspectors will be appointed by the Executive, some by local authorities. Inspectors are each given a written document specifying the power they may exercise (including powers of entry, examination and investigation). Such powers could vary from inspector to inspector.

Some of the powers of inspectors listed in the Act are:

1. To enter premises at any reasonable time, in the performance of his duties; to be accompanied by a police officer, or anyone else duly authorized, if he feels it necessary.

2. To require a workplace to be undisturbed (e.g. after an accident) so that he can make his investigations; to take measurements, photographs, etc.
3. To inspect premises—including aircraft, tents and movable structures.
4. Where anything is identified by the inspector as being a probable hazard to health or safety, he can test it, cause it to be dismantled, or even destroyed in certain circumstances.
5. To question employees, and require them to sign a declaration of the truth of their replies; to see relevant documents (including the general register or accident book).

An inspector could prosecute an organization or an individual for breach of the Act or the general duties, but as we noted the Robens Report felt that prosecution should not be the first and final resort. Accordingly inspectors have been given the power to issue Notices, obliging employers to remedy a contravention of a regulation, or cease operating in a particular way.

Entry to the Inspectorate today is at graduate level, with normally a requirement for appropriate industrial experience. Its total force is about 850 inspectors and in the last decade they have been making some 200 000 inspections annually.

24.4.10   Improvement Notice

If a person is thought by an inspector to be breaking the law (HASAWA or some safety regulation), he may issue an Improvement Notice, requiring that person to remedy the situation-within a given, stated period. In effect, the inspector is saying, 'I believe that you are breaking the law (or might do so), but I am giving you time to put things right'.

Notices can be served on employers, employees or the self-employed. Appeals can be made against Improvement Notices (provided that they are made within 21 days) to an industrial tribunal, who may agree to modify or cancel notices. While an appeal is pending, the Improvement Notice is suspended.

24.4.11   Prohibition Notice

An inspector can serve a Prohibition Notice on a person 'in control of activities', which in the inspector's opinion involve a serious risk of personal injury. The Notice will specify the opinion and direct the activities listed to cease unless and until the matters specified are put right. The inspector can delay the effect of the notice so that things can be put right, for a period of 21 days. If the risk is serious enough, and imminent, the Act provides the Notice shall be effective immediately.

Appeals can be made against Prohibition Notices, but unless the tribunal so orders there is no suspension pending the appeal.

24.4.12 Prosecutions

Failure to comply with a Notice past the appeal period (or where an appeal has been made and is lost), could lead to a prosecution in a Magistrates Court (in Scotland a Sheriff's Court). Serious breaches or repeated breaches could lead to a Crown Court case, with unlimited fines and/or imprisonment for up to two years.

24.5 FACTORIES ACT 1961

This Act will eventually be completely superseded by Regulations issued under the HASAWA. Included below are some important features of particular relevance to supervisors. In any event the Factories Act specifically states that an abstract of the Act and certain prescribed information must be kept posted at the principal entrance of a factory, and factory supervisors should already be aware of the detailed provisions, or be able to check on them.

24.5.1 General provisions—health

Cleanliness. Every factory is to be kept clean and free from drain smells; dirt and refuse is to be removed daily, workroom floors to be cleaned weekly.

Overcrowding. The minimum standard is 400 cubic feet per worker, no space higher than 14 feet from the floor to be taken into account. (A notice specifying the number of people who can be employed in a workroom is to be posted up.) Space taken up by benches is not, however, taken into account.

Temperature. Where work people sit down most of the time, a temperature of 60°F (15.5°C) is to be maintained after the first hour.

Ventilation. This is to be adequate, *lighting* suitable and sufficient: glazed windows and skylights to be kept clean and free of obstruction.

Sanitary conveniences. Sufficient and suitable conveniences must be provided; kept clean and lighted, with separate accommodation for each sex.

24.5.2 General provisions—safety

Many of these provisions refer to the fencing of machinery, and vessels containing scalding, poisonous, or corrosive liquids; and others cover hoists and lifts; chairs, ropes and lifting tackle; cranes and lifting machines. The precise details should be checked if such provisions apply in your workplace.

All floors, steps, stairs, passages, gangways and ladders are required to be of sound construction, adequately maintained, kept free from obstruction. Staircases need handrails, and, if open, lower guardrails. Safe means of access must be provided to every workplace.

A *fire certificate* must be obtained approving fire escapes provided, where more than 20 people are employed (and in some cases where there are only 10 employees). The certified means of escape is to be maintained and kept free from obstruction. Exit doors must not be locked or fastened, so they can be easily opened; the doors should slide or open outwards; all escape doors should be clearly marked, and in every room a free passageway must be kept to the means of escape.

In most cases fire instructions must be given to all employees where more than 20 are employed.

24.5.3 General provisions—welfare

Adequate drinking water. This must be provided together with facilities for washing (plus hot/cold running water), soap, towels, or other similar means of cleaning and drying.

Cloakroom facilities. Accommodation for clothing not worn during working hours must be made available, plus facilities for drying it out. Sitting facilities should be available for all workers who could sit at their work.

A first-aid box. First-aid equipment must be provided and maintained (if more than 150 people are employed more than one is needed). Every box should be put in the charge of a 'responsible' person; and in a factory of more than 50 employees, the responsible person should have first-aid qualifications.

24.5.4 Other provisions

Other provisions include the provisions of goggles or screens when there is danger to the eyes; no-one is to be employed in lifting or moving loads which could cause them injury. There were provisions covering the complex rules governing the employment of women and young persons, including restrictions on hours of work or overtime. These provisions were removed by the Sex Discrimination Act 1986.

Details of young people engaged to work who are under 18 are to be forwarded to the local careers office, and subsequently firms may be required to permit the employee to be medically examined in working hours.

24.5.5 Accidents

If an accident occurs and an employee is killed, or so disabled that he is absent from his normal work as a result, for more than three days, written notice is to be sent to the local inspector. There are also other occasions when the inspector is notified: these are in connection with illnesses a doctor believes to be a result of poisoning con-tracted at work—'industrial disease'.

Records must be kept of all accidents and cases of industrial disease notified to the inspector. (Many organizations insist on every accident, however slight, being reported on an official accident form. Supervisors should be well acquainted with their own forms.)

24.6   OFFICES, SHOPS AND RAILWAY PREMISES ACT 1963

Many of the provisions relating to health, safety and welfare are very similar to those in the Factories Acts.

Differences are: *drinking water* must be provided which, if not piped, must be con-tained in suitable vessels and changed at least once daily; and if not delivered in a jet, drinking vessels are to be provided, with facilities for rinsing them.

The *overcrowding* provisions are similar, except that height over 10 feet is ignored; the minimum temperature to be achieved after the first hour's work is 16°C (60.8°F); thermometers are to be provided.

All premises to which the Act applies must be provided with suitable *means of escape* in case of fire. Many of the other details are similar to the Factories Act, with the exception of a requirement for a three-monthly test of fire alarms and a require-ment than all employees should be made aware of the means of escape and the route to be followed in case of fire. Fire-fighting equipment is to be provided and main-tained, and placed ready for use.

24.7   DEVELOPMENTS IN HEALTH AND SAFETY IN THE LATE 1980s AND EARLY 1990s
(Particular reference is made to The Control of Substances Hazardous to Safety and Health 1988 (popularly known as the COSHH Regulations); and the 'Six Pack', new European set of related Regulations including the Management of Health and Safety at Work Regulations – MHSWR – 1992)

We can think of the Heath and Safety at Work etc. Act 1974 as being a foundation upon which further safety legislation could be built. Some of this more recent legisla-tion was devised in Britain – the COSHH Regulations; the remainder – the 'Six Pack' – whilst being approved by Parliament, were based on European Union Directives.

24.7.1   The COSHH Regulations

The Health and Safety at Work Act 1974 briefly touches on the notion of safety as a *complete system*. But there is no guidance as to what *exactly a safe system is*. No modern organization can eliminate the use of 'hazardous' substances (even a humble bottle of bleach qualifies); or eliminate the force of gravity, or stop a bottle from breaking – nor, indeed, can an organization ensure it only recruits staff who never do anything silly, never have accidents. Thus it is vital to have a system capable of anticipating, reacting to, and dealing with emergency situations which accidents produce.

These Regulations have the effect of extending the responsibility of each and every employer to every health hazard which could arise from the use of all substances and materials to be found in the workplace, especially those which are toxic, corrosive or irritant. Thus a control system needs to be set up. There are four stages in the setting up the process:

Preparation

To begin with a *Risk Assessment* survey needs to be undertaken. In every part of the organization the employer has the responsibility to assess what hazards are present in respect of all substances used by the organization; to establish what health risks exist; to decide who might be harmed by such risks (and in what way); to evaluate the risks and determine whether existing policies and procedures are satisfactory; and then to prepare a plan of a complete system to minimize the risks identified as far as practicable. (See Regulations 6 and 7.)

Implementation and System Maintenance

Risk Assessments form the basis for written procedure documents and safety codes of practice. This can, in effect, place the onus on every manager, supervisor or team leader to check on the safety aspects of the work practices of every employee for whom they are responsible.

After these plans and codes of practice have been produced, the next responsibility for employers is to implement the appropriate systems and controls. To minimize yet further the possibility of accident or failure, a checking system must be created, to monitor the control system; and where necessary, the health of employees. Supervisors are intimately involved in both system implementation and maintenance. (See Regulations 8, 9, 10 and 11.)

Being prepared for emergencies

The COSHH Regulations not only lay down duties for employers to prevent employees being exposed to hazardous substances, but, where exposure does happen, to have a detailed set of rules and procedures worked out to minimize as far as possible the effects of such exposure. Whether due to a system failure, deliberate sabotage, or a totally unforeseen occurrence, employers must be ready to provide means of reducing risks to all personnel involved (see Approved Code of Practice, issued with the Regulations). (It should also be noted that the Pressure Systems and Mobile Gas Containers Act 1989, and the Environmental Health Act, both have the effect of re-inforcing the need to have written plans for the control of all hazards to health and safety.)

Monitoring the controls

The fourth stage is that of checking to see the control system is working properly. This includes, for example, keeping meticulous records of a variety of tests: for example, those of the work environment, of extraction equipment; of any personal equipment used in alien environments. Regular health checks made on any employee who may encounter hazardous situations at work also need to be recorded and put on file. Such records can be looked at by factory or similar inspectors. (See Regulation 12.)

24.7.2 The supervisor and COSHH

Managers, supervisors and team leaders have responsibilities under the Health and Safety at Work etc. Act, even though the ultimate responsibilities lie with the employer. The same applies to the COSHH Regulations. As well as ensuring their staff are fully conversant with every safety procedure to be followed in the normal course of work, supervisors must also make sure staff are aware of all possible hazards relating to any substance in use, how to minimize risks where there are hazards, and what to do if an emergency arises. Naturally managers and supervisors will need to lead by example by following any safety rules and procedures applicable to them to the letter.

24.7.3 The 'Six Pack' Regulations

This set of six separate but related Regulations came into force at the beginning of 1993.

1. Management of Health and Safety at Work Regulations (1992) as amended in 1994 by the Management Health and Safety at Work (Amendment) Regulations, 1994

These Regulations set the scene for the other five. They have a great deal in common with the COSHH Regulations, and are directly related to the basic functions of a manager's/supervisor's job discussed in Chapter 5.
   Four major responsibilities can devolve on supervisors in varying degrees:

— identifying safety hazards, assessing the risks involved, and recording findings
— preparing and recording the details of the arrangements for planning, organizing, controlling and monitoring the health and safety system
— setting up and operating health surveillance of employees (where this is necessary)
— training their own staff.

   The supervisor could well become a 'competent person' to assist the employer in fulfilling these responsibilities. The Approved Code of Practice accompanying MHSWR should be used as a guide to supervisors involved in any of the areas covered by the Regulations.

The 1994 Amendments require employers to assess the risks to health and safety of women who are either pregnant or have recently given birth and/or are breast feeding, and to ensure that such women are not exposed at work to any risks identified by the risk assessment.

2. Workplace (Health, Safety and Welfare) Regulations (1992)

Many of the areas covered by these Regulations will be familiar to those well versed in the Health and Safety at Work etc. Act (which in part, these Regulations replace). They set out legal requirements in respect of the work environment (e.g. temperature, lighting, ventilation); safety aspects (relating to doors, windows, floors); welfare provision (such as rest areas, toilets, seating arrangements); and good housekeeping (keeping the workplace clean, removal of rubbish and waste). Again supervisors are recommended to follow the Approved Code of Practice.

3. Manual Handling Operations Regulations and Guidance (1992)

Under these enactments which cover the lifting and movement of every kind of load, consideration has to be given to whether an activity can be carried out by non-manual means. If this is not possible, it will be necessary to assess what risks manual handling would entail, and record the findings. To meet the requirements, supervisors need to be trained in manual handling. The aim (as in other work situations) is to minimize any risk of injury.

4. Personal Protective Equipment Regulations (1992), and Guidance

'Personal protective equipment' means any equipment or clothing assisting in personal safety such as goggles, life jackets or weather protection clothing. Where normal provision more than meets the requirements of the Regulations, there is still a need to check the equipment's suitability, see it is suitably stored, ready and fit for use and to ensure staff are properly trained in its use. Provision and training are normally easily achieved: the more difficult aspect for supervisors is getting staff actually to use such equipment.

5. Provision and Use of Work Equipment Regulations (1992), and Guidance

These complex Regulations apply *now* to all new equipment; and to that existing and in current use, after 1 January 1997. 'Work equipment' covers anything used in a work situation, not just machinery. Again Risk Assessments need to be done on all existing equipment, to establish whether any work or modifications are required to bring it into line; and what regular maintenance is needed.

When purchasing new equipment, thought must be given as to how it will fit into the work environment; what potential hazards could be created by its introduction; what training will be required for those who are to operate it.

6. Health and Safety (Display Screen Equipment) Regulations (1992), and Guidance

Problems resulting from looking at computer monitors, VDUs, and display screens of all kinds for long periods include eye strain and headaches. These Regulations require the assessment of all risks associated with using such equipment; and employers have the duty of minimizing such risks. For example, training in the correct use of the equipment; planned breaks from display screens, or changes to different activities; and the provision of eye and eyesight tests will need to be arranged. As with other Regulations, the Health and Safety Executive's 'Guidance' is an extremely helpful document to all concerned.

24.7.4   Other Relevant Regulations

1. The Reporting of Injuries, Diseases and Dangerous Occurrences Regulations, 1995

These regulations specify occasions when reports, in writing, to the Health & Safety Executive (HSE) must be made. These include: a death as a result of a work-related accident (up to one year after the occurrence), the suffering by any person at work of certain kinds of injury, including various types of fractures; loss of parts of limbs, serious eye injuries; electric shocks, effects of contact with substances (requiring medical attention), and any injury requiring hospitalization for more than 24 hours. Supervisors, particularly those working in a production environment, should make themselves fully aware of every detail of this set of Regulations.

2. Environment Protection Act, 1990 (EPA); Environment Act, 1995 (EA)

The EPA covers such areas as air pollution, waste management and noise. The EA, while establishing strategies for air quality and various pollutants, introduced regulations which imposed responsibilities on waste producers to increase the re-use, recovery or recycling of such waste.

24.8   THE SUPERVISOR AND SAFETY

From what we have seen in this chapter, there are obviously many legal obligations placed on managers and supervisors (which are too numerous to reiterate) whether as agents for the employer, or as employees. But, in addition to the strictly *legal* role, the

supervisor has the task of promoting and maintaining a high level of safety consciousness among the workforce. Safety is not an exciting topic: indeed it can be greeted
with indifference or even open hostility, particularly where safety practices may be
time-consuming and/or inconvenient, or might limit earnings.

The safety minded supervisor will not only do what the law says, but try to involve
his workforce either by direct action, or in collaboration with other supervisors, or
where this would be more appropriate, through participation in company-wide programmes, devised perhaps by the personnel department.

Suggestions to improve safety consciousness amongst employees include:

1. Role-playing simulated accidents, with workers observing, and themselves trying
    to establish the causes and possible ways of prevention.
2. Competitions. These could vary from each employee being asked to find as
    many safety faults in his working environments as he can; to running a sugges-
    tion scheme to produce ideas for safer ways of working; or to organizing RoSPA
    poster competitions, with a prize for the employee finding the greatest number
    of hazards.
3. Departmental or shop safety committees, or even the involvement of every worker
    in safety discussions at regular intervals (this would have to be considered in the
    light of union-management relations).
4. Films—a selection of safety films is available.
5. Visits from inspectors, fire brigade, ambulance officers, etc., to advise and instruct
    employees in safety methods, the use of appliances, elementary first-aid. Possibly
    consideration should be given to a monetary award for possession of say a First-
    Aid Certificate.

Organizations are required to prepare and circulate safety policies as applying to
the whole organization (provided more than five people are employed). Supervisors
would do well to create a similar working document applicable to their own departments. The Accident Prevention and Advisory Unit of the HSE have produced a
useful check list to help organizations plan the overall policy (too long to include
here), and to act as a safety audit document.

Supervisors would do well to read it and pick out appropriate entries (e.g. 'Are all
walkways, gangways, paths and roadways marked?') and make up a departmental
safety audit check list. All employees could be involved in regular checks, with perhaps some recognition for those not only pointing out inadequacies or hazards but
how they may be overcome. No workplace can be entirely hazard free.

Finally, remember that your example is important. One factory inspector stated
that he often visited premises where management complained that employees would
not wear eye-shields on the shop floor. In one case the manager concerned took the
inspector into the shop to prove his statement, failing *himself* to wear an eye-shield.
As the inspector comments, how can workers be expected to be safety conscious when
managers are not?

SUMMARY

1. Although the Victorian attitude to safety can be severely criticized, Britain's safety record has not been satisfactory in recent years either.

2. Previous legislation consisted of a series of codes and regulations, applicable to the workplace, and inspectors could only prosecute precise offences. Punishments were petty, and individual managers or officials were not themselves prosecuted.

3. Lord Robens chaired a committee which reported that the law was too complex, technical and its enforcement was impossible; it concentrated too much on the workplace when visitors also needed protection and did not involve the workforce in safety measures.

4. The Health and Safety at Work etc. Act (HASAWA) of 1974 attempted to remedy the situation. It laid down duties (many taken from the common law duty of care) for:

    (a) *Employer–employee*. To ensure, as far as reasonably practicable, the health, safety and welfare of employees at work, by maintaining safe plant and systems of work; by providing adequate supervision and training; providing for the safe handling, storage and transport of articles and substances. To ensure safe places of work and a safe working environment; and to consult on safety with the workforce. (All 'as far as reasonably practicable'.)
    (b) *Employer–persons other than employees.* To conduct the undertaking so that persons not employed by him are not at risk; that premises, plant and machinery do not endanger them.
    (c) *Manufacturer/supplier–user/employer*. To ensure that which is supplied is safe when delivered, and safe to use with full instructions. Designers are also included in this duty of care. (Users would have to ensure instructions are followed, especially when bulk is broken, and that staff are properly trained in the use of that which is supplied.)
    (d) *Employee–employer*. To take reasonable care of himself and of others affected by his acts or omissions at work; to co-operate with his employer over safety matters; not to interfere with safety equipment.

5. The Health and Safety Commission is the controlling national safety body to whom the Health and Safety Executive reports. The latter body took over many of the previous inspectors and is empowered to issue codes of practice on safety.

6. Inspectors have written evidence of their authority, can enter premises, inspect, investigate, interrogate; destroy dangerous items or substances and issue notices.

7.   An Improvement Notice requires a person to remedy a safety hazard within a given period. Appeals suspend the Notice, but must be made within 21 days.

8.   A Prohibition Notice requires a person 'in control of activities' to have them stopped—either at the time or in the future; or if a serious risk of injury is imminent, immediately. Appeals do not suspend the notice, and have to made within 21 days.

9.   Failure to comply with notices can lead to prosecution.

10. The Factories Act 1961 (to be eventually phased out by the issue of appropriate regulations) covered aspects such as cleanliness, overcrowding, the maintenance of a warm working environment, ventilation and sanitary arrangements. The technical aspects dealt with fencing regulations, access and movement around the workplace and fire regulations.
     Welfare aspects involved provision of drinking water, accommodation for clothing, first-aid box, etc.

11. Accidents—those fatal and those resulting in an employee being away from his normal work for three days or more have to be reported to the inspector, and recorded in the accident register.

12. The Shops, Offices and Railways Premises Act 1963 contains many similar provisions, as applicable to shops and offices.

13. Supervisors have a positive duty to promote safety consciousness among their workforce.

14. The most recent legislation has amplified what was there previously. The 1998 COSHH Regulations extend the notion of employer liability to any health hazard that can or could possibly arise from the use of substances or materials in the workplace. Four steps in compliance are set out:

     Preparation—with Risk Assessment surveys, followed by a look at all existing procedures, leading to the preparation of modified or supplementary risk minimizing plans.

     Implementation and System Maintenance—involving the introduction and implementation of plans to cope with potential risks and codes of practice (being in essence a control system). Also developing a checking system to monitor the effectiveness of the control system.

     Being prepared for emergencies—to ensure that if control systems fail (for whatever reason), a set of rules and procedures exist to minimize the effects of the system failure.

Monitoring the controls—checking to see that the control systems are working properly.

Supervisors will need to ensure staff are fully conversant with safety procedures; are aware of all possible hazards in relation to substances in use at works; know how to minimize risks identified, and how to cope in an emergency.

15.   The 'Six Pack' set of related regulations was issued in 1992.

1.   The management of Health and Safety at Work Regulations include the duties of identifying safety hazards; preparing the details for planning, organizing, controlling and monitoring the health and safety system; setting up and operating an employee health surveillance system; and the training of staff in health and safety.

2.   Workplace (Health, Safety and Welfare) Regulations deal with the work environment.

3.   Manual Handling Operations Regulations and Guidance cover the manual lifting and handling of any kind of load.

4.   Personal Protection Equipment at Work Regulations relate to all aspects of protective clothing and equipment used in potentially hazardous situations.

5.   Provision and Use of Work Equipment Regulations and Guidance. These deal with any equipment (including machinery) used at work.

6.   Health and Safety (Display Screen Equipment) Regulations cover hazards arising from intensive looking at computer (and related equipment) screens at work.

16.   The Reporting of Injuries, Diseases and Dangerous Occurrences sets out the occasions when it is mandatory for written reports to be compiled and sent to the HSE.

REVIEW QUESTIONS

1.   What is:

(a)   Enabling legislation?

(b)   A statutory instrument?

2.   What were the disadvantages of the legislation passed prior to the Health and Safety at Work etc. Act?

3.   What was the Robens Report? What were its conclusions?

4.   What were the four basic objectives of the HASAWA? Who are 'persons other than persons at work'?

5.   What are employer's duties towards employees?

6.   What are the employee's duties under the HASAWA?

7.   What is the position with regard to suppliers of equipment?

8.   List the powers of inspectors under the Act. Who appoints them?

9.   Compare and contrast Improvement and Prohibition Notices. Which would be more appropriate in a case where poisonous gas seems to be leaking from a pipe in a workplace?

10.   List all the responsibilities now resting with employers in relation both to the COSHH and 'Six Pack' Regulations.

11.   What action must an organization take if an employee is away from work through a work accident related injury for over three days?

DISCUSSION TOPICS

1.   Safety is often considered a 'boring' topic by both management and supervisors on the one hand, and the workforce on the other. Consider the reasons why there should be so much indifference.

2.   Can an act like HASAWA do anything to improve the situation? Does involving the workforce—which is encouraged in some ways by the Act—help?

3.   Discuss how you as a supervisor could increase the safety consciousness of your work group.

4.   Discuss the view that all safety matters should be left to safety officers—after all it is their job!

ASSIGNMENTS

A24.1   From organizations represented on the course two or three safety policy documents should be obtained. Class members should be divided into two or three groups to evaluate and comment on one document and report back.

A24.2   Alternatively, each class member could obtain a copy of (preferably) his own organization's safety policy, and prepare a short report to read to the course. The report should outline the policy briefly and explain how it meets the organization's particular circumstances.

A24.3   In groups (as A24.1) the class should compare and evaluate the risks assessment procedures in two or three organizations.

A24.4   Noting *all* accidents should be reported (in case an injury today causes an absence in the future), however slight, design an accident report form suitable for office workers. (Firms' existing reports could be pooled to compile a joint effort.)

Case studies

A24.5   Fred Peerless was proud of his firm, the Tortoise Bus Company, for which he worked as a depot manager of the Slackville bus station. The safety record of his depot was good—three years without a single reportable accident. Indeed, Fred was also the depot's safety officer and had attended no less than six courses in the last two years.

He was, however, concerned about making his men more safety conscious. They had seen six films in the first half of the current year; and he had laid on innumerable talks and lectures for them. Lately, he had noticed a reluctance to attend; Joe Smith and 'Speedy' Price always seemed to have priority jobs to do when lectures were held.

Yesterday he had a shock when he glanced at Joe working under the newest Leyland addition to the fleet. A box of matches lay on the tool box, and a packet of cigarettes was beside it. Depot rules expressly forbade smoking on the job because besides diesel engined vehicles, several petrol driven vans were stationed in the depot, and petrol cans were lying about. Fred wondered what he should do: suspend Joe, or let the matter pass? After all, it was Saturday and if he blew himself up, Joe would only have himself to blame; no-one else was about.

(a)   Should Fred take any action? If he does not, discuss the legal position.
(b)   If Fred does decide to act, what might he do?
(c)   How can a manager cope with the lack of safety consciousness, after he has made as much effort as Fred?

A24.6   Terry Keene, the chief divisional safety officer of the Tortoise Bus Company
visited head office recently to discuss the revised company safety policy with
the general manager. The safety officer had visited all the depots, reviewed
all the procedures, agreed the necessary changes: indeed he was well satisfied with what he had done. Just as he was leaving he bumped into Albert
Staffe, the office manager.

'I'm glad I've seen you Bert,' Keene smiled, 'I might have forgotten about
the offices: after all I spend most of my time in the workshops or on the
road. Safety is as important in the office as it is on the factory floor.'
'Rubbish,' snapped Staffe. 'In your workshops I agree that a great deal can
go wrong, but my offices are well-run, ventilated, lighted and we don't need
your people poking round in smelly overalls. My environment is perfectly
safe: we've got all the fire certificates we shall ever need.'

(a) Is it true that an office environment is safer than the workshop?
(b) Whatever the answer to (a), work out a possible list of dangers or
     hazards which could exist in an office; or unsafe practices which
     could occur (such as opening more than one drawer of a filing cabi-
     net at a time).
(c) Does Staffe appear to be fulfiling his legal obligations?
(d) Why did Staffe snap back at Keene? Is Keene really a good safety
     officer?

The Supervisor and Industrial Relations

'Managers at the highest level should give, and show that they give, just as much attention to industrial relations as to such functions as finance, marketing, production or administration.... All managers should receive training in the industrial relations implications of their jobs. This is as necessary for line managers, including supervisors, as for personnel managers.'

(Industrial Relations Code of Practice Paragraphs 2 and 7)

25
The Background to Trade Unionism

Industrial relations (increasingly called 'employee relations' at organizational level, especially where unions play little or no part in management–worker relations) has long been a complex topic to consider, whether on a national or organizational level. However, a short introduction to trade unionism makes a useful beginning.

25.1   THE INDUSTRIAL REVOLUTION AND THE BIRTH OF TRADE UNIONISM

One of the many consequences of the Industrial Revolution (from say 1740 onwards), particularly in England, was the shift of population from countryside to towns; and instead of lots of small groups working on the land, fewer, but larger, groups of people were recruited to work in factories. At the workplace, groups of workers were employed on very similar tasks (and those tasks would often be similar to those done by other groups of workers in other, nearby firms). Rows of 'back to back' housing were built close to the factories, so that workers lived and worked in close proximity. Working conditions were dangerous and unpleasant. Thus the following conditions existed for union formation:

— economic factors such as the presence of energy (e.g. coal and water) and raw materials, caused similar types of industry to congregate in a particular place
— fewer employers
— easier communication between workers (as they lived and worked close together)
— the goals of individual workers were very similar, as they did (dangerous and unpleasant) work of a similar kind, in close proximity
— improvements in public transport (especially, in the beginning, the railways) meant people could travel around the country and meet others in similar work and compare experiences.

25.2   THE PERIOD OF GROWTH

After 1824 what were called 'trade societies' were legalized, and they began to proliferate. Those with similar aims began to federate, then amalgamate. (The Amalgamated Engineering and Electrical Union can trace part of its origins back to 1851.)

To begin with, unions were composed of the brighter, cleverer, more skilled workers. Indeed, the skilled workers' unions refused applications from those who were not 'craftsmen'. The rejected workers looked elsewhere, and a crop of 'new' unions (who were not interested in the 'friendly society' aspects of unionism) emerged. These new unionists were more militant, more political, with talk of 'capitalist exploiters'. Out of the association between these unions and those others with a more political outlook was eventually born the Labour Party.

25.2.1   Membership trends

From 1900 onwards there was an overall rise in union membership from some 2 million at the turn of the century (with a sharp increase between 1910 and 1920 when a 'high' of 8 million was reached), to a total of some 6.3 million by 1939.

Since 1939, there has been, first a steady fall in the number of unions, and in contrast, during the war years and beyond, a rise in membership which peaked in 1978 at 13.28 million. Since then there has been a fall in membership. Some possible reasons for this decline are mentioned in the following section.

Union membership could well be expected to fall when employment levels are also falling, but the downward trend has continued steadily from 1979 during which time employment has at times increased as well as decreased. A careful examination of labour market statistics does, however, reveal the number of members in service (i.e. 'non-manual') unions has remained broadly stable since 1988; the total decline since then (of over one million) is virtually due to a falling manual union membership. It is also worth noting the number of part-time workers who are union members increased slightly in the early 1990s, mirroring the recent general increase in part-time employment.

25.2.2   Some comments on the trends

The last few years have seen a continuing decline in the total number of unions, an initial growth in union membership and a corresponding increase in union size, followed by a slow, continuing decline in membership. There is no doubt that this trend to fewer, larger unions will continue, despite the reluctance of some smaller unions to give up their independence. The tendency for wage negotiations to become more centralized (in larger, manufacturing organizations, for example,); the concentration of employers into larger groupings (by merger or amalgamation); or by the centralized effect of employers' associations); and the TUC's policy of encouraging 'competing' unions to merge, all are factors in the situation.

In fact, there are two kinds of union mergers: amalgamations (two or more unions merging to form a larger union); and transfers of engagements (a sort of 'take-over' of one union by another). Amalgamations in recent times have included that of the Amalgamated Engineering Union and the Electrical Electronic and Plumbing Union to form the Amalgamated Engineering and Electrical Union (with effect from May 1992).

Indeed may of the larger unions today are the result of amalgamations, sometimes several of them. The Manufacturing Science and Finance Union (MSF) was originally formed from part of the Amalgamated Union of Engineering Workers and the Association of Scientific Technical and Managerial Staff. Since then another 6 unions have transferred to MSF. At the time of writing the largest union of all, UNISON (with 1.5 million members), could be described as a 'super union'. UNISON is the result of a 1993 amalgamation of three public service unions: NALGO (local government officers); NUPE (local government manual employees), and COHSE (health service employees). Unusually, the majority of UNISON members are female.

The general decline in union membership, and particularly in the unskilled manual sector, is partly a reflection of the immense restructuring that has gone on in British industry in the last two decades. Labour-intensive methods of working have been replaced by automated assembly lines; those workers remaining have had to learn new skills, and indeed, where 'empowering' has been introduced, to take on some of the responsibilities previously held by charge-hands or even supervision. In other areas, the demand for particular products has declined significantly (for example in coal mining: in 1979 the NUM had 372 122 members, but by 1994 there were a mere 18 227), and large numbers of workers previously employed in these areas have retired early or taken redundancy. If they have found work in smaller organizations, the chances are there was no union to join: only 18% of workplaces with less than 25 employees were unionized in 1993.

25.2.3 Looking to the future

Obviously concerned about the trends mentioned above in 1994, the Trades Union Congress initiated a study called *The Future of the Trade Unions*. Based on evidence submitted to the House of Commons Employment Committee, it concluded further contraction was not inevitable. Opportunities were available: the hope was workers could be recruited from developing industries and services. However it was necessary for unions to be pragmatic and take up the causes of all workers, whether or not they were union members. Unions could be relevant to workers on individual contracts, to those in small firms; and even to the self-employed. Time alone will tell if these aspirations can be achieved.

25.3   UNIONS AND POLITICS

Already mentioned above (section 25.2), unions were involved with the birth of the Labour Party. Over the years the majority of unions have not only supported the party with financial contributions, but have had considerable influence within in the party, especially with the use of the 'block vote' at Party Conferences when party policy was being discussed.

However the 1990s have seen some significant changes in that relationship: more power (for example, in the election of the Party Leader) has gone to both individual party members, and union members, rather than union executive committees exercising the power of the 'block vote'.

By 1994 the newly appointed TUC General Secretary, John Monks, had decided to broaden the unions' base of influence aiming to establish contacts widely with politicians of all parties (including speaking at 'fringe meetings' at each of the major party conferences), senior civil servants, and employers' associations. He wished to promote the idea of unions as being responsible social and industrial partners, co-operating with business and all political parties. Further, he saw no likelihood of (or call for) any formal TUC links with any future Labour government. His immediate aim was to improve the standing and respect given to unionism in general; and to the TUC in particular.

SUMMARY

1.   The Industrial Revolution changed the lives of the work force: there was a population shift from countryside to town. Conditions were then ripe for unions to come into existence: large concentrations of workers doing similar jobs with common dangers, with similar interests, who were able easily to communicate with each other.

2.   Legal recognition of unions first came in 1824, and despite setbacks, the growth of unionism can be traced back to this time.

3.   Initially, the unions formed were for skilled workers; and those without particular skills could not gain entry to them. Eventually new unions catering for the unskilled emerged. Politically inclined members were instrumental in the birth of the Labour Party.

4.   The numbers of workers who were union members rose from 1900 onwards; and doubled from 1939 to 1980. Since then there has been a steady decline in membership, particularly in the manual sector. Throughout the century, the number of individual unions has progressively declined through mergers and amalgamations. This trend has resulted in the emergence of a small number of very large unions with great influence.

5. Despite the long period of decline, the TUC came to the conclusion in 1994 that the time was opportune for a relaunch of unionism and the TUC. The policy became one of broadening contacts in politics and industry with a view to restoring the high respect the union movement had enjoyed in the past.

REVIEW QUESTIONS

1. What sorts of changes did workers leaving the countryside (from jobs connected with the land) face when they took up jobs in towns in the new factories?
2. What conclusions can we come to about trade union membership since 1939, as recorded in Table 25.1? In particular, can you account for the significant drop in the numbers of unions since 1939?
3. What is the distinction between 'union amalgamations' and 'transfers of engagement'?
4. Why is it UNISON aptly described as a 'super union'?
5. How far can it be said that unions are political?

DISCUSSION TOPICS

1. Discuss why you think trade unions arose. Were they formed to put pressure on employers, to squeeze as much as possible from them; or to improve working conditions? What do you think their role is (or should be) *today*, after such a long period of decline in membership? Is there, in fact, a case for letting them fade into history?
2. In 1994 a considerable debate was in progress as to the relationship of unions in general, and the TUC in particular, with the Labour Party and other political parties. Do you feel the union movement should associate itself with any particular party? If so, suggest which one, and why. On the other hand should the TUC maintain dialogues with all major parties?
3. A strong union movement depends upon a large and vigorous membership. Suggest ways in which individual unions could broaden their membership bases, other than by amalgamation.

ASSIGNMENTS

A25.1 Either in groups, or as individual course members, research into a particular union. Prepare a report on when it was first formed, and what kind of workers were invited to join it; what amalgamations have taken place during its history, and how its membership has grown or declined. (Where appropriate, course members' own unions should be chosen.)

A25.2 Using information gained from your own place of work, and/or those to which you have access, and that available in college, school or public libraries, look at the growth of part-time or job-share employment within the organization. Assess the problems unions might have in recruiting employees who work less than full-time.

26
Unions: Their Structure, Purpose and Objectives

Several definitions have been offered as to what a trade union is. Here are a few taken from various sources:

1. *Oxford English Dictionary:*
    'An association of the workers in any trade, or an allied trade, for the protection and furtherance of their interests in regard to wages, hours and conditions of labour, and for the provision, from their common funds of pecuniary assistance to the workers during strikes, sickness, unemployment, old age, etc.'
2. *Legal* (Trade Union Amendment Act 1876):
    'The term "Trade Union" means any combination, whether temporary or permanent, for regulating the relations between workmen and masters, or between workmen and workmen, *or between masters and masters*, or for imposing restrictive conditions on the conduct of any trade or business whether such combinations would or would not . . . have been deemed to have been an unlawful combination by reason of one or more of its purposes being in restraint of trade.'
    (Note: under this definition, what we would call employers' associations are trade unions: no one now would want to subscribe to this wider definition.)
3. *Academic*:
    The Webbs in 1920 defined a union as: 'A continuous association of wage earners for the purpose of maintaining or improving the conditions of their working lives.' Professor G. Cole thought they were: 'Vocational associations representing man in his capacity as a producer.'
    Professor J. Henry Richardson thought that unions were 'essentially associations of manual and/or non-manual work people, formed to safeguard and improve the working conditions of their members and more generally to raise their status and promote their vocational interests.'
4. *Trade Union and Labour Relations (Consolidation) Act 1992 (TULRA):*
    Lists of trade unions are kept by the Certification Office of Trade Unions and Employers' Associations under TULRA. To be entered on the statutory list a union body must satisfy a definition, the essential requirement of which is that it is an organization composed wholly or mainly of workers, and which has the regulation of relations between those workers and employers as one of its main purposes.

These definitions bring out the essential points that unions are associations or bargaining organizations, bargaining on behalf of their members for better wages and conditions. They are also organizations which 'impose restrictive conditions on the conduct of any trade or business'—'take industrial action'—as we would say today. A further function of unions is to collect funds to provide help to members in need. Missing from all these definitions is any reference to union political activity, which we mentioned in the previous chapter.

26.1   CATEGORIES OF UNIONS

In the past it was generally agreed there were four distinct types of unions, each of which had its own history, outlook, and set of values; and on occasions what might be called 'characteristic behaviour'. Whilst the amalgamations mentioned in Chapter 25 have greatly blurred the historical distinctions between these categories, it is still useful on occasions to use them. For example, during the 1994 dispute with Railtrack, the signalworkers (by then one set of members of the amalgamated Rail, Marine and Transport Union—RMT) were keen to lay emphasis on their special skills and expertise, and the way in which they had adapted to the introduction of modern technology. This stress on special skills was reminiscent of the characteristic behaviour of craft union members over the years.

26.1.1   Craft unions

The concept of a craft union was basically that *craftsmen* (women were not originally eligible to become members) skilled in a trade or trades should belong to a union representative of that trade or trades, irrespective of the firms or industries for which the craftsmen worked. (The beginnings of craft unions can be traced back to 1851 when skilled workers in a variety of metal trades formed the then named Amalgamated Society of Engineers and Machinists (ASEM).)

Craft unions were very concerned with preserving not only the status but also the jobs of their members. The ASEM's rules showed its exclusiveness through strict control over membership qualifications—only time-served apprentices, for example, could apply to be members. Considerable attention was also paid to the content of various skilled jobs to try and ensure only members of a particular craft union were employed to fill such posts. (This resulted at times in unions competing for the rights of their members to carry out particular tasks; even resorting to strike action. Such arguments were called 'demarcation disputes'.) Even as recently as during the 1994 RMT signalworkers' pay dispute, doubt was cast on more than one occasion on the ability of supervisory and other Railtrack staff to carry out signalling duties to the standards followed by signalworkers.

Change has, however, been inevitable: the clear distinctions between skilled workers and those less skilled have become blurred. Many craft unions now do allow semi-skilled, or even unskilled workers to join; women are now eligible to become members. Yet other craft unions have amalgamated with larger, less specialized, or even general unions.

26.1.2 General unions

These unions emerged as opportunities for the less skilled, not permitted to join craft unions, to combine. The result was that such unions were general in character: they drew members from every level of skill, and from more than one industry. An inevitable consequence was that such unions had to deal with the many differing problems of their members, coming as they did from many diverse industries and trades.

The current picture is even more blurred in that some unions, previously craft or white-collar/professional unions (see below), have amalgamated with these large general unions. In 1989 for example, the General Municipal Boilermakers and Allied Trades Union (GMB) joined up with the Association of Professional Executive Clerical and Computer Staff (APEX) to form an enlarged GMB.

26.1.3 Industrial unions

A definition of a true industrial union would have to make it clear that such a union would have as members *all* (or the majority of) workers in a particular industry, irrespective of occupation or level of skill. Such a union would *confine its activities to the one industry:* and not wish to expand elsewhere.

Whilst there have been numerous examples of industrial unions in the USA and (since the end of the Second World War) in Germany, few industries have been organized in this way in Britain. The National Union of Mineworkers was perhaps the most high profile industrial union. It represented a wide spectrum of interests amongst mine employees, but lost its position as an industrial union when, as a consequence of the mineworkers' strike of the early 1980s, the Union of Democratic Mineworkers was registered in 1985, with a claimed membership of 40 000.

It would seem, with both the break-up of large nationalized industries such as coalmining, and the ever-increasing growth of multinational organizations, there is little future for industrial unions in Britain.

26.1.4 White-collar unions

The term 'white-collar unions' is commonly used to mean non-manual unions catering for a wide spectrum of occupations and professions. Thus we find unions for teachers and lecturers, and people working in the banking and financial sector. However, as with the other categories of union, there has been a trend towards amalgamation, producing unions with a broader membership than in the past; even including manual grades as well. In this respect, we have already noted UNISON (a merger of NALGO—national and local government officers; NUPE—other national and local government employees, and COSHE—health service employees).

What is interesting to note is that the number of non-manual union members has been broadly stable since 1989. Indeed, some like the Royal College of Nursing (RCN) have increased membership over this period. This is probably accounted for by the fact that many of the white-collar unions serve employees in the public sector.

26.2   THE ORGANIZATION OF UNIONS

With such diverse categories of unions—craft, general, industrial, 'white-collar' and even more so where amalgamations between different types have taken place—it would be dangerous to pretend that any model or organization chart could represent the structure of all, or indeed most unions. Craft unions tend to have a strong central leadership, but policy is vested in a National Committee drawn widely from the various areas of the country: general unions have to reflect the different interest groups as well as regional representation.

The principle of delegation exists in unions, but in reverse to the way in which it operates in the formal industrial or commercial enterprise that we considered in Unit I. That is to say power is delegated *upwards* from the ordinary member: the leaders' powers depend upon the consent of the members. Thus, instead of starting with the shareholders, or board, we must begin with the ordinary member. (There is, however, a crucial difference between the *operation* of this delegation: in a company the delegated authority can be *quickly* withdrawn if the job holder's behaviour meets with the disapproval of the delegator. It is rather more difficult for individual union members to withdraw their delegated authority from elected officials; even more so from appointed ones.)

25.2.1   The member

Every paid-up member of a union belongs to a union branch, but on the whole is not noted for his liking to attend meetings. John Goldthorpe, in a survey in the 1960s of Luton car workers, discovered that 60% of branch members never attended meetings: only 2% attended regularly. A more recent survey amongst NUPE (National Union of Public Employees representing the manual side of local government and the public services) branches showed 67% of them reporting that no more than 5% attended branch meetings. Among teachers attendance is much higher, but there are instances here where the branch membership is drawn from just one work unit, i.e. one college, and branch meetings are held *at the workplace*. However, the problem of low attendances has been compared by one trade union official with falling church attendances. Indeed, there are probably factors common to both: not only 'agnosticism', but also the myriad attractions competing for everyone's leisure time, including of course, the 'telly'.

26.2.2   The shop steward

Because of low branch attendances, the union is personified for the majority of members at the place of work by the (unpaid) shop steward or union (or staff) representative. The exact number of such officials is in doubt: figures of 250 000 have been quoted, and a recent estimate put the number as high as 370 000. The beginning of the shop stewards' movement goes back to the 19th century, but the First World War saw a considerable increase in the numbers and power of stewards. A further impetus was given as unions became more bureaucratic, and began to negotiate wages and conditions at a national level. The individual work group felt that it had little influence on such negotiations, and there was plenty of scope (and support) for stewards who complemented national agreements with local bargaining.

The shop stewards do a great deal of the unions' work for them, at the workplace; additional duties in recent years have included health and safety work, and redundancy negotiations. There does not seem to be great competition to take on a steward's job: in 1968 a Government survey found that 71% of stewards were elected unopposed and only 8% actually beat an existing steward in an election. Other, later surveys seem to suggest an even higher percentage of unopposed elections. (Elections, where they take place, are usually held annually, by a show of *hands.*) To be a steward does call for unstinted devotion to union work, many extra hours of work; and, for some, a loss of earnings when on shop steward's duties.

These duties include representing the union at work, for example, in negotiations with management, and both representing and serving the membership. Routine checks are made on members' union cards, and when subscriptions are collected from members, the steward will do this. Further duties are:

1. To increase union membership. Except where a closed shop exists, the need to recruit members is always important. Stewards are often involved in an organization's induction procedure to inform newcomers about the union.
2. To keep in general contact with members. This is particularly important where subscriptions are deducted from pay, and sent direct to union headquarters (the 'check-off' system). The steward keeps members informed about union matters, distributes union publications and helps with the distribution and collection of ballot papers at elections for senior union posts.
3. To represent members as individuals over grievances or disciplinary matters.
4. To represent his work group as a whole, monitoring pay arrangements, rate fixing, distribution of work; perhaps even the introduction of new methods and/or machinery.
5. To represent the union as a whole (as well as his own group) as a member of a joint negotiating committee, or other body involved in company or plant-wide negotiation.

In many large organizations, grades of steward are to be found—stewards, senior stewards, chief stewards and convenors. The latter, in a firm of any size, will usually work full-time on union business and may have their own office and telephone. Bonded together as a group, a shop stewards' committee is a powerful influence in negotiations. Committees of shop stewards of *different* unions (Joint Shop Steward Committees) are even more powerful, and cause anxiety not only to employers, but to senior union officials. They are outside the control of any particular union, and there have been unfortunate consequences of these 'unions within unions' acting autonomously with control over their own funds, defying official union instructions, and forming 'strike committees' overnight.

There is no doubt that much power has passed from branches to stewards in the last 50 years.

Stewards do not have a good public image and often get a bad press. However, supervisors should remember that for every infamous steward or conveyor featured in the popular press as militant, aggressive or devious, there are hundreds quietly going about their business resolving disputes and defusing potentially explosive situations rather than creating them.

26.2.3 The branch

As we have seen, every member of a union is a branch member. In the earlier years of unionism, most members lived close to their work: it made sense to establish branches on a geographical basis therefore near workplaces. Now industries are staffed by workers travelling many miles to get to work: to drive back into a town left only an hour or two previously is not attractive. We have already examined the attendance problem, but some unions, notably in the printing industry, fine members for non-attendance. At one time the branch was, in the words of Sidney and Beatrice Webb, the local centre of the union's intellectual life; certainly it was a social occasion, it is hardly so now.

Each branch will have a chairman (sometimes called a 'president') and a secretary at least, probably a treasurer and other committee members who are normally unpaid, though the secretary might get more in total than his expenses (that is a commission based on membership size). Elections are annual, usually by a show of hands (though some unions stipulate ballots for some posts).

The branch will deal with membership applications, consider union policy, make recommendations upwards (in the form of resolutions) about policy; appoint delegates to outside bodies such as trades councils (associations of trade union branches in a locality to promote the interests of affiliated unions); and hear reports from delegates on other bodies, especially those belonging to committees at a higher level in the union. Where the branch members all work at the same place of employment, a technical college, for example, even matters such as deciding whether or not to take industrial action at that college could be voted on locally, under certain circumstances.

26.2.4 District level

Most unions group branches into districts: at this level we have district committees, elected directly by branch members (and possibly shop stewards) by ballot. They are serviced by district secretaries who might be also directly elected; or equally often, appointed just like any other employee, possibly for life. These district secretaries or organizers are therefore full-time, paid officials, who not only service the committee meetings, but spend most of their time dealing with problems in the district—disputes, wages and overtime queries, hours of work, and piece-work—and will need both to be in touch with the union stewards and employers. It is essential that the district secretary is a good communicator and negotiator.

District committees will be closely involved with every agreement signed between the union and employers within the district.

26.2.5   Division (regional) level

Where unions are large, even at district level further groupings are convenient and several districts will be brought under a division (or region). The committees are again elected by branch members (and possibly shop stewards) and again they have a full-time secretary, usually called a 'divisional organizer'. Not only does this body oversee the divisions, but members of the committee can be involved in the running of the union itself, sending representatives to the National Committee.

26.2.6   Union headquarters

The overall policy of a union is decided at the annual[3] delegate conference. The delegates are there to represent the union 'grassroots', that is those who care to attend branch meetings and elect the delegates. The business of the conference revolves mainly around voting on a series of motions (originating theoretically from branches, but often modified by districts and divisions, and by a conference steering committee), which are held to be representative of members' views. It is not uncommon for factions with conflicting views to be in evidence at conferences, but unionists are great negotiators, and the usual result is a compromise with trade-offs for each group, and the emergence of a modified 'composite' motion which incorporates what has been agreed.

Conferences are expensive and cannot sit all year. The day to day affairs of the union have to be carried on. In some unions there is a national committee which, following conference guidelines, can put flesh on the bones of policy. In all unions there is some form of executive committee or council comprised of the principal figures of the union, including the president or secretary, plus members elected by the membership as a whole. This latter committee may meet frequently and may even be full time.

26.2.7   Union leaders

Union leaders are constantly in the limelight as each strike, wage bargaining round and crisis runs its course. We think of them as the democratically elected leaders of their interest groups, but amazingly some of them in the past have not faced contested

---

[3] In smaller unions conferences may be held at intervals longer than one year.

elections; and those who have, have been elected with the positive votes of a small minority of the membership. Union officials in white-collar unions, even general secretaries, tend to be appointed by union committees. While Jack Jones (TGWU) and Joe Gormley (NUM) were elected in high polls, others have been elected on remarkably few votes. Even with postal voting, unions are lucky to get one-third of the electorate taking part. Some unions only accept votes cast at branch meetings, here total votes cast can be very low.

In an attempt to promote more member involvement within unions, the 1984 Trade Union Act requires the principal union executive committee (and other office holders in the union such as secretary/president with a vote or casting vote on the executive) to be elected by *secret ballot* of the union's members. The effect to be that every voting member of the executive would owe his position to an election within the last five years. (Any term in the contract of employment of an employee of a union, say the general secretary, preventing him being elected as required under the Act would be disregarded.)

All union members are entitled to vote (but with some very special exceptions); voting must be the marking of a postal ballot form in secret, returnable by post at no direct cost; and the votes cast fairly counted. The only permitted alternative to a postal ballot is one secret and free from any interference or constraint at the workplace. In such instances, union members would be given a convenient opportunity to vote during, or immediately before or after work—again at no direct cost to themselves.

The cost of such ballots could be met out of public funds.

Who emerges as the significant figure in a union, president or general secretary is sometimes a matter of personality, but in the majority of unions the post of general secretary is regarded as the most important: he will, even where he faces re-election, have a longer tenure of office than most other senior officers; will appoint the office staff, and have considerable influence in the recruitment of research assistants and the like. The media demand from him 'instant' responses on every topic from the increased minimum lending rate to troubles in the Labour Party, as well as on union matters.

26.3 THE TRADES UNION CONGRESS

Another federation is the Trades Union Congress (TUC), founded in 1868, to which individual unions are 'affiliated'. As with individual unions a key annual event is the delegate conference which settles general policy for the ensuing year, and elects a general council to carry out its decisions (the candidates are nominated by various different groups of trades). The duties of the general council include: keeping a watching brief on the economy and on government legislation which it feels will affect unions and their members; attempting to adjust differences or disputes between unions (guided by the principles adopted at the Bridlington Conference of 1939, which, for example, discourage 'poaching' by one union of other unions' members and encourage the demarcation of work); conducting propaganda on behalf of the trade union movement, and entering into relations with overseas and international labour organizations.

The TUC is often in the news, especially during its annual conference in early September. The general Secretary leads the TUC's full-time staff, which is much more extensive than that of an individual union. (There are separate TUC organizations in Scotland and Wales.)

In 1980s the TUC was faced with the problems of the miners' strikes, inter-union disputes, and (as we have seen) falling union membership. The influence of unions in collective bargaining (where industry-wide employers do formal deals with unions to set their workers' wages and conditions for a specific period of time ahead) was declining. Worse, partly self-inspired, the TUC began to lose its voice in national policy making.

Mr Monks showed himself determined to attempt to halt, and possibly reverse these trends. His aim was to modernize and update the TUC when he took office in 1992; and to return it to a more centre-stage position. He presided over an internal reorganization, and formed a campaigns unit. An aim would be for the TUC to speak out for all employed people, whether they were union members or not, particularly in a time (as he saw it) of increasing job insecurity. This could encourage more workers to become union members. A parallel objective was to increase employer recognition.

26.4 UNION PURPOSES AND OBJECTIVES

At this stage, whilst noting the new stance of the TUC, we should consider whether unions are necessary or relevant in the current, rapidly changing industrial and commercial scene. In doing so, shall need to look first quite briefly at how people in the past viewed union objectives; and then at how some have adapted to what may be called the 'new realism'.

26.4.1 Earlier views

Discounting some unusual views which assumed the existence or possibility of a socialist, Marxist or syndicalist society in which unions might operate, many earlier commentators would agree with the Webbs' definition listed at the beginning of this chapter. (The Webb definition is in fact no longer strictly accurate as increasingly large numbers of union members earn salaries and 'fringe benefits' beyond the wildest dreams of workers in the 1920s.)

A contemporary United States' view from R. F. Hoxie was much more explicit: he described the 'principles of action' of a union which were to oppose the aims of the employer, who wanted to get out of the workforce the greatest amount of production at the lowest possible cost. It was necessary for a union to aim for the opposite: the 'continuous employment' of all its members at the highest possible (standardized) level of wages, and conditions (e.g. reasonable hours of work, safe working environment, comfort etc.).

In the immediate post Second World War era of relatively high levels of employment, with a significant proportion of the workforce engaged in relatively routine, unskilled or semi-skilled work, such objectives seemed still to be appropriate.

By 1970, Alan Flanders (then a leading commentator on unionism) was summarizing the overall purpose of unions as 'the welfare of their members'. The unions' primary commitment was, then, to the members: not to any organization for which the members worked; not to any industry, not to any country. He did however recognize that the *activity* in which unions most indulged was collective bargaining (discussed in more detail in Chapter 27), which he saw as rule-making process. The unions, then, operated on behalf of their members by limiting the ability of the employers to make rules about wages, work practices, hours of work, and so on. 'One of the principal purposes of trade unions in collective bargaining is regulation or control,' was an accurate summary of the thinking at that period. Life could become difficult for employers who had to deal with several different unions – each with its own agenda – within one workplace.

26.4.2 The decades of change

The information technology evolution, begun in the early '70s, was an all-embracing change, as it affected such areas as design procedures, production methods, information storage and retrieval; and spurred on equipment standardization, and the automation of many labour-intensive processes. As the demand for skilled labour increased, the market for the less-skilled people decreased.

The 'Thatcher years' saw large state-owned utilities being sold off, and being transformed into profit-orientated organizations, but dispensing with significant proportions of their workforces in the processes.

Perhaps the greatest change agents were foreign companies (some European, Japanese, American: others multinational) who set up in Britain, or took over existing British companies. They brought with them new industrial cultures; and new ideas about quality and service to customers, and labour relations. Whilst willing to purchase materials, components and services within the UK, they laid down strict conditions on their suppliers including those of quality of output and assured rates of delivery. In turn, these suppliers had to rethink their cultures, in an endeavour more nearly to match those of their customers.

The 'new wave' of incoming organizations did not have a common strategy for dealing with labour relations. Some choose to recognize unions, but instead of carrying on the practice of negotiating on a multi-union basis they opted for 'single-union' deals: negotiating with one union representing the whole workforce. However reluctantly, unions fell into line. 'No strike' agreements (essential where continuity of supply was an integral part of contracts with important customers) were negotiated and accepted by the unions concerned.

Other newcomers who wished either to diminish union involvement in the relationship between employers and employees or avoid union recognition entirely, opted for 'commitment strategies' such as 'Quality Circles' or the more sophisticated notions such as 'Empowerment', 'Total Quality Management' (TQI), or 'Total Quality Involvement' (TQI) (concepts discussed in detail in Chapter 28).

Any marked degree of commitment by employees to a work-group and the wider organization obviously conflicts with the original concept of the union–employer relationship being that of opponent. Thus unions have had to approach bargaining bearing in mind the realities of the market, the demand of customers, and their own weakened position. The number of disputed, and high profile strikes has declined dramatically. The new realism of the TUC mentioned earlier fits quite well into the current market-led industrial and commercial climate.

SUMMARY

1.   Various definitions of a trade union exist: the consensus would seem to indicate that unions are bargaining associations, bargaining on behalf of members over wages and conditions, associations which can take industrial action, take part in political activity, and have funds to help members in need.

2.   Prior to the 1980s it was possible to describe four main and reasonably distinct categories of union: craft, general, industrial and white-collar. These distinctions between categories have become very blurred latterly, particularly due to amalgamations.

3.   Craft unions were exclusive and élitist, but now admit semi-skilled and other workers: women can be members. They were originally formed to protect the status, differentials and jobs of skilled craftsmen.

4.   General unions were formed for those workers ineligible to join craft unions: they were much more militant and aggressive. A big drawback was their size and mixed trade membership.

5.   Industrial unions (now virtually non-existent in Britain) served all the workers in a particular industry.

6.   White-collar unions cater for a wide number of clerical, professional and supervisory workers; though even these have tended to lose their original identities.

7.   Starting with the union member, his or her first contact with the union is likely to be the (unpaid) shop steward, staff or office representative. There are variously estimated to be 250 000–370 000 stewards in office, many of whom were elected unopposed. Their duties include:

(a)   Checking members' cards, keeping in contact with members.
(b)   Collecting subscriptions (where this is still done).
(c)   Increasing union membership.
(d)   Representing members in grievances.
(e)   Monitoring pay agreements, rate fixing, etc.
(f)   Sitting on committees.

8.   Every member belongs to a branch, though few attend regularly. Each branch has a chairman, secretary (possibly a treasurer) and committee. Not only dealing with membership applications, the branch will discuss policy and send resolutions to district, divisional (regional) branch or even for transmission to conference.

9.   Both at district and divisional level there are paid officials (who act as secretary of the district or division) plus an elected committee.

10.   At national level the annual delegate conference is the supreme policy-making body; with a national committee, and executive committee to guide affairs between conferences. The general secretary is usually the dominant figure (but sometimes the president is the more powerful).

11.   Unions amalgamate by agreement; federate in larger unions to form larger negotiating bodies, affiliate to bodies such as the Trades Union Congress (TUC), which attempts to co-ordinate the activities of the union movement generally.

12.   Particularly from the union movement's point of view, the original objectives of unions were to regard themselves as opponents of management; and by collective bargaining to attempt to influence the regulation of the conditions of work; and limit the ability of employers to make and enforce rules at work.

13.   The many changes in the work climate since the early 1980s, and the declining influence of the union movement have brought about modifications to the earlier perceived role. Unions tend to bargain now more on a local level; and are seen to be more flexible in their dealings with management.

REVIEW QUESTIONS

1.   Do any of the definitions at the beginning of the chapter usefully describe the existing position of unions? (If not why not?)

2.   What are the duties of a typical shop steward? Why is he so powerful now?

3.   Describe the various levels of a union organization from ordinary member to national level.

4.   What is the function of the annual delegate conference?

5.   What is the TUC; what are its functions?

6. Is it true that unions are now less strong than they were in the 1960s? If so, why?

DISCUSSION TOPICS

1. In view of small branch attendances could unions be said to be democratic? What could happen to a union with an apathetic, non-attending membership?

2. Were the craft unions right to defend their status and members' jobs; or should they have campaigned on behalf of the worse-off, the unskilled workers?

3. Do you agree with the view that there is a basic contradiction in any union organization between the desire for democratic control by the members and the need for unity of action dictated by officials, the regions or the centre?

ASSIGNMENTS

A26.1 Course members, whether as individuals or in groups, should research into the structure of a union, to which at least one course member belongs, and produce a short, written report with an appropriate structure chart. Qualifications for election to union posts should be established (these can be found usually in union rule books).

A26.2 The course members are to form an appropriate union, elect a chairman and secretary, and hold a meeting. On the agenda are to be at least two further items:

(a) Drafting of a short set of rules.
(b) Discussion of a motion: 'That this union apply for affiliation to the TUC'.

(This activity could span several weeks: a sub-committee could be delegated to look at union rule books; another could establish what benefits could accrue from joining the TUC—the advice of union officials might be sought.)

27
Collective Bargaining

27.1 DEFINITION

Where all the conditions of work, pay and other benefits are laid down by the employer, without any possibility that employees will be able to influence the employment contract, there is said to be *employer regulation* of wages and conditions; where individuals can (and do) bargain with their employers, we have *individual bargaining;* and where the Government lays down 'minimum rates', or some strict rules about pay, e.g. an incomes policy, we call this *statutory regulation.*

Collective bargaining is none of these methods of wage determination: it is joint regulation under which wages and conditions of service are settled by a bargain struck between employers (or employers' associations), on the one hand, and workers' associations (unions or groups of unions) on the other. A consequence of collective bargaining is that all employers and employees covered by an agreement are guaranteed equality of treatment where settlements are industry wide or cover a whole sector of public employees. Employers also realize (all other things being equal) that in a competitive situation labour costs are likely to be similar.

An agreement arrived at by collective bargaining may have a wider influence than just upon those employees covered by it: non-union labour doing similar jobs to union members will be awarded the same pay—a sore point with unionists who say such people get the benefits of unionism without paying for it. Employers who are not members of the associations involved in the bargain might well agree to the same conditions.

27.2 THE SCOPE OF COLLECTIVE BARGAINING

Originally pay and hours were the major topics of collective bargaining: nowadays the list is long, and includes rates and differentials, holidays, shift working and overtime; work and method study arrangements, health and safety; disciplinary procedures, redundancy, welfare, and union recognition. In fact, very few of the work relationships and elements of the employment contract are not now regular elements of bargaining.

Besides the two major parties to an agreement, other influences in collective bargaining have been the Government, ACAS, industrial tribunals, pay research consultants, and even public opinion spurred on, some would say, by television and newspaper coverage. Economic conditions and the levels of unemployment are still significant in that in bad times union targets will tend to be less ambitious: when the economy and companies are doing well, demands will increase.

27.3   THE BASIS OF COLLECTIVE BARGAINING

Two principles can be clearly distinguished in collective bargaining: voluntary association and mutual consent. There is no legal compulsion on employers and employees to bargain, though, as we have seen, the Government has since 1916 actively encouraged it. Any resulting bargain must be agreed *mutually*, that is, by both parties. Further, agreements between employers and employees arrived at through collective bargaining are not legally binding, although the Confederation of British Industry, at the time of the publication of the Code of Practice issued with the Employment Act, called for legal binding agreements, accountability in law, notice before striking and a completely new framework for industrial relations.

27.4   THE NEED TO BARGAIN

When do unions and management need to bargain? The old answer was that the bargaining process began with a *dispute*, a *dispute procedure* was activated, and *agreement* was eventually reached (even if the interim period was tough, there was a strike, and so on). But many bargaining situations do *not* begin with a dispute: perhaps one side wants to put a deal to the other: management may wish to negotiate a productivity deal, or a revision for work practices; the union might wish for more money, and/or less hours or a revision of work practices. Sometimes the need to negotiate is simultaneous on both sides: more often one side wants to take the initiative.

Thus, we may say that the need to negotiate arises when one side or the other wishes to change the existing state of affairs at the work place. It is true that if the second party *refuses* to listen to, or accept the arguments put forward by the first party, a dispute will exist.

27.5   PROCEDURE AGREEMENTS

Procedure agreements can be negotiated at one extreme by national associations of employers and large unions or groupings of unions; at the other, by an employer and an individual union. The procedures so agreed normally turn out to be first a solemn statement of the parties' rights (that of the employer 'to manage': that of the union 'to exercise its functions'), followed by a long series of 'steps' to be carefully adhered to in the case of a dispute arising. (Procedure agreements are often called 'disputes procedures'.)

An agreement signed in 1922 for manual workers in the engineering industry sets out the rules very clearly: if a worker has a problem he discusses it with a foreman. An inability to reach a settlement entails the matter being taken to the second level of management, with the shop steward present. Failure here could lead to discussion of the problem either at a works' committee or works' conference (the permanent union official may enter at this stage).

Higher 'steps' in the procedure involve the dispute being 'taken out' of the factory: discussed at a local conference attended by local union and employer representatives; and a central conference at which attempts are made to resolve the matter once and for all by national representatives of unions and employers' associations.

Other industries have rather different agreements, all, of course, tending to the same end—the avoidance of industrial action and some, like the agreement in the quarrying industry, allow for arbitration as a solution.

27.6   THE PROCESS OF NEGOTIATION

A clear distinction must be made between problem-solving activity, and a bargaining exercise. The problem-solvers normally work together. Even if they argue, they argue over means not ends; normally they trust each other. They certainly do not trip, trap or trick one another. The bargainers, on the other hand, are generally aware of the fact that each side has a different target, at least at the start, and attempt to blackmail or bring subtle pressures to bear on the other party, using bluff and counterbluff, and the presentation of 'facts' in a biased way. There is less trust in the bargaining environment.

A dispute, or conflict, can be resolved by:

1. *Avoiding the issue.* This is a common strategy when we cannot be bothered, or feel we have not got a good case. It is generally unsatisfactory, particularly when the other party insists on some action being taken.
2. *Defusing the situation.* Shop stewards may be involved in this tactic. Essentially a stalling device, in the hope that by soothing the angry with some concessions, their demands will cool with their anger. As with avoiding the issue, the basic problem does not go away.
3. *Collaborating with the other party.* Here we move into the region of joint problem-solving, which, as we have seen above, calls for co-operation and a relatively high degree of trust: the conflict is seen as something to be resolved by a partnership. This implies that one side at least has totally to abandon its position, or accept entirely new goals or targets. It is pleasant when you can succeed in getting total collaboration, but this is not a normal outcome of a dispute.
4. *Negotiating.* This is a method of resolving a dispute (or conflict) to the satisfaction of both parties, and is the most common of methods used in collective bargaining.

27.6.1 The 'trade-off'

Negotiation is primarily a strategy which can be used by two parties who recognize each other's existence, recognize each other's power, realize that their strengths are almost equal and accept that each is 'going to be around' for some time to come. Of course, the balance of power is never going to remain constant: when demand is high, orders are flowing in, and production is behind, a strike (or even the *bluff* of threatening one) is a much more effective weapon, than when, for example, the management might secretly be considering a temporary lay-off. The timing of bargaining is, therefore, important.

Many negotiations, particularly when power is roughly equal, can 'polarize', that is the two parties can take up even more extreme positions. They each refuse to budge and talk about 'rights', 'duties', and 'principles'. Then, mysteriously, after perhaps days or weeks of impasse, the whole dispute is quickly settled—often on terms quite close to those totally rejected at an earlier stage. The general public can be forgiven for being mystified by such behaviour. What happens is a series of 'swaps' or 'trade-offs'. The union concedes new work arrangements, the employer a higher hourly rate: one dismissal notice is withdrawn, another is allowed to stand. Both sides can claim a 'victory', or at least point to gains achieved, or to a successful stand taken. (A typical example of this was the 1994 signalworkers' dispute with Railtrack.)

27.6.2 The formalities and strategies of bargaining

Particularly where procedure agreements exist, and there is a history of bargaining in an organization, the whole process has an air of formality, even of ritual. We have, in fact, a formal meeting with a chairman. (Possibly too, a secretary to record what has been said 'officially'.) Each side makes a considered move, then waits for a response. Speeches can be long, and old ground may be covered several times, although the keen observer may note slight changes in what is stressed or emphasized each time the position is outlined. All this activity has been likened to tennis, but probably a chess game is a closer analogy. For example, from time to time there are adjournments (but without 'sealed moves'!) and each side consults its team.

Supervisors should try to get involved, even on a supernumerary basis, in this more formal bargaining if it takes place at work. It would give them more insight into the way that people behave, and perhaps improve the way in which they bargain with the union representatives in their daily work. As with debating, putting a case to a superior, or writing a project, a bad case is often the result of inadequate planning and preparation. So it is with negotiation.

As in chess, the opening moves are crucial. Does the union claim all, and allow a certain amount of whittling down (to what perhaps they reasonably felt was possible to attain)? Should the union be flexible, be imprecise or ambiguous at the start—ask for a 'substantial' wage increase without naming a figure? Does the management give way, stand firm, express surprise (or even appear hurt), ask for an adjournment? Should either side walk out, and when? In allowing the union to state its case first, management can, in reply, attack the union's case rather than defend its own; on the other hand, if the union's case is brilliantly argued and documented, this *could* force management into a defensive position at the start.

Even the formalities, rituals and conventions can be used to advantage: an adjournment proposed before one side has properly completed its case; the fact that management is required to sit unruffled despite abuse, but never to retaliate in like coin; the polite request for 'clarification' of what someone has spent twenty minutes outlining; all have a part to play. Negotiating calls for a thousand skills, most of which are 'interpersonal', that is negotiators need to be acceptable people, good communicators, and able, while speaking, to detect the reactions of the other side. The slight hesitation, the shared glance, the whispered aside, the shuffling of papers, all must be noted and evaluated.

27.6.3   Closing the deal

Negotiating and selling have much in common: finalizing negotiations could be considered similar to the closing of a sale. Useful tactics are:

1. *Summarizing areas of agreement.* While this does entail highlighting the areas of dispute which are left, at least it reduces the discussion range. 'We seem now only to have the overtime problem to deal with.'
2. *Suggesting the trade-off.* Here we use a positive suggestion disguised to look like a conditional one, and one which commits neither side to anything. 'Now if you were to resubmit your claim on the basis of a £1 per hour increase, we would be prepared to review the overtime premium payment.'
3. *A free gift.* Sales are sometimes clinched with 'free gifts'. A definite concession, with no strings attached, could be a way of demonstrating your reasonableness and good faith. The problem is the gift could be snapped up without a concession in return.
4. *Time is running out.* Either side could use this ploy. Sales staff win sales by drawing attention to material shortages, or an impending price increase. The negotiators' equivalents are hints of reminders of the approach of Christmas, the peak demand season, the worsening economic climate, or impending national wage freezes.

27.7   INDUSTRIAL ACTION

By 'industrial action' we mean some action taken by a union or its members in furtherance of a trade dispute, usually before or during negotiations, or when negotiations have broken down. The objective is usually to try to tip the balance of power in favour of the union. Of course, industrial action is sometimes used as a warning to employers not to take a certain line, or as a protest, e.g. underground train drivers protesting against vandalism.

The commonest forms of industrial action are:

1. *Overtime ban.* By banning overtime the union members are restricting output or the provision of services, causing disruption to the delivery schedules, and possibly increasing unit costs. The workers still get their basic weekly wage. A significant form of action because overtime is still worked regularly, even in the climate of current employment levels, particularly in the engineering industry.
2. *Non-co-operation.* This means refusing to help the employer when in difficulties and doing no more than the actual job itself. Teachers refusing to cover for absent colleagues would be an example.
3. *Working-to-rule.* It can be much more obstructive to obey rules than to break them! Many organizations have complicated sets of rules, which if they were all obeyed would, in fact, cause chaos. (Many of the rules refer to overcautious safety practices.) As railway managements have discovered over the years, the imposition of union work-to-rules have quickly resulted in disruption of services and delays to passengers. Some years ago, 60 plant health inspectors at the Ministry of Agriculture, angered by an attempt to re-categorize them (which would have resulted in loss of status and salary), searched the rule book and found many little-used regulations which they determinedly began to obey, such as inspecting *every furrow* in a field. The Ministry quickly agreed to negotiate—provided that the inspectors started to disobey the rules!
4. *Go-slow.* Very much akin to working-to-rule, but would apply where no work rule book exists. More difficult for piece-workers, but people on time rates still receive full pay. Much disruption can be caused by *indirect* workers who might reduce the quantity of material brought at a time to work benches, take longer over drawing tools or processing documentation, or transport goods from one area to another slowly. At the extreme, very little work might be done at all, and a virtual strike exists.
5. *Strikes.* A strike is a total withdrawal of labour. Discussed in detail below.
6. *Lock-out.* A lock-out is where the employer closes his place of work, if he gives the usual period of notice normal in the trade. In the past, lock-outs were a method of 'trying to tip the balance' the employer's way. A lock-out by coal mine owners was a factor in the miners' request for a General Strike in 1926.
7. *Sit-ins and work-ins.* A typical example of industrial 'interaction' took place in 1972 in the Manchester area: the Confederation of Shipbuilding and Engineering Unions (CSEU) having decided to pursue a wage claim (which had not been accepted by the employers) used overtime bans and work-to-rules. The employers in the factories concerned replied by locking out the workers. In about 30 factories workers moved in and 'took over'. They 'sat in'.

    Sit-ins are obviously worse for an employer than strikes: he does not have the use of his plant; even his offices may be occupied. Work-ins take the process a stage further: workers continue working in a factory after it has been closed in the hope of saving jobs. The Govan (in the Upper Clyde area) Shipyard workers' work-in was probably the most famous but a later sit-in at Norton Villiers Triumph factory (near Meriden) went a stage further with the formation of a workers' co-operative. This venture subsequently received Government assistance.
8. *Picketing.* In its simplest form, picketing is merely an attempt to *persuade* workers from attending work. However, in recent years, *mass picketing* (discussed in the

next section) has included organized attempts to *prevent* the inward flow of finished products. In addition to its effect in discouraging or preventing workers going into work, the other restrictions can seriously threaten the future survival of an organization.

27.8 STRIKES

Strikes are, as we have seen, withdrawal of labour by the workforce, but often not the *whole* unionized workforce. If manual workers are in dispute they may strike, but management and office workers still continue working. This does not mean striking is confined to manual workers: in recent years we have seen teachers, civil servants, social workers, and (in the Republic of Ireland) bank staff on strike.

27.8.1 Official and unofficial strikes

An official strike is one which has been called by, or approved by a union: an unofficial one is one *not* officially approved by a union. Strikes which start as unofficial can later be declared 'official'. Unofficial strikes are usually also 'unconstitutional',[2] that is they take place before all the 'steps' in the official procedure agreement have been exhausted or completed. This distinction between the two kinds of strike is important: provided that the union rules so lay down, strike pay—a weekly grant from union funds—is payable to those on official strike. Unofficial strikers do not receive union strike pay.

The Trade Union Act 1984 attempted to democratize (and possibly make more difficult) the calling of strikes. Section 10 removes immunity from legal action in cases where trade unions do not hold a ballot before authorizing or endorsing a strike call (or any other action which breaks or interferes with the contracts of employment of those called upon to join in). In fact there can be no immunity unless the ballot is held no more than four weeks before the strike begins, and there is a majority in favour (amongst those voting) for strike action. Immunity will also be lost if any member is called upon to strike after being denied entitlement to vote.

The Employment Act 1988 gave the right to a trade union member to obtain a court order requiring his union to withdraw its authorization of a strike if it were given without the support of a ballot of members; and further, gave the right to a trade union member to continue working during a strike (even one approved by members in a ballot) without fear of union discipline.

There was evidence, even in the 1990s, if ever Labour took office in the future, strike ballots would be retained: they have become accepted practice now. However, one possible reason for their retention is that the majority of ballots on some kind of industrial action end up in *support* of such action.

---

[2] It is also possible in some cases for official strikes to be unconstitutional.

Official strikes are usually called over *national* issues, or where, for example, large numbers of workers are affected by redundancy; unofficial strikes tend to be *organization based*, over local disputes or grievances. They could be quite short—almost protests against, for example, over-hot or over-cold working conditions, which when remedied result in the workers going back to their jobs.

27.8.2 Where strikes occur

Contrary to popular belief, many organizations never have strike problems: only about 7% of establishments employing under 500 people suffer strikes; but when we examine the situation in large industrial units, e.g. those employing over 1000 people, about half *do* have strikes. The causes of strikes are too complicated and numerous to consider here, but it would seem that the *size* of an organization is an important factor.

27.8.3 Picketing—a restricted immunity

Picketing is a very emotive topic, depending on your point of view. The sight on television, of massed miners causing the gates of Saltley gasworks to be closed in 1972, or in 1984, pickets preventing miners getting to work, might be greeted as a triumph for the workers on the one hand; a breakdown of law and order on the other.

The legal position is complicated: TULRA (Section 15) states that picketing in contemplation of a trade dispute is lawful at or near the place where another person works or carries on his business, or happens to be (except where he resides—picketing the managing director's home is not allowed!). Picketing, TULRA adds, may be for the purpose only of 'communicating information', or peacefully persuading others to work or abstain there from. This immunity is not as wide as it looks: a trade union official who stood in the way of a lorry and tried to persuade the driver not to deliver his load was charged with obstructing the highway and convicted (*Broome v. Director of Public Prosecutions* 1974). Besides this case, there are others where pickets have been charged with public nuisance (which arises when anyone interferes unreasonably with the freedom of others), obstructing the police in their duties, criminal damage and insulting behaviour.

'Flying pickets' emerged in the 1972 miners' strike: this new tactic involved sending out bus and coach loads of pickets to descend suddenly on a particular place chosen in advance (not always pit-heads, e.g. Saltley gasworks), where police were either few in number, or even absent. In the 1973 building workers' dispute, flying pickets gained notoriety by allegedly using violence, or threatening it. The charges against three pickets included conspiracy to intimidate; and the others charged were convicted of unlawful assembly.

On the face of it, the only lawful pickets are those who are reasonably few in number, and keep themselves to themselves, making the odd, polite enquiry of persons intending to enter the place being picketed.

27.8.4   Secondary picketing

From picketing the place of work, i.e. workers in Factory A picketing Factory A and nowhere else, the practice of picketing *other* premises (not forbidden by the TULRA which was so worded that secondary picketing was quite possible) grew up. These other premises included suppliers and customers and users of the products of Factory A. Miners 'picketing' Saltley gasworks were far away from the nearest mine. The strike in the nationalized steel industry even extended picketing to steel producers in the private sector (Hadfields, for example), and to the docks to prevent foreign steel from being landed.

27.8.5   Picketing—developments in 1980

The Employment Act 1980, and the accompanying draft Code of Practice dealt with picketing in detail. The code is discussed below: here we note the 1980 Act provisions which:

1.   Replaced the TULRA provisions with some new ones.
2.   Stated that it was still lawful to picket at or near a place of work; allowed a union official,[3] who accompanied his members, to picket at or near their place of work.
3.   Restated the purpose of picketing: to give and receive information; to persuade (peaceably) workers to abstain from working, provided that the picketing is in furtherance of a *trade* dispute (i.e. this would seem to exclude 'political strikes' from the protection of the Act).
4.   Allowed a worker who works in more than one place (e.g. an out-worker) to picket the premises from which he worked; or from which his work was administered.
5.   Allowed an *ex-employee* (whose employment was ended as a result of a trade dispute), provided that he had not started a new job, to picket his last place of work.
6.   Granted immunity to picketers from actions in tort only if the picketing were lawful (i.e. in accordance with the provisions of the legislation).
7.   Further added that *secondary* picketing was only lawful in two instances: the first where the picketing occurred of premises which were the immediate customers or suppliers of the employer. (In practice, this implies that pickets would have to be very sure of the targets of secondary action, and be sure that such action would achieve the aim of preventing or disrupting the supply of goods and services from immediate suppliers or to immediate customers of the employer.) Secondly, similar provisions applied to the employees of a company *associated* with the company where the primary dispute occurs. They would be permitted to picket if the principal purpose was to disrupt supplies, products or services between the associated company's suppliers or customers where such goods or services are *in*

---

[3] From the Act and Code of Practice it is clear that a trade union official under this provision must be said to represent the members on strike: he may be either a specific shop steward of the work group striking; a branch official—only when his members are lawfully picketing; or a national official of the union wherever his members are picketing.

substitution for goods or services, which (but for the dispute) would have been supplied to or by the employer involved in the primary dispute.

8. Stated that a person in employment had a right not to be unreasonably expelled from a specified trade union: the code adds that exclusion or expulsion from a trade union on the mere grounds that a member crossed a picket line could be held to be unreasonable; pickets were to respect the right of any individual, even before a picket put his case (including a trade union member), to decide whether or not he crossed a picket line.

9. Declared that any act done or carried out in the course of picketing not within the strict guidelines laid out above could be actionable in tort: for example, the draft code stated that to picket on or inside any part of the premises belonging to the employer 'would constitute trespass'. (The implication here is that pickets must be clearly stationed *outside* the employer's premises.)

27.9   THE CLOSED SHOP

For many years, unions have aimed to secure the situation where all workers in a particular place of work belong to an appropriate trade union, i.e. 100% union membership where unions are in existence and recognized by the employer at a place of work. Of course, this aim does not in itself imply that in a particular place of work *all* workers have to belong to the *same* union (to the exclusion of all other unions), but as a matter of fact there are many places of work where all workers employed there *do* belong to the same union.

A 100% membership is one thing, to keep it that way permanently is another. A 'closed shop' is just such an attempt. A closed shop is said to exist where not only a 100% membership of recognized unions at a place of work obtains, but there is also an agreement between the unions concerned and the employer that being a member of one of the unions mentioned in the union-management agreement (UMA) is a necessary condition of a job applicant being offered a job there.

Two kinds of closed shop have existed in the past. First, the *pre-entry* closed shop only allowed employees to join the work group covered by the UMA, if they had already held a union card (of one the unions mentioned in the UMA) *before* they started work. Possession of an appropriate union card was therefore a prerequisite to getting the job. A *post-entry* closed shop arrangement did allow a non-union member (or a member of another union not specified in the UMA) to be appointed and start work, provided that he joined (or transferred his union membership to) a union specified in the UMA within a given time, e.g. 14 days.

27.9.1   The present position

In August 1980 about 5 million workers were estimated to be working with closed shop agreements, but it is clear that there is no law which says that closed shops must exist in any organization, and while ACAS can suggest, after being approached by a union, that recognition rights should be extended, namely by a UMA, such suggestions do not have to be taken up and implemented.

Since 1980, the position has changed greatly: various Acts have modified the protection closed shops had at one time. In particular, the Employment Act 1988 seemed to suggest that legal support for the closed shop was on the way out: this Act made industrial action to enforce a closed shop unlawful; and provided that any dismissal on the grounds of non-membership of a union was unfair—even if the UMA had been approved by a valid ballot.

These legal moves, and the kinds of changes in employer–union relationships discussed in Chapter 26 (including the arrival of overseas-based organizations with distinctly different cultures) are partly responsible for the fact that issues related to closed shops do not feature greatly in current industrial relations.

27.9.2 Ballots

The way decisions are taken in unions has varied enormously over time and with the unions concerned. In the past shop stewards in a union could be elected by a show of hands by those present at the election meeting, and senior union officials in the same union by postal (secret) ballot. Decisions to strike might be taken at national level, or by shop stewards' committees at local level, or by individual union branches either in open vote or secret ballot.

Concern was expressed by many especially during the 1984-5 miners' strike that decisions on important matters of policy in unions are not made with the participation of the grassroots membership. Voting at branches, by those present, meant that only a small percentage of the members were involved. It is significant therefore that the very first section of the Employment Act 1980 related to trade union ballots.

The Government has revised the scheme to fund trade union postal ballots so that unions can claim towards the costs of all secret postal ballots held under the Trade Union Act 1984.

The Regulations issued under the Act revise the scheme, set up under the Employment Act 1980, to cover a wider range of union elections and the ten-yearly ballots which unions must hold to review their political funds. Ballots before industrial action are already covered. The conditions which ballots must meet to qualify for funds have also been revised following the 1984 Act.

The scheme in detail

The new scheme provides public funds for ballots held by independent trade unions for the following purposes:

1. Calling or ending a strike or other industrial action.
2. To decide whether unions with political funds should continue to spend money on party political matters.
3. Elections to the principal executive committee of a trade union.
4. Elections provided for by the rules of a trade union to the positions of president, chairman, secretary, or treasurer of the union or to any position which the person elected will hold as an employee of the union.

5. Amending the rules of a trade union.
6. Obtaining a decision in accordance with the Trade Union (Amalgamations, etc.) Act 1964 on a resolution to approve an instrument of amalgamation or transfer.
7. Accepting or rejecting a proposal by an employer relating to remuneration, hours of work, level of performance, holidays or pensions.

The specific conditions which a ballot must meet to qualify for funding depend on its purpose. Broadly speaking *all* ballots must satisfy the following requirements:

1. Voting must be by the marking of a ballot paper and in secret.
2. Every voter must be allowed to vote without interference or constraint on the part of the union or any of its members, officials or employees.
3. Every voter must, so far as is reasonably practicable, be sent a ballot paper by post and be given a convenient opportunity to return it by post—but ballot papers can be distributed at the workplace and only *returned* by post if the ballot is about industrial action or remuneration.
4. Every voter must be allowed to vote without any direct cost to himself.
5. 'Block vote' systems of voting must not be used, the votes cast must be fairly and accurately counted—although payment may still be made, for example, if there was an accidental inaccuracy in counting which did not affect the result of the ballot.

The scheme is run by the independent Certification Officer, who has the power to make payment towards postage, printing and stationery costs. Unions must apply to the Certification Officer within six months of the date of the ballot.

However, unions are not *compelled* to use such schemes and could use less rigidly organized ballots, but union members are becoming more and more critical of the way ballots are run—an example being the 're-run' of the Transport and General Workers' Union General Secretary ballot in 1985, after pressure from some branches, and the media.

27.10   THE ROLE OF ACAS

Finally, in this survey of collective bargaining, we must consider the significant and important role of ACAS, the Advisory, Conciliation and Arbitration Service, set up under Section 1 of the EPA 1974. The brief is that the Service operates under the direction of its Council (a chairman and nine members; three of whom are nominated by the CBI, three nominated by the TUC, plus three independent members). It was given the general duty of promoting the improvement of industrial relations.

27.10.1   Advisory activities

ACAS can be called in to advise employers (or their associations), workers, and trade unions on any matters concerned with industrial relations. The remit is a wide one and could cover investigations into shift working and training programmes (with subsequent advice); sick pay schemes; problems in companies of high LTO or absenteeism; self-financing productivity schemes, and communications problems. The advisory service is free. Advisory visits carried out are some 6000 annually; and 'in depth' exercises nearly 1000.

27.10.2   Conciliation

Conciliation is the act of promoting goodwill between people, by actions which create a friendly feeling. As far as ACAS is concerned, there are two distinct areas of conciliation: individual and collective.

Individual conciliation deals with those employees who consider that one or other of their statutory rights in employment have been infringed in such a way that they are entitled to make a complaint to an industrial tribunal. However, it should be noted that ACAS 'approval' has to be obtained in 'out-of-court' settlements—that is, settlements arrived at between employer and employee *after* the time application has been made for a Tribunal Hearing, and the Hearing itself. (There is also some evidence that cases are sometimes brought by complainants, especially in alleged unfair dismissal cases, in the hope the employers concerned will 'buy off' the claimant. The cost of defending the case, even if successful, could be high to an employer in time, legal expenses etc. and is an incentive to persuade the employer to settle at a figure below the expected expenses.) The ACAS 'rubber stamping role' is largely a non-positive one here. There is a statutory obligation on ACAS to provide a conciliation officer to try to get the complaint settled by mutual agreement *before* it ever gets to the tribunal hearing.

27.10.3   Trade union recognition

Collective bargaining cannot take place where one of the potential parties to the bargain refuses to acknowledge the existence or competence of the other to bargain. In industrial relations jargon we say that an employer recognizes a union when the employer is prepared to accept that union as bargaining agent on behalf of some or all the workers involved. Prior to 1980, ACAS had the task of dealing with any union complaint that an employer had refused to recognize it as a bargaining agent. However, the Employment Act 1980 repealed this procedure. Trade union recognition is therefore no longer part of ACAS's work.

27.10.4   Arbitration

Voluntary arbitration has had a long history in collective bargaining. The basic conditions are that both sides disagree, and cannot see any way in which they will agree on the dispute; but both sides agree on a third party who will make a decision, which both sides undertake to accept whatever it turns out to be.

ACAS's responsibilities are to facilitate arbitration if asked to do so, and it considers arbitration to be the most appropriate way of resolving a dispute. Usually ACAS calls in the Central Arbitration Committee, but can appoint an individual (independent of ACAS, e.g. a lawyer, academic, or a retired conciliation officer) as arbitrator.

27.10.5 Mediation

Mediation is described by ACAS as a 'half-way house' method. It is conciliation plus an active intervention by the mediator who puts forward proposals for acceptance or discussion. He does not however enforce them, nor do the parties undertake in advance to accept them.

27.10.6 Publications

Supervisors are advised to obtain ACAS Annual Reports, and other publications which set out the Service's work in greater detail. Additionally, individual conciliation officers are usually very co-operative and it is a useful addition to a residential weekend to invite one to talk about ACAS's work at first hand.

27.10.7 The future of ACAS

It is now clear that ACAS is likely to continue for many years. Its involvement in helping to settle high profile disputes in the 1970s and 1980s built and established a national reputation. More latterly in the Ambulance dispute at the beginning of this decade, and by the great assistance given to both sides in the 1994 signalworkers' dispute, ACAS reinforced its collective conciliation, arbitration and mediation reputation.

It is interesting to note that whilst this reputation was built on collective conciliation, there is an ever-increasing caseload of individual conciliation (up from 45 000 annually in the late 1980s to over 60 000 in the mid 1990s). The majority of claims were over unfair dismissal; though race or sex discrimination and wages or equal pay claims also involved substantial case work.

ACAS provide a very large range of publications in respect of most aspects of employer–employee relations. Managers and supervisors needing help could benefit from getting appropriate copies. One booklet '*Supervision*' is of particular interest. ACAS can also be contacted by telephone for advice.

SUMMARY

1. Collective bargaining is a procedure in which changes in wages, conditions and other employment-related matters are settled by discussion between employers and unions (or groups of unions).

2.   Agreements arrived at by collective bargaining can affect non-union work-
       ers, as well as union members, in the organizations involved; and also affect
       employees in firms not party to the agreement (where their employers, as a
       matter of policy, decide to pay the increase, or concede the claim).

3.   Collective bargaining agreements (originally dealing with pay and hours)
       now cover a wide range of work-related matters including, for example,
       disciplinary, grievance or redundancy procedures, welfare and health and
       safety.

4.   The need for collective bargaining arises when either the employer or union
       wishes to change the existing order of things at the workplace.

5.   The process of negotiation or dispute resolution is often regulated by the use
       of a procedure agreement which sets out the series of steps to be taken in
       trying to resolve a dispute, deal with a grievance, or negotiate a change—all
       in the interests of avoiding (or at least postponing the possibility of) a
       deterioration in the relationship between the two sides.

6.   Negotiation is often a complicated game (even in those cases where the rules
       are well defined). It is, however, the most common method used in collec-
       tive bargaining, rather than those of avoiding the issue, defusing the situa-
       tion, or collaborating with the other party.

7.   Both sides often begin negotiations from extreme positions and later make
       concessions which form the basis of the agreement. The whole process calls
       for a great deal of skill on the part of the negotiators; the choice of effective
       strategies and tactics, and the ability to gauge the effect of arguments and
       points on the other side.

8.   Negotiating and selling have much in common, and certain ploys in
       closing the sale can be used in negotiation: summarizing areas of agree-
       ment, suggesting a trade-off, the offer of a free gift (i.e. a concession
       'without strings'), or a reminder of an impending event which could
       influence the negotiations.

9.   Industrial action can take various forms, including:

       (a)   Overtime ban.
       (b)   Non-co-operation.
       (c)   Working-to-rule.
       (d)   Go-slow.
       (e)   Strike.
       (f)   Sit-in or work-in.

       All these are actions which the *employees* can take: employers can shut the
       workplace, so workers are prevented from working there.

10. Strikes which receive official union 'blessing', are called *official* strikes; those without such approval are called *unofficial*. Where union rules so provide, members on official strike get strike pay (from the union funds).

11. Most strikes occur in larger work units (employing over 1000 employees).

12. Picketing is for the purpose of communicating or seeking information, or peacefully persuading others to work or abstain there from. Besides picketing the actual workplace where a dispute exists, recent years have seen secondary picketing (picketing at a place *other* than those at which the dispute is centred); and the further extension of secondary picketing 'flying pickets'.

13. A closed shop is said to exist where there is 100% membership of an independent recognized trade union (or unions), and this situation is maintained permanently by an agreement between the union(s) and the employer that only union labour will be recruited (or that new employees are taken on, on condition they join the appropriate union). A *pre-entry* closed shop is where prior union membership is required before an employee can take up employment in the work group covered by the closed shop; a *post-entry* closed shop allows non-union workers to take up employment, provided that they join the appropriate union within a given time.

14. Issues relating to closed shops do not feature greatly in current industrial relations.

15. Ballots, particularly secret ballots, were considered by the Government to be desirable for elections of union officials, and local representatives, as well as for ascertaining union members' views on the calling of a strike. Money would be provided by the Government for such ballots. In 1984 the Trade Union Act revised and extended the scheme.

16. ACAS—the Advisory, Conciliation and Arbitration Service, set up under the EPA 1974—*advises* employers and/or unions on a wide variety of industrial relations matters; *conciliates* between individuals and their employers, or between unions and employers (automatic when an individ-ual makes a complaint to an industrial tribunal); deals with recognition disputes; *arbitrates* (or arranges for arbitration) when both sides agree to disagree, but seek a ruling from a third party, which both sides agree to accept; *mediates* when proposals for discussion are put to both sides in a dispute.

17. There is little doubt ACAS will continue for the foreseeable future to provide a useful service to British industrial relations.

REVIEW QUESTIONS

1. What is meant by:

   (a) Employer regulation of wages and conditions?
   (b) Individual bargaining?
   (c) Statutory regulation of wages and conditions?
   (d) Collective bargaining?

2. When is there a need to bargain?

3. What is procedure agreement?

4. Distinguish between problem-solving and negotiation.

5. What is a 'trade-off'?

6. Explain the differences between a:

   (a) Strike and lock-out.
   (b) Overtime ban and work-to-rule.
   (c) Sit-in and work-in.

7. What is the difference between an official and an unofficial strike?

8. What is the purpose of picketing, as stated in the Employment Act 1980 and the Code of Practice on Picketing 1983?

9. What is secondary picketing? When is it lawful now?

10. What is a 'closed shop'? Distinguish between pre-entry and post-entry closed shops.

11. Why were secret ballot of members relating to the elections for union officer posts, or to the possibility of strike action considered to be desirable?

12. What conditions must a proposed ballot meet, to qualify for government funding?

13. What are the functions of ACAS?

DISCUSSION TOPICS

1.   A statement is made in this chapter that negotiation is the most common way of carrying out collective bargaining and resolving disputes. Is it, in fact, the best way? (Points to consider: in what other ways could a dispute be settled—evaluate the gains and losses to both sides *and* to the general public/customers/consumers.)

2.   'Strikes should be made illegal. All they do is weaken our industrial muscle, cause loss of jobs, bring Britain into disrepute abroad, and weaken foreign confidence in our ability to produce, or provide services. In fact, strikes benefit no-one.'
      Discuss this statement. (Points to consider: are strikes ever effective in getting *justified* change (e.g. Poland, August 1980); is a company or the economy really *permanently* damaged by strikes; are there occasions when employers actually *welcome* strikes?)

3.   'Despite its occasionally unpleasant and violent overtones, picketing is essentially the weapon of the weak. For this reason alone, it is difficult to justify its suppression.' Discuss this statement by Lord McCarthy. Could, in fact, picketing *ever* be suppressed by law?

4.   The class should divide into two groups: Group A should make out the case for allowing non-union members to cross a picket line; Group B should make out the contrary case.

5.   Can legislation actually be effective if unions (and their rank-and-file membership) either (a) refuse to co-operate with it; (b) actually oppose it?

6.   Are closed shops (a) useful; (b) desirable? (This question could be discussed from various viewpoints: that of the union(s), a potential employee, or of an employer.) Why do you think the Thatcher Administration disliked closed shops 'on principle'?

7.   How democratic are trade unions? Do you consider union members are satisfied with present arrangements for election of union officers and officials? Should the law be changed once again?

8.   Should ACAS be abolished?

ASSIGNMENTS

A27.1   Students in employment should investigate and prepare a short report on the collective bargaining arrangements in their own places of work. Full-time students should carry out a similar activity in the college or school in which they are studying.

A27.2   ACAS has built itself an excellent reputation in the industrial relations field, right from the start. Students should divide into appropriate groups, each researching into a different strand of ACAS's work such as individual conciliation, advisory activities, arbitration, or mediation. The groups can then make formal presentations of their findings.

Case study

A27.3   A firm of consultants has been investigating the refuse collection services provided by the North Middlewick District Council's Public Health Committee, and has come up with a series of findings and recommendations, some of which are detailed below, together with the Environmental Health Officer's comments.

CONSULTANT'S REPORT—EXTRACTS

1. The study was taken on an 'activity sampling' basis, including some 9000 domestic and 500 trade bin carriers.
2. Currently the Council uses *12* vehicles, each crewed with a driver and two loaders, except for three vehicles which each have a driver and three loaders, all on a $33^1/_3\%$ bonus rate.
3. Taking into account the work, usual allowances, rest periods and travelling, the consultants conclude that it should be possible to carry out the same service using *10* vehicles (three with a driver and three loaders; the remainder with two loaders), all to earn a bonus of 41.27%.
4. Bearing in mind the economies in wages by 'slimming down' the workforce up to a maximum of six employees, and the maintenance and running costs of the two (now surplus) vehicles; costs can be cut by an amount of some £30 000 in the first year.
5. In addition, both surplus vehicles, Leyland Musketeers, will not now need replacing: saving about £60 000.
6. Because of present overmanning the men cannot earn full bonus; adopting the new system proposed a considerably higher bonus can be earned.
7. Staff reductions will be from the present 39, plus 6 spare men (including 2 foremen) to 33 plus the 6 spare men. Of the present staff, 5 are in their late 50s or early 60s; and one man's health is under investigation.

ENVIRONMENTAL HEALTH OFFICER'S EXTRACTS

1. Regrettably there is no other work available for surplus labour, although there is one vacancy for a labourer at the Council tip.
2. The driver of one of the two vehicles to be withdrawn is Sam Binns, the UNISON shop steward. Neither he nor the area officer of UNISON have any criticism of the fairness or objectivity of the consultant's report. In a letter from the area officer he says he will press for:

   (a) Guarantees that there will be no loss of earnings for existing men.
   (b) A guarantee that there will be no loss of jobs.
   (c) Any savings to be shared with the men.
   (d) Provision for voluntary early retirement with enhanced retirement pay until aged 65.

3. *All* 'bin men' are UNISON members.

   (a) Dividing into two groups, one representing the Council's Personnel Sub-Committee, the other the union side, prepare a case for your side for a meeting to be held to consider the implementation of the consultant's proposals.
   (b) *Either* report back the strategies for discussion by the whole class, *or* (under the chairmanship of a student) hold the meeting, role playing four committee members, the area officer, Mr Binns, and two other collectors. (The remaining students should note the progress of the meeting, and comment afterwards on the effectiveness of both sides' presentation of the arguments.)
   Note: there is no right outcome of the negotiations. The final position may well reflect the skill of the participants to argue their case. Any other facts or information required can either be assumed or supplied by the course tutor, e.g. where the meeting is to be held, etc.

(Note: Due to changes in legislation many councils now employ private contractors to do this work. For the purposes of this case study please assume the workers remain council employees.)

28
Employee Participation

28.1 DEFINITION

As with other terms we have met, 'employee participation' presents difficulties. It can mean very different things to different people. To some, the aim is *involvement* in determining the conditions of one's working life: to others *control*—a stronger term—is the important objective. This is reflected in the many terms besides employee participation which are used, and the following list cannot claim to be exhaustive:

1. Worker participation.
2. Industrial democracy/workers on the board.
3. Co-determination.
4. Workers' control.
5. Empowerment.
6. Total Quality Involvement.
7. Participation (by itself).

Common to all these terms, and definitions of them, is the central idea of 'involvement in decision-making'. Depending on one's viewpoint, there are, however, differences of opinion concerning *which* decisions workers should be involved in; whether participation should mean *control* as well, and indeed what *degree* of involvement or control there should be. Finally, there are also differences as to whether individuals, or all workers should be involved, or just union members, or even more remotely, persons elected by union members.

Worker participation is probably the most frequently used term. However, it probably gives too much of an impression that we are only considering the manual or factory worker, bearing in mind the commonly recognized distinction between works and staff personnel. *Employee participation* gets over this problem. *Industrial democracy* has a more formal ring about it, now that contemporary Western democracies are so institutionalized; and so does *co-determination*—taken from the German system of participation discussed later. *Workers' control* is a term favoured by those militants with perhaps more radical, socialist aspirations. *Empowerment* is a 1990s modish term, which has been defined as giving every employee all the information needed to make decisions at work; as well as the responsibility to implement such decisions. *Total Quality Involvement (TQI)* is where empowerment is incorporated into Total Quality Management (TQM) schemes. These topics are discussed later. *Participation* on its own has fewer extra implications, so this term will be used from now on, for convenience.

Reviewing what has necessarily been a very brief survey of an extremely complex collection of views we see, at the one extreme, those who would consider participation as a rather high grade and formalized version of consultation. In this scenario, while referring downwards matters of policy, working conditions and the like, for opinions (or advice), management would retain the right to make the final decision. The opposing extreme would be typified by views stressing that places of work should be run by those employed there—or their elected representatives. This could be called *undivided control*, and would imply that whoever occupied a 'management' role would be expected to carry out workers' decisions, and be answerable to them.

In between lies a whole variety of views; and of these, a very important one to note is that of workers' representatives 'on the board', i.e. the notion of *shared control*.

28.2 LEVELS OF PARTICIPATION

Before people began to look at participation in a formal way—and most of this chapter is devoted to the more formal means of involving the workforce in decision-making— participation *did* exist. Workers, including operatives, salesmen, clerks, drivers and supervisors, have been able to make decisions about, even control the way they worked, and what work they did. They had, as we say, areas of discretion. Boardroom decisions are often based on reports presented at meetings; those preparing the reports are going to have a profound influence on the final decisions.

In fact, we can distinguish three levels of participation in the organization: *governmental* participation concerning overall policy decisions; *management* participation involving decisions made below board level; both of these could be called policy- (or power-) centred participation, to be contrasted with participation in the job itself— *job-(or task-) centred* participation.

28.2.1 Job-centred participation

Job-centred participation has already been considered at length in the context of motivation, McGregor's Theory 'Y', and Likert's participative management. Job enrichment and job enlargement aim to involve individual workers or work groups in decision-making on how to do the job, thus restoring self-reliance to workers.

Many examples of job enlargement can be found in the literature about participation, and Scandinavia provides some interesting cases. With jobs involving machine-tending, production-line and assembly work, there is a particularly high degree of repetition, a low degree of personal responsibility, and little scope for a feeling of achievement, let alone self-realization. Group working schemes (variously called 'cell systems', 'flexible team systems', or 'team work structuring') have been advocated as solutions, besides the well-known Volvo experiments in this direction, Saab have 'production groups' which discuss methods of doing jobs, the work environment and safety matters.

In Norway, a paper mill changed a traditional, foreman-directed production system to one where shift groups, after receiving appropriate training in quality control and information-handling techniques, made decisions formerly taken by management. Production and productivity increased, workers became more contented and versatile. Another Norwegian firm, in light engineering, arranged work groups in which team members took turns to be 'foreman' (or 'contact men' as they were called). Besides increases in productivity, forward-planning skills were developed.

More recent developments under this heading are covered in Section 28.5.

28.2.2   Policy-centred participation

Policy-centred participation, even control, is not new in British industry, even at the highest levels. Every time a group of workers manages to block or modify a management policy, by whatever means, it can be argued that the workers concerned have been involved in that policy's final formation—even if they were unwelcome and uninvited contributors! The situation has been likened to a Government and Opposition; but as the union is more likely to win more concessions more often than the average Opposition, perhaps the analogy is not exact.

The success of unions in gaining a foothold in the decision-making process has, of course, been variable; and the areas in which *some* influence has occurred are all aspects of the production system, organization and allocation of work, pay, production levels or promotion rules. A closed shop places constraints on a company's employment policy, so does a seniority rule for promotion; work allocation rules could give a supervisor real problems, and so could negotiated overtime schemes. However, some areas are not usually part of the collective bargaining process: five year plans (and planning generally); investment policies, mergers and acquisitions.

Participation at the 'management' level, where it occurs, is likely to involve the shop steward, convenor, or more junior levels of management. The average worker is, as we have seen, not very interested in union affairs: the same apathy extends to participation even in more 'local' decisions, particularly because employees are used to collective bargaining in such situations.

Joint consultation, a much more formal procedure, is still to be found in British industry: in a 1972 survey, one-third of the workplaces sampled had a consultative arrangement. However, this could encompass everything from small briefing meetings to works councils. The problem for those who seek a much wider influence is that the consultations are joint: the decisions are not. Even when consultation exists, management may still 'by-pass', and deal direct with a union.

28.2.3 Worker directors

The introduction of the worker director as a full member of the board of a company is an attempt to involve the workforce—even though at a distance, through one or more elected representatives—in the central decision-making process. Worker directors are justified by those who feel that union power is ineffective at the centre, no matter how effective it is in the work environment. Some people feel union power at present to be merely negative: only a power to stop things happening, not to initiate events.

In the UK, the number of well researched and documented cases of organizations with worker directors is very limited: the three most quoted are the Post Office, the British Steel Corporation, and the Belfast shipyard of Harland and Wolff. The start of the latter experiment was well documented in an Open University programme. Reactions to the scheme were very mixed, and especially interesting are the comments of those who felt that the job of the union was collective bargaining and not being involved, however indirectly, in running the company.

Employee directors in the British Steel Corporation were first appointed in March 1968; and the original scheme was later modified in April 1972, to allow greater involvement of steel workers, trade unions and the TUC Steel Committee in the selection process. Employee directors were then allowed to hold union office and to be involved in joint consultation. The directors in 1972 included a departmental manager, a loco driver, shop steward/convenor, furnace bricklayer, a chief clerk, and two foremen. Unfortunately for the experiment, the employee directors were appointed to 'second-level' boards below the main BSC board, and the decision-making powers of the divisional boards were somewhat constrained.

Other interesting evidence emerged from a study carried out by an independent research team into the original (1968–72) experiment, which seems relevant to any discussion on worker directors:

1. Decision-making does not all take place in the boardroom—we have already noted that.
2. Over time, the relationship between the employee director and his co-workers on the shop floor becomes increasingly strained (also felt by some to be a problem at Harland and Wolff).
3. It was felt that employee directors could over time become more and more 'management-men' (a point related to 2 above) especially if they were not 'accountable' to an electorate.
4. Important decisions were not significantly influenced by employee directors.

To these points must be added the thought that a real conflict could occur if an employee director were party to a decision which he honestly felt was in the workers' best interest and which was subsequently opposed by his or any other union. It would also be difficult for an employee director to consider making colleagues redundant.

28.2.4 Worker co-operatives

There is no accepted *legal* definition, but a *worker co-operative* is essentially a business owned and controlled by those who work in it. The absence of a precise definition results in a wide variety of forms of such co-ops. Most lay down that every 'employee' must be a member; but some work on the idea the majority are. It has attractions to those not totally fired with the idea of working for a private enterprise firm to help someone else make and use a profit. It offers an alternative way of organizing the workplace, all participating in and benefiting from the firm. Seemingly it offers, too, a way out from the eternal conflict between managers and workers.

The past history of co-operatives is not on the face of it encouraging: despite the efforts of Robert Owen and many who followed, co-ops have been isolated, short-lived and sometimes spectacularly unsuccessful. The drama of the Meriden Co-op, born to rescue an ailing motor-cycle company, resulted in a worthy dream becoming a bitter memory. Co-ops often lack sufficient working capital; run up against the prejudices of suppliers and customers; and decision-making, with everyone having a say and a vote, becomes slow and commercially inappropriate. However, co-ops continue to be formed; and some have had remarkable success.

The advocates of co-ops suggest having a share in a business is a motivator, makes workers more committed, and willing to work harder. The evidence does not fully bear out this supposition: co-ops can be areas of conflict. On the positive side, many workers in co-ops see advantages for themselves: 'having a say' at members' meetings, being involved in decision-making, getting more job satisfaction, making shared pro- fits, a 'democratic' environment, all these are motivators for dedicated co-operators. For them, worker participation is not an optional extra; it's a major aspect of the job.

28.3 PARTICIPATION IN EUROPE

In order to understand more clearly an important British landmark in participation, the publication of the 1977 Bullock Report, it is useful to have some knowledge of European participation practice. Certain key concepts are important, and need some explanation:

1. *Unitary Board.* The Unitary Board system means that each company has *one* main board of directors. This board exercises overall supervision over the managing director and the business, makes overall policy and plans for the future. Unitary Boards are found, for example, in Britain, Belgium, France (though French law does provide for a two-tier system), Ireland, Italy and Sweden.
2. *Two-tier system.* Here a company has two boards. The typical model is shown in Fig. 28.1.

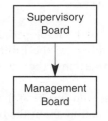

Figure 28.1 Two-tier board system.

The precise powers and composition of the two boards vary from country to country, but basically the Supervisory Board appoints the Management Board, and takes major policy decisions including manpower planning. The Management Board deals with all the day to day problems of the business, gratifies official contracts, etc. This dual system can be found, for example, in Germany, Holland and Denmark; and also in Norway, where the Supervisory Board emerged as the 'Corporate Assembly'.

3. *Works Councils*. The Works Council is the most common feature of Western European participation systems. Councils are established by legislation in most countries including Germany, Holland, Belgium, Luxembourg and Italy. In contrast, Scandinavian councils were set up by employer-union agreement soon after the Second World War. (For reasons outside our present scope, the continental approach to industrial relations has ended up with a concentration on implant participation systems, and the institutions involved are Supervisory Boards and Works Councils, rather than the British collective bargaining pattern.)

Councillors do not have to be union members (though *in practice* most are), and are elected by the *whole* workforce. It will be quickly seen that if, in addition, Works Councils have teeth, can discuss and even share control over a wide range of issues, then the role and power of organized unions are much less significant. The result is that unions seek to increase their power by pushing for increased representation: in Germany, for example, unions may submit lists of their own candidates for election now. The unions are still engaged in wage bargaining both at national and plant level, where 'conflict' can occur, but at the Works Council level the emphasis is on 'co-determination', and councils are expected to keep the peace, and do all they can to assist the smooth functioning of the organization. As the Department of Employment Research Paper No. 4[1] (which is a survey of, continental practice) points out, this results in a 'neutralization' of the workplace, as far as the unions are concerned. No wonder the TUC in the 1970s felt that the Works Council system was inappropriate for Britain.

---

[1] David Marsden, *Industrial democracy and industrial control in West Germany, France and Great Britain.* London, Dept of Employment, 1978. p. 11.

28.3.1   The German participation system

Not only is the German system a highly-developed one, but much quoted; and it was obviously in the minds of the members of the Bullock Committee, even though the majority *rejected* certain aspects. In a sense the Bullock proposals were a reaction to German experiences.

The official German government view has been that workers do not only have rights to be consulted, and be given information about the firms they work for, but to have an equal voice with management over employment policies and work organization. In a modified way what is legislated for the private sector of the economy also applies to the public sector.

28.3.2   Works Councils in Germany

Council members are elected by the whole workforce, have special privileges and serve for three years. The size of each council varies with the numbers employed; and in large organizations with several plants, divisions or groups, a hierarchy of councils is set up.

Besides a list of general tasks—keeping an eye on how the firm is complying with current legislation; looking after the young, the old, the disabled, and foreign workers, etc.—councils have 'areas of co-determination'. This means they have an *equal voice* with management on such matters as recruitment and selection (even individual posts), promotion; working conditions—hours, overtime, etc; job evaluation, redundancy provisions, including levels of compensation. The whole adds up to a fairly formidable list of activities formerly in the control of management, now with shared control.

There are some exclusions, in respect of economic and financial policies. A fall-off in demand is a reality hardly likely to be remedied by a resolution of a Works Council, nor can the council prevent resulting redundancies, though the employer will have to agree on how the consequences of redundancies will have to be handled.

The 1972 Act relating to Works Councils lays down that they should be set up in every firm employing more than five people. Workers' powers at shop floor and management levels can be seen to be significant, therefore, right across the industrial scene.

28.3.3   Board level participation

Co-determination is also found at board level, in the Supervisory Board. This body meets about once a quarter, is responsible for overall policy and appoints the Management Board members. Three different schemes exist:

1. *Coal and steel industry*. Five shareholder representatives face five on the workers' side, in a typical example (numbers vary with company size but parity is constant).

    Shareholder representatives are elected at the AGM, but one of the five must be completely independent of the shareholders or the company: he represents the 'public interest'.

Workers' representatives consist of two from the Works Council; two nominees of trade unions represented in the firm (agreed by the Works Council); and on nominated by the German equivalent of the TUC.

The chairman is co-opted as an 'eleventh man', for casting vote purposes, and represents the 'public interest'.

The personnel director on the Management Board is elected by the employee directors and is usually a union person.

2. *Medium-sized companies.* Outside the coal and steel industry, companies with 500-2000 employees have a composition of one-third worker representatives elected by secret ballot; and the remaining two-thirds are shareholder representatives. It will be seen the parity rule does not operate here.

3. *Larger firms.* Firms (outside the coal and steel industry) employing over 2000 members are covered by the 1976 Co-determination Act. Nearly three-quarters of workers are employed by firms in this category. Ostensibly the parity rule operates with six board members elected by each group at the lower end of the scale; and ten each in the largest enterprises.

Workers' representatives are mostly elected from shop floor and office workers; with the rest going to (outside) trade union officials. One elected representative from the workforce must be a senior manager. Non-union members could (in theory) be elected.

Shareholder representatives are directly elected at their AGM. As the chairman (for built-in and very technical reasons) is likely to be a shareholder representative (and one worker director is a senior manager) it is obvious that the parity rule is not really as effective as it might seem at first view.

28.4 THE BULLOCK REPORT

The Government set up a Committee of Inquiry in 1975 to examine the most effective ways of extending industrial democracy, 'accepting the need for a *radical* extension' of it, 'by means of representation on boards of directors'; and the report the Committee issued has ever since been called the 'Bullock Report', after the name of its chairman, Lord Bullock.

Part of the background to the formation of this Committee was the European Parliament's (Draft) Fifth Company Law Directive (1972). Had it become law, European Community members would have had to accept two-tier boards, with a one-third employee, two-thirds employer membership for the Supervisory Board. For this reason alone, it was not surprising to find that the terms of reference assume industrial democracy could be achieved by worker directors (as opposed to any other method). The TUC had already made representations to the (then Conservative) Government stressing trade union involvement in such a scheme; and the terms of reference accept 'the essential role of trade union organization in the process'.

The Committee was also to take into account the European experience of industrial democracy.

28.4.1 Majority report

This report made a series of recommendations, the most important of which were:

1. *Companies to be involved.* Only companies employing over 2000 personnel would be subjected to the provisions of the report (if made law). (738 enterprises employing 6-7 million people were thought to be involved.)
2. *Starting the 'worker director' process.* Before the scheme described below is activated, an official request for a secret ballot of *all* full-time employees would have to be made by the unions recognized by the company. A majority in favour would be required of at least one-third of the eligible employees.
3. *Choosing the 'worker directors'.* The report laid on *the unions* in the company the responsibility to 'devise whatever method of selection was appropriate', but suggests that seats could be divided up among unions in relation to membership; or the worker directors could be chosen by and from the joint shop stewards' committee (or an equivalent body).
4. *The board and its composition.* The board to which the employee directors would be elected would be composed of the given number of shareholders' representatives; exactly the same number of workers' representatives, and a small number of co-opted members. (This became known as the $2x + y$ formula.) The third group, the y in the formula, were to be co-opted by both sides together and to be an uneven number greater than one, but a smaller number than either of the other two groups: y is smaller than x. These people *could* be insiders, but the report suggested that they should be senior personnel from other organizations connected in some business way with the company: professionals—solicitors, bankers, etc.; or local trade union officials.
5. *The unitary board to be supreme.* No two-tier system was envisaged: the present unitary board system was to be retained.
6. *Works Councils were out.* The report expressed surprise at the emphasis placed (in evidence to it) on Works Councils. In particular, it rejected the German model, as the functions it performed were a duplication of those carried out by shop stewards' organizations in Great Britain. (The majority of the Committee obviously felt that the collective bargaining system would be menaced and both unions and shop stewards weakened by Works Councils.) Thus it would be 'singularly inappropriate' to introduce them.

   (The whole essence of the report is revealed here: the accent is *control* at the centre, rather than *participation* at the management or shop floor level. Ultimate control could pass to the workers' representatives eventually, as in time the chairmanship could pass to a worker director.)

28.4.2 Minority report

The three industrialist members entered a Minority Report, in which they plumped for a Supervisory Board. This body would have three equal groups of directors, one group representing and elected by shareholders; the second representing employees and directly elected by them; and the third independent members who have no direct relationship with the other two groups, but are co-opted by them: a $3x$ system. Preconditions to the setting up of this system would include the formation of an Employee (Consultative) Council, elected by the workforce.

The Council would consult with, and would be consulted by a Management Board (elected by the shareholders, but appointments approved by the Supervisory Board), which would carry out most of the functions that the present unitary board does. The Management Board would, therefore, be accountable to shareholders (as at present); to the Supervisory Board; and have obligations to the Employee Council to discuss its proposals.

28.4.3 Reaction to the reports

The Government considered the reports, and eventually in May 1978, issued a White Paper, the proposals of which in effect contained considerable modifications. The supreme body was to be a 'Policy Board' (with a one-third employee representation to start with) and this would appoint a Management Board, approve its strategic plans, generally monitor its performances and its conduct of financial affairs; and would oversee employment policies. Although the White Paper still stuck to a lower limit of 2000 employees required to have this two-tier system, companies with over 500 employees would be required to set up Joint Representation Committees, broadly representative of union membership in the company.

It was envisaged that the Management Board would be composed of senior executives and the chairman would be the chief executive (i.e. managing director).

28.4.4 Subsequent developments

There was much less criticism of the White Paper, but hardly any enthusiasm either, and the whole subject seemed to languish; and finally die after the Labour Government's defeat.

Later, in 1979, the two-tier (Draft) Fifth Company Law Directive was thrown out by the European Parliament, and a new directive to be considered calls for a unitary system which could include a 'Consultative Council' . This body would be elected by *all* employees, and would consider the Unitary Board's policy proposals over a wide range of topics.

The Thatcher administration did however decide that a voluntary approach to employee involvement was better, and indeed at Brussels in 1983 resisted legislation (in the Council of Ministers) *on principle*. In a roundabout way, however, the Government has got the question of participation moving on two fronts. First, the Employment Act 1982 requires directors' reports to shareholders of larger companies (these with over 250 employees) to include a statement reporting what action has been taken during the previous twelve months to introduce, maintain or develop arrangements aimed at furthering employee development.

The idea behind this provision is to force companies at least to think about involvement, and to report what they are doing about it—whether a little or a great deal. John Selwyn Gummer, the then Employment Secretary, said he would be disappointed if there were even a small minority of firms opting out. Such inertia would provide ammunition for those that argued legislation (from the EC) is the only way of achieving progress.

Secondly, the Government produced a consultative document expressing 'profound reservations' on EC draft directives, and on worker directors with a 'supervisory' function. The CBI's attitude largely reflected these views, whilst the TUC felt what was needed was a framework for workers' rights covering information and consultation which would benefit both sides of industry.

In 1989, another twist to the story was the European Commission's adoption of the 1990 Action Programme on the Community Charter of Fundamental Social Rights of Workers. This Charter was intended as a general statement of minimum workers' social rights throughout the Community.

In fact, the Charter failed to receive the necessary unanimous support at Council of Ministers level. Eventually, in April 1994, the Commission put forward a proposal for a Council Directive based on earlier initiatives, the opinions of the European Parliament and the discussions of the Council. The Draft Directive renames the 'Works Council' the 'European Committee' and states the objective of the Directive to be 'To improve the right to information and to consultation of employees in Community-scale undertakings (i.e. at least 1000 employees; and at least 100 of those employees in each of two member states), or Community-scale groupings.'

(The 'shorter' version of the document runs to many pages, and covers membership—3 to 30 members; and more importantly the right to meet central management at least annually; to be informed and consulted upon the progress of the undertaking under a wide set of headings, including the probable development of the business, production and sales; and be given details of any possible cut-backs and closures.)

When adopted, the Directive would apply to all member states, except the UK. However, it *would* apply to UK undertakings as far as their activities in other member states were concerned. It is also thought that EU companies with UK subsidiaries might well want to set up European Committees.

28.5 OTHER FORMS OF PARTICIPATION

There can never be a balanced view of participation, as all involved—government, management, workforce, shareholders and outside advisers all start from different assumptions (and prejudices). The following points (looked at mainly from a management viewpoint) are however worthy of some consideration.

Pros—participation

1. Helps satisfy a need for involvement (where it exists) in matters which are of workers' concern, and gives them an opportunity to influence events in a

greater or lesser degree. Involvement can lead to commitment, and to a reduction in alienation.

2. Can better utilize skills and abilities of the workforce (Theory 'Y'). See *Quality Circles,* and the sub-sections on empowerment and TQI.
3. Recognizes the change in social values (particularly in the young) which tends to challenge authority-based systems which call for unquestioning obedience.
4. Is to be preferred (especially if it is the result of a voluntary, agreed and tailor-made scheme) to a system imposed upon the organization from outside (national or European Parliament).

Cons—participation

1. Can threaten (or be seen as a threat by) managers, to their ability to manage and take decisions.
2. Can threaten (or be seen as a threat by) union officers, to their negotiating role.
3. Implies information will have to be made much more freely available within the organization. This could lead to 'leaks', and other confidentiality problems.
4. Could fall flat if attempts to introduce it are mismanaged, leading to apathy or even resentment towards participation.

(It will be seen how important it is that any scheme of participation should be devised, sold and introduced to the workforce with careful preparation and a high degree of skill.)

28.5.1 Quality Circles

The idea of Quality Circles (or 'QCs' as they are popularly known) is rather more than just another gimmick to be taken up by management, and discarded after a year or two. As with any scheme of participation it will only be effective if it is designed and managed properly.

Popularly thought to be a Japanese idea, QCs originated in America,[2] but were quickly recognized by the Japanese as vital in their quest to win post-war markets for their goods in the West (their pre-war image being rather that of suppliers of shoddy goods). QCs were eventually re-exported to America, and thence to Europe. Admittedly Japanese culture had a lot to do with the success in Japan of QCs, but equally successful experiences have been achieved in the West, including the UK.

The basic idea is very simple: a Circle Leader (often a work-team supervisor) sits down with his or her workforce, as a group meeting voluntarily, to tackle a work problem, with the basic aim of improving quality and productivity. It has (as with other participation schemes) profound implications for supervisors, managers and the organization. QCs are typical of the kinds of changes mentioned elsewhere in the book—matrix organizations, project teams, job enrichment, breaking down of departmental barriers—which threaten to modify the rigid, compartmentalized traditional

---

[2] That is the verdict of most writers on QCs.

bureaucratic structure in which power, influence and decision making are found at the top rather than the bottom of the organization.

QCs can take many forms, but one often encountered is where a Circle is formed of about ten members who are doing similar work, or who work in the same department. Circles meet (voluntarily) in paid work time on a regular basis, usually at fixed times (with provision for other meetings in special circumstances). Circle Leaders are normally (but need not be) group supervisors. The 'agenda' comes from circle members, and is usually closely related to the immediate group work environment—the problems the workforce actually have identified. Brainstorming or similar techniques are often used at these meetings.

Not only are problems discussed, but ways of overcoming them. Perhaps the solution could be entirely in the workers' hands. Where 'outside' assistance is needed the circle leader/supervisor will act as a link man. Thus QCs enable employees at the lowest levels in the organization not only to initiate ideas, *but to communicate them upwards.* As the problems and ideas raised are (probably) well appreciated by management, management will usually be ready to respond, and a real dialogue results. The fact that members of the workforce at *different levels* are all involved with the same problems, breaks down barriers, enhances mutual respect and reduces mistrust.

QC members in their work quickly learn that problems (and their solutions) are rarely found to exist in isolation within one department. The causes and effects of a machine producing over-sized parts could be found or experienced in different departments, and at various levels in the organization. Design, maintenance, inspection, re-work sections could all be involved. The discovery of the wider implications of problems can lead to the formation of links between QCs, as well as with specialized service departments (maintenance, purchasing, sales for example). Workers begin to get a broader view of the organization through the problems they are trying to solve. The Facilitator (the name given to the overall controller of QCs in an organization) may help with such links and set up appropriate contacts.

Introducing QCs to an organization—on the face of it to improve quality and productivity—becomes much more than that. Work problems with only remote connections with quality are tackled, morale improves, personal relationships become co-operative and trusting, and workers enrich their own jobs.

It should however not be forgotten that QC introduction is a major and significant change in itself. All the considerations outlined in Chapter 9 apply. Like any change its introduction needs careful planning, selling and implementing. The case study at the end of Chapter 9 brings out this point clearly enough.

Three major conditions are essential for QCs to succeed:

1. A firm commitment, publicly made, by senior management to introduce Quality Circles. A firm commitment by supervisory managers to support QCs and to participate actively (possibly as Circle Leaders).
2. The appointment of a single individual (not tied to any particular part, division or department of the organization) to initiate and co-ordinate the whole programme—the Facilitator. Special training is required for this post. He or she persuades, advises, suggests, assists.

3. QCs are introduced gradually, starting in one department as a pilot scheme. Extension should be steady, with no attempt to impose QCs on unwilling, or uncommitted workers.

Like many initiatives which went before, QCs have rather lost favour with forward-looking organizations in the 1990s. More emphasis is currently being given to empowerment and TQM, dealt with next.

28.5.2 Empowerment

One of the 'in-flavours' of the early 1990s, the notion of empowerment, like many other 'participation' philosophies, is ultimately derived from McGregor's 'Theory Y'. Empowerment builds on the 'Quality Circle' approach we have just examined. Instead of looking at people at work as isolated extensions to production equipment, with very narrow skill ranges and needing close supervision, empowerment views the workforce as people who complement plant and machinery, who are a resource to be developed, with the emphasis on self-inspection, self-supervision and problem-solving abilities. All the information needed by the workforce to carry out their tasks must be available to them.

The process of empowerment is essentially first to find the best way of designing (or redesigning) the organization, and then to establish the best mix of practices that should operate within it. Commitment to a high level of customer care and service is a central theme, and considerable training and responsibility is given to those front-line staff who work closely with external customers. It also recognizes *internal* customers (who are the other parts of the organization one section or department serves in the normal course of work) who need the same kind of customer care and service.

Thus the members of the 'empowered' workforce have considerable influence over their working environment, take responsibility for the quality of their output (or the service they provide), use their initiatives to find solutions to the problems they face, and freely share their skills, knowledge (and their problems) with their colleagues.

Such a state of affairs is not easily achieved overnight by what was originally a 'traditional' organization. It requires not only a rethink by the 'empowered' workforce, but by management and supervision. After all, you cannot *order* people to be empowered: they must want to be.

Thus managers and supervisors need to have a broad vision of the goals and objectives of the redesigned organization, understand the need to change, be 'change agents'—as discussed in Chapter 9. Often, faced with the idea that the workforce 'supervisors itself', managers and supervisors in particular, feel they have been 'done out of a job': empowering not only *needs* managers; it cannot operate without them. Supervisors will need to be able, in particular to:

— advise and coach their team members to develop and improve the skills and knowledge they will need to cope with new approaches and responsibilities
— help team members to focus on one goal to start with; once accomplished, encourage them to establish and plan further goals on their own; and accomplish them one by one

— be available to listen to what their staff have to say; and respond to any suggestions or proposals for innovation from them
— provide continual feedback, support and guidance
— practice self-development to cope with their role (see Chapter 36).

Individual workers can have their own action plans (one goal to be agreed at a time,
to begin with), on which progress and achievement can be recorded. Agreeing goals in
this fashion is a way of managing resources which simultaneously releases and
increases employees' potential, and effectively accomplishes organizational objectives.
Goals should not be so easy to accomplish that they cease to be challenging; nor so
challenging that the risk of failure is high.

In the same way, teams can formulate team objectives, and record their achievements for all to see: I have seen this in action, and the pride teams involved had in
explaining their progress to visitors was impressive. In Maslow terms, they had certainly achieved a degree of self-fulfilment.

What does have to be understood, however, is that an organization cannot change a
workforce overnight into an empowered set of employees: a great deal of hard and
careful preparatory work is required to integrate these new ways of managing and
developing people into its overall strategy.

28.5.3 Total Quality Involvement

Total Quality Involvement (TQI) is an extension of Total Quality Management, a
Japanese-inspired management technique. On close inspection TQI turns out to be
a specialized version of empowerment, which makes a priority of involving workers
in the continuous search for, and improvement of the quality of the outputs of an
organization; whether those outputs are primarily goods or services, or a combination
of both.

The simple idea behind TQM/TQI initiatives is that every aspect, every department
of an organization in the public or private sector has 'clients' or 'customers'; and what
customers want/need/deserve is 'quality'. (As we noted above, customers can be external or internal.)

A basic maxim of marketing is 'identify exactly what your customer wants (not
only the goods/services needed, but when they are required, in what format, at what
kind of price, etc.), and then set about meeting those requirements'. 'Meeting those
requirements' can be regarded as providing customers with quality. (It is interesting to
note the British Standard Institution defines 'quality' as the 'totality of features of a
product or service that bears on its ability to satisfy stated or implied needs'.)

Thus, in essence, the customer comes first: the customer needs quality. If an organization decides to follow the TQM path, to try and ensure all parts of an organization
know precisely what its customers want, can be a major, time-consuming and costly
undertaking in itself; and every department must be involved—from design to marketing, purchasing to distribution, sales to accounts. Successful implementation of TQM

requires the preparation of a well organized quality management system to function across departments. Supporters of TQM also accept the need for teamwork, and suggest the starting point is to not to try to change people's knowledge, attitudes and beliefs, but to create for them new roles and responsibilities. The new situation will change the culture. Groups will see the need to co-operate.

TQI goes even further and can involve employees not just in making local decisions and monitoring their own performance: I have been present at meetings of groups made up of employees from all levels and from different departments in the same organization, enthusiastically considering broader, company-wide problems; and formulating proposals for dealing with them. (Additionally, each employee there brought along his or her own action plan, and was able to discuss it with others to generate ideas.) At a later date there would be a report-back session.

However, it must be said that all schemes have their differences, and it cannot be supposed that any one way of involving the workforce could be successful everywhere. Organizations should only adopt those practices which they really feel meet both the demands of their customer, and the needs of their workforce.

28.5.4 The wish to participate

How far workers want to participate, at what levels they really feel they would like to have a say in what goes on at work has long been a matter of debate. My own view has always been that whilst workers generally welcome 'job-centred' participation, participation at policy-making levels was less important to them. Workers understand their own work situation only too well, and have views on their work problems. They have much to offer and much to gain from participation at this level.

Research by Paul Rathkey[3] in four firms in the North of England supports this view. More interesting is his list of those areas in which workers had a widespread desire for consultation or participation. Virtually all revolve round anxieties of one kind or another derived from change, or the threat of change. Typical examples given include reorganization of work layouts; introduction of new machinery, new work methods; closing down part or all of a factory; changing company rules, payment schemes etc. It does seem that participation here could help dispel some of these anxieties.

28.6 THE FUTURE OF PARTICIPATION

Looking first at the more formal, mandatory proposals, so many have been considered, it is difficult to predict the final format of any participation scheme.

If the EU does eventually agree on its Directive, then worker directors in the UK may never become a reality: I am convinced that increasing participation at management

---

3 Paul Rathkey, 'Participation and Industrial Democracy—the Shop Floor View'. Jim Conway Foundation, Stockton-on Tees, 1984.

level (however difficult it is for managers and supervisors) and on the shop floor is not only possible but desirable. It was interesting to note that whatever workers felt in the Harland and Wolff documentary about worker directors (including indifference), there was, in the programme, coverage of a well-attended, lively meeting between management and workers at sub-board level.

Voluntary formalized participation has been seen to work in some companies (Glacier Metal, Scott Bader and the John Lewis Partnership are often quoted in this respect), but Parliament itself provides an interesting model which could be a basis for consideration. Ministers do have certain decision-making powers, formulate policy, initiate legislation; but an excellent system of select committees of back-benchers enables them to call upon these Ministers to explain, justify and defend their proposals. Perhaps directors should be called upon *individually* to explain their own specific policies and decisions to sub-committees of a Works Council with powers to request information, and to make its own comments and suggestions.

Two areas are missing from EU and British proposals; the smaller firm, and mostly the public sector. Some form of participation could be envisaged in the smaller manufacturing unit, but obviously would be very difficult to consider in the corner shop. The public sector presents a host of difficulties, particularly bearing in mind the role of the elected representative; but the German system does allow the civil servant co-determination in conditions of work; recruitment and training; work breaks and holiday schedules through 'Personnel Councils'. The chief administrator (e.g. a Chief Executive/Clerk to the Council in local government) has to meet this body for discussion at least once every month.

Finally we should note the increase in the so-called redesigning (sometimes called 're-engineering') of organizations to permit the introduction of one form or another of the empowerment of the workforce. It is still too early to judge whether this approach will become widely adopted in the UK.

SUMMARY

1. It is difficult to define participation: some see it as involvement; others as control.

2. Besides worker participation, other terms used include: employee participation, industrial democracy, workers on the board, co-determination, workers' control, empowerment, Total Quality Involvement, participation.

3. Views about participation vary from formal consultation with the workforce to outright or undivided control by workers or their representatives. Shared control implies a balanced board with worker directors.

4. *Governmental* participation is at board level; *management* participation at managerial level; and *job-centred* participation at shop floor level.

5.   Job-centred participation is the kind of involvement advocated by the American organizational psychologists of the 1960s, implied by, for example, participative management.

6.   Worker directors have had a limited trial in the UK, and probably because of the rules and constraints placed on them, the results are less than encouraging. Real problems such as conflicts of interest and even of conscience are inherent in the job of a worker director.

7.   European participation has taken various forms: some countries with Unitary Boards (one board only), others with a two-tier system (two boards), with worker directors sitting on them. Proportions of shareholders' and workers' representatives vary, even in the same country, in different industries.

8.   Common to most Western European countries is the Works Council: a body entirely composed of worker representatives. In some countries it consults with management; in Germany there is co-determination over a wide range of employment matters.

9.   The German coal and steel industry sees genuine parity between shareholders' and workers' representatives on the Supervisory Board; and workers also elect the personnel director on the Management Board.

10.   Outside these industries, in medium-sized firms (500–2000 employees), Supervisory Boards have a one-third worker and two-thirds shareholder representation.

11.   Larger German firms are covered by the Co-determination Act. The parity rule operates on the Supervisory Board, but the chairman's vote can be decisive (the chairman is a shareholder representative normally).

12.   The Bullock Report (1977) recommended:

(a)   Companies with over 2000 employees be subject to the recommendations.
(b)   The process to start after a union request, followed by a secret ballot.
(c)   The method of choosing worker directors to be left open to unions to decide.
(d)   The formula for the Unitary Board should be $2x + y$: equal numbers of directors to be elected by shareholders and the workforce, with the balance of power being held by a smaller group of outside independent directors co-opted by the two larger groups.
(e)   No Works Councils.

13.   A Minority Report recommended a two-tier system with a 3x formula
        for the Supervisory Board—equal groups of representatives elected by
        shareholders and workers, plus a co-opted group of the same size. An
        employee Council would consult with the Management Board (elected
        by shareholders).

14.   After adverse criticism the Government issued (1978) a White Paper recom-
        mending a two-tier system (Policy and Management Boards). The lower
        limit of 2000 employees stayed, but industrial democracy was extended to
        firms of 500 employees only in regard to Joint Representation Committees
        being set up representing all union membership, to consult with manage-
        ment. The Management Board would be composed of senior executives.

15.   Governmental opinion in the mid-1980s seemed to be against EC direc-
        tives, but to demand that companies report on what they are doing to
        encourage participation.

16.   From management's viewpoint, participation allows worker involvement,
        leading (hopefully) to increased commitment; uses workforce skills to
        better advantage, and is to be preferred (on a voluntary basis) to some
        scheme forced upon it from outside. It can, however, also be seen as a chal-
        lenge to managers as decision makers, and to union officers as negotiators,
        it can be very counter productive if introduced badly.

17.   Quality Circles, voluntary groups of workers meeting regularly during
        working hours to consider work problems which have been identified by
        group members, are a further development of job-centred participation.
        A variation of the project team, except that the team come from the
        same working group. QCs need a catalyst, an overseeing co-ordinator—
        a ' facilitator'.

18.   Empowerment sees the workforce, not as something to be controlled and
        regimented, but as a resource to be developed. Self-determination and self-
        motivation are to be encouraged. Responsibility for a wide range of
        decision-making is delegated to the workforce. Supervisors in such a situa-
        tion will need to develop a new range of skills, including advising, coaching,
        supporting and guiding their teams. Such changes in culture cannot take
        place without a great deal of planning and preparation.

19.   Total Quality Involvement (a specialized version of empowerment) concen-
        trates on involving the workforce in the continuous search for, and
        improvement of the quality of an organization's outputs. Employees in TQI-
        orientated concerns are often given a chance to participate in considering
        wider matters than the functioning of their immediate work environment.

20.   However, from my experience, employees seem to prefer job-centred
        participation to other forms.

REVIEW QUESTIONS

1. Distinguish between consultation and workers' control; between undivided and shared control.

2. What is job-centred participation? Why is McGregor's Theory 'Y' relevant to this concept?

3. What is meant by saying job-centred participation is not a new feature of British industrial relations?

4. Define the idea of a 'worker director'. What are some of the problems a worker director could face in doing his job (as a director)?

5. What is the difference between a Unitary Board and a two-tier system?

6. What is a Works Council (in a continental European context)? Can all workers (or just union members) participate in elections to this body?

7. Explain the constitution of Works Councils in Germany.

8. How does the 'parity' system operate (or *not* operate) in the German coal and steel industry; in medium-sized and large-sized firms?

9. Outline the principal recommendations of the (1977) Bullock Reports (Majority and Minority).

10. What are the differences between Quality Circles and empowerment? Which of these initiatives is the more participative?

11. If empowering means the workforce 'manages itself', are supervisors or team leaders still needed? If so, why?

12. Explain the main features of Total Quality Management.

DISCUSSION TOPICS

(Note: The whole question of participation is so involved and controversial that almost any given topic can lead on to others; and it may be difficult (and unnecessary) to restrict discussion to the specific topics suggested.)

1. Should shop floor workers, clerks, shop assistants, nurses, civil servants, policemen, have:

(a)   No say at all;

(b)   Some say;

(c)   A complete say in how the enterprises for which they work shall be run?

(Points to consider: shareholders, the state or local authorities have *ownership* rights: does ownership imply control? Even if it does, has not control actually passed to managers? Workers give up potential leisure time to work for an enterprise. Does the money/benefit package they receive settle the matter completely, or should they acquire participation (or even control) rights by working there?)

2.   Which system do you consider most appropriate to introduce or improve in the UK (assuming you are in favour of participation):

(a)   A formal, policy-centred system;

(b)   A management level participation system;

(c)   A job-centred participation system on the shop floor;

(d)   A formalized TQI type of scheme?

Or is it *none* of these, or a combination of two or more? (Points to consider: the practicalities of any scheme, possible TUC/union reactions and management relations.)

3.   How would you, as a manager or supervisor, like to have to stand up (at fixed intervals) and explain the decisions you have made, and to justify them to your workforce?

4.   How do you see participation at the job level:

(a)   Management initiating ideas, asking for comments, suggestions;

(b)   Management delegating the 'how' of the job to the worker;

(c)   The complete job, and the management of it being left to the worker (e.g. the Scandinavian experiments or some versions of empowerment/TQI)?

5.   Does the supervisor's job disappear if 4(c) is the solution? If not, what is left then for supervisors to do?

6.   If a 'parity' system operates at board level, what would happen if a complete deadlock occurred in the company? How could such a situation be avoided?

7.   Discuss how Total Quality Involvement could be useful to:

(a) An engineering company (making car components);
(b) A processed foods manufacturer;
(c) A hospital;
(d) A supermarket;
(e) A Job Centre.

ASSIGNMENTS

A28.1 Each course member should ascertain what consultative/participative arrangements exist in his organization (including 'nil returns'!):

(a) At job level;
(b) At management level;
(c) At policy-making level;

and prepare a short report to read out to the group.

Note: Full-time students should examine their college/school participation arrangements, if they have had no suitable work experience to go on.

A28.2 As a class, or in groups, take an organization with which you are familiar (it could be a firm, local authority, club, school or college, for example) and discuss how it could be made more 'participative'. Draw up a set of proposals to achieve what you feel is possible; and outline the kinds of changes to the organization that would be necessary.

UNIT VI

Management and Supervisory Competences

With every passing day the need for better trained and qualified people at all levels becomes ever more important and urgent. The coincidental increase of competition following the establishment of the Single European Market, the opening of the Channel Tunnel, and the relentless challenge from the Far East demands not only skilled producers and givers of service, but trained and competent managers and supervisors, to sustain and enhance the performance of the organization.

In this unit we shall look briefly at the work and philosophy of the National Council for Vocational Qualifications, and then go on to consider some key skills and competences, the possession of which is vital to every successful manager at any level.

29
The Qualified Workforce

'A National Vocational Qualification . . . is awarded to people who have achieved employment-led competence, and who have demonstrated that they can perform in employment, through assessment either in the workplace or in a realistic simulated work environment.'

NCVQ Update No. 1 (1989)

29.1 THE BACKGROUND TO NATIONAL VOCATIONAL QUALIFICATIONS

Over many years a large number of different educational bodies have been established (City and Guilds, RSA, EDEXEL/BTEC, for example), as well as professional associations in banking, accountancy, marketing, engineering and similar fields. Most of them have designed, offered and administered, formal courses of vocational study leading to specific qualifications. Students attained these specific qualifications after finishing a formal course, usually completing assignments and possibly passing written examinations. The theory has been successful students, by passing, have indicated their potential for further study; or for employment, relocation or promotion within their work unit. The reverse has often been implied for those who did not pass, or who had never even started out on the study route, regardless of their work performance.

There were, indeed, many problems with a system such as this. At one time awarding bodies numbered approximately 300, many with highly individual qualifications. It was frequently difficult to relate one qualification to another.

Assessment methods varied widely, and course philosophies ranged from some with highly practical approaches, to those more concerned with the acquisition of large amounts of factual information and/or theoretical knowledge. Whilst some courses of study were available through open learning, many required attendance away from work on a regular basis for typically nine months. Whole modules of a course may have been inappropriate for some students. Entry qualifications might have excluded suitable potential students from even enrolling.

The National Council for Vocational Qualifications (NCVQ) was set up by the Government in 1986 to undertake the reform of the whole national vocational qualification system. Its remit was to 'hallmark' qualifications which met the needs of people at work and to introduce a new, simple structure which everyone could understand and make use of.

This Council was replaced in 1997 by the Qualifications and Curriculum Authority (QCA), which is a statutory regulator now spanning the whole of the education area in the UK—from the 'rising fives' to the highest level vocational qualifications (e.g. NVQs, see below) and national occupational standards. The QCA sees its task as both developing appropriate curricula and qualifications (in partnership with the business and education sectors) and overseeing their assessment. Only those qualifications meeting the QCA's criteria will be admitted to their network of formal, approved qualifications.

In particular, with vocational qualifications, the intention was that there would be dialogue between the QCA and advisory groups based on related occupational sectors. Such groups would have a majority of members coming from related businesses, plus some coming from further and higher education. The QCA would look to these groups to identify not only current training needs but those which will emerge in the foreseeable future. The paramount aim is to marry maximum flexibility of form (to suit differing work environments) with maximum rigour. A particular award of an NVQ, then, wherever, whenever and by whomsoever made, must always reflect the same level of competence and knowledge.

29.2   NATIONAL VOCATIONAL QUALIFICATIONS

By 1988 the NCVQ had established the criteria for those awards which would carry their 'hallmark'. These awards were called 'National Vocational Qualifications' (NVQs). From the start it was laid down that these qualifications were only to be gained by those who had achieved work-based competences and were able to prove or demonstrate them (through some form of assessment either in the workplace or in a realistic simulated work environment). The differing areas of work in which the candidate's competences were to be demonstrated were called 'units'. Units were further divided into separate activities called 'elements'.

It should be noted that NCVQ's definition of a competence was 'the ability to perform work activities to the standards required in employment'. In no way was an NVQ to be regarded as a 'training course'. The pertinent standards were then set by various examining bodies such as City & Guilds, RSA and, in the case of management, by the Management Charter Initiative (MCI). Earlier forms of NVQs—of all kinds, not just management ones—merely listed 'performance criteria' (PCs), which defined what was required to be done to perform the task concerned well. The current management NVQs, including the Supervisory level 3 (see *Levels of competence accreditation*, below), not only set out for each element the PCs to be achieved but two other important aspects: 'knowledge requirements' (which specify what you as a supervisor will need to know *and* understand to be able to do your job properly) and 'personal competences' (which you will need to be able to demonstrate in the process of achieving each complete Unit).

Thus an essential aspect of gaining a management NVQ qualification is the ability of a supervisor to demonstrate that he or she has acquired both those knowledge requirements and competences relating to the NVQ in question.

Assessment is rarely a 'one-off' activity: candidates, working closely with their assessors, can produce the required evidence, can discuss progress on an ongoing basis and confirm the appropriateness of the next piece of evidence to be acquired. Each element can be assessed and certified separately over a period of time. Thus any given candidate can accumulate certified units until sufficient have been acquired to merit the full qualification.

After NVQs had been running for some years the Department for Education and Employment commissioned a review which recommended that individual training and development via NVQs should relate to (a) a candidate's previous learning and experience and (b) a candidate's specific needs. It was also felt important that appropriate learning opportunities were agreed upon by both candidate and assessor. Thus NVQ-related training and development now enable a candidate to undertake a totally 'customized' programme, both *person-related* and *job-related*. Such a programme can not only help a candidate to become more competent in a current job but develop skills which could meet future challenges.

To summarize: a well-run organization needs competent employees and managers who are prepared to follow a planned approach to continuous development. The NVQ framework and its emphasis on standards to be achieved are an ideal way of ensuring the qualified workforce can become a reality. It is now generally agreed that NVQs have opened up the acquisition of qualifications to many more people at work than previously.

Levels of competence accreditation

Currently there are five levels of accreditation for competence-based qualifications:

1. Level 1. This is appropriate to jobs whose requirements are limited. The areas of competence are solely the ability to perform varied activities (most being routine and predictable) which are normally done under strict supervision.
2. Level 2. Appropriate to jobs on the shop floor, office work and working in a retail environment. This level demands competence in a significant range of varied work activities performed in a variety of contexts. Some activities are complex or non-routine; there is usually some individual responsibility and autonomy. Being a team member or collaborating with others may be a requirement.
3. Level 3. This is a more advanced level; appropriate to many fully skilled apprenticeship-entry jobs and where skills required are indicative of supervisory responsibilities. Competence is required in a broad range of varied work activities performed in a wide range of contexts. Most are complex and many are non-routine. There is considerable responsibility and autonomy. Control and guidance of others are required.

4. Level 4. Covers jobs undertaken by more senior/specialist staff. Areas of competence required include the ability to perform to specified standards a comprehensive range of specialized tasks, in a wide variety of contexts. This implies a considerable emphasis on a degree of personal responsibility and autonomy. In addition, responsibility for the work of others and the acquisition and use of resources is often present.
5. Level 5. This covers the responsibilities, jobs and tasks undertaken by very senior staff/top management personnel. At this level there is very substantial personal autonomy and often significant responsibility for the work of others. The allocation of substantial resources can feature strongly, as well as personal accountability for analysis, diagnosis, design, planning, execution and evaluation.

Progression

Each NVQ is complete in itself. From the beginning it was felt it would be a mistake to build into an NVQ award any extra study or learning needed towards progression to a higher level. Thus, progression from one level to another is made solely by building upon attainments achieved at the lower level; and acquiring the knowledge, understanding and competences necessary to achieve the higher award. In short, an NVQ is awarded for the ability to *do* certain things, and for the possession of relevant knowledge and understanding. It does not demonstrate a potential to do anything else.

Assessment and evidence requirements

Assessment of NVQs is normally delegated to an 'assessor', someone in close contact with the candidate and who is qualified to assess after gaining the necessary Training and Development Lead Body (TDLB) NVQs. When assessing a candidate's worthiness to receive an NVQ award assessors will always ask themselves 'can the candidate do what is being assessed?' There are only three possible answers to such a question: 'yes, competent'; 'no, not yet competent'; 'or 'insufficient evidence available currently upon which to make a judgement'.

Assessments are monitored and countersigned by a (qualified) internal verifier (IV). Periodically, the work of an NVQ-awarding centre is monitored and verified by an external verifier (EV), who is responsible to the awarding body to ensure the assessment procedures used by the centre are being properly carried out.

Evidence examined at level 3 (i.e. supervisory) could be *performance evidence* from natural observation in the workplace; tests, projects or assignments carried out by candidates; *supplementary evidence* from oral questioning; written reports and *evidence from (relevant) prior achievements*, including reports and certificates from various sources. In arriving at a decision assessors will be looking for 'occupational competence'. This includes the candidate's ability to *apply* knowledge and understanding (in conjunction with practical and thinking skills). (The latest versions of the management NVQs contain evidence requirements for each element; and examples of acceptable evidence are given for each and every element.)

Action planning

Candidates aiming to gain an NVQ (at any level) will each need to create an 'action plan' for achieving the award. Such a plan should reflect their individual learning and development needs. Carefully prepared, stages of such a plan could well cover more than one element or unit at a time. Particular activities managed well by a given supervisor could, for example, simultaneously provide evidence towards the creation of effective working relationships, the development of teams and individuals and the supervisor's own time-management skills. Such a widely 'evidence-based' approach can save time and paperwork and also remind candidates no job is a mere collection of discrete activities, but an integrated whole.

29.3   GENERAL NATIONAL VOCATIONAL QUALIFICATIONS (GNVQs)

Originally announced in 1991, GNVQs are aimed primarily at those not yet in work, the majority of whom will be 16–19 year-olds at school or college. They were devised to offer a broad-based vocational preparation for work; and enable those learning to acquire the kind of skills, knowledge and understanding needed to work in an occupational area (e.g. manufacturing, leisure and tourism, science, business). The new qualifications would be at levels 1, 2 and 3. The aim was to have GNVQs covering 15 broad areas by September 1995.

Managers and supervisors will, increasingly, come across employees—particularly younger ones—who have been through the 'GNVQ system'. Additionally, current students could be encountered undergoing work experience.

It should be noted that in late 1994, detailed criticisms were made by the Office for Standards in Education (OFSTED) about GNVQs run in schools, particularly in course design and assessment (where OFSTED felt more rigour was required).

At the same time, industry and commerce showed a positive endorsement of these new qualifications. Fifteen major companies (including McDonald's, J. Sainsbury, Peugeot, American Express (Amex) and United Biscuits) offered assistance towards qualifications in their particular employment areas. For example, Amex undertook to sponsor work experience in local businesses for students taking GNVQ in leisure and tourism. Travel bursaries were on offer for the best student in each region.

By the time of the publication of this edition it was envisaged that a new series of GNVQ modules would have been issued. One intention was to reduce the amount of paperwork to be completed by teaching staff and to concentrate on unit (as opposed to element) assessment.

29.4   FINAL REMARKS

The rest of Unit VI is devoted to specific skills or activities, many of which are mentioned as 'personal competences' in various Units of the NVQ level 3 in (Supervisory)

Management. In particular, a completely revised Chapter 36 looks at different aspects of the non-specialist optional units, (a) personal competences (PCs) not mentioned elsewhere in this book, and (b) the knowledge and understanding (K&U) called for in both mandatory and the non-specialist units. (A special index dealing with these areas can be found at the end of Chapter 36. It should, however, be noted that this chapter does not cover in any specific detail the requirements of the specialist Optional Units relating to Energy Efficiency, Quality Systems or Quality Audits.)

In the following chapters, in which key skills are dealt with in some detail, you will find at the end of the appropriate section a Skill-Building Programme which serves three purposes; as an 'action plan' to help guide you through the process; as a 'checklist' to 'tick-off' each item as it has been completed; and as a record of what you have achieved. If you make your own copy, you can then add your own notes and comments.

SUMMARY

1.   Qualifications have been offered in the past by a large number of bodies. The normal method of obtaining such a qualification was a formal course of study with examinations at the end. The qualification was taken rather to indicate potential than to certify ability.

2.   There were over 300 awarding bodies, and it was difficult to relate their awards to each other.

3.   Assessment methods vary; course philosophies differ widely; study is usually by attendance on a taught course. Some material might be irrelevant. Entry qualifications can deter potential students.

4.   The NCVQ was set up to reform and rationalize the system; encourage people to develop work-based competences; and make available more, better and more appropriate qualifications. The QCA (which has succeeded it) has expanded and clarified its role to ensure maximum flexibility alongside maximum rigour.

5.   As an alternative to previous study-related routes to qualifications, NVQs can be gained by people who can demonstrate their mastery of work-based competences. These can be assessed over time, credits being awarded for individual elements achieved which add up to the full NVQ qualification when all the elements in a unit have been achieved. The current view is that any individual's training and development via NVQs should be based on the candidate's learning, experience and specific needs.

6.   At present there are five levels (numbered 1–5) of competence: (1) routine and predictable; (2) with a wider range of activities, some non-routine and/or complex; (3) fully skilled, with competence in a wide range of activities and supervisory responsibilities; (4) competences required by senior/specialist staff; and (5) those required of the most senior staff in the organization.

7. The achievement of any particular level can be made only by acquiring the necessary skills, knowledge and understanding and competences needed for that level. The only way to progress to a higher level is by acquiring the skills, knowledge, understanding and competences necessary to achieve the higher award.

8. NVQ assessment is made is by qualified assessors. The process is monitored by qualified internal verifiers and ultimately by verifiers appointed by the awarding body.

9. Candidates aiming to achieve an NVQ will need to create and follow a personal 'action plan'. Such a plan could be wide-ranging and cover a variety of evidence-generating activities.

10. GNVQs are mostly intended for the 16–19 age group and form a set of broad-based vocational qualifications for levels 1, 2 and 3. Despite initial criticisms leading firms have sponsored students and offered prizes.

11. The rest of Unit VI is devoted to exploring different aspects of personal competence at Management NVQ level 3 standard (with the exception of the topics of energy efficiency, quality systems and quality audits).

REVIEW QUESTIONS

1. What are NVQs?

2. List some of problems of the British qualification system before the introduction of NVQs.

3. Explain what is meant by (a) a 'competence', (b) 'knowledge and understanding'.

4. Describe the five 'levels of competence' (as related to NVQs). To which levels(s) of competence do you think the following jobs might be allocated:

   (a) that of a senior nurse in charge of a ward (and other nurses)?
   (b) an office junior of two-weeks' standing?
   (c) the personnel office of a district council?
   (d) the chairman of a large public company?

5. What is the key question an assessor will have to ask when assessing an employee's competence in a given area?

6. Distinguish between 'performance evidence', 'supplementary evidence' and 'evidence from prior achievement'.

7. What is an 'action plan'? Explain why such a plan would be very useful to produce before undertaking an NVQ qualification.

8. Why is this chapter headed *The Qualified Workforce*?

DISCUSSION TOPICS

1.   Why, do you think, did the Government feel in the late 1980s that the quali-
          fication system needed a review and restructuring?

2.   Discuss the view that workers in routine, basic jobs don't need any train-
          ing—even less do they need a certificate to prove they can do their job. (You
          could also go on to consider whether people who have been in more senior
          posts for some years don't need training either.)

3.   Should, in your view, the successful execution of a job over a period of time
          merit being taken into consideration when awarding a qualification relevant
          to that job?

4.   What do you think may well happen in the future to people at work who
          seek promotion but, at the same time, decline to become trained and quali-
          fied to a level appropriate to the job they aspire to?

ASSIGNMENT

A29. 1   Find out as much as you can about NVQs, and how far your organization
          has become involved in NVQ training. Put your findings into a short report.
          Be prepared to report back to the class or study group.

30
Project Planning and Report Writing

'The project will be an investigation of a problem or situation with the object of collecting information, analysing it, arriving at logical conclusions and making recommendations.'

NEBSM

30.1 INTRODUCTION

As all those studying for the Certificate in Supervisory Management (run by NEBSM) are aware, students are required to undertake, during the course, a *project*, that is a major assignment which takes the form of a critical investigation into such areas as a work-related problem, difficulty, or an impending change to the working environment. The results of the investigation are then to be submitted for assessment in the form of a concise report in writing. Other examination bodies may require something very similar, involving a structured approach to a problem, task or topic, and some kind of written report.

The work involved in tackling the project and the subsequent report is so interrelated that you will in this skill-building programme be following an integrated process. This does not mean a manager or supervisor who is more concerned with improving report-writing skills cannot use this programme: all you will need to do is to concentrate on the second half of the *six stages*, and take note of the relevant points in the overall programme review.

30.2 AIMS OF THIS PROGRAMME

The aims of the programme are to help you.

1. To choose, research into, and complete a work-based project.

2. To write a well-presented and useful report, setting out your conclusions and recommendations.

30.3   THE FUNCTION OF PROJECTS

The project is seen to fulfil the following functions:

1. As a demonstration you have acquired or enhanced a series of skills (see Section 30.4 below), and put those skills into practice.
2. As a major learning situation. You are asked to work out how to solve a challenging problem in meticulous detail, possibly for the first time.
3. As a testing exercise in communication.
4. As a challenge in thinking, then doing. Many of your projects will contain recommendations relevant to your workplace, even your own job. If your recommendations are accepted, you will have to put them into practice and live with the results.
5. As a method of assessment. From reading it, your tutor (with some input from your employer) can assess your level of skill, your grasp of principles studied, your ability to put principles into practice. NEBSM have always placed considerable store on successful completion of the project in the award of a certificate.
6. As a way of repaying the employer. Most students on management or supervisory courses are sponsored by their employers: fees are paid, and part or whole paid day-release is granted, a residential week-end subsidised. A total sum in excess of £1000 could be involved.

If your completed project, for example, aids productivity, or saves waste; reduces costs, or makes something complicated simpler and safer to use; reduces conflict, or increases motivation, then your employer not only has a more alert, better trained supervisor, but other, quantifiable advantages.

30.4   THE SKILLS YOU WILL NEED

It is difficult to predict all the skills you will need to complete your project successfully, but at least some of the following skills will be needed, many of which we have already looked at:

Creating (using your imagination in problem-solving)
Planning (the project as a whole; scheduling; setting terms of reference)
Organizing (the material, information, ideas; the report itself)
Communicating (during research; discussing ideas; writing the report)
Controlling (the progress of the work; keeping to schedule)
Working with people (getting co-operation in obtaining data and ideas)
Identifying and tackling problems (spotting system weaknesses)

Numeracy (using statistical techniques; quantifying problems and/or solutions)
Gathering and analysing data (from many sources: records, people, personal observation, libraries)
Being objective (eliminating personal prejudices; having an open mind)
Generating alternatives (looking for more than one solution to a problem)
Choosing (the project itself; the best of the alternative solutions)
Evaluating (weighing pros and cons; costs and benefits; assessing effects)
Devising and designing (cover; layout generally; diagrams, charts, etc.)
Selling/persuading (presenting the evidence to back your case; presenting your recommendations persuasively)

A formidable list: but each item in its way contributes to a successful final report.

30.5   THE SIX STAGES OF PROJECT PREPARATION

There are six distinct stages in project preparation. Work through each in turn, and review your progress against the checkpoints at the end of each section.

30.5.1   Stage 1: Making a beginning—choosing a project

Some students start a course with a good idea of what they want to explore in a project. Others cannot choose from several ideas; a few have no ideas at all. Remembering that your organization should endorse your eventual choice, if you have a firm proposal you need to get confirmation to go ahead from your superiors (and/or training officer), as well as getting the blessing of your course tutor. Similarly, those with several possible projects will need to talk the ideas through with superiors and tutor, and normally the topic chosen will be the one which appeals most to the organization.

What do you do if you have no ideas? Your course tutor can help you here. By discussion the two of you can often arrive at a suitable project to put to your employer. Think about your job, and those who work with (or against) you.

Finding a topic begins at the workplace. I have met very few managers or supervisors who haven't got any problems at all! Some problems are self-evident: repeated errors in handling materials, or excessive waste of food in a catering establishment, for example. Others are less so: where an inefficient way of doing things has been around for a long time, everyone—including supervisors—develops a mental blindness to it. Try, when you go to your workplace tomorrow, to imagine you are a consultant visiting the department for the very first time; look at everything which is going on with a critical eye.

Another way to find a suitable project is to ask yourself what annoys you at work: inefficient paperwork routines, wrong material deliveries, out-of-date equipment holding up the work, lack of vital information? You will soon be driven to admit there is, in every situation, at least *one* job where a different method would be more efficient, or would save time and money, or would achieve a safer working environment.

If you are a full-time student at college or school who is required to complete a similar kind of project (perhaps it's called an assignment), you could, with the help of your tutor, find a local firm or public-sector organization willing to let you investigate a suitable project; and possibly give you work experience at the same time.

Projects are everywhere.

30.5.2 Some successful projects

What makes a 'good' project? Ideally your project should be job-related, course-related, be 'integrated' (that is, bring in all the knowledge and skills you have acquired from the different aspects of the course: money, supervisory principles, technical matters, communication, and possibly even legal aspects). It should not be too biased in one area, e.g. highly technical without considering the effects that the proposed technical change might have on people—staff, customers, the public at large. The project, too, must require more demanding research then delving into a few books in the library.

The following short list of successful projects is to give you an idea of the sort of topics which you can choose or adapt:

1. Accounting methods in a technical stores.
2. Reorganizing health and safety inspection procedures.
3. Better use of existing equipment.
4. Need to replace ageing equipment.
5. Critical examination of an organization's induction procedure.
6. Designing a procedure manual (for a job, section, or whole department).
7. Introduction of a breakfast service at BP International HQ, London.

This last quoted one won an NEBSM award in 1989: so many employees brought breakfast to work, a catering staff member felt there might be a market for putting breakfast on the menu. The project researched into what staff wanted, local competition, and what would be the implications for the facilities. The idea was given a (successful) trial, and then fully adopted.

30.5.3 Types of projects

Projects fall into categories. The most important are:

Problem-solving

Here you set out to explain a problem facing you and/or your section; and put forward your recommendations for dealing with it.

Cost-saving

As a spin-off, the proposed solutions to problem-solving projects often do save money; but there are some projects where saving money is the primary objective. Does the organization carry out its own vehicle maintenance, or contract out the work; engage part-time workers on a permanent basis, or use a temporary staff bureau; make certain components within the works, or buy them elsewhere? The *comparative costs* of taking either course of action are most important considerations in any final recommendations made.

Increased safety or improved working environments

With the ever-increasing accent on both health and safety in the workplace, and the need to make working conditions as pleasant as possible, many useful projects fall into this category. Does the organization's safety policy need updating when it moves premises, buys new machinery, uses new materials? Does it need to review office lay-outs, and working conditions?

Procedure review

This type of project is primarily method-study based. The idea is to look at an existing procedure (goods inwards documentation, raising of internal sales orders, purchasing routines, induction of new staff) critically, particularly if some technology change is envisaged. The recommendations will take the form of a revised procedure. Be careful here to think of the effect of proposed change on people (see Chapter 9).

Procedure (descriptive) reports

Sometimes you may come across a different problem: the need to set out a procedure for the first time. Perhaps some job or routine has never been officially documented previously, and the present job-holder retires soon; or a new job and/or set of routines needs working out in detail. This is more demanding than revising an existing document. Be careful about choosing this kind of project unless you have plenty of help and advice to hand.

30.5.4 Terms of reference (TOR)

Before you can start on the project proper there is one vital job for you to complete: working out and agreeing the project's *terms of reference*. By this phrase we mean the purposes, aims and objectives of the project; what is to be investigated, and what topics covered. They show the reader of the final report what can be found in it; and they show the way to proceed, like signposts as you work through the project.

Signposts on a road need to be clear and unambiguous: so do your terms of reference. What does it mean if you say you are 'looking into Health and Safety'? Are you doing a report on the Health and Safety at Work Act, the safety policy of your employers, the current way that policy is working out in practice, or the need for more safety training? TORs, then, must be very precise.

Good practice is to list the terms of reference numerically—1, 2, 3, etc.—and move logically along the road you have chosen. Many projects are about *change*, doing something differently, changing work routines, moving departments, using new equipment. TOR usually, then follows this pattern:

1. To investigate and describe our present appraisal system (or whatever is being investigated).
2. To comment on and evaluate the usefulness of this system.
3. To draw conclusions from this evaluation (usually the present method unsatisfactory).
4. To suggest amendments to, or alternatives to the present system.
5. To make recommendations (usually to choose one or more of the alternatives in 4); and to spell out the implications (in financial, production, legal, human, etc. terms) of what you have recommended.

Example: Accessibility for Disabled Users at Borchester Leisure Centre

1. To investigate the needs of disabled users of the Centre.
2. To establish how far those needs are being met currently, and where the Centre is lacking.
3. To draw conclusions about our service to disabled users.
4. To suggest various ways in which we could more closely meet their needs.
5. To make firm recommendations, bearing in mind both the potential benefits to disabled users, and the financial implications of the changes.

Checkpoint Stage I

In preparing your project or report have you:

1. Chosen a suitable topic, based upon an existing problem or situation, after consultation with your tutor, your work superior, or training officer, as appropriate?
2. Chosen a topic which is job-related, course-related, integrated, not wholly technical in content?
3. Made sure your proposed project or report is problem-solving, cost-saving, safety related, descriptive, or is a procedure review; or a combination of several of these?
4. Clarified your terms of reference: do they state what is to be investigated, the way in which you propose to proceed, and whether you are drawing any conclusions or making recommendations?
5. Agreed the TOR with your tutor, work superior, training officer as required?

30.5.5 Stage 2: Planning the project

Your project is going to involve you in a great deal of work, and occupy considerable time (in the NEBSM Certificate course, some 40 hours). To make effective use of this time you will need to draw up a timetable or schedule of the various stages involved. Because many courses no longer stick rigidly to the academic year (i.e. September-June), suggested times are quoted in the example below in months after the course starts.

Stage of project/report	*Target completion date by*	*Actual completion date*
Discuss possible topics project areas with tutor, superiors, training staff; making final choice	1 month at latest	[Fill in actual date]
Finalize terms of reference	$1^{1}/_{2}$ months	
Decide on methods of investigation	2 months	
Fact-finding and groundwork	5 months	
Organize and analyse data and information obtained	6 months	
Formulate conclusions, recommendations, first draft	7 months	
Revise, check report; final consultations with advisers	$7^{1}/_{2}$ months	
Complete report ready	8 months	

(Please note, however, specific rules or timetables may be set out by examining bodies, or your employer, in the case of projects or investigations carried out as a part of your job, and your plan must reflect such requirements.)

Planning the collection of data and information

By *data* we mean raw, plain, unprocessed facts about a routine, situation, or people. The term *information* is used when the data have been processed in some way (e.g. have been checked, collated, sorted, classified, selected, turned into charts, graphs, tables, etc.) so that the transformed data become useful and significant in decision-making.

First you must ask, what kind of data and information do I need for this project/report? If you are looking at a routine, you will need to find out all the background to it, why the routine was established originally, who carries out the work, how often, in what sequence, etc. Investigating a material calls for data and information about its properties, characteristics, capabilities, limitations, availability and cost. Projects or reports on experiments and tests will demand that you specify what was tested, why and how it was done, and what the results were.

Then you need to decide, if the data or information you need are not readily available, where to find them. Perhaps you can get what you want from reading other people's reports; trade magazines, books, newspaper articles, company balance sheets and other records, say in your department—clock cards, overtime details; absence or accident reports.

Or, again, asking experts inside and outside the organization for advice or information could be useful (e.g. local council officers, librarians, people working for research units). Sometimes you will want to find out colleagues' or customers' views about a product, service or procedure; perhaps here you should prepare a questionnaire to make sure you ask everyone the same questions, and can evaluate the data you obtain.

Special techniques such as method study, O&M, sampling or value analysis can be used as appropriate.

What you must have is plenty of data, information and evidence to back up any conclusions or recommendations you want to make. Just saying 'We never get deliveries on time' is not enough: a list of *every* occasion when deliveries were late over the last year, with supporting documentation, will make your point.

Checkpoint Stage 2

In preparing your plan have you:

1. Worked out a timetable for your project/assignment based on the rules of the course, or on deadlines set by yourself, or others?
2. Got clear in your mind the difference between data and information?
3. Sorted out what kinds of data and information you will need?
4. Established where you will find such data and information?
5. Considered whether any particular techniques (e.g. work study) will help?

30.5.6 Stage 3: Fact-finding and groundwork

As soon as you have finished planning what to investigate, and how you propose to go about it, you can start on what will normally be the most active part of the project: gathering and accumulating data and information which will act as supporting evidence for your conclusions and recommendations.

Wherever possible try to *quantify* (that is, express in numerical terms) the data you collect. Don't write 'The office is quite large': do record 'The office is 20 m × 15 m'. The first statement is not very precise: 'large' may mean different things to different people; but 20 m × 15 m means the same to everyone. You may also wish to record people's opinions: check their comments with them after you have written them down.

Jot down the facts and ideas as they emerge. Carry round a 'little black book', or something similar. As soon as you notice something, or have a flash of inspiration; you can write it down *at once* before you have forgotten it. Sometimes people have a set of folders into which they can put copies of records, reports, newspaper cuttings as they come to hand. Make sure you have *more* material than you will eventually use, so your final report will be truly complete.

Note refusals to help, and mention them in your report. In any event, you will need to make a note of data and information sources—you may want to mention them. Check to see that what you have collected is relevant to the investigation, and see where it points. Perhaps the indications are more detailed investigations are needed; or the trends emerging are not what you expected. (You might even find your original TOR require modification.)

If you are examining a process you may have to collect data regularly over a long period (e.g. workplace temperatures during the day from October to February): draw up a suitable chart on which to record the figures as they become available.

Checkpoint Stage 3

With each item of data, information, comment or opinion, have you

1. Recorded it promptly in a systematic way (e.g. using a chart or form)?
2. Quantified it as accurately as you can?
3. Noted the source of the item recorded?
4. Checked the item is relevant to the investigation?
5. Looked at any implications revealed?

30.5.7 Stage 4: Organizing and evaluating the material

Once you have obtained all the data and information you reasonably can find in the time available, your first job is to review and sort it into topic headings. Does it refer to the background of the project? Then you could sort it under *Background Information*; or when it covers facts about a procedure or process, you could use an appropriate heading such as *Calibration Readings, Accident Reports, or Turnover Comparisons*, and so on.

Now you can start to analyse and evaluate the data and/or information. The kinds of things you should be looking for are *significance* (how important the data are); *trends* or *similarities* (can you see patterns, correlations, repeating cycles); *differences* (or irregularities, deviations, variances, anomalies); or *danger* or *problem* areas (rising costs, error occurrences, falling ouput, high turnover of staff, for example). Wherever possible try and convert data into pictorial or visual information; it is much easier to understand when you have done it. (You will need to do this in any event when writing the final report, as the reader will require help in understanding what you have dis-covered: remember, 'a picture is worth a thousand words'.) Illustrations, maps, charts, photographs, graphs, tables, all of. these can be helpful to you and your (even-tual) readers.

Coming to conclusions

As you progress with your analysis and evaluation, you should begin to assess the implications of your findings. Perhaps you will conclude what you have looked at is *not* satisfactory, safe, acceptable, desirable, profitable and so on. Change, modification or improvement in a lesser or greater degree is then needed. On the other hand, you might conclude what is being investigated is satisfactory, safe, acceptable, etc., and really little or no change is required.

Developing possible solutions or ideas for change

At this stage you will be considering all the possible courses of action open to you (or the organization). You can get ideas from:

1. Lateral thinking and brainstorming (see Chapter 6, Sections 6.1.1 and 6.1.2 for a full account of what to do here).
2. Asking other people for their suggestions.
3. Asking yourself what the causes and symptoms of the original problem were: a fruitful line could be to generate possible 'mini-solutions' for dealing with each cause or symptom identified.

Remember the purpose of the conclusions is to interpret your findings.

Evaluating alternatives

Any possible solution must pass three tests to be considered in depth: is it *practicable;* is it *cost-effective* (with appropriate benefits); and what are the *overall risks and implications* (particularly in terms of the people involved) for the organization? Obviously a proposal which cannot for one reason or another be put into effect must be ruled out; and similarly, one whose costs (in terms of people, money, time and physical resources) outweigh the potential advantages will probably be unacceptable. The most difficult to quantify are overall implications: what price to set against improved industrial relations, increased safety, or greater motivation.

Making recommendations

Your eventual report should consider more than one possible solution (two or three at least). You might well consider, too, the option of leaving things as they are, if none of the alternatives you have come up with seems to offer much in the way of improvement.

However, in the end, you will almost certainly have to recommend *one* course of action. You will need to consider in some depth all the implications of adopting it, both beneficial and adverse, and be prepared to defend your recommendation(s) with the facts and expert advice you have gathered in your research.

Remember that when recommendations are required in a report, or thought by you to be of some value, they should *always* be developed logically from the conclusions (which in turn have been based on your findings).

Checkpoint Stage 4

In respect of organizing and evaluating the material, have you:

1. Continually kept in mind the terms of reference of your investigations?
2. Gathered all the data you need to prepare a comprehensive report?
3. Sorted the data under appropriate headings?
4. Analysed what you have discovered, looking for patterns, similarities, variances, anomalies?
5. Thought of how any data obtained could be shown graphically, pictorially, or in any other visual form?
6. Considered all possible solutions or ideas and evaluated each thoroughly (from the practicality viewpoint, cost-benefit angles, and overall implications)?
7. Chosen eventually several alternative solutions to consider in your report; and evaluated them in depth not only in terms of costs, benefits but also in respect of staffing implications, and the people involved?
8. Arrived at a final recommendation, or set of recommendations?

30.5.8   Stage 5: Writing your report

Reports of any size become more attractive to the reader, are more easily read, and have a better chance of being accepted if they are well laid out. There is a saying 'hard writing makes easy reading'—the trouble you take in organizing and setting out your material will pay real dividends in the end. Think of the trouble newspaper layout staff go to in presenting the news: the use of headlines, different sizes and styles of type, subheadings, pictures, spaces. All this effort has one major objective: to make the information set out easy to read.

You may find your organization has its own rules for report layouts: these should be respected, provided they are consistent with your needs. Layouts should help your reports to become successful; and in the last resort, the report should dictate the layout, not the other way round.

What follows is a model based on best practice.

Title page.   This page is the first the reader will see: lay it out attractively, using large, well-spaced out print. The title itself is a short, snappy summary of the central topic, though brevity should take second place to clarity. Include the date, and the author's name (i.e. your name), and as appropriate the name(s) of those to whom it is addressed.

Course detail. For NEBSM projects, it is useful to have a page with a short paragraph stating the year of the course, the name of your organization, and your job title within it.

Contents page (or Table of Contents). This lists section numbers and/or alphabetical references; section (and possibly sub-section) titles; appendices, figures and tables, with the page number of each. It is very useful for readers to be able to refer to a particular point quickly. This page can only be finalized when the report is complete.

Glossary of terms. The more technical a report is or the more specialized the subject, the more likely are technical terms, abbreviations or jargon to be used. The glossary gives, in alphabetical order, definitions of these if there is a possibility and potential readers (including a course tutor!) may not understand terms you have used. Some people prefer to leave glossaries to the end of a report: I feel it better to reassure readers from the start they will understand your text!

Summary. Whilst not essential, or even desirable in a short report, for a report of say five pages or more in length, a summary will help the reader—often a busy person—to grasp quickly what a report is about. It should normally not exceed a single paragraph. Simply state the problem, or purpose of the report, the important findings, conclusions and recommendations as briefly as you possibly can. No arguments or supporting facts are required. It is a good test of a report, because if it is easy to read and seems to make good sense, it is likely the rest of the report will do also.

Terms of reference. These have been discussed above. It is preferable to list them on a single page containing no other text.

Introduction. In this section you will need (in the case of a Certificate report) to describe the organization for which you work or at which you are studying, and the work of your own section, before proceeding further. Remember the people reading your report include your tutor, and an outside assessor, who lives miles away, and possibly has never heard of your employer. This section should then detail the scope of the report, why it was written, and the sources of the data and information you have used. The reader should be told how much of the topic is to be covered; and what you do *not* propose to cover. The problem or situation involved needs defining, and the chosen methods of investigation explained and justified. The choice of material in this section will depend a great deal on how much the potential readers already know.

Facts discovered. This section should be titled to suit the report. Some use terms like *Information, Discussion,* or *Present Situation* in a standardized way, but a specific heading relating to the topic under review is preferable. You will be well advised to order what you have found under a series of subheadings, especially if you have several pages of text in this section. This ordering is first to make the readers' task easier, but you will find the discipline will help *you* to marshal your evidence.

Conclusions, findings, evaluations. The purpose of this section is for you to interpret the facts revealed in the previous section. Each conclusion must only relate to previous data and/or information: you must be careful at this stage not to introduce new facts in support of conclusions. It is usual to present findings as a list of numbered points.

Recommendations.   These are required to follow on logically from the conclusions. Recommendations are best put forward in a positive though polite and tactful way: you do not want to be seen to be bullying or blackmailing the reader! Recommendations should also be numbered individually; and, as mentioned earlier, you will need to include all the implications of implementing each and every one of them.

Appendices (sometimes called *Annexes*).   These are reserved for material which supports the more summarized information in the main body of the report. Basically this means data or information too detailed to include in the main text: parts lists, charts, graphs, plans, calculations, verbatim statements, etc., each clearly labelled as a separate appendix, and in the order in which they are first mentioned in the text. Photographs, tapes, even video cassettes can now be used as appendices. It is advisable to keep this type of data/information quite separate from the body of the report, especially where readers are non-specialists.

References (sometimes called *Bibliography*).   Some reports make reference to other reports, to books, magazines, newspaper articles, or speeches. A reader of your report may wish to look at the original document; and at the same time you may wish to put on record, as an act of respect to the author, the original source of a point you have made. Where a number of references are used, list them (numbered in sequence) in the order they are mentioned in the text. References may not only record author and publisher, but also page numbers. (Some writers prefer footnotes: these have the advantage of tying references and the text closely.)

Acknowledgments (sometimes called *Credits*).   It is customary to express your thanks and appreciation to the people and organizations who have given significant help in preparing your report. Many students with assignments or projects to complete like to mention their partners who may have had to put up with many evenings spent on the work, and who may even have had to type the report.

Index.   An index (at the conclusion of a report) is only needed if the report is a long one. It serves the same function as the index at the back of this book: listing the topics covered in alphabetical order to help a reader searching for a particular point raised.

Style and layout

A report is a piece of communication: as such it should be clear, concise and precise. Any device—such as different type faces, use of spaces, underlining—which helps to make your report attractive as well, and easier to read, is to be welcomed.

Try and keep your sentences short. Experience has shown a sentence over 25 words in length is somewhat difficult to read; over 40 words, and it is *very* difficult. To provide some variety the use of an occasional short sentence can be very effective.

However, if you stuck to short sentences all the time, a reader could get very irritated. Keep jargon to a minimum, and *never* use a word the meaning of which you are not sure about.

Finally, the use of charts, maps, diagrams and photographs may eliminate the need for hundreds of words. These visual devices provide the reader with a change from the text, and make for easier understanding. A report on the condition of a stores is all the more compelling with a few, stark black-and-white photographs showing a mess on the shelves and clutter in the gangways.

Checkpoint Stage 5

Concerning the writing of your report, have you:

1. Checked to see if your organization has its own 'house style' for report writing, and then taken this into account in designing your layout?
2. Laid out the title page attractively, with a snappy title, used large-sized lettering, included your name, the date, and the name of the person to whom the report is addressed?
3. (particularly for assignments or projects) Stated on the first page the course title and year, the name of your organization, and your job title?
4. Included a Table of Contents, a Glossary of terms (if one is required), and (for larger reports) a Summary?
5. Set out clearly your terms of reference?
6. Defined clearly the problem or situation in the Introduction?
7. Checked, ordered and recorded accurately all the facts discovered and opinions obtained under a series of headings and subheadings?
8. Ensured your conclusions are based on the data and/or information in the report?
9. Listed and numbered your recommendations, and included all the implications of implementing each and every recommendation?
10. Included the details of references to other publications?
11. Expressed in the Acknowledgement section your appreciation of people and organizations who have given you significant help in your project/report?
12. Added an index (in the case of long reports only)?
13. Paid careful attention to style and layout?

30.5.9   Stage 6: Drafting and editing

Particularly with long reports, it is advisable to write out an initial draft, or drafts, before committing yourself to the final copy for presentation. In any event, it is worth going through the second draft with another person qualified to give constructive criticism—possibly your tutor—who may have some advice on presentation. Please note, however, your tutor is *not* there to write the report for you.

At this stage you have to change your role and become an editor/critic, impartially and ruthlessly reading through the report in as impersonal a fashion as possible.

Checkpoint Stage 6

Questions to ask yourself, when editing and reviewing your report, include:

1. Will the reader understand all you write?
2. Is there too much technical language?
3. Have you eliminated vague generalizations; can you justify your conclusions? Do they follow from the facts presented?
4. Have you correctly identified the problem or situation under review?
5. Does the text come over easily and smoothly, when read aloud?
6. Have you checked *every* fact; *all* your figures, graphs and illustrations?
7. Have you covered both cost implications and the effects on people?
8. What are the chances of your solution being successful?
9. What are the implications and risks of implementing your chosen solution?
10. Have you checked your report over with someone with appropriate knowledge?
11. *Have you completed all the tasks contained in your terms of reference?*

30.6 FINAL REMARKS—PROJECT ASSESSMENT

In the Certificate in Supervisory Management your assessor will take into account when deciding whether to award a PASS:

1. General presentation and layout.
2. Methods of investigation (including the identification of the problem).
3. Relevance of the material used.
4. Adequacy of information.
5. Charts, diagrams, etc. (Are they used at all, and used well?)
6. Conclusions and recommendations. (Are they adequate?)
7. Degree of completeness of the report.

It is obvious that if you follow carefully the guidelines set out in this chapter, you should go a long way in satisfying the assessor on every point.

Lastly, always remember that the *readers* are the people for whom the report is written. The more it is made simple for them to understand, the more successful your report will be. I wish you every success.

31
Managing Time

'Time is the scarcest resource, and unless it is managed, nothing else can be managed.'
Peter Drucker

'There is never any time like the present to make a start on a task.'

Tony Wilson

31.1   INTRODUCTION

Time is a basic characteristic of the universe: it is often called the 'fourth dimension' (coming after length, breadth and height). Whenever time began [the Creation or the 'Big Bang'] one inescapable fact emerges: time only goes one way; and any given time only comes once. Once experienced, it disappears; and, unlike a used car or an empty bottle it cannot be saved or subsequently be recycled.

Thus time is a sort of capital, just as money is, to be spent and used in the most effective way. But, as with money, people both waste time and misuse it, despite the fact time is such a valuable and limited resource. In this chapter we will be looking at ways of helping you to acquire some of the skills of *time management*, that is of *controlling* time through a series of planned strategies.

31.2   AIMS OF THIS PROGRAMME

The aims of the programme are to help you:

1. To appreciate the importance of time as a key resource of managers and supervisors.
2. To identify the consequences of poor time management.
3. To become aware of how time can be wasted.
4. To assess your own time management behaviour.
5. To develop strategies to improve your own time management.

31.3 THE IMPORTANCE OF TIME MANAGEMENT

Money management is not only about keeping track of the money we have or for which we are responsible ('keeping accounts', we often call it), but is also about planning its use (budgeting), avoiding wasteful expenditure, getting the best value for the money, and so on. In other words, it is a money control system.

So it is with *time management* (TM). TM implies planning the best use of time, including cutting down on time-wasting, devoting more time to the really important issues, or jobs on hand, and completing more in the time available.

If you don't plan properly the way your *money* is managed you may find yourself short of capital just when you need it most: failure to manage your *time* can leave you so short of it that you have a 'last minute rush' to get a really important job done. Inevitably, something gets overlooked, causing yet another crisis, which, in turn, takes yet more time to put right.

An essential objective of looking at time management is to enable you both to save at least some of the time you presently waste in one way or another at work, and to use this time better in tackling jobs which really require your undivided attention and effort. It is of course unlikely you will never waste time in the future, but even a 10% saving in the first year could give you up to 4 hours a week extra productive time.

You always have the choice: let time manage you, or manage your own time. Which is it to be?

31.4 THE CONSEQUENCES OF POOR TIME MANAGEMENT

The following are possible consequences of poor TM:

Activity mania. Because every day begins without a proper plan, jobs became fragmented, are left unfinished, and have to be picked up again and again. In the end, the manager/supervisor is left rushing from one crisis to another, without a moment left for thought and reflection. The law of diminishing returns begins to operate, and yet more activity is required to keep things going.

Reacting to, and not controlling, events. Instead of being able to take the initiative, having plans to meet emergencies (so that they are dealt with in the way he or she prefers), the supervisor spends much time fending off customers and superiors, or dealing with telephone calls from all and sundry. In what time is left, the supervisor tries to cope with the problems which have emerged.

Living in the present, rather than the future. Charles Handy in his Penguin book *Understanding Organizations* points out that the manager (and by inference the supervisor) is above all responsible for the future. Managers, then, need to devote time to anticipating and planning for the future: marshalling resources, creating the best possible working environment, recruiting, training and developing staff. Living in the present means the future is neglected, and more potential problems remain undetected.

Becoming less effective.   Because the supervisor with poor TM skills is seen to be inefficient by senior management, advancement and promotion become less likely.

Work overload.   Being pressed for time as a result of poor TM generally leads to an ever-increasing list of jobs yet to be tackled. Too often, the only perceived way out is to work overtime.

Less leisure time.   The more time spent at work the less is available for sport, leisure activities, or for home and family. Interpersonal relationships can be threatened, and job satisfaction diminished.

Stress.   All the above consequences of poor TM can lead to stress. This has implications for the supervisor, the work team, the organization at large, as well as family and friends.

31.5   WHERE DOES TIME GO?

Given the consequences listed above, it is a useful exercise for any manager or supervisor to consider what happens during time available for work. All activities are *time consumers*, but many, often too many, are *time wasters*. Here are some of the latter which can take big slices of time if you do not control them properly.

Lack of forward planning.   As you have already seen, this can result in 'crisis management', rushing from one fire-fighting situation to the next.

The telephone.   Agreed, if your telephone rings it has to be answered. But many people, by poor telephone technique, let conversations go on far too long. On the other hand, when making calls, it is easy for you to prolong conversations, or 'hang on' for long periods.

Visitors.   These can be from within the organization as well as from without. As with telephone calls, visitors can take up valuable time if they are handled badly, and encouraged to stay too long.

Paperwork.   Sadly, the paperless office has not yet arrived. It is all too easy to dawdle over dealing with routine forms and correspondence, especially when the alternative is to deal with a more demanding job.

Deadlines.   Whilst these are usually set by other people, and you may get to know about them well in advance, it is all too easy to leave things to the last minute! The later you initiate action to meet a deadline, the more critical any unforeseen delay becomes, and the more time may have to be taken to ensure it is met.

Doing it yourself (DIY). This takes several forms: failing to delegate is the worst. Doing jobs which subordinates could do equally well is generally inexcusable; taking on jobs voluntarily from others could be a recipe for overwork. Don't be one of those who can't say 'No'!

Taking on too much work. A variation on DIY, this is particularly difficult to avoid for those who are not very assertive, or those who want to please or impress. The worst version of this is offering to take on extra jobs which realistically can't be finished in the time available.

Taking work home. Whether you go home with a bulging briefcase, or a carrier-bag full of paperwork, this is a sure sign of bad TM. When you do get home there are bound to be many other legitimate activities for you to carry out: how sad it is to go back to work next day, with the work taken home largely untouched!

Meetings. Meetings should be a tool in helping things to get done efficiently and in good time. Frequently, meetings are badly run, and what you put into them is not matched by the outcomes. A lot depends upon how much preparation people are prepared to make before a meeting starts; and the amount of participation individuals are willing to undertake during meetings (including listening to what others have to say!).

Communication problems. Communication failures abound in most organizations. Time is wasted in clarifying obscure messages, checking on missing facts, chasing overdue statistics or reports. Poor filing systems or inefficient documentation preparation and transmission systems assist in yet more time wasting within the organization.

Lack of self-discipline. Supervisors and managers of all kinds can find some jobs more attractive than others. It is much more difficult to motivate yourself to tackle the less interesting tasks, or those demanding much effort, for example, making out complicated returns. The choice often made is to 'put things off', especially where no immediate deadlines are involved. The inevitable consequence yet again is uncompleted work piles up, creating problems for the future.

Not assessing priorities. Generally a result of not sitting back, sorting through, and thinking about what work is on hand. Instead of the really important tasks being completed, the ones on the top of the pile, or those someone makes a fuss about, are tackled first.

Checkpoint No. I

Few of us could truthfully claim not to have committed at least one of the errors mentioned above. Check carefully what you did (or did not do) at work recently against the list, and ask yourself how many errors you made. If you score FIVE or more, then you have a real TM problem. Even a score of ONE indicates a need to examine your TM behaviour carefully.

31.6   ASSESSING YOUR OWN TIME MANAGEMENT BEHAVIOUR

Everyone can benefit from a little self-analysis. Time spent on considering the following twenty questions will help you develop ways of improving your TM. You must answer truthfully (no-one but you will be checking your replies!), and make sure you choose the most appropriate heading each time.

	Question	*Never*	*Rarely*	*Sometimes*	*Regularly*
1.	Do you make 'to do today' lists, every working day, and use them?				
2.	Do you put the most important items first in your lists?				
3.	Is your desk tidy and organized?				
4.	Have you a place for everything?				
5.	Do you deal effectively with callers and visitors?				
6.	Can you easily find papers and documents you need?				
7.	Do you deal with paperwork quickly?				
8.	Do you deal with unpleasant jobs as soon as they need to be done?				
9.	Do you begin and finish jobs on time?				
10.	Do people know the best times to see you?				
11.	Do you meet deadlines with time to spare?				
12.	Do you delegate when appropriate?				
13.	Do you allow yourself 'free' or quiet time during the day when you can work undisturbed?				
14.	Do you try to prevent problems arising, rather than solve them after they crop up?				
15.	Do you get to work/meetings/ events on time?				
16.	Do you find it easy to say 'no' to requests from others?				
17.	Do you prepare properly for meetings?				
18.	Do you avoid taking work home?				
19.	Do you review the way you spend your time at work?				
20.	Do you tackle the most demanding tasks at your 'peak energy' times?				

Scoring: NEVER—0, RARELY—1, SOMETIMES—2, REGULARLY—3.

Interpretation: 0–10 You do very little or no conscious TM, and are at the mercy of events. A fresh start *now* is imperative!

11–20 You do some TM, but you do need to review your weak areas in a planned fashion one at a time.

21–40 You have generally good TM behaviour, but there is still some room for improvement where you have low-rated scores.

41–60 Well done! You seem to have very good TM skills, but do look critically at any low-rated answer.

These questions do not cover *every* facet of TM behaviour, but are sufficiently representative to take account of its more important aspects. The questions are so worded as to give you a clue to twenty positive strategies for good TM, but in the next section you will find some of the ideas developed further.

31.7 IMPROVING YOUR TIME MANAGEMENT

Now you have completed assessing the current quality of your TM, the final, action stage is considering how to make improvements. What follows is a list of practical suggestions and hints to help you do this. Individually, all of them have varying degrees of merit: taken as an interrelated package, they will assist you in becoming more time-conscious, and hopefully more efficient in its use.

1. Cost your time

Take your annual salary, and divide it by the number of working days in a calendar year (365 less weekends, holidays, etc.) to give a daily rate. Add say 20% for administrative and other overheads, then divide by the number of working hours in the day (say $7^1/_2$). The resultant figure is the hourly cost of your time to your employers. Every occasion when you 'save' an hour, or put it to better use, you become more cost-effective.

2. Identify significant job elements (SJEs)

To start this process, examine your job description. (If you are unlucky enough not to have one, draw one up for yourself, and get it checked out by a superior or a colleague.) Select from it three or four key activities, or *significant job elements* (SJEs). These could be, for example, *organizing staff, maintaining a constant flow of materials to a given point, recording or storing information, developing and maintaining a healthy and safe working environment*. (These will all be 'job elements' in NVQ terms.)

List the tasks and duties falling under each SJE.

Estimate the time taken each month to complete the tasks and duties under each SJE. Cost this time.

Assess the corresponding 'payback' to you and the organization of the time spent on each SJE.

This exercise will help you identify the SJEs, and estimate their value to you and the organization, as well as the time you presently spend on each. After reviewing the figures, you may decide to increase or decrease this amount of time based upon the costs incurred, and the corresponding payback achieved.

Later on, you can take another batch of SJEs, and repeat until you have covered all of them.

3.   *Assess your long-term priorities (LTPs)*

There are two kinds of priorities you will need to take into account: long-term (LTP) and short-term (STP). LTPs are clearly recognized by those organizations who have corporate plans, company objectives, mission statements and the like. Much less often are LTPs set for individual employees. Even more rarely do individual employees sit down and assess their *own* long-term plans and objectives in detail. Having them clarified helps you with your priorities.

If you desire promotion, for example, and this entails getting a further qualification, then not only may some work time be set aside for study, but a considerable part of your own time as well. Study time becomes a priority activity. Thus you become committed to prioritizing your use of time over a *long* period.

This applies to all LTPs, except that in an emergency, you can postpone an LTP for a day or so. However, if no action is taken to further an LTP over a period of time, then you will be faced with having to pull out all the stops to catch up.

4.   *Consider your short-term priorities (STPs)*

Short-term priorities are very different. They have the advantage of being newer, easier to remember, easier to achieve. The big temptation is to spend more time and effort on the STPs. What is required is for you to strike a balance between the two, on any given day (but see point 6).

5.   *Use a planning aid*

You may well have gathered by now that you will need a planning aid of some sort (a time/appointments diary, a work-planner or daily schedule form) to assist in planning the day's activities. Only by using such a device will you be able to plan ahead successfully, allocate time, and keep an overall check on what you are doing. However this is not all: in subsequent sections you will find other hints on planning.

6. *Prioritize on the 'MOP' principle*

If you do decide to use a planning medium like a daily work schedule, facing you at the start of any one day will be a mixture of activities to sort out. Some will be LTPs, some STPs, and yet more will have much lower priorities still.

Additionally, some activities will be imposed upon you by others: meetings, visitors, routine tours of the workplace. These will obviously go into your schedule from the start.

The question now is: of the items under your control, what to do first? A simple guide is to follow the 'MOP', or the 'Must', 'Ought' and 'Prefer' principle.

This entails listing all the tasks, duties and activities you need to do within a given day, and assessing (a) the approximate time each is likely to take, and (b) to which one of three categories to allocate each task.

Category A is a 'must' task, one which simply has to be completed in whole or part on that day, (and probably by a particular time, too)—ensuring, for example, a batch of products are ready for collection by a customer by 11 am. Category A jobs are best tackled *first* in any given day, when you have sufficient discretion over your time. When you are under time constraints imposed by others, Category A jobs should be done at the earliest opportunity.

Category B, or 'ought', tasks, are those which you decide are highly desirable to be completed during the day, but as a last resort could be delayed. These need to be attempted after the Category A tasks are under way.

Category C, or 'preferred', tasks are those jobs you like doing because you find them pleasurable and satisfying. Additionally, such jobs will normally contribute to the good of the organization—provided too much time is not spent on them.

However, by the very nature of Category C tasks, the tendency is to spend time on them to the detriment of As and Bs, unless you have carried out the approximate time assessment mentioned above (a Category A task!), and kept to it.

After working out all the tasks and jobs to be done during a day, you may want to add 'cushion time', a further period of time to cover for unscheduled interruptions, and breaks for tea, coffee and lunch. Now you may find the total time available is insufficient to do every job listed! Several strategies might help here.

One way out is to start work earlier (but to do this regularly goes against good TM). Another is to enter only the As and Bs into the schedule, then reassess the Cs. Perhaps some can wait; others be delegated sideways, downwards or upwards. Yet others will just not get done at all. Don't think you are *inefficient* if you can't complete in a day every job you can think of: you will be *effective* if you do all the As and Bs well, and just some of the Cs.

7. Work through the day in an orderly way

Now you have a plan for the day: the jobs and tasks to be done have been established, and the order in which they are to be done. You have made sufficient time available to accomplish the work. You can now focus on *one job at a time*, giving your whole attention to the task in hand. Avoid whenever you can, lots of short work periods. Spend say two hours with A jobs, two with Bs, and the rest of the time with fixed appointments (e.g. regular meetings), interruptions and C tasks.

The advantage of this type of approach is that, provided the tasks determined by others do not come too often in the early part of the day, the 'must' ones are done when you are fresh, and more able to cope with demanding activities. At the end of the day, when your energy level is lower, it is easier for you to have to deal with the preferred tasks.

8. Distinguish between the URGENT and the IMPORTANT

This is a classic dilemma: choosing between doing jobs which are *urgent* (to be done within a given time in the near future), and those which are *important* (significant or critical to the organization in the long term). Too often the urgent and unimportant jobs get done to the detriment of the important.

One way of resolving the dilemma is to use the Urgent v. Important matrix. The best advice is: tasks which are both important and urgent should get top priority (A). Those which are urgent but not very important (B) need to be done soon, but spend as little time as possible on each. Important but not urgent tasks (C) should be started as soon as possible, as they have *disaster potential*—that is they could suddenly become both important *and* urgent. Tasks which are neither important nor urgent (D) go to the back of the queue.

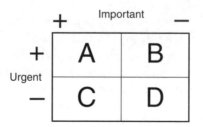

Figure 31.1 The Urgent v. Important matrix.

9. Review each day's work

At the end of each day, take five minutes to review what you have done, and how successful the day has been. Make a note of anything not achieved, or which still needs completion. Put it on the list for tomorrow. Clear your desk before you leave.

10. Book time for yourself: make yourself 'unavailable'

When you have a task on hand which is both urgent and important, use any subterfuge to prevent interruptions. Even senior managers hesitate to intrude upon subordinates entertaining visitors. One supervisor invented a fictitious visitor, whose appointment was always 'officially' booked in his diary whenever that supervisor had a high-priority job to finish.

11. Learn to speed-read

Many supervisors and managers spend a great deal of time reading forms, returns, reports, memos or other paperwork. Savings can be made if you learn to read faster. Read whole phrases (or even whole lines) at a time rather than individual words. Skim quickly through the conventional or routine parts of the document. Practice reading, say a section of this chapter, carefully first, then rereading it two or three times at a quicker speed each time. Now take a fresh piece of text and try and read it at the new speed. You will be surprised how much you can improve.

The average person reads at about 300 words per minute. Even if you only reach 400 wpm, you will save 15 seconds for every 300 words read!

12. Learn to delegate whenever you can

Every job, each task you do should be subjected to a critical examination from time to time, similar to that used in method study. Key questions in the list are '*Who* does the job?' (answer—*you*!), 'Why *that* person?' (indeed, why you?); 'Who else *could* do it?' (think of alternative people), and 'Who *should* do it?' (choose someone).

Not every supervisor or manager has an official assistant, deputy or stand-in, though this is highly desirable. However, by using one of your team from time to time to take on a routine task for you, you both save time for yourself, and develop and motivate staff. Many of your 'preferred' jobs are candidates for delegation: let someone else enjoy doing them!

13. Stop 'putting things off'

If you are a procrastinator—a 'putter-offer'—ask yourself, why are you one? Perhaps it is the fear of doing the wrong thing, making a mistake, especially where the activity is high risk or high profile. Perhaps it is the wish always to do the right thing, so you only want to bet on certainties. Maybe it's a feeling of inadequacy due to lack of information, lack of a particular skill or lack of training.

In each of these cases the remedy lies in your own hands: all can be dealt with if you face the underlying fear in the situation. Start by tackling a minor risk area, asking someone for the information you lack, establish how you can acquire the skills you don't have at the moment.

14. Limit the time you are prepared to talk to colleagues

Provided you put it politely ('Sorry, Fred, I can only spare you five minutes now, but do fire away'), people will see why you want to keep the interaction brief. If they still persist, you will have to say 'Look, Fred, I really must go and see to that other job now....'

    If you go to see your boss, do be fully prepared beforehand: by so doing you can save his or her time as well as yours.

15. Motivate yourself to save time

When you have done a good job, or completed a top priority task before time, give yourself a treat. Have a break, have a fresh cup of tea or coffee, take an early lunch. Promising yourself a treat or reward will help to keep you motivated.

16. Study recurrent crises and disasters

Take a hard look at problems, crises, or mistakes which keep cropping up. Think of ways of planning ahead to prevent them happening.

Checkpoint No. 2

Whilst you can read this now, why not try and improve your TM for a week, and come back to this section?

1. Have you read through the text carefully, and completed the twenty questions? Have you identified any shortcomings in your TM?
2. Have you an up-to-date job description/specification now?
3. Are you certain now you know how to estimate the time taken to complete various tasks?
4. Can you identify your priorities clearly now?
5. Can you place various jobs into appropriate categories?
6. Can you decide now on which tasks could be delegated?
7. Will you be spending less time now on Category C tasks?
8. Will you be concentrating on doing one job at a time now?
9. Have you stopped putting things off?

31.8 FINAL COMMENTS

Something else to remember is always to take advantage of any unusual situation. The series of one and two-day rail strikes in 1994 forced many people to think carefully about time management. One woman compelled to stay at home on strike days decided to take home her A and B tasks: to her amazement she finished her A tasks by mid-morning. Next, she realized being at home allowed her to start work much earlier than normal, to the extent she completed even the B tasks before lunch. Her new No. 1 A task was now how to use this experience to alter her normal working day habits.

During the whole of this chapter you have been concentrating on what you can do about time management. It is appreciated that what your colleagues do (or fail to do) and the culture of the organization can affect your ability to manage your time effectively. Perhaps one of your Category A tasks could be to alert others to the need to strive for better TM!

32
Building and Leading a Work Team

'A team is a medium through which work gets done.'

Unknown

32.1 INTRODUCTION

The process known as *team building* is not a new one, but in the latter part of the 20th century it has become an important element in helping organizations to function more effectively. As you saw in Chapter 1, there are many virtues and considerably higher returns from working in groups as opposed to working in isolation. In fact it is becoming impossible for many individuals to cope alone with the kind of complex problems that arise with the use of expensive and sophisticated equipment.

With an ever-increasing emphasis on the involvement of the workforce in decision-making, there has been a considerable growth in group meetings and committee work. As a result, supervisors and managers are being called upon to take on new tasks, and be involved with more than one group of people in the workplace. Additionally, the supervisor has to work *with* the assistance of groups in a leadership role; and *within* other groups (say a committee of managers and supervisors) as an ordinary group member.

In this chapter we will be looking at ways of helping you to get an understanding of how teams and groups operate, and to acquire some of the skills of *team building* and *team maintenance*, as well as being a useful team member. Those of you tasked with forming/leading work teams under a 'participation' scheme (see Chapter 28), should find the information in this chapter particularly useful.

32.2 AIMS OF THIS PROGRAMME

The aims of this programme are to help you:

1. To appreciate exactly what is meant by a 'work team', 'team building' and 'team maintenance'.
2. To identify when team building or team maintenance is needed, and how team building programmes can be organized.
3. To examine the features of an effective team, and to recognize the differing roles team members fulfil.
4. To explore ways in which you can assist the team building and team maintenance processes.
5. To consider how you can become a more effective team leader.

32.3 DEFINING THE TERMS

Work team.   One definition of a work team is a department, section or 'gang', with a set of common tasks. It is part of a larger organization, and has just one person in charge of it, though every member of the team has some input into the way the team operates. Thus people belonging to a work group who merely do as they are told, accept instructions as they receive them, and make no contribution to deciding how the work is to be done, do not on this definition qualify as a team.

A second kind of work team is the 'project group' (see Chapter 2, Section 2.7) 'sub-committee', or 'working party', comprising a number of people from different sections, and with different backgrounds, complementary skills and knowledge, who work together on some precisely defined project or task. A good example would be a plant-wide health and safety committee, or a team responsible for the relocation of a business from one town to another.

Team building, or perhaps more accurately *team development*, is the process of removing obstacles that prevent the team functioning effectively, and planning how to improve the team's overall performance. This process can be inward-looking (team members examine and evaluate the ways in which they work, and act upon each other); or outward-looking (the team leader sets out to focus the team's efforts on real, existing problems facing the group; and helps the team to realize by removing certain barriers acceptable solutions can be found).

Because teams decline in effectiveness over time, or change their membership, the process may have to be a revitalizing one rather than starting from scratch every time.

Team maintenance is the process of keeping what is already a good team at a constant (if not improving) level of competence and effectiveness.

32.4 WHEN IS TEAM BUILDING NEEDED?

First, before any successful team building can even be started, there has to be a recognition—at least by the supervisor/manager/group leader—that 'something must

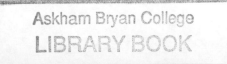

be done' to form a team or to improve the way an existing team is working. Better still, group members (or potential members) should also feel this need otherwise they may well not be properly motivated to get involved wholeheartedly in the work effort required.

Secondly, there are several activity or behaviour indicators within a group which can point to a need for some team building work:

> decrease in output or productivity, group underachieving
> decrease in quality of work; decline in professional standards
> decrease in job satisfaction
> increase in cost of production or provision of service (other than inflation, etc.)
> increase in people leaving, applying for transfers
> increase in either formal or informal grievance complaints
> reluctance to change methods of doing jobs, use new equipment
> reluctance to accept instructions
> reluctance to share information
> meetings that get nowhere
> competing sub-groups, internal conflict
> low morale, lack of enthusiasm, poor individual motivation

In addition some team building activity is advisable when forming a new group from scratch, or when the group's overall aims and objectives are seemingly not clear to all group members.

A useful exercise at this stage would be (provided in your present job you are a leader of a group) to consider your group against the list above. You may well decide team building would be useful. You could also evaluate any team in which you are an ordinary member against the list.

32.5   THE OBJECTIVES OF TEAM BUILDING

Assuming that the need to convert a work group into a work team has been agreed, for a group to function as a team, it must:

1.   Have a reason, or set of reasons, for working together.
2.   Have members who depend upon each other for the output of the group, whether the output is a product or a service.
3.   Have members who are committed to the idea that working together is more productive than working on their own.
4.   Be able to work with other groups within the organization.

Any set of objectives for team building must take into account these preconditions, as do the following set:

1.   To promote a better understanding of each team member's role in the work group.

2. To promote a better understanding of the role and function of the work group, and commitment to its goals.
3. To promote a better understanding of how the work group relates to the rest of the organization.
4. To improve the ability of the group to work with other departments, sections and groups in the organization.
5. To develop and improve the interpersonal, communication and other skills of group members.
6. To give group members a greater understanding of the behaviour of and the interacting forces within the group.
7. To promote the idea that group members give support to and trust each other.
8. To foster the notion that group members are dependent upon each other, and need to collaborate.
9. To help group members develop more effective ways of working at task-related problems and interpersonal issues.
10. To show how conflict can be used constructively in planning and problem-solving.

The overall long-term objective is to enable the team to become as far as possible self-reliant and flexible, capable of responding and adapting to change. Shorter-term objectives may be added to meet particular identified needs, such as trying to find a better way of doing a particular task, or solving a problem which has implications for more than one work group. Desired outcomes such as the formulation of 'action plans' for the group and individual members should be considered carefully too.

32.6   CHOOSING AND ORGANIZING A TEAM-BUILDING PROGRAMME

Having sorted out the objectives for a particular programme there are some important preliminaries to cover before the programme can start:

1. There must be commitment from the organization to allow the team building approach to be used; if the senior management feel that problem-solving and making decisions are what supervisors and other managers are paid to do, alone, then a supervisor could well shy away from even considering the process. Paid time for all the participants—and other expenses—are almost certainly going to be involved, time during which more widgets could be produced, invoices despatched or patients visited.
2. There must be a specific peg to hang the event on: the reason for embarking on a programme could be you have spotted the need from the list in Section 32.4, above; or some unplanned change is thrust upon the organization. People are not going to be involved if they don't see the significance (to them) of spending time off-the-job.
3. The timing and length of the programme are relevant. An impending change (for example in markets, equipment, technology, or procedures) with definite dates

involved, would indicate some months before the change. The formation of a new group from scratch calls for immediate activity, the purpose of which is to try and develop as much teamwork feeling as possible before the group starts being productive.

4. Accurate data must be available if the purpose is to look at an existing system, or any problems that can be quantified.

5. A choice has to be made of programme styles, of which the following are possible versions:

(a) A non-work-based task as the mainspring of the programme, probably an 'outward bound' type of course, all participants being involved with quite physical tasks with a need for the group members to help each other, say to cross a river, scale a steep slope or find 'buried treasure'.

Other versions are less physical, like building bungalows with Lego in competitive groups. Whatever the format, these events have positive aspects: failure by a team to get to the top or finish the building correctly does not mean the *exercise* is a failure. A 'debriefing' stage is an essential part of any team building exercise, and 'How did we perform as a team?', or 'Where did we go wrong?' are the key kinds of questions to consider. Once this review stage has become established as part of the activity, by extension it can become an ongoing aspect of the way the group functions from week to week. The team has begun to learn about itself.

Many lessons can be learned though this medium, and objectives (from the list above) 5, 6, 7, 8, 9 and 10 can be attempted. The problems are first the expense, and secondly, some staff object to 'playing games'.

(b) A work-related task, tackled away from the workplace. Departmental re-organization, planning the launch of a new service, introducing Total Quality Involvement (TQI) to a company or section—all these make good candidates around which to plan team building. This type of 'real' task has a greater immediate appeal to staff than a 'pretend' one. Being away from distractions—visitors, the telephone, all the normal work environment—means (if the event is properly organized and run) specific group goals can be achieved, as well as team building. A 'residential' element means there will be considerable interaction during meal times and during any free time, which hopefully enhances the 'team spirit', and encourages more informal types of relationships between group members.

This format is also expensive, but the outcomes are more easily quantified.

(c) A work-related task, tackled within the organization (though away from the actual workplace, perhaps). Whilst all the kinds of things you can do with version (b) are possible, time is usually limited; and there is always the possibility—and the temptation—for people to find reasons for slipping away. Obviously, much less costly, and provided commitment is high, and team building is part of the group's way of life, this will become the normal mode. Indeed, it could become part of *team maintenance*, helping to keep the group or team in being on a routine basis.

6. Each event requires careful preplanning. The success of a programme will be made more certain if the objectives have been identified, the sequence of activities time tabled, and ensuring the direct involvement of group members from the beginning. Small sub-groups may be needed to carry out subsidiary tasks (finding more information, questioning whether the chosen objectives are attainable, finding the root causes of increased product failure, and so on), and decisions made as to the mechanism of 'choosing' who tackles what. Reporting-back sessions, debriefing ('What worked best?', 'How well did we tackle the problem?') and even self-evaluation by group members have their place. In a sense the group is appraising itself.

7. Consideration as to who runs the programme could include using outside helpers who could be consultants (expensive but useful when setting the whole process going in the organization) or staff from other departments. However a key figure is always the supervisor or group leader, who will essentially be responsible for fostering and utilizing the members' talents, and developing and guiding the group.

32.7   TEAMS AND TEAM MEMBERS

Assuming you are now the leader/supervisor of a *team* you should try to review both the work and personality of your team members twice a year—even if you don't have a formal appraisal system in your organization. The work aspect is one for you to consider, but on the personality side considerable work has been done on the roles of team members.

Of the different views I prefer those of R. M. Belbin of Henley Management College, who in the mid '70s researched this area for seven years. He suggested, from his discoveries, that in teams there were eight distinct and specific roles. Accepting his research was done with teams of *managers*, most teams seem to contain the kinds of characters he portrays. All eight have both positive and negative qualities, but all are useful people to have in a team.

Chairperson: calm, self-controlled, self-confident. Talks easily, easy to talk to. Welcomes contributions on their merits. Listens, sums up, announces the general view. Takes decisions when necessary. Not especially creative.

Company worker: conservative, follows instructions, predictable. Hard working and self-disciplined. Not very flexible; doesn't like unproven ideas.

Team worker: stable, very sociable, mild-mannered, low in dominance. Very sensitive to undercurrents in the team. Popular, loyal and a promoter of team spirit. Could be indecisive in a crisis.

Shaper: highly strung, takes on specific jobs, challenges. Dynamic, doesn't like inertia, complacency or ineffectiveness in others. Prone to impatience and irritation.

Plant: very much an individual, serious, unorthodox. Ideas person, not too concerned with detail, nor rules and regulations. Doesn't like criticism.

Resource investigator: digs out facts, information, others' ideas. A 'contact person'. Often out and about looking for things. May get bored and ditch tasks.

Monitor/evaluator: serious and down to earth. Checks and examines carefully. Lacks inspiration, warmth, humour, imagination.

Finisher: painstaking, orderly, anxious to 'get it right'. Basically a perfectionist. Meets deadlines. Worries too much, often about nothing.

You might like to think about the members of either the team you lead, or of one of which you are a member. Can you identify in the chosen team individuals who resemble those in Belbin's list? How can the attributes of each member be put to better use than they are at present?

32.8   TEAM LEADERS

You will remember from Chapter 8 (Section 8.2 and Fig. 8.1) that in his theory of leadership John Adair singles out the core responsibilities of the group/team leader, which here you can think about in more detail:

1. *Achieving the task*: which entails defining the objectives(s), aims, goals, etc. In the case of the groups you are likely to lead now, or in the future, tasks could include allocating jobs, setting standards, and controlling the work; problem-solving and decision-making; collecting data, information and opinions, and passing them on as required; promoting involvement and commitment; evaluating ideas and performance; negotiating, and resolving conflicts.
2. *Developing each individual member:* which includes ensuring he is aware of his targets. (The targets might be in quantity or output terms, time scales or quality for example.) The best targets should be:

    (a) Able to be clearly stated.
    (b) Preferably measurable (against some standard).
    (c) Achievable within a specified period of time.
    (d) Challenging.
    (e) Appropriate to the individual.

3. *Building and maintaining the team*: which includes all the kinds of activities discussed in previous sections of this chapter.

   These three core responsibilities overlap, but all must be taken care of by the team leader, even if individual members, or the team as a whole, is delegated to undertake part of the responsibilities.

32.8.1 Being a team leader

A team leader will, however, have to consider more than the brief outline above of the core responsibilities. He or she will want to take into account other important factors, such as:

1. *Personal viewpoint*: how he feels about life, the world, the job; the amount of confidence in the ability of team members to do their jobs; his current personal needs and ambitions.
2. *Obligations*: to the organization, to customers or clients, and the team. Concerning the latter, particularly to individuals who seek independence or to be dependent; those who want more, or less, responsibility; who want help and counselling; who have grievances and who may need representing; and to the members generally by equality of treatment (having no favourites, for example).
3. *Work environment*: these being factors external to the team. They include the known future of the organization; the expectations of senior colleagues and groups; time and demand pressures; the past history of the organization; the relationship with others outside the team; how the remainder of the organization is structured; the destinations of any of the team's outputs, and the consequences of its decisions.

Checkpoint

As a group leader do you try to ensure that:

1. There is a relaxed, informal and friendly atmosphere?
2. There is a shared purpose, an overall objective to unite members and shape behaviour?
3. All members can have their say, and the others listen?
4. Issues affecting the group are faced and dealt with?
5. Members support each other, and develop a high degree of trust in each other?
6. Tasks are clearly understood by all members?
7. Members enjoy being involved, and take pride in their work?
8. The team evaluates its own progress, and learns from this process?
9. You make the best use of the different skills of the group members, and see each person is properly trained in his job?
10. You take advice from and consult with group members?
11. You take every opportunity to build teamwork into jobs?
12. You brief them regularly on past performance, current progress and plans for the future?
13. The group's relationships with other work groups are cordial and constructive?

If you can safely answer 'yes' to most of these questions, you will be well on the way to be leading a very effective team! You probably find you have increased levels of output, increased co-operation, higher motivation, and less absenteeism than when you started team building.

32.9   SOME FINAL CONSIDERATIONS

Action plans

Action plans are statements by team members about their work plans for a given period (say 6 or 12 months ahead). They should be drawn up (with help particularly in the beginning—another exercise at a team building event!) by the individuals concerned. In 1990 I visited a busy factory where every single employee had one. Many were concerned about work methods, improving safety, or the work environment. All were challenging and motivating, and part of the team building process. It was a resoundingly successful scheme.

Win/lose situations

We live in a competitive society: indeed we have to compete to stay in business, and the urge to compete is very strong within us, even in recreation activities (like sports and games). Unfortunately the work team needs co-operation, not internal struggles ending with someone 'winning'. The implication is someone else loses. Regrettably, more time and effort is spent (and wasted?) within some organizations in internal win-or-lose rivalries than in the production of goods, or provision of services. Win-or-lose situations within the group should be avoided. The effect can be the opposite of team building: group disintegration.

A team base

Human beings are very territory minded: teams are no exception. Try to give your team a physical base for its operations, a place to 'call home'. For staff normally working away from the organization (sales staff, for example) this is even more important, even if it is only one desk in a representatives' room.

   Give the team a name: perhaps it will choose its own!

Splinter groups

Over a certain size (I suggest over sixteen, though others suggest a larger figure), groups tend to 'splinter' into two or more sub-groups. These then develop their own internal structure and challenge the solidarity of the total group. The first possibility is to accept the situation if it makes sense to do so, possibly creating official sub-groups reporting back to the parent group on a regular basis. Failing this, to identify the 'breakaway' team leader, and work with him to bring back the 'deserters'.

The elite group

A group can become so cohesive and successful that the members come to view themselves as being 'special'; and other groups may even resent this. They may even develop additional group objectives which may not fit in with the remainder of the organization. They may try to restrict the entry of new members, or even reject them.

Do not discourage high cohesiveness, but identify the minus factors in the situation, and discuss them with the group. Again it is essential to get the group to reaffirm its original objectives, and place within the total organization.

Teams may not be perfect, but they have one thing in common: they are all different!

33
Managing Conflict

'Conflict and co-operation are two sides of the same coin.'

Tony Watson

33.1 INTRODUCTION

Conflict is part of the human makeup, and so embedded in our basic nature that from early childhood out interactions with others are full of disagreements. Life at work is no different, and as we spend nearly half our waking life at work, it is not surprising that conflict is an ever-present feature in all organizations.

Consequently, you as a supervisor or manager will undoubtedly not only come into conflict at work with others at your level or above, but also have to deal with conflict within the team or work group you lead. Indeed, at times, managing conflict can represent a significant part of a week's work.

It is therefore essential for managers at every level to try to understand how conflict can arise, and what strategies might be used to cope with it. In this chapter we will be looking closely at conflict, hopefully with an open mind, as conflict can have positive value to the work of a group in the right circumstances.

33.2 AIMS OF THIS PROGRAMME

The aims of this programme are to help you:

1. Appreciate the positive as well as the negative aspects of conflict.
2. Identify the kinds of people or groups of people engaged in conflict with whom the supervisor/manager will come into contact.
3. Examine the possible causes of conflict at work.
4. Consider the various strategies for responding to and dealing with conflict.
5. Evaluate your own conflict-handling style.

These aims are related to the NVQ element 'Identify and minimize interpersonal conflicts'.

33.3 WHAT IS CONFLICT?

The word 'conflict' at first sight has a very warlike and unpleasant sound about it: its synonyms are words like 'battle', 'clash' and 'fight'; and 'discord', 'friction' and 'dissension'. You could be easily led to believe all conflict was bad. However, there are different degrees of conflict, and there are those (and I am one) who feel that without conflict many problems would remain unresolved; and that an organization in which there was no active debate, no contrary views about future plans, no difference of opinion would be a dull, unimaginative and probably boring place to work in. Indeed the 'ideal' work team (of the kind described in Chapter 32) would be the home of active, constructive conflict.

So conflict can be considered as a continuum (see Fig. 33.1). At the one extreme there is the divisive and destructive kind of conflict; at the other the energetic debate, with contrasting ideas, opposing views and alternative strategies being put forward. Somewhere in the middle is the chronic, low-grade conflict which is neither so developed as to be divisive, nor particularly constructive.

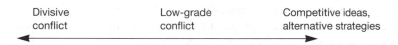

| Divisive conflict | Low-grade conflict | Competitive ideas, alternative strategies |

Figure 33.1 The conflict continuum.

33.4 CATEGORIES OF CONFLICT

Classifying conflicts between human beings is not an easy task: we can do it in a variety of ways. One useful approach is to single out the participants or players in conflict situations. Those I can identify in the workplace include the following:

1. One single group member (SGM) versus another SGM.
2. One SGM versus a group of people (GP), i.e. more than one person.
3. Sub-groups (SGs) within a GP (i.e. in conflict with each other).
4. One GP versus another GP.
5. An organization-wide group (OWGP) versus another OWGP.

The kind of conflict which occurs most often in the majority of organizations is *one SGM versus another SGM*. Such conflicts take many forms: a 'clash of personalities' (two people who profoundly dislike each other); a fight over the allocation of resources (e.g. money and equipment); a dispute over the relative status of the two, or changes in procedures (which favour one or the other).

592 Management and supervisory competences

There is also the question of 'territory'. Well known in the animal world as well as the human, the defence of a worker's territory (desk, workspace, equipment; power held; job description, job title; freedom of action, having special access to places, people, information, and so on) is a very powerful motivator. Anyone 'trespassing' on what an individual feels is his territory, will provoke resentment, which if bitter enough will lead to a high level of conflict.

Less frequently conflicts arise between *an SGM and a GP*. Perhaps a group member falls out of line with the rest: works harder, or is perceived as a slacker; or perhaps, violates some unwritten rule the group has. In an extreme case, the offending SGM is 'sent to Coventry', by the group; in effect ignored and cold-shouldered.

A fruitful field for conflict is between *a sub-group and the main group* to which it belongs. You will remember looking at this problem in Chapter 32 (Section 32.9) under the *elite group.*

Groups versus other groups are a significant area of conflict. The causes can be similar to conflicts between two individuals: allocation of resources, status, procedures, and, of course, territory. However, a further element can be a *clash of objectives.*

The sales department might (possibly legitimately) take the view that its prime objectives were to satisfy customers and maximize sales. A result could be an increasing number of small orders, 'specials', bringing forward of agreed delivery dates, part supplies virtually on demand. Against this, production might (again legitimately) strive for low unit costs, planned batch or large-run output patterns, scheduled delivery of orders. Both these sets of laudable objectives taken together are a recipe for arguments, complaints and much hostility.

Similar problems can be found in the stores-versus-finance field (high stocks being good for production continuity versus keeping the cost of stocks and stock management as low as possible); and production and inspection, where there is plenty of opportunity for conflict.

An example of an *organization-wide group* clash would be a trade union in conflict with an employer. As problems at this level are usually not in the supervisor's remit we will not consider them here.

You are also reminded of the discussion in Chapter 2 on *Line and staff organization* and *Functional authority*; and their attendant problems (see Sections 2.3.2 to 2.3.4.) to which you should refer.

33.5 CAUSES OF DIVISIVE CONFLICT

These can now be summarized so far as:

1. Perceived inequitable allocation of resources.
2. Interpersonal friction.
3. Differences in status, prestige, power.
4. Clashing objectives.
5. Differing sets of values, beliefs.
6. Functional authority being exercised incorrectly.

We can identify other causes which originate from the organization and its structure, rather than from its employees directly. *Too many rules and regulations* (these can be created by staff personnel—the specialist groups); *poor communication systems* (leading to ambiguities and misunderstandings) and *the total value system of the organization* (as discussed in reference to C. Argyris, Chapter 3, Section 3.9.6.).

33.6   THE CONSEQUENCES OF CONFLICT

When we think of conflict in terms of argument, debate, competition between individuals and/or groups, then positive consequences flow:

1. Different ideas, suggestions, strategies, plans of action can be highlighted and compared.
2. With open discussion and debate on these differences, there is a good chance they can be resolved, and a consensus set of strategies and plans can be agreed.

Conflict of the kinds discussed in the previous section has generally negative outcomes:

1. The misuse of resources, time, energy and creativity.
2. An increase in hostility.
3. A decrease in trust and openness.
4. A decrease in the ability of groups and the organization as a whole to achieve the objectives set.

At this stage you could usefully make a list of the kinds of conflict you have encountered at work within the recent past. Endeavour to categorize them using the analysis in Section 33.4; to establish what the causes were (noting that more than one cause may be found in any particular conflict situation); and to assess what the consequences were to you (if any), to your group, and to the organization generally.

33.7   MANAGING NEGATIVE CONFLICT

There are two major strategies for managing negative conflict:

1. To convert the conflict into a positive kind by a team building process (see Chapter 32).
2. To respond to the conflict by trying to ignore it (avoidance); calm it (defusion), or resolve it (confrontation).

33.7. 1 Avoidance

You may find you always want to avoid conflict altogether, or possibly just avoid certain kinds—conflict with your boss, perhaps! You might:

1. Bottle up your feelings, turn the other cheek, swallow your pride.
2. Slip away, or just 'not notice it'.
3. Pretend to yourself—and others—the situation doesn't exist.

You may well adopt these strategies because you cannot bring yourself to face the difficulties, unpleasantness and bother that actually dealing with the situation might cause; or because you feel you lack the appropriate skills needed.

Not only may you be left with a guilty feeling caused by your inaction, but the conflict you shield away from may still be out there. Leaving it may indeed make it worse in the future.

Not recommended.

33.7.2 Defusion

Defusing conflict means essentially 'smoothing things over'. By trying to calm everyone involved down you may buy some time. During the following period small issues may well go away or be resolved. However, the danger is the problem may tick away like a time bomb, then suddenly reappear—much more urgent next time.

Again not recommended.

33.7.3 Confrontation

This procedure requires the whole set of conflicting issues being faced and brought out into the open. Where members of your group might be involved, then they too need confronting. It's time to say, 'Let's get to the bottom of this.'

A difficult strategy because it is high-risk, and people—including yourself—may get hurt emotionally by adopting it. But you may be sure, this is the *only* certain and dependable way to resolve conflict.

There are two versions of confrontation, though:

1. The use of *power*.
2. The *negotiation approach*.

The *power* strategy is only available if the 'conflict manager' has adequate real power in his armoury. The occupation of the Falkland Islands provoked a conflict solved by *physical* power—that of the armed forces. Having enough money to buy people off— the power of bribery—could resolve an union/management confrontation being settled. However, the power option means one party, the one with the greater power, wins. The other party loses.

As you saw in Chapter 32, win-or-lose situations can be less than satisfactory. The loser may well hang around waiting for the day when revenge is possible. Certainly resentment and loss of motivation on the loser's part are potential minus outcomes.

33.7.4 Confrontation by negotiation

Negotiation is not an easy option, but the potential outcomes are much more positive than with the other two approaches to dealing with conflict. Assuming you are engaged in attempting to resolve a conflict situation, you must first get the parties concerned to trust you. Next you try and find as much common ground as there is between the parties, and encourage them to arrive at an acceptable middle ground. Ideally, the aim would be for everyone to be satisfied by the deal or arrangement suggested, though the best that can be managed is usually a compromise where each party 'trades off', that is wins *something*.

Managing a negotiation is a tricky activity: no two situations are the same. You may have to steer things along if no one is willing to take the first step; but if the parties start negotiating between themselves, you need to slip into more of an encouraging, supporting and advisory role. Skills required of you are very similar to those mentioned in Chapter 6 (Section 6.1.20) in connection with *Six-step problem-solving*. These include ascertaining all the facts (diagnosing the situation), arranging the negotiations (initiating the process), listening, and assisting in the problem-solving process.

The whole activity can be a team building or team maintenance one.

33.8 ASSESSING YOUR OWN CONFLICT MANAGEMENT STYLE

Scenario

You are the Pool Manager at Borchester Leisure Centre. You have three deputies, and the rule is no more than one of them can be away on holiday or attend a course at any one time. All three approach you; John (single, and keen to go on holiday with his friends from the Scouts, and who is the most senior of the three), Mary (married, and whose husband can only have two specific weeks when the factory closes for the summer shut-down), and Tom (who has been waiting for six months to hear about the dates to go on a special course to enhance his promotional prospects) all want to be off in the same two weeks.

Each of them hears about the others' applications and all three have a furious row in the staff room. None of them will talk to the other two, except about work-related matters.

The two weeks in question are three months away.

Checkpoint

As the Pool Manager would you:

1. Call them all together and explain they must sort the matter out themselves, but if they don't you will sort the matter out for them by exercising your right to fix the holiday rota, but no one will be allowed to go that fortnight anyway?
2. Call them all together and tell them they must sort the matter out themselves?
3. Talk the matter over with each of them separately to discuss the facts with them. Make a decision as to whose need is the most pressing, get them all together and announce your decision?
4. Tell them individually not to be silly, and suggest they take an afternoon off and talk the matter over with their families/friends/training officer?
5. Discuss all the problems the situation raises with each fully, and if the matter still cannot be sorted out, go to the training officer and see if there is an alternative course; and the Chief Officer to see if one this occasion two deputies can be allowed on holiday at the same time. Bring them all back to hear the outcome?

Comment

If you go for the first option, you are choosing the *power* route. Fine if jobs are scarce, but highly risky. If you win, they all lose! Letting them sort it out themselves is *avoiding* the situation. Number three is an attempt at a *compromise*, though not allowing very much input from them. Patting them on the head and telling them to talk to others is trying to *defuse* the situation. Only the last option begins to address the problems. Even though there is no knowing there will be a successful outcome you are trying to resolve *all* the conflicting needs.

Remember the team building approach, and if you can promote openness and discussion of problems like these, there will be fewer divisive conflicts to cope with.

Finally you could return to the confrontation situation you looked at the end of Section 33.6. Consider the way this situation was dealt with. Did you agree with the method that was chosen then? Thinking about it now, what different strategies could have been used?

34
Briefing a Work Group

'Don't talk unless you can improve the silence.'

Vermont Proverb

34.1 INTRODUCTION

Being in contact with other people at work forms a significant part of the job of supervising or managing others. Whilst you may spend considerable time talking to superiors, colleagues, visitors, customers or the general public, contact with the members of your own work group or team is normally your prime responsibility.

One-to-one communication with group members is the most common method, but there are occasions when it is more suitable or appropriate to speak to all of your work group at the same time. When the situation is such that you need to fill them in as a group, this activity is often called *briefing*.

Some supervisors and managers prefer to avoid this type of communicating at all costs, because perhaps they lack confidence in themselves or are not sure how this kind of job is best done. Indeed, if you think back on the last time you talked to a group of people in some 'official' capacity, no doubt some of you will agree you didn't do as well as you would have liked. In this chapter we will be looking at ways of helping you to prepare yourself beforehand; and in acquiring some of the skills of putting the message over.

34.2 AIMS OF THIS PROGRAMME

The aims of this programme are to help you:

1. To appreciate what is meant by 'briefing'.
2. To identify when it is appropriate to brief a work group, rather than pass on information individually to people.

3.   To consider the benefits—and drawbacks—of group briefings.
4.   To plan the format and structure of a briefing session.
5.   To plan how to get the message across.
6.   To cope with replying to questions.

34.3   DEFINING THE TERM 'BRIEFING'

The term *briefing* is derived here from a legal usage, the word 'brief' originally being a short account of a client's case for consideration by a barrister. Later, in military practice it became the term for a set of instructions with appropriate background information given to pilots and others about to carry out a mission against the enemy.

Today *briefing* is widely used at work to mean something very similar when, for example, telling a work group or, say, a party of visitors about some aspect of the organization, or how they are going to spend the next few hours. As opposed to *making a presentation,* which is dealt with in Chapter 35, *briefing* still carries with it the idea of something fairly short and self-contained.

34.4   WHEN TO BRIEF A GROUP

Obviously, as a supervisor or manager, you will spend much of your working day talking to, and occasionally writing to, individual members of work groups, and other colleagues. If what you have to say is only relevant to one or two individuals, then it makes sense to communicate with just those individuals. However, there are occasions when it makes sense to talk to several people at the same time, of which the following are examples:

1.   When all staff are only present in the same area at set times.
2.   When the work group needs to be updated on minor changes in work arrangements on a regular basis.
3.   When it would be very time-consuming to explain something to every group member personally.
4.   Warning the group before visitors come round the department.
5.   Explaining to visitors to the organization what the programme of the visit is going to be.
6.   When what you have to say is of interest to a committee.

In effect, when something important has to be passed on, you should weigh up the pros and cons of talking to a whole group, as opposed to seeing its members separately. Very often a big plus is *saving time* (your time, that is). Again, where everyone needs to have exactly the same details or set of instructions a briefing session for all is an ideal solution. Regular meetings of the group are helpful in team building (see Chapter 32).

On the other hand, especially where the work group is very mixed in terms of jobs to be done, skill levels, or the ability to grasp anything at all complicated, to talk to the group as a whole might be less productive than in ones or twos. If the supervisor or manager who is to give the briefing is in any way nervous, unprepared, or unsure of the true situation, more harm than good may come of an attempt, however well intentioned. Hopefully, after you have completed this short programme, you will be more confident in your ability to tackle the job.

34.5   THE FOUR STAGES OF GIVING A BRIEFING

There are four stages in giving a briefing:

1. Preparation.
2. Structure.
3. Delivery.
4. Follow-up.

It is suggested, when preparing for a briefing, that you go through these stages in the order given in this chapter. They follow a logical sequence. If you have any doubts or apprehensions about 'speaking in public' (even though the audience is your own team), to keep to this sequence will help you to gain confidence and help to lessen your anxieties.

34.5.1   Preparation

Preparation is the key to a successful briefing. A few questions to you to start with:

1. What group are you going to talk to (e.g. a work group, visitors, management)?
2. Have you something definite to say to them, a specific purpose in briefing the group? What, in fact, do you want to tell them?
3. How much do they know about the topic already?
4. How much do *you* know already?
5. How much time have you got?

The *makeup of the group* is going to be important. Knowing their personalities or abilities is useful in assessing *at what level* to pitch the briefing: is it to be full of technical phrases (talking to the experts), down to earth (an unskilled work group), or informative (an intelligent but uninformed group)? The latter could entail a much longer briefing than in the case of the experts. Visitors will need a general introduction to the organization, as well as the visit-specific information. Even the general *tone* of the briefing (formal or informal) will depend on the type of group you have. Find out as much as you can about the group before hand.

A *specific purpose* entails having aims, goals and objectives in briefing the group in question. A briefing for its own sake is a waste or everyone's time. Do you want to inform, persuade, exhort, train, motivate, or prepare for change? If you don't know what the purpose of your briefing is, it is hardly likely your audience will, after you have finished.

Knowing in advance where you can start from is important: if the group are well informed about events up to last Monday, bringing them up to date can start with the events of Tuesday. If the group know very little about the topic at all, then you may have to go back months, or even longer, to put people in the picture.

Your own knowledge (or ignorance) is a key factor: preparation means finding out all you can about the topic, especially if what data you have are misleading, incomplete, or inconsistent. (It could be useful for you to refer back to Chapter 30 on project preparation if you need some guidance on finding appropriate data.)

The *time available* for the briefing will affect you in two ways: it will put a limit on the amount of information you can pass on, and encourage you to concentrate on the key points. (You should ensure you can have sight of a clock or watch when you come to the briefing itself. It will help you to leave time for the final, essential summary; and a 'question time' period if this is needed. A normal briefing is unlikely to last more than 10 minutes; 15 at most.)

Checkpoint No. I

In preparing for your presentation, have you:

1. Given thought to the kind of group you will be speaking to?
2. Become clear in your own mind what the objective of the presentation is going to be?
3. Checked or clarified the amount of knowledge the group has already?
4. Checked you own knowledge, and made good any deficiencies?
5. Established the time available, and how you propose to use it?

34.5.2   Structure

There is the legendary story of an American preacher from Haarlem who, when asked how he prepared his sermons, is alleged to have replied: 'First I tells 'em what I'm going to tell 'em; then I tells 'em, and then I tells 'em what I told 'em!' He had mastered the art of structuring his homilies with a *beginning,* a *middle piece*, and an *end.* So must you, though you might want to call the three parts:

Introduction
Main subject matter
Conclusion

Let us consider planning each of these parts in turn.

The introduction

The *introduction* is where you will want to tell the group the purpose of the briefing: perhaps about the new work rotas for the forthcoming season; a health and safety training session, or a new project the group will be working on. A simple, brief statement is best.

Getting people's attention at the start can sometimes be difficult in the workplace, and some writers advocate you should plan unusual gimmicks to get attention. If you have an appropriate visual aid, such as an example of the new equipment being introduced, or copies of the new requisition form to circulate, all well and good. If not, you will have to rely on speaking clearly, simply and to the point. Let the group feel you have a worthwhile reason for speaking to them.

Main subject matter

When you finish the introduction, you can then move on to the main subject matter. Putting the points you want to make in a logical order, in a series of separate, well-defined stages (like this chapter), will help the group grasp the message, and keep their attention.

For example, if you are covering a proposed new emergency evacuation procedure in case of fire, you might need to explain to your group:

1. How they will be made aware of a fire.
2. What the procedure for evacuation is, and how it affects different individuals (for instance those people responsible for checking that all their sub-group has reached the marshalling point safely).
3. Which evacuation routes apply to the group.
4. The date when the new procedure will come into effect.

You may also plan to hand out a written version of the procedure at the end.

It is unlikely you will remember all the points you will want to make, so you will probably benefit from preparing notes (as memory joggers) on pieces of stiff card, listing and setting out the main ideas in the order you have planned to make them, with short comments. It is fatal, unless you are very skilled at doing this, to write the whole text, to be read out. The chances are you will lose yourself as you try to read and speak at the same time.

Conclusion

You can then either plan to move on to the conclusion straight away, or break for questions. Waiting until the very end is more effective, as you can leave a brief summary in the minds of the group as they break up.

The summary, containing all the key points you want to stress, can also be set out on your collection of cards.

Checkpoint No. 2

In planning your briefing session, have you:

1. Worked out how you are going to state the purpose of the briefing?
2. Considered any useful way of getting the group's undivided attention?
3. Sorted out the points you want to make in an easily understood and appropriate, logical order?
4. Prepared a series of easily readable notes, to remind you of the points you want to make, in the order you have planned?
5. Similarly prepared your summary/conclusion?

You should by now have a clear-cut structure for your briefing.

34.5.3 Delivery

You have just organized what you want to say: now you need to look at *how* you propose to put it over. Careful preparation is again essential, and some more questions need to be answered:

1. Where are you giving the briefing; are there any difficulties to be overcome (noise, other people working, not everyone being able to be present)?
2. What equipment or visual aids, paperwork to be handed out will you require to support your verbal briefing?
3. How much do you plan to involve the group: by asking them questions, or inviting questions from them?
4. What personal fears or anxieties do you face?
5. What vocabulary do you propose to use?
6. How will you ensure the group understands the information you give them?
7. Will you be keeping an eye on yourself, and any distracting habits or mannerisms you may admit to?

These may seem a daunting list, but a little extra effort will really put the final polish on your briefings.

Place.   Try hard to find a place away from obvious distractions: noise, movement, telephones. Perhaps you will prefer your group to sit down whilst you brief them: chairs will be have to be available. If you use an overhead projector (OHP), then you will want to be near an electric plug-in point.

Time.   Try hard to find a time to hold the briefing when everyone can be present. Should this not be possible, make sure you do talk to those who can't attend either before or after your briefing.

Visual aids.   If you use an OHP, flipchart, blackboard or other visual aid make sure you have everything prepared beforehand, plus pens, chalk, or erasers. Make sure you have enough copies of any hand-out for everyone present.

Questions.   Briefings can become exercises in one-way communication if the members of the group are not involved. Questions help the two-way flow, help to keep people interested, and improve the understanding of your message. You can ask the *group*, or *individuals* within the group, questions as you proceed: 'How many of you have had experience of using this type of fire extinguisher?' . . . 'Perhaps, Tracey, you could let us know how often you had fire drills in the other office block?'

Inviting questions *from* the group also helps the feedback process. You will need to be prepared for questions, but if you can't answer there and then, admit you can't, and promise to find out the answer as soon as possible.

Fears and anxieties.   Most people are nervous and tense when they have to speak in public for the first time. Do not be worried by this. If you feel apprehensive before a briefing session, you are in good company. There are few of us who don't get anxious before 'making an appearance' in front of others. I certainly do. The good news is, you are more likely to perform better if you are keyed up at the start—and have prepared yourself well, in advance!

Two or three deep breaths before you begin, and relaxing your face with a smile are highly recommended!

Vocabulary.   The words you use need to be those the group will understand. You are not out to impress the group with technical jargon or long words like 'marketing mix', or 'interpersonal communication'. Keep your words short, simple and direct. Avoid repeating your favourite phrases of the moment ('right!'; 'actually'; shortage situation'; 'lastly'—for the third time!—and the like).

Feedback.   It is important you monitor how well your message is getting over. Shuffling feet, whispering, gazing through the window, yawning—these are all danger signals to indicate your listeners are switching off. You will have to counter this by the energy and enthusiasm of you presentation.

Never forget to maintain eye contact with every member of your group. Not all at the same time, of course, but sweeping across the group at regular intervals. Fix each individual for a second or two. This will help you keep their attention.

Afterwards, it can be useful during one-to-one conversations to check back and see how much was learned from a briefing.

Distracting habits.   These can be many and varied: pacing up and down (which normally entails losing eye contact); fiddling with a pen, money, spectacles; 'umming and erring'. All have the fatal effect of distracting your group. Ask someone you can trust to be honest with you, to attend one of your briefings and assess if you have any off-putting mannerisms.

Checkpoint No. 3

When delivering the briefing message, do you:

1. Make sure that you choose the best available place in which to brief your group?
2. Ensure you bring along the appropriate visual aids and/or hand-outs?
3. Try and involve the group in the communication process, say by using questions, or encouraging them to question you?
4. Take care to relax and smile before you start?
5. Keep the message as simple as possible, using words the group will understand?
6. Ensure your message has been heard and understood?
7. Take care to eliminate distracting habits or mannerisms?

Now the message has been put over there is just one more task to complete.

34.5.4 Follow-up

The idea behind a follow-up stage is to both to check that the briefing message is being acted upon, and to reinforce it, perhaps by repetition. This stage can be done at a subsequent 'debriefing' session—where the group brief *you* on what they have done—or during face-to-face contact in the normal course of work.

34.6 FINAL REMARKS

By now you will have realized that just as with writing a report or preparing a schedule, briefing a work group involves a logical planned approach and a lot of preparation—particularly the first few times you do it. Always bear in mind that whilst the group are listening to you, they could have been doing their usual jobs. It is up to you to make sure they make the best use of the time set aside for briefing.

35
Making a Presentation

'The finest eloquence is that which gets things done.'

David Lloyd George

35.1   INTRODUCTION

The idea of giving a presentation fills many people with apprehension, and brings to mind addressing a large group, using all the latest in electronic gadgetry. Most presentations, however, are given to quite small groups, and sometimes even just to a single individual. There are some similarities with briefing a work group, which is covered in Chapter 34, though the essential differences lie in the *audience*, the *overriding purpose*, and the *formality of the occasion*.

In this chapter we will be looking at the skills required for making effective business, commercial and specialized audience presentations, including techniques such as voice control and the use of audio-visual aids, and the essential groundwork you will need to cover before you can put over your message confidently.

You are strongly advised, if you have not done so already, to work through Chapter 34, *Briefing a Work Group*, as this chapter builds upon many of the ideas discussed in the last one.

35.2   AIMS OF THIS PROGRAMME

The aims of this programme are to help you:

1. To appreciate what is meant by 'giving a presentation'.
2. To plan the format and structure of your presentation.
3. To plan the organization of your presentation.
4. To develop and prepare audio-visual aids.

5. To prepare for the delivery of your presentation.
6. To deliver your presentation effectively.

35.3 DEFINING THE TERM 'PRESENTATION'

The term *presentation* has been used for 400 years to mean an address to a group, but in recent times has been specifically applied to a semi-formal or formal talk to one person (e.g. a sales representative to a customer), or a small group (say up to twenty people) which will either *inform* and/or *motivate* the audience *to take some kind of action*. The desired action from the audience could be, for example, a changing of attitudes towards equipment or systems; the buying of a product or service; the giving of money to a charity; the setting up of a Total Quality Involvement programme in an organization; or the recognition by top management of the achievements of your department in the last twelve months. In effect, putting over the information, and/or getting the desired action will be the most important objective of the presentation. Business presentations are more likely to be persuasive rather than being purely informative.

You cannot proceed any further until you have decided upon your objectives.

35.4 PREPARING FOR YOUR PRESENTATION

You will remember from Chapter 34 that the first stage in giving a briefing was *preparation*. So it is in making a presentation. The work involved can be set out under the following headings:

1. Preparing for your audience.
2. Gathering data and information.
3. Preparing and structuring the material.
4. Developing and preparing visual or audio-visual aids.
5. Delivering the presentation.

35.4.1 Preparing for your audience

You will naturally want to think about your audience. They are less likely to be members of your immediate work group than would be the case with briefing. They could be, for example, other colleagues, your superiors, customers, people from other organizations, trainees, or members of the general public.

With your colleagues you will need to be technically competent; with superiors well prepared and positive; with customers and outsiders friendly and courteous (acting as an ambassador for the organization you represent); and with trainees careful not to overload them with new ideas and material.

Where your audience might contain people from different backgrounds, with widely differing levels of knowledge and experience, it is best to pitch your approach to those with least knowledge, though towards the end you can dwell shortly upon more advanced or detailed points. By inviting questions or comments at the end, you can cater for the more well-informed, and make them feel they have got something out of attending.

Whoever the audience are likely to be, the more you can find out about them the better able you will be to angle or slant your material.

35.4.2 Gathering data and information

The first step is to gather material for the main body of the presentation. (The introduction and conclusion can be sorted out later.) The process is very similar to that you looked at in Chapter 30, dealing with project work (read through Sections 30.5.5, 30.5.6 and 30.5.7). The general idea is to obtain as much information on your chosen topic as possible. It doesn't matter if you have too much in the end: it is much easier to discard the surplus than to find too late you are short of material.

Basically you are going to make a presentation because you are in some way qualified to do so, usually because of a combination of knowledge and experience. You may need to *add* to your store of knowledge, perhaps to fit what you want to say into a broader context. Thus you may need to do some research by asking others, looking something up in a scientific paper or topical newspaper or magazine article (to become an OHP transparency).

35.4.3 Preparing and structuring the material

Once you have the material you require, you need to plan the length of your presentation. You remember from Chapter 34 a briefing should ideally not go on longer than 15 minutes at the most, and the target time is 10 minutes. Presentations can go on a little longer, but not much: 20 minutes is about the maximum time you can expect people to concentrate on a new idea, product or way of doing things. Everything you want to say must fit into the allotted time which—if others are also speaking—could be restricted to less than 20 minutes.

Even within a 20-minute period you would be advised to attempt to cover only three to five main themes or points. Agreed, each main point can have sub-points, but never more than four or five. Selecting the main points must be done carefully, so that you can stress all the important aspects of your chosen topic.

Taking an example, suppose you, as a local government supervisor, have to persuade a committee of councillors to spend more money in your section during the coming year on computer systems and software than that originally budgeted. You would start by identifying the structure of what you want to say (see Fig. 35.1). The audience are not computer experts, thus a deluge of 'computerspeak' would be counter-productive. What is needed here are plain, general assertions as the main points, backed up with real and well-researched reasons for the extra expenditure.

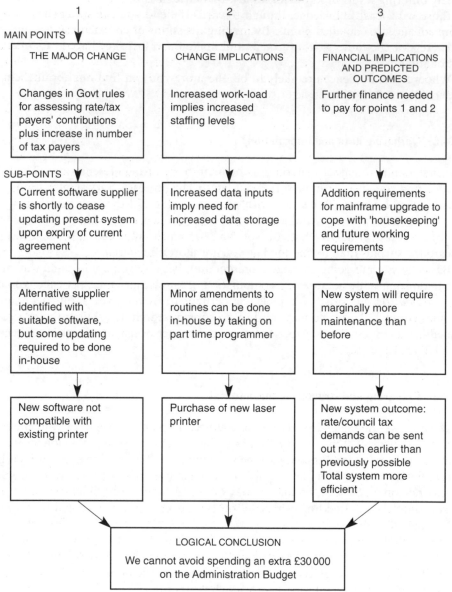

PRESENTATION OUTLINE: SUPPLEMENTARY ESTIMATE
RATES/COUNCIL TAX SOFTWARE

1   2   3

MAIN POINTS

THE MAJOR CHANGE	CHANGE IMPLICATIONS	FINANCIAL IMPLICATIONS AND PREDICTED OUTCOMES
Changes in Govt rules for assessing rate/tax payers' contributions plus increase in number of tax payers	Increased work-load implies increased staffing levels	Further finance needed to pay for points 1 and 2

SUB-POINTS

Current software supplier is shortly to cease updating present system upon expiry of current agreement	Increased data inputs imply need for increased data storage	Addition requirements for mainframe upgrade to cope with 'housekeeping' and future working requirements
Alternative supplier identified with suitable software, but some updating required to be done in-house	Minor amendments to routines can be done in-house by taking on part time programmer	New system will require marginally more maintenance than before
New software not compatible with existing printer	Purchase of new laser printer	New system outcome: rate/council tax demands can be sent out much earlier than previously possible Total system more efficient

LOGICAL CONCLUSION
We cannot avoid spending an extra £30 000
on the Administration Budget

Figure 35.1 Presentation planning chart.

All you have left to do at this stage is to consider the Introduction, in which you will state the main theme or purpose of the presentation, and outline the areas and topics you propose to cover. Your Conclusion (finish) will summarize the main points, and stress (in the case of the example) how vital it is for the extra expenditure to be incurred to enable the council to undertake its statutory duties.

35.4.4 Preparing your notes and memory joggers

There are three possible ways of preparing for the delivery of the presentation: have it all in your head before you start—that's only for the very practised speaker; have every word written or typed out—just the way to lose contact with your audience when you start reading it out; or make notes or memory joggers of some kind. These have the advantage of keeping you to the points you have planned to make, and making the points in the order you have already worked out (see the previous section).

Some people like to use stiff cards to write their notes upon. The big advantage of cards is that they come in various sizes, and you can choose a size which you can hold easily in one hand. Some cards are punched with a centred hole close to the top edge, and once you have put them into the correct order, you can pass a length of thin cord through them. When tying the cord, ensure there is a little slack in the loop. They are now both secured in your chosen sequence, and capable of being turned over when you wish to move on to the next card.

All you need to put on each card are a few short words or phrases (very like, in fact, the main and sub-points illustrated in Fig. 35.1), plus any instruction you have for yourself; 'Show OHP No. 6', or 'Pass round first hand-out' in the top right hand corner. (The use of visual aids is discussed in the next section.)

Others prefer to use A4 or A5 sheets of plain paper for their notes. Obviously less expensive, but more difficult to hold. Avoid using both sides of the sheets, and number the sequence clearly. They are most useful if you have a lectern or raised ledge upon which to place them, leaving your hands free to operate a projector or use a flipchart.

Checkpoint No. 1

In preparing your presentation have you:

1. Given thought to the type of group you will be speaking to?
2. Established the purpose of the presentation: to inform, motivate, or get a particularly desired outcome?
3. Gathered *all* the material you will need: not only for the formal presentation, but to cope with possible questions or discussion?
4. Prepared and structured the material, with three to five main topics or themes, and appropriate subsidiary points for each topic?
5. Transcribed the points you wish to make in note or memory-jogging format onto cards or sheets of suitable size in a logical sequence?
6. Ensured there is a 'signposting' Introduction; and a 'summarizing' Conclusion, which, when appropriate, indicates the kind of action you are inviting the audience to take?

35.4.5 Developing and preparing visual aids

When the term 'visual aids' is used, people often tend to think of slides, overhead transparencies, or something to write on such as black or whiteboards, and flipcharts.

In fact, people can be visual aids (think of the mannequin modelling clothes or new hair-styles), pieces of equipment (when, say, we want to sell, explain or describe them), or even ordinary things like forms or documents. We can extend the idea to other senses than that of sight: a presentation of something eatable (a new type of cake, say), could involve handing round samples; or of something smelling nice could require dabbing a little perfume on the wrists of those volunteering to try it. Almost anything can be used to demonstrate a point: using your imagination and ingenuity you can enliven most presentations.

At this stage, ask yourself the following questions about your presentation: Is your chosen topic or theme, for the audience you have in mind:

1. Theoretical, abstract or academic?
2. Complex, or difficult to understand?
3. Probably a new or unusual one to them?
4. Not easy for you to put over verbally without illustration?
5. One of vital importance to them?
6. Full of detailed information?

If the answer to any of these questions is 'yes', then visual aids of some kind are essential. In any event, such aids will help you to increase your audience's attention; help you to emphasize and underline your message, and ensure it is better remembered. Note that visual aids are *supplementary* to the spoken message, and not substitutes for it.

Dealing with the more traditional kinds of visual aids: *OHP transparencies.* Ideally these clear, acetate sheets should be carefully prepared beforehand, using commercially produced letters and symbols or marker pens; or else they can be typed on a good machine, the text enlarged and the transparency produced using a photocopier. The more 'professional' the overhead, the better the chance of the message getting accepted by the audience.

Care must be taken to keep the message short and simple: avoid an overload of data or information. Under a main heading set out, say four or five numbered points with perhaps a chart, graph or similar diagram (see Fig. 35.2) Each acetate sheet should be carefully numbered in sequence.

ENLIVENING A TRANSPARENCY

1. Keep the message short and simple

2. Use diagrams, graphs, pie charts, maps (not detailed ones), cartoons

3. Use colour where you can

4. Use material which can be clearly seen by those furthest away from you

5. Always use 'permanent ink' marker pens

Figure 35.2 Example of the 'Keep it short' word-based transparency.

By using 'overlays' (flaps taped on the original transparency), a basic diagram such as that of an office or workshop can be built up in stages; or by using pieces of appropriately shaped card, kept loose, to represent workbenches, machines, desks, filing cabinets, etc., you can move them around to illustrate various layouts in a department.

Overhead projector. There are a few important points when using an OHP:

1. Never use a projector for a presentation without trying it out first.
2. Make sure you can switch it on and off; and are able easily to adjust the focus to cope with any transparencies you intend to use.
3. Always have a spare bulb handy, if your OHP hasn't got a second bulb to switch over to; and a spare extension lead in case the power socket you want to use fails (it also allows you to change the position of the OHP if this becomes necessary).
4. Make sure the lens and the surface on which you place your transparencies are clean and free from dust.
5. Photocopied extracts from handouts are not recommended, as the words are likely to be too small to read properly. As with the flipchart you will need to write quite large (or use some kind of commercial lettering), and stick to headings and key points
6. You are strongly recommended to protect transparencies with commercially available card frames. You can then number the frames, and keep them in the order you need.

Very important for you is to make sure before you start where you will be positioning the OHP, and your screen (sometimes you can use a wall if it is white or cream-coloured). You will have to be careful not to site the screen so that part of the audience cannot see it, as you are in the way!

Other major faults you must plan to avoid are:

1. Leaving the OHP on for a long time during extended explanation or discussion. The fan is quite noisy, and can be a distraction eventually.
2. Having the room too bright, or casting a shadow on the screen.
3. Exposing all the points on a sheet at once: uncovering one point at a time is preferable. You will need a handy piece of card to blank off points not yet covered in the presentation.
4. Pointing to the image on the screen. If you use a pen or short ruler and point it close to the *transparency* on the OHP, the image of the pointer will seen on the screen. In any event use the pointer quickly, and do not leave it pointing as it will turn attention away from you.

Black- or whiteboards. These days blackboards are being phased out, and are being supplanted by the more environmentally friendly whiteboard. Whichever you use there are problems:

1. The board must be perfectly clean at the start and you will have to learn to write very clearly in large letters, so that everyone can see your message.

2. Bright sunlight or spot lamps shining on the board can make it difficult for some people to see at acute angles.
3. Plenty of chalk or spare pens must be available in case you run out.

Additionally, you can, if you are like me, misspell simple words if you are not very careful! Writing whilst you are talking is quite difficult.

Flipcharts. Flipcharts are now very common in organizations, and are often used in other work situations (like brainstorming sessions) as well as for presentations. The virtues of this medium are:

1. You can carefully prepare what you want to write, before the event.
2. When you have finished with a set of ideas, all you have to do is to 'flip over' the page you have finished with, and the next one is now revealed.
3. You can always recap by turning back.
4. You can move the flipchart to the best place for the audience to see it.
5. You can use different coloured pens to stress particular main points.

Videotapes.   There are many suitable videotapes on the market which you can use to enhance a presentation. However, few of them are as short as 5 or 10 minutes, which is as long as you can use a videotape when 20 minutes is your limit. Thus you will have to be selective, and choose the most appropriate section of the tape. You will want to have everything set up, so all you have to do is to switch on, *after* your introduction. Suggest some points the audience should be looking out for: this will encourage their attention.

Using the 'pause' button, and freezing the tape for a short while, can be useful to make a telling point, as long as you don't overdo it.

Hand-outs.   Hand-outs have advantages: they summarize what you have to say, and for those who normally don't take notes, your hand-outs will be their only record of the event. Points to avoid include:

1. Using poorly typed or badly prepared notes.
2. Spelling mistakes.
3. Giving them out *before* you start: all that will happen is people will start reading the material, and lose interest in what you have to say!

Checkpoint No. 2

In preparing your presentation, have you:

1. Considered your chosen topic might be complex, new, difficult to understand, and/or could be easier for the audience to take in if visual aids were used?
2. Thought over carefully which of the possible visual aids are the most appropriate to enhance your presentation?

3. Looked at the advantages and disadvantages of your choices, and taken into account the availability of suitable sitings for any equipment, the equipment's expense and reliability, and any difficulties in transporting it about?
4. Made sure vital services and backup, such as power points, extension leads, spare bulbs, flipchart packs, marker pens, chalk, dusters, etc. are available?
5. Carefully planned exactly at which stage in your presentation each visual aid will be used?
6. Worked out how to put the visual messages over in a clear, lively, short and professional fashion?

35.5 DELIVERING YOUR PRESENTATION

A successful presentation depends upon concentrating hard on the 'four P's': *preparing*, *practising*, *polishing* and *persuading*. You will need to look carefully at each stage.

35.5.1 Preparing for the presentation delivery

By now, you should know what you are proposing to put over to your audience, and what visual and other aids you will be using. Following on from the previous section (i.e. checking on the visual aid equipment and spares), the next area to look at is the presentation environment. Leave nothing to chance. Points that should be dealt with, preferably well in advance, are:

1. Electrical power points and leads, overhead and wall lighting. Can you dim the lights from a dimmer control close to your speaking position? Or perhaps someone can control the lights for you, on request?
2. Microphone. In large rooms a microphone may be available: use it. (Except, that is, the hand-held variety—you will need both hands free for notes, pointers and gestures.) Try it out first for volume and clarity with someone sitting far away from you.
3. Acoustics. Can you be heard everywhere in the room (i.e. when there is no microphone system)?
4. Presenter's table or lectern. Is where your notes are to be put too low, high or just right for you? Can you adjust this to suit? Is there sufficient room for you to put out your other papers, transparencies, hand-outs or samples? A portable, folding lectern can be a great help: many of the 'extras' can be hidden underneath it.
5. Seating arrangements. Try and ensure you are going to be well away from an entrance or exit; and you will not be upset by those entering late. A horseshoe seating set-up is better than straight rows. More people can see you clearly.
6. Temperature and ventilation. The last thing you want is either a cold room—everyone wanting to get away as quickly as possible—or a hot, stuffy one, and the audience only half awake. Even just opening a window a little could solve this problem.

35.5.2   Rehearsing the presentation

Practice makes perfect; at least that's the theory! Effective rehearsal can begin at home or anywhere convenient. (Note: to begin with do not practise in front of a mirror; you may only distract yourself.) Some suggestions:

1.   Rehearse standing up. Imagine the audience is sitting in front of you, and speak as loudly as you would on the day. The first runs-through should cover the verbal presentation; trying out with visual aids comes after you have mastered the idea-sequence. A final rehearsal, ideally, should be checked by someone else, using a checklist like that in the next section. Take note of the comments, and be prepared to adapt your presentation.
2.   A 'dress rehearsal' in the actual room you will be using is a real bonus if it can be arranged. In any event, four or five rehearsals at least are recommended for those who are new to presentations.
3.   Work at the beginning (introducing yourself as well as your topic), and try linking what you have to say with something topical.
4.   Polish your conclusion. Summarize clearly, and ask for any action that you are there to try and get. Do not prolong this part of the presentation.

35.5.3   Checking your presentation

If you can get a colleague or friend to check your final version, ask him or her to use a simple checklist based on the one in Fig. 35.3, next page. Score each section from, say, 10 (excellent) to 1 (found wanting). If you can score 5 (average) or more in most sections before your first presentation, you are well on the way. You should aim at higher scores as you improve with practice.

35.5.4   Putting it over

Once the preparation is finished, you are then faced with the actual presentation itself. As you may have noted from the delivery checklist some quite new ideas are involved here: they centre on the way in which the message is put over.

General appearance.   A presentation is a formal or semi-formal occasion, and as such, demands you spend time on your appearance. Both men and women are recommended to wear a dark or grey business-type suit, with a crisp white shirt or blouse (keeping away from fancy trimmings), all clean and pressed. Hair, at the least, should be clean and tidy.

   Keep bulky items out of your pockets, and anything that jingles. Shoes should be clean; and where appropriate, polished.

Manner. Your manner should be warm and friendly. Smile when you are introduced, and try to maintain eye contact with every individual in the audience at regular

PRESENTATION CHECKLIST

ITEM	SCORE	COMMENTS

1. INTRODUCTION
   Pleasant, polite introduction of self?
   Was presentation's purpose made clear?
   Did the introduction attract attention?

2. MAIN CONTENT
   Was material interesting/suitable for this audience?
   Were main points identified, and subsidiary ideas arranged
      logically
   Was each section adequately covered?
   How well did the speaker know his/her subject?
   Was sufficient evidence used to back up the views expressed?

3. CONCLUSION
   Did the conclusion arise naturally from the evidence given?
   Was the conclusion convincing/asking for what action was required?

4. DELIVERY
   Was the speaker's dress/appearance suitable?
   Did the speaker maintain 'eye contact' throughout?
   Was the speaker enthusiastic?
   Did the gestures and hand movements add to the
      understanding?
   Was the speaker's voice pleasant/clear?
   Was there sufficient variety of tone, pitch and volume in the
      delivery?
   Did the words used suit the audience and subject?

Figure 35.3 Example of a 'Presentations Delivery Checklist'.

intervals. Show your interest in your chosen topic: there is nothing better than an enthusiastic speaker for grabbing and keeping an audience's attention.

Movement. Your success as a presenter/speaker is largely dependent upon your body language. Always stand up straight in front of the audience, and never slouch; if you have to move, move quickly. Keep your hands out of your pockets; and never cross your arms in front of you (this signifies you are on the defensive).

Voice. Your message must be heard, otherwise all your efforts will be in vain. The key word is *projection*, that is getting your voice to the back row without actually shouting. To project your voice you will have to breath a little more deeply than you do normally, and open your mouth wider. Speak somewhat more slowly, too, and this will assist you in speaking clearly. Try, in fact, to speak to people in the back row, and you will instinctively keep your head up.

If you speak in a monotone (i.e. at the same level and pitch), all the time, you will soon lull the listeners into semi-sleep: keep them alert by changing the pitch and tone, and vary the pace from time to time. Emphasizing key words in your presentation ('efficiency' or 'quality', say) helps to stress them, as does repetition.

Language. Remember the advice given earlier: suit the language used to the listeners. Avoid jargon and too many technical words.

Questions. You are bound to get questions. The golden rules are:

1. Prepare for the obvious ones beforehand: have the facts available.
2. Repeat the question out loud to the whole audience; some may not have heard the questioner speaking.
3. Address the reply to the whole gathering; not just to the questioner.
4. Never make up an answer: if you don't know, say so, and undertake to find out and let the questioner have the full details later.

Checkpoint No. 3

In delivering your presentation, do you plan to:

1. Check the venue beforehand for services such as power points, leads, room lighting, microphone and acoustics?
2. Ensure your notes will be available for you at the right height; and there will be room for your other papers, transparencies, etc.?
3. Make sure the seating arrangements are appropriate for the occasion?
4. Have a well-regulated and ventilated environment?
5. Rehearse the presentation beforehand several times; using a 'critic' to monitor your performance?
6. Use a checklist to assist the assessment?
7. Pay attention to your grooming and general appearance, manner, movement, voice and language used?

35.6 WHEN YOU HAVE FINISHED

After the presentation, and you have been thanked, you will still need to attend to some outstanding matters. Ensure you pack everything you have brought with you, thank those who have helped *you*, and particularly the organizer of the event, if this was not one of your duties.

Some of the audience may want speak to you to ask you questions or make their comments. Politeness dictates you do deal with them courteously, though you would be advised not to enter into any prolonged discussions.

36

Personal Competence, Knowledge and Understanding

'Anyone who keeps learning stays young. The greatest thing in life, is to stay young.'
Henry Ford

'Manage yourself'
NVQ Level 3, Unit C1

36.1   INTRODUCTION

Those of you who have read and thought about the chapters in this book (and particularly in this unit) will have realized that the contemporary supervisor or manager cannot stand still. Every day there are new challenges to face, new situations to cope with. A wide variety of skills and knowledge are needed to meet these challenges successfully.

Occupational competence has been defined as 'the ability to perform to the standards of best current employment practice, and to have the adaptability to meet foreseeable future requirements'. In order to maintain and increase your effectiveness as a manager, training and development are a means of improving your existing skills and knowledge; and as a basis for acquiring new skills. The current (NVQ) management standards recognize this. They call for supervisors and managers not only to gain a general and basic knowledge of the essential areas of supervision and management, but also to acquire, practise and refine appropriate skills.

Further, they point to the need to identify personal strengths and weaknesses; and to acquire the confidence required to engage in continuous self-development within the job. The earlier versions of the management NVQs listed, element by element, the 'performance criteria' (PCs) which defined exactly what was to be performed by candidates and demonstrated to an assessor. Additionally, details were given of the range of evidence ('range standards') and the 'knowledge and understanding' (K&U) required for each element. Then, from 1990, these management NVQs were published with the addition of 13 separate 'personal competences', listed in four clusters, but not specifically related to particular units or elements.

The latest management NVQs, issued in 1997, are much more specific and helpful, both to candidates and assessors. These standards set out, for each and every element, the PCs to be demonstrated and the appropriate K&U required. They also include the relevant personal competences needed to be acquired before being assessed for competence in the whole unit in question.

In this chapter we shall be reviewing both the personal competences and the K&U involved in the current level 3 management NVQ. (While these are scattered among 24 separate elements, in this chapter we shall be looking at particular competences and the K&U under general headings. A special index at the end of this chapter relates both the personal competences and the K&U headings to the units/elements where they are found.)

You will soon realize that a number of these competences and areas of K&U have already featured in earlier chapters of this book. Whenever this is the case, specific reference is made in the text to the relevant chapters and sections concerned to help you to refer back to the relevant material.

Additionally, to help your self-development, you will find after each item of personal competence, or particular area of K&U discussed, some suggested activities for you to undertake. These activities can be useful as self-development in your present job as well as creating some evidence towards an NVQ or other management-related award.

36.2 AIMS OF THIS PROGRAMME

The aims of this programme are to help you:

1. To identify the various areas of personal competence and the associated knowledge and understanding expected of a manager or supervisor.
2. To become more aware of your training and development needs.
3. To establish achievable objectives for self-development and/or for working towards a formal award.
4. To create and use opportunities for furthering your development and that of the team you lead.
5. To ensure that progress and performance towards your objectives are regularly monitored and reviewed by yourself and others.
6. To ensure any feedback received from others is compared with your own assessment of your progress and performance; and is then used to help improve your future performance and that of your team.

36.3 PERSONAL COMPETENCES AND KNOWLEDGE & UNDERSTANDING

Excluding the specialist units, at least nine distinct sets of personal competence and 22 different areas of K&U are identified in the level 3 management NVQ. While we will be looking at each of these in the following two sections, we need to be clear about both the differences and similarities between these two main classifications. Many years ago my attention was drawn to what was felt (then) to be a major distinction between 'knowing how' and 'knowing that'. 'Knowing how' was interpreted as 'the ability to do things': 'knowing that' was said to imply you had possession of facts, or were very familiar with routines or procedures.

I am now no longer so sure these are two distinct activities or abilities. Looking at what is mentioned under particular competences and K&U in the NVQ it is easy to see how both knowledge and personal competence can be intertwined: 'knowing how' can often imply 'knowing that' as well. While we will be considering what is listed under personal competences and K&U separately, it is inevitable that there will be areas of overlap (e.g. 'communicating' under competences, 'communication' included in K&U).

36.4 PERSONAL COMPETENCES

These are dealt with in alphabetical order to help you refer to them when you need to.

Acting assertively

'Assertive' can mean 'aggressive', 'dogmatic' or 'pushy', but the clear emphasis in the NVQ is on being 'confident', 'decisive' and 'positive', with a determination to be successful. Rather than sitting back whenever there is a problem, a manager at any level needs to be able to take the initiative without hesitation, as and when it is appropriate; and to take control of situations and events (or at least playing a leading role in making things happen). It also implies, particularly in a conflict situation, that managers should maintain their point of view strongly and defend it against criticism.

All managers need to be tough at times: someone has to give orders, spell out the possible consequences of non-compliance. The need to see every job is done and finished off correctly is the over-riding consideration.

Suggested self-development activity. Identify (and make notes about) an occasion at work when you (or another manager) failed to act in an assured and positive fashion when this was needed. Evaluate the outcomes of the incident, then work out a possible, alternative, more 'assertive' strategy which you feel could have improved the eventual outcome of the incident.

Behaving ethically

Recently there has been an increasing emphasis on fair, honest and principled behaviour in business, commerce, the state sector and national and local government. Many professional bodies now have their own 'codes of ethics' by which members agree to abide. Again, some organizations have similar sets of rules, systems or conventions for their staff. In this NVQ the accent is not only on following these but fully complying with the law (and associated regulations)—such as, for example the law relating to health and safety—and industry-wide codes of practice. Principled behaviour requires a balanced and honest approach to decision-making by managers, with every attempt being made to deal with all those involved in an open and sensible way.

It is not just a question of obeying the letter of the law, but the spirit.

Suggested self-assessment/development activity. Methodically review the way in which you make decisions, particularly those relating to health and safety, personnel selection, grievance or disciplinary matters. Do you fully understand (and comply with) all the legislation, and codes of practice involved? Do you honestly feel you make suggestions or take decisions relating to appointments, promotions or disciplinary matters which can be considered as fair and objective? Where you feel you need to build on your current competence you can, as necessary, take advice from colleagues, your line manager, safety officer or the personnel function.

Building teams

Chapter 32 of this book is entirely devoted to team building and team maintenance. As a team leader, you will be well advised both to re-read this chapter from time to time, and consider some further relevant competences highlighted in the NVQ. Many centre on the need to improve the performance both of yourself and of every team member: this promotes both cohesion and motivation.

Considerable stress in the NVQ is laid on keeping team members informed at all times; making sure everyone knows exactly what has to be done; making time to give individual support to team members and providing them with (ongoing) feedback about their progress. (In doing this, you are recommended to adopt communication styles and strategies appropriate both to the team members themselves and to the situation they are in; and to choose a suitable time and place to talk to them.)

Chapter 32, Section 32.8, 'Team leaders', stresses the need to develop every team member; this same message comes over very clearly in the NVQ. The emphasis on promoting involvement and commitment in Chapter 32 is also found in the NVQ. Both advise team members being involved in a variety of work-based activities (such as individual members being encouraged to contribute to the planning and review of the team's progress). You can find useful references in the *Checkpoint* list to be found in Section 7.1 of Chapter 7.

Suggested self-assessment/development activity. As a start, review as objectively as you possibly can how you function as a group leader, using the 13 points under the *Checkpoint* heading in Chapter 32. (Where you feel unsure as to your evaluation about any point, do not hesitate to discuss it with colleagues or team members and get their views.)

Where you find there could room for improvement, work out how you could upgrade your future performance.

Communicating

Chapter 5 (Section 5.2.5) explains the communication process, and Chapter 7 looks in detail at the supervisor's part in the process. (Section 7.1 refers to this role when a supervisor is acting as a team leader and developer: Questions 1, 2, 6, 7, 8 and 9 of the checklist are very relevant here. Section 7.2 specifically looks at the supervisor as a communicator.)

The NVQ adds to all this by drawing attention to the need to use a variety of different communication methods in a given situation, both to drive home points and maintain interest. It rightly stresses that the supervisor should be able to converse effectively with a wide range of people other than team members. Examples would be the organization's customers and suppliers, the supervisor's colleagues, line managers and, indeed, top management.

Emphasis is given in the NVQ to being an 'active listener' by, for example, the use of questions, particularly when it is essential to establish a situation accurately. Again, to confirm mutual understanding, it could be useful to rephrase what others have said (and getting their agreement to your version) and to interpret any non-verbal signals they may give. Thus the feedback obtained during a conversation can help you to modify your communication style appropriately. (You will also find useful references to these points in Section 7.2.1; and the rest of Section 7.2 covers communicating in a variety of situations.)

Suggested self-assessment/development activity. As this competence area is both extensive and diverse, it is clearly impossible to review every aspect in a short period of time. Chapter 7 (Section 7.2) is a good place to start from, particularly the two checklists already mentioned. Look through these and choose two or three areas where you think you could improve on what you are doing now and prepare an 'action plan' to enhance your current skills. Only when you are confident you have addressed these adequately should you attempt to tackle further aspects.

Focusing on results

Many managers in the past behaved as if their role was 'reactive', one of seeing things ticked over reasonably well, without too many errors or problems emerging. Now the focus has shifted to that of planning for the future, the setting of objectives (to enable the planned future to become reality) and a continuous monitoring of progress towards planned results.

Some of your objectives may be set by others, some you will need to set yourself. (Regarding the latter, you would be well advised to look at existing longer-term aims—those of your organization, other departments, or the team you lead—to ensure your chosen objectives are consistent with the wider aims.) In both cases you will need to prioritize and schedule work to make the best use of time and resources.

Additionally, the NVQ stresses you (as a team leader) should have high expectations of the team's individual and collective performance, which expectations you will want to pass on to all the members. You are looking for excellence. (Naturally, you will want to set them an example first!)

Further advice is to tackle problems as they arise (rather than hoping they will sort themselves out sooner or later) and similarly to take advantage of any opportunities which come your way. (Chapter 9 dealt with change and its implications: change must always be regarded both as an opportunity for improvement and as an occasion for a fresh look at desired results.)

To summarize: you should always be trying to ensure that you and your team do things tomorrow in a better way than they have done today.

Suggested self-assessment/development activities. Review objectively how you see your present role—as an 'maintenance manager', or as a striver for continuous improvement in every area of work, or somewhere in between. Make lists of: (a) all the areas (of the work of your department or section) where you feel you really focus on results and look for excellence; (b) where you have to admit you only intermittently maintain such a focus; and (c) the areas where you seemingly have never ever set any clear objectives.

Tackle list (c) first. Attempt to set appropriate objectives (consulting the team as necessary) for each area in question and consider how progress should be monitored and recorded. Next, move on to list (b) and see how you can actively ensure a planned focus on all objectives. Finally, check through list (a) carefully. You may find it useful to re-prioritize what are probably the most important activities for which you are responsible, and to take a fresh look at the way the work is monitored and controlled.

(Note: you way find it useful during these exercises both to re-read Chapter 31 on time management and to refer to Table 36.1 whose questions were originally developed for a factory/production situation but which can easily be adapted to suit your own work environment.)

Influencing others

'Influencing' in the context of this NVQ implies being a good, positive, persuasive and helpful influence, rather than a biased or manipulative one. This competence is related to 'acting assertively' in that you will need to present yourself positively to be able to influence others at work. To do this effectively, you will require to know a great deal about the organization to which you belong, the people in it and its prevailing culture. This information will help you devise suitable strategies with which to influence your colleagues or work group.

Suggested self-assessment/development activities. Reassess the ways in which you have attempted to influence others (e.g. members of your team, fellow team leaders or senior management) in the past. Have you really presented yourself in an actively assertive way; chosen the best approach, the right time and place, or tried to take account of the culture of your organization? Make notes of your self-assessment and sketch out ways in which you feel you could improve this competence.

Assume you wished to impress on your colleagues and superiors the need to place a much greater emphasis on quality in every area of the organization's outputs: e.g. products, services, advertising, customer/supplier relations. Work out how you might plan to do this effectively.

Table 36.1 Critical examination questions (for any job, task, activity, etc.).

A	Purpose of job	1. *What* is achieved?	*Why* is it achieved?
		2. What else *could* be achieved? (Is achievement really necessary? Could it be eliminated/modified?)	What *should* be achieved? (Consider alternatives.)
B	Means of doing job	1. *How* is it done? (Consider materials, equipment, methods employed, etc.)	*Why* that way? (Consider pros and cons.)
		2. How else *could* it be done? (Formulate alternatives.)	How *should* it be done? (Pros and cons of alternatives, including costs, considered.)
C	Sequence position of job	1. *When* is it done? (How does it fit in with sequence of operations?)	*Why* then?
		2. When else *could* it be done? (Earlier/later stage in sequence? Combined with another job?)	When *should* it be done? (Pros and cons of alternatives, including costs, considered.)
D	Place in which job is done	1. *Where* is it done? (Consider place, distances from previous and subsequent activities.)	*Why* there? (Pros and cons considered.)
		2. Where else *could* it be done? (Consider layout, distances, people involved.)	Where *should* it be done? (Pros and cons of alternatives, including costs, considered.)
E	People involved in job	1. *Who* does the job? (Consider numbers, grades, pay, etc.)	*Why* that person? (Pros and cons considered.)
		2. Who else *could* do it? (Consider alternative people, grades, types of workers.)	Who *should* do it? (Is work properly balanced balanced between staff concerned?)

Managing self

It is no accident that a whole unit of this NVQ is called 'Manage yourself'. Clearly, if you can't manage yourself, how can you manage anybody else? While the NVQ concentrates on the management of your own behaviour in the work environment, there are many good reasons why you should try to extend the good practice recommended to other areas of your life.

Managing your own personal learning and development is clearly of prime importance: just because the organization you work for has a personnel, human or training department, you cannot be sure all your personal needs will automatically be identified by that department, and appropriate training arranged for you.

Before you can start on any programme you will need first to assess your strengths and weaknesses (getting feedback from others where necessary), then to discuss your training needs (as you see them) with your immediate manager, and any personnel/training specialist who may be involved. When doing so, it is advisable to bring along with you your thoughts about a career development plan (related to your current or next projected role) to talk over. (For the NVQ you will need, in particular, to be able to show how you propose to improve your skills (a) in relation to work and personal objectives and (b) the organization's overall policies.)

It would not normally be the case that all self-development would take place in working hours: most supervisors and managers would be expected to use off-duty time, especially if any formal training is involved. So you could spend evenings and week-ends in building up your portfolio.

A totally different dimension is self-management in awkward circumstances: the ability to remain cool, collected and composed in difficult or unpredictable situations; being able to cope with highly emotional people in a caring but detached fashion, or accepting valid criticism without resentment. (Indeed you can take advantage from such criticism and learn from your mistakes.)

Suggested self-assessment/development activities. A good starting point is the 'strengths and weaknesses' list mentioned above. This activity could entail your finding out from your team, colleagues or superiors how they view your performance as well as undertaking an (honest) self-assessment. If you identify a glaringly obvious weakness, you can make a start with that, but don't forget to build on your strengths as well. Make sure your progress is recorded.

You can then look at how you manage others' personal emotions. Well-proven advice is to avoid getting personally involved: the implication is, in such situations, you should always act as an independent counsellor and adviser, without appearing to take sides.

Searching for information

The saying 'information is power' often causes people in organizations to hoard and hang on to it—possibly with the hope of gaining themselves some advantage. The level 3 NVQ advises the opposite and stresses the need actively to encourage the free exchange of information. This advice, if followed, not only ensures that all who require information to do their jobs properly have all the information they need, but also helps to promote a greater feeling of co-operation and trust. The positive aspects of information searching entail setting up and maintaining 'information networks'. These (hopefully) ensure you can (a) find the information you require, when it is needed and (b) gather it in a suitable format. (This emphasizes the importance of keeping in regular contact with your fellow employees at all levels.) However, be careful of the 'grapevine' (see Section 5.2.5.).

While you should make good use of existing sources, even better is to have additional, alternative ones as back-up. (You should never assume every one of your sources is always automatically reliable.) In any event, having more than one source helps (a) to create a broader picture of any situation, and (b) to highlight any deficiencies of information coming from any given source. The need to challenge will not arise on every occasion, but where you feel what you have been told 'doesn't quite fit', checking things out with other sources is no bad thing.

Suggested self-assessment/development activities. Review the information networks you access and use most frequently. Rate each of them for availability (i.e. as and when required), for accuracy and being up-to-the-minute; for containing enough detail, in an appropriate and convenient format for your immediate use. (An effective aid here is to use Table 36.1.)

Against each make notes as to how you feel any or all of these fall short of the ideal. Again with Table 36.1 as a prompt, set out how the quality of the information needed could be improved.

Thinking and taking decisions

Problem-solving and decision-making are related activities: you are first recommended to read Chapter 6, Section 6.1.2, particularly the text under the heading of 'Problem-solving and decision-making'. It is a useful introduction to this NVQ competence.

A variety of skills are needed here. Those related to thinking about a problem prior to taking a decision include the abilities to: (a) analyse systems or processes and break them down into individual tasks or activities; (b) look at a given situation, identify its various elements, perspectives, implications and possible consequences; (c) identify patterns, causal relationships (or other meaning) from data, information or events which—on the face of it—are not related.

Skills associated with the decision-making process itself include: (a) working out alternative solutions to any given problem before becoming committed to a particular decision—which must be a realistic choice, given the situation; (b) the ability to make a decision based on past experience (of yourself and/or of others)—this would usually refer to the more routine decisions; (c) where there might be an 'emotional' element in any decision-making, focusing yourself entirely on the facts and the problems involved in the situation, when making the relevant decision.

Finally, whatever choices you make—particularly with the more important decisions—you will naturally want to evaluate, later, how things actually worked out in practice.

Suggested self-assessment/development activities. Choose and review examples of decisions you have made in the recent past in the following categories: (a) very routine ones; (b) those with some degree of complexity; and (c) very complex decisions.

With each decision evaluate (a) to what degree (and how well) you employed each of the individual skills mentioned above, relating to the 'pre-decision' stage (such as analysing the initial situation and the background to it) and (b) those associated with the decision-making process itself. Finally, assess whether had you done more 'thinking' before taking each decision you could have made a more effective one.

36.5 KNOWLEDGE & UNDERSTANDING (K&U)

As with the Personal Competences, the different aspects of the K&U discussed in this section are in alphabetical order.

Analytical techniques

The word 'analysis' was originally used to describe the separation of the parts of a substance to determine its structure or make-up. It now has the wider meaning of examining and interpreting ideas, systems, methods, decisions and events. Often this is done with a view to modifying what has been analysed (e.g. a system) and, hopefully, improving it in some way.

 The level 3 NVQ expects knowledge of analytical techniques, particularly as applied to a manager's responsibilities: the use of resources, the state of the workplace environment, working practices, and the acquisition and storage of data and information. The emphasis is on using what you find by analysis to help you improve the use of resources, provide a better working environment, devise a better set of working practices, identify/eliminate discrepancies, and establish more efficient ways of data/information storage.

Suggested self-assessment/development activities. Take one of the suggested areas mentioned above (e.g. a particular working practice in your department) and (a) submit it to a careful analysis and (b) set out on paper your suggestions for improvement. (You will find Table 36.1 a useful prompt sheet at this stage.) Then work out how you would introduce the revised work practice, including the necessary consultations with your line manager and your work team.

Communication

You will have already realized from Chapters 5, 7, 30, 33, 34 and 35 that communicating is a key role of supervisors and managers. The particular aspects of communication mentioned in the level 3 NVQ include effective communication with others (e.g. with team members, colleagues, or people outside the organization) in a way which encourages a frank exchange of views); the presentation of an argument for change (both Chapter 9, Section 9.6 and Stages 4 and 5 of Chapter 30 are useful here); and the usefulness of getting feedback from your readers/listeners not only to check their understanding but also the quality and relevance of what you have written or said.

 In fact, feedback features very strongly in this area of K&U, not only for its own sake but for the purposes of encouraging team members, gaining their respect, co-operation, support and commitment; enhancing working relationships and putting your immediate superior into the picture about your activities, progress, results and achievements.

Chapter 30 deals with report writing, which ties in with the NVQ's stress on the ability to present proposals which are unambiguous and practical and which will most probably gain your manager's approval. Indeed the written word is as important as the spoken.

Finally, there is mention of the importance of being able to recognize (a) lines of reasoning (put forward by others) which are less than helpful, and (b) plain digressions. In either instance, you will need to be able to devise appropriate ways of discouraging such interventions.

Suggested self-assessment/development activities. Communication has so many different aspects that even the limited range mentioned in the NVQ requires a wide variety of knowledge, understanding and competence. You will do well to assess your K&U of communication (plus any related skills) against the areas mentioned above and make notes of where you feel you need to improve them. Sort your findings into those areas where (a) you feel you already have adequate knowledge (and experience), (b) you would like to build on your existing K&U and (c) where you have to admit you need some help and assistance.

Where both (b) and (c) are concerned, the best advice is to discuss your findings with your line manager, training or personnel officer to help you map out a suitable (work-related) training programme for improving your knowledge and skills on a continuous basis.

Continuous improvement

This is an objective already alluded to in the previous section under the heading of 'Focusing on results', where managers are urged 'actively to seek to do things better'. Here you are additionally asked to appreciate why this is not only desirable but essential, particularly with regard to the management of activities under your control. In addition, stress is laid on 'team development', and your contribution towards it. The ultimate aim is to enhance the continuing effectiveness of the organization to which you belong. To this end, you are asked to recognize the importance of an ongoing and systematic programme of work review (which can help to highlight where improvement is both needed and possible).

Suggested self-assessment/development activities. Consider whether you have arranged any team development activities within the last 12–18 months. If so assess: (a) how successful these were and why, and (b) how far these activities contributed to the continuing effectiveness of the organization. Based on your findings, plan further, improvement-related activities covering the next 12–18 months and discuss them with your line manager.

Where there have not been any team-development activities recently, work out (a) what kind of programme you consider would contribute to your organization's continuing effectiveness and (b) what the immediate objectives should be for the first two. Discuss your proposals with your line manager.

Customer relations

While it would be silly to believe that until recently organizations took no notice of customers, the development of the *marketing concept—the customer is central*—is a recent one. In the early eighteenth century the accent was on technology, the design of products, and not selling. However, when eventually mass-produced goods hit the markets, active selling became a necessity. Later still, customers and their needs began to take centre-stage. Now they are paramount. Customer expectations about the quality of the product or service provided must be continuously focused upon. Every employee has a role in this, and managers (at whatever level) have responsibilities to ensure customer expectations are met. You will therefore need to learn how to identify precisely customers' requirements, not only for planning your team's work but also to ensure that those needs are satisfied fully.

Organizations have now come to realize that their various sites, departments, sections (and individual employees) act as *internal* suppliers and/or customers to each other, whenever they supply or receive a service of some kind. While we would all agree that serving the ultimate (external) customer is the number one concern, any failure of a department to provide the appropriate service required to another function could well mean not only problems for that function, but for the external customer as well—with the possible loss of future business. It is therefore essential that we all realize internal customers are important too.

Suggested self-assessment/development activities. List separately all the internal and external 'supplier' and 'customer' roles undertaken by your own office, section or department. Note carefully with every entry the precise nature of the service and/or product you and your staff receive or supply; and the quality standards set or expected. Now, starting from the internal customer standpoint, assess how well your 'suppliers' meet your requirements and what might be done to improve their service to you. Then turn the spotlight on yourself, and your department, and your dealings with your internal customers. After you have carried out this second review, you may need to discuss your findings with both your staff and your customers to ensure you are doing everything to keep them happy.

(You can then repeat the assessment with any external customers with whom you may deal direct.)

Disciplinary and grievance procedures

In the previous section you will remember the stress laid on behaving ethically and the need to comply with industrial legislation. The specific emphasis here is on managers having: (a) a good K&U of disciplinary and grievance procedures (especially as relating to the NVQ Unit C15); (b) ensured all team members have been made fully aware of these procedures; and (c) the ability to apply those procedures fairly, impartially and quickly when they see the need arising. Chapter 23 covers employment contract-based legislation: Section 23.3 is particularly relevant here.

Suggested self-assessment/development activities. If you have had occasion (in the last year or so) either to dismiss or to be involved in the dismissal of an employee in your organization, review carefully how this was done; and check against the appropriate official procedure, that each item of that procedure was followed. In hindsight, do you think that the matter could have been handled differently, and how?

Alternatively, if you have not been involved recently (or ever) in an employee dismissal, assume two employees (Tom and Bill, for whom you are directly responsible) were discovered in your organization's showroom, fighting in full view of potential customers. Referring as necessary to your organization's disciplinary procedures, consider what action you would take. (Assume it transpired that Bill had hit Tom first!)

Health & Safety (H&S)

This is another area of the law that managers must be fully aware of. H&S legislation (discussed at length in Chapter 24) has a double implication for you in relation to your role as a line manager: first, your legal responsibilities of being a person 'in control of activities', and secondly as representing the employer (see Section 24.4.2). Thus your job as a manager will normally include providing a healthy, risk-free and productive environment for staff, and being capable of keeping an ongoing watch on that environment to make sure it meets all the requirements of H&S legislation.

The job can also involve taking an active role in training staff in health and safety matters. This could include providing both relevant H&S information and active support to people both within and outside your organization.

Suggested self-assessment/development activities. 'Risk-assessment' is a key activity (see Section 24.7.1). Even though others (or even yourself) may have in the past carried out risk-assessments (e.g. on particular activities or processes, or even of everything done), circumstances can change over time.

Identify first the most obvious/important safety hazards (both actual and potential) in your department. Assess the risks which are/could be involved and how they are monitored currently. See if you can find ways of: (a) minimizing those risks even further; (b) improving the monitoring systems in use; and (c) motivating your team to be more vigilant.

Another activity could be to refer to the Workplace (Health, Safety and Welfare) Regulations (1992) which set out the legal requirements relating to the work environment (see Section 24.7.3). Take each of the items mentioned in the section and check that each of them fulfils the relevant legal requirements.

Information handling

The task of *searching* for information is mentioned under Personal Competencies (Section 36.4). This area of K&U concentrates more on how to gather and handle information once it has been located.

An obvious—but very important—initial requirement is to be able to assess exactly how much information you need in any given situation. This applies whether you are involved with decision-making, or the assessment and evaluation of others, or are just immersed in your daily routine.

Information which is secret, classified or confidential (whether relating to colleagues, other individuals, team members, or to the organization) should be treated with great care; and you will need to ensure you both understand and follow all the applicable rules, procedures and principles of confidentiality followed by your organization.

Chapter 33 is devoted to managing conflict at work. As you read it, you will doubtless see the merits of carefully recording the progress and outcomes of any conflicts with which you are in some way involved.

Other important aspects of information handling to know about include: (a) the types of information (e.g. factual and that concerned with quality) needed to enable you to do your job; (b) the ways of collecting that information (confirming both its value and validity); (c) how to overcome any problems arising during collection; and (d) how to assess any information about your work team's progress (and that of the organization as a whole) and your part in it. Finally, you will need to become familiar with the most efficient ways of recording and storing all the information you will need for the future.

Suggested self-assessment/development activities. Review your information handling profile. Work through the paragraphs above and assess yourself against each area of information handling in turn. Note the areas where you feel you could build on your existing K&U, and decide which aspects need tackling first.

(You may wish to discuss both your findings and proposed course of action with others, including those responsible for your training.)

Involvement and motivation

The current level 3 management standards reflect the changes (mentioned in Chapter 7) in the approach of managers to the managed. The old model of (sometimes innumerable) hierarchies of managers—who (in theory) knew everything and made all the decisions—in charge of squads of workers who were paid for doing exactly as they were told has more or less disappeared. Networks are now replacing hierarchies. The accent is on empowerment and team-work, with everyone working to common, agreed aims.

This area of K&U centres on how to encourage team members to identify their own training needs, undertake new responsibilities, assess their own performance and put forward their own suggestions on improving their contributions. The manager's role as a helper (including making recommendations, guiding, giving feedback on performance to or encouraging team members) is a vital one. The skills of empathy, persuasion, leadership and the ability to sense when and where to delegate are vital here.

Involvement can be for and by individuals (e.g. team members identifying their own development needs, assessing their own progression towards meeting these, working out and asking for the resources they need to carry out their functions) and by the team as an entity (working out ways of improving efficiency, contributing to both the planning and organizing of the work of the team). Whatever the kind of involvement, you will need to know how to encourage and enable your team and its members. (See also Chapter 8, especially Section 8.8.)

Leadership styles

While leadership styles are discussed in Chapter 8 (Sections 8.5 to 8.9), the K&U listed under this heading in the level 3 management NVQ are restricted to those relating to the conduct of meetings (see Chapter 7, especially Sections 7.2.16 and 7.2.17).

(Note: further information on this topic (as well as appropriate self-assessment/development activities) is given under the heading *Meetings*, below. For the moment, note that for the NVQ you will be expected (a) to understand the various leadership styles applicable to running meetings and (b) for any given meeting where you are in the chair, to be able to choose the leadership style most appropriate to that meeting. Whatever your choice, you will want to ensure that meeting members are (a) encouraged to make useful and positive contributions and (b) discouraged from wandering off the point or generally being unhelpful.)

Legal requirements

The need for K&U relating to particular aspects of employment law was mentioned earlier in this chapter (see *Behaving ethically* under 'Personal Competences': *Disciplinary and grievance procedures* and *Health & Safety*, earlier in this section). This area of K&U is also relevant to *Meetings* and *Recruitment and selection*, discussed later; and obviously to other areas of work where the law operates. However, in this NVQ 'legal requirements' relate only to some features of industrial and employment legislation.

There are, indeed, other areas of employment law about which you should be aware. Again, as you will have realized when reading Unit IV—'The Supervisor and the Law'—keeping up to date with changes in the law is essential, especially where you as a manager could be in the firing line. (An example of such a change in employment law which could affect you was the adoption by the UK government (October 1998) of the EU directive on 'working time'—limiting the weekly hours of work of employed persons. A further complication is the list of exceptions to the directive.)

Suggested self-assessment/development activities. While you could not possibly be expected to know everything in Unit IV (which in any event only highlights some aspects of the law), it is useful to read through the unit carefully. Further, it is worthwhile to ensure you have a good knowledge of every legal point which you think could affect you and your team at work. Where you feel you are not as fully briefed as you would like to be, ensure you do know where to go, and whom to ask—particularly if you have a problem at work with possible legal implications.

Managerial competence

This relates specifically to Unit Cl of the NVQ. The K&U required is that relating to (a) the principal skills required to perform effectively as a manager and (b) the interpersonal skills you need for effective team work.

One of these skills—time management—is specifically listed in the NVQ and is discussed nearer the end of this section. By implication, many of the remainder can be related to the Personal Competences already examined in the previous section.

While Unit I of this book concentrates on management theory, Unit II looks at a range of management competences: creating, planning, organizing and leading (a work-group); and planning, introducing and managing change. Unit III not only describes the personnel function, but also the competences required by supervisors/line managers in such activities as recruitment and selection, induction, performance appraisal and training.

The previous chapters in this Unit (i.e. Unit VI) are also particularly pertinent, dealing with such diverse activities as planning projects, writing reports, building and leading a work team, managing conflicts, briefing a work group and making a presentation.

Suggested self-assessment/development activities. Taking each competence mentioned above in turn, candidly rate how well you perform each one. Note particularly those areas in which you feel you could become even more competent. Work out how you would go about working towards such a goal.

Meetings

Meetings (and yet more meetings!) are another inevitable consequence of the trend away from autocratic management and towards that of the involvement and empowerment of the whole workforce. Unfortunately, there are many meetings in organizations which are both unnecessary and inappropriate; which go on too long, and which are inefficiently run. As noted in Chapter 7 (Sections 7.2.14–7.2.17), a supervisor or manager will inevitably spend time at work attending some meetings as an 'ordinary' member and others as the person calling and running the meeting.

Meetings are often thought of as extremely useful ways of exchanging ideas, information and coming to decisions. There can, however, be some occasions where one-to-one conversations, written communications or immediate decisions by management are more relevant. 'Calling a meeting' is not a universal problem-solver. Thus, you should be able to identify both the benefits and drawbacks of meetings as methods of information dissemination and decision-making.

It is important that you are familiar with all the conventions followed by your organization in (a) planning, (b) determining the purpose and objectives of and (c) calling meetings. You should also be aware of the duties and responsibilities involved in chairing meetings, and of the need to ensure that what has to be achieved is accomplished within the allotted time.

Suggested self-assessment/development activities. While you will benefit from a self-assessment of your own knowledge of meetings, their purposes, procedures and the task of chairing or leading a meeting (see Section 7.2.17 as a guide), you will do well to find out how others regard your abilities—particularly the members of your own team, and other colleagues who might attend your meetings from time to time. (This might well reveal small matters which can be easily dealt with as well as highlighting future training needs.)

Monitoring and evaluation

Keeping a continuous check on the work of a section or department (and intervening where work requirements are seen not to be met) has long been part of a manager's job. Additionally, for the level 3 NVQ, you are required to understand how to do this methodically and consistently. You will therefore need to be be aware of how to undertake periodic and systematic reviews of work progress. Such reviews will enable you to check that planned targets are being met; and to take steps to reschedule work if this is not the case. (This, in turn, entails you knowing how to assess correctly, fairly and objectively the outputs of both work teams and individual workers.)

A particular aspect of this latter activity is appreciating when teams or individuals are performing well below expectations (described as 'poor performance' in the language of the NVQ), and quickly bringing this to the attention of those concerned.

Suggested self-assessment/development activities. Carefully assess how often and well you (a) monitor the work of your department (the checklist in Chapter 6, Section 6.2.3—especially step 7 and the general review process which follows—could be helpful here) and (b) work out what you need to do to remedy any shortcomings in your performance. Where you are unsure of precisely when you carried out such checks (through, say, lack of record keeping in the past) you will need, for the future, to ensure you record such events in your work diary.

Organizational context

In Chapter 1 (Section 1.3) you were introduced to systems theory and how organizations (as systems) interact with their environments. Reading that text, you will have become aware that the way an organization behaves is greatly influenced by its surroundings. The 'organizational context' area mentioned here shifts the emphasis down one degree, that is to the interactive relationship between *you* and the

organization for which you work. It is the detail of this interactive relationship that you must be fully aware of.

A good starting point is the K&U of the internal management structure of the organization, lines of authority, accountability and control. Next are the policies, strategies, procedures followed, ways of operating and plans and activities adopted by the organization. (These may impose various constraints on your decision-making, such as the way disciplinary matters or the selection of personnel are dealt with, the need to follow laid down procedures for recommending the use of resources—and how these might be influenced by future trends—and the actual use of such resources.)

Other areas to be aware of are the organization's perceived (internal) strengths and weaknesses, the (external) threats to it and opportunities currently available. (Your immediate manager or colleagues may need to have their attention drawn to these, particularly to the opportunities.)

Then there are other aspects such as Health & Safety (discussed earlier), especially if there are any conflicts (actual or potential) between the law and the organization's needs and constraints; and the environmental implications of resources used. Even closer to you are matters such as team objectives and how these fit into the organization; the handling and resolution of conflicts; record keeping (and how this should be done, especially where there are legal requirements to do so); the ways of consulting with your line manager about work-related problems, and where (and from whom) you should get feedback about your performance.

Finally, there are the current (and possible future) requirements of your own job. You will need to know how to assess your competence and performance against these: any shortcomings identified could be the basis of further self-development.

Suggested self-assessment/development activities. Besides making a start by assessing your level of competence in your current job, review carefully how much you know about your organization, particularly those aspects mentioned in the second and third paragraphs of this topic area. You will then be able to prepare a 'learning agenda' covering those aspects of the organizational context you still need to know more about.

Planning

This activity is mentioned in Chapters 5 (see 5.2.2), 6 (Section 6.2), 7 (part of 7.3.9), 15 (in relation to training plans) and 30 (with reference to planning a project). Consulting these will give you some insight into the principles and practice of planning.

In the context of the level 3 NVQ you will have to prove you understand both the principles and practice of planning work-based activities (with the objective of enhancing organizational effectiveness). This includes knowing how to (a) set clear-cut, feasible and assessable work objectives for yourself, (b) prepare short- and medium-term, feasible and practical work plans for both teams and individuals, (c) prioritize both your work and that of others for whom you are responsible and (d) forecast how long planned activities will take. You should also be able to assess how well your plans succeed in meeting your team's objectives.

You will also want to know how to anticipate possible problems which may arise during the lifetime of any planned activity and to be able to prepare contingency plans which can be acted upon as needed.

Suggested self-assessment/development activities. Take one area of work for which you are now responsible and review the way it was initially planned out, especially if this was done by someone else. Check that specific objectives were set for the team leader and the team; that you and the team now work to feasible and practical objectives and work plans. Where you feel improvements could be made, consulting with the team as necessary, work out a revised programme. (You may well want to discuss your ideas with both your line manager and other colleagues as well.)

Providing support

An important aspect of any manager's job is knowing how to support others and be a source of strength to them. Part of your job, then, involves helping team members, colleagues and other managers in the organization to achieve their work-related objectives. This is especially so in respect of team members when they are experiencing work-related problems. (Chapter 19, Section 19.2, covers counselling skills, which are very relevant here.) The importance of this support role is underlined in the NVQ units relating to creating effective working relationships and responding to poor performance within the team.

You should, therefore, be ready to identify and deal appropriately with the types of problems team members may encounter at work. (Note that some of these problems may prove to be outside your level of competence or responsibility: in such cases you should then be able to decide where, or to whom, such problems should be referred. This implies knowledge of the relevant support services available both within and without the organization.)

Where you *are* able to assist with a problem you have identified, you must know how to make a suitable response, such as agreeing with the staff concerned any proposed programme of action to be followed. With regard to colleagues (though this can apply equally well to team members), you should be able to provide them with useful help, encouragement and guidance in, for example, presenting, negotiating and agreeing their plans (and associated monitoring and checking procedures).

In essence, you should be able to create a work climate which encourages ongoing feedback from teams and colleagues. They should feel they can request help from you whenever it is needed.

Suggested self-assessment/development activities. Review carefully how you go about counselling and giving support to your team and colleagues. Reflect on two or three recent instances and assess how well you (a) identified the problems involved, (b) devised suitable responses, (c) came up with reasonable, workable solutions and agreed appropriate courses of action with those concerned, and (d) monitored their implementation. (You could also use the checklists in Chapter 19—Sections 19.2.3, 2.4, and 2.5—to help you assess how well you managed the interaction between those counselled and yourself.)

In addition, you could read through case study A19.3 and plan how you would deal with André's predicament. (While on the face of it, the problem is not a work-related one, the employee's work has suffered because of it. Note also the possible need to call on outside services.)

Recruitment and selection

While this area of K&U in the NVQ concentrates on the supporting role in recruitment and selection played by level 3 managers, increasingly such managers are having a greater say in selection. (In some small organizations they may have a major, if not the sole, influence both on the selection and promotion of their own staff.) Chapter 12 defines and explains both recruitment and selection in sufficient detail to be useful to all managers whatever role they may play in the processes involved.

First, as a manager, you must be fully aware of the legal implications of recruitment and selection (particularly those relating to 'equal opportunities' and employee specifications).

Identifying personnel needs can involve both collecting and analysing pertinent information and taking into account any work and team objectives (and constraints) which may influence the situation. Where there is (or might be) a vacancy in the team, or need for an increase in the team's size, you should be able to put together a good case for the replacement or new team member. This implies having a good knowledge of those work objectives (and constraints on them) which have a bearing on your team's personnel needs. Based on this information, you should then be able to identify and specify the job roles of team members, the competences they need to possess and any particular personal attributes which would be relevant.

When it comes both to the ongoing staff assessment and the selection process for new appointments, you must be fully aware of your organization's methods (and their comparative merits and weaknesses as applied to your team). You must be able to make honest and unbiased assessments (against the agreed criteria) during the selection process itself.

Finally, you will naturally need to ensure you exercise the proper degree of confidentiality throughout the whole process.

Suggested self-assessment/development activities. Where you are currently faced with an actual or potential recruitment or selection situation, review carefully how you propose to contribute to it. Using both Chapter 12 as a series of discrete tasks—e.g. job analysis, job description, recruitment and selection—and the related K&U discussed above, work out on paper exactly how you would assist (or even manage) the process. When the matter has been resolved, and the appointment(s) made, review how well things went and make notes of any lessons learnt for the future.

If there are no vacancies currently, reflect on the last recruitment and selection activity with which you were involved. Make notes of where you performed well and where you feel (in hindsight) you could have done better. Prepare an action plan to help you cope more successfully in the future.

Resource management

Every organization has resources (which can include both skills and physical assets like computers, machines and motor vehicles, information, materials and finance; see also *Time management*, below). Such resources require managing. There are very few managers who can escape being held responsible for at least some resources, and how they are utilized.

The overriding objectives of resource management include minimizing costs while simultaneously maximizing resource use. There may be constraints such as storage space or customers' needs, so that the actual resource usage can be dictated, wholly or partly, by the situation.

The level 3 NVQ puts considerable emphasis on the knowledge of the principles underlying the management of resources with a view to maximizing their efficiency and maintaining the quality of the goods and services offered. (This could involve scheduling skills and/or materials management techniques being needed in the office, on the shop floor or in despatch, for example.) The need to be able to keep careful and exact records on resource use is also very important.

Suggested self-assessment/development activities. Carry out an audit of all the resources for which you are responsible. Taking each resource area in turn, review how carefully you have managed it in the past, taking into account the points made in the preceding paragraph. Make notes of where you feel you could improve the use of that resource and make suitable plans to do so. Finally, check on the suitability and relevance of your recording systems.

Time management

As suggested at the beginning of Chapter 31 (*Managing Time*) time is the scarcest resource of all. Many would also say it is the resource which is the least well managed of all. (The possible consequences of poor time management are considered in Section 31.4.)

The rest of Chapter 31 contains the K&U you need to help you to (a) appreciate that competent managers are aware of the need for, and the importance of, good time management, (b) carry out a self-diagnosis on your current time management skills, and (c) go about the job of improving those skills. (The checklist in Section 31.6 and the 'improvement regime' in 31.7 are particularly relevant here.) Having done all this you will then be in a better position to manage your own time, rather than being at the mercy of unwanted interruptions.

Suggested self-assessment/development. Work carefully and honestly through Chapter 31, with particular attention to Sections 31.5 (checkpoint 1), 31.6 (self-assessment questionnaire), and 31.7 (checkpoint 2). Arrange to put into practice as soon as possible any suggested improvements which are relevant to you. Review your progress at three-monthly intervals.

Training and development (T&D)

It is no surprise to find training and development (T&D) is allocated a specific element (C1.1) in this NVQ. Every NVQ implies some T&D before and/or while the qualification is being achieved. Those aiming at level 3 management are expected to progress their own T&D on an ongoing basis.

In many organizations managers are additionally expected to contribute to the T&D of (a) the teams they lead and (b) each individual team member (see optional module C9). (Chapter 15 is very relevant here.)

Although the K&U in this area is very carefully spelt out, there might have been more explicit emphasis on the important role of annual performance appraisals (see Chapter 14); and especially that of the formal appraisal interview in helping to identify the training and development needs of others (see Section 14.4.4).

Dealing with your own T&D first, you will undoubtedly accept the need for continuing self-development towards full competence as a manager. Having first assessed how competent you actually are against the desired degree of competence, you will then be in a good position to map out a self-development action plan. (This might well be largely or wholly related to the level 3 management NVQ or some other qualification.) It may be useful to discuss the plan with others, including your line manager. Finally, you will need regularly to review your progress. This could also involve setting fresh targets as earlier ones are achieved.

The T&D of the team (and the individuals within it) is a more complex matter. (Chapter 32 covers the topic in some detail.) Sometimes both the planning and execution of such T&D can be a joint effort between yourself and others, and sometimes everything may depend upon you. Whatever the arrangements, you must be aware of (a) what you need to know in order to be able to identify the team's development needs and (b) what development activities seem to be relevant and suitable to meet those identified needs (taking into account any organizational and team constraints). Next, you will want to be fully aware to what extent and in what way you will contribute to both the planning and delivery of the eventual T&D. You also need to understand how important it is that any activities arranged should be suitably designed to cater for *all* team members, whatever their jobs, aptitude for learning or individual circumstances. This includes being able to pin-point the knowledge and skills required by particular individuals.

Further K&U needed covers (a) how to present your contributions during the initial planning of development activities; and (b) how to ensure your training contributions to the development activities comply with agreed objectives and plans; and also know how they are relevant to the team members, and to your own goals and capabilities.

When the T&D activities are complete, obviously there should be a careful review to assess how suitable and effective they have been. You need to be aware of the importance of this process and the methods used to carry it out. When the purpose of such assessment has been agreed upon, you should then be able to assess individual team members' performance against the development activities.

User-feedback contributes a useful extra dimension to the assessment process. An essential skill, then, is knowing how to encourage trainees to voice their opinions on any T&D in which they have participated.

Suggested self-assessment/development activities. If you are not currently involved in any ongoing and structured self-development activities, list all the requirements of your present job. By each requirement note carefully both the degree of K&U called for and the personal competences needed. Then draft an action plan to remedy any deficiencies noted in either knowledge or competence. You are advised to discuss your conclusions with others, such as your line manager, colleagues and those responsible for training and development. This could well help you structure any subsequent T&D you may undertake.

If you are already involved with continuous development, as well as endeavouring to carry out your current job more effectively, consider the possibilities of your taking on a more demanding role and the T&D implications of doing so. This, too, can lead to an action plan for the future.

Working relationships

Left on its own, a group may function well, but it is more likely to go its own way or even disintegrate. As a group leader, one of your tasks is to ensure this does not happen to your group.

From the discussion in Chapter 7 (Section 7.1) it is clear that good working relationships have a key role in establishing and maintaining a satisfactory climate in the workplace, and in contributing much towards the smooth running of a section, department or work group. You should, therefore, strive to adopt ways of working which aim to stimulate effective working relationships.

The K&U you need to create and preserve such relationships starts with knowing how people can (and do) work in groups. Much of this knowledge can be gained by careful observation and analysis of how groups operate in your organization. (Bear in mind group behaviour can be affected by an organization's principles, values or sense of mission, as well as those of the group leader.)

Potentially, conflicts can arise in all groups. You must accordingly be well aware of the kinds of circumstances, personal behaviour and interactions between group members which can encourage or lead to conflict. This implies the ability to spot impending conflicts between individuals. (One useful way of attempting to minimize potential conflict is to ensure all of your team are fully aware of the kinds and standards of behaviour you expect from them.)

When conflicts do arise, ideally you will sort them out in ways which will create the least possible disruption to the work of the group. (Chapter 33 not only explains the nature and categories of conflict but also how you can devise strategies for coping with them.) A typical example could be finding yourself in a potential conflict situation (labelled a 'disagreement' in the NVQ) with your line manager. The message here is to transform confrontation into negotiation (see Section 33.7.4).

Group members can encounter problems directly affecting their work. They will need your help. Providing them with opportunities to discuss their problems with you can consolidate good working relationships. (Note, however, you will need to be conscious of the limits beyond which you should not go when dealing with a team member's problem.)

Treating people with respect (and as individuals in their own right, whatever their position or job in the organization) at all times is essential. (This particularly applies when dealing with staff in disciplinary or grievance situations.) Promoting and sustaining good working relations between you and your colleagues are also part of your remit. You should always deal with them with respect, honouring any commitments you may have to them.

Finally, you should be able clearly to distinguish between *line* and *functional* staff (the latter also called variously 'element' and 'staff' in Chapter 2, Sections 2.3.1, 2.3.2 and 2.3.3, to which you are referred). The working relationship with these specialist members of staff for whom you have functional responsibility can well be different from that which exists between those who come directly under you (i.e. 'line' personnel). This can have implications for work planning.

Suggested self-assessment/development activities. Analyse carefully (and as honestly as you can!) the quality of the working relationships you have with (a) your team as a whole, (b) each individual team member, (c) any functional staff for whom you are responsible, (d) colleagues, (e) your line manager and (f) senior managers. Make notes of any areas where you feel you should concentrate on building on existing working relationships and make them more effective.

Review your progress at regular intervals.

Workplace organization

This aspect of K&U requires you, first, to be fully aware of the kinds of conditions and working environments most likely to promote productive work. The closer your section can get to an appropriate working environment, the more effective it can become. Obviously, such 'ideal' conditions will vary in relation to the type of work involved (such as those found in retail, administrative or manufacturing environments, for example).

Next, you must know how to organize both yourself and those for whom you are responsible. This entails knowing how to set yourself objectives or targets which are clear-cut, quantifiable and attainable within a given time; and having the ability to prioritize work activities in accordance with your organization's goals and procedures. Similarly, with those working under you, you must be aware of how to devise short- and medium-term work programmes for both the team and individual workers.

Finally, you must be able to plan for and cope with any emergencies or contingencies, as and when they may arise.

Suggested self-assessment/development activities. Carefully review the major aspects of your department's physical environment, the equipment used—whether for the production of goods, the provision of services or as office equipment—and current working practices and procedures. This review should cover all the major functions of your department.

For example in a production area you could consider how well it met H&S requirements and other legal requirements; the characteristics of materials used (and the actual or potential effects these may have on the work team), noise and other distractions encountered and the amount of open space available for the safe movement of staff between machinery or other equipment.

In an office-based environment you may want to look at the current layout, considering its good and bad points. While much can be said in favour of 'open plan' layouts, these, too, have their drawbacks such as distraction from background noise (especially the constant ringing of telephones). Lighting, heating, ventilation and the work flow are other considerations.

Whatever the purpose of your work area, carefully attempt to identify problems (both actual or potential) with the current working conditions which do (or could) impinge the productivity of your work teams.

As appropriate, involve some or all of your work team in this task.

Ideally, you could draw up a report covering the whole physical environment, equipment and materials used and the working practices currently followed, with suggestions which you feel would help improve both morale and productivity.

INDEX NO. 1: KNOWLEDGE AND UNDERSTANDING

As noted earlier in this chapter, for candidates to be assessed as being competent in the revised Management level 3 qualification they will need to be able to demonstrate they have the necessary (underpinning) knowledge and understanding (K&U).

In this index you will find the different categories of the K&U listed alphabetically. With respect to each individual entry, the Units which make reference to that category of K&U are recorded alongside in strict alphanumeric order. (It should be noted, however, that (a) the published Units do not always follow this order and (b) no account is taken in this index of the specialist Units relating to Energy Efficiency or Quality Systems and Audits.)

INDEX NO. 2: PERSONAL COMPETENCE

As noted earlier in this chapter, for candidates to be assessed as being competent in the revised level 3 qualification they will need to be able to demonstrate they have the necessary personal competences (PCs).

In this index you will find the different categories of the PCs listed alphabetically. With respect to each individual entry, the Units which make reference to that category of PC are recorded alongside in strict alphanumeric order. (It should be noted, however, that (a) the published Units do not always follow this order and (b) no account is taken in this index of the specialist Units relating to Energy Efficiency or Quality Systems and Audits.)

Acting assertively	C1, C4, C7, C9, C12, C15; D1
Behaving ethically	C7, C15
Building teams:	
(a) the management of others	C4, C9, C 12, C15; D1
(b) relating to others	A1; C4, C9, C12, C15; D1
Communicating	A1; B1; Cl, C4, C7, C9, C12, C15; D1
Focusing on results	A1; B1; Cl, C15
Influencing others	C7; D1
Managing self	C1, C4
Searching for information	C7; D1
Thinking and making decisions:	
(a) being analytic	A1; Cl, C7, C9, C12
(b) dealing with concepts	C7
(c) making and taking decisions	A1; B1; Cl, C4, C7, C9, C12

Appendix A

EXAMPLE OF A JOB DESCRIPTION

Job Description	—Home Sales Manager
Department	—Sales
Division	—Marketing
Company	—Electrical Goods Ltd

No. Employed in position—1

1. Purpose and duties

Purpose

To build, maintain and direct an efficient, well-trained and effective field turnover sales organization in the UK, so that adequate sales and profit margins are achieved to maintain the company's profitable operation.

Duties

(a) To establish and execute sales programmes in accordance with approved policies laid down by the board.

(b) To assign sales objectives to district, branch and other sales territories; periodically to evaluate performance in their attainment; and to take appropriate remedial action as necessary to bring results into line with objectives.

(c) To organize, recommend to the proper executives, and administer procedures affecting sales, prices, terms, discounts, allowances on returned goods sales service and field engineering services.

(d) To plan, organize and conduct periodic sales meetings for the purpose of instructing, training and motivating the whole sales organization.

(e) To liaise with the Personnel Manager in the formulation and maintenance of an adequate recruitment, selection, training and development programme for sales personnel.

(f)　To lay down policies on travel and selling expenses, and approve individual claims of Field Sales Managers and other sales staff for such expenses, in conjunction with their monthly sales reports.

(g)　To review monthly sales reports of Field Sales Managers, and their Sales Representatives.

(h)　To recommend the addition of new products to existing lines; or the modification, or elimination of existing items.

(i)　To assist the Marketing Director in the preparation of advertising and promotion programmes and to supervise the execution of such programmes by sales personnel.

(j)　To supervise the preparation and production of sales forecasts; the preparation and production of reports on actual sales; and the comparison of forecasts with actual sales. Additionally, to keep the board informed of all significant sales developments that would affect the company.

(k)　To correspond with customers (and company personnel) as required. To deal with all customer complaints in the first instance.

(l)　To travel in the field, to supervise, and evaluate the effectiveness of the Field Sales Managers.

(m)　To attend such industry trade fairs and conventions, and assist the Marketing Director to prepare and staff the company sales areas, as the Marketing Director may direct.

2. Responsibilities

(a)　To develop and recommend to the Marketing Director, for his or her approval, policies and programmes relating to:

> Size and type of sales organization
> Product lines
> Distribution channels
> Prices
> Sales objectives (based on sales forecasts)
> Salary and commission sales for sales staff
> Promotions, personnel development, training and general career advancement of sales staff
> Sales department budgets

(b)　To control a staff of 6 Field Sales Managers, 35 Sales Representatives; and Sales Office Staff (approx. 25), Advertising Staff (5), Sales Promotion (3).

3. Relationships

Accountable to the Marketing Director, the job holder has close relationships with all company central, head office departments, including Production, Research and Development, Accounts and Personnel; attends weekly Senior Executives Meeting.

4. Physical conditions

A private office is provided on the fourth floor of office block. Office hours will be 9.30 am to 5.00 pm Monday–Friday, but the job holder will be expected to work longer hours as required from time to time.

5. Economic conditions

Salary range £30 000–£35 000 plus overriding commission of $\frac{1}{2}$% on all sales over £1 million per year. Eligible for superannuation and non-contributory pension schemes, membership of BUPA.
  Suitable car is provided, and private mileage is allowed. Expense account.
  Annual leave: 30 days plus all public holidays (or time off in lieu).

6. Prospects

This is a Senior Company appointment. No promotion would be envisaged for three years, but a successful job holder could be rewarded with a seat on a subsidiary company board within two years.

Appendix B

SAMPLE APPLICATION FORM

POSITION APPLIED FOR:			
CONFIDENTIAL **EXPLODING CHEMICAL COMPANY** APPLICATION FOR STAFF EMPLOYMENT			
ALL QUESTIONS SHOULD BE ANSWERED IN THE APPLICANT'S OWN HANDWRITING			JOB REF NO.
SURNAME	FORENAMES	MALE/ FEMALE	AGE
SURNAME AT BIRTH (IF DIFFERENT)			DATE OF BIRTH
HOME ADDRESS	TEMPORARY ADDRESS (IF APPLICABLE)		
TEL. NO.	TEL. NO.		
PLACE OF BIRTH (TOWN/COUNTRY)	NATIONALITY		
MARITAL STATUS	FULL NAME/ADDRESS OF NEXT OF KIN		RELATIONSHIP
CHILDREN (IF ANY) BOYS AGES GIRLS AGES	OTHER DEPENDANTS		

HEALTH

HEIGHT: Ft   Ins   WEIGHT: St   Lbs

GIVE DETAILS OF ANY PHYSICAL OR
MENTAL DISABILITY, OR SERIOUS ILLNESSES

ARE YOU REGISTERED AS DISABLED? (DISABLED EMPLOYMENT ACT 1944)   YES/NO
IF YES GIVE BRIEF DETAILS

                              CERT. NO.   EXPIRY DATE

HAVE YOU LOST MORE THAN FIVE WORKING
DAYS THROUGH ILLNESS IN THE LAST TWO YEARS?   YES/NO
IF YES, GIVE BRIEF DETAILS

NOTE: IT IS A CONDITION OF EMPLOYMENT THAT ALL SUCCESSFUL CANDIDATES
        SHALL AGREE TO BE MEDICALLY EXAMINED BY THE COMPANY DOCTOR

EDUCATION (from the age of 11 years)			
SCHOOL/COLLEGE/UNIVERSITY	FROM	TO	EXAMINATIONS PASSED (with grades)

POSITIONS HELD: SCHOOL PREFECT, COLLEGE POSTS, etc.

SCHOLARSHIPS/PRIZES

FURTHER/HIGHER EDUCATION, TRAINING COLLEGE	FROM	TO	TITLE OF COURSE P.T., F.T., Block, etc.

EXAMINATIONS PASSED	SUBJECTS AND GRADES
1. DETAILS OF ANY OTHER TRAINING COURSE UNDERTAKEN (IN-PLANT, RESIDENTIAL, CORRESPONDENCE, etc.) STATE NAME OF COURSE, DATE SUBJECTS STUDIED. 2. PROFESSIONAL QUALIFICATIONS OBTAINED (state if by examination)	

-2-

EMPLOYMENT EXPERIENCE

(Please complete in chronological order. Include
any experience you may have had in H.M. Forces)

FROM	TO	NAME AND ADDRESS OF EMPLOYER NATURE OF BUSINESS	POSITION(S) HELD	FINAL SALARY AND REASONS FOR LEAVING

Have you been dismissed or asked to resign?   YES/NO
If yes, please state circumstances

Please describe your present or most recent post, indicating to whom you are/were responsible, and who is/was responsible to you. What do you consider to have been your major contribution in this appointment and why? What are your 'main' duties and activities?
(Continue on a blank sheet if necessary)

HOBBIES AND INTERESTS

Please give details of any hobbies or leisure
interests you may have.

REFERENCES

Give two references, both preferably from past employers, or
college tutors or school headteacher

Name _____   Name _____

Address _____   Address _____

_____   _____

_____   _____

_____   _____

Status _____   Status _____

(REFERENCES WILL ONLY BE TAKEN UP WITH YOUR PERMISSION)

SUPPLEMENTARY DETAILS

Please use this space to record any other information which you consider relevant—
languages spoken/read, etc. (Continue on a blank sheet if necessary)

I certify that the statements made on this application form are strictly accurate in every detail.
I have not wittingly withheld any information which might be to my disadvantage in this application.
I agree, if engaged, to accept all the conditions of the rules and regulations of the company.
I also undertake, if engaged, to observe secrecy in respect of all matters of a confidential nature
which may come to my knowledge whilst in the company's employ.

Signature _____ Date _____

Index